# Lecture Notes in Computer Science 4807

*Commenced Publication in 1973*
Founding and Former Series Editors:
Gerhard Goos, Juris Hartmanis, and Jan van Leeuwen

Zhong Shao (Ed.)

# Programming Languages and Systems

5th Asian Symposium, APLAS 2007
Singapore, November 29-December 1, 2007
Proceedings

Springer

Volume Editor

Zhong Shao
Yale University
Department of Computer Science
51 Prospect Street
New Haven, CT 06520-8285, U.S.A.
E-mail: shao-zhong@cs.yale.edu

Library of Congress Control Number: 2007938893

CR Subject Classification (1998): D.3, D.2, F.3, D.4, D.1, F.4.1

LNCS Sublibrary: SL 2 – Programming and Software Engineering

ISSN 0302-9743
ISBN-10 3-540-76636-7 Springer Berlin Heidelberg New York
ISBN-13 978-3-540-76636-0 Springer Berlin Heidelberg New York



Springer is a part of Springer Science+Business Media

springer.com


Printed in Germany

Typesetting: Camera-ready by author, data conversion by Scientific Publishing Services, Chennai, India
Printed on acid-free paper SPIN: 12187423 06/3180 5 4 3 2 1 0

# Preface

This volume contains the proceedings of the Fifth Asian Symposium on Programming Languages and Systems (APLAS 2007), which took place in Singapore, November 29 – December 1, 2007. The symposium was sponsored by the Asian Association for Foundation of Software (AAFS) and School of Computing, National University of Singapore.

In response to the call for papers, 84 full submissions were received. Each submission was reviewed by at least three Program Committee members with the help of external reviewers. The Program Committee meeting was conducted electronically over a 2-week period. After careful discussion, the Program Committee selected 25 papers. I would like to sincerely thank all the members of the APLAS 2007 Program Committee for their excellent job, and all the external reviewers for their invaluable contribution. The submission and review process was managed using the EasyChair system.

In addition to the 25 contributed papers, the symposium also featured three invited talks by Vincent Danos (University of Paris VII and CNRS, France), Sriram Rajamani (Microsoft Research India), and Vijay Saraswat (IBM T.J. Watson Research Lab, USA).

Many people helped to promote APLAS as a high-quality forum in Asia to serve programming language researchers worldwide. Following a series of well-attended workshops that were held in Singapore (2000), Daejeon (2001), and Shanghai (2002), the first four formal symposiums were held in Beijing (2003), Taipei (2004), Tsukuba (2005), and Sydney (2006).

I am grateful to the General Chair, Joxan Jaffar, for his invaluable support and guidance that made our symposium in Singapore possible and enjoyable. I am indebted to our Local Arrangements Chair, Wei-Ngan Chin, for his considerable effort to plan and organize the meeting itself. I thank Eijiro Sumii for serving as the Poster Chair and Alexandru Stefan for his help with the conference Web site and posters. Last but not least, I would like to thank the AAFS Chair Tetsuo Ida, and the program chairs of the past APLAS symposiums, especially Naoki Kobayashi, for their advice.

September 2007 Zhong Shao

# Organization

## General Chair

Joxan Jaffar (National University of Singapore, Singapore)

## Program Chair

Zhong Shao (Yale University, USA)

## Program Committee

Lars Birkedal (IT University of Copenhagen, Denmark)
Martin Hofmann (University of Munich, Germany)
Kohei Honda (Queen Mary, University of London, UK)
Atsushi Igarashi (Kyoto University, Japan)
Suresh Jagannathan (Purdue University, USA)
Annie Liu (State University of New York at Stony Brook, USA)
Shin-Cheng Mu (Academia Sinica, Taiwan)
Henrik Nilsson (University of Nottingham, UK)
Michael Norrish (NICTA, Australia)
Jens Palsberg (University of California, Los Angeles, USA)
G. Ramalingam (Microsoft Research, India)
Zhendong Su (University of California, Davis, USA)
Martin Sulzmann (National University of Singapore, Singapore)
Eijiro Sumii (Tohoku University, Japan)
Jérôme Vouillon (CNRS, France)
Kwangkeun Yi (Seoul National University, Korea)
Jian Zhang (Chinese Academy of Sciences, China)

## Local Arrangements Chair

Wei-Ngan Chin (National University of Singapore, Singapore)

## Poster Chair

Eijiro Sumii (Tohoku University, Japan)

## External Referees

Andreas Abel
Tomoyuki Aotani
Kenichi Asai
Earl Barr
Josh Berdine
Lennart Beringer
Bodil Biering
Maria Paola Bonacina
Michele Boreale
Sugwoo Byun
Pavol Cerny
Supratik Chakraborty
Yiyun Chen
Troels Damgaard
Abhishek Das
Jeremy Dawson
Søren Debois
Yuxin Deng
Daniel Dougherty
Gregory Duck
Steven Eker
Hyunjun Eo
Manuel Fahndrich
Xinyu Feng
Cedric Fournet
Mark Gabel
Michael Gorbovitski
Hermann Gruber
Sumit Gulwani
Ichiro Hasuo
Si-Min He
Daniel Hirschkoff
Haruo Hosoya
Katia Hristova
Barry Jay
Bertrand Jeannet
Alan Jeffrey
Lingxiao Jiang
Jan Johannsen
Yungbum Jung
Deokhwan Kim
Satoshi Kobayashi
Elliot Kolodner
Soonho Kong
Martin Lange
Julia Lawall
Jimmy Lee
Oukseh Lee
Heejong Lee
Sorin Lerner
Lei Liu
Brian Logan
HW Loidl
Lunjin Lu
Wolfgang Lux
Roman Manevich
Mircea Marin
Aart Middeldorp
Matthew Might
Arjan Mooij
Mayur Naik
Koji Nakazawa
Hakjoo Oh
Luke Ong
Sungwoo Park
Daejun Park
Benjamin Pierce
Herbert Prähofer
Murali K. Ramanathan
Julian Rathke
Tamara Rezk
Andreas Rossberg
Tom Rothamel
Abhik Roychoudhury
Alejandro Russo
Ondřej Rypáček
Andrei Sabelfeld
Chieri Saito
Davide Sangiorgi
Ulrich Schoepp
Xipeng Shen
Christian Stefansen
Scott Stoller
K. Tuncay Tekle
Rene Thiemann
Alwen Tiu
Seiji Umatani
Tarmo Uustalu
Kapil Vaswani
Alexander Vaynberg
Maria Grazia Vigliotti
Mirko Viroli
Walter Vogler
Razvan Voicu
David Walker
Liqiang Wang
Meng Wang
Bow-Yaw Wang
Gary Wassermann
Jun Wei
Tao Wei
Ye Yang
Hongseok Yang
Shoji Yuen
Gianluigi Zavattaro
Naijun Zhan

## Sponsoring Institutions

Asian Association for Foundation of Software (AAFS)
National University of Singapore

# Table of Contents

## Session 4



## Session 5



## Session 6



## Invited Talk 3



## Session 7

## Session 8



## Session 9

# X10: Concurrent Programming for Modern Architectures

Vijay Saraswat

IBM TJ Watson Research Center
PO Box 704, Yorktown Heights, NY 10598

**Abstract.** Two major trends are converging to reshape the landscape of concurrent object-oriented programming languages. First, trends in modern architectures (multi-core, accelerators, high performance clusters such as Blue Gene) are making concurrency and distribution inescapable for large classes of OO programmers. Second, experience with first-generation concurrent OO languages (e.g. Java threads and synchronization) have revealed several drawbacks of unstructured threads with lock-based synchronization.

X10 is a second generation OO language designed to address both programmer productivity and parallel performance for modern architectures. It extends the sequential Java programming language with a handful of constructs for concurrency and distribution: a clustered address space (with global data-structures) to deal with distribution; lightweight asynchrony to deal with massive parallelism; recursive fork-join parallelism for structured concurrency; termination detection for sequencing, and atomic blocks for mutual exclusion.

Additionally, it introduces a rich framework for constraint-based dependent types (and annotations) in OO languages. Specifically, the framework is useful for statically specifying the shape of various data-structures (e.g. multidimensional arrays) and the location of objects and distribution of arrays in the clustered address space.

X10 is being developed jointly with several colleagues (at IBM and elsewhere) as part of the DARPA-IBM high performance computing project, PERCS. X10 is being developed under the Eclipse open-source licence. A first implementation of the language is available at `http://x10.sf.net`. It compiles X10 source programs to Java class files and calls to a runtime. A distributed implementation suitable for clusters is currently under development.

This material is based upon work supported by the Defense Advanced Research Projects Agency under its Agreement No. HR0011-07-9-0002.

Z. Shao (Ed.): APLAS 2007, LNCS 4807, p. 1, 2007.

# The Nuggetizer: Abstracting Away Higher-Orderness for Program Verification

Paritosh Shroff[1], Christian Skalka[2], and Scott F. Smith[1]

[1] The Johns Hopkins University, Baltimore, MD, USA
{pari,scott}@cs.jhu.edu
[2] The University of Vermont, Burlington, VT, USA
skalka@cs.uvm.edu

**Abstract.** We develop a static analysis which distills first-order computational structure from higher-order functional programs. The analysis condenses higher-order programs into a first-order rule-based system, a *nugget*, that characterizes all value bindings that may arise from program execution. Theorem provers are limited in their ability to automatically reason about higher-order programs; nuggets address this problem, being inductively defined structures that can be simply and directly encoded in a theorem prover. The theorem prover can then prove non-trivial program properties, such as the range of values assignable to particular variables at runtime. Our analysis is flow- and path-sensitive, and incorporates a novel *prune-rerun* analysis technique to approximate higher-order recursive computations.

**Keywords:** program analysis, higher-order, 0CFA, program verification.

## 1 Introduction

Higher-order functional programming is a powerful programming metaphor, but it is also complex from a program analysis standpoint: the actual low-level operations and the order in which they take place are far removed from the source code. It is the simpler first-order view that is easiest for automated verification methods to be applied to. In this paper we focus on defining a new form of program abstraction which distills the first-order computational structure from higher-order functional programs. The analysis is novel in how it condenses higher-order programs into a first-order inductive system, a *nugget*, which characterizes all value bindings that can result from program execution. Nuggets can be extracted automatically from the program source of any untyped functional language, and without any need for programmer annotation.

A major advantage of the nuggets is that they are inductively defined structures which can be directly expressed as inductive definitions in a theorem prover. So in effect, our analysis produces an output, a *nugget*, which is ideally suited as input to a theorem prover. We use Isabelle/HOL [1] to reason about nuggets in this paper since it has built-in mechanisms to define and reason about inductively defined first-order entities (although other provers with a similar mechanism, e.g. ACL2 [2], could be employed as well). The theorem prover can then be used to

Z. Shao (Ed.): APLAS 2007, LNCS 4807, pp. 2–18, 2007.

automatically prove desirable properties of the corresponding program. Putting these steps together gives a method for automatically proving complex inductive properties of higher-order programs. The alternative approach to formally prove program properties in a theorem prover involves writing an operational or denotational semantics for the programs and proving facts about those definitions, or using an existing axiomatized programming logic. While these approaches are effective, there is a high user overhead due to all of the program features such as higher-order functions that clutter up the semantics or axioms, and a great deal of time and effort is thus required. Nuggets are not complete in that some program information is abstracted out, but enough information remains for a wide class of program properties to be verified. So, we are trading off the completeness of full verification for the speed and simplicity of partial verification. For concreteness, we focus here on solving the *value range* problem for functional programs—deducing the range of values that integer variables can take on at runtime. While this is a narrow problem it is a non-trivial one, and it serves as a testbed for our approach. Our analysis grew out of a type-and-effect constraint type system [3], and is also related to abstract interpretation [4].

## 2 Informal Overview

In this section we give an informal description of our analysis. We start by showing the form of the nuggets, their expressiveness, and the technique to prove properties they encapsulate. Then we describe the nugget-generation algorithm. Consider the following simple untyped higher-order program which computes the factorial of 5, using recursion encoded by "self-passing",

$$\begin{array}{l}\mathsf{let}\ f = \lambda fact.\,\lambda n.\,\mathsf{if}\ (n\ != 0)\ \mathsf{then}\ n * fact\ fact\ (n-1)\ \mathsf{else}\ 1 \\ \mathsf{in}\ f\ f\ 5\ .\end{array} \quad (1)$$

We want to statically analyze the range of values assignable to the variable $n$ during the course of computation of the above program. Obviously this program will recurse for $n$ from 5 down to 0, each time with the condition $(n\ != 0)$ holding, until finally $n = 0$, thus the range of values assignable to $n$ is $[0, \ldots, 5]$. The particular goal of this paper is to define an analysis to automatically infer basic properties such as value ranges. For non-recursive programs it is not hard to completely track such ranges; the challenge is to track ranges in the presence higher-order recursive functions.

### 2.1 Nuggets

There is a huge array of potential program abstractions to consider: type systems, abstract interpretations, compiler analyses, etc. All of these can be viewed as abstracting away certain properties from program executions. Type systems tend to abstract away the control-flow, that is, flow- and path-sensitivity, but retain much of the data-flow including infinite datatype domains; abstract interpretations, on the other hand, generally make finitary abstractions on infinite datatype domains, but tend to preserve flow- and path-sensitivity. Our approach is somewhat unique in that we wish to abstract away only the higher-order nature of functional programs, and preserve as much of the other behavior as possible, including flow- and path-sensitivity, infinite datatype domains, and other inductive program structure.

The core of our analysis is the *nuggetizer*, which automatically extracts *nuggets* from source programs. We begin with a description of the nuggets themselves and their role in proving program properties; subsequently, we discuss the nuggetizing process itself.

Nuggets are purely first-order inductive definitions; they may contain higher-order functions but in a nugget they mean nothing, they are just atomic data. All higher-order flows that can occur in the original program execution are reduced to their underlying first-order actions on data by the *nuggetizer*, the algorithm for constructing nuggets described in the next subsection. We illustrate the form and the features of nuggets by considering the nugget produced by the nuggetizer for program (1),

$$\text{Nugget: } \left\{ n \mapsto 5, n \mapsto (n-1)^{n\,!=0} \right\} . \tag{2}$$

(We are leaving out the trivial mappings for $f$ and *fact* here.) As can be seen, nuggets are sets of mappings from variables to simple expressions—all higher-order functions in program (1) have been expanded. The mapping $n \mapsto 5$ represents the initial value 5 passed in to the function $(\lambda n. \ldots)$ in program (1). The mapping $n \mapsto (n-1)^{n\,!=0}$ additionally contains a *guard*, $n \,!= 0$, which is a precondition on the usage of this mapping, analogous to its role in dictating the course of program (1)'s computation. Note the inductive nature of this mapping: $n$ maps to $n-1$ given the guard $n \,!= 0$ holds. The mapping can then be read as: during the course of program (1)'s execution, $n$ may be also bound to $(n_i - 1)$, for some value $n_i$, such that $n \mapsto n_i$ is an already known binding for $n$, and the guard $n_i \,!= 0$ holds. It corresponds to the fact that the recursive invocation of function $(\lambda n. \ldots)$ at call-site '(*fact fact*) $(n-1)$' during program (1)'s computation results in $(n_i - 1)$ being the new binding for $n$, given $n$ is currently bound to $n_i$ and the guard $n_i \,!= 0$ holds.

*Denotational semantics of nuggets.* Nuggets are in fact nothing more than inductive definitions of sets of possible values for the variables—the least set of values implied by the mappings such that their guards hold. So, the denotational semantics of a nugget is nothing more than the values given by this inductive definition. The above nugget has the denotation

$$\{n \mapsto 5, n \mapsto 4, n \mapsto 3, n \mapsto 2, n \mapsto 1, n \mapsto 0\} .$$

This is because $n \mapsto 0$ does not satisfy the guard $n \,!= 0$, implying it cannot be inlined in the right side of mapping $n \mapsto (n-1)^{n\,!=0}$, to generate the mapping $n \mapsto (-1)$ for $n$. Notice that the above nugget precisely denotes the range of values assignable to $n$ during the course of program (1)'s computation.

The key soundness property is: a nugget $N$ for a program $p$ must denote each variable $x$ in $p$ to be mapping to *at least* the values that may occur during the run of $p$. Thus the nugget (2) above serves to soundly establish the range of $n$

to be $[0, \ldots, 5]$ in program (1), which is also precise in this case: $n$ will take on exactly these values at runtime.

*Defining and reasoning about nuggets in Isabelle/HOL.* Properties of a nugget can be manually computed as we did above, but our goal is to automate proofs of such properties. Since nuggets are inductive definitions, any nugget can be automatically translated into an equivalent inductive definition in a theorem prover. The theorem prover can then be used to directly prove, for example, that $0 \leq n \leq 5$ in program (1). The Isabelle/HOL encoding of the above nugget is presented in Section 5. Theorem proving aligns particularly well with nuggets for two reasons: 1) since arbitrary Diophantine equations can be expressed as nuggets there can be no complete decision procedure; and, 2) theorem provers have built-in mechanisms for writing inductive definitions, and proof strategies thereupon.

*Two more complex examples.* To show that the nuggets can account for fancier higher-order recursion, consider a variation of the above program which employs a fixed-point combinator $\mathsf{Z} = \lambda f.\, (\lambda x.\, f\ (\lambda y.\, x\ x\ y))\ (\lambda x.\, f\ (\lambda y.\, x\ x\ y))$ to perform recursion. Z is a version of the Y combinator, given by $\eta$-expansion on a part of it, to be used in call-by-value evaluations.

$$\mathsf{let}\ f' = \left(\lambda \mathit{fact}.\lambda n.\, \mathsf{if}\ (n \mathrel{!=} 0)\ \mathsf{then}\ n * \mathit{fact}\ \ (n-1)\ \mathsf{else}\ 1\right)\ \mathsf{in}\ \mathsf{Z}\ f'\ 5\ . \tag{3}$$

The nugget at $n$ as extracted by the nuggetizer is $\{n \mapsto 5, n \mapsto y, y \mapsto (n-1)^{n\,!=0}\}$ which, by transitive closure, maps $n$ equivalently as in nugget (2). The more complex higher-order structure of the above program proves no more demanding to the nuggetizer.

Now, consider another variation of program (1), but with higher-order mutual recursion,

$$\begin{array}{l}\mathsf{let}\ g = \lambda \mathit{fact}'.\, \lambda m.\, \mathit{fact}'\ \mathit{fact}'\ (m-1)\ \mathsf{in} \\ \mathsf{let}\ f = \lambda \mathit{fact}.\, \lambda n.\, \mathsf{if}\ (n \mathrel{!=} 0)\ \mathsf{then}\ n * g\ \mathit{fact}\ n\ \mathsf{else}\ 1 \\ \mathsf{in}\ f\ f\ 5\ .\end{array} \tag{4}$$

The nugget at $n$ and $m$ as extracted by the nuggetizer is,

$$\text{Nugget: } \{n \mapsto 5, m \mapsto n^{n\,!=0}, n \mapsto (m-1)\}\ . \tag{5}$$

The mutually recursive computational structure between the functions $(\lambda n.\ \ldots)$ and $(\lambda m.\ \ldots)$ in the above program is reflected as a mutual dependency between the mappings of $n$ and $m$ in the extracted nugget above. The denotational semantics at $n$ and $m$ for the above nugget are,

$$\begin{array}{l}\{n \mapsto 5, n \mapsto 4, n \mapsto 3, n \mapsto 2, n \mapsto 1, n \mapsto 0\} \text{ and} \\ \{m \mapsto 5, m \mapsto 4, m \mapsto 3, m \mapsto 2, m \mapsto 1\},\end{array}$$

respectively. Note the binding $m \mapsto 0$ is not added because the guard $n \mathrel{!=} 0$ on the mapping $m \mapsto n^{n\,!=0}$ fails—even though the mapping $n \mapsto 0$ is present, it does not satisfy the guard $n \mathrel{!=} 0$ and hence cannot be used to generate the mapping $m \mapsto 0$.

*External inputs.* The above examples assume a concrete value, such as 5, to be flowing into functions. In general the value can come from an input channel, and properties can still be proven. Since we do not have input statements in our language, we only sketch how inputs can be handled. Imagine a symbolic placeholder, **inp**, corresponding to the input value. Now consider the nugget, $\{n \mapsto \mathbf{inp}^{\mathbf{inp} \geq 0}, n \mapsto (n-1)^{n\,!=0}\}$, extracted from a program which invokes the factorial function, from the above examples, on **inp** under the guard $\mathbf{inp} \geq 0$. The bindings for $n$ in the denotation of this nugget lie in the *symbolic* range $[0, \ldots, \mathbf{inp}]$, which, along with the guard $\mathbf{inp} \geq 0$, establishes that $n$ is never assigned a negative number over any program run.

### 2.2 The Nuggetizer

We now describe the process for creating nuggets, the *nuggetizer*. It constructs the nugget via a collecting semantics—the nugget is incrementally accumulated over an abstract execution of the program.

*The challenge.* Our goal is to abstract away only the higher-orderness of programs and preserve as much of the other behavior as possible including flow- and path-sensitivity, and infinite datatype domains. In other words, we aim to define an abstract operational semantics (AOS) which structurally aligns very closely with the concrete operational semantics (COS) of programs. This is a non-trivial problem as concrete executions of programs with recursively invoked functions may not terminate; however, abstract executions must always terminate in order to achieve a decidable static analysis. Further, recursive function invocations need not be immediately apparent in the source code of higher-order programs due to the use of Y-combinators, etc., making them hard to detect and even harder to soundly approximate while preserving much of their inductive structure at the same time.

*The AOS.* Our AOS is a form of environment-based operational semantics, wherein the environment collects abstract mappings such as $n \mapsto (n-1)^{n\,!=0}$; the environment is monotonically increasing, in that, mappings are only added, and never removed from the environment. The AOS closely follows the control-flow of the COS, that is, the AOS is flow-sensitive. Further, the AOS keeps track of all guards that are active at all points of the abstract execution, and tags the abstract mappings with the guards in force at the point of their addition to the environment; the AOS is path-sensitive. So for example, when analyzing the then-branch of the above programs, the AOS tags all mappings with the active guard $n \mathrel{!=} 0$, before adding them to the environment, as for mappings $n \mapsto (n-1)^{n\,!=0}$ and $m \mapsto n^{n\,!=0}$ in nuggets (2) and (5), respectively.

*The prune-rerun technique.* A novel *prune-rerun* technique at the heart of the nuggetizer is pivotal to ensuring its convergence and soundness in presence of a flow-sensitive AOS. All recursive function invocations are *pruned*, possibly at the expense of some soundness, to ensure convergence of the AOS. The AOS is then repeatedly *rerun* on the program, a (provably) finite number of times, while accumulating mapping across subsequent runs, until all soundness lost by way of pruning, if any, is regained.

*Finiteness of the abstract environment.* The domain and range of all mappings added to the environment during abstract execution, e.g. $n$, $y$, $m$, 5, $(n-1)$, $(m-1)$ and $(n \mathrel{!=} 0)$ in the above shown nuggets, are fragments that *directly* appear in corresponding source programs—no new subexpressions are *ever* created in the nuggets, either by substitution or otherwise. For this reason, the maximum number of distinct mappings in the abstract environment of the AOS is finite for any given program. Since the nuggetizer accumulates mappings across subsequent runs of the AOS on a given program, all feasible mappings must eventually appear in the environment after some finite number of reruns. Thus the environment must stop growing and the analysis must terminate, producing the nugget of the program.

*An Illustration.* We now discuss the abstract execution of program (1) placed in an A-normal form [5], for technical convenience, as follows:

$$\begin{array}{l}\mathsf{let}\ f = \lambda fact.\,\lambda n.\,\mathsf{let}\ r = \mathsf{if}\ (n \mathrel{!=} 0)\ \mathsf{then}\ \mathsf{let}\ r' = fact\ fact\ (n-1)\\ \qquad\qquad\qquad\qquad\qquad\qquad\qquad\qquad\quad \mathsf{in}\ n * r'\\ \qquad\qquad\qquad\qquad\qquad\qquad\qquad\quad \mathsf{else}\ 1\\ \qquad\qquad\qquad\quad \mathsf{in}\ r\\ \mathsf{in}\ f\ f\ 5\ .\end{array} \tag{6}$$

The abstract execution of the above program closely follows the control-flow of its concrete execution. It is summarized in Fig. 1. The column labeled "Stack" indicates the state of the abstract stack at the corresponding step. The "Collected Mappings" column indicates the mappings collected by the nuggetizer, if any, during the indicated step. The collected mappings are added to the environment of the nuggetizer, and so the environment at any step is the union of all collected mappings up to the current step. The environment is initially empty. The "Curr. Guard(s)" column , where "Curr." is short for "Current", indicates the guard(s) in force, if any, at the corresponding step. The "Redex" column holds the redex of the abstract execution at the end of the corresponding step. We now highlight the significant steps in Fig. 1.

*Setup and forking the branches.* During step 1, the mapping of $f$ to $(\lambda fact.\,\lambda n \ldots)$ is collected in the environment, and then the function $(\lambda fact.\,\lambda n \ldots)$ is invoked during step 2 by placing it in the abstract stack and collecting the mapping $fact \mapsto f$. Step 3 pops the stack and results in the function application '$(\lambda n \ldots)\ 5$' being the redex at the end of step 3. Step 4 invokes the function $(\lambda n \ldots)$ by placing it in the abstract stack and collecting the mapping $n \mapsto 5$. At step 5 the abstract execution is forked into two, such that the then- and else-branches are analyzed in parallel under their corresponding guards, that is, $(n \mathrel{!=} 0)$ and $(n == 0)$, and under the subcolumns labeled 'T' and 'F', respectively; since the abstract stack remains unchanged during each of these parallel executions, only one column labeled 'T/F' is used for brevity.

Now, as $n$ is bound to only 5 in the environment, the guard $(n \mathrel{!=} 0)$ is resolvable to only true, and we could have chosen to analyze only the then-branch at step 5; however, that would have required invocation of a decision

| # | *Stack* | *Collected Mappings* | | *Curr. Guard(s)* | | *Redex* | | *Next Action* | |
|---|---|---|---|---|---|---|---|---|---|
| 0 | | | | | | let $f =$ $(\lambda fact.\lambda n\ldots)$ in $f\ f\ 5$ | | collect let-binding | |
| 1 | | $f \mapsto (\lambda fact.\lambda n\ldots)$ | | | | $f\ f\ 5$ | | invoke $f$ | |
| 2 | $(\lambda fact.$ $\lambda n\ldots)$ | $fact \mapsto f$ | | | | $((\lambda n\ldots))\ 5$ | | pop $(\lambda fact.\lambda n\ldots)$ | |
| 3 | | | | | | $(\lambda n\ldots)\ 5$ | | invoke $(\lambda n\ldots)$ | |
| 4 | $(\lambda n\ldots)$ | $n \mapsto 5$ | | | | let $r =$ (if $(n\,!{=}\,0)$ ...) in $r$ | | fork execution | |
| | T/F | T | F | T | F | T | F | T | F |
| 5 | $(\lambda n\ldots)$ | | | $n\,!{=}\,0$ | $n{=}{=}0$ | let $r' =$ $fact\ fact\ (n-1)$ in $n * r'$ | 1 | invoke $fact$ | nop |
| 6 | $(\lambda n\ldots)$ | $fact \mapsto fact^{n\,!=0}$ | | $n\,!{=}\,0$ | $n{=}{=}0$ | let $r' =$ $(\lambda n\ldots)\ (n-1)$ in $n * r'$ | 1 | prune re-activation of $(\lambda n\ldots)$ | nop |
| 7 | $(\lambda n\ldots)$ | $n \mapsto (n-1)^{n\,!=0}$ $r' \mapsto r$ | | $n\,!{=}\,0$ | $n{=}{=}0$ | $n * r'$ | 1 | merge executions | |
| 8 | $(\lambda n\ldots)$ | $r \mapsto (n * r')^{n\,!=0}$ $r \mapsto 1^{n==0}$ | | | | $(r)$ | | pop $(\lambda n\ldots)$ | |
| 9 | | | | | | $r$ | | | |

**Fig. 1.** Example: Abstract Execution of Program (6)

procedure at the branch site to decide on the branch(es) needing analysis given the current environment. Since the environment can have multiple bindings for the same variable, it is likely that a branching condition will resolve to both true and false in which case both branches would have to be analyzed in any case. So, for efficiency we forgo the decision procedure and always analyze both branches in parallel. Note that this does not lead to a loss in precision as all mappings collected during the abstract execution of each of the branches are predicated on their respective guards, thus preserving the conditional information in the nugget. Step 6 under subcolumn labeled 'T', is similar to step 2, except the collected mapping, $fact \mapsto fact^{n\,!=0}$, is now tagged with the current guard, $n\,!= 0$.

*Pruning recursion.* The redex $(\lambda n\ldots)\ (n-1)$ at the end of step 6 entails a recursive invocation of the function $(\lambda n\ldots)$, which is already on the stack. The abstract execution has two options at this point: i) follow the recursive invocation, as the concrete execution would, opening the possibility of divergence if later recursive invocations are followed likewise, or ii) *prune*, that is, ignore, the recursive invocation in order to achieve convergence, while (possibly) losing soundness. The first option is obviously infeasible to obtain a convergent analysis, hence we choose the second option. We show later that soundness can be achieved by simply rerunning the abstract execution. The pruning of the function invocation, $(\lambda n \ldots)\ (n-1)$, involves (a) collecting the mapping, $n \mapsto (n-1)^{n\,!=0}$, which captures the flow of the symbolic argument $(n-1)$, under the guard $n\,!=0$, to the parameter variable $n$, and (b) skipping over the abstract execution of the body of $(\lambda n \ldots)$ by collecting the mapping $r' \mapsto r$, simulating the immediate return from the recursive invocation. Now, since the function was *not* in fact recursively invoked, the abstract execution is yet to collect any binding for $r$, hence, at this point in the abstract execution, $r$ only serves as a *placeholder* for the return value of the recursive call, to be filled in by later analysis. We say return variables $r$ and transitively, $r'$, are *inchoate* as of the end of step 7 since they have no mappings in the environment. Consequently, later invocations of $r$ and $r'$, if any, would be skipped over as well until they are choate (this example, however, has no such invocations). (Note, the mapping $r' \mapsto r$ is not tagged with any guard so as to allow any binding for $r$, that may appear later, to be transitively bound to $r'$ as well.)

This pruning technique was in fact inspired by the type closure rule for function application in type constraint systems (which is itself isomorphic [6] to 0CFA's [7] handling of function application): $\tau_1 \rightarrow \tau_2 <: \tau_1' \rightarrow \tau_2'$ implies $\tau_1' <: \tau_1$ and $\tau_2 <: \tau_2'$. The recursive invocation at step 7 can be thought of as generating a type constraint $n \rightarrow r <: (n-1) \rightarrow r'$ (punning by using program point expressions as type variables) which by the above function type closure rule would give $(n-1) <: n$ and $r <: r'$, which are in turn isomorphic in structure to the mappings collected in step 7, minus the guard. So, this work can be viewed as a method of extending type constraints or 0CFA to incorporate flow- and path-sensitivity while preserving infinite datatype domains. The close alignment of the AOS with the COS imparts flow-sensitivity to our analysis, while the guards on the mappings furnish path-sensitivity.

*Merging branches and completing.* Step 8 merges the completed executions of the two branches by collecting the resulting values tagged with their corresponding guards, that is, adding mappings $r \mapsto (n * r')^{n\,!=0}$ and $r \mapsto 1^{n==0}$, respectively, depicting the flow of each of the tagged resulting values into the outer let-binding $(\mathsf{let}\ r = \ (\mathsf{if}\ \ldots)\ \mathsf{in}\ r)$. Now $r$ and, by transitivity, $r'$ are no longer inchoate. The redex at the end of step 8 is $(r)$. Step 9 pops the stack, and the abstract execution terminates.

*Environment has a fixed-point.* The environment at the end of this abstract execution is,

$$\begin{aligned}\{f \mapsto (\lambda \mathit{fact}.\, \lambda n \ldots), \mathit{fact} \mapsto f, \mathit{fact} \mapsto \mathit{fact}^{n\,!=0}, \\ n \mapsto 5, n \mapsto (n-1)^{n\,!=0}, r' \mapsto r, r \mapsto (n * r')^{n\,!=0}, r \mapsto 1^{n==0}\}\ ,\end{aligned} \tag{7}$$

which is, in fact, the nugget for program (6). It is identical to (2) but with the mappings elided there now shown. In general, the nugget is the least fixed-point of the symbolic mappings collectable by the AOS for a given program. A *rerun* of the AOS on the program (6), but this time using the above environment as its initial environment, will yield the same environment at its end *i.e.*, it is a fixed-point. In general, however, the initial run need not result in a fixed-point of the environment.

*The need for rerunning* The above example does not need to be rerun other than to observe that a fixed-point has been reached. To show the need for rerunning, consider the following variation of program (6) where the return value of the function $(\lambda n \ldots)$ is changed to be a function,

$$\begin{aligned}
&\mathsf{let}\ f = \lambda fact.\,\lambda n.\,\mathsf{let}\ r = \mathsf{if}\ (n\ != 0)\ \mathsf{then}\ \mathsf{let}\ r' = fact\ fact\ (n-1)\ \mathsf{in} \\
&\qquad\qquad\qquad\qquad\qquad\qquad\qquad\quad \mathsf{let}\ r'' = r'()\ \mathsf{in} \\
&\qquad\qquad\qquad\qquad\qquad\qquad\qquad\qquad \lambda y.\,(n * r'') \\
&\qquad\qquad\qquad\qquad\qquad\qquad\quad \mathsf{else}\ \lambda x.\,1 \\
&\qquad\qquad\qquad\quad \mathsf{in}\ r \\
&\quad \mathsf{in}\ f\ f\ 5\ ()\ .
\end{aligned} \tag{8}$$

During the initial run of the AOS on the above program, the return variable $r'$ is inchoate in the analysis of the then-branch, as in the previous example. Hence, when the redex is '$r'()$', the environment of the abstract execution has no known function mapping to $r'$. So the abstract execution simply skips over the call site '$r'()$' and proceeds without adding any mapping for $r''$, either. At the merging of the branches the abstract execution adds the mappings $r \mapsto (\lambda y.\, n * r'')^{n\,!=0}$ and $r \mapsto (\lambda x.\,1)^{n==0}$ to the environment, finally giving mappings to $r$ and $r'$. Since the AOS is flow-sensitive it must *not* now jump back, out of context, to the skipped-over call-site '$r'()$' and reanalyze it with the now-known bindings for $r'$—if it were to do so it would lose flow-sensitive information. Although the pruning step was inspired by flow-insensitive type constraint systems, as discussed above, the closure process in a constraint system is flow-*in*-sensitive and can ignore the order of steps; we cannot follow that lead here and must instead align the closure step order with the computation itself. The way we achieve this alignment is by continuing with and finishing the current run, and then *rerunning* the AOS on the same program, but with an initial environment of the one at the end of the just concluded run. This rerun will collect the new bindings for the call $r'()$ in proper execution order, and the environment at the end of the rerun will be

$$\begin{aligned}
&\{f \mapsto (\lambda fact.\,\lambda n \ldots), fact \mapsto f, fact \mapsto fact^{n\,!=0}, n \mapsto 5, n \mapsto (n-1)^{n\,!=0}, \\
&\ x \mapsto ()^{n\,!=0}, y \mapsto ()^{n\,!=0}, r' \mapsto r, r \mapsto (\lambda y.\, n * r'')^{n\,!=0}, r \mapsto (\lambda x.\,1)^{n==0}, \\
&\ r'' \mapsto 1^{n==0}, r'' \mapsto (n * r'')^{n\,!=0}\}\ ,
\end{aligned}$$

This is in fact the least fixed-point of the mappings collected for program (8), that is, the *nugget*; the AOS is run one last time to verify a fixed-point has indeed been reached. As pointed out earlier, the maximum size of the environment is strongly bound by the number of program subexpressions, and the environment itself is monotonically increasing in size during the course of nuggetizing, thus it must always converge at a fixed-point nugget. The number of reruns required by the nuggetizer depends on the level of nesting of higher-order recursive functions which themselves return functions; we believe it will be small in practice.

*Value range of return values.* The core analysis tracks function argument values well, but loses information on values returned from recursive functions. The part of the nugget (7) at the return variable $r$ of the function $(\lambda n \ldots)$ is,

$$\{n \mapsto 5, n \mapsto (n-1)^{n\,!=0}, r \mapsto 1^{n==0}, r \mapsto (n * r)^{n\,!=0}\} \ . \tag{9}$$

Note the mapping $r' \mapsto r$ is inlined into mapping $r \mapsto (n * r)^{n\,!=0}$ for simplicity. Observe that $r$ in the range of the mapping $r \mapsto (n * r)^{n\,!=0}$ is not guarded—in effect allowing *any* known value of $r$ to be multiplied with *any* known non-zero value of $n$ in order to generate a new value for $r$. The denotational semantics at $n$ and $r$ of the above nugget is,

$$\{n \mapsto 0, n \mapsto 1, n \mapsto 2, n \mapsto 3, n \mapsto 4, n \mapsto 5\} \text{ and}$$

$$\{r \mapsto 1, r \mapsto 2, r \mapsto 6, r \mapsto 24, r \mapsto 120, r \mapsto 5, r \mapsto 8, r \mapsto 18, r \mapsto 48, \ldots\}$$

which is sound but not precise at $r$: $r$ maps to 5 because $n \mapsto 5$ and $r \mapsto 1$ are present, but 5 is not in the range of runtime values assignable to $r$. The correlation between the argument and return values of recursive function invocations is not captured by the nuggetizer while pruning re-activations of a function, as shown in step 7 of Fig. 1 for $(\lambda n \ldots)$; hence, precision for the analyzed return value is lost. The nuggetizer can, however, be extended to capture the above mentioned correlation and thus perform a precise analysis on the range of return values as well; this extension is presented in [8].

*Incompleteness.* To better show the scope of the analysis, we give an example of an incomplete nugget, the handling of which is beyond the scope of this paper. The following program is inspired by a bidirectional bubble sort.

$$\begin{array}{l} \mathsf{let}\ f = \lambda sort.\, \lambda x.\, \lambda limit.\, \mathsf{if}\ (x < limit)\ \mathsf{then}\ sort\ sort\ (x+1)\ (limit-1) \\ \qquad\qquad\qquad\qquad\qquad\qquad\qquad\qquad\quad \mathsf{else}\ 1 \\ \mathsf{in}\ f\ f\ 0\ 9\ . \end{array} \tag{10}$$

The nugget at $x$ and *limit* as extracted by the nuggetizer is,

$$\{x \mapsto 0, x \mapsto (x+1)^{x < limit}, limit \mapsto 9, limit \mapsto (limit-1)^{x < limit}\}$$

and their corresponding denotational semantics are,

$$\{x \mapsto 0, x \mapsto 1, \ldots, x \mapsto 9\}, \text{ and } \{limit \mapsto 9, limit \mapsto 8, \ldots, limit \mapsto 0\},$$

respectively; while the exact ranges of values assigned to $x$ and *limit* during the computation of the above program are $[0, 5]$ and $[4, 9]$ respectively. The nuggetizer does not record the correlation between the order of assignments to $x$ and *limit* in the computation of the above program, that is, the fact that the assignment of $(x+1)$ to $x$ is immediately followed by the assignment of $(limit-1)$ to *limit*, and vice-versa. Note, however, that the analysis still manages to bound $x$ to a narrow range—if $x$ had been used as an index into an array of length 10, then the above nugget could have been used to prove that all accesses to such an array would be in-bounds.

## 3 Language Model and Concrete Operational Semantics

Our programming language model is an untyped pure higher-order functional language with variables $x$, integers $i$, booleans $b \in \{\mathsf{true}, \mathsf{false}\}$, and

| | | |
|---|---|---|
| $\oplus$ | $::= + \mid - \mid * \mid / \mid == \mid != \mid < \mid >$ | *binary operator* |
| $F$ | $::= \lambda x.\, p$ | *function* |
| $\eta$ | $::= x \mid i \mid b \mid F \mid x \oplus x$ | *lazy value* |
| $\kappa$ | $::= \eta \mid p \mid x\ x$ | *atomic computation* |
| $p$ | $::= x \mid \mathsf{let}\ x = \kappa\ \mathsf{in}\ p$ | *A-normal program* |
| | $\langle \eta, \mathrm{E} \rangle$ | *concrete closure* |
| $\mathrm{E}$ | $::= \{\overline{x \mapsto \langle \eta, \mathrm{E} \rangle}\}$ | *concrete environment* |

The grammar assumes expressions are already in an A-normal form [5], so that each program point has an associated program variable. $\langle \eta, \mathrm{E} \rangle$ represents a closure, for a lazy (discussed below) value $\eta$, and an environment E. The overbar notation indicates zero or more comma separated repetitions and $\{\cdot\}$ denotes a set, so for example '$\{\overline{x \mapsto \langle \eta, \mathrm{E} \rangle}\}$' is shorthand for the set '$\{x \mapsto \langle \eta, \mathrm{E} \rangle, x \mapsto \langle \eta, \mathrm{E} \rangle, \ldots\}$'; while the subscripted overbar notation denotes a fixed number of repetitions, such that, for example, '$\{\overline{x_k \mapsto \langle \eta_k, \mathrm{E}_k \rangle}\}$' where $k \geq 0$, is shorthand for the set '$\{x_1 \mapsto \langle \eta_1, \mathrm{E}_1 \rangle, x_2 \mapsto \langle \eta_2, \mathrm{E}_2 \rangle, \ldots, x_k \mapsto \langle \eta_k, \mathrm{E}_k \rangle\}$'. Fig. 2 gives the COS for our language. The semantics is *mixed-step*, that is, a combination of both small- and big-step reductions; it allows for an elegant alignment with the AOS. The COS is otherwise standard. The mixed-step reduction relation $\longrightarrow$ is defined over configurations, which are tuples, $(\mathrm{E}, p)$; while $\longrightarrow^n$ is the $n$-step reflexive (if $n = 0$) and transitive (otherwise) closure of $\longrightarrow$. The environment lookup function on variables is the partial function defined as, $\mathrm{E}(x) = \langle \eta', \mathrm{E}' \rangle$ iff $x \mapsto \langle \eta', \mathrm{E}' \rangle$ is the only binding for $x$ in E. The transitively closed environment $\lambda$-lookup function on variables and function values is inductively defined as, $\mathrm{E}(x)^{+\lambda} = \mathrm{E}'(\eta')^{+\lambda}$ iff $\mathrm{E}(x) = \langle \eta', \mathrm{E}' \rangle$, and $\mathrm{E}(F)^{+\lambda} = \langle F, \mathrm{E} \rangle$, respectively. The binary operations $(x \oplus x)$ are evaluated in a maximally lazy fashion; hence the term *lazy values*. So for example, the reduction of the abstract value $x + y$, given its environment $\{x \mapsto \langle 1, \emptyset \rangle, y \mapsto \langle 2, \emptyset \rangle\}$, to integer 3, is postponed until it is absolutely essential to do so for the computation to proceed, that is, the branching condition of the `if` rule needs to be resolved. Again, lazy values allow for a closer alignment between the COS and the AOS. The following function reduces a closure to its smallest equivalent form, or as we say "grounds" it.

**Definition 1 (Ground of a Concrete Closure).** *The function* $\llbracket \cdot \rrbracket : \{\overline{\langle \eta, \mathrm{E} \rangle}\} \rightarrow \{\overline{\langle \eta, \mathrm{E} \rangle}\}$ *is inductively defined as,*

1. $\llbracket \langle x, \mathrm{E} \rangle \rrbracket = \llbracket \mathrm{E}(x) \rrbracket$; $\llbracket \langle i, \mathrm{E} \rangle \rrbracket = \langle i, \emptyset \rangle$; $\llbracket \langle b, \mathrm{E} \rangle \rrbracket = \langle b, \emptyset \rangle$; $\llbracket \langle F, \mathrm{E} \rangle \rrbracket = \langle F, \mathrm{E}' \rangle$, *where* $\mathit{free}(F) \cap \mathit{dom}(\mathrm{E}) = \{\overline{x_k}\}$ *and* $\mathrm{E}' = \{\overline{x_k \mapsto \llbracket \langle x_k, \mathrm{E} \rangle \rrbracket}\}$; *and,*
2. $\llbracket \langle x_1 \oplus x_2, \mathrm{E} \rangle \rrbracket = \langle \eta, \emptyset \rangle$, *if* $\llbracket \langle x_1, \mathrm{E} \rangle \rrbracket = \langle i_1, \emptyset \rangle$, $\llbracket \langle x_2, \mathrm{E} \rangle \rrbracket = \langle i_2, \emptyset \rangle$, *and* $i_1 \oplus i_2 = \eta$; *else,* $\llbracket \langle x_1 \oplus x_2, \mathrm{E} \rangle \rrbracket = \langle x_1 \oplus x_2, \mathrm{E}' \rangle$, *where* $\mathrm{E}' = \{x_1 \mapsto \llbracket \langle x_1, \mathrm{E} \rangle \rrbracket, x_2 \mapsto \llbracket \langle x_2, \mathrm{E} \rangle \rrbracket\}$.

A program $p$ is said to be canonical iff all its local variables are distinct. The canonicality of programs allows new mappings to be simply appended to the environment in the semantics rules, as opposed to overwriting any previous bindings—by keeping local variables distinct we reduce the amount of renaming needed in the COS to zero. The function $\lfloor \cdot \rfloor : \{\overline{p}\} \rightarrow \{\overline{x}\}$ returns the variable $x$ serving as a placeholder for the result value of a program $p$; it is inductively defined as $\lfloor \mathsf{let}\ x = \kappa\ \mathsf{in}\ p \rfloor = \lfloor p \rfloor$, and $\lfloor x \rfloor = x$.

$$\frac{}{(\mathrm{E}, \mathsf{let}\ x = \eta\ \mathsf{in}\ p) \longrightarrow (\mathrm{E} \cup \{x \mapsto \langle \eta, \mathrm{E}\rangle\}, p)}\ \texttt{let}$$

$$\frac{\llbracket \langle x, \mathrm{E}\rangle \rrbracket = \langle b_i, \emptyset\rangle \qquad (b_1, b_2) = (\mathsf{true}, \mathsf{false}) \qquad (\mathrm{E}, p_i) \longrightarrow^n (\mathrm{E}', y')}{(\mathrm{E}, \mathsf{let}\ y = (p_2)\ \mathsf{in}\ p) \longrightarrow (\mathrm{E}' \cup \{y \mapsto \langle y', \mathrm{E}'\rangle\}, p)}\ \texttt{if}$$

$$\frac{\mathrm{E}(f)^{+\lambda} = \langle \lambda x.p, \mathrm{E}_f\rangle \qquad (\mathrm{E}_f \cup \{x \mapsto \langle x', \mathrm{E}\rangle\}, p) \longrightarrow^n (\mathrm{E}', r')}{(\mathrm{E}, \mathsf{let}\ r = f\ x'\ \mathsf{in}\ p_{next}) \longrightarrow (\mathrm{E} \cup \{r \mapsto \langle r', \mathrm{E}'\rangle\}, p_{next})}\ \texttt{app}$$

**Fig. 2.** Concrete Operational Semantics (COS) Rules

## 4 Abstract Operational Semantics and Nuggetizer

The additional syntax needed for the AOS is as follows:

$\mathcal{P} ::= b \mid \eta = \eta \mid \mathcal{P} \wedge \mathcal{P} \mid \mathcal{P} \vee \mathcal{P}$ — *predicate*
$\langle \eta, \mathcal{P}\rangle$ — *abstract closure*
$\mathcal{E} ::= \{\overline{x \mapsto \langle \eta, \mathcal{P}\rangle}\}$ — *abstract environment*
$\mathcal{S} ::= \{\overline{\langle F, \mathcal{P}\rangle}\}$ — *abstract "stack"*

The abstract environment $\mathcal{E}$ is a set of mappings from variables to abstract closures; it may have multiple mappings for the same variable. Unlike concrete closures, abstract closures $\langle \eta, \mathcal{P}\rangle$ do not come with full environments but with their abstracted forms, the predicates $\mathcal{P}$, which are simple propositional formulae. The predicate $\mathcal{P}$ was informally called a "guard" in Section 2, and notated slightly differently: for example, $n \mapsto (n-1)^{n\,!=0}$ in Section 2 is formally $n \mapsto \langle (n-1), n\ != 0\rangle$. The abstract "stack" $\mathcal{S}$ is a set of abstract function closures; this stack is not used as a normal reduction stack, it is only used to detect recursive calls for pruning. Fig. 3 presents the AOS rules; observe how the AOS rules structurally align with the COS rules of Fig. 2. The AOS reduction $\longrightarrow$ is defined over configurations which are 4-tuples, $(\mathcal{S}, \mathcal{E}, \mathcal{P}, p)$. The predicate $\mathcal{P}$ in abstract configurations indicates the constraints in force *right now* in the the current function activation. The transitively closed abstract environment $\lambda$-lookup function on variables, $\mathcal{E}(x)^{+\lambda}$, is inductively defined to be the smallest set $\{\overline{\langle F_k, \mathcal{P}_k\rangle}\}$, such that $\forall x \mapsto \langle y, \mathcal{P}\rangle \in \mathcal{E}.\ \mathcal{E}(y)^{+\lambda} \subseteq \{\overline{\langle F_k, \mathcal{P}_k\rangle}\}$, and $\forall x \mapsto \langle F, \mathcal{P}\rangle \in \mathcal{E}.\ \langle F, \mathcal{P}\rangle \in \{\overline{\langle F_k, \mathcal{P}_k\rangle}\}$.

The *let* rule collects the let-binding as an abstract closure $x \mapsto \langle \eta, \mathcal{P}\rangle$, analogous to the `let` rule collecting it as a concrete closure. The current predicate is then updated to reflect the just-executed let-assignment by conjoining the equality condition $(x = \eta)$, which is the new constraint in force, hereafter, in the current function activation. The equality predicates were ignored in Section 2 for simplicity of presentation.

The *if* rule performs abstract execution of the then- and else-branches in parallel under the current predicate appended with their respective guards, as discussed in Section 2.2, and then merges their resulting environments and predicates.

The *app* rule performs abstract execution of all possible function invocations at the corresponding call-site in parallel under their respective predicates (recall

$$\frac{}{(\mathcal{S},\mathcal{E},\mathcal{P},\mathsf{let}\ x=\eta\ \mathsf{in}\ p)\longrightarrow\Big(\mathcal{S},\mathcal{E}\cup\{x\mapsto\langle\eta,\mathcal{P}\rangle\},\mathcal{P}\wedge(x=\eta),p\Big)}\ \textit{let}$$

$$\frac{\begin{array}{c}\mathcal{P}_1=\mathcal{P}\wedge(x=\mathsf{true})\qquad \mathcal{P}_2=\mathcal{P}\wedge(x=\mathsf{false})\\ (\mathcal{S},\mathcal{E},\mathcal{P}_1,p_1)\longrightarrow^{n_1}(\mathcal{S},\mathcal{E}_1,\mathcal{P}_1',y_1')\qquad(\mathcal{S},\mathcal{E},\mathcal{P}_2,p_2)\longrightarrow^{n_2}(\mathcal{S},\mathcal{E}_2,\mathcal{P}_2',y_2')\\ \mathcal{E}'=\mathcal{E}_1\cup\{y\mapsto\langle y_1',\mathcal{P}_1'\rangle\}\cup\mathcal{E}_2\cup\{y\mapsto\langle y_2',\mathcal{P}_2'\rangle\}\\ \mathcal{P}'=(\mathcal{P}_1'\wedge(y=y_1'))\vee(\mathcal{P}_2'\wedge(y=y_2'))\end{array}}{\Big(\mathcal{S},\mathcal{E},\mathcal{P},\mathsf{let}\ y=(p_2)\ \mathsf{in}\ p\Big)\longrightarrow(\mathcal{S},\mathcal{E}',\mathcal{P}',p)}\ \textit{if}$$

$$\frac{\begin{array}{c}\mathcal{E}(f)^{+\lambda}=\{\overline{\langle F_k,\mathcal{P}_k\rangle}\}\qquad\overline{F_k=\lambda x_k.\,p_k}\\ \forall 1\le i\le k\qquad \textit{CALL}(\mathcal{S},\langle F_i,\mathcal{P}_i\rangle)=p_i'\qquad \mathcal{S}_i=\mathcal{S}\cup\{\langle F_i,\mathcal{P}_i\rangle\}\\ \Big(\mathcal{S}_i,\mathcal{E}\cup\{x_i\mapsto\langle x',\mathcal{P}\rangle\},\mathcal{P}_i,p_i'\Big)\longrightarrow^{n_i}(\mathcal{S}_i,\mathcal{E}_i,\mathcal{P}_i',r_i')\end{array}}{(\mathcal{S},\mathcal{E},\mathcal{P},\mathsf{let}\ r=f\ x'\ \mathsf{in}\ p_{next})\longrightarrow\Big(\mathcal{S},\mathcal{E}\cup\bigcup_{1\le i\le k}\mathcal{E}_i\cup\{r\mapsto\langle r_i',\mathcal{P}_i'\rangle\},\mathcal{P},p_{next}\Big)}\ \textit{app}$$

**Fig. 3.** Abstract Operational Semantics (AOS) Rules

that $\mathcal{E}$ may map a variable multiply), and then merges their resulting environments and values. Observe various analogies between the app and *app* rules—for example, the app rule pulls the concrete environment $\mathrm{E}_f$ from the concrete closure of the corresponding function being invoked, while the *app* rule pulls its abstracted form, that is, the predicate $\mathcal{P}_i$, from the corresponding abstract closure. The function $\textit{CALL}:\{\overline{\mathcal{S}}\}\times\{\overline{\langle F,\mathcal{P}\rangle}\}\rightarrow\{\overline{p}\}$ returns the redex $p$ to be executed when an abstract function closure $\langle F,\mathcal{P}\rangle$ is invoked given an abstract stack $\mathcal{S}$—if it is not a recursive call, the body of $F$ is returned, while if it is a recursive call, it should be pruned, and only the return variable of $F$ is returned, as discussed in Section 2.2. Formally, for $F=\lambda x.p$, $\textit{CALL}(\mathcal{S},\langle F,\mathcal{P}\rangle)=p$ if $\langle F,\mathcal{P}\rangle\notin\mathcal{S}$, and $\textit{CALL}(\mathcal{S},\langle F,\mathcal{P}\rangle)=\lfloor p\rfloor$ if $\langle F,\mathcal{P}\rangle\in\mathcal{S}$. If $\mathcal{E}(f)^{+\lambda}=\emptyset$, that is, $f$ is *inchoate* in $\mathcal{E}$, the *app* rule simply skips over the call-site and steps the AOS over to $p_{next}$; as discussed in Section 2.2 this skipping over call-sites is sound from the point of view of the nuggetizer as later steps will fill in the appropriate values which will then be used for analysis in later rerun(s).

We now formally define the nugget and state that it is computable. The formal proofs can be found in [8].

**Definition 2 (Nugget).** *The nugget of a 3-tuple $(\mathcal{E},\mathcal{P},p)$ is the the smallest set $\mathcal{E}'$ such that $(\emptyset,\mathcal{E},\mathcal{P},p)\longrightarrow^n(\emptyset,\mathcal{E}_n,\mathcal{P}_n,r)$, for some $n$, $\mathcal{P}_n$ and $r$, and either $\mathcal{E}=\mathcal{E}_n=\mathcal{E}'$, or inductively, $\mathcal{E}'$ is the nugget of 3-tuple $(\mathcal{E}_n,\mathcal{P},p)$.*

The nuggetizer is then defined as the function that builds a nugget starting from an empty environment.

**Definition 3 (Nuggetizer).** *$nuggetizer(p)=\mathcal{E}$, where $\mathcal{E}$ is the nugget of 3-tuple $(\emptyset,\mathsf{true},p)$.*

As discussed in Section 2.2, the combination of guaranteed termination of the AOS, monotonic growth of the abstract environment during nuggetizing, and existence of a finite upper bound on the abstract environment, implies the abstract environment of the nuggetizer is guaranteed to reach a fixed-point after a finite number of reruns.

**Lemma 4 (Computability of the Nugget).** *The function nuggetizer* : $\{\overline{p}\} \rightarrow \{\overline{\mathcal{E}}\}$ *is computable.*

In theory, the worst-case runtime complexity of the nuggetizer is $O(n! \cdot n^3)$, where $n$ is the size of a program; we expect it to be significantly less in practice.

### 4.1 Towards Automated Theorem Proving

In this subsection we provide "glue" which connects the notation of the formal framework above with the syntax of the Isabelle/HOL theorem prover, and then we prove the soundness of the nuggetizer. We relax the grammar for lazy values, atomic computations and programs to be used in this subsection as follows: $\eta ::= x \mid i \mid b \mid F \mid \eta \oplus \eta$, $\kappa ::= \eta \mid p \mid \eta\ \eta$, and $p ::= \eta \mid \mathsf{let}\ x = \kappa\ \mathsf{in}\ p$, respectively. We write $p[\eta/x]$ to denote the capture-avoiding substitution of all free occurrences of $x$ in $p$ with $\eta$. The following function then reduces a lazy value to its smallest equivalent form, or as we say grounds it.

**Definition 5 (Ground a Lazy Value).** *The function* $\llbracket \cdot \rrbracket : \{\overline{\eta}\} \rightarrow \{\overline{\eta}\}$ *is inductively defined as,* $\llbracket x \rrbracket = x$; $\llbracket i \rrbracket = i$; $\llbracket b \rrbracket = b$; $\llbracket F \rrbracket = F$; *and,* $\llbracket \eta_1 \oplus \eta_2 \rrbracket = \eta$, *if* $\llbracket \eta_1 \rrbracket = i_1$, $\llbracket \eta_2 \rrbracket = i_2$, *and* $i_1 \oplus i_2 = \eta$; *else,* $\llbracket \eta_1 \oplus \eta_2 \rrbracket = \llbracket \eta_1 \rrbracket \oplus \llbracket \eta_2 \rrbracket$.

We now define a new concrete environment, denoting the environment in the theorem prover, as $\mathbb{E} ::= \{\overline{x \mapsto \eta}\}$. Further we write $p[\mathbb{E}]$, for $\mathbb{E} = \{\overline{x_k \mapsto \eta_k}\}$, as shorthand for $p[\eta_k/x_k]$.

**Definition 6 (Predicate Satisfaction Relation: $\mathbb{E} \vdash \mathcal{P}$).** $\mathbb{E} \vdash \mathsf{true}$; $\mathbb{E} \vdash \eta_1 = \eta_2$, *iff* $\llbracket \eta_1[\mathbb{E}] \rrbracket = \llbracket \eta_2[\mathbb{E}] \rrbracket$; $\mathbb{E} \vdash \mathcal{P} \wedge \mathcal{P}'$, *iff* $\mathbb{E} \vdash \mathcal{P}$ *and* $\mathbb{E} \vdash \mathcal{P}'$; *and* $\mathbb{E} \vdash \mathcal{P} \vee \mathcal{P}'$, *iff either,* $\mathbb{E} \vdash \mathcal{P}$ *or* $\mathbb{E} \vdash \mathcal{P}'$.

**Definition 7 (Denotational Semantics of $\mathcal{E}$: $[\![\mathcal{E}]\!]$).** $[\![\mathcal{E}]\!]$ *is smallest set* $\mathbb{E}$ *such that,*

1. $x \mapsto \eta' \in \mathbb{E}$, *if* $x \mapsto \langle \eta, \mathcal{P} \rangle \in \mathcal{E}$, $\emptyset \vdash \mathcal{P}$, $\llbracket \eta \rrbracket = \eta'$, *and* $\eta'$ *is closed; and,*
2. $x \mapsto \eta' \in \mathbb{E}$, *if* $x \mapsto \langle \eta, \mathcal{P} \rangle \in \mathcal{E}$, $\mathbb{E}' \subseteq \mathbb{E}$, $\mathbb{E}' \vdash \mathcal{P}$, $\llbracket \eta[\mathbb{E}'] \rrbracket = \eta'$ *and* $\eta'$ *is closed.*

Given the relaxed grammar, we redefine the ground of a concrete closure as,

**Definition 8 (Ground of a Concrete Closure).** *The function* $\llbracket \cdot \rrbracket : \{\overline{\langle \eta, \mathrm{E} \rangle}\} \rightarrow \{\overline{\eta}\}$ *is inductively defined as,* $\llbracket \langle x, \mathrm{E} \rangle \rrbracket = \llbracket \mathrm{E}(x) \rrbracket$; $\llbracket \langle i, \mathrm{E} \rangle \rrbracket = i$; $\llbracket \langle b, \mathrm{E} \rangle \rrbracket = b$; $\llbracket \langle F, \mathrm{E} \rangle \rrbracket = F[\mathbb{E}]$, *where* $free(F) \cap dom(\mathrm{E}) = \{\overline{x_k}\}$ *and* $\mathbb{E} = \{\overline{x_k \mapsto \llbracket \langle x_k, \mathrm{E} \rangle \rrbracket}\}$; *and,* $\llbracket \langle \eta_1 \oplus \eta_2, \mathrm{E} \rangle \rrbracket = \eta$, *if* $\llbracket \langle \eta_1, \mathrm{E} \rangle \rrbracket = i_1$, $\llbracket \langle \eta_2, \mathrm{E} \rangle \rrbracket = i_2$, *and* $i_1 \oplus i_2 = \eta$; *else,* $\llbracket \langle \eta_1 \oplus \eta_2, \mathrm{E} \rangle \rrbracket = \llbracket \langle \eta_1, \mathrm{E} \rangle \rrbracket \oplus \llbracket \langle \eta_2, \mathrm{E} \rangle \rrbracket$.

The following theorem then shows that all values arising in variables at runtime will be found in the denotation of the nugget, meaning the latter is a sound reflection of the runtime program behavior.

**Theorem 9 (Soundness of the Nuggetizer).** *For a closed canonical program $p$, if $nuggetizer(p) = \mathcal{E}$, $(\mathrm{E}', p')$ is a node in the derivation tree of $(\emptyset, p) \longrightarrow^n (\mathrm{E}_n, p_n)$, and $x \mapsto \langle \eta, \mathrm{E} \rangle \in \mathrm{E}'$ then $\lfloor\!\lfloor \langle \eta, \mathrm{E} \rangle \rfloor\!\rfloor = \eta'$, for some $\eta'$, such that $x \mapsto \eta' \in [\![\mathcal{E}]\!]$.*

## 5 Automated Theorem Proving

In this section we discuss how we use the Isabelle/HOL proof assistant [1] to formalize and prove properties of the nugget. Isabelle/HOL has a rich vocabulary that is well-suited to the encoding of nuggets, and has a number of powerful built-in proof strategies. We translate each nugget into an inductively defined set in the prover. For any such definition, Isabelle/HOL automatically generates an inductive proof strategy which can be leveraged to prove properties of programs.

For brevity we elide formal details of the encoding here, but they can be found in [8]. In summary, the encoding of a given nugget $\mathcal{E}$, denoted $[\![\mathcal{E}]\!]_{\mathrm{HOL}}$, is defined inductively as a set of (var, nat) pairs called "abstractenv", where the elements of var are of the form $X(n)$ with $n \in$ nat, representing variables $x_n$ from a given nugget domain. Each mapping $x_i \mapsto \langle \eta, \mathcal{P} \rangle$ in $\mathcal{E}$ defines a separate clause in the inductive definition, where $\mathcal{P}$ defines a set of preconditions. The encoding is straightforward, the main trick being that any variable $x_j$ referenced in $\eta$ and $\mathcal{P}$ needs to be changed to an Isabelle/HOL variable $v_j$, and associated with $x_j$ via the precondition $(X(j), v_j) \in$ abstractenv. If $\eta$ is variable-free, then it is a basic clause, otherwise the clause is inductive.

Our main result for the encoding is that the Isabelle/HOL least fixpoint interpretation of $[\![\mathcal{E}]\!]_{\mathrm{HOL}}$ is provably equivalent to the interpretation of $\mathcal{E}$, i.e. $[\![\mathcal{E}]\!]$. Thus, by Theorem 9, any property of $[\![\mathcal{E}]\!]_{\mathrm{HOL}}$ verified in Isabelle/HOL for all values of variables is a property of the runtime variables of the corresponding program $p$ whose nugget is $\mathcal{E}$. For example, consider the nugget $\{x_0 \mapsto 5, x_0 \mapsto (x_0 - 1)^{x_0 \,!= 0}\}$ for program (1) from Section 2, assuming $x_0$ in place of $n$. The encoding of this nugget will generate the following Isabelle/HOL definition:

inductive abstractenv intros
"$(X(0), 5) \in$ abstractenv"
"$((X(0), v_0) \in \text{abstractenv} \wedge v_0 \neq 0) \Longrightarrow (X(0), v_0 - 1) \in \text{abstractenv}$"

To prove that $x_0$ falls in the range $[0, 5]$, we state the following theorem in Isabelle/HOL: "$(X(0), v_0) \in \text{abstractenv} \Longrightarrow (v_0 \leq 5 \ \wedge \ v_0 \geq 0)$". Following this, a single application of the elimination rule abstractenv.induct will unroll the theorem according to the inductive definition of abstractenv, and the resulting subgoals can be solved by two applications of the arith strategy. While we have proved this and other more complicated examples in an interactive manner, the strategy in each case is the same: apply the inductive elimination rule, followed by one or more applications of the arith strategy. This suggests a fully automated technique for proof. We note that the nugget encoding itself is fully automated. In a deployed system we could imagine writing statements such as $\texttt{assert}(x_0 \geq 0)$ in the source code of the function, and such asserts would then be compiled to theorems and automatically proved over the automatically generated nugget. This yields a general, powerful, end-to-end programming logic.

## 6 Related Work

We know of no direct precedent for an automated algorithm that abstracts arbitrary higher-order programs as inductive definitions; however, our work is both related to other verification efforts and to previous techniques in program analysis. We address these two topics in turn.

There is a wide class of research also aimed at partial, more automated verification of program properties than that obtained by full formal verification with a theorem prover. Examples that we would consider more close to our work include systems with dependent and refinement types [9,10,11,12]. Our approach has a good combination of expressiveness and automation in comparison to the aforementioned works in that it gives precise, automatic answers to verification questions. Several projects also similarly aim to combine a program analysis with a theorem prover in a single tool, *e.g.* [9,12,13]; we believe this general approach has much promise in the future.

This work is an abstract interpretation [4] in the sense that an abstraction of an operational semantics is defined. It differs from abstract interpretation in that we are not interested in abstracting away any of the (infinite) structure of the underlying data domains, and that we wish to derive an inductive structure. The most related abstract interpretation is LFA [13], which addresses a similar problem but by a different technical means. LFA is more a proposal in that it has no formal proofs. Further, it does not generate inductive definitions (like our nuggets) to be fed into a theorem prover at the end of the analysis; rather it relies on invoking a theorem prover on-the-fly to verify first-order logical propositions about the program. We are concerned about the feasibility of implementing LFA in practice, as it fundamentally relies on an initial CPS transformation step which removes the join points of conditional branching statements; hence LFA must explore nearly all paths of the conditional tree in parallel. Our work evolved from attempts to incorporate flow- and path-sensitivity into a type constraint system [3]. Since simple type constraint systems are closely related to 0CFA [7], our work is also a logical descendant of that work.

## 7 Conclusion

We have defined a static analysis which distills the first-order computational structure from untyped higher-order functional programs, producing a *nugget*. We believe this work has several novel aspects. Most importantly, the analysis produces nuggets which are simple inductive definitions. Inductive definitions provide the best abstraction level for modern theorem-provers—modern provers do their best when reasoning directly over inductively defined structures since that gives a natural induction principle. There are several other features of our approach which make it appealing. The nuggets include guards indicating dependencies. The analysis is fully supportive of higher-order programs—nuggets reflect the higher-order flow of the original program, but expressed as a first-order entity. The *nuggetizer* algorithm which collects a nugget is completely automated and always terminates. The *prune-rerun* technique, a synthesis of existing ideas in type constraint systems and abstract interpretation, provides a new method for soundly interpreting higher-order functions in presence of flow- and path-sensitivity. We show how the meaning of nuggets can be easily formalized in the HOL theorem-prover.

While in this paper we focus on value range analysis for a pure functional language, our general goal is much broader. We have done initial work on extensions to incorporate flow-sensitive mutable state and context-sensitivity.

## References

1. Nipkow, T., Paulson, L.C., Wenzel, M.: Isabelle/HOL. LNCS, vol. 2283. Springer, Heidelberg (2002)
2. Kaufmann, M., Moore, J.S.: ACL2. University of Texas at Austin (2007)
3. Skalka, C., Smith, S.: History effects and verification. In: Chin, W.-N. (ed.) APLAS 2004. LNCS, vol. 3302, pp. 107–128. Springer, Heidelberg (2004)
4. Cousot, P., Cousot, R.: Abstract interpretation: a unified lattice model for static analysis of programs by construction or approximation of fixpoints. In: POPL (1977)
5. Flanagan, C., Sabry, A., Duba, B.F., Felleisen, M.: The essence of compiling with continuations. In: PLDI (1993)
6. Palsberg, J., Smith, S.: Constrained types and their expressiveness. In: TOPLAS, ACM Press, New York (1996)
7. Shivers, O.G.: Control-flow analysis of higher-order languages. PhD thesis, Carnegie Mellon University, Pittsburgh, PA, USA (1991)
8. Shroff, P., Skalka, C., Smith, S.F.: The nuggetizer: Abstracting away higher-orderness for program verification. Technical report, Johns Hopkins University (2007), `http://www.cs.jhu.edu/~scott/pll/papers/nuggetizer-TR.pdf`
9. Chen, C., Xi, H.: Combining programming with theorem proving. In: ICFP (2005)
10. Jones, S.L.P., Vytiniotis, D., Weirich, S., Washburn, G.: Simple unification-based type inference for GADTs. In: ICFP (2006)
11. Xi, H., Pfenning, F.: Eliminating array bound checking through dependent types. In: PLDI (1998)
12. Gronski, J., Knowles, K., Tomb, A., Freund, S.N., Flanagan, C.: Sage: Hybrid checking for flexible specifications. In: Workshop on Scheme and Functional Programming (2006)
13. Might, M.: Logic-flow analysis of higher-order programs. In: POPL (2007)

# Local Reasoning for Storable Locks and Threads

Alexey Gotsman[1], Josh Berdine[2], Byron Cook[2], Noam Rinetzky[3,⋆], and Mooly Sagiv[2,3]

[1] University of Cambridge
[2] Microsoft Research
[3] Tel-Aviv University

**Abstract.** We present a resource oriented program logic that is able to reason about concurrent heap-manipulating programs with unbounded numbers of dynamically-allocated locks and threads. The logic is inspired by concurrent separation logic, but handles these more realistic concurrency primitives. We demonstrate that the proposed logic allows local reasoning about programs for which there exists a notion of dynamic ownership of heap parts by locks and threads.

## 1 Introduction

We are interested in modular reasoning, both manual and automatic, about concurrent heap-manipulating programs. Striking progress in this realm has recently been made by O'Hearn [10], who proposed concurrent separation logic as a basis for reasoning about such programs. Concurrent separation logic is a Hoare logic with two novel features: the assertion language of the logic contains the $*$ connective that splits the program state into disjoint parts, and the proof system has two important rules:

$$\frac{\{P\}\ C\ \{Q\}}{\{P * R\}\ C\ \{Q * R\}}\ \textsc{Frame} \qquad \frac{\{P_1\}\ C_1\ \{Q_1\} \quad \{P_2\}\ C_2\ \{Q_2\}}{\{P_1 * P_2\}\ C_1 \parallel C_2\ \{Q_1 * Q_2\}}\ \textsc{Par}$$

According to the FRAME rule, if $P$ includes the part of the program state that $C$ accesses, then executing $C$ in the presence of additional program state $R$ results in the same behavior, and $C$ does not touch the extra state. The PAR rule says that if two processes access disjoint parts of the program state, they can safely execute in parallel and the final state is given by the $*$-conjunction of the postconditions of the processes. Therefore, to reason about a command (or a process) in a program, it is sufficient to consider only the part of the program state that the command actually accesses, a feature that greatly simplifies program proofs and is referred to as the principle of *local reasoning* [9].

In the PAR rule it is intended that the processes access a finite set of shared resources using conditional critical regions to synchronize access. Process interaction is mediated in the logic by assigning to every resource an assertion – its

⋆ Supported by the German-Israeli Foundation for Scientific Research and Development (G.I.F.).

Z. Shao (Ed.): APLAS 2007, LNCS 4807, pp. 19–37, 2007.

*resource invariant* – that describes the part of the heap owned by the resource and must be respected by every process. For any given process, resource invariants restrict how other processes can interfere with it, and hence, the process can be reasoned about in isolation. In this way the logic allows local reasoning about programs consistent with what O'Hearn terms the Ownership Hypothesis ("A code fragment can access only those portions of state that it owns.") [10], i.e., programs that admit a notion of ownership of heap parts by processes and resources. At the same time, the ownership relation is not required to be static, i.e., it permits ownership transfer of heap cells between areas owned by different processes and resources. The resource-oriented flavor of the logic makes it possible to use it as a basis for thread-modular program analysis [7]: certain classes of resource invariants can automatically be inferred by an abstract interpretation that analyzes each process separately in contrast to a straightforward analysis that just enumerates all execution interleavings.

However, concurrent separation logic [10], its derivatives [1,12,3], and a corresponding program analysis [7] all suffer from a common limitation: they assume a bounded number of non-aliased and pre-allocated locks (resources) and threads (processes) and, hence, cannot be used to reason about concurrency primitives present in modern languages and libraries (e.g., POSIX threads) that use unbounded numbers of *storable* locks and threads. Here "storable" means that locks can be dynamically allocated and destroyed in the heap; threads can be dynamically created and can terminate themselves, and moreover, thread identifiers can be stored and subsequently used to wait for termination of the identified thread.

Reasoning about storable locks is especially difficult. The issue here is not that of expressiveness, but of modularity: storable locks can be handled by building a global invariant describing the shared memory as a whole, with all locks allocated in it. However, in this case the locality of reasoning is lost, which kicks back in global invariants containing lots of auxiliary state, proofs being extremely complex and program analyses for discovery of global invariants being infeasible. Recent efforts towards making proofs in this style of reasoning modular [4,15] use rely-guarantee reasoning to simplify the description of the global invariant and its possible changes (see Section 9 for a detailed comparison of such techniques with our work).

What we want is a logic that preserves concurrent separation logic's local reasoning, even for programs that manipulate storable locks and threads. To this end, in this paper we propose a logic (Section 3), based upon separation logic, that treats storable locks along with the data structures they protect as resources, assigning invariants to them and managing their dynamic creation and destruction. The challenges of designing such a logic were (quite emotionally) summarized by Bornat et al. in [1]:

> ...the idea of semaphores in the heap makes theoreticians wince. The semaphore has to be available to a shared resource bundle:[1] that means a bundle will contain a bundle which contains resource, a notion which

[1] Here the term "resource bundle" is used to name what we, following O'Hearn's original paper, call "resource invariant".

> makes everybody's eyes water. None of it seems impossible, but it's a significant problem, and solving it will be a small triumph.

Less emotionally, stored locks are analogous to stored procedures in that, unless one is very careful, they can raise a form of Russell's paradox, circularity arising from what Landin called knots in the store. Stored locks can do this by referring to themselves through their resource invariants, and here we address this foundational difficulty by cutting the knots in the store with an indirection.

Our approach to reasoning about storable locks is to represent a lock in the assertion language by a *handle* whose denotation cuts knots in the store. A handle certifies that a lock allocated at a certain address exists and gives a thread owning the handle a permission to (try to) acquire the lock. By using the mechanism of permissions [1] the handle can be split among several threads that can then compete for the lock. Furthermore, a handle carries some information about the part of the program state protected by the lock (its resource invariant), which lets us mediate the interaction among threads, just as in the original concurrent separation logic. Handles for locks can be stored inside resource invariants, thereby permitting reasoning about the situation described in the quote above. In this way we extend the ability of concurrent separation logic to reason locally about programs that are consistent with the Ownership Hypothesis to the setting with storable locks and threads. As we show in Section 4, the class of such programs contains programs with coarse-grained synchronization and some, but not all, programs with fine-grained synchronization, including examples that were posed as challenges in the literature.

We prove the logic sound with respect to an interleaving operational semantics (Section 7). It happens that even formulating the soundness statement is nontrivial as we have to take into account resource invariants for locks not mentioned directly in the local states of threads.

The technical issues involved in reasoning about storable locks and storable threads are similar. To make the presentation more approachable, we first present a logic for programs consisting of one top-level parallel composition of several threads. In Section 8 we extend the logic to handle dynamic thread creation.

## 2 Technical Background

In this section we review some technical concepts of (sequential) separation logic that we reuse in ours. We consider a version of separation logic that is a Hoare logic for a heap-manipulating programming language with the following syntax:

| | | |
|---|---|---|
| $V$ | $::= l, x, y, \ldots$ | variables |
| $E, F$ | $::= \mathsf{nil} \mid V \mid E + F \mid \ldots$ | expressions |
| $G$ | $::= E = F \mid E \neq F$ | branch guards |
| $C$ | $::= V = E \mid V = [E] \mid [E] = F \mid V = \mathbf{new} \mid \mathbf{delete}\ E$ | primitive commands |
| $S$ | $::= C \mid S; S \mid \mathbf{if}\ G\ \mathbf{then}\ S\ \mathbf{else}\ S\ \mathbf{fi} \mid \mathbf{while}\ G\ \mathbf{do}\ S\ \mathbf{od}$ | commands |

Here square brackets denote pointer dereferencing; the meaning of the rest of the language is standard.

Formulae in the assertion language of separation logic denote program states represented by stack-heap pairs and have the following syntax:

$$\Phi ::= \mathsf{false} \mid \Phi \Rightarrow \Phi \mid \exists X.\Phi \mid \Phi * \Phi \mid \Phi \mathrel{-\!\!*} \Phi \mid \mathsf{emp_s} \mid \mathsf{emp_h}$$
$$\mid\ E = F \mid \pi = \mu \mid \mathsf{Own}_\pi(x) \mid E \mapsto F$$

We can define usual connectives not mentioned in the syntax definition using the provided ones. Note that we treat variables as resources [12] to avoid side conditions in proof rules, i.e., we treat the stack in the same way as the heap, Thus, the assertion $E \mapsto F$ denotes the set of stack-heap pairs such that the heap consists of one cell allocated at the address $E$ and storing the value $F$, and the stack contains all variables mentioned in $E$ and $F$. The assertion $\mathsf{Own}_1(x)$ (the general form $\mathsf{Own}_\pi(x)$ is explained later) restricts the stack to contain only the variable $x$ and leaves the heap unconstrained. We can separate assertions about variable ownership $\mathsf{Own}_1(x)$ with $*$ in the same way as assertions $E \mapsto F$ about ownership of heap cells. $\mathsf{emp_s}$ describes the empty stack and $\mathsf{emp_h}$ the empty heap. We distinguish integer program variables $x, y, \ldots$ (which may appear in programs) and logical variables $X, Y, \ldots$ (which do not appear in programs, only in formulae). In the assertion language definition $E$ and $F$ range over expressions, which are the same as in the programming language, but can contain logical variables. We write $E \mapsto \_$ for $\exists X. E \mapsto X$ where $X$ does not occur free in $E$.

The assertion language includes fractional permissions [1] for variables, which are necessary for getting a complete (in the sense of [12]) proof system when variables are treated as resources. For clarity of presentation we omit the treatment of permissions for heap cells. Permissions are denoted with permission expressions (ranged over by $\pi$ and $\mu$), which are expressions evaluating to numbers from $(0, 1]$. A permission shows "how much" of a variable is owned by the assertion. For example, variable $x$ represented by $\mathsf{Own}_1(x)$ can be split into two permissions $\mathsf{Own}_{1/2}(x)$, each of which permits reading the variable, but not writing to it. Two permissions $\mathsf{Own}_{1/2}(x)$ can later be recombined to obtain the full permission $\mathsf{Own}_1(x)$, which allows both reading from and writing to $x$. We make the convention that $\Vdash$ binds most loosely, use $\pi_1 x_1, \ldots, \pi_k x_k \Vdash P$ to denote $\mathsf{Own}_{\pi_1}(x_1) * \ldots * \mathsf{Own}_{\pi_k}(x_k) \wedge P$ and abbreviate $1x$ to $x$.

The proof rules (see [6]) are the same as in [13,12] modulo treating variables as resources in heap-manipulating commands. In the rules and the following, $O$ ranges over assertions of the form $\pi_1 x_1, \ldots, \pi_k x_k$. We also allow $O$ to be empty, in which case we interpret $O \Vdash P$ as $\mathsf{emp_s} \wedge P$.

## 3 Logic

We now consider a concurrent programming language based on the sequential one presented in Section 2:

| | |
|---|---|
| $C ::= \ldots \mid \mathbf{init}(E) \mid \mathbf{finalize}(E) \mid \mathbf{acquire}(E) \mid \mathbf{release}(E)$ | primitive commands |
| $P ::= S \parallel \ldots \parallel S$ | programs |

We assume that each program consists of one parallel composition of several threads. Synchronization is performed using locks, which are dynamically created and destroyed in the heap. **init**$(E)$ converts a location allocated at the address $E$ to a lock. After the completion of **init**$(E)$ the thread that executed it holds the lock. **acquire**$(E)$ and **release**$(E)$ try to acquire, respectively, release the lock allocated at the address $E$. **finalize**$(E)$ converts the lock into an ordinary heap cell containing an unspecified value provided that the lock at the address $E$ is held by the thread that is executing the command.

As in concurrent separation logic [10], with each lock we associate a resource invariant – a formula that describes the part of the heap protected by the lock. (This association is considered to be part of the proof, rather than of the program.) To deal with unbounded numbers of locks we assume that each lock has a *sort* that determines its invariant. Formally, we assume a fixed set $\mathcal{L}$ of function symbols with positive arities representing lock sorts, and with each $A \in \mathcal{L}$ of arity $k$ we associate a formula $I_A(L, \vec{X})$ containing $k$ free logical variables specified as parameters – the resource invariant for the sort $A$. The meaning of the first parameter is fixed as the address at which the lock is allocated. Other parameters can have arbitrary meaning. In Sections 5 and 7 we give certain restrictions that resource invariant formulae must satisfy for the logic to be sound.

We extend the assertion language of separation logic with two extra forms: $\Phi ::= \ldots \mid \pi A(E, \vec{F}) \mid \mathsf{Locked}_A(E, \vec{F})$. An expression of the form $A(E, \vec{F})$, where $A \in \mathcal{L}$, is a *handle* for the lock of the sort $A$ allocated at the address $E$. It can be viewed as an existential permission for the lock: a thread having $A(E, \vec{F})$ knows that the heap cell at the address $E$ is allocated and is a lock, and can try to acquire it. $A(E, \vec{F})$ does not give permissions for reading from or writing to the cell at the address $E$. Moreover, it does not ensure that the part of the heap protected by the lock satisfies the resource invariant until the thread successfully acquires the lock. We allow using $A(E, \vec{F})$ with fractional permissions [1] writing $\pi A(E, \vec{F})$. The intuition behind the permissions is that a handle for a lock with the full permission 1 can be split among several threads, thereby allowing them to compete for the lock. A thread having a permission for the handle less than 1 can acquire the lock; a thread having the full permission can in addition finalize the lock. We abbreviate $1A(E, \vec{F})$ to $A(E, \vec{F})$. Assertions in the code of threads can also use a special form $\mathsf{Locked}_A(E, \vec{F})$ to represent the fact that the lock at the address $E$ is held by the thread in the surrounding code of the assertion. $\mathsf{Locked}_A(E, \vec{F})$ also ensures that the cell at the address $E$ is allocated and is a lock of the sort $A$ with parameters $\vec{F}$.

Our logic includes the proof rules of sequential separation logic and four new rules for lock-manipulating commands shown in Figure 1. We do not provide a rule for parallel composition as our programs consist of only one top-level parallel composition, and in Section 8 we instead treat dynamic thread creation. We write $\vdash \{P\}\ C\ \{Q\}$ to denote that the triple $\{P\}\ C\ \{Q\}$ is provable in our logic.

Initializing a lock (Init) converts a cell in the heap at the address $E$ to a lock. Upon completion of **init**$(E)$ the thread that executed it gets both the ownership (with the full permission) of the handle $A(E, \vec{F})$ for the lock and the knowledge that it holds the lock, represented by $\mathsf{Locked}_A(E, \vec{F})$. Note that for

$$\frac{(O \Vdash E \mapsto \_) \Rightarrow \vec{F} = \vec{F}}{\{O \Vdash E \mapsto \_\}\ \mathbf{init}_{A,\vec{F}}(E)\ \{O \Vdash A(E,\vec{F}) * \mathsf{Locked}_A(E,\vec{F})\}}\ \text{INIT}$$

$$\frac{}{\{O \Vdash A(E,\vec{F}) * \mathsf{Locked}_A(E,\vec{F})\}\ \mathbf{finalize}(E)\ \{O \Vdash E \mapsto \_\}}\ \text{FINALIZE}$$

$$\frac{}{\{(O \Vdash \pi A(L,\vec{X})) \wedge L{=}E\}\ \mathbf{acquire}(E)\ \{(O \Vdash \pi A(L,\vec{X}) * \mathsf{Locked}_A(L,\vec{X})) * I_A(L,\vec{X})\}}\ \text{ACQUIRE}$$

$$\frac{}{\{((O \Vdash \mathsf{Locked}_A(L,\vec{X})) * I_A(L,\vec{X})) \wedge L{=}E\}\ \mathbf{release}(E)\ \{O \Vdash \mathsf{emp_h}\}}\ \text{RELEASE}$$

**Fig. 1.** Proof rules for lock-manipulating commands

the precondition $O \Vdash E \mapsto \_$ to be consistent $O$ must contain variables mentioned in $E$. In this and other rules we use $O$ to supply the permissions for variables necessary for executing the command. For $\mathbf{init}_{A,\vec{F}}(E)$ commands to be safe the stack must contain variables mentioned in $E$ and $\vec{F}$, hence, the premiss $(O \Vdash E \mapsto \_) \Rightarrow \vec{F} = \vec{F}$ additionally requires that variables be contained in $O$ (see [12]). An implicit side condition in the INIT rule is that in all branches of a proof of a program, the sort $A$ of the lock and the values of parameters $\vec{F}$ have to be chosen consistently for each **init** command (as otherwise the conjunction rule of Hoare logic becomes unsound). This is formally enforced by annotating each **init** command with the sort of the lock that is being created and its parameters (defined by arbitrary expressions $\vec{F}$ over program variables). In general, the lock sort can also be computed as a function of program variables. To simplify notation we assume the sort of the lock is fixed for each **init** command in the program. We note that although we use the sort of the lock and its parameters for conceptually different purposes (see the examples in Section 4), technically they are merely pieces of auxiliary state associated with the handle for the lock that carry some information about the resource invariant of the lock. Therefore, the annotations of lock sorts and parameters at **init** commands can be viewed as just assignments to auxiliary cells in memory.

Finalizing a lock results in it being converted into an ordinary cell. To finalize a lock (FINALIZE) a thread has to have the full permission for the handle $A(E,\vec{F})$ associated with the lock. Additionally, the lock has to be held by the thread, i.e., $\mathsf{Locked}_A(E,\vec{F})$ has to be in its local state.

A thread can acquire a lock if it has a permission for the handle of the lock. Acquiring a lock (ACQUIRE) results in the resource invariant of the lock (with appropriately instantiated parameters) being $*$-conjoined to the local state of the thread. The thread also obtains the corresponding Locked fact, which guarantees that it holds the lock. A thread acquiring the same lock twice deadlocks, which is enforced by $\mathsf{Locked}_A(E,\vec{F}) * \mathsf{Locked}_A(E,\vec{F})$ being inconsistent (see Section 5). Conversely, a thread can release a lock (RELEASE) only if it holds the lock, i.e., the corresponding Locked fact is present in the local state of the thread. Upon releasing the lock the thread gives up both this knowledge and the ownership of the resource invariant associated with the lock. The fact that resource invariants

```
struct RECORD {
  LOCK Lock;
  int Data;
};

main() {
  RECORD *x;
  {x ⊩ emp_h}
  x = new RECORD;
  {x ⊩ x↦_ * x.Data↦_}
  init_R(x);
  {x ⊩ x.Data↦_ * R(x) *
   Locked_R(x)}
```

```
  x->Data = 0;
  {x ⊩ x.Data↦0 * R(x) *
   Locked_R(x)}
  release(x);
  {x ⊩ R(x)}
  // ...
  {x ⊩ R(x)}
  acquire(x);
  {x ⊩ x.Data↦_ * R(x) *
   Locked_R(x)}
  x->Data++;
  {x ⊩ x.Data↦_ * R(x) *
   Locked_R(x)}
```

```
  release(x);
  {x ⊩ R(x)}
  // ...
  {x ⊩ R(x)}
  acquire(x);
  {x ⊩ x.Data↦_ * R(x) *
   Locked_R(x)}
  finalize(x);
  {x ⊩ x↦_ * x.Data↦_}
  delete x;
  {x ⊩ emp_h}
}
```

$$I_R(L) \triangleq \mathsf{emp_s} \wedge L.Data \mapsto \_$$

**Fig. 2.** A very simple example of reasoning in the logic

can claim ownership of program variables complicates the rules Acquire and Release. E.g., in the postcondition of Acquire we cannot put $I_A(L, \vec{X})$ inside the expression after ⊩ as it may claim ownership of variables not mentioned in $O$. This requires us to use a logical variable $L$ in places where the expression $E$ would have been expected.

## 4 Examples of Reasoning

We first show (in Example 1 below) that straightforward application of rules for lock-manipulating commands allows us to handle programs in which locks protect parts of the heap without other locks allocated in them. We then present two more involved examples of using the logic, which demonstrate how extending the logic with storable locks has enabled reasoning more locally than was previously possible in some interesting cases (Examples 2 and 3).

Instead of the minimalistic language presented in Section 3, in our examples we use a language with some additional C-like syntax (in particular, C structures) that can easily be desugared to the language of Section 3. For an address $x$ of a structure, we use $x.F$ in the assertion language as syntactic sugar for $x + d$, where $d$ is the offset of the field $F$ in the structure. We assume that each field in a structure takes one memory cell. We also use an obvious generalization of **new** and **delete** that allocate and deallocate several memory cells at once.

*Example 1: A simple situation.* Figure 2 shows a proof outline for a program with a common pattern: a lock-field in a structure protecting another field in the same structure. We use a lock sort $R$ with invariant $I_R(L)$. The proof outline shows how the "life cycle" of a lock is handled in our proof system: creating a cell, converting it to a lock, acquiring and releasing the lock, converting it to an ordinary cell, and disposing the cell. For simplicity we consider a program with only one thread.

*Example 2: "Last one disposes".* This example was posed as a challenge for local reasoning in [1]. The program in Figure 3 represents a piece of multicasting code:

```
struct PACKET {
  LOCK Lock;
  int Count;
  DATA Data;
};

PACKET *p;

initialize() {
  {p ⊩ emp_h}
  p = new PACKET;
  {p ⊩ p↦_ ∗ p.Count↦_ ∗ p.Data↦_}
  p->Count = 0;
  {p ⊩ p↦_ ∗ p.Count↦0 ∗ p.Data↦_}
  init_{P,M}(p);
  {p ⊩ p.Count↦0 ∗ p.Data↦_ ∗ P(p, M) ∗
   Locked_P(p, M)}
  // ...Initialize data...
  release(p);
  {p ⊩ P(p, M)}
}
```

```
thread() {
  {(1/M)p ⊩ (1/M)P(p, M)}
  acquire(p);
  {(1/M)p ⊩ ∃X.0 ≤ X < M ∧ p.Count↦X ∗
    p.Data↦_∗((X+1)/M)P(p, M)∗Locked_P(p, M)}
  // ...Process data...
  p->Count++;
  {(1/M)p ⊩ ∃X.1 ≤ X ≤ M ∧ p.Count↦X ∗
    p.Data↦_ ∗ (X/M)P(p, M) ∗ Locked_P(p, M)}
  if (p->Count == M) {
    {(1/M)p ⊩ p.Count↦M ∗ p.Data↦_ ∗
      P(p, M) ∗ Locked_P(p, M)}
    // ...Finalize data...
    finalize(p);
    {(1/M)p ⊩ p.Count↦M ∗ p.Data↦_ ∗ p↦_}
    delete p;
  } else {
    {(1/M)p ⊩ ∃X.1 ≤ X < M ∧ p.Count↦X ∗
      p.Data↦_ ∗ (X/M)P(p, M) ∗ Locked_P(p, M)}
    release(p);
  }
  {(1/M)p ⊩ emp_h}
}
```

$$I_P(L, M) \triangleq \mathsf{emp_s} \wedge \exists X.X < M \wedge L.Count \mapsto X * L.Data \mapsto \_ * \\ ((X = 0 \wedge \mathsf{emp_h}) \vee (X \geq 1 \wedge (X/M)P(L, M)))$$

**Fig. 3.** Proof outline for the "Last one disposes" program

a single packet $p$ (of type *PACKET*) with *Data* inside the packet is distributed to $M$ *threads* at once. For efficiency reasons instead of copying the packet, it is shared among threads. A *Count* of access permissions protected by *Lock* is used to determine when everybody has finished and the packet can be disposed. The program consists of a top level parallel composition of $M$ calls to the procedure *thread*. Here $M$ is a constant assumed to be greater than 0. For completeness, we also provide the procedure *initialize* that can be used to initialize the packet and thereby establish the precondition of the program.

To prove the program correct the resource invariant for the lock at the address $p$ has to contain a partial permission for the handle of *the same lock*. This is formally represented by a lock sort $P$ with the resource invariant $I_P(L, M)$. Initially the resource invariant contains no permissions of this kind and the handle $P(p, M)$ for the lock is split among $M$ threads (hence, the precondition of each thread is $(1/M)p \Vdash (1/M)P(p, M)$). Each thread uses the handle to acquire the lock and process the packet. When a thread finishes processing and releases the lock, it transfers the permission for the handle it owned to the resource invariant of the lock. The last thread to process the packet can then get the full permission for the lock by combining the permission in the invariant with its own one and can therefore dispose the packet.

*Example 3: Lock coupling list.* We next consider a fine-grained implementation of a singly-linked list with concurrent access, whose nodes store integer keys. The program (Figures 4 and 5) consists of $M$ operations *add* and *remove* running

```
locate(int e) {
  NODE *prev, *curr;
  $\{O \Vdash -\infty < e \wedge (1/M)H(head)\}$
  prev = head;
  $\{O \Vdash -\infty < e \wedge prev = head \wedge (1/M)H(head)\}$
  acquire(prev);
  $\{O \Vdash \exists V'.-\infty < e \wedge -\infty < V' \wedge (1/M)H(head) * \mathsf{Locked}_H(prev) *$
   $\exists X.prev.Val \mapsto -\infty * prev.Next \mapsto X * N(X, V')\}$
  curr = prev->Next;
  $\{O \Vdash \exists V'.-\infty < e \wedge -\infty < V' \wedge (1/M)H(head) * \mathsf{Locked}_H(prev) *$
   $prev.Val \mapsto -\infty * prev.Next \mapsto curr * N(curr, V')\}$
  acquire(curr);
  $\{O \Vdash \exists V'.-\infty < e \wedge -\infty < V' \wedge (1/M)H(head) * N(curr, V') * \mathsf{Locked}_H(prev) *$
   $\mathsf{Locked}_N(curr, V') * prev.Val \mapsto -\infty * prev.Next \mapsto curr * curr.Val \mapsto V' *$
   $((curr.Next \mapsto \mathsf{nil} \wedge V' = +\infty) \vee (\exists X, V''.curr.Next \mapsto X * N(X, V'') \wedge V' < V''))\}$
  while (curr->Val < e) {
    $\{O \Vdash \exists V, V'.V' < e \wedge (1/M)H(head) * N(curr, V') * \mathsf{Locked}_N(curr, V') *$
     $(\mathsf{Locked}_H(prev) \wedge V = -\infty \vee \mathsf{Locked}_N(prev, V)) * prev.Val \mapsto V * prev.Next \mapsto curr *$
     $\exists X, V''.curr.Val \mapsto V' * curr.Next \mapsto X * N(X, V'') \wedge V < V' < V''\}$
    release(prev);
    $\{O \Vdash \exists X, V', V''.V' < e \wedge V' < V'' \wedge (1/M)H(head) * \mathsf{Locked}_N(curr, V') *$
     $curr.Val \mapsto V' * curr.Next \mapsto X * N(X, V'')\}$
    prev = curr;
    curr = curr->Next;
    $\{O \Vdash \exists V, V'.V < e \wedge V < V' \wedge (1/M)H(head) * \mathsf{Locked}_N(prev, V) *$
     $prev.Val \mapsto V * prev.Next \mapsto curr * N(curr, V')\}$
    acquire(curr);
    $\{O \Vdash \exists V, V'.V < e \wedge V < V' \wedge (1/M)H(head) * \mathsf{Locked}_N(prev, V) *$
     $\mathsf{Locked}_N(curr, V') * N(curr, V') * prev.Val \mapsto V * prev.Next \mapsto curr * curr.Val \mapsto V' *$
     $((V' = +\infty \wedge curr.Next \mapsto \mathsf{nil}) \vee \exists X, V''.curr.Next \mapsto X * N(X, V'') \wedge V' < V'')\}$
  }
  $\{O \Vdash \exists V, V'.V < e \leq V' \wedge (1/M)H(head) * \mathsf{Locked}_N(prev, V) * \mathsf{Locked}_N(curr, V') * N(curr, V') *$
   $prev.Val \mapsto V * prev.Next \mapsto curr * curr.Val \mapsto V' * ((V' = +\infty \wedge curr.Next \mapsto \mathsf{nil}) \vee$
   $\exists X, V''.curr.Next \mapsto X * N(X, V'') \wedge V' < V'')\}$
  return (prev, curr);
}
```

$$I_H(L) \triangleq \mathsf{emp_s} \wedge \exists X, V'.L.Val \mapsto -\infty * L.Next \mapsto X * N(X, V') \wedge -\infty < V'$$

$$I_N(L, V) \triangleq \mathsf{emp_s} \wedge ((L.Val \mapsto V * L.Next \mapsto \mathsf{nil} \wedge V = +\infty) \vee (\exists X, V'.L.Val \mapsto V * L.Next \mapsto X * N(X, V') \wedge V < V'))$$

**Fig. 4.** Proof outline for a part of the lock coupling list program. Here $O$ is $e$, *prev*, *curr*, $(1/M)head$.

in parallel. The operations add and remove an element with the given key to or from the list. Traversing the list uses lock coupling: the lock on one node is not released until the next node is locked. The list is sorted and the first and last nodes in it are sentinel nodes that have values $-\infty$, respectively, $+\infty$. It is initialized by the code in procedure *initialize*. We only provide a proof outline for the procedure *locate* (Figure 4), which is invoked by other procedures to traverse the list. We use lock sorts $H$ (for the head node) and $N$ (for all other nodes) with the invariants $I_H(L)$ and $I_N(L, V)$. In this example the resource invariant for the lock protecting a node in the list holds a handle for the lock protecting the next node in the list. The full permission for $N(X, V')$ in the invariants above essentially means that the only way a thread can lock a node is by first locking its predecessor: here the invariant enforces a particular locking policy.

```
struct NODE { LOCK Lock;
              int Val;
              NODE *Next; }

NODE *head;

initialize() {
  NODE *last;
  last = new NODE;
  last->Val = INFINITY;
  last->Next = NULL;
  init_{N,+∞}(last);
  release(last);
  head = new NODE;
  head->Val = -INFINITY;
  head->Next = last;
  init_H(head);
  release(head);
}
```

```
add(int e) {
  NODE *n1, *n2, *n3, *result;
  (n1, n3) = locate(e);
  if (n3->Val != e) {
    n2 = new NODE;
    n2->Val = e;
    n2->Next = n3;
    init_{N,e}(n2);
    release(n2);
    n1->Next = n2;
    result = true;
  } else {
    result = false;
  }
  release(n1);
  release(n3);
  return result;
}
```

```
remove(int e) {
  NODE *n1, *n2, *n3;
  NODE *result;
  (n1, n2) = locate(e);
  if (n2->Val == e) {
    n3 = n2->Next;
    n1->Next = n3;
    finalize(n2);
    delete n2;
    result = true;
  } else {
    release(n2);
    result = false;
  }
  release(n1);
  return result;
}
```

**Fig. 5.** Lock coupling list program. The procedure *locate* is shown in Figure 4.

$$
\begin{array}{ll}
\mathsf{nil} = 0 & \text{Values} = \{\dots, -1, 0, 1, \dots\} \\
\text{Perms} = (0, 1] & \text{Vars} = \{x, y, \dots\} \\
\text{Stacks} = \text{Vars} \rightharpoonup_{\text{fin}} (\text{Values} \times \text{Perms}) & \text{Locs} = \{1, 2, \dots\} \\
\text{LockPerms} = [0, 1] & \text{ThreadIDs} = \{1, 2, \dots\} \\
\text{LockVals} = \{\mathsf{U}, \mathsf{0}\} \cup \text{ThreadIDs} & \text{States} = \text{Stacks} \times \text{Heaps}
\end{array}
$$

$$
\text{Heaps} = \text{Locs} \rightharpoonup_{\text{fin}} (\mathsf{Cell}(\text{Values}) \cup \mathsf{Lock}(\mathcal{L} \times \text{LockVals} \times \text{LockPerms}) \setminus \mathsf{Lock}(\mathcal{L} \times \{\mathsf{U}\} \times \{0\}))
$$

**Fig. 6.** Model of the assertion language

We were able to present modular proofs for the programs above because in each case we could associate with every lock a part of the heap such that a thread accessed the part only when it held the lock, that is, the lock owned the part of the heap. We note that we would not be able to give modular proofs to programs that do not obey this policy, for instance, to optimistic list [14] – another fine-grained implementation of the list from Example 3 in which the procedure *locate* first traverses the list without taking any locks and then validates the result by locking two candidate nodes and re-traversing the list to check that they are still present and adjacent in the list.

## 5 Model of the Assertion Language

As usual, assertion language formulae denote sets of pairs of a stack and a heap, both represented by finite partial functions. They are interpreted over the domain in Figure 6. However, in contrast to the standard domain used in separation logic, here cells in the heap can be of two types: ordinary cells ($\mathsf{Cell}$) and locks ($\mathsf{Lock}$). A lock has a sort, a value, and is associated with a permission from $[0, 1]$. To simplify notation, here and in the further semantic development we assume that lock sorts have no parameters other than the address of the lock. Our results can straightforwardly be adjusted to the general case (parameters can be treated in

$$
\begin{array}{ll}
(s,h,i) \models_k E \mapsto F & \Leftrightarrow [\![E]\!]_{(s,i)}\downarrow \wedge [\![F]\!]_{(s,i)}\downarrow \wedge h = [[\![E]\!]_{(s,i)} : \mathsf{Cell}([\![F]\!]_{(s,i)})] \\
(s,h,i) \models_k \mathsf{Own}_\pi(x) & \Leftrightarrow \exists u.[\![\pi]\!]_{(s,i)}\downarrow \wedge s = [x : (u, [\![\pi]\!]_{(s,i)})] \wedge 0 < [\![\pi]\!]_{(s,i)} \leq 1 \\
(s,h,i) \models_k \pi A(E) & \Leftrightarrow \\
\quad [\![E]\!]_{(s,i)}\downarrow \wedge [\![\pi]\!]_{(s,i)}\downarrow \wedge h = [[\![E]\!]_{(s,i)} : \mathsf{Lock}(A, \mathsf{U}, [\![\pi]\!]_{(s,i)})] \wedge 0 < [\![\pi]\!]_{(s,i)} \leq 1 & \\
(s,h,i) \models_k \mathsf{Locked}_A(E) & \Leftrightarrow [\![E]\!]_{(s,i)}\downarrow \wedge h = [[\![E]\!]_{(s,i)} : \mathsf{Lock}(A, k, 0)] \\
(s,h,i) \models_k \mathsf{emp_s} & \Leftrightarrow s = [\,] \\
(s,h,i) \models_k \mathsf{emp_h} & \Leftrightarrow h = [\,] \\
(s,h,i) \models_k E = F & \Leftrightarrow [\![E]\!]_{(s,i)}\downarrow \wedge [\![F]\!]_{(s,i)}\downarrow \wedge [\![E]\!]_{(s,i)} = [\![F]\!]_{(s,i)} \\
(s,h,i) \models_k \pi = \mu & \Leftrightarrow [\![\pi]\!]_{(s,i)}\downarrow \wedge [\![\mu]\!]_{(s,i)}\downarrow \wedge [\![\pi]\!]_{(s,i)} = [\![\mu]\!]_{(s,i)} \\
(s,h,i) \models_k P \Rightarrow Q & \Leftrightarrow ((s,h,i) \models_k P) \Rightarrow ((s,h,i) \models_k Q) \\
(s,h,i) \models_k \mathsf{false} & \Leftrightarrow \mathsf{false} \\
(s,h,i) \models_k P * Q & \Leftrightarrow \\
\quad \exists s_1, h_1, s_2, h_2. s = s_1 * s_2 \wedge h = h_1 * h_2 \wedge (s_1, h_1, i) \models_k P \wedge (s_2, h_2, i) \models_k Q & \\
(s,h,i) \models_k P -\!\!* Q & \Leftrightarrow \\
\quad \forall s', h'. s \sharp s' \wedge h \sharp h' \wedge ((s', h', i) \models_k P) \Rightarrow ((s * s', h * h', i) \models_k Q) & \\
(s,h,i) \models_k \exists X.P & \Leftrightarrow \exists u.(s, h, i[X : u]) \models_k P
\end{array}
$$

**Fig. 7.** Satisfaction relation for the assertion language formulae: $(s, h, i) \models_k \Phi$

the same way as lock sorts). The permission 0 is used to represent the existential permission for a lock that is carried by $\mathsf{Locked}_A(E, \vec{F})$. Locks are interpreted as follows: 0 represents the fact that the lock is not held by any thread (i.e., is *free*), values from ThreadIDs represent the identifier of the thread that holds the lock, and U means that the status of the lock is unknown. U is not encountered in the states obtained in the operational semantics we define in Section 6, but is used for interpreting formulae representing parts of complete states. The semantics of formulae and commands never encounter locks of form $\mathsf{Lock}(A, \mathsf{U}, 0)$ for any $A$, and so the definition of Heaps removes them in order to make the $*$ operation on states cancellative [3].

Note how Heaps in the domain of Figure 6 is not defined recursively, but instead uses an indirection through $\mathcal{L}$, whose elements are associated with resource invariants, and hence indirectly to Heaps. It is this indirection that deals with the foundational circularity issue raised by locks which may refer to themselves.

In this paper we use the following notation for partial functions: $f(x)\downarrow$ means that the function $f$ is defined on $x$, $f(x)\uparrow$ that the function $f$ is undefined on $x$, and $[\,]$ denotes a nowhere-defined function. Furthermore, we denote with $f[x : y]$ (defined only if $f(x)\uparrow$) the function that has the same value as $f$ everywhere, except for $x$, where it has the value $y$. We abbreviate $[\,][x : y]$ to $[x : y]$.

We now define $*$ on states in our domain, which interprets the $*$-connective in the logic. We first define the $*$ operation on values of locks in the following way: $\mathsf{U} * \mathsf{U} = \mathsf{U}$, $k * \mathsf{U} = \mathsf{U} * k = k$, and $k * j$ is undefined for $k, j \in \{0\} \cup \text{ThreadIDs}$. Note that $k * k$ is undefined as it arises in the cases when a thread tries to acquire a lock twice (recall that we specify that a thread deadlocks in this case).

For $s_1, s_2 \in$ Stacks let

$$s_1 \sharp s_2 \Leftrightarrow \forall x. s_1(x)\downarrow \wedge s_2(x)\downarrow \Rightarrow (\exists v, \pi_1, \pi_2. s_1(x) = (v, \pi_1) \wedge s_2 = (v, \pi_2) \wedge \pi_1 + \pi_2 \leq 1)\ .$$

If $s_1 \sharp s_2$, then

$$s_1 * s_2 = \{(x,(v,\pi)) \mid (s_1(x) = (v,\pi) \wedge s_2(x)\uparrow) \vee (s_2(x) = (v,\pi) \wedge s_1(x)\uparrow) \vee \\ (s_1(x) = (v,\pi_1) \wedge s_2(x) = (v,\pi_2) \wedge \pi = \pi_1 + \pi_2)\} ,$$

otherwise $s_1 * s_2$ is undefined. For $h_1, h_2 \in$ Heaps let

$$h_1 \sharp h_2 \Leftrightarrow \forall u. h_1(u)\downarrow \wedge h_2(u)\downarrow \Rightarrow ((\exists v. h_1(u) = h_2(u) = \mathsf{Cell}(v)) \vee (\exists A, v_1, v_2, \pi_1, \pi_2. \\ h_1(u) = \mathsf{Lock}(A, v_1, \pi_1) \wedge h_2(u) = \mathsf{Lock}(A, v_2, \pi_2) \wedge v_1 * v_2\downarrow \wedge \pi_1 + \pi_2 \leq 1)) .$$

If $h_1 \sharp h_2$, then

$$h_1 * h_2 = \{(u, \mathsf{Cell}(v)) \mid h_1(u) = \mathsf{Cell}(v) \vee h_2(u) = \mathsf{Cell}(v)\} \cup \\ \{(u, \mathsf{Lock}(A,v,\pi)) \mid (h_1(u) = \mathsf{Lock}(A,v,\pi) \wedge h_2(u)\uparrow) \vee (h_2(u) = \mathsf{Lock}(A,v,\pi) \wedge h_1(u)\uparrow) \\ \vee (h_1(u) = \mathsf{Lock}(A, v_1, \pi_1) \wedge h_2(u) = \mathsf{Lock}(A, v_2, \pi_2) \wedge \pi = \pi_1 + \pi_2 \wedge v = v_1 * v_2)\} ,$$

otherwise $h_1 * h_2$ is undefined. We lift $*$ to states and sets of states pointwise.

The satisfaction relation for the assertion language formulae is defined in Figure 7. A formula is interpreted with respect to a thread identifier $k \in \{0\} \cup$ ThreadIDs, a stack $s$, a heap $h$, and an interpretation $i$ mapping logical variables to Values. Note that in this case it is convenient for us to consider 0 as a dummy thread identifier. We assume a function $[\![E]\!]_{(s,i)}$ that evaluates an expression with respect to the stack $s$ and the interpretation $i$. We consider only interpretations that define the value of every logical variable used. We omit $i$ when $s$ suffices to evaluate the expression. We let $[\![P]\!]_i^k$ denote the set of states in which the formula $P$ is valid with respect to the thread identifier $k$ and the interpretation $i$ and let $\mathcal{I}_k(A,u) = [\![I_A(L) * \mathsf{Locked}_A(L)]\!]_{[L:u]}^k$.

We say that a predicate $p \subseteq$ States is *precise* [10] if for any state $\sigma$, there exists at most one substate $\sigma_0$ (i.e., $\sigma = \sigma_0 * \sigma_1$ for some $\sigma_1$) satisfying $p$. We say that a predicate $p$ is *intuitionistic* [8] if it is closed under stack and heap extension: if $p$ is true of a state $\sigma_1$, then for any state $\sigma_2$, such that $\sigma_1 * \sigma_2$ is defined, $p$ is also true of $\sigma_1 * \sigma_2$. We say that a predicate $p$ *has an empty lockset* if the value of any lock in every state satisfying $p$ is U. A formula is precise, intuitionistic, or has an empty lockset if its denotation with respect to any thread identifier and interpretation of logical variables is precise, intuitionistic, or has an empty lockset. We require that formulae representing resource invariants be precise and have an empty lockset, i.e., that for each $u$ and $k$ the predicate $[\![I_A(L)]\!]_{[L:u]}^k$ be precise and have an empty lockset. The former requirement is inherited from concurrent separation logic, where it is required for soundness of the conjunction rule. The latter requirement is necessary for soundness of our logic and stems from the fact that in our semantics we do not allow a thread that did not acquire a lock to release it (in agreement with the semantics of mutexes in the POSIX threads library). If we were to allow this (i.e., if we treated locks as binary semaphores rather than mutexes), then this requirement would not be necessary. It is easy to check that the invariants for lock sorts $R$, $P$, $H$, and $N$ from Section 4 satisfy these constraints.

$$\begin{array}{lll}
x = E, (s[x:(u,1)], h) & \rightsquigarrow_k & (s[x:(\llbracket E \rrbracket_{s[x:(u,1)]}, 1)], h) \\
x = [E], (s[x:(u,1)], h[e:\mathsf{Cell}(v)]) & \rightsquigarrow_k & (s[x:(v,1)], h[e:\mathsf{Cell}(v)]), e = \llbracket E \rrbracket_{s[x:(u,1)]} \\
[E] = F, (s, h[\llbracket E \rrbracket_s : \mathsf{Cell}(u)]) & \rightsquigarrow_k & (s, h[\llbracket E \rrbracket_s : \mathsf{Cell}(\llbracket F \rrbracket_s)]) \\
x = \mathbf{new}, (s[x:(u,1)], h) & \rightsquigarrow_k & (s[x:(v,1)], h[v:\mathsf{Cell}(w)]), \text{ if } h(v)\uparrow \\
\mathbf{delete}\ E, (s, h[\llbracket E \rrbracket_s : \mathsf{Cell}(u)]) & \rightsquigarrow_k & (s, h) \\
\mathbf{assume}(G), (s,h) & \rightsquigarrow_k & (s,h), \text{ if } \llbracket G \rrbracket_s = \mathsf{true} \\
\mathbf{assume}(G), (s,h) & \not\rightsquigarrow_k & \qquad \text{if } \llbracket G \rrbracket_s = \mathsf{false} \\
\mathbf{init}_A(E), (s, h[\llbracket E \rrbracket_s : \mathsf{Cell}(u)]) & \rightsquigarrow_k & (s, h[\llbracket E \rrbracket_s : \mathsf{Lock}(A,k,1)]) \\
\mathbf{finalize}(E), (s, h[\llbracket E \rrbracket_s : \mathsf{Lock}(A,k,1)]) & \rightsquigarrow_k & (s, h[\llbracket E \rrbracket_s : \mathsf{Cell}(u)]) \\
\mathbf{acquire}(E), (s, h[\llbracket E \rrbracket_s : \mathsf{Lock}(A,0,\pi)]) & \rightsquigarrow_k & (s, h[\llbracket E \rrbracket_s : \mathsf{Lock}(A,k,\pi)]) \\
\mathbf{acquire}(E), (s, h[\llbracket E \rrbracket_s : \mathsf{Lock}(A,j,\pi)]) & \not\rightsquigarrow_k & \qquad \text{if } j > 0 \\
\mathbf{release}(E), (s, h[\llbracket E \rrbracket_s : \mathsf{Lock}(A,k,\pi)]) & \rightsquigarrow_k & (s, h[\llbracket E \rrbracket_s : \mathsf{Lock}(A,0,\pi)]) \\
C, (s,h) & \rightsquigarrow_k & \top, \qquad \text{otherwise}
\end{array}$$

**Fig. 8.** Transition relation for atomic commands. $\not\rightsquigarrow_k$ is used to denote that the command does not fault, but gets stuck. $\top$ indicates that the command faults.

## 6 Interleaving Operational Semantics

Consider a program $S$ consisting of a parallel composition of $n$ threads. We abstract away from the particular syntax of the programming language and represent each thread by its control-flow graph (CFG). A CFG over a set $\mathcal{C}$ of atomic commands is defined as a tuple $(N, F, \mathsf{start}, \mathsf{end})$, where $N$ is the set of program points, $F \subseteq N \times \mathcal{C} \times N$ the control-flow relation, $\mathsf{start}$ and $\mathsf{end}$ distinguished start and end program points. We note that a command in our language can be translated to a CFG. Conditional expressions in **if** and **while** commands are translated using the **assume**$(G)$ statement that acts as a filter on the state space of programs – $G$ is assumed to be true after **assume**$(G)$ is executed. We let the set of atomic commands consist of primitive commands and the **assume** command. Let $(N_k, F_k, \mathsf{start}_k, \mathsf{end}_k)$ be the CFG of thread with identifier $k$ and let $N = \bigcup_{k=1}^{n} N_k$ and $F = \bigcup_{k=1}^{n} F_k$. First, for each thread $k = 1..n$ and atomic command $C$ we define a transition relation $\rightsquigarrow_k$ shown in Figure 8.

The interleaving operational semantics of the program $S$ is defined by a transition relation $\rightarrow_S$ that transforms pairs of program counters (represented by mappings from thread identifiers to program points) $\mathsf{pc} \in \{1, \ldots, n\} \rightarrow N$ and states $\sigma \in \text{States} \cup \{\top\}$. The relation $\rightarrow_S$ is defined as the least one satisfying:

$$\frac{(v, C, v') \in F \quad k \in \{1, \ldots, n\} \quad C, (s,h) \rightsquigarrow_k \sigma}{\mathsf{pc}[k:v], (s,h) \rightarrow_S \mathsf{pc}[k:v'], \sigma} \, .$$

We denote with $\rightarrow_S^*$ the reflexive and transitive closure of $\rightarrow_S$. Let us denote with $\mathsf{pc}_0$ the initial program counter $[1 : \mathsf{start}_1] \ldots [n : \mathsf{start}_n]$ and with $\mathsf{pc}_\mathsf{f}$ the final one $[1 : \mathsf{end}_1] \ldots [n : \mathsf{end}_n]$. We say that the program $S$ is *safe* when run from an initial state $\sigma_0$ if it is not the case that for some $\mathsf{pc}$ we have $\mathsf{pc}_0, \sigma_0 \rightarrow_S^* \mathsf{pc}, \top$.

$\{x, y \Vdash x \mapsto \_ * y \mapsto \_\}$
`init`$_{A,y}$`(x);`
`init`$_{B,x}$`(y);`
$\{x, y \Vdash A(x, y) * \mathsf{Locked}_A(x, y) * B(y, x) * \mathsf{Locked}_B(y, x)\}$
`release(x);`
$\{x, y \Vdash A(x, y) * \mathsf{Locked}_B(y, x)\}$
`release(y);`
$\{x, y \Vdash \mathsf{emp_h}\}$

$$I_A(X, Y) \triangleq \mathsf{emp_s} \wedge B(Y, X) \quad \text{and} \quad I_B(X, Y) \triangleq \mathsf{emp_s} \wedge A(Y, X)$$

**Fig. 9.** A pathological situation

## 7 Soundness

As it stands now, the logic allows some unpleasant situations to happen: in certain cases the proof system may not be able to detect a memory leak. Figure 9 shows an example of this kind. We assume defined lock sorts $A$ and $B$ with invariants $I_A(X, Y)$ and $I_B(X, Y)$. In this case the knowledge that the locks at the addresses $x$ and $y$ exist is lost by the proof system: the invariant for the lock $x$ holds the full permission for the handle of the lock $y$ and vice versa, hence, local states of the threads are then left without any permissions for the locks whatsoever.

Situations such as the one described above make the formulation of the soundness statement for our logic non-trivial. We first formulate a soundness statement (Theorem 1) showing that every final state of a program (according to the operational semantics of Section 6) can be obtained as the $*$-conjunction of the postconditions of threads and the resource invariants *for the free locks allocated in the state.* Note that here a statement about a state uses the information about the free locks allocated in the same state. We then put restrictions on resource invariants that rule out situations similar to the one shown in Figure 9 and formulate a soundness statement (Theorem 4) in which the set of free locks in a final state is computed solely from the postconditions of threads.

For a state $\sigma$ let $\mathsf{Free}(\sigma)$, respectively, $\mathsf{Unknown}(\sigma)$ be the set of pairs from $\mathcal{L} \times \mathsf{Locs}$ consisting of sorts and addresses of locks allocated in the state that have value 0, respectively, $\mathsf{U}$. We denote with $\circledast$ iterated separating conjunction [13]: $\circledast_{j=1}^{k} P_j = (\mathsf{emp_s} \wedge \mathsf{emp_h}) * P_1 * \cdots * P_k$. The soundness of the logic with respect to the interleaving operational semantics from Section 6 is established by:

**Theorem 1.** *Let $S$ be the program $C_1 \parallel \ldots \parallel C_n$ and suppose $\vdash \{P_k\}\, C_k\, \{Q_k\}$ for $k = 1..n$. Then for any interpretation $i$ and state $\sigma_0$ such that $\sigma_0 \in \left(\circledast_{k=1}^{n} [\![P_k]\!]_i^k\right) * \left(\circledast_{(A,u)\in\mathsf{Free}(\sigma_0)} \mathcal{I}_0(A, u)\right)$ the program $S$ is safe when run from $\sigma_0$ and if $\mathsf{pc}_0, \sigma_0 \to_S^* \mathsf{pc_f}, \sigma$, then $\sigma \in \left(\circledast_{k=1}^{n} [\![Q_k]\!]_i^k\right) * \left(\circledast_{(A,u)\in\mathsf{Free}(\sigma)} \mathcal{I}_0(A, u)\right)$.*

The proof is given in a companion Technical Report [6]. We do not follow Brookes's original proof of soundness of concurrent separation logic [2]. Instead, we prove soundness with the aid of an intermediate thread-local semantics defined by fixed-point equations that can be viewed as the scheme of a thread-modular program analysis in the style of [7]. This method of proving soundness should facilitate designing program analyses based on our logic. The idea of our proof, however, is close to that of Brookes's and consists of establishing what is called the Separation Property in [10] and is formalized as the Parallel Decomposition Lemma in [2]:[2] At any time, the state of the program can be partitioned into that owned by each thread and each free lock. As a direct consequence of the Separation Property, we can also show that provability of a program in our proof system ensures the absence of data races (see [6] for details).

We now proceed to formulate a soundness statement in which the component $\circledast_{(A,u)\in\mathsf{Free}(\sigma)} \mathcal{I}_0(A,u)$ from Theorem 1 representing the resource invariants for free locks in the final state is obtained directly from the thread postconditions $Q_k$. To this end, we introduce an auxiliary notion of closure. Intuitively, closing a state amounts to $*$-conjoining it to the invariants of all free locks whose handles are reachable via resource invariants from the handles present in the state.

**Definition 2 (Closure).** *For* $p \subseteq \mathrm{States}$ *let* $c(p) \subseteq \mathrm{States}$ *be the least predicate such that* $p \cup \{\sigma_1 * \sigma_2 \mid \sigma_1 \in c(p) \wedge \sigma_2 \in \circledast_{(A,u)\in\mathsf{Unknown}(\sigma_1)} \mathcal{I}_0(A,u)\} \subseteq c(p)$. *The closure* $\langle p \rangle$ *of* $p$ *is the set of states from* $c(p)$ *that do not contain locks with the value* $\mathsf{U}$.

In general, the closure is not guaranteed to add invariants for all the free locks allocated in the state. For example, the closure of the postcondition of the program in Figure 9 still has an empty heap while in the final states obtained by executing the operational semantics there are locks allocated at addresses $x$ and $y$. The problem is that there may exist a "self-contained" set of free locks (containing the locks at the addresses $x$ and $y$ in our example) such that the corresponding resource invariants hold full permissions for all the locks from the set. Local states of threads are then left without any permissions for the locks in the set, and hence, closure is not able to reach to their invariants. The following condition on resource invariants ensures that this does not happen.

**Definition 3 (Admissibility of resource invariants).** *Resource invariants for a set of lock sorts* $\mathcal{L}$ *are admissible if there do not exist non-empty set* $L \subseteq \mathcal{L} \times \mathrm{Locs}$ *and state* $\sigma \in \circledast_{(A,u)\in L} \mathcal{I}_0(A,u)$ *such that for all* $(A,u) \in L$ *the permission associated with the lock at the address* $u$ *in* $\sigma$ *is* $1$.

Definitions 2 and 3 generalize to the case when resource invariants have more than one parameter in the obvious way. Revisiting Example 3 of Section 4, we can check that any state satisfying the closure of $[\![O \Vdash (1/M)H(\mathit{head})]\!]^k$ for any thread identifier $k$ represents an acyclic sorted list starting at *head*. It is easy to check that resource invariants for the set of lock sorts $\{R, P, H, N\}$ from Section 4 are admissible whereas those for $\{A, B\}$ from this section are not. The admissibility of $N$ is due to the fact that $I_N$ implies sortedness of lists built out of resource invariants for $N$, hence, the invariants cannot form a cycle.

We say that a state is *complete* if permissions associated with all the locks allocated in it are equal to 1. Note that according to the semantics in Section 6,

[2] We call it the Over-approximation Lemma in [6] due to the analogy between our proof and proofs of soundness of program analyses based on abstract interpretation.

if $\sigma_0$ is complete and $\mathsf{pc}_0, \sigma_0 \to_S^* \mathsf{pc}, \sigma$, then $\sigma$ is also complete. We can now formulate and prove the desired soundness statement.

**Theorem 4.** *Let $S$ be the program $C_1 \parallel \ldots \parallel C_n$ and suppose $\vdash \{P_k\}\ C_k\ \{Q_k\}$ for $k = 1..n$. Suppose further that either at least one of $Q_k$ is intuitionistic or resource invariants for lock sorts used in the proofs are admissible. Then for any interpretation $i$ and complete state $\sigma_0$ such that $\sigma_0 \in \langle \circledast_{k=1}^n [\![P_k]\!]_i^k \rangle$ the program $S$ is safe when run from $\sigma_0$ and if $\mathsf{pc}_0, \sigma_0 \to_S^* \mathsf{pc}_\mathsf{f}, \sigma$, then $\sigma \in \langle \circledast_{k=1}^n [\![Q_k]\!]_i^k \rangle$.*

*Proof.* Consider an interpretation $i$ and a complete state $\sigma_0 \in \langle \circledast_{k=1}^n [\![P_k]\!]_i^k \rangle$. Therefore $\sigma_0 \in \left(\circledast_{k=1}^n [\![P_k]\!]_i^k\right) * \left(\circledast_{(A,u)\in\mathsf{Free}(\sigma_0)} \mathcal{I}_0(A,u)\right)$ from the definition of closure. Then by Theorem 1 the program $S$ is safe when run from $\sigma_0$ and if $\mathsf{pc}_0, \sigma_0 \to_S^* \mathsf{pc}_\mathsf{f}, \sigma$, then $\sigma \in \left(\circledast_{k=1}^n [\![Q_k]\!]_i^k\right) * \left(\circledast_{(A,u)\in\mathsf{Free}(\sigma)} \mathcal{I}_0(A,u)\right)$. Hence, by the definition of closure, we have $\sigma \in \sigma_1 * \sigma_2$ where $\sigma_1 \in \langle \circledast_{k=1}^n [\![Q_k]\!]_i^k \rangle$ and $\sigma_2 \in \circledast_{(A,u)\in L} \mathcal{I}_0(A,u)$ for some $L \subseteq \mathsf{Free}(\sigma)$. If one of $Q_k$ is intuitionistic, then from this it directly follows that $\sigma \in \langle \circledast_{k=1}^n [\![Q_k]\!]_i^k \rangle$.

Suppose now that $L \neq \emptyset$ and the resource invariants for lock sorts mentioned in $L$ are admissible. Consider any $(A,u) \in L$. The state $\sigma$ is complete, therefore, the permission associated with the lock at the address $u$ in $\sigma$ is 1. Besides, since $L \subseteq \mathsf{Free}(\sigma)$, the value associated with $u$ in $\sigma$ is 0. Hence, if the permission associated with $u$ in $\sigma_2$ were less than 1, then $u$ would have to be allocated in $\sigma_1$ with a non-zero permission and the value $\mathsf{U}$, which would contradict the definition of closure (a state in a closure cannot contain locks with the value $\mathsf{U}$). So, for any $(A,u) \in L$ the permission associated with $u$ in $\sigma_1$ is 1, which contradicts the admissibility of resource invariants for lock sorts used in the proof of the program. Therefore, $L = \emptyset$ and, hence, $\sigma \in \langle \circledast_{k=1}^n [\![Q_k]\!]_i^k \rangle$. □

Note that for garbage-collected languages we can use the intuitionistic version of the logic [8] (i.e., one in which every assertion is intuitionistic) and, hence, do not have to check admissibility. Also, admissibility does not have to be checked if we are not interested in detecting memory leaks, as then Theorem 1 can be used.

## 8 Dynamic Thread Creation

We now extend the programming language with dynamically created threads:

$$\begin{array}{ll} T ::= f, f_1, f_2, \ldots & \text{procedure names} \\ C ::= \ldots \mid V = \mathbf{fork}(T) \mid \mathbf{join}(E) & \text{primitive commands} \\ P ::= \mathbf{let}\ T = S,\ \ldots,\ T = S\ \mathbf{in}\ S & \text{programs} \end{array}$$

We represent the code of threads by parameterless procedures (passing parameters to threads at the time of their creation is orthogonal to our concerns here and can be handled in a way similar to the one used for handling procedure calls when variables are treated as resources [12]; see [6] for details). A program consists of several procedure declarations along with the code of the main thread. We consider only well-formed programs in which all declared procedure names are distinct and all procedures used are declared. $x = \mathbf{fork}(f)$ creates a new thread executing the code of the procedure $f$ and stores the corresponding thread identifier into the variable $x$. **join**$(E)$ waits until the thread with the identifier $E$ finishes executing. In our semantics we allow at most one thread to wait for the termination of a given thread.

We add two new forms to our assertion language: $\Phi ::= \ldots \mid \mathsf{tid}_f(E) \mid \mathsf{emp_t}$. A formula $\mathsf{tid}_f(E)$, which we call a thread handle, represents the knowledge that the thread with the identifier $E$ exists and executes the code of the procedure $f$, and gives its owner a permission to join the thread. $\mathsf{emp_t}$ denotes that the assertion does not contain any permissions of this kind. Note that a thread is deallocated (only) when it is joined.

Judgements are now of the form $\Gamma \vdash \{P\}\ C\ \{Q\}$ where $\Gamma$ is a context consisting of a set of procedure specifications, each of the form $\{P\}\ f\ \{Q\}$. We consider only contexts in which there is at most one specification for each procedure. As procedures are parameterless, we restrict our attention here to contexts in which pre- and postconditions do not contain free logical variables. We add $\Gamma \vdash$ to all the triples in the rules from Figure 1 as well as in the standard rules of separation logic. In addition, we $\wedge$-conjoin $\mathsf{emp_t}$ to every pre- and postcondition in the axioms for primitive commands (except for the postcondition of ACQUIRE and the precondition of RELEASE: in the postcondition of ACQUIRE and the precondition of RELEASE we $\wedge$-conjoin $\mathsf{emp_t}$ right after $\mathsf{Locked}_A(L, \vec{X})$). To reason about **fork** and **join** we introduce two new axioms:

$$\overline{\Gamma,\ \{P\}\ f\ \{Q\} \vdash \{(x \Vdash \mathsf{emp_h} \wedge \mathsf{emp_t}) * P\}\ x = \mathbf{fork}(f)\ \{x \Vdash \mathsf{emp_h} \wedge \mathsf{tid}_f(x)\}}\ \textsc{Fork}$$

$$\overline{\Gamma,\ \{P\}\ f\ \{Q\} \vdash \{O \Vdash \mathsf{emp_h} \wedge \mathsf{tid}_f(E)\}\ \mathbf{join}(E)\ \{(O \Vdash \mathsf{emp_h} \wedge \mathsf{emp_t}) * Q\}}\ \textsc{Join}$$

That is, upon creating a new thread executing the code of procedure $f$, the thread that executed **fork** obtains the thread handle $\mathsf{tid}_f(x)$ for the newly-created thread and gives up ownership of the precondition of $f$. Joining a thread with the identifier $E$ requires the joining thread to own the handle $\mathsf{tid}_f(E)$. When **join** succeeds, the thread exchanges the handle for the postcondition of $f$.

The model of the assertion language has to be adapted to account for thread handles. A state of the program is now represented by a triple of a stack, a heap, and a thread pool, the latter represented by a finite partial function from thread identifiers to procedure names. Now a lock can be free, held by the main thread, held by a thread, or its status may be unknown. Assertions are then interpreted with respect to a thread identifier, a stack, a heap, a thread pool, and an interpretation of logical variables. We define the $*$ operation on thread pools as disjoint union of the partial functions representing them, and the semantics of $P * Q$ and $P \mathrel{-\!\!*} Q$ are then straightforwardly adjusted so as to partition thread pools. In addition, we add clauses for the new forms in our assertion language such that $\mathsf{tid}_f(E)$ describes singleton thread pools and $\mathsf{emp_t}$ describes the empty thread pool. The satisfaction relation for all other formulae just ignores the thread pool. The notion of precision of formulae does not change.

Due to space constraints, we omit the detailed development of semantics and soundness for the extended logic, which can be found in [6]. Instead, we just state the conditions under which the logic is sound. A proof of the program **let** $f_1 = C_1, \ldots, f_n = C_n$ **in** $C$ is given by triples $\Gamma \vdash \{P_1\}\ C_1\ \{Q_1\}, \ldots, \Gamma \vdash \{P_n\}\ C_n\ \{Q_n\}, \Gamma \vdash \{P\}\ C\ \{Q\}$, where $\Gamma = \{P_1\}\ f_1\ \{Q_1\}, \ldots, \{P_n\}\ f_n\ \{Q_n\}$. For the proof to be sound, $P_k$ must be precise, and $P_k$ and $Q_k$ must have empty locksets, for all $k = 1..n$. We note that the operational semantics of Section 6 can be adjusted to our setting and a soundness statement similar to Theorem 1 can then be formulated. The proof of soundness is then done in the same style as that of Theorem 1. The notions of closure and admissibility can also be generalized to the new setting and a theorem similar to Theorem 4 can be proved.

## 9 Conclusions and Related Work

We have presented a logic that allows reasoning about concurrent heap-manipulating programs with realistic concurrency primitives including unbounded numbers of locks dynamically allocated and destroyed in the heap and threads dynamically created and terminating themselves. We have demonstrated that the logic makes it possible to reason locally about programs with a notion of dynamic ownership of heap parts by locks and threads. We believe that in the future this aspect of the logic will produce some additional pay-offs. First, the resource-oriented flavor of the logic should make it easy to design program analyses on the basis of it following the lines of [7]. In fact, the fixed-point equations defining the thread-local semantics used in the proof of soundness of our logic can be seen as a scheme of a thread-modular program analysis in the style of [7]. Second, lock handles in our logic's assertion language are somewhat reminiscent of abstract predicates used for modular reasoning in separation logic about object-oriented programs [11]. This is not a coincidence as object-oriented programs use information hiding extensively in their locking mechanisms, and hence, often satisfy the Ownership Hypothesis. For this reason, we believe that our logic, combined with the techniques from [11], should be convenient for reasoning about concurrent object-oriented programs. Note, however, that lock handles and abstract predicates are different, in particular, we cannot see a way in which the former can be encoded in terms of the latter.

Two papers [4,15] have recently suggested combinations of separation logic and rely-guarantee reasoning that, among other things, can be used to reason about storable locks. For example, in [15] locks are not treated natively in the logic, but are represented as cells in memory storing the identifier of the thread that holds the lock; rely-guarantee is then used to simplify reasoning about the global shared heap with locks allocated in it. The logic allows modular reasoning about complex fine-grained concurrency algorithms (e.g., about the optimistic list mentioned in Section 4), but loses locality of reasoning for programs that allocate and deallocate many simple data structures protected by locks, which results in awkward proofs. In other words, as the original concurrent separation logic, the logics in [4,15] are designed for reasoning about the concurrent control of bounded numbers of data structures whereas our logic is designed to reason about the concurrent control of unboundedly many data structures that are dynamically created and destroyed. Ideally, one wants to have a combination of both: a logic in which on the higher-level the reasoning is performed in a resource-oriented fashion and on the lower-level rely-guarantee is applied to deal with complex cases. Achieving this is another direction of our future research.

Feng and Shao [5] presented a rely-guarantee logic for reasoning about concurrent assembly code with dynamic thread creation. They do not have analogs of our rules for ownership transfer at **fork** and **join** commands. On a higher level, our logic for storable threads relates to theirs in the same way as separation logic relates to rely-guarantee reasoning: the former is good at describing ownership transfer, the latter at describing interference. As in the case of storable locks, investigating possible combinations of the two approaches would be fruitful.

*Acknowledgments.* We would like to thank Richard Bornat, Cristiano Calcagno, Peter O'Hearn, and Matthew Parkinson for comments and discussions that helped to improve the paper.

## References

1. Bornat, R., Calcagno, C., O'Hearn, P.W., Parkinson, M.: Permission accounting in separation logic. In: POPL (2005)
2. Brookes, S.D.: A semantics of concurrent separation logic. Theoretical Computer Science 375(1-3), 227–270 In: Gardner, P., Yoshida, N. (eds.) CONCUR 2004. LNCS, vol. 3170, pp. 227–270. Springer, Heidelberg (2004)
3. Calcagno, C., O'Hearn, P., Yang, H.: Local action and abstract separation logic. In: LICS (2007)
4. Feng, X., Ferreira, R., Shao, Z.: On the relationship between concurrent separation logic and assume-guarantee reasoning. In: ESOP (2007)
5. Feng, X., Shao, Z.: Modular verification of concurrent assembly code with dynamic thread creation and termination. In: ICFP (2005)
6. Gotsman, A., Berdine, J., Cook, B., Rinetzky, N., Sagiv, M.: Local reasoning for storable locks and threads. Technical Report MSR-TR-2007-39, Microsoft Research (April 2007)
7. Gotsman, A., Berdine, J., Cook, B., Sagiv, M.: Thread-modular shape analysis. In: PLDI (2007)
8. Ishtiaq, S., O'Hearn, P.W.: BI as an assertion language for mutable data structures. In: POPL (2001)
9. O'Hearn, P., Reynolds, J., Yang, H.: Local reasoning about programs that alter data structures. In: CSL (2001)
10. O'Hearn, P.W.: Resources, concurrency and local reasoning. Theoretical Computer Science 375(1-3), 271–307 (2007) Preliminary version appeared in CONCUR 2004
11. Parkinson, M., Bierman, G.: Separation logic and abstraction. In: POPL (2005)
12. Parkinson, M., Bornat, R., Calcagno, C.: Variables as resource in Hoare logics. In: LICS (2006)
13. Reynolds, J.C.: Separation logic: A logic for shared mutable data structures. In: LICS (2002)
14. Vafeiadis, V., Herlihy, M., Hoare, T., Shapiro, M.: Proving correctness of highly-concurrent linearisable objects. In: PPoPP (2006)
15. Vafeiadis, V., Parkinson, M.J.: A marriage of rely/guarantee and separation logic. In: CONCUR 2007. LNCS, vol. 4703, Springer, Heidelberg (2007)

# Monadic, Prompt Lazy Assertions in Haskell*

Olaf Chitil[1] and Frank Huch[2]

[1] University of Kent, UK
[2] University of Kiel, Germany

**Abstract.** Assertions test expected properties of run-time values without disrupting the normal computation of a program. We present a library for enriching Haskell programs with assertions. Expected properties can be specified in a parser-combinator like language. The assertions are lazy: they do not force evaluation but only examine what is evaluated by the program. They are also prompt: assertion failure is reported as early as possible. The implementation is based on lazy observations and continuation-based coroutines.

## 1 Introduction

Assertions are parts of a program that, instead of contributing to the functionality of the program, express properties of run-time values the programmer expects to hold. It has long been recognised that augmenting programs with assertions improves software quality. An assertion both documents an expected property (e.g. a pre-condition, a post-condition, an invariant) and tests this property at run-time. For example, an assertion may express that the argument of a square root function has to be positive or zero and likewise the result is positive or zero. Assertions can be an attractive alternative to unit tests. Assertions simplify the task of locating the cause of a program fault: in a computation faulty values may be propagated for a long time until they cause an observable error, but assertions can detect such faulty values much earlier.

We can easily define a combinator for attaching assertions to expressions:

```
assert :: Bool -> a -> a
assert b x = if b then x else error "Assertion failed."
```

The assertion is an identity function when the expected property holds, but raises an exception otherwise[1]. Then, assertions can be defined as normal Haskell functions to express expected properties, for example

```
ordered :: Ord a => [a] -> Bool
ordered []         = True
ordered [_]        = True
ordered (x:y:ys) = x<y && ordered (y:ys)
```

* This work has been partially supported by the German Research Council (DFG) under grant Ha 2457/5-2 and by the United Kingdom under EPSRC grant EP/C516605/1.

[1] The Glasgow Haskell Compiler provides a variant that produces a more informative error message that includes the source location of the failed assert call.

Z. Shao (Ed.): APLAS 2007, LNCS 4807, pp. 38–53, 2007.

and use them to assert for example a pre-condition:

```
checkedInsert :: Ord a => a -> [a] -> [a]
checkedInsert x xs = assert (ordered xs) (insert x xs)

insert :: Ord a => a -> [a] -> [a]
insert x [] = [x]
insert x (y:ys) = if x < y then x:y:ys else y : insert x ys
```

In many applications such assertions work fine

```
> checkedInsert 4 [1,3,2,5]
Assertion failed.
```

but sometimes they do not, as the following non-terminating expression shows:

```
> take 4 (checkedInsert 4 [1,2..])
```

In our example the function `ordered`, which expresses our expected property, is fully strict and thus forces evaluation of the whole infinite list. Programming with assertions as above results in strict programs and thus a loss of the expressive power of laziness, for example, the use of infinite data structures and cyclic definitions. As long as an assertion does not fail, a program augmented with assertions should have exactly the same input/output behaviour as the one without assertions. Hence assertions for a lazy language should be lazy, that is, a property should only be checked for the part of a data structure that is evaluated during the computation anyway.

Our example above also demonstrates that using Boolean functions for specifying properties is rather limiting in expressiveness. We want to say that any list containing two neighbouring elements in the wrong order should raise an assertion failure, also when most of the rest of the list has not been evaluated. However, `ordered` only decides on totally evaluated finite lists. We present a parser-combinator like monadic language for expressive lazy assertions. Parser combinators are a well-known tool for describing a set of token sequences. Similarly our assertion combinators describe a set of possibly partial expected values.

Whenever a part of a value is evaluated that violates an asserted property, the assertion immediately fails. We say our assertions are *prompt*. Promptness ensures that the reported unexpected value is as unevaluated as possible and thus smaller to read. Furthermore, a program fault usually violates many assertions, but promptness ensures that the assertion that is closest to the fault with respect to data flow is reported. In summary, our assertions have the following properties:

- Lazy: They do not modify the lazy behaviour of a program.
- Prompt: The violation of an assertion is reported as early as possible, before a faulty value is used by the surrounding computation.
- Expressive: Complex properties can be expressed using full Haskell.
- Portable: Assertions are implemented as a library and do not need any compiler or run-time modifications; the only extension to Haskell 98 used for the implementation are `unsafePerformIO` and `IORefs`.

## 2 Using the Assertion Monad

Expected properties are specified in an assertion monad `Try a` that combines pattern matching and non-deterministic computations. The combinators are used very similarly to standard monadic parser combinators [8].

Here is a specification of the ordered property from the Introduction:

```
ordered :: Ord a => Lazy [a] -> Try ()
ordered xs = pNil xs
         ||| (do (_,ys) <- pCons xs; pNil ys)
         ||| (do (x,ys) <- pCons xs; (y,_) <- pCons ys;
                ((do rx <- pVal x; ry <- pVal y; guard (rx < ry))
                 &&& ordered ys))
```

The tested argument is wrapped within a new type constructor `Lazy` and the result type has to be `Try ()`. Together these two types enable prompt and lazy evaluation of assertions. To specify the three different cases for lists of length zero, one, and longer lists, the assertion monad `Try a` provides the non-deterministic choice operator `(|||) :: Try a -> Try a -> Try a`. For a fair evaluation, that is, there is no fixed order in which the different cases are evaluated. Similarly, we provide a fair, parallel[2] conjunction operator `(&&&) :: Try () -> Try () -> Try ()`, which here allows independent testing at every position within the list.

For pattern matching we provide the following pattern combinators within the assertion monad:

```
pNil :: Lazy [a] -> Try ()
pCons :: Lazy [a] -> Try (Lazy a,Lazy [a])
pVal :: Lazy a -> Try a
```

For each data constructor we provide a pattern combinator that matches only the constructor and that yields the sub-structure as a tuple within the `Try` monad. For example, for the empty list it returns the empty tuple and for `(:)` it returns a pair consisting of the element and the remaining list. The combinator `pVal` matches every value and directly corresponds to a variable in a Haskell pattern. Finally, the function `guard` is the standard Haskell function that integrates a Boolean test into a `MonadPlus`.

To attach an assertion to an expression we provide the function `assert :: String -> (Lazy a -> Try ()) -> a -> a`. The first parameter is a label naming the assertion. When an assertion fails, the computation aborts with an appropriate message that includes the assertion's label. As further parameters `assert` takes the property and the value on which it behaves as a partial identity.

For expected values an assertion is an identity function. For partial values that are smaller than expected values (in the standard ordering where unevaluated/undefined is less than any value) the assertion cannot be decided and hence it is also the identity function. For any unexpected value the assertion raises an exception.

---

[2] That is, it has no fixed sequential evaluation order for the two arguments.

To prevent an assertion from evaluating too much, the property has to be defined as a predicate on the tested data structure. The implementation of `assert` uses a class `Observe` to ensure that only the context in which the application of `assert` appears determines how far the tested data structure is evaluated and only that part is passed to the predicate.

```
insertWithPre :: (Ord a,Observe a) => a -> [a] -> [a]
insertWithPre x xs = insert x (assert "insert input ordered" ordered xs)
```

The assertion is evaluated in a prompt, lazy manner, as the following call shows:

```
> take 4 (insertWithPre 4 ([3,4] ++ [1,2..]))
[3,4,
Assertion (insert input ordered) failed: 3:4:1:_
```

Beside reporting the failed assertion, we also present the wrong value to the user and highlight those parts that contribute to the failure. Here these are, beside the unordered values, all `(:)` constructors above the unordered values, because the assertion would not have failed if any of them was `[]`.

Similar to this precondition, we can add a postcondition specifying that the result of `insert` is ordered. However, this is not exactly what one would like to specify as a property of `insert`. In case `insert` is called with an unordered list, this fault should not be blamed on `insert`, but on the function applying `insert` to an unordered list. A better specification for `insert` is: if the argument list is ordered, then the result is ordered as well. In contrast to the first assertion, this property is defined for a function. It specifies properties for an argument and the result. Functional assertions can be expressed by means of function `fun`$n$ [3] for functions of arity $n$:

```
insertChecked :: (Ord a, Observe a) => a -> [a] -> [a]
insertChecked = assert "insert preserves ordered property"
                       (fun2 (\ _ ys zs -> ordered ys ==> ordered zs))
                       insert
```

To express the dependence between the two ordered properties, we can use an implication (simply defined as `x ==> y = notAssert x ||| y`). Executing `insertChecked` yields the following behaviour:

```
> insertChecked 3 [5,3,4]
[5,3,3,4]
> insertChecked 3 [2,3,4]
[2,3,
Assertion (insert preserves ordered property) failed:
3 -> (2:3:4:[] -> 2:3:3:4:_)
```

In the second case highlighting shows that for the ordered input list [2,3,4] the duplicate occurrence of `3` in the result list does not meet the specification. To correct the program, we could omit duplicated elements.

---

[3] `fun2 :: (Lazy a -> Lazy b -> Lazy c -> Try ()) -> Lazy (a->b->c) -> Try ()`.

## 3 The Idea of Respecting Laziness

This section outlines how the types `Try a` and `Lazy a` enable Haskell computations to respect how far arguments are evaluated. We introduce the data type

```
data EvalTree = Eval [EvalTree] | Uneval
```

An `EvalTree` represents how far a corresponding data structure is evaluated. It has the same tree structure as the data structure itself except that parts may be cut off by the constructor `Uneval`; that is, if the data structure contains an $n$-ary evaluated constructor, then the corresponding `EvalTree` contains an `Eval` node with $n$ `EvalTree`s in the argument list. For instance, the evaluation of list `[1,2,3]` in the call of `[1,2,3]!!1` is represented by the `EvalTree`: `Eval [Uneval,Eval [Eval [],Uneval]]`. In later sections we will refine the definition of `EvalTree` further. Now we can introduce the type synonym

```
type Lazy a = (EvalTree,a)
```

in which values are paired with their corresponding evaluation information. Because in Haskell pattern matching works from left to right, some of our later definitions are simplified by having the evaluation information as first component of the pair. The `Lazy a` type enables us to define an assertion that respects the evaluation state of the tested value, for example a function `checkOrdered` that checks whether a given list is ordered with respect to its evaluated parts:

```
checkOrdered :: Lazy [Int] -> Maybe Bool
checkOrdered (Eval [], [])          = Just True
checkOrdered (Eval [_,Eval []], [_]) = Just True
checkOrdered (Eval [eX,eYXs@(Eval [eY,eXs])], (x:yxs@(y:xs))) =
                          leq (eX,x) (eY,y) &|& checkOrdered (eYXs,yxs)
checkOrdered _                      = Nothing

leq :: Lazy Int -> Lazy Int -> Maybe Bool
leq (Eval [],x) (Eval [],y) = Just (x <= y)
leq _           _           = Nothing

(&|&) :: Maybe Bool -> Maybe Bool -> Maybe Bool
(Just True)  &|& (Just True)  = Just True
(Just False) &|& _            = Just False
_            &|& (Just False) = Just False
_            &|& _            = Nothing
```

The result type of `checkOrdered` reflects that besides being ordered or not, there is a third alternative (`Nothing`), namely that at this stage of evaluation it is not possible to decide whether the list is ordered or not. For comparing two elements of the list we use a variation of `(<=)` that also respects the `EvalTree`. Finally, the results of each comparison of two elements are combined by a modified version of `(&&)`. Besides using the extended type `Maybe Bool` this function also implements a parallel version of `(&&)` by means of its third rule. Independent of the other argument, `(&|&)` propagates an argument `Just False` as a result.

How can this approach be generalised to arbitrary computations on lazy values? Although, assertions have to return Boolean values as result, subcomputations may return other result types. Here we can also use the `Maybe a` type to express that we either obtain a result of type `a` or have a suspension.

## 4 Non-determinism

Looking ahead, we do want to restart suspensions when more parts of a tested data structure have been evaluated. Hence we need to keep track of all separate suspensions and cannot simply conflate several into one (`Nothing &|& Nothing = Nothing`). The solution is to use a list of `Maybe` values as result for computations on lazy values. Each individual result may not be computable because of insufficient evaluation.

```
newtype Try a = Try [Maybe a]

failT = Try []
suspT = Try [Nothing]
```

The type constructor `Try` forms a monad, namely the standard combination of the non-determinism list monad and the Maybe monad, in which functions are applied to all list elements.

```
instance Monad Try where
  (Try as) >>= f = Try $ concatMap (applyRes (fromTry . f)) as
    where fromTry (Try x) = x
          applyRes :: (a -> [Maybe b]) -> Maybe a -> [Maybe b]
          applyRes f (Just x) = f x
          applyRes f Nothing = [Nothing]

  return x = Try [Just x]
```

For non-deterministic branching we define a parallel disjunction operator, which collects all possible results[4]:

```
(|||) :: Try a -> Try a -> Try a
(Try xs) ||| (Try ys)  = Try (xs++ys)
```

Within the `Try` monad we can now define pattern combinators for matching lazy values. For example:

```
pCons :: Lazy [a] -> Try (Lazy a,Lazy [a])
pCons (Eval [eX,eY],(x:xs)) = return ((eX,x),(eY,xs))
pCons (Eval _,_) = failT
pCons (Uneval,_) = suspT

pNil :: Lazy [a] -> Try ()
pNil (Eval _,v) = if null v then return () else failT
pNil (Uneval,_) = suspT
```

[4] In fact, `Try` can also be made an instance of `MonadPlus` with `mplus = (|||)` and `mzero = failT`.

These pattern combinators respect the evaluation of a given argument. If the argument is not evaluated at all, then the result is a suspension. If the constructor is evaluated and it is the wrong constructor, then matching fails. Finally, if the constructor matches, then we succeed and return the sub-terms together with their evaluation information. Similarly we define a pattern combinator that strictly matches any value.

```
pVal :: Lazy a -> Try a
pVal (et,v) = condEval et (return v)

condEval :: EvalTree -> a -> a
condEval (Eval ets) tv = foldr condEval tv ets
condEval Uneval _ = suspT
```

The combinator `pVal` is mostly used for flat data types such as `Int` or `Char`.

Next we define the parallel `(&&)` function within our framework. We start with a more general function, which applies arbitrary result functions to `Try` results:

```
(***) :: Try (a -> b) -> Try a -> Try b
(***) (Try fs) (Try xs) = Try [res | fRes <- fs, xRes <- xs,
                                     let res = do f <- fRes
                                                  x <- xRes
                                                  return (f x)]
type Assert = Try ()

(&&&) :: Assert -> Assert -> Assert
t1 &&& t2 = (return (\x1 x2 -> ()) *** t1) *** t2
```

Whereas our old `(&|&)` on type `Maybe Bool` could produce only one of three values, the new `(&&&)` may produce a value representing many successful and suspended computations.

Now it is possible to define the `ordered` assertion from Section 2. For a complete implementation it remains to show how the `EvalTree` can successively be constructed during the computation.

## 5 Generating EvalTrees

To generate evaluation information for data structures we use the idea of *observations*, first introduced by Hood [6]. All values for which an assertion is specified are *observed.* An observation constructs a corresponding `EvalTree` representing how far the data structure has been evaluated. The key idea is that the context of a computation demands head normal forms (*hnf*). Whenever such an hnf is computed we extend its `EvalTree` by means of a side effect. This means an `Uneval` leaf is replaced by `Eval [Uneval,...,Uneval]` where the number of `Uneval`s within the list is equal to the arity of the constructor of the hnf.

Because we construct and use `EvalTree`s in program parts that are not linked by data-flow and for efficiency reasons, we use mutable references (`IORef`s) in our new EvalTree representation:

```
data EvalTree = EvalR [EvalTreeRef] | UnevalR
type EvalTreeRef = IORef EvalTree
```

With this representation it is not necessary to descend into the whole data structure, when extending it in a leaf position. Instead, we can directly update the leaf.

Observable data types are represented by the following class:

```
class Observe a where
  obs :: a -> EvalTreeRef -> a
```

We demonstrate how an instance of this class can be defined by means of the list data type:

```
instance Observe a => Observe [a] where
  obs (x:xs) r = unsafePerformIO $ do [aRef,bRef] <- mkEvalTreeCons r 2
                                      return (obs x aRef : obs xs bRef)
  obs []     r = unsafePerformIO $ do mkEvalTreeCons r 0
                                      return []
```

Whenever the context demands the evaluation of an observed value, the corresponding node in the `EvalTree` is extended by means of the function

```
mkEvalTreeCons :: EvalTreeRef -> Int -> IO [EvalTreeRef]
mkEvalTreeCons r n = do refs <- sequence (replicate n emptyUnevalRef)
                        writeIORef r (EvalR refs)
                        return refs

emptyUnevalRef :: IO EvalTreeRef
emptyUnevalRef = newIORef UnevalR
```

Furthermore, observers are added to the (not yet evaluated) arguments of the resulting constructor. These observers extend on demand the `IORef`s returned by `mkEvalTree` (`aRef` and `bRef`), which are also added to the new `EvalR` node within the `EvalTree`. The initial observer can be added with the function

```
observe :: Observe a => a -> IO (EvalTreeRef,a)
observe x = do r <- emptyUnevalRef
               return (r,obs x r)
```

This function is called whenever an assertion is added to a data structure, as discussed in the next section.

On top of these functions, it is possible to define a late (in contrast to prompt) implementation of our lazy assertions. Such an implementation stores all assertions of the program within a global state. At the end of the execution, all checks within this state are executed. Failed assertions are reported to the user.

## 6 Promptness

So far, our assertions meet two major goals. They respect the laziness of the program and they provide non-determinism by means of the operators `(|||)`,

`(***)`, and `(&&&)`. However, we still want our assertions to be *prompt* for the following reasons:

- Currently substantial memory is consumed, because the assertions themselves and the underlying data structures have to be kept until the final check can be performed. The more assertions are added the more memory is needed, although some data structure is fully evaluated or the assertion can be decided already by the evaluated part. When checking assertions directly at run-time large parts of the memory would become garbage and could be reused.
- Evaluating assertions at the end of the computation means the assertion is checked on maximally evaluated data structures. If a failed assertion would be reported earlier, then smaller data structures would be presented to the user. It will often be easier to understand why an assertion was violated.
- It will often be the case that in the end not only one assertion fails. There may be many consecutive faults. But how can a user know which was the initial fault to detect the bug in the program? The order in which the assertions are printed at the end of the execution does not reflect how different assertions depend on each other. Having prompt assertions, the computation can directly stop after reporting the first violated assertion. Consecutive faults are not reported anymore.
- In non-terminating systems such as most reactive applications (e.g. a web-server or a web-browser) it is inconvenient to stop the application just for checking assertions. Users want them to be checked in parallel in the background, without effecting the run-time behavior of the program.

The implementation shall suspend checks on unevaluated parts of data structures and directly awake them when these parts are evaluated to hnf.

### 6.1 Preparing the EvalTrees

For checking an assertion many checks have to be executed concurrently on different parts of the tested data structure. Many of these checks will have to suspend, because specific parts of the data structure are not yet evaluated. We store each suspended check in the `Uneval` leaf associated with the part of the data structure that it is suspended on, so that the checks can be executed when that data part is demanded. Several checks may be associated with the same part and hence many suspended checks may have to be stored in one `Uneval` leaf. A check does not return any value (it may just raise an exception), but it reads `IORefs` to read the growing `EvalTree` and hence it is of type `IO ()`. Checks may be added to an `Uneval` leaf at different times. We simply compose all checks for one `Uneval` leaf sequentially as an `IO` action stored within an `IORef`. Arbitrary sequential composition works, because we assume that all checks terminate.

We redefine the `EvalTree` with a reference containing an `IO` action:

```
data EvalTree = Eval [EvalTreeRef] | Uneval (IORef (IO ()))
type EvalTreeRef = IORef EvalTree
```

For the construction of the new `EvalTree` only two modifications have to be made:

```
mkEvalTreeCons :: EvalTreeRef -> Int -> IO [EvalTreeRef]
mkEvalTreeCons r n = do refs <- sequence (replicate n emptyUnevalRef)
                        Uneval aRef <- readIORef r
                        action <- readIORef aRef
                        writeIORef r (Eval refs)
                        action
                        return refs

emptyUnevalRef :: IO EvalTreeRef
emptyUnevalRef = do aRef <- newIORef (return ())
                    newIORef (Uneval aRef)
```

The function `mkEvalTreeCons` is called whenever an observed expression is evaluated to hnf. Then we read the suspended assertion checks (`action`) and execute them before we return the list of new sub-references. The `emptyUnevalRef` contains an `IORef` with no action, since there is no lazy computation to be performed for that sub-value yet.

### 6.2 Coroutines

In our outline in Section 3 we defined the data type `Try` as a list of `Maybe` values. However, for implementing promptness we have to compute the assertion checks step by step whenever the `EvalTree` is extended. Hence non-determinism or coroutines through continuation passing style is a more appropriate means of implementation. We have a success continuation and a fail continuation, just like continuation-based parser combinators [9]. The success continuation must take a fail continuation as argument to support non-determinism. We already established that checks are of type `IO ()`.

```
type FailCont = IO ()
type SuccCont a = FailCont -> a -> IO ()

newtype Try a = Try (SuccCont a -> FailCont -> IO ())
```

If there exists an alternative for a failed assertion, for example by non-deterministic branching in `(|||)`, then the `SuccCont` can discard the current `FailCont`.

Now we are ready to define the `Monad` instance for the new type `Try`:

```
instance Monad Try where

  (Try asIO) >>= f =
     Try (\sc fc -> asIO (\sfc x -> fromTry (f x) sc sfc) fc)

  return x = Try (\sc fc -> sc fc x)

fromTry :: Try a -> SuccCont a -> FailCont -> IO ()
fromTry (Try x) = x
```

```
failT :: Try a
failT = Try (\sc fc -> fc)
```

Similar to constructing success continuations by means of `return`, it is handy to have a function `failT` for constructing fail continuations.
To see how this lazy `Try` monad works, we first redefine the list patterns:

```
pNil :: Lazy [a] -> Try ()
pNil (Eval _ _,[]) = return ()
pNil (Eval _ _,(_:_)) = failT
pNil rx@(Uneval ref,v) = Try (suspTIO ref (pNil rx))
```

If the data structure is already evaluated, then we either succeed or fail. If the data structure is not yet evaluated, we add a suspended computation to the corresponding `IORef` within the `EvalTree`. The action to be performed when the constructor is evaluated to hnf is the same matching again (`pNil rx`). In the definition of `suspTIO` the action within the `IORef` is extended accordingly:

```
suspTIO :: IORef (IO ()) -> Try a -> SuccCont a -> FailCont -> IO ()
suspTIO ref try c fc = do io <- readIORef ref
                          writeIORef ref (io >> (fromTry try) c fc)
```

Similarly we can define the pattern combinator `pCons`:

```
pCons :: Lazy [a] -> Try (Lazy a,Lazy [a])
pCons (Eval _ [eX,eY],(x:y)) = return ((eX,x),(eY,y))
pCons (Eval _ _,[])          = failT
pCons rx@(Uneval ref,v)      = Try (suspTIO ref (pCons rx))
```

Next we define the operator `(|||)` which allows a parallel, independent execution of two `Try` computations:

```
(|||) :: Try a -> Try a -> Try a
(Try x) ||| (Try y) = Try (\c fc -> do
  ref <- newIORef True
  x c (orIORef ref fc) >> y c (orIORef ref fc))

orIORef :: IORef Bool -> FailCont -> IO ()
orIORef ref fc = do v <- readIORef ref
                    if v then (writeIORef ref False)
                         else fc
```

Both computations have to be performed in parallel because they may compute different results of type `a`. The whole computation only fails if both subcomputations fail. For this purpose we create a synchronisation `IORef` which is set to `False` by the first failing alternative. If the other alternative fails too this alternative continues with the fail continuation `fc`. The fail continuation is passed to both alternatives, but only the second failing alternative (with respect to time, not order in the code!) executes this continuation.

We define the parallel conjunction `(&&&)` again in terms of the more general operator `(***)`:

```
(***) :: Try (a -> b) -> Try a -> Try b
(***) (Try f) (Try x) = Try $ \sc fc -> do
  fRef <- newIORef []
  xRef <- newIORef []
  ref <- newIORef True
  f (\ffc f' -> do updateIORef ((ffc,f'):) fRef
                   xs <- readIORef xRef
                   mapM_ (\(xfc,x) -> sc (ffc >> xfc) (f' x)) xs)
    (andIORef ref fc)
  x (\xfc x' -> do updateIORef ((xfc,x'):) xRef
                   fs <- readIORef fRef
                   mapM_ (\(ffc,f) -> sc (ffc >> xfc) (f x')) fs)
    (andIORef ref fc)

(&&&) :: Assert -> Assert -> Assert
t1 &&& t2 = (return (\x1 x2 -> ()) *** t1) *** t2

andIORef :: IORef Bool -> IO () -> IO ()
andIORef ref fc = do v <- readIORef ref
                     if v then writeIORef ref False >> fc
                          else return ()
```

The computation of both arguments of `(***)` may introduce non-determinism, that is, multiple values. Whenever a new value is produced within the success continuation we extend the corresponding list in `fRef` and `xRef`. Besides the different values, this list also contains the corresponding fail continuations within a pair. Furthermore, we directly apply a new function to every already computed argument in the success continuation of `f`, as well as every stored function to a new argument in the success continuation of `x`. Thus every function is applied to every argument exactly once.

If any computation fails, we update the Boolean value in `ref` to `False` and directly continue with the fail continuation. Then, if the other coroutine fails as well, the `IORef` already contains `False` and it stops immediately. Like for the disjunction operator, the fail continuation is executed at most by one coroutine.

Finally we need the definition of `assert`:

```
assert :: Observe a => String -> (Lazy a -> Assert) -> a -> a
assert label p x = unsafePerformIO (do
  (eT,x') <- observe x
  let Try check = p (eT,x)
  check (const (putStrLn ("Assertion succeeded: "++label)))
        (fail ("Assertion failed: "++label))
  return x')
```

After installing an observer for `x`, we directly start the coroutine `check` for the asserted property `p`. Usually this coroutine directly suspends itself. Its `SuccCont` ignores its current `FailCont` and simply prints that the assertion succeeded. The `FailCont` aborts the whole computation reporting the failed assertion. We have to pass `x`, not the observer-wrapped variant `x'`, to the property `p`, because a partial value of `x'` is only available after all necessary assertion checks have been performed on it. As shown in Section 2, the real implementation reports a failure with a highlighted presentation of the wrong value, which we will discuss in the next section. Furthermore, success messages are written to a file to avoid conflicts with the program output.

To provide a comfortable library, we provide some further functions on assertions, like negation, implication, and assertion variations of standard Haskell function such as `elem` and `any`.

## 7 Failure Highlighting

As presented in Section 2, the data structure violating an assertion is also presented to the user. All parts responsible for the failure are marked such that the problematic sub-structures can easily be detected. This section gives a brief overview of how this highlighting is realised in our implementation.

So far the `EvalTree` does not contain any information about the names of the constructors inside the data structure. Hence it is not possible to print data structures at all. Therefore we add a `String` parameter to the constructor `Eval` that can easily be set in `obs`. Knowing all constructor names of the observed data structure, it is straightforward to generate a string representation of the data structure containing underscores for unevaluated parts.

For syntax highlighting we have to collect some more information while checking assertions. We identify every node in the `EvalTree` with a position `Pos`:

```
data EvalTree = Eval Pos String [EvalTreeRef] | Uneval (IORef (IO ()))
```

While checking an assertion, we can then collect sets of positions (`PosSet`), representing the nodes visited during the check. We extend the success and the fail continuations with a set of positions as additional parameter:

```
type SuccCont a = PosSet -> FailCont -> a -> IO ()
type FailCont   = PosSet -> IO ()
```

When a check splits into (parallel, independent) sub-checks, both checks generate their own sets of positions which are later combined according to the branching operator. For `(|||)` both sub-checks have to fail and, hence, the sets of positions are joined. For `(***)` (e.g. `(&&&)`) only the set of positions of the failing sub-check has to be considered.

In our implementation `Pos` and `PosSet` are defined as abstract data types with functions for set manipulation. Internally, a `Pos` is implemented as a list of `Ints` where the `Ints` successively express which branch in the `EvalTree` is chosen. The set of positions is implemented as a Trie [10] over lists of `Ints`.

Although the Trie of positions has the same structure as the `EvalTree`, it is not possible to directly integrate the position information into the `EvalTree`. Many assertions are checked in parallel and for each of these parallel checks different positions have to be considered. Parts of these assertions may have succeeded and their position sets should be discarded since this part of the data structure was not responsible for the failure.

## 8 Assertions for Functions

One of the most important features of our library is the ability to assert properties of functions. This allows programmers to express pre- and postconditions as well as invariants of functions. It is possible to express arbitrary relations between arguments and results.

The basic idea of the implementation is to represent a function as its graph, as far as it is used/constructed during the program execution. At each application of the function the graph is extended with a new pair of lazily constructed values. Functional assertions usually contain checks applied to function arguments or results which have to be checked by the mechanism described so far.

In the data type `EvalTree` we add a representation for functions

```
data EvalTree = ... | Fun Pos EvalTreeRef EvalTreeRef () () EvalTreeRef
```

where the first two `EvalTreeRef`s represent the argument and result value of the (curried) function and the last `EvalTreeRef` represents the next application of the function. The two arguments of type `()` are used to store the concrete argument and result value (of arbitrary type) by means of a type-cast[5] inside the monomorphic data structure `EvalTree`. An instance of the class `Observe` is defined to construct and extend `EvalTree`s for functions.

In the `Try` monad we give access to the graph of an observed function through a function which converts the observed function into a lazily constructed (infinite) list of argument-result pairs:

```
pFun ::  Lazy (a -> b) -> Try (Lazy [(a,b)])
```

Assertions defined on this lazily constructed list are stepwise evaluated whenever the list is extended by a new function application. Functional assertions have to hold for each application. We apply them to all list elements by means of the assertion variant of the Haskell function `all`.

This conversion through a lazily constructed list is hidden in functions for a convenient construction of functional assertions of arbitrary arity:

```
fun1 :: (Lazy a -> Lazy b -> Assert) -> Lazy (a -> b) -> Assert
fun2 :: (Lazy a -> Lazy b -> Lazy c -> Assert) -> Lazy (a -> b -> c)
        -> Assert
...
```

An example for a functional assertion is presented in Section 2.

## 9 Related Work

The first systematic approach to adding assertions to a functional language targets the strict language Scheme [5]. It provides convenient constructs for expressing properties of functions, including higher-order functions, and augmenting

[5] A function `coerce :: a -> b` can be defined using the Haskell 98 extension `IORefs` in combination with `unsafePerformIO`.

function definitions with assertions. Laziness is irrelevant and promptness trivial for strict functional languages. Instead a major concern of this work is which program part to blame when an assertion fails. The approach to blaming cannot directly be transferred to a lazy language, because there the run-time stack does not reflect the call structure. Instead a cooperation with the Haskell tracer Hat [11] may provide a solution in the future. The Scheme approach has been transferred to Haskell [7], but without taking its lazy semantics into account.

The first paper on *lazy* assertions for the lazy language Haskell [2] uses normal functions with Boolean result for expressing properties and hence the assertions are not prompt. The paper gives several examples of where the lack of promptness renders the assertions useless. Furthermore, expressibility of properties of functions is limited and the implementation requires concurrency language extensions as provided only by GHC.

In the first paper on *lazy and prompt* assertions for Haskell [1] properties are expressed in a pattern logic. The logic provides quantifiers and context patterns that allow referring to substructures of the tested value. However, most Haskell users find this logic hard to understand and many simple properties, such as that two lists have the same lengths, require complex descriptions. The implementation of the pattern logic is only sketched.

QuickCheck is a library for testing Haskell functions with random data [3]. Normal Boolean functions express expected properties, for example

```
prop :: Int -> [Int] -> Property
prop x xs = ordered xs ==> ordered (insert x xs)
```

where `ordered :: [Int] -> Bool` states that the function `insert` preserves order. Normal Boolean functions can be used, because only total, finite data structures are tested. An extension for (finite) partial values [4] has fundamental limits whereas our assertions fully support laziness. It can be very hard to generate random test data, for example input strings for a parser that are likely to be parseable. QuickCheck can only test top-level functions whereas an assertion can be attached to any local definition or subexpression. So testing with random data and testing with real data as our assertions do are two different methods which complement each other.

## 10 Conclusions

We have presented a new approach to augmenting lazy functional programs such as Haskell with assertions. The implementation is based on a technically interesting combination of continuation-based non-determinism, explicit scheduling of concurrent processes and HOOD-like observation of values. However, it is a portable library that requires only two common extensions of Haskell 98, `unsafePerformIO` and `IORefs`, which are supported by all Haskell compilers. The assertions are lazy and prompt. Most importantly, the combinator language for expressing asserted properties is easy to use, because it is similar to familiar parser combinator libraries. It combines pattern matching and non-deterministic computations. Furthermore, it is very expressive, allowing the formulation of any imaginable computable property. Assertions for functional values are easy to write and syntax highlighting simplifies the identification of parts of a value that are relevant for a failure.

The library does not prevent the user from writing assertions that change the program semantics by causing non-termination or raising an exception; after all, an asserted property may evaluate any Haskell expression, including `undef` or `error`. However, the library enables the user to formulate complex properties for partial and infinite values.

In the future we intend to investigate a theoretical formalisation of our assertions and to import ideas from strict assertions for Haskell [7].

## References


1. Chitil, O., Huch, F.: A pattern logic for prompt lazy assertions in Haskell. In: Horvath, A.B.Z. (ed.) IFL 2006. LNCS, vol. 4449, Springer, Heidelberg (2007)
2. Chitil, O., McNeill, D., Runciman, C.: Lazy assertions. In: Trinder, P., Michaelson, G.J., Peña, R. (eds.) IFL 2003. LNCS, vol. 3145, pp. 1–19. Springer, Heidelberg (2004)
3. Claessen, K., Hughes, R.J.M.: QuickCheck: a lightweight tool for random testing of Haskell programs. In: Proc. 5th Intl. ACM Conference on Functional Programming, pp. 268–279. ACM Press, New York (2000)
4. Danielsson, N.A., Jansson, P.: Chasing bottoms, a case study in program verification in the presence of partial and infinite values. In: Kozen, D. (ed.) MPC 2004. LNCS, vol. 3125, pp. 85–109. Springer, Heidelberg (2004)
5. Findler, R.B., Felleisen, M.: Contracts for higher-order functions. In: ICFP 2002, pp. 48–59. ACM Press, New York (2002)
6. Gill, A.: Debugging Haskell by observing intermediate datastructures. Electronic Notes in Theoretical Computer Science 41(1) (2001) (Proc. 2000 ACM SIGPLAN Haskell Workshop)
7. Hinze, R., Jeuring, J., Löh, A.: Typed contracts for functional programming. In: Hagiya, M., Wadler, P. (eds.) FLOPS 2006. LNCS, vol. 3945, pp. 208–225. Springer, Heidelberg (2006)
8. Hutton, G., Meijer, E.: Monadic parsing in Haskell. J. Funct. Program. 8(4), 437–444 (1998)
9. Okasaki, C.: Functional pearl: Even higher-order functions for parsing or Why would anyone ever want to use a sixth-order function? Journal of Functional Programming 8(2), 195–199 (1998)
10. Okasaki, C.: Purely Functional Data Structures. Cambridge University Press, Cambridge (1998)
11. Wallace, M., Chitil, O., Brehm, T., Runciman, C.: Multiple-view tracing for Haskell: a new Hat. In: ACM Workshop on Haskell, ACM Press, New York (2001)

# Translation Correctness for First-Order Object-Oriented Pattern Matching

Burak Emir[1,*], Qin Ma[2], and Martin Odersky[1]

[1] EPFL, 1015 Lausanne, Switzerland
[2] OFFIS, Escherweg 2, Oldenburg, Germany

**Abstract.** Pattern matching makes ML programs more concise and readable, and these qualities are also sought in object-oriented settings. However, objects and classes come with open class hierarchies, extensibility requirements and the need for data abstraction, which all conflict with matching on concrete data types. Extractor-based pattern matching has been proposed to address this conflict. Extractors are user-defined methods that perform the task of value discrimination and deconstruction during pattern matching. In this paper, we give the first formalization of extractor-based matching, using a first-order object-oriented calculus. We give a direct operational semantics and prove it sound. We then present an optimizing translation to a target language without matching, and prove a correctness result stating that an expression is equivalent to its translation.

## 1 Introduction

Algebraic datatypes and pattern matching render ML programs more concise, easier to read, and amenable to mathematical proof by structural induction [1]. Match expressions are high-level constructs with good properties: Compilers can translate them very efficiently [2,3,4,5,6]. However, ML style pattern matching is often incompatible with data abstraction.

To see why, consider the ML **datatype** definition in Fig. 1 which introduces a type name and its constructors. Constructors play the double role of tags and functions that aggregate data. Every list instance is tagged with either Nil or Cons. In match expressions, values are distinguished by their tag to recover their data. In the example, the append function concatenates lists by *matching* its argument xs: if it is the empty list, we return the second argument zs. If xs is a Cons cell, a non-destructive update appends zs to its tail via a recursive call.

This style of programming is concise and readable. The programs can be efficient, since tags can be translated to integers and match expressions to cascaded switch statements. However, note that the set of constructors as well as the arrangement of data items is fixed once and for all. Furthermore, the grouping of data items for the Cons constructor (e.g. **int** $*$ list) exposes the representation of the data, making it harder to change.

Representation independence forms the basis for data abstraction. Researchers have suggested to reconcile pattern matching and data abstraction [7,8]. However, slow

* Present address: Google Switzerland GmbH, Freigutstr. 12, 8002 Zürich, Switzerland.

Z. Shao (Ed.): APLAS 2007, LNCS 4807, pp. 54–70, 2007.

```
datatype list = Nil | Cons of int * list

fun append (xs,zs) = case xs of
  Nil          ⇒ zs
| Cons(y,ys)  ⇒ Cons(y,append(ys,zs));
```

**Fig. 1.** Algebraic Matching in ML

adoption suggests that data abstraction, while desirable, is not considered essential for functional programming. In object-oriented programming, data abstraction is essential: it is one of the principles that permit object-oriented programmers to describe systems using class hierarchies.

Pattern matching in object-oriented systems is appropriate when the set of operations cannot be anticipated (cf. the Visitor design pattern [9]). Like functional pattern matching, the Visitor pattern breaks encapsulation: the internal object representation has to be exposed in order for operations like append to access them.

In order to use pattern matching without tying it to a closed set of types that expose their representation, a semantics for pattern matching based on user-defined functions has been proposed independently by Emir, Odersky and Williams [10], and Syme, Neverov and Margetson [11]. A pattern is interpreted as the invocation of a so-called extractor method, which discriminates and deconstructs the input value. This decouples the type of an accepted value from the representation extracted from it.

A short example of matching with extractors is given in Fig. 2. It defines a List class, three subclasses Nil, Cons, and Singleton as well as two extractors cons and nil. These extractors are methods, which here use test expressions $a?\{\mathsf{x}\colon C \Rightarrow d\}/\{e\}$. Such a test expression is the contraction of the Java code

$$\textbf{if}\ (a\ \ \textbf{instanceof}\ \ C)\ \{\ C\,\mathsf{x} = (C)a; d\ \}\ \textbf{else}\ e\,.$$

The append implementation demonstrates the use of extractors. A pattern invokes an extractor method with an implicit argument — the List().cons(y, ys) pattern expresses two steps:

1. invoke method List().cons with the input value xs of the match expression as *single* argument
2. if the method returns null, the input value is rejected. Otherwise, it is accepted: bind the first field of the result to y and the second one to ys.

The return value of the extractor is a representation object that groups data items, which can be matched against subpatterns or bound to local variables. The type Cons is the result type of method cons, so it is used internally and externally to represent lists. Representation can be chosen independently though: note that lists that contain only one element can internally be represented with class Singleton, which is never exposed through pattern matching. This class could have been added later, without breaking client code that references cons and nil extractors.

We are interested in the question whether algorithms for optimized translation of pattern matching can be applied to extractors and the object-oriented context. Also, the

```
class List() ◁ Obj {
  def nil(x: Obj): Nil = {                                    /* extractor */
    x?{y: Nil ⇒ y}/{null}
  }
  def cons(x: Obj): Cons = {                                  /* extractor */
    x?{y: Cons ⇒ y}/{x?{y: Singleton ⇒ Cons(y.i, Nil())}/{null}}
  }
}
class Nil() ◁ List {}
class Cons(hd: int, tl : List) ◁ List {}
class Singleton(i: int) ◁ List {}       /* internal representation class */

def append(xs: List, zs: List): List = {
  xs match {
   case List().nil() ⇒ zs
   case List().cons(y, ys) ⇒ Cons(y, append(ys, zs))
}}
```

**Fig. 2.** Extractor-based Matching in the FPat Calculus

question arises which conditions (if any) have to be satisfied by extractors in order to prove that optimizing translation preserves the meaning of the program.

In this paper, we present possible answers to these questions. For this purpose, we adapted the translation to decision-trees described by Pettersson [4] to extractors. Using a formal calculus based on Featherweight Java (FJ) [12], we define a first-order object-oriented calculus FPat that offers runtime type inspection and pattern matching. A generic version is presented elsewhere [13]. We give a direct operational semantics and then show a straightforward translation algorithm to compile match expressions down to the fragment without pattern matching. This translation is proven correct, under the hypothesis that extractor methods do not diverge and do not throw exceptions. To the best of our knowledge, this hypothesis was never mentioned in the literature, though its necessity is easily justified in our development.

Extractor-based pattern matching has been implemented independently in F♯ (there called "active recognizer") and Scala. In contrast to previous work [10], this paper aims to shed light on its formal underpinnings. In summary, we contribute:

- a formal calculus that precisely describes extractor-based pattern matching,
- a formal definition and correctness proof of an optimized translation of match expressions,
- and formal conditions extractors have to satisfy in order for optimization to be correct.

The rest of the paper is organized as follows. We define FPat in Section 2. We present the translation of pattern matching in Section 3. We describe the correctness proof in Section 4. Section 5 discusses related work and Section 6 concludes.

## 2 An Object-Oriented Calculus with Pattern Matching

The syntax and operational semantics of FPat are given in Fig. 3, and the typing rules and auxiliary definitions are given in Fig. 4 and Fig. 5. The calculus is based on FJ, but with semantics defined using a strict, left-to-right big-step semantics. We will briefly review the definitions. We then define divergent programs and show type soundness.

### 2.1 Syntax

What follows is a short presentation of the rules and notation. A sequence $\alpha_1..\alpha_n$ is abbreviated as $\alpha_\star{}^{1..n}$, where $\alpha$ can be an expression, a name-type binding, or a judgment. The empty sequence is written $\bullet$. Multiple occurrence of the $\star$ indicate that the same index appears at multiple positions. Moreover, we shall need to express sequences with holes, so $\alpha_\star, \beta, \alpha_\star{}^{1..]i[..n}$ stands for $\alpha_\star^{1..i-1}, \beta, \alpha_\star^{i+1..n}$.

An FPat program $cd_\star{}^{1..n}; e$ is a set of class definitions and a top-level expression. Class definitions are kept in a class table, which we leave implicit throughout the paper and which satisifies the important properties that inheritance cycles and duplicate entries are absent. Classes have an explicit superclass as well as field declarations and method definitions, all publicly accessible. Methods can have an **@safe** annotation to indicate that they terminate without throwing an exception. The class hierarchy induces a subtype relation <:, of which the magic class Obj forms the largest element and the magic class Exc forms the smallest. These two types are magic because they do not have definitions in the class table. We also have a least upper bound $C \sqcup D$ operation, which is the least type $E$ in the hierarchy that satisfies $C{<:}E$ and $D{<:}E$.

There are 8 expression forms: **null**, variables x, field selection $e$.f, method invocation $e.\mathsf{m}(e_\star{}^{1..n})$, object construction $C(e_\star{}^{1..n})$, exception **throw**, test expressions $a?\{\mathsf{x}\colon C \Rightarrow d\}/\{e\}$ and match expressions $e_\star{}^{1..n}$ **match** $\{c_\star{}^{1..k}\}$. The calculus does not model assignment nor object identity. The free variables $fv$ and the defined variables $dv$ are defined in the straightforward manner.

### 2.2 Semantics

We briefly describe operational semantics of the fragment without pattern matching, in order to be self-contained. Semantics specific to pattern matching are deferred to a separate section below.

Terminating computation of meaningful expressions is modeled by a big-step evaluation relation $e \Downarrow q$ that takes expressions $e$ to results $q$. A result $q$ is either a value $v \in$ Values, the **null** result or the exception **throw**. Note that substitutions are all restricted to map variables only to values or **null**. A dotted metavariable $\dot{v}$ indicates either a value $v$ or **null**.

A value is the outcome of an object construction $C(\dot{v}_\star{}^{1..n})$, which is written without **new**. There is no explicitly declared constructor, instead the field order determined by the inheritance hierarchy (specified in the auxiliary judgment fields($C$)) is used. The following correct program illustrates how arguments in object construction relate to fields in class definitions:

$$\begin{array}{l}\textbf{class}\ D(\mathsf{f}\colon A) \lhd \mathsf{Obj}\,\{\ldots\}\\ \textbf{class}\ C(\mathsf{g}\colon B) \lhd D\,\{\ldots\}\\ C(A(), B())\end{array}$$

Rules (Rfld), (Rinvk), (Rnew) in Fig. 3 describe field access, method invocation and object construction. The auxiliary judgment $\mathsf{mbody}(\mathsf{m}, C)$ specifies how to lookup method bodies. Rules (Cfld), (Crcv), (Carg), (Cnew) throw or propagate exceptions.

The only significant use of **null** happens in test expressions. Their behavior is specified in rules (Rcst) and (Rskp): if the tested expression, or *scrutinee*, is not **null** and its type is lesser than the required type, it is bound to a local variable and the first branch is evaluated (Rcst). Otherwise, the second branch is evaluated (Rskp). If the scrutinee throws, the exception is propagated (Ctst).

The relation $\Downarrow$ does not specify the behavior of meaningless or non-terminating programs. To show type soundness, divergent programs are defined using a relation $\Uparrow$ in Fig. 6. Meaningless expressions are then precisely those that neither terminate nor diverge.

### 2.3 Semantics of Matching

Pattern matching expressions contain one or more case clauses, each of which compares the $n$ input values against $n$ patterns. The last clause may only have variable patterns. This excludes pathological expressions of the form $e_\star{}^{1..k}$ **match** {} and ensures that the behavior is defined for any possible combination of input values. It is easy to enforce this convention in a compiler.

Matching depends on judgments describing acceptance and rejection of patterns and cases. Rule (Rmch) describes evaluation of cases according to the first match policy: an accepting case is evaluated only if all preceding cases rejected the input.

Two separate judgments describe acceptance for cases $\dot{v}_\star{}^{1..n}; c \Downarrow q$ and patterns $\dot{v} \curvearrowright p \dashv \sigma$. We explain the judgments for case clauses first. A case accepts and evaluates to result $q$ if each input value is accepted by the corresponding pattern (mcase). Analogously, a case rejects $\dot{v}_\star{}^{1..n}; c \Downarrow \textbf{reject}$ if an initial segment of patterns accept and the following pattern rejects its input (rcase). Together, these rules describe a left-to-right evaluation of patterns. If a pattern accepts, it yields a substitution, and if all patterns accept, the combined substitution is applied to the body of the case (the merging of substitutions is indicated by juxtaposition).

The judgment $\dot{v} \curvearrowright p \dashv \sigma$ describes that pattern $p$ accepts $\dot{v}$ and yields substitution $\sigma$. Analogously, the judgment $\dot{v} \curvearrowright p \dashv \textbf{reject}$ describes rejection. A variable pattern always accepts its input (mvar), yielding the obvious substitution. An extractor pattern $C(\hat{v}_\star{}^{1..n}).\mathsf{m}(p_\star{}^{1..n})$ accepts (mextr) if:

1. evaluation of the extractor call returns a value $w$, yielding so-called case fields $\dot{w}_\star{}^{1..k}$
2. all subpatterns accept the case fields, yielding substitutions $\sigma_\star{}^{1..k}$

The extractor pattern rejects if the call returns **null** (rnull) or if one of its subpattern rejects its input (rchild). Case fields $\mathsf{casefld}(E, w)$ are determined for the return type $E$ of the extractor method, as specified in the auxiliary judgment $\mathsf{xtype}(\bullet, \hat{v}, \mathsf{m})$. They are the fields declared in the class definition of $E$ itself. Note that we will often abbreviate $C(\hat{v}_\star{}^{1..n})$ with $\hat{v}$.

**Subtyping** $C<:D$

$$\frac{}{C<:\mathsf{Obj}}\ (\mathsf{Sobj}) \qquad \frac{}{\mathsf{Exc}<:C}\ (\mathsf{Sthr})$$

$$\frac{}{C<:C}\ (\mathsf{Sref}) \qquad \frac{C<:D \quad D<:E}{C<:E}\ (\mathsf{Stran})$$

$$\frac{\mathbf{class}\ C(\mathsf{f}_\star : C_\star^{1..n}) \triangleleft D\,\{md_\star^{1..m}\}}{C<:D}\ (\mathsf{Sext})$$

$C \sqcup D \overset{\text{def}}{=}$ smallest $E$ such that $C<:E$ and $D<:E$.

**Computation** $e \Downarrow q$

$$\frac{e \Downarrow C(\dot{v}_\star^{1..n}) \quad \mathsf{fields}(C) = \mathsf{f}_\star : C_\star^{1..n}}{e.\mathsf{f}_i \Downarrow \dot{v}_i}\ (\mathsf{Rfld})$$

$$\frac{\begin{array}{c} e \Downarrow C(\dot{v}_\star^{1..l}) \quad e_\star \Downarrow \dot{w}_\star^{1..n} \\ \mathsf{mbody}(\mathsf{m}, C) = (\mathsf{x}_\star^{1..n})d \\ d\,\{\mathsf{this} \mapsto C(\dot{v}_\star^{1..l}),\ \mathsf{x}_\star \mapsto \dot{w}_\star^{1..n}\} \Downarrow q \end{array}}{e.\mathsf{m}(e_\star^{1..n}) \Downarrow q}\ (\mathsf{Rinvk})$$

$$\frac{e_\star \Downarrow \dot{v}_\star^{1..n}}{C(e_\star^{1..n}) \Downarrow C(\dot{v}_\star^{1..n})}\ (\mathsf{Rnew})$$

$$\frac{e \Downarrow C(\dot{v}_\star^{1..l}) \quad C<:D \quad e_1\{\mathsf{x} \mapsto C(\dot{v}_\star^{1..l})\} \Downarrow q}{e?\{\mathsf{x}\!:D \Rightarrow e_1\}/\{e_2\} \Downarrow q}\ (\mathsf{Rcst})$$

$$\frac{e \Downarrow \mathbf{null}\ \mathit{or}\ \left[e \Downarrow C(\dot{v}_\star^{1..l}) \quad C \not<: D\right] \quad e_2 \Downarrow q}{e?\{\mathsf{x}\!:D \Rightarrow e_1\}/\{e_2\} \Downarrow q}\ (\mathsf{Rskp})$$

$$\frac{\begin{array}{c} e_\star \Downarrow \dot{v}_\star^{1..n} \quad \forall j < i\,.\,\dot{v}_\star^{1..n}; c_j \Downarrow \mathbf{reject} \\ \dot{v}_\star^{1..n}; c_i \Downarrow q \end{array}}{e_\star^{1..n}\ \mathbf{match}\ \{c_\star\} \Downarrow q}\ (\mathsf{Rmch})$$

$$\frac{}{\mathbf{throw} \Downarrow \mathbf{throw}}\ (\mathsf{Cthr}) \qquad \frac{}{\mathbf{null} \Downarrow \mathbf{null}}\ (\mathsf{Rnul})$$

$$\frac{e \Downarrow \mathbf{throw}\ \mathit{or}\ e \Downarrow \mathbf{null}}{e.\mathsf{f} \Downarrow \mathbf{throw}}\ (\mathsf{Cfld})$$

$$\frac{e \Downarrow \mathbf{throw}\ \mathit{or}\ e \Downarrow \mathbf{null}}{e.\mathsf{m}(e_\star^{1..n}) \Downarrow \mathbf{throw}}\ (\mathsf{Crcv})$$

$$\frac{e_\star \Downarrow \dot{v}_\star^{1..i-1} \quad e_i \Downarrow \mathbf{throw}}{e.\mathsf{m}(e_\star^{1..n}) \Downarrow \mathbf{throw}}\ (\mathsf{Carg})$$

$$\frac{e_\star \Downarrow \dot{v}_\star^{1..i-1} \quad e_i \Downarrow \mathbf{throw}}{C(e_\star^{1..n}) \Downarrow \mathbf{throw}}\ (\mathsf{Cnew})$$

$$\frac{e \Downarrow \mathbf{throw}}{e?\{\mathsf{x}\!:C \Rightarrow e_1\}/\{e_2\} \Downarrow \mathbf{throw}}\ (\mathsf{Ctst})$$

**Syntax**

$$\begin{array}{lll}
cd & ::= & \mathbf{class}\ C(\mathsf{f}_\star : C_\star^{1..n}) \triangleleft D\,\{md_\star^{1..k}\} \\
md & ::= & an\ \mathbf{def}\ \mathsf{m}(\mathsf{x}_\star : C_\star^{1..n})\!: C = \{e\} \\
an & ::= & \mathbf{@safe} \mid \text{(empty)} \\
a, b, d, e & ::= & \mathbf{null} \\
 & \mid & \mathsf{x} \\
 & \mid & e.\mathsf{f} \\
 & \mid & e.\mathsf{m}(e_\star^{1..n}) \\
 & \mid & C(e_\star^{1..n}) \\
 & \mid & \mathbf{throw} \\
 & \mid & e?\{\mathsf{x}\!: C \Rightarrow e\}/\{e\} \\
 & \mid & e_\star^{1..n}\ \mathbf{match}\ \{c_\star^{1..m}\} \\
 & & (\text{convention: } c_m \equiv \mathbf{case}\ \mathsf{x}_\star^{1..n} \Rightarrow e) \\
c & ::= & \mathbf{case}\ p_\star^{1..n} \Rightarrow e \\
p, \pi & ::= & \mathsf{x} \mid C(\hat{v}_\star^{1..n}).\mathsf{m}(p_\star^{1..k}) \\
q & ::= & v \mid \mathbf{throw} \mid \mathbf{null} \\
u, v, w & ::= & C(\dot{v}_\star^{1..k}) \\
\hat{v} & ::= & \mathsf{x} \mid C(\hat{v}_\star^{1..k}) \\
\dot{v} & ::= & v \mid \mathbf{null}
\end{array}$$

$$\frac{e_\star \Downarrow \dot{v}_\star^{1..i-1} \quad e_i \Downarrow \mathbf{throw}}{e_\star^{1..n}\ \mathbf{match}\ \{c_\star^{1..k}\} \Downarrow \mathbf{throw}}\ (\mathsf{Cmch})$$

**Acceptance** $\dot{v}_\star^{1..n}; c \Downarrow q$, $\dot{v} \curvearrowright p \dashv \sigma$

$$\frac{\begin{array}{c} c \equiv \mathbf{case}\ p_\star^{1..n} \Rightarrow b \\ \dot{v}_\star \curvearrowright p_\star \dashv \sigma_\star^{1..n} \quad b\,\sigma_\star^{1..n} \Downarrow q \end{array}}{\dot{v}_\star^{1..n}; c \Downarrow q}\ (\text{mcase})$$

$$\frac{}{\dot{v} \curvearrowright \mathsf{x} \dashv \{\mathsf{x} \mapsto \dot{v}\}}\ (\text{mvar})$$

$$\frac{\begin{array}{c} v.\mathsf{m}(\dot{u}) \Downarrow w \quad \mathsf{xtype}(\bullet, v, \mathsf{m}) = E \\ \mathsf{casefld}(E, w) = \dot{w}_\star^{1..k} \quad \dot{w}_\star \curvearrowright p_\star \dashv \sigma_\star^{1..k} \end{array}}{\dot{u} \curvearrowright v.\mathsf{m}(p_\star^{1..k}) \dashv \sigma_\star^{1..k}}\ (\text{mextr})$$

**Rejection** $\dot{v}_\star^{1..n}; c \Downarrow \mathbf{reject}$, $\dot{v} \curvearrowright p \dashv \mathbf{reject}$

$$\frac{\begin{array}{c} c \equiv \mathbf{case}\ p_\star^{1..n} \Rightarrow b \\ \dot{v}_\star \curvearrowright p_\star \dashv \sigma_\star^{1..i-1} \quad \dot{v}_i \curvearrowright p_i \dashv \mathbf{reject} \end{array}}{\dot{v}_\star^{1..n}; c \Downarrow \mathbf{reject}}\ (\text{rcase})$$

$$\frac{v.\mathsf{m}(\dot{u}) \Downarrow \mathbf{null}}{\dot{u} \curvearrowright v.\mathsf{m}(p_\star^{1..k}) \dashv \mathbf{reject}}\ (\text{rnull})$$

$$\frac{\begin{array}{c} v.\mathsf{m}(\dot{u}) \Downarrow w \quad \mathsf{xtype}(\bullet, v, \mathsf{m}) = E \\ \mathsf{casefld}(E, w) = \dot{w}_\star^{1..k} \quad \dot{w}_\star \curvearrowright p_\star \dashv \sigma_\star^{1..i-1} \\ \dot{w}_i \curvearrowright p_i \dashv \mathbf{reject} \end{array}}{\dot{u} \curvearrowright v.\mathsf{m}(p_\star^{1..k}) \dashv \mathbf{reject}}\ (\text{rchild})$$

**Fig. 3.** FPat Syntax and Semantics

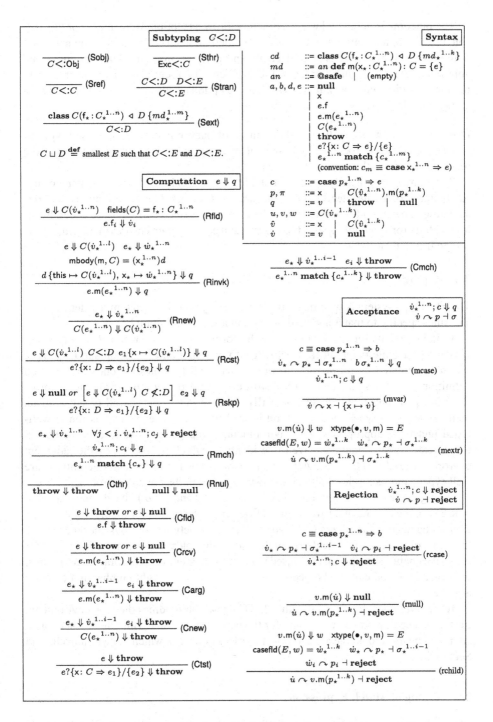

The outcome is undefined when extractors throw exceptions or diverge. For this reason, the **@safe** annotation is required on any method that is referenced as an extractor. Safety in the above sense is an undecidable property or programs, but restrictions and approximations are available to tackle this problem. Our focus in this paper is on justifying the condition, not checking it. Avoiding exceptions is also the reason for excluding extractor calls x.m(...).

*Discussion.* In any statically-typed definition of pattern matching, order and types of subpatterns must be specified. The benefit of using extractors lies in decoupling the matched type from the representation type.

Pattern matching usually includes matching on literals like 42, **true** and named constants like foo. While literal expressions are constructors without arguments, a corresponding convention for extractors can be assumed. Named constants are added by allowing tests for *singleton types* $v$.type. Structural equality then ensures that $C(\dot{w}_\star{}^{1..k}) \in$ $v$.type if $v \equiv C(\dot{w}_\star{}^{1..k})$.

### 2.4 Typing

The FPat type system is specified through a set of syntax-directed typing rules in Fig.4. The rules specific to matching are described in a separate section below.

Type judgments for expressions have the form $\Gamma \vdash e \in C$ where $\Gamma$ is a type environment (a finite mapping from variables to types), $e$ an expression and $C$ a class. The judgments $cd\ \diamond$ and $an\ md\ \diamond$ in $C$ assert well-typedness of class and method definitions. Methods annotated with **@safe** are assumed to terminate and never throw exceptions for any input (including **null**). A class definition is well-typed if all its methods are well-typed, and a method is well-typed if its return expression is well-typed under the appropriate type environment. If the method overrides a method in a superclass, their signatures have to be identical, which is asserted by the judgment override$(an(B_\star{}^{1..n})B, \mathsf{m}, D)$. A program is well-typed if all its class definitions are well-typed, and its top-level expression is well-typed in the empty environment.

Typing expressions is straightforward. Rules (Tthr) and (Tnul) give the most specific type Exc to the **throw** and **null** results. (Tvar) takes the type of a variable from the type environment, and field access (Tfld) and object construction (Tnew) is checked against the fields of the class as calculated by the judgment fields$(C)$. A similar judgment for method signatures mtype$(\mathsf{m}, C)$ is used to type-check method invocation (Tinvk). Thus, well-typed method calls and objects constructions have the right number and types of arguments.

Test expressions are checked with rule (Ttst), which modifies the type environment for the succeeding branch to account for the new local variable. Binding in test expressions can be used to define a derived form **val** x: $C = a; b$, which we will introduce in Section 3.1.

### 2.5 Typing of Match Expressions

Match expressions are well-typed if all their clauses are well-typed (Tmch), using the least upper bound to combine the clauses' result types. To type-check a single

**Expression Typing** $\Gamma \vdash e \in C$

$$\frac{}{\Gamma \vdash \mathsf{x} \in \Gamma(\mathsf{x})}\ (\mathsf{Tvar}) \qquad \frac{}{\Gamma \vdash \mathbf{null} \in \mathsf{Exc}}\ (\mathsf{Tnul}) \qquad \frac{}{\Gamma \vdash \mathbf{throw} \in \mathsf{Exc}}\ (\mathsf{Tthr})$$

$$\frac{\Gamma \vdash e \in C \quad \mathsf{fields}(C) = \mathsf{f}_\star : C_\star^{1..n}}{\Gamma \vdash e.\mathsf{f}_i \in C_i}\ (\mathsf{Tfld}) \qquad \frac{\Gamma \vdash e \in C \quad \mathsf{mtype}(\mathsf{m}, C) = an(D_\star^{1..n})E \quad \Gamma \vdash e_\star \in C_\star^{1..n} \quad C_\star <: D_\star^{1..n}}{\Gamma \vdash e.\mathsf{m}(e_\star^{1..n}) \in E}\ (\mathsf{Tinvk})$$

$$\frac{\mathsf{fields}(C) = \mathsf{f}_\star : D_\star^{1..n} \quad \Gamma \vdash e_\star \in C_\star^{1..n} \quad C_\star <: D_\star^{1..n}}{\Gamma \vdash C(e_\star^{1..n}) \in C}\ (\mathsf{Tnew}) \qquad \frac{\Gamma \vdash e \in A \quad \Gamma, \mathsf{x}: C \vdash a \in D \quad \Gamma \vdash b \in E}{\Gamma \vdash e?\{\mathsf{x}: C \Rightarrow a\}/\{b\} \in D \sqcup E}\ (\mathsf{Ttst})$$

$$\frac{\Gamma \vdash e_\star \in C_\star^{1..n} \quad \Gamma; C_\star^{1..n} \vdash c_\star \in D_\star^{1..m}}{\Gamma \vdash e_\star^{1..n}\ \mathbf{match}\ \{c_\star^{1..m}\} \in \bigsqcup D_\star^{1..m}}\ (\mathsf{Tmch})$$

**Pattern and Case Typing** $\Gamma; C_\star^{1..n} \vdash c \in D$, $\Gamma; C \ni p \dashv \Delta$

$$\frac{}{\Gamma; D \ni \mathsf{x} \dashv \mathsf{x}: D}\ (\mathsf{TPvar})$$

$$\frac{\mathsf{xtype}(\Gamma, \hat{v}, \mathsf{m}) = E \quad \mathbf{class}\ E(\mathsf{f}_\star : C_\star^{1..m}) \lhd E'\ \{an_\star md_\star^{1..k}\} \quad \Gamma; C_\star \ni p_\star \dashv \Gamma_\star'^{1..m} \quad \Gamma' \equiv \Gamma_\star'^{1..m}}{\Gamma; D \ni \hat{v}.\mathsf{m}(p_\star^{1..m}) \dashv \Gamma'}\ (\mathsf{TPext}) \qquad \frac{\Gamma; C_\star \ni p_\star \dashv \Delta_\star^{1..n} \quad \Gamma, \Delta_\star^{1..n} \vdash b \in D}{\Gamma; C_\star^{1..n} \vdash \mathbf{case}\ p_\star^{1..n} \Rightarrow b \in D}\ (\mathsf{Tcase})$$

**Method Typing** $md \diamond \text{ in } C$

$$\frac{\mathsf{this}: C, \mathsf{x}_\star : C_\star^{1..n} \vdash e \in E \quad E <: B \quad \mathbf{class}\ C(\mathsf{f}_\star : D_\star^{1..m}) \lhd D\ \{md_\star^{1..k}\} \quad \mathsf{override}(an(C_\star^{1..n})B, \mathsf{m}, D)}{an\ \mathbf{def}\ \mathsf{m}(\mathsf{x}_\star : C_\star^{1..n}) : B = \{e\} \diamond \text{ in } C}$$

**Extractor Type** $\mathsf{xtype}(\Gamma, \hat{v}, \mathsf{m})$

$$\frac{\Gamma \vdash \hat{v} \in B \quad \mathsf{mtype}(\mathsf{m}, B) = \mathsf{@safe}(\mathsf{Obj})E}{\mathsf{xtype}(\Gamma, \hat{v}, \mathsf{m}) = E}$$

**Class Typing** $cd \diamond$

$$\frac{an_\star md_\star \diamond \text{ in } C^{1..k}}{\mathbf{class}\ C(\mathsf{f}_\star : D_\star^{1..n}) \lhd D\ \{an_\star md_\star^{1..k}\} \diamond}$$

**Fig. 4.** Typing Rules

clause **case** $p_\star^{1..n} \Rightarrow b$ (Tcase), each pattern in $p_\star^{1..n}$ is type-checked w.r.t. the type environment $\Gamma$ and an "expected type" $C_\star$, yielding a type environment $\Delta_\star$ as in $\Gamma; C_\star \ni p_\star \dashv \Delta_\star^{1..n}$. Then, the body is type-checked against the combined type environments as in $\Gamma, \Delta_\star^{1..n} \vdash b \in D$. Variables introduced in patterns must be pair-wise different and may not clash with $\Gamma$, which is implicit in the juxtaposition of environments.

Pattern typing $\Gamma; E \ni p \dashv \Delta$ is type-checked as follows: For variable patterns (TPvar), the expected type $E$ is used to produce a singleton environment. For extractor patterns (TPextr), the judgment $\mathsf{xtype}(\Gamma, \hat{v}, \mathsf{m})$ looks up the type of receiver and the

**Field Lookup** $\mathsf{fields}(C)$

$$\frac{}{\mathsf{fields}(\mathsf{Obj}) = \bullet}$$

$$\frac{\mathsf{fields}(D) = \mathsf{f}_\star : {C_\star}^{1..m} \qquad \textbf{class}\ C(\mathsf{g}_\star : {D_\star}^{1..n}) \lhd D\ \{an_\star md_\star{}^{1..k}\}}{\mathsf{fields}(C) = \mathsf{f}_\star : {C_\star}^{1..m}; \mathsf{g}_\star : {D_\star}^{1..n}}$$

**Case Field Lookup** $\mathsf{casefld}(C, v)$

$$\frac{\mathsf{fields}(D) = \mathsf{f}_\star : {C_\star}^{1..m} \qquad \textbf{class}\ C(\mathsf{g}_\star : {D_\star}^{1..n}) \lhd D\ \{an_\star md_\star{}^{1..k}\}}{\mathsf{casefld}(C, C({v_\star}^{1..m+n})) = v_\star^{m+1..m+n}}$$

$$\frac{E \not\equiv C \quad \mathsf{fields}(D) = \mathsf{f}_\star : {C_\star}^{1..m} \qquad \textbf{class}\ C(\mathsf{g}_\star : D_\star^{1..n}) \lhd D\ \{an_\star md_\star{}^{1..k}\}}{\mathsf{casefld}(E, C({v_\star}^{1..m+n})) = \mathsf{casefld}(E, D({v_\star}^{1..m}))}$$

**Overriding** $\mathsf{override}(an({B_\star}^{1..n})B, \mathsf{m}, D)$

$$\frac{\mathsf{mtype}(\mathsf{m}, D) = an({B_\star}^{1..n})B \text{ or undefined}}{\mathsf{override}(an({B_\star}^{1..n})B, \mathsf{m}, D)}$$

**Method Lookup** $\mathsf{mtype}(\mathsf{m}, C)$ $\mathsf{mbody}(\mathsf{m}, C)$

$$\frac{\textbf{class}\ C(\mathsf{f}_\star : {C_\star}^{1..m}) \lhd D\ \{an_\star md_\star{}^{1..k}\} \qquad an_i \equiv an \qquad md_i \equiv \textbf{def}\ \mathsf{m}(\mathsf{x}_\star : {B_\star}^{1..n}) : B = \{e\}}{\mathsf{mtype}(\mathsf{m}, C) = an({B_\star}^{1..n})B \qquad \mathsf{mbody}(\mathsf{m}, C) = ({x_\star}^{1..n})e}$$

$$\frac{\textbf{class}\ C(\mathsf{f}_\star : {C_\star}^{1..m}) \lhd D\ \{an_\star md_\star{}^{1..k}\} \qquad \mathsf{m} \not\equiv md_\star{}^{1..k}}{\mathsf{mtype}(\mathsf{m}_i, C) = \mathsf{mtype}(\mathsf{m}, D) \qquad \mathsf{mbody}(\mathsf{m}, C) = \mathsf{mbody}(\mathsf{m}, D)}$$

**Fig. 5.** Auxiliary Definitions

signature of the extractor method in order to recover the representation type. It also ensures that extractors are @**safe**. The case field types are then used as expected types to check the subpatterns. Finally, the environments ${\Delta_\star}^{1..m}$ obtained from the subpatterns are merged into one environment $\Delta$.

## 2.6 Divergent Programs

Our approach to type soundness, following Leroy and Grall [14], is to characterize meaningless programs as those that neither terminate nor diverge. Divergent programs are defined coinductively by the set of divergence rules in Fig. 6. These rules are tailored to establish that any well-typed term that does not terminate necessarily diverges. Their coinductive nature is indicated by horizontal double lines: coinductive derivations are infinite trees with the root being the assertion to derive and the successors of each node being determined by a derivation rule.

Let us consider the rules one by one. Rule (Dfld) and (Drcv) express that accessing a field or invoking a method on a divergent expression yields a divergent expression. Rules (Darg) and (Dnew) say that object construction and method invocation diverges if one of their arguments diverge. Note that a strict call-by-value, left-to-right evaluation order is followed also here. Rule (Dinvk) says that calling a method with arguments that make the method body diverge yields a divergent expression. Similarly, (Dtst), (Dcst) and (Dskp) characterize divergent test expressions by locating divergence in the respective subexpression.

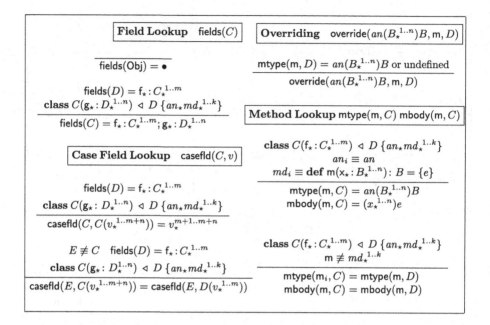

**Divergent Computation** $e \Uparrow$

$$\frac{e \Uparrow}{e.\mathsf{f} \Uparrow}\ (\mathsf{Dfld}) \qquad \frac{e \Uparrow}{e.\mathsf{m}({e_\star}^{1..n}) \Uparrow}\ (\mathsf{Drcv}) \qquad \frac{e \Downarrow v \quad e_\star \Downarrow {\dot{v}_\star}^{1..i-1} \quad e_i \Uparrow}{e.\mathsf{m}({e_\star}^{1..n}) \Uparrow}\ (\mathsf{Darg})$$

$$\frac{\begin{array}{c} e \Downarrow C({\dot{v}_\star}^{1..m}) \quad e_\star \Downarrow {\dot{w}_\star}^{1..n} \\ \mathsf{mbody}(C, \mathsf{m}) = ({\mathsf{x}_\star}^{1..n})b \\ b\,\{\mathsf{this} \mapsto C({\dot{v}_\star}^{1..m}), \mathsf{x}_\star \mapsto {\dot{w}_\star}^{1..n}\} \Uparrow \end{array}}{e.\mathsf{m}({e_\star}^{1..n}) \Uparrow}\ (\mathsf{Dinvk}) \qquad \frac{e_\star \Downarrow {\dot{v}_\star}^{1..i-1} \quad e_i \Uparrow}{C({e_\star}^{1..n}) \Uparrow}\ (\mathsf{Dnew})$$

$$\frac{e \Uparrow}{e?\{\mathsf{x}\colon C \Rightarrow a\}/\{b\} \Uparrow}\ (\mathsf{Dtst}) \qquad \frac{e \Downarrow D({\dot{v}_\star}^{1..n}) \quad D{<:}C \quad a\{\mathsf{x} \mapsto D({\dot{v}_\star}^{1..n})\} \Uparrow}{e?\{\mathsf{x}\colon C \Rightarrow a\}/\{b\} \Uparrow}\ (\mathsf{Dcst})$$

$$\frac{e \Downarrow \textbf{null}\ \textit{or}\ \left[e \Downarrow D({\dot{v}_\star}^{1..n}) \quad D \not<: C\right] \quad b \Uparrow}{e?\{\mathsf{x}\colon C \Rightarrow a\}/\{b\} \Uparrow}\ (\mathsf{Dskp})$$

$$\frac{e_\star \Downarrow {\dot{v}_\star}^{1..i-1} \quad e_i \Uparrow}{{e_\star}^{1..n}\ \textbf{match}\ \{{c_\star}^{1..m}\} \Uparrow}\ (\mathsf{Dmch}) \qquad \frac{\begin{array}{c} e_\star \Downarrow {\dot{v}_\star}^{1..n} \quad \forall j < i\,.\, {\dot{v}_\star}^{1..n} \curvearrowright c_j \dashv \textbf{reject} \\ {\dot{v}_\star}^{1..n}; c_i \Uparrow e \end{array}}{{e_\star}^{1..n}\ \textbf{match}\ \{{c_\star}^{1..m}\} \Uparrow}\ (\mathsf{Dcase})$$

**Divergent Cases and Patterns** ${\dot{v}_\star}^{1..n}; c \Uparrow e$

$$\frac{c = \textbf{case}\ {p_\star}^{1..n} \Rightarrow b \quad \dot{v}_\star \curvearrowright p_\star \dashv {\sigma_\star}^{1..n} \quad b\,{\sigma_\star}^{1..n} \Uparrow}{{\dot{v}_\star}^{1..n}; c \Uparrow b\,{\sigma_\star}^{1..n}}\ (\mathsf{Dbdy})$$

**Fig. 6.** Divergent Programs

In match expressions, a divergent match expression can be traced back to some (possibly empty) initial segment of rejecting case clauses followed by a divergent case clause. A case clause may only diverge because its body diverges (Dbdy).

*Discussion.* If we did not rely on the **@safe** annotation, divergence could also be caused by extractor calls during pattern match evaluation. It is possible but tedious to omit the **@safe** hypothesis, give divergence and exception propagation rules for extractor calls and adapt the soundness proof accordingly. Moreover, we discover that **@safe** is actually needed for correctness of the optimizing translation (see section 3.2). As a consequence, we chose the simpler route by defining only those divergent programs that are needed for **(Progress)**. Here and in the proofs, bold-face names and phrases in parentheses refer to lemmata and theorems.

## 2.7 Soundness

We now prove type soundness using big-step versions of the standard lemmata.

**Lemma 1 (Uniqueness).** *For all $a$, if $a \Downarrow q$ then for all $q'$, if $a \Downarrow q'$ then $q = q'$.*

**Lemma 2 (Termination).** *For all $a$ and all $q$, it holds that if $a \Downarrow q$ then $a \not\Uparrow$.*

**Lemma 3 (Subtypes have all Fields)**
*If $C{<:}D$, $C \neq \mathsf{Exc}$ then $\mathsf{fields}(C) = \mathsf{fields}(D); \mathsf{g}_\star : E_\star{}^{1..m}$.*

**Lemma 4 (Subtypes have all Methods).** *If $C{<:}D$, $C \neq \mathsf{Exc}$ and $\mathsf{mtype}(\mathsf{m}, D) = an(C_\star{}^{1..n})B$, then $\mathsf{mtype}(\mathsf{m}, C) = an(C_\star{}^{1..n})B$.*

The following two lemmata are needed to prove the substitution lemma for pattern matching expressions. We have to deal with the typing rule for variables which might end up producing a "better" environment for input values whose type has become more precise after substitution. We write $\Delta'{<:}\Delta$ when $\mathsf{dom}(\Delta) = \mathsf{dom}(\Delta')$ and $\mathsf{x}\colon B \in \Delta$ implies $\mathsf{x}\colon A \in \Delta'$ with $A{<:}B$.

**Lemma 5 (Subtypes yield Refined Environment)**
*If $C{<:}D$ and $\Gamma; D \ni p \dashv \Gamma'$ then $\Gamma; C \ni p \dashv \Gamma''$ for some $\Gamma''{<:}\Gamma'$.*

**Lemma 6 (Refined Environment preserves Typing)**
*If $C_\star{<:}D_\star{}^{1..n}$ and $\Gamma, \mathsf{x}_\star : D_\star^{1..n} \vdash e \in B$ then $\Gamma, \mathsf{x}_\star : C_\star^{1..n} \vdash e \in A$ for $A{<:}B$.*

**Lemma 7 (Weakening)** *If $\Gamma \vdash d \in S$ and $\mathsf{x} \notin fv(d)$, then $\Gamma, \mathsf{x}\colon T \vdash d \in S$ for any $T$.*

**Lemma 8 (Substitution Lemma).** *If $\Gamma, \mathsf{x}_\star : B_\star^{1..n} \vdash b \in D$ and $\bullet \vdash \dot{u}_\star \in A_\star{}^{1..n}$ for $A_\star{<:}B_\star{}^{1..n}$, $\dot{u}_\star \in \mathsf{Values} \cup \{\mathbf{null}\}$ then $\Gamma \vdash b\,\{\mathsf{x}_\star \mapsto \dot{u}_\star{}^{1..n}\} \in C$, for $C{<:}D$.*

**Lemma 9 (Preservation)**
*If $a \Downarrow q$ and $\bullet \vdash a \in C$, then $\bullet \vdash q \in C'$ for some $C'{<:}C$.*

The big-step version of the progress lemma uses coinduction.

**Lemma 10 (Progress)**
*If $\bullet \vdash a \in C$ and $a \not\Downarrow q$ for all $q$, then $a \Uparrow$.*

**Theorem 1 (Type Soundness)**
*If $\bullet \vdash a \in C$ then either $a \Uparrow$ or $a \Downarrow q$ for some $q$ with $\bullet \vdash q \in C'$, $C'{<:}C$.*

## 3 Translation

### 3.1 Rewriting Match Expressions

An elegant way to describe translation is to give a set of rewrite rules, which are applied successively until all match expressions are replaced with lower-level operations. Apart from being easy to understand and implement, correctness can then be established for each rule separately.

There are two approaches to the compilation of pattern matching, one based on decision-trees and the other based on backtracking automata [6,5]. We chose the translation to decision trees, which in the functional setting guarantees that no input value is tested more than once. Our presentation of the algorithm follows Pettersson's [4].

The central idea is to remove a top-level pattern of a case clause, lifting its subpatterns to the top-level. Consider the two expressions below, for fresh $\mathsf{y}, \mathsf{y}_1, \mathsf{y}_2, \mathsf{y}_3$

```
//recall xtype(Γ, List(), cons) = Cons      List().cons(x)?{y: Cons ⇒
x match {                                      (x, y.hd, y.tl) match {
    case List().cons(π1, π2)   ⇒ a                 case y1 , π1 , π2 ⇒ a
    case y0                    ⇒ b                 case y0 , y2 , y3 ⇒ b
}                                           }}/{  x match {case y0 ⇒ b}}
```

Some scrutiny reveals that these are actually equivalent. The extractor of the first pattern $\mathsf{List}().\mathsf{cons}(\pi_1, \pi_2)$ in the first case has been pulled out and a test is done on the outcome: if it is non-null, it is bound to the fresh variable $\mathsf{y}$ and the subpatterns are matched against the case fields $\mathsf{y.hd}, \mathsf{y.tl}$. Note that the width of the original match is augmented by lifting the nested patterns to the top-level. Since $\pi_1, \pi_2$ can potentially reject the input, all cases of the original match are copied to the new one. Some entries need to be *expanded* to match the arity of the new match, which is done by using fresh variable patterns $\mathsf{y}_1, \mathsf{y}_2, \mathsf{y}_3$. If the extractor returns **null**, the first clause rejects and so the second branch of the test expression deals with the remaining cases of the match.

The algorithm performs optimization by reusing results of an extractor call: calls to the same extractor in the same column are replaced with clauses that match subpatterns (if the call succeeded), or discarded altogether (if the result was null). We illustrate the optimization with an example.

```
                                         List().cons(x)?{y : Cons ⇒
                                           (x, y.hd, y.tl) match {
x match {                                      case y1              , π1 , π2 ⇒ a
    case List().cons(π1, π2) ⇒ a               case List().nil()    , y2 , y3 ⇒ b
    case List().nil()        ⇒ b               case y4              , π3 , π4 ⇒ d
    case List().cons(π3, π4) ⇒ d               case y0              , y5 , y6 ⇒ e
    case y0                  ⇒ e         }}/{
}                                          x match { case List().nil() ⇒ b
                                                     case y0           ⇒ e }}
```

Here, the first and third case (on the left) test the same extractor $\mathsf{List}().\mathsf{cons}$. This extractor call has been pulled out into a test expression. If it succeeds (then-branch), the resulting value is deconstructed and matched against the subpatterns. Again, since patterns $\pi_1, \pi_2$ may fail, we include all other cases, but we do not need to repeat the extractor call. If the extractor call returns **null**, then (else-branch) the remaining test cases are those that have extractor patterns *other* than $\mathsf{List}().\mathsf{cons}$. This suggests a recursive algorithm that identifies common patterns and translates them into test expressions and new, smaller match expressions.

Figure 7 contains the rewrite rules used by the algorithm. The translation relies on the static types of expressions, and is thus expressed as a translation of type derivations. The rules use a derived form **val** $\mathsf{x}\colon C = a; b$ which has the double purpose of simplifying the presentation and catching divergent and exception-throwing input values. The derived form is only used when $a$ is of static type $C$, and abbreviates $a?\{\mathsf{x}\colon C \Rightarrow b\}/\{b'\}$ where $b' = b\,\{\mathsf{x} \mapsto \textbf{null}\}$ .

**Translation** $[\![\Gamma \vdash a \text{ match } \{c_\star^{1..m}\} \in D]\!] = e$

(Tmp)

$$[\![\frac{\ldots \quad \Gamma \vdash a_\star \in C_\star^{1..n}}{\Gamma \vdash a_\star^{1..n} \text{ match } \{c_\star^{1..m}\} \in D}]\!] = \textbf{val } \mathsf{z}_\star : C_\star = a_\star^{1..n}; \mathsf{z}_\star^{1..n} \textbf{ match } \{c_\star^{1..m}\}$$

condition: – $a_\star$ are not all variables

---

(Var)

$$[\![\frac{\ldots \quad \Gamma \vdash \mathsf{z}_\star \in C_\star^{1..n}}{\Gamma \vdash \mathsf{z}_\star^{1..n} \text{ match } \{c_\star^{1..m}\} \in D}]\!] = b\,\{\mathsf{x}_\star \mapsto \mathsf{z}_\star^{1..n}\}$$

condition: – $c_1$ has the shape **case** $\mathsf{x}_\star^{1..n} \Rightarrow b$

---

(Mix)

$$[\![\frac{\ldots \quad \Gamma \vdash \mathsf{z}_\star \in C_\star^{1..n}}{\Gamma \vdash \mathsf{z}_\star^{1..n} \text{ match } \{c_\star^{1..m}\} \in D}]\!] = \hat{v}.\mathsf{m}(\mathsf{z}_i)?\{\mathsf{y} : C \Rightarrow \textbf{val } \mathsf{y}_\star : D_\star = \mathsf{y}.\mathsf{f}_\star^{1..k}; d\}/\{e\}$$

condition: – $c_1$ has the shape **case** $\mathsf{x}_\star^{1..i-1}\ \hat{v}.\mathsf{m}(p_\star'^{1..k})\ p_\star^{i+1..n} \Rightarrow b$

translation steps:

- $\hat{v}.\mathsf{m}(\mathsf{z}_i)$ has pattern typing $\dfrac{\mathsf{xtype}(\Gamma, \hat{v}, \mathsf{m}) = C \quad \ldots}{\Gamma; C_i \ni \hat{v}.\mathsf{m}(p_\star'^{1..k}) \dashv \Delta}$ (TPext)
- the definition of $C$ is **class** $C(\mathsf{f}_\star : D_\star^{1..k}) \lhd E\,\{md_\star^{1..n}\}$
- $\mathsf{y}, \mathsf{y}_\star^{1..k}$ are fresh variables
- $d = \mathsf{z}_\star, \mathsf{y}, \mathsf{y}_\star^{1..k}, \mathsf{z}_\star^{1..]i[..n}$ **match** $\{expand_{\hat{v}.m}(c_\star^{1..m})\}$
- $e = \mathsf{z}_\star^{1..n}$ **match** $\{other_{\hat{v}.m}(c_\star^{1..m})\}$
- where $expand_{\hat{v}.m}$ and $other_{\hat{v}.m}$ are defined for arbitrary patterns $p_\star, p'_\star$, as (subscript omitted):

  $expand(\bullet) = \bullet$

  $expand(\textbf{case } p_\star\ \hat{v}.\mathsf{m}(p_\star^{1..k})\ p_\star^{1..]i[..n} \Rightarrow b;\ c_\star^{1..m}) =$
  $\quad \textbf{case } p_\star\ \mathsf{z}'\ p_1' \cdots p_k'\ p_\star^{1..]i[..n} \Rightarrow b;\ expand(c_\star^{1..m}) \qquad \mathsf{z}'\ fresh$

  $expand(\textbf{case } p_\star\ p\ p_\star^{1..]i[..n} \Rightarrow b;\ c_\star^{1..m}) =$
  $\quad \textbf{case } p_\star\ p\ \mathsf{z}_1' \cdots \mathsf{z}_k'\ p_\star^{1..]i[..n} \Rightarrow b;\ expand(c_\star^{1..m}) \qquad \mathsf{z}_\star'^{1..k} fresh \quad p \neq \hat{v}.\mathsf{m}(p_\star^{1..k})$

  $other(\bullet) = \bullet$

  $other(\textbf{case } p_\star\ \hat{v}.\mathsf{m}(p_\star'^{1..k})\ p_\star^{1..]i[..n} \Rightarrow b;\ c_\star^{1..m}) = other(c_\star^{1..m})$

  $other(\textbf{case } p_\star\ p\ p_\star^{1..]i[..n} \Rightarrow b;\ c_\star^{1..m}) =$
  $\quad \textbf{case } p_\star\ p\ p_\star^{1..]i[..n} \Rightarrow b;\ other(c_\star^{1..m}) \qquad p \neq \hat{v}.\mathsf{m}(p_\star^{1..k})$

**Fig. 7.** FPat Translation Rules

Rule (Tmp) introduces **val** definitions, so that input values are always variables. Rule (Var) handles matches that are known to accept. The essential rule is (Mix) which performs the optimizing translation described above. If the extractor returns value $w$, then the subvalues $\mathsf{casefld}(C, w)$ can be obtained with field accesses $w.\mathsf{f_\star}^{1..k}$, and the return value as well as the subvalues are bound to fresh local variables $\mathsf{y}, \mathsf{y_\star}^{1..k}$. The function *expand* adapts the width of case clauses as mentioned before. If the extractor returns **null**, we continue matching on those clauses that have a different extractor, computed by function *other*.

In contrast to functional pattern matching, we cannot assume that e.g. a rejecting extractor cons means that nil will necessarily accept the input value. The user-defined methods could be annotated to supply this information, an extension that we do not pursue in this paper. We shall call *rewrite* the function that applies a rule to a suitable term (with its typing derivation).

### 3.2 Why Must Extractors Be @safe to Allow Optimized Translation?

Recall the example above. Suppose $\pi_1$ was a variable pattern and $\pi_2, \pi_4$ test the same extractor. Optimizing for the failing pattern $\pi_2$ causes omission of the entire third case clause.

When omitting this case clause, we are already assuming that $\pi_3$ will either accept or reject its input. However, if $\pi_3$ were allowed to throw an exception or diverge, it would not be possible to omit its evaluation without changing the meaning of the program. For this reason, the semantics does not cover these anomalous situations (if we included them, we could not prove our optimization correct). Any semantics for pattern matching that involves user-defined code depends on this assumption if optimized translation of matching is to preserve the meaning of programs, since we usually do not expect divergent or exception throwing programs to turn into normally terminating ones. A correct translation without the **@safe** assumption would have to include case clauses that are *known* to fail for the sole purpose of preserving their exception-throwing or divergent behavior.

The assumption that extractors are **@safe** complements the assumptions formulated by Syme *et al* [11] and Okasaki [8] that informally require extractors to be side-effect free and return the same result in all execution contexts in order for optimization to work. Of course in this calculus, absence of side-effects is guaranteed by the absence of assignment.

### 3.3 The Algorithm

We define a function *transform* that recursively traverses expressions, rewriting any match statements it finds.

$$
\begin{aligned}
&\mathit{transform}(\mathbf{null}) &&= \mathbf{null}\\
&\mathit{transform}(\mathsf{x}) &&= \mathsf{x}\\
&\mathit{transform}(\mathsf{e.f}) &&= \mathit{transform}(\mathsf{e}).\mathsf{f}\\
&\mathit{transform}(\mathsf{e.m}(\mathsf{e_\star}^{1..n})) &&= \mathit{transform}(\mathsf{e}).\mathsf{m}(\mathsf{e'_\star}^{1..n})\\
& &&\quad \text{where } \mathsf{e'_\star} = \mathit{transform}(\mathsf{e_\star})^{1..n}\\
&\mathit{transform}(\mathbf{throw}) &&= \mathbf{throw}
\end{aligned}
$$

$$transform(a?\{\mathsf{x}\colon C \Rightarrow d\}/\{e\}) \quad = a'?\{\mathsf{x}\colon C \Rightarrow d'\}/\{e'\}$$
$$\text{where } a' = transform(a)$$
$$\text{and } d' = transform(d)$$
$$\text{and } e' = transform(e)$$

$$transform(e_\star{}^{1..n} \textbf{ match } \{c_\star{}^{1..k}\}) = transform(rewrite(e_\star{}^{1..n} \textbf{ match } \{c_\star{}^{1..k}\}))$$

The *transform* function is then naturally extended to method definitions and class definitions. A program is translated by translating all class definitions and the top-level expression. Note that a single application of a rewrite rule takes place in one of the following contexts:

**Definition 1 (Target Context).** *A target context is defined by the following grammar:*

$$\xi, \zeta ::= [\,] \mid \xi.\mathsf{f} \mid \xi.\mathsf{m}(b_\star{}^{1..n}) \mid a.\mathsf{m}(b_\star, \xi, b_\star{}^{1..]i[..n})$$
$$\mid \xi?\{\mathsf{x}\colon C \Rightarrow d\}/\{e\} \mid a?\{\mathsf{x}\colon C \Rightarrow \xi\}/\{e\} \mid a?\{\mathsf{x}\colon C \Rightarrow d\}/\{\xi\}$$

By the reasoning in the next section, this rewrite preserves the meaning of the program. A subsequent call of *transform* performs the same for subexpressions of $a'$, until all match expressions are translated away.

## 4 Correctness

We define a formal notion of equivalence. Recall that a substitution always satisfies $\mathsf{x}\sigma \equiv$ **null** or $\mathsf{x}\sigma \in \mathsf{Values}$ for all $\mathsf{x} \in \mathsf{dom}(\sigma)$. We proceed in two steps, following the *démarche* of [15]: we define a notion of equivalence and show that it is stable under contexts. Then we show that an expression is equivalent to its translation.

### 4.1 Equivalence and Open Equivalence

**Definition 2 (Equivalence).** *For $d, e$ expressions with $fv(d) = fv(e) = \emptyset$, $d$ is equivalent to $e$ (written $d \approx e$), if both of these conditions hold: 1. for all $q$, if $d \Downarrow q$ then $e \Downarrow q$, and 2. if $d \Uparrow$ then $e \Uparrow$.*

Showing that $\approx$ is an equivalence relation is easy using **(Uniqueness)**,**(Termination)**. Equivalence alone is not enough for our purpose, since rewrite rules take place in context. We now define an equivalence on open terms and show it is stable under contexts.

**Definition 3 (Open Equivalence).** *For expressions $d, e$ with $fv(d) \cup fv(e) \subseteq X$, $d$ is open-equivalent to $e$ (written $X \Vdash d \approx e$) if $d\sigma \approx e\sigma$ for all substitutions $\sigma$ with $X \subseteq \mathsf{dom}(\sigma)$.*

**Lemma 11 (Substitution preserves Equivalence).** *If $X \Vdash d \approx e$, then for any substitution $\sigma$ with $\mathsf{dom}(\sigma) \subseteq X$, it holds that $X \backslash \mathsf{dom}(\sigma) \Vdash d\sigma \approx e\sigma$.*

**Theorem 2 (Congruence).** *If $X \Vdash d \approx e$, then $Y \Vdash \xi[d] \approx \xi[e]$ for $Y = fv(\xi[d]) \cup fv(\xi[e])$.*

We now have everything we need for proving the correctness theorem. Since equivalence is a congruence, it is enough to show correctness of the rewrite rules. The proof of the following theorem references the **@safe** assumption, to derive case clause rejection for clauses omitted by $other_{\hat{v}.\mathsf{m}}$ – this requires normal termination of extractor calls to the left of the $\hat{v}.\mathsf{m}$.

**Theorem 3 (Correctness of $[\![\,]\!]$).** *For* $a \equiv a_\star{}^{1..n}$ **match** $\{c_\star{}^{1..m}\}$, $fv(a) = X$, *typing* $\Gamma \vdash a \in A$, *translation* $a' = [\![\Gamma \vdash a \in A]\!]$ *it holds that* $X \ \Vdash a \approx a'$.

**Corollary 1 (Complete Algorithm)** *The algorithm described in Section 3.3 is correct.*

***Proof*** Consequence of the above theorem, applied sequentially to every application of a rewrite rule $[\![\,]\!]$, and transitivity of $\approx$. For termination, observe that each match expression produced by a rewriting rule is smaller than the original match expression using the lexicographically ordered tuples $\langle i, j, k\rangle$ where $i$ is the number of non-variable input values, $j$ the number of case clauses, and $k$ the number of extractor patterns in $c_\star{}^{1..j}$. This ordering shows that for any $e$, all chains of dependency-pairs $\langle transform(e), transform(rewrite(e))\rangle$ must be finite. □

## 5 Related Work

Pettersson [4] and Ramsay and Scott [5] describe a matrix-based algorithm for translating match expressions to decision trees (the latter allowing heuristics other than left-to-right). Since an algebraic data type defines a closed set of constructors, different optimizations are available. Maranget [16] treats clause matrices and incompleteness checking in more detail.

If extractors came with coverage annotations, then more optimizations and incompleteness checking could be integrated. Syme, Neverov and Margetson [11] use *structured names* for this purpose. The authors also introduce parameterized patterns and give strong informal guidelines to restrict extractors (there called recognizers) in order to allow optimizations.

Extractors are rooted in Wadler's work on views [7], which Okasaki adapted to ML [8]. The design in a functional language context that comes closest to ours is Gostanza [17]. A more detailed discussion of the literature on views is presented in [10,13].

Zenger and Odersky use pattern matching and algebraic datatypes in an object-oriented setting to handle the extensibility problem [18]. Liu and Myers add pattern matching to a Java like language by introducing forwards and backwards modes of evaluation [19].

## 6 Conclusion

We presented a formal object-oriented calculus with pattern matching. We proved the calculus sound, and gave an optimizing translation algorithm. We then proved the translation correct, revealing an important assumption required for correctness: that extractor patterns may not throw exceptions or diverge. We emphasize that non-optimizing translation is not affected by this requirement – yet, optimizing pattern matching by factoring out common test seems essential for good performance.

In future work, we would like to extend our formalization to support incompleteness checking and further optimizations as known from algebraic data types. The Scala language offers matching on specific types (case classes) and the **sealed** keyword to this end. Specifying the completeness of a set of extractors for a given domain would be possible through source annotations. Apart from this, further study is necessary to analyze how the backtracking approaches to pattern match translation can be adapted.

## References

1. Burstall, R.M.: Proving properties of programs by inductive definitions. Computer 41–48 (1969)
2. Wadler, P.: Pattern Matching. In: ch. 4 of Peyton Jones, Wadler "Implementation of Functional Programming Languages", Prentice Hall, Englewood Cliffs (1987)
3. Field, A., Harrison, P.: Functional Programming. Addison-Wesley, Reading (1988)
4. Pettersson, M.: A term pattern-match compiler inspired by finite-automata theory. In: Pfahler, P., Kastens, U. (eds.) CC 1992. LNCS, vol. 641, Springer, Heidelberg (1992)
5. Scott, K., Ramsey, N.: When do match-compilation heuristics matter? Technical Report CS-2000-13, University of Virginia (2000)
6. Fessant, F.L., Maranget, L.: Optimizing pattern matching. In: ICFP, pp. 26–37 (2001)
7. Wadler, P.: Views: A way for pattern matching to cohabit with data abstraction. In: POPL (1987)
8. Okasaki, C.: Views for Standard ML. In: Proceedings of SIGPLAN Workshop on ML, pp. 14–23 (1998)
9. Gamma, E., Helm, R., Johnson, R., Vlissides, J.: Design Patterns. Addison-Wesley, Reading (1995)
10. Emir, B., Williams, J., Odersky, M.: Matching objects with patterns. In: ECOOP 2007. LNCS, vol. 4609, Springer, Heidelberg (2007)
11. Syme, D., Neverov, G., Margetson, J.: Extensible Pattern Matching via a Lightweight Language Extension. In: ICFP (2007)
12. Igarashi, A., Pierce, B., Wadler, P.: Featherweight Java. In: OOPSLA (1999)
13. Emir, B.: Object-Oriented Pattern Matching. PhD thesis, EPFL Lausanne (2007)
14. Leroy, X., Grall, H.: Coinductive big-step operational semantics. Theoretical Computer Science (submitted)
15. Ma, Q.: Concurrent Classes and Pattern Matching in the Join Calculus. PhD thesis, INRIA-Rocquencourt and University Paris 7 (2005)
16. Maranget, L.: Warnings in pattern matching. Journal of Functional Programming 17(3), 387–421 (2007)
17. Gostanza, P.P., Pena, R., Nunez, M.M.: A new look at pattern matching in abstract data types. In: ICFP (1996)
18. Zenger, M., Odersky, M.: Extensible algebraic datatypes with defaults. In: ICFP (2001)
19. Liu, J., Myers, A.C.: JMatch: Iterable Abstract Pattern Matching for Java. In: Dahl, V., Wadler, P. (eds.) PADL 2003. LNCS, vol. 2562, pp. 110–127. Springer, Heidelberg (2002)

# Persistent Oberon: A Programming Language with Integrated Persistence

Luc Bläser

Computer Systems Institute, ETH Zürich, Switzerland
blaeser@inf.ethz.ch

**Abstract.** This paper presents the programming language Persistent Oberon, which offers persistence as a naturally inbuilt concept. Program data is automatically kept durable and stored in non-volatile memory, without the programmer having to write explicit code for the interactions with an external database system. In the case of a system interruption or failure, the program can directly continue from its latest consistent state. In contrast to other existent persistent programming languages, this language does not need any artificial programming interfaces or commands to use persistence. The programming language is completely implemented and offers a high scalability and performance.

## 1 Introduction

As a consequence of the traditional computer architecture with volatile main memory, programming languages also only support a volatile memory model. Unless the programmer takes extra efforts, the state of a program is lost when the system or application is terminated. As a result of performance advantages on current machines, this design may be reasonable for applications which only perform temporary computations. However, many practical programs work on data that should be persistent and remain present even if the system is interrupted. For this area of application, programming languages currently leave the programmer unsupported and require them to explicitly employ a separate persistence system, such as a database, a serialization framework, or a file system. Even with the help of existing software tools, the programming work and error proneness for managing persistent data within a program are still immense. Complicated and time-consuming work is typically involved in the effective mapping of the program data to the persistent secondary memory (e.g. a disk) and in programming the necessary interactions with the persistence system, for storing and loading the data at the right moments. Especially for object-oriented programs, the intricacy is particularly high, as the dynamic reference-linked object structures need to be efficiently represented in the persistent storage and a memory-safe runtime support with garbage collection has to be provided on all levels of the memory (main memory and disk).

In order to improve the support of persistent data in a program, various approaches have been taken to directly provide persistence as an inbuilt feature

Z. Shao (Ed.): APLAS 2007, LNCS 4807, pp. 71–85, 2007.

of the programming language [3,4,5,6,12,14,15,19,20,22,24,34]. Although this approach seems to be the most obvious step towards simple and efficient programming with persistent data, none of these programming models have received widespread recognition in practice. A reason for this fact is certainly, that various fundamental problems are still open in this field, such that the programmer may decide against using a persistent language:

- *Language-support*
  To the best of our knowledge, no programming language exists that really features data persistence as a fully integrated concept. Existing persistent programming languages still require artificial programming interfaces when working with persistent data.
- *Interoperability*
  The range of practical applicability can be substantially widened for a persistent programming language by introducing a more general data model, which facilitates consistent and uniform interoperability with data of arbitrary longevity and already existing software.
- *Safety*
  The runtime support for object-oriented persistent programs is often not fully memory safe. Many persistent languages for example, require that garbage collection has to be performed when the system is turned off.
- *Efficiency*
  Persistent programming languages are often less efficient than a conventional solution which uses customized interactions with a database or a persistent storage.

A sustainable solution to these issues seems to be a prerequisite for a potential successful prevalence of the persistent programming vision. For this purpose, we have developed the new programming language Persistent Oberon that aims to address these open problems. The language offers the following key features:

- *Language-integrated persistence*
  The programming language supports data persistence as an elementary feature, without requiring any persistence-specific programming interfaces and thinking about a separate external persistence system.
- *General data longevity*
  The programming language is based on a data model, which uniformly covers data of arbitrary longevity, i.e. persistent, volatile and cached data can be used in a consistent way.
- *Effective and safe memory management*
  The runtime system incorporates effective non-disruptive and complete garbage collection with simultaneous caching in volatile main memory. To our knowledge, none of the existing systems is capable of such effective caching for persistent garbage-collection, which works for this general programming model.

While Persistent Oberon has already been very briefly presented in a poster session [11], here we describe the language in more detail, explain its rationale and also report on its implementation. The programming language has been completely implemented on the basis of Active Oberon [16,28,32], which is the object-oriented descendant of Oberon [37,38]. The system supplies the entire infrastructure that is necessary for persistent programming, including a compiler and runtime system, as well as a disk storage and program evolution facility. By means of an experimental evaluation, we also show that the new language offers a high scalability and performance.

The remaining paper is organized as follows: Section 2 motivates the idea of persistent programming and identifies the main shortcomings of existing persistent languages. Section 3 then describes the new programming language Persistent Oberon. In Section 4, the design and implementation of the runtime system is presented together with a performance evaluation. Section 6 reports on related work, before we conclude this paper in Section 7.

## 2 State of the Art

For object-orientation, concrete criteria of a seamless integration of persistence within a language have already been postulated by the principles of *orthogonal persistence* [8,7]:

- *Persistence independence*
  All program operations look the same irrespective of the lifetime of the accessed data.
- *Type orthogonality*
  An object type does not predetermine the lifetime of its instances.
- *Persistence identification*
  The concepts of object identification and implicit object lifetimes remain unchanged.

The main idea of orthogonal persistence is to avoid any special handling, which is only applicable to persistent data and to preserve the philosophy of the underlying programming paradigm. Although many persistent languages [3,12,24,19,6] (including non object-oriented ones) are claimed to be orthogonally persistent, regrettably none of them fulfils this goal of language-institutionalized persistence:

- Special program functions and explicit interfaces are required in these languages, to query and fix a root of the persistent object graph, something that is clearly contradicting the principle of persistence independence. Persistent roots have to be handled entirely differently in comparison to the transient ones (such as static variables in Java, module variables in Persistent Modula-3). Figure 1 illustrates how cumbersome it is to set up the initial persistent state in these languages. As an implication of the special persistent roots, a program also has to explicitly determine whether it is started for the first time or is simply resumed after interruption.

- To maintain consistency for the interruptible execution, the abovementioned languages often require explicit stabilization (checkpointing) or starting and stopping database transactions via a dedicated persistence interface. These mechanisms also form persistence-specific artifacts that are quite unnatural and complicated to use. More especially, the approach of global checkpoints necessitates the knowledge over the entire program, in order not to prematurely save the temporary modifications of a non-completed logical transaction.

Persistent Modula 3 (PM3)

```
INTERFACE MyModule;
 IMPORT Database;
 DataEntry = OBJECT (* ... *) END;
 VAR myData: DataEntry; p: Database.Public
BEGIN
   TRY
     p := NARROW(Database.Open("MyModuleData"),
                    Database.Public);
     myData := NARROW(p.getRoot(), DataEntry)
   EXCEPT
    Database.DatabaseNotFound =>
      Database.Create("MyModuleData");
      p := NARROW(Database.Open("MyModuleData",
                    Database.Public)
      NEW(myData); p.SetRoot(myData)
   END
END MyModule.
```

PJama

```
import org.opj.store;
class DataEntry { /* ... */ }
class MyProgram {
  static DataEntry myData;
  public static void main(String args[]) {
    PJStore p = PJStoreImpl.getStore();
    if (p.existsPRoot("MyProgramData")) {
      myData =
           (DataEntry) p.getPRoot("MyProgramData"));
    }
    else {
      myData = new DataEntry;
      p.newPRoot("MyProgramData, myData);
    }
  }
}
```

**Fig. 1.** Explicit accesses to the persistent state

## 3 Persistent Oberon

Persistent Oberon is based on a modular object-oriented programming model, which combines the notion of conventional objects with the concept of modules, as they are known in Oberon [37,38] and Modula [36]. Modules thereby turn out to be a key concept for introducing persistence in a natural way. Besides being a static compilation and deployment unit, a module represents a singleton instance at runtime that maintains an individual data state. A module is dynamically loaded by the system, as soon as it is used for the first time by the user or another importing module. In the following sections, we explain the main language concepts that are related to persistence support.

### 3.1 Modules

In our language, a module is designed to live infinitely long in the system. Once loaded and initialized, the module and its contained state stays permanently alive and survives all system restarts. Naturally, references also belong to this persistent state and by default, remain valid at system restart. In other words, modules constitute the persistent roots, implicitly making all transitively reachable objects of the modules persistent. To illustrate the meaning of this, Figure 2 outlines a persistent bank system, together with an exemplary runtime topology of the corresponding object instances. Notably, the code of the module is

```
MODULE Bank;
  TYPE
    Account = OBJECT
      VAR
        customer: Customer;
        balance: REAL;
    END Patient;
    Customer = OBJECT (* ... *) END Customer;
    AccountList = OBJECT (* ... *) END AccountList;
  VAR accounts: AccountList;
END Bank.
```

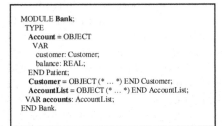

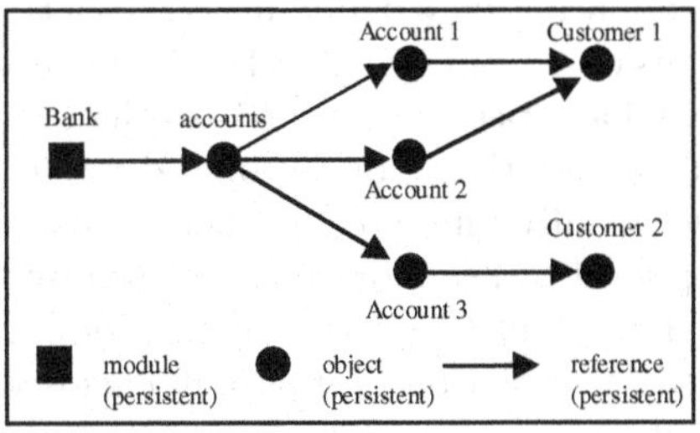


**Fig. 2.** A persistent program

identical to a conventional transient program and no persistence-specific programming constructs are involved here. In Persistent Oberon, a module can only be unloaded for the reason of changing the program definition. In this case, the runtime system provides an evolution facility that supports the programmer to migrate the persistent data of the former module version to the newer one.

In ordinary languages, a seamless integration of persistence is usually not so simple because of the absence of the module concept. Though class variables (*static* keyword) may represent a part of the persistent root set, a program is usually completely executed by the *main*-method without a separation between the initialization phase and the actual main program activity. Hence, the program state that ought to be valid during the entire program is not necessarily contained in the (*static*) class variables but may just as well be contained as local variables of procedures invoked by the *main*-method (including the *main*-procedure itself).

### 3.2 Transactions

As the persistent state should always be available in a consistent way when the system is resumed after an interruption or failure, the program execution has to necessarily reflect the states of consistency. For this purpose, the language features the concept of transactions, which define statement sequences that change the program from one consistent state to another. In Persistent Oberon, a normal statement sequence (BEGIN-END block) can be annotated by the TRANSACTION-attribute in order to represent a transaction, see Figure 3. All modifications, which are performed by the execution of a transaction (including the code of directly or indirectly called procedures), are either completely applied or not at all. During the unfinished transactions, these changes are only temporarily valid and are discarded at a system interruption. A transaction may also be prematurely stopped by the programmer by way of the ABORT-statement. In this case, the corresponding transaction statement block is immediately exited and none of its modifications to the program state become effective.

Naturally, a transaction may also execute statement sequences which are defined as transactions. Such transactions (executed as part of another transaction) are called sub-transactions [25]. A sub-transaction can be aborted without terminating its surrounding transaction. However, an abort of the surrounding transaction always cancels all the sub-transactions and discards all the effects that have been performed by the sub-transactions. Therefore, the effects of a sub-transaction only become durable when the surrounding procedure is also successfully finished. In other words, only the changes of a successfully finished top-level transaction (not enclosed by another transaction) are made persistent. In Persistent Oberon, a single modifying operation automatically forms an implicit transaction if it is not enclosed by an explicit transactional statement sequence.

Figure 3 explains the use of transactions through the bank example. The *Transfer* procedure contains a transactional statement block, which runs as a top-level transaction. The transactional statement blocks within the procedures *Withdraw* and *Deposit* are called by the *Transfer* procedure and hence only represent sub-transactions.

```
Account = OBJECT
  VAR balance: REAL;

  PROCEDURE Withdraw(amount: REAL): BOOLEAN;
  BEGIN {TRANSACTION}
    IF balance >= amount THEN
      balance:= balance - amount; RETURN TRUE
    ELSE RETURN FALSE
    END
  END Withdraw;

  PROCEDURE Deposit(amount: REAL);
  BEGIN {TRANSACTION}
    balance:= balance + amount
  END Deposit;
END Account;
```

```
PROCEDURE Transfer(from, to: Account; amount: REAL);
VAR success: BOOLEAN;
BEGIN
  BEGIN {TRANSACTION}
    success := from.Withdraw(amount);
    IF success THEN
      to.Deposit(amount)
    END
  END;
  ReportStatus(success)
END Transfer;
```

**Fig. 3.** Transactions

Both top-level and sub-transactions feature isolation with respect to serializability[9], of read- and write-accesses on the granularity of objects and modules. This means that concurrent transactions can only see effects of others as if the transactions were executed in a strictly serial order. A sub-transaction is however not isolated from its enclosing transactions, as it has access to the temporary state of its surrounding transactions.

It should be noted that the transactional statement block is a language-integrated feature that is not only applicable for persistence but it is also useful for volatile data due to the rollback-possibility and the isolation. Contrary to other persistent languages, the begin and end points of a transaction is implicitly defined by the transactional statement block and no explicit invocation of database methods such as *Transaction.Begin* and *Transaction.Commit* is needed.

### 3.3 Interoperability

To allow interoperability with existing non-persistent programs, Persistent Oberon also supports references to objects that do not necessarily have to be persistent but can be of shorter longevity. For example, this could be transient objects, which are only available during an uninterrupted system phase, or cached objects, which can even vanish during the running system when memory space becomes scarce. To enable such shorter object lifetimes, a reference can be declared as *transient* or *weak*, to deviate from the default semantics of a usual persistent reference. The meaning of a transient reference is that the target data does not need to be retained at system interruptions. Analogously, a weak reference permits the disposal of the target reference at any time during program execution. However, transient or weak references do not force shorter lifetime for the referenced objects but merely figure as a suggestion for the runtime system. The value of transient references is safely reset to NIL on system restart and a weak reference is cleared on removal of the referenced object. Significantly, object lifetimes are still determined by transitive reachability, such that in combination with an appropriate runtime system, memory safety can be completely ensured. This may be illustrated by Figure 4, showing an extension of the previous bank example. Everything that is not explicitly declared as transient or weak should be persistent, that is particularly true for all data associated with accounts. The list of account managers, which are currently logged in the system, can be maintained as transient, since they have to logon again after a system interruption. Furthermore, the module also maintains an object cache of the least recently accessed accounts, which are only retained as long as free memory space is not sought by automatic garbage collection. The right-hand side of Figure 4 shows the potential states of the program object graph in different stages, the initial topology, after garbage collection and at system restart. Thereby, the object lifetimes are specified as follows: All objects being transitively reachable from a module via persistent references, are persistent. The other non-persistent objects are transient, if they are reachable via persistent or transient references from a module or the transient state of a running procedure (or transaction). All remaining objects form garbage, which are possibly used as cached data, and are eventually removed from the system.

As a result, the introduced reference semantics enable a general data model, safely interoperable with other preexisting transient programs, such as with low-level operating system modules. Modules written in the persistent programming language may then import classical transient modules and reuse the therein provided logic, with the restriction that the persistent program part only interacts with the data of the imported module by using transient (or weak) references.

### 3.4 Particular Functionality

We deliberately do not provide the same amount of functionality as a database system offers. The presented model is rather designed for general-purpose programming with a minimum set of fundamental concepts for persistence. Advanced functionality, such as special querying languages, mechanism of data distributions and security policies, can be individually provided by customized program logic.

```
MODULE Bank;
  TYPE
    Account = OBJECT
      VAR
        customer: Customer;
        balance: REAL;
    END Account;

    Customer = OBJECT (* ... *) END Customer;
    AccountList = OBJECT (* ... *) END AccountList;
    BankManager = OBJECT (* ... *) END BankManager;
    ManagerList = OBJECT (* ... *) END ManagerList;
  VAR
    accounts: PatientList;
    managers: ManagerList;

    loggedInManagers: {TRANSIENT} ManagersList;

    leastRecentlyAccessed: {WEAK} AccountList;
END Bank.
```

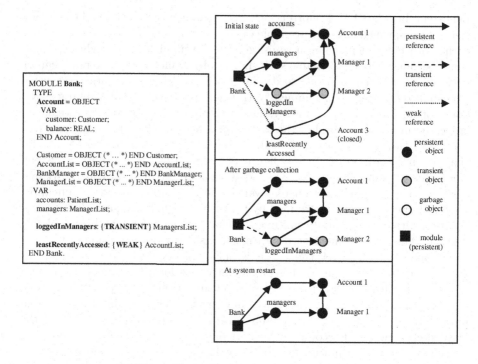

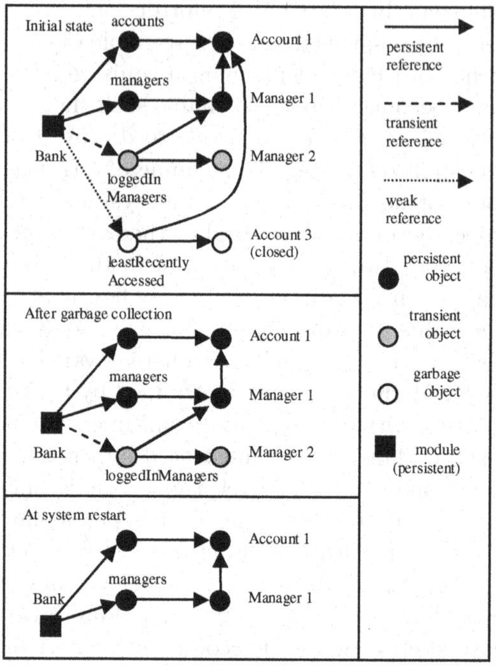


**Fig. 4.** Using data with shorter lifetimes

## 4 Runtime System

We have implemented an entire execution platform Persistent Oberon, to provide evidence that the proposed persistent programming model can be efficiently realized on conventional computer machines. As a fundament, we have chosen the operating system AOS [28], which employs Active Oberon as the native programming language.

### 4.1 Memory Management

The basic infrastructure of the memory system is the persistent object store (POS), managing the non-volatile memory heap on a disk and enabling fault-tolerant atomic updates or allocations. Furthermore, the system supports main memory caching with a lazy-loading mechanism, where an object is only loaded into memory, when requested for the first time after a system restart. As the normal main memory addresses depend on a system run, synthetic unique object identifiers are used for the reference values, also allowing flexible memory movement of the objects. Consequently, these identifiers need to be mapped to both main memory addresses and locations in the POS. This translation is realized by a residency object table, implemented as a high-scalable and efficient hash table with splay-trees as table entries [17]. Automatic garbage collection is another decisive issue, in continuously ensuring the following memory safety requirements:

- Durability of the latest committed states of each persistent object and module at any time. (Only the top-level transactions change the stable state).
- Exclusion of dangling pointers, i.e. a reference pointing to an object with shorter lifetime than the source object or module.
- Absence of memory leaks, where each non-persistent object is eventually freed from the persistent store and each garbage object is removed from all memory spaces with finite delay.

For this purpose, modules and objects are conceptually classified into two disjoint sets $P$ and $T$. The set $P$ contains at least all modules and persistent objects and furthermore, forms a transitive closure of reachability via persistent references in the stable states. All transient objects, which are not contained in $P$, belong to $T$. The union of $P$ and $T$ represents the transitive closure of reachability via non-weak references in all states (persistent store and main memory). It is essential for correctness that the latest stable states of modules and objects of $P$ always reside in the POS, whereas for all other objects, the POS does not hold a value state. The accuracy of these two sets can be established by two independent automatic garbage collectors: One, called the POS garbage collector, removes objects from $P$ and frees the occupied space in the POS; the other is only responsible for disposing of garbage in the main memory and is hence named the main memory garbage collector.

At system startup, $P$ is initialized with the set of all objects in the POS and $T$ is empty. When a module is activated for the very first time, an empty state is immediately allocated for this module in the POS and the module is added to $P$. Subsequently, each state modification has to be performed within a transaction. Each transaction has an associated set, called the write-object-set (WOS), recording all objects and modules, which have been modified or allocated during the execution of the transaction. The write-object-set is implemented as a combination of a bucketed list for rapid iteration and a hash-splay [17] for fast searching.

On the commit of a top-level transaction, the system collects all object states that have to be propagated to the persistent store, as specified on the left-hand side of Figure 5. Thereby, it tracks the stable states for the entities unmodified by the current transaction and otherwise, the current states in the transaction's WOS. Transactions cannot commit concurrently, implying that the commit process always maintains a coherent view of the stable states. Conversely, the commit of a subtransaction (in the context of nested transactions [25]) causes each entry of its WOS to be transferred to the super-transaction, if the entry is not yet contained in the super-transaction's WOS. In addition, each transaction maintains a backup of the original states of its modified objects or modules. In the case of a transaction abort, the corresponding backup states are restored in main memory.

The POS garbage collector detects non-persistent objects in the POS and safely reclaims the corresponding free space. Therefore, the collector also has to

```
PROCEDURE Commit(top-level transaction A);
  AcquireLock(TopLevelTransactionCommit);
  NewP := {}; MarkStack := Empty;
  FOREACH x ∈ WOS(A) with x ∈ P DO
   RefSet := persistent references in current state of x
   FOREACH reference in RefSet pointing to y ≠ NIL DO
    MarkStack.Push(y)
   END
  END;
  WHILE MarkStack is not empty DO
   x := MarkStack.Pop();
   IF x is in main memory and x ∉ P and x ∉ NewP THEN
    NewP := NewP ∪ {x};
    IF x ∈ WOS(A) THEN
     RefSet := persistent references in current state of x
    ELSE
     RefSet := persistent references in stable state of x
    END;
    FOREACH reference in RefSet pointing to y ≠ NIL DO
     MarkStack.Push(y)
    END
  END;
  Begin atomic POS update;
  FOREACH x ∈ WOS(A) with (x ∈ P or x ∈ NewP) DO
   Store current state of x in POS and set it as the stable state
  END;
  FOREACH x ∈ (NewP \ WOS(A)) DO
   Promote stable state of x to POS.
  END;
  P := P ∪ NewP;
  End atomic POS update;
  ReleaseLock(TopLevelTransactionCommit);
END Commit;
```

```
PROCEDURE RemoveNonPersistentData(object set S);
AcquireLock(TopLevelTransactionCommit);
FOREACH object x ∈ S DO
 IF x is not present in main memory THEN
  Load x into main memory
 END
END;
P := P \ S; T := T ∪ S
Delete S in the POS
ReleaseLock(TopLevelTransactionCommit);
END RemoveNonPersistentData;
```

**Fig. 5.** Cache interaction mechanism

correctly interact with the simultaneous main memory object cache. To do so, all objects that are detected as non-persistent by the POS garbage collector, are atomically moved to set $T$ under exclusion of intermediate concurrent transactions. As the non-persistent objects may still have transient lifetime, they are loaded to main memory before removal from the persistent storage. The right-hand side of Figure 5 shows the detailed cache interaction by the disposal process of the persistent garbage collector. The described cache interaction mechanism is combinable with any correct (and thus necessarily complete) persistent garbage collector. Because of the characteristics of the non-volatile disk storage, such a collector should specifically support incremental execution, fault-tolerance, minimal I/O-overheads and maximum progress on each collection run [23,2]. For these requirements, we have chosen the persistent mature object space (PMOS) [26], as a suited underlying garbage collector. It allows incremental and complete collection by using a partitioned object space. A disadvantage of PMOS is however the overhead involved in storing small partitions, because each partition records all incoming references. On the other hand, longer disruptions of the POS result from larger partitions, since the POS is locked during a collection and thus blocks concurrent transaction commits. We have abandoned this trade-off by using larger partitions and only blocking the POS during the evacuation of a small amount of objects per partition. The disposal of non-persistent objects is done within a single blocking period.

The main memory collector has only the task of reclaiming garbage objects in the set $T$ by immediately removing them from the main memory space. As for garbage objects of $P$, the POS collector first moves them to $T$, before they can be definitively discarded. This two-step disposal process is necessary because objects in $P$ may still be reachable from a root in the POS, even though they are not so in main memory. Therefore, objects of $P$ are considered as additional root elements for main memory garbage collection. All states must be traced for references and the collector can ignore references pointing to not yet loaded objects. Before garbage is finally deleted, weak references on these objects are reset to NIL, to avoid dangling references.

Transactional isolation can be supported by different concurrency control mechanisms. The transaction scheduling may be serial or relaxed, by using *strict two-phase locking* or *optimistic concurrency control* (such as *software transactional memory* [33]). However, the relaxed mechanisms possibly abort transactions, in order to prevent deadlocks or unserializable accesses, respectively. In such a case, the unexpectedly aborted transactions need to be restarted. The problem of this approach is that long running transactions may suffer from starvation, since they could be continuously aborted by the scheduler. Therefore, we currently use a serial transaction scheduler as default mechanism in the runtime system. *Preclaiming two-phase locking* would be less strict but require static analysis to conservatively determine the potentially accessed objects of a transaction.

### 4.2 Experimental Evaluation

To give an impression of our system's functionality and efficiency, we have measured the performance by the OO7 benchmark [13]. The results are compared to a classical approach, which a user would probably take if they have to develop this persistent application (i.e. the benchmark) within a similar time frame. Such an alternative could be JDO [35], which has been recently advertised as a transparent persistence framework for Java, interacting with a normal database system. Regrettably, the framework does not entirely fulfill this ideal: A programmer has to interact with special persistence API's and needs to provide additional XML-metadata for database mapping[1]. An even greater drawback is that objects are not automatically managed by the runtime system but must be explicitly deleted or made transient. This disagrees with the conventional Java programming model and allows violations of the referential integrity. All tests were run on a PC with Intel Pentium 4, 3GHz, 8KB L1 and 512KB L2 cache, as well as 1GB main memory. The hard disk was a Seagate ST3200822AS with 200GB capacity, 8.5ms average read seek time, 7200 rpm and about 16MB/s transfer-bandwidth. In Persistent Oberon, the data store space resided on a 10GB partition with POS-partition size of 4KB. The garbage collector was continuously active to measure the real efficiency. The JDO system is based on

[1] For some JDO implementations, one must even account for foreign key constraints in the database: An acyclic data topology first needs to be allocated in the database, before cyclic references may be set in the program.

Windows XP with JDK 1.5SE, JDO 1.0, JPOX 1.0.4 vendor implementation, and MySQL 4.0 database[2]. Initially, the measurements should be performed with the small OO7 configuration (about 53,000 objects inclusive collection entries). However, this amount already exceeds the capabilities of the JDO implementation, whereas our system runs perfectly with this configuration[3]. Therefore, we had to scale down the configuration to make the comparison possible (8,300 objects inclusive collection entries, see the right-hand side of Figure 6). The results are restricted to the most interesting traversals, each forming a single top-level transaction. The remaining tests gave no further information nor did they show up any contradictions. The left-hand side of Figure 6 summarizes the average execution times including the commit overheads, rounded to two significant figures. T1 is a read-only traversal, whereas T3C updates the data set. Both traversals are distinguished by whether the transaction operates on a cold main memory cache (meaning it is empty) or a warm cache, which already contains all needed objects. CU resembles the costs of solely updating the warm main memory cache. As a result, our system is not only scaling well for higher data loads but also greatly outperforms the JDO system by a factor of about 30 to 80. As for the cache updates, the discrepancy is not that high but this time only accounts for a small part of the total runtime cost. More details about the benchmark implementation, as well as the complete experimental results can be found in [10].

| | Persistent Oberon | | JDO | |
|---|---|---|---|---|
| | cold | warm | cold | warm |
| T1 | 91 ms | 23 ms | 3400 ms | 1800 ms |
| T3 C | 390 ms | 300 ms | 13000 ms | 11000 ms |
| CU | | 81 ms | | 115 ms |

| | |
|---|---|
| NumAtomicPerComp | 10 |
| NumConnPerAtomic | 3 |
| DocumentSize bytes | 200 |
| ManualSize bytes | 1024 |
| NumCompPerModule | 30 |
| NumAssmPerAssm | 3 |
| NumAssmLevels | 3 |
| NumCompPerAssm | 3 |
| NumModules | 1 |

**Fig. 6.** OO7 performance comparison

## 5 Related Work

Persistent programming has a long tradition and therefore, our language is related to various existing works.

**Persistent programming languages.** One of the earliest programming languages with support of persistence is PS-algol [3]. It already features persistence by referential reachability, as well as a transactional execution model. Napier88 [24] is a successor of PS-algol. Pointer type annotations were already introduced

[2] Many other database systems and JDO vendor implementations could not be used because corresponding license contracts forbid the publication of performance results.

[3] The JDO system fails with stack overflow errors even for very high stack sizes, or runs out of connection ports (increasing the system parameters only helped to a certain degree).

in object-oriented Persistent Modula-3 [19] for fine-granular specification of persistence reachability [18]. In Persistent Modula-3, a reference can also be declared to refer to an object that ought to be always transient, even if it could be reached over persistent references [27]. This is different to our model, where a chain of persistent references from a persistent root cannot be broken by an object explicitly forced to always be transient, which implies the risk of dangling persistent references in Persistent Modula-3. [21] shows the integration of transitive persistence into classical non-concurrent Oberon but does not support any transactional features. Optional custom internalization and externalization functions are proposed by [21], to ignore certain references for persistence reachability, which is solved in our work using transient or weak references. PJama [5,6] is a system providing persistence for Java, also based on reachability from a persistent root. Checkpoints may be performed under PJama, to update modifications of a program in the persistent store but no fine-grained transaction model exists for threads within an application. All of the mentioned languages do not offer a fully language-integrated persistence. They still require artificial programming constructs to deal with persistent roots or to define transactions or checkpoints. Software transactional memory [33] supports isolated transactions on the granularity of memory reads and writes. While we do not prejudice a specific implementation of transactional isolation, software transactional memory is realized by optimistic concurrency control (possibly leading to continuous aborts of transactions).

**Caching-aware garbage collection.** We have designed our own cache mechanism for simultaneous garbage collection in the persistent store, because we could not find another such cache mechanism, which is applicable to our general data model. A series of work on garbage collectors for persistent object systems points out this issue of cache-coordination but does not address it [31,23,29]. An interesting collector is reported by [1,2], which allows concurrent modifications in main memory. The system is however not designed (and does not work) in the presence of non-persistent references, since only reference cuts and newly allocated objects are recorded. In our model, a transient or garbage object can become persistent again, by converting a transient reference to a persistent one. The collector of [30] manages both a transitory and persistent memory heap but does not discard objects from the disk space without system restart. The copying collector of Persistent Modula-3 [20] works in the presence of caching but computes all persistent objects for the entire system with a global stabilization. This is unsuited for our system, since an atomic transaction should only update its own modified objects and should not save the temporary state of other objects used by a different concurrent transaction. To ensure that our caching algorithm is correct, we have formally proved the memory safety of it [10].

## 6 Conclusion

We have demonstrated that data persistence can be featured as a naturally inbuilt concept of a programming language, enabling the uniform, flexible and safe use of data with arbitrary longevity. Such a language eventually facilitates the development of persistent applications without bothering programmers to write cumbersome and vulnerable code for database interactions. The programming model is intentionally kept to a minimum of fundamental concepts and therefore, does not provide inbuilt mechanisms for special purposes. Instead, one can individually augment this functionality by using customized logic or interoperating with classical non-persistent program modules. The runtime system and its source code are available at [10].

## Acknowledgments

I am especially grateful to Prof. Dr. Jürg Gutknecht for many helpful discussions during the entire work, leading to several improvements of conceptual aspects. Many thanks also go to Raphael Güntensperger and Dr. Thomas Frey for their important remarks regarding the design and implementation of the runtime system.

## References

1. Amsaleg, L., Franklin, M., Gruber, O.: Efficient Incremental Garbage Collection for Workstation/Server Database Systems. In: VLDB (September 1995)
2. Amsaleg, L., Franklin, M., Gruber, O.: Garbage Collection for a Client-Server Persistent Object Store. ACM Transactions on Computer Systems 17(3), 153–201 (1999)
3. Atkinson, M.P., Bailey, P.J., Chisholm, K.J., Cockshott, W.P., Morrison, R.: PS-algol: A Language for Persistent Programming. In: Austrian National Computer Conference (September 1983)
4. Atkinson, M.P., Daynès, M.J., Spence, S.: Design Issues for Persistent Java. A Type-Safe Object-Oriented Orthogonally Persistent System. In: POS (May 1996)
5. Atkinson, M.P., Daynès, L., Jordan, M.J., Printezis, T., Spence, S.: An Orthogonally Persistent Java. ACM SIGMOD Record 25(4), 68–75 (1996)
6. Atkinson, M.P., Jordan, M.J.: A Review of the Rationale and Architecture of PJama: A Durable, Flexible, Evolvable and Scalable Orthogonally Persistent Programming Platform, Sun Labs Technical Report TR-2000-90, Sun Microsystems Laboratories (June 2000)
7. Atkinson, M.P., Morrison, R.: Orthogonally Persistent Object Systems. VLDB Journal 4(3), 319–402 (1995)
8. Atkinson, M.P.: Programming Languages and Databases. VLDB Journal, 408–429 (1978)
9. Bernstein, P.A., Hadzillacos, V., Goodman, N.: Concurrency Control and Recovery in Database Systems. Addison Wesley, Reading (1987)
10. Bläser, L.: The Persistent Oberon System, `http://www.jg.inf.ethz.ch/persistence`
11. Bläser, L.: A Programming Language with Natural Persistence, Poster Session. In: OOPSLA (October 2006)
12. Boyapati, C.: JPS: A Distributed Persistent Java System, Department of Electrical Engineering and Computer Science, Massachusetts Institute of Technology (September 1998)
13. Carey, M.J., De Witt, D.J., Naughton, J.F.: The OO7 Benchmark. In: ACM SIGMOD Conference, Washington, D.C (May 1993)

14. Carey, J., DeWitt, D.J., Franklin, M.J., et al.: Shoring up persistent applications. ACM SIGMOD Record 23(2), 383–394 (1994)
15. Dearle, A., di Bona, R., Farro, J., et al.: Grasshopper: An Orthogonally Persistent Operating System. Computing Systems 7(3), 289–312 (1994)
16. Gutknecht, J.: Do the Fish Really Need Remote Control? A Proposal for Self-Active Objects in Oberon. In: JMLC (March 1997)
17. He, Z., Blackburn, S.M., Kirby, L., Zigman, J.: Platypus: Design and Implementation of a Flexible High Performance Object Store. In: POS (September 2000)
18. Hosking, A.L., Moss, J.E.B.: Towards Compile-Time Optimisations for Persistence. In: POS (September 1990)
19. Hosking, A.L., Chen, J.: PM3: An Orthogonally Persistent Systems Programming Language – Design, Implementation, Performance. In: VLDB (1999)
20. Hosking, A.L., Chen, J.: Mostly-Copying Reachability-Based Orthogonal Persistence. ACM SIGPLAN Notices 34(10) (1999)
21. Knasmüller, M.: Adding Persistence to the Oberon System. In: JMLC (March 1997)
22. Lewis, B., Mathiske, B., Gafter, N.: Architecture of the PEVM: A High-Performance Orthogonally Persistent Java(tm) Virtual Machine. In: POS (September 2000)
23. Maheshwari, U., Liskov, B.: Partitioned Garbage Collection of a Large Object Store. In: ACM SIGMOD, pp. 313–323 (1997)
24. Morrison, R., Connor, R.C.H., Cutts, Q.I., et al.: The Napier88 Persistent Programming Environment, School of Mathematical and Computational Sciences, University of St. Andrews, Scotland (1999)
25. Moss, J.E.B.: Nested Transactions: An Approach to Reliable Distributed Computing. MIT Press, Cambridge Mass (1985)
26. Moss, J.E.B., Munro, D.S., Hudson, R.L.: PMOS: A Complete and Coarse-Grained Incremental Garbage Collector for Persistent Object Stores. In: POS (May 1996)
27. Moss, J.E.B., Hosking, A.L.: Expressing Object Residency Optimizations Using Pointer Type Annotations. In: POS (September 1994)
28. Muller, P.J.: The Active Object System. Design and Multiprocessor Implementation, PhD thesis 14755, Department of Computer Science, ETH Zurich (2002)
29. Munro, D.S., Brown, A.L., Morrison, R., Moss, J.E.B.: Incremental Garbage Collection of a Persistent Store using PMOS. In: POS (September 1998)
30. O'Toole, J., Nettle, S., Gifford, D.: Concurrent Compacting Garbage Collection of a Persistent Heap. In: SOSP (December 1993)
31. Printezis, A.: Management of Long-Running High-Performance Persistent Object Stores, PhD Thesis, Department of Computing Science, University of Glasgow (May 2000)
32. Reali, P.: Active Oberon Language Report, Institute of Computer Systems, ETH Zurich (March 2002), `http://www.bluebottle.ethz.ch/languagereport/ActiveReport.pdf`
33. Shavit, N., Touitou, D.: Software Transactional Memory. In: Symposium on Principles of Distributed Computing (August 1995)
34. Skoglund, E., Ceelen, C., Liedtke, J.: Transparent Orthogonal Checkpointing through User-Level Pagers. In: POS (September 2000)
35. Sun Microsystems. Java Data Objects (JDO),`http://java.sun.com/products/jdo`
36. Wirth, N.: Modula: A Language for Modular Multiprogramming. Software - Practice and Experience 7(1), 3–35 (1977)
37. Wirth, N.: The Programming Language Oberon. Software - Practice and Experience 18(7), 671–690 (1988)
38. Wirth, N., Gutknecht, J.: The Oberon System. Software - Practice and Experience 19(9), 857–893 (1989)

# More Typed Assembly Languages for Confidentiality

Dachuan Yu

DoCoMo Communications Laboratories USA
yu@docomolabs-usa.com

**Abstract.** We propose a series of type systems for the information-flow security of assembly code. These systems extend previous work $\text{TAL}_C$ with some timing annotations and associated judgments and rules. By using different timing rules, these systems are applicable to different practical settings. In particular, they can be used to prevent illicit information flow through the termination and timing channels in sequential programs as well as the possibilistic and probabilistic channels in multi-threaded programs. We present the formal details of these as a generic type system $\text{TAL}_C^+$ and prove its noninterference. $\text{TAL}_C^+$ is designed as a core target language for certifying compilation. We illustrate its use with a formal scheme of type-preserving translation.

## 1 Introduction

Language-based techniques are promising in enforcing information-flow security [19]. An information-flow problem typically concerns a program which operates on data of different security levels, *e.g., low* and *high*. Low data are public data that may be disclosed to all principals; high data are secret data whose access must be restricted. An information-flow policy, such as noninterference, typically requires that no information about high input data can be inferred from observing low output data. In practice, the security levels can be generalized to a lattice [26].

Whereas most existing work on information flow has focused on high-level languages, low-level languages are gradually receiving more attention, especially from the perspective of typed assembly languages [13] and for the purpose of certifying compilation [10,21]. In recent work [12,31], type annotations are used to restore the missing abstraction in assembly code, and type-preserving translation is used to preserve security evidence from the source to the target. By security-type checking directly at the target level, the compiler is lifted out of the trusted computing base, yielding higher confidence on the code behavior. In addition, in the context of mobile code security where code providers are potentially malicious and source code is typically not available for analysis, certifying compilation allows code producers to provide security evidence in the form of types and other annotations to accompany the target code for separate verification on the code consumer's side.

Although a good start, such low-level information-flow analysis only investigated relatively simple settings. In particular, only sequential programs were considered, and attackers were assumed to be unable to observe beyond the regular machine states (*e.g.,* heaps and register files). In practice, however, attackers may also be able to observe some timing behaviors, either by observing physically the execution time of a program

Z. Shao (Ed.): APLAS 2007, LNCS 4807, pp. 86–104, 2007.

(external timing) or by exploiting thread interaction (internal timing). Such timing behaviors, unfortunately, provide some covert channels of information flow.

This paper presents solutions that address information-flow security for low-level languages in more practical settings. For sequential programs, we propose type systems for closing up some covert channels, namely termination [25] and timing [1] channels. For multi-threaded programs, we propose type systems that guarantee possibilistic [23] and probabilistic [20] noninterference. Our solutions are inspired by source-level security-type systems which account for program timing behaviors. Based on our previous work [31] on a typed assembly language for confidentiality ($\text{TAL}_C$), we introduce additional annotations to document the timing of program execution. These timing annotations are used to express various source-level constraints, such as the absence of loops in high security contexts.

We observed that different timing annotations were needed to address different information-flow channels. Nonetheless, there was much similarity between the underlying type systems. We have formulated a generic type system $\text{TAL}_C^+$, which addresses different information-flow channels when given different "timing rules." The formal results of this paper is given in terms of the generic $\text{TAL}_C^+$. By giving $\text{TAL}_C^+$ different "parameters," we obtain specialized systems for different situations. As expected, the trivial "empty" parameter reduces the generic $\text{TAL}_C^+$ to the original $\text{TAL}_C$.

An advantage of the generic treatment, and of $\text{TAL}_C^+$, lies in simplicity. The extensions we propose are self-contained and easy to understand, yet they suffice in addressing all the above mentioned practical settings. They also interact naturally with advanced features of typed assembly languages. These enable the potential use of $\text{TAL}_C^+$ in a more sophisticated typed assembly language, which in turn may serve as a general target for certifying compilation. The smooth transition from $\text{TAL}_C$ to $\text{TAL}_C^+$ also serves as a validation that $\text{TAL}_C$ is a good platform for low-level information-flow analysis.

The remainder of this paper is organized as follows. Section 2 provides background on security-type systems at a source level and at a target level. Section 3 illustrates the problems introduced by termination channels and outlines the ideas behind our solution. A rigorous treatment is given in Section 4, where we present our type system for closing up termination channels, prove its noninterference, and outline a certifying compilation scheme targeting it. Although focusing on termination channels for ease of understanding, the formal details in Section 4 are organized generically so that later sections simply provide different "parameters" to obtain type systems and certifying compilation schemes for addressing other information-flow channels. Following this generic treatment, Section 5 discusses timing channels, and Section 6 discusses possibilistic and probabilistic noninterference in multi-threaded programs. Finally, Section 7 discusses related and future work, and Section 8 concludes.

## 2 Background

### 2.1 Security-Type System

Suppose we introduce two security levels, `low` and `high`, into a simple imperative language. Variables of this language are classified into low and high variables, meaning that they hold low and high data respectively. For convenience, we use `l` as a low variable and `h` as a high variable. We wish to enforce a policy that there should be no flow of information from high variables to low variables. More specifically, we must prevent, among others, the following two kinds of illicit information flow:

1. Explicit flow through assignments, such as `l` := `h`.
2. Implicit flow through program structures (conditionals and while-loops), such as `if h then l := 1 else l := 0`.

A security-type system typically addresses these requirements by:

1. To track security levels in the types of expressions. This helps preventing information leak through explicit flow—mismatch of security levels in assignments will be disallowed.
2. To mark the program counters (PC) with security levels. If a conditional expression has a high guard, its branches will be type-checked under a high PC. This essentially marks the branches as falling in a "sensitive region," under which updates to low variables are disallowed. This idea applies also to other program structures such as while-loops.

## 2.2 TAL$_C$

TAL$_C$ [31] adapts source-level information-flow analysis for assembly code. The main challenge is that assembly code does not present as much abstraction as does source code. Whereas the program structures of source code help to determine the security levels of various program points, such structures are not available in assembly code.

For example, a conditional statement in a source program can be type-checked so that both branches respect the security level of the guard expression. Such checks become difficult in assembly code, where the "flattened" control flow provides little help in identifying the program structure. A conditional is typically translated into a branching instruction and some code blocks, where the ending points of the two branches are no longer apparent. Although control-flow analysis can be used to compute such information [3], it expands the trusted computing base substantially—the analysis itself would be trusted.

TAL$_C$ recovers the missing structure using type annotations. These annotations provide explicit information on the security levels of instructions as well as the ending points of the security levels. Two new security operations are introduced to manipulate the annotations, and appropriate typing rules are used to make sure that the annotations faithfully reflect the actual structure of the code.

The syntax of a simplified version of TAL$_C$ is given in Figure 1. Compared with the original TAL$_C$, we have omitted stacks and polymorphism because they are mainly for supporting functions and procedures in source programs and their handling is orthogonal to the TAL$_C$ extensions in this paper. We use $\theta$ to represent security levels. A security context $\theta \triangleright l$ indicates that the security level of the PC will be no less than $\theta$ until the program point $l$ is reached.

A `raise` $\kappa$ operation is used to increase the security level, which corresponds to the beginning of a sensitive region such as those introduced by a high conditional. A

$$
\begin{array}{rl}
(\textit{contexts}) & \kappa ::= \bullet \mid \theta \rhd l \\
(\textit{pre-types}) & \tau ::= \texttt{int} \mid \langle \sigma_1, \ldots, \sigma_n \rangle \mid \forall[].\langle \kappa \rangle \Gamma \\
(\textit{types}) & \sigma ::= \tau_\theta \\
(\textit{heap ty}) & \Psi ::= \{l_1 : \sigma_1, \ldots l_n : \sigma_n\} \\
(\textit{reg file ty}) & \Gamma ::= \{r_1 : \sigma_1, \ldots r_n : \sigma_n\} \\
(\textit{registers}) & r ::= r_1 \mid r_2 \mid \ldots \\
(\textit{word val}) & w ::= l \mid i \\
(\textit{small val}) & v ::= r \mid w \\
(\textit{heap val}) & h ::= \langle w_1, \ldots, w_n \rangle \mid \texttt{code}[]\langle \kappa \rangle \Gamma.I \\
(\textit{heaps}) & H ::= \{l_1 \mapsto h_1, \ldots, l_n \mapsto h_n\} \\
(\textit{reg files}) & R ::= \{r_1 \mapsto w_1, \ldots, r_n \mapsto w_n\} \\
(\textit{instr}) & \iota ::= \texttt{add}\ r_d, r_s, v \mid \texttt{ld}\ r_d, r_s(i) \mid \texttt{st}\ r_d(i), r_s \mid \texttt{mov}\ r_d, v \mid \texttt{bnz}\ r, v \mid \texttt{raise}\ \kappa \\
(\textit{instr seq}) & I ::= \iota; I \mid \texttt{lower}\ l \mid \texttt{jmp}\ v \mid \texttt{halt}\ [\sigma] \\
(\textit{prog}) & P ::= (H, R, I)_\kappa
\end{array}
$$

**Fig. 1.** Syntax of a simplified TAL$_C$

`lower` $l$ is used to restore the security level and transfer the control to label $l$, which marks the end of a sensitive region. These two security operations can be placed into the target code by a certifying compilation process based on the structures and the typing of source programs.

Given these, the security levels of all program points become apparent through the annotations. The adaptation of the source level solutions is then straightforward. High branching must happen in high contexts, and updates to low data in high contexts are disallowed. In addition, every pointer is given two security levels, one for the pointer, the other for the data or code being referenced.

This concludes our introduction to TAL$_C$. Interested readers are referred to previous work [30,31] for more details, including the support for functions and pointers, the exact semantics and noninterference proof, and a certifying compilation scheme.

## 3 Termination Channels

TAL$_C$ assumes that the only means for observing program behaviors is by inspecting the content of certain program variables (or heap and register file for assembly code). In practice, termination channels enable some attacks not prevented by TAL$_C$. In the following two examples, no low variable is updated. However, the values of the high variable `h` can be learned by observing whether the programs terminate.

1. Nonterminating high loop: `while h do skip;`
2. Nonterminating loop in a high branch: `if h then {while true do skip} else skip`.

Volpano and Smith [25] close termination channels by putting restrictions on program constructs that could potentially lead to nontermination. In essence, if a program construct is potentially nonterminating, then it must have the minimum typing (one that corresponds to the lowest security level). For example, all while-loops are restricted to have the type `low`. This is reflected in the type system as allowing a while-loop only under a low PC. In the first example earlier, the high loop is now disallowed, because the high loop guard cannot be typed under a low PC. In the second example, the loop in the high conditional is now also disallowed, because the body of the high conditional has a high PC, but a loop is allowed only under a low PC.

The correctness of this approach with respect to termination is intuitive. Consider executing a program twice on different high variables but same low variables. Upon a high conditional, both executions will terminate because of the absence of loops in the conditional body. Upon a low conditional, both executions will follow the same path, resulting in the same behavior on termination.

### 3.1 Idea at an Assembly Level

In a typed assembly language, one cannot easily identify loops, because both loops and conditionals are implemented using branching instructions. Nonetheless, the essence of the source-level approach is that high branches must be terminating. The security annotations of $\text{TAL}_C$ are handy for identifying such branches—a branch is high if and only if it has a high context. On top of this, we attach to high branches some new timing annotations that mark the upper bound of their execution steps before returning to low regions. The solution of $\text{TAL}_C$ guarantees that terminating high branches will meet eventually in a low region with matching low variables. The new timing annotations introduced here are to guarantee that high branches do terminate.

More specifically, we introduce a timing tag $t$ for this purpose, where $t$ is either a natural number (indicating that the execution will leave the current high region in at most this number of steps) or $\infty$ (indicating "unknown" or "potentially infinite"). Under a high context, the type system allows a branching instruction only if both branches have finite timing tags. This prevents potentially nonterminating "backward jumps" later on. Note that when giving a timing tag to the branching instruction itself (needed for nested branches), one must take the longer branch into account.

The correctness intuition of this approach is similar to that of the minimum typings at a source level—upon a high branching, two executions of a program may split but will meet in a low region in a finite number of steps.

These timing annotations can come from the compilation of security-typed source code. A conditional will be compiled with finite timing if and only if both branches yield finite timing. A loop can be compiled conservatively with infinite timing. By accepting only finite timing annotations in high regions, a type system would reject the two counter examples given earlier. Such timing annotations also work naturally with functions and abnormal termination (see the companion technical report [29]).

### 3.2 Allowing Terminating Loops

The key idea above conservatively disallows potentially nonterminating constructions in high contexts. It is sometimes useful to relax this restriction by allowing terminating loops (or well-founded recursions). This can be achieved using singleton types.

$$
\begin{array}{ll}
l : \forall[t:\mathtt{nat} \mid t \geq 1].\ \langle 2t \rangle\ \{r_1 : \mathtt{int}(t)\} & \\
\quad \mathtt{sub}\ r_1, r_1, 1 & \%\ r_1 \leftarrow r_1 - 1 \\
\quad \forall[t:\mathtt{nat} \mid t \geq 1].\ \langle 2t-1 \rangle\ \{r_1 : \mathtt{int}(t-1)\} & \\
\quad \mathtt{bnz}\ r_1, l & \%\ \text{to branch if } r_1 \neq 0 \\
\quad \langle 0 \rangle\ \{r_1 : \mathtt{int}(0)\} & \\
\quad \mathtt{halt}\ [\mathtt{int}] &
\end{array}
$$

The above example code demonstrates some simple concepts of singleton types. In the type annotations, $t$ is a type variable of kind (or sort) nat mimicking natural numbers, and $t \geq 1$ is a constraint. The initial type annotation at label $l$ essentially means that there exists a natural number $t$ satisfying $t \geq 1$ such that the "clock" (timing annotation) is $2t$ and $r_1$ has type $\mathtt{int}(t)$ (an integer of value $t$). Note how the clock depends on the value in $r_1$. In the next program point, the annotation reflects the execution of the subtraction instruction (sub). Interesting manipulation happens when type-checking the branching instruction (bnz), where the result of the comparison is used in establishing the typing of the next program points. In the case where $r_1$ is not zero, a newly introduced constraint $(t-1 \neq 0)$ would be used in establishing the typing annotation at the target $l$ of the branching, with the type variable at $l$ now instantiated with $(t-1)$. In the case where $r_1$ is zero, a constraint $(t-1=0)$ would be used in establishing the typing annotation at halt.

In essence, singleton types are used here to connect the clock, a type-level concept, with values. More generally, the applications of singleton types have been detailed both in the context of resource bounds certification [7] and for a typed assembly language [28]. The work is applicable here with little adaptation. Since the use of singleton types is orthogonal to our main contribution (certifying compilation for information-flow analysis in certain practical settings), we omit its formal handling for a simpler exposition, instead briefly pointing out the potential use when introducing the typing rule of the branching instruction. In any case, the formal contents of this paper already suffice in supporting certifying compilation from related source-level systems.

# 4 $\mathrm{TAL}_C^+$

Now we present a typed assembly language $\mathrm{TAL}_C^+$ following the above idea. In particular, we present $\mathrm{TAL}_C^+$ as an extension to $\mathrm{TAL}_C$ (the version in Figure 1 is used, where features orthogonal to timing behaviors are omitted as explained in Section 2.2). For ease of reading, we put the new additions in shaded boxes. By removing the shaded boxes, we get exactly $\mathrm{TAL}_C$.

Although we are focusing on termination channels for now, $\mathrm{TAL}_C^+$ can also be used to prevent illicit flow through other channels. The details will follow in later sections.

## 4.1 Type System

Following $\mathrm{TAL}_C$, we assume security labels form a lattice $\mathcal{L}$. We use $\theta$ to range over elements of $\mathcal{L}$. We use $\bot$ and $\top$ as the bottom and top of the lattice, $\cup$ and $\cap$ as the lattice join and meet operations, and $\subseteq$ as the lattice ordering.

$$\begin{array}{rl} (\textit{timing anno}) & t ::= n\ (\textit{natural numbers}) \mid \infty \\ (\textit{pre-type}) & \tau ::= \texttt{int} \mid \langle \sigma_1, \ldots, \sigma_n \rangle \mid \forall [].\langle \kappa; t \rangle\, \Gamma \\ (\textit{heap val}) & h ::= \langle w_1, \ldots, w_n \rangle \mid \texttt{code}[]\langle \kappa; t \rangle \Gamma.I \end{array}$$

**Fig. 2.** $\text{TAL}_C^+$ syntax

The syntax extension is given in Figure 2. Timing annotations $t$ are either natural numbers $n$ or the special $\infty$. They accompany security contexts $\kappa$ in code types and code values.

| Judgment | Meaning |
|---|---|
| $\Gamma_1 \subseteq \Gamma_2$ | Register file type $\Gamma_1$ weakens $\Gamma_2$ |
| $\vdash H : \Psi$ | Heap $H$ has type $\Psi$ |
| $\Psi \vdash R : \Gamma$ | Register file $R$ has type $\Gamma$ |
| $\Psi \vdash h : \sigma$ | Heap value $h$ has type $\sigma$ |
| $\Psi \vdash w : \sigma$ | Word value $w$ has type $\sigma$ |
| $\Psi; \Gamma \vdash v : \sigma$ | Small value $v$ has type $\sigma$ |
| $\Psi; \Gamma; \kappa; t \vdash I$ | $I$ is a valid sequence of instructions |
| $\Psi; \Gamma; t \vdash P$ | $P$ is a valid program |
| $\lvert comm \rvert = n$ | Command $comm$ requires time $n$ |
| $\theta \vdash t \xrightarrow{t'} t''$ | Timing may change from $t$ to $t''$ after $t'$ |
| $\theta \vdash t$ | Timing $t$ is OK under security level $\theta$ |
| $\theta \vdash t \sim t'$ | $t$ and $t'$ match under security level $\theta$ |

**Fig. 3.** $\text{TAL}_C^+$ typing judgments

In Figure 3, typing judgments are extended for the timing annotations. Instruction sequences and programs are further checked with respect to $t$. We introduce four new judgment forms on timing annotations. By using different definitions of these four judgment forms, we obtain type systems for closing different information channels. For termination channels, the definitions are in Figure 4.

$$\frac{comm \in \{\texttt{add}, \texttt{ld}, \texttt{st}, \texttt{mov}, \texttt{bnz}, \texttt{raise}, \texttt{lower}, \texttt{jmp}, \texttt{halt}\}}{\lvert comm \rvert = 1}$$

$$\frac{}{\bot \vdash t \xrightarrow{t'} t''} \qquad \frac{t \geq t' + t''}{\theta \vdash t \xrightarrow{t'} t''}$$

$$\frac{}{\bot \vdash t} \qquad \frac{t \neq \infty}{\theta \vdash t} \qquad \frac{}{\theta \vdash t \sim t'}$$

**Fig. 4.** Timing rules on termination channels

$\lvert comm \rvert$ is designed to track the progress of time during program execution. With respect to termination, it suffices to consider any assembly command (or security operation) as consuming one unit of time. The time passage $\theta \vdash t \xrightarrow{t'} t''$ is irrelevant in low security contexts $\bot$. In other security contexts, it requires that $t$ be no less than the sum of $t'$ and $t''$; it is used in the typing rules to ensure that the timing tag is monotonically decreasing with respect to the control flow. Here the addition $+$ is extended straightforwardly to work with $\infty$. This judgment may seem unwieldy when $\infty$ is involved. Fortunately, a premise in a rule of well-typed programs, to be shown later, will prevent $\infty$ from being used in high contexts for well-typed programs.

Two rules are used for establishing the judgment of valid timing $\theta \vdash t$. Any timing is valid under a low security context $\bot$. In contrast, under high security contexts, a timing is valid if and only if it is finite. Finally, we define matching timing $\theta \vdash t \sim t'$ to hold trivially, since it does not play a role for termination channels. It is a placeholder for the extensions in later sections.

$$\frac{m \leq n}{\{r_1{:}\sigma_1 \ldots r_m{:}\sigma_m\} \subseteq \{r_1{:}\sigma_1 \ldots r_n{:}\sigma_n\}}$$

$$\frac{\Psi = \{l_1 : \sigma_1, \ldots l_n : \sigma_n\} \qquad \Psi \vdash h_i : \sigma_i}{\vdash \{l_1 \mapsto h_1, \ldots, l_n \mapsto h_n\} : \Psi}$$

$$\frac{\Gamma = \{r_1 : \sigma_1, \ldots r_n : \sigma_n\} \qquad \Psi \vdash w_i : \sigma_i}{\Psi \vdash \{r_1 \mapsto w_1, \ldots, r_n \mapsto w_n\} : \Gamma}$$

$$\frac{\Psi \vdash w_i : \sigma_i}{\Psi \vdash \langle w_1, \ldots, w_n \rangle : \langle \sigma_1, \ldots, \sigma_n \rangle_\theta}$$

$$\frac{\Psi; \Gamma; \kappa; t \vdash I}{\Psi \vdash \mathsf{code}[](\kappa; t)\Gamma.I : (\forall[].(\kappa; t)\ \Gamma)_\theta}$$

$$\Psi \vdash i : \mathtt{int}_\theta \qquad \frac{\Psi(l) = \sigma}{\Psi \vdash l : \sigma}$$

$$\frac{\Gamma(r) = \sigma}{\Psi; \Gamma \vdash r : \sigma} \qquad \frac{\Psi \vdash w : \sigma}{\Psi; \Gamma \vdash w : \sigma}$$

$$\frac{\vdash H : \Psi \qquad \Psi \vdash R : \Gamma \qquad \Psi; \Gamma; \kappa; t \vdash I \qquad SL(\kappa) \vdash t}{\Psi; \Gamma; t \vdash (H, R, I)_\kappa}$$

**Fig. 5.** $\mathrm{TAL}_C^+$ typing rules: non-instructions

The extended typing rules are in Figures 5 and 6. For understanding the timing related aspects, it suffices to focus on the shaded boxes. Interested readers are referred to previous work [31] for details of the $\mathrm{TAL}_C$ type system.

In $\mathrm{TAL}_C^+$, only a few changes are made to $\mathrm{TAL}_C$ on the rules for non-instructions. Notably, there is an extra invariant in the rule for checking programs, namely the timing $t$ must be valid with respect to the security level of the context $\kappa$. Here we use $SL(\kappa)$ to refer to the security label component of $\kappa$; $SL(\bullet)$ is defined to be $\bot$. This timing invariant ensures that $\infty$ cannot be used to type program points in high contexts, even though the previously shown judgment of time passage is permissive in the case of $\infty$.

$$\frac{SL(\kappa)=\theta \quad \Gamma(r_s)=\mathtt{int}_{\theta_1} \quad \Psi;\Gamma\vdash v:\mathtt{int}_{\theta_2} \quad \Psi;\Gamma\{r_d:\mathtt{int}_{\theta\cup\theta_1\cup\theta_2}\};\kappa;t'\vdash I \quad \theta\vdash t\xrightarrow{|\mathtt{add}|}t'}{\Psi;\Gamma;\kappa;t\vdash \mathtt{add}\ r_d,r_s,v;I}$$

$$\frac{SL(\kappa)=\theta \quad \Gamma(r_s)=\langle\sigma_1,\ldots,\sigma_n\rangle_{\theta_1} \quad \sigma_i=\tau_{\theta_2} \quad \Psi;\Gamma\{r_d:\tau_{\theta\cup\theta_1\cup\theta_2}\};\kappa;t'\vdash I \quad \theta\vdash t\xrightarrow{|\mathtt{ld}|}t'}{\Psi;\Gamma;\kappa;t\vdash \mathtt{ld}\ r_d,r_s(i);I}$$

$$\frac{SL(\kappa)=\theta \quad \Psi;\Gamma\vdash v:\tau_{\theta'} \quad \Psi;\Gamma\{r_d:\tau_{\theta\cup\theta'}\};\kappa;t'\vdash I \quad \theta\vdash t\xrightarrow{|\mathtt{mov}|}t'}{\Psi;\Gamma;\kappa;t\vdash \mathtt{mov}\ r_d,v;I}$$

$$\frac{\begin{array}{l}SL(\kappa)=\theta \quad \Gamma(r)=\mathtt{int}_{\theta_1}\\ \Psi;\Gamma\vdash v:(\forall[].\langle\kappa;t'\rangle\,\Gamma')_{\theta_2}\\ \theta_1\cup\theta_2\subseteq\theta \quad \Gamma'\subseteq\Gamma \quad \Psi;\Gamma;\kappa;t''\vdash I\\ \theta\vdash t\xrightarrow{|\mathtt{bnz}|}t' \quad \theta\vdash t\xrightarrow{|\mathtt{bnz}|}t'' \quad \theta\vdash t'\sim t''\end{array}}{\Psi;\Gamma;\kappa;t\vdash \mathtt{bnz}\ r,v;I}$$

$$\frac{\begin{array}{l}SL(\kappa)=\theta \quad \Gamma(r_d)=\langle\sigma_1,\ldots,\sigma_n\rangle_{\theta_1} \quad \sigma_i=\tau_{\theta'}\\ \Gamma(r_s)=\tau_{\theta_2} \quad \theta\cup\theta_1\cup\theta_2\subseteq\theta' \quad \Psi;\Gamma;\kappa;t'\vdash I\\ \theta\vdash t\xrightarrow{|\mathtt{st}|}t'\end{array}}{\Psi;\Gamma;\kappa;t\vdash \mathtt{st}\ r_d(i),r_s;I}$$

$$\frac{\begin{array}{l}SL(\kappa)=\theta \quad \kappa'=\theta'\rhd w' \quad \theta\subseteq\theta'\\ \Psi\vdash w':(\forall[].\langle\kappa;t_1\rangle\,\Gamma')_{\theta_1} \quad \Psi;\Gamma;\kappa';t'\vdash I\\ \theta\vdash t\xrightarrow{|\mathtt{raise}|}t' \quad \theta'\vdash t'\end{array}}{\Psi;\Gamma;\kappa;t\vdash \mathtt{raise}\ \kappa';I}$$

$$\frac{\begin{array}{l}\kappa=\theta\rhd w \quad \Psi\vdash w:(\forall[].\langle\kappa';t'\rangle\,\Gamma')_{\theta_1}\\ \theta_1\subseteq SL(\kappa') \quad \Gamma'\subseteq\Gamma\\ \theta\vdash t\xrightarrow{|\mathtt{lower}|}t_1 \quad \text{where } t_1=\begin{cases}0 \text{ if } SL(\kappa')=\bot\\ t' \text{ otherwise}\end{cases}\end{array}}{\Psi;\Gamma;\kappa;t\vdash \mathtt{lower}\ w}$$

$$\frac{SL(\kappa)=\theta \quad \Psi;\Gamma\vdash v:(\forall[].\langle\kappa;t'\rangle\,\Gamma')_{\theta_1} \quad \theta_1\subseteq\theta \quad \Gamma'\subseteq\Gamma \quad \theta\vdash t\xrightarrow{|\mathtt{jmp}|}t'}{\Psi;\Gamma;\kappa;t\vdash \mathtt{jmp}\ v}$$

$$\frac{\kappa=\bullet \quad \Gamma(r_1)=\sigma}{\Psi;\Gamma;\kappa;t\vdash \mathtt{halt}\ [\sigma]}$$

**Fig. 6.** $\mathrm{TAL}_C^+$ typing rules: instructions

The rules for add, ld, mov and st are all extended in the same way. An extra check on the time passage is used to ensure that the timing annotations match the instructions.

Instruction bnz has two potential successors. Therefore, both branches must be checked with respect to the time passage. The matching judgment trivially holds for now. Note that if singleton types are used to allow terminating loops, an instantiation of the timing annotation at the code label $v$ would be required, and the comparison result on the register $r$ (whose type may be dependent on a value related to the timing annotation) would be used together with existing constraints to establish the judgments on time passage.

Upon entering a new security context marked by raise, we check that the new timing $t'$ is valid under the new security level $\theta'$. In addition, the time passage is also checked; this is useful in a multi-level security lattice where the current security level $\theta$ might not be $\bot$. There is no need to check the timing $t_1$ of the end point $w'$ of the new context $\kappa'$ directly at this point.

For lower, we make sure that the time passage is valid under $\theta$. In the case of going to the lowest security level, this trivially holds. For jmp, we simply check the time passage. Finally, nothing special is needed for halt. TAL$_C$ allows halt only in the empty security context. In such a context, all timing annotations are valid.

## 4.2 Soundness

The noninterference proof of TAL$_C^+$ extends that of TAL$_C$. We first define the equivalence of two programs with respect to a security level $\theta$. Intuitively, two programs (heaps and register files) are equivalent if and only if they agree on low-security contents.

**Definition 1 (Heap Equivalence).** *$\Psi \vdash H_1 \approx_\theta H_2 \iff \forall\, l \in \mathrm{dom}(\Psi)$, if $\Psi(l) = \tau_{\theta'}$ and $\theta' \sqsubseteq \theta$ then $H_1(l) = H_2(l)$.*

**Definition 2 (Register File Equivalence).** *$\Gamma \vdash R_1 \approx_\theta R_2 \iff \forall\, r \in \mathrm{dom}(\Gamma)$, if $\Gamma(r) = \tau_{\theta'}$ and $\theta' \sqsubseteq \theta$, then $R_1(r) = R_2(r)$.*

**Definition 3 (Program Equivalence).** *$\Psi; \Gamma \vdash P_1 \approx_\theta P_2 \iff P_1 = (H_1, R_1, I_1)_{\kappa_1}$, $P_2 = (H_2, R_2, I_2)_{\kappa_2}$, $\Psi \vdash H_1 \approx_\theta H_2$, $\Gamma \vdash R_1 \approx_\theta R_2$, and either:*

1. *$\kappa_1 = \kappa_2$, $SL(\kappa_1) \sqsubseteq \theta$, and $I_1 = I_2$, or*
2. *$SL(\kappa_1) \not\sqsubseteq \theta$, $SL(\kappa_2) \not\sqsubseteq \theta$.*

The above relations are all reflexive, symmetrical, and transitive. Our noninterference theorem relates the executions of two equivalent programs that both start in a low security context (relative to the security level of concern). In TAL$_C$, we showed that if both executions terminate, then the result programs are equivalent. The extra timing annotations now guarantee that nontermination can only happen in a context at the lowest security level.

The idea of the proof is intuitive. Given a security level of concern, the executions are phased into "low steps" and "high steps." It is easy to relate the two executions under a low step, because they involve the same instructions. Under a high step, the two executions are no longer in lock step. Recall that raise and lower mark the beginning and end of a secured region. We relate the program states before the `raise` and after the `lower`, circumventing directly relating two executions under high steps. In addition, there would be no nontermination in the secured region.

We give the formal details in three lemmas and a noninterference theorem. Lemma 1 indicates that a security context in a high step can be changed only with `raise` or `lower`. Lemma 2 says that a program in a high context will eventually reduce to a step that discharges the current security context with a `lower`. Lemma 3 articulates the lock step relation between two equivalent programs in a low step. Theorem 1 of noninterference then follows: given two equivalent programs, if one terminates, then the other terminates in a state equivalent to the first. As a corollary, if one does not terminate, then the other does not either.

In the following, $\longmapsto^*$ represents the reflexive and transitive closure of a single-step relation $\longmapsto$ of the operational semantics. $\Gamma \succeq_\theta \Gamma'$ means that $\Gamma(r) = \Gamma'(r)$ for every $r$ such that $\Gamma'(r) = \tau_{\theta'}$ and $\theta' \subseteq \theta$. We use $Q$ in addition to $P$ to denote programs when comparing two executions. The proofs are given in the companion TR [29].

**Lemma 1 (High Step).** *If $P = (H, R, I)_\kappa$, $SL(\kappa) \not\subseteq \theta$, $\Psi; \Gamma; t \vdash P$, then either:*

1. *there exists $\Gamma_1$, $t_1$ and $P_1 = (H_1, R_1, I_1)_\kappa$ such that $P \longmapsto P_1$, $\Psi; \Gamma_1; t_1 \vdash P_1$, $\Gamma \succeq_\theta \Gamma_1$, $t_1 < t$, and $\Psi; \Gamma_1 \vdash P \approx_\theta P_1$, or*
2. *$I$ is of the form $(\mathtt{raise}\ \kappa'; I')$ or $(\mathtt{lower}\ w)$.*

**Lemma 2 (Context Discharge).** *If $P = (H, R, I)_{\theta \rhd w}$, $\theta \not\subseteq \theta'$, $\Psi; \Gamma; t \vdash P$, then there exists $\Gamma'$, $t'$ and $P' = (H', R', \mathtt{lower}\ w)_{\theta \rhd w}$ such that $P \longmapsto^* P'$, $\Psi; \Gamma'; t' \vdash P'$, $\Gamma \succeq_{\theta'} \Gamma'$, $t' \leq t$, and $\Psi; \Gamma' \vdash P \approx_{\theta'} P'$.*

**Lemma 3 (Low Step).** *If $P = (H, R, I)_\kappa$, $SL(\kappa) \subseteq \theta$, $\Psi; \Gamma; t \vdash P$, $\Psi; \Gamma; t \vdash Q$, $\Psi; \Gamma \vdash P \approx_\theta Q$, $P \longmapsto P_1$, $Q \longmapsto Q_1$, then exists $\Gamma_1$ and $t_1$ such that $\Psi; \Gamma_1; t_1 \vdash P_1$, $\Psi; \Gamma_1; t_1 \vdash Q_1$ and $\Psi; \Gamma_1 \vdash P_1 \approx_\theta Q_1$.*

**Theorem 1 (Noninterference).** *If $P = (H, R, I)_\kappa$, $SL(\kappa) \subseteq \theta$, $\Psi; \Gamma; t \vdash P$, $\Psi; \Gamma; t \vdash Q$, $\Psi; \Gamma \vdash P \approx_\theta Q$, and $P \longmapsto^* (H_p, R_p, \mathtt{halt}\ [\sigma_p])_\bullet$, then exists $H_q$, $R_q$, $\sigma_q$ and $\Gamma'$ such that $Q \longmapsto^* (H_q, R_q, \mathtt{halt}\ [\sigma_q])_\bullet$, and $\Psi; \Gamma' \vdash (H_p, R_p, \mathtt{halt}\ [\sigma_p])_\bullet \approx_\theta (H_q, R_q, \mathtt{halt}\ [\sigma_q])_\bullet$.*

### 4.3 Certifying Compilation

We now outline a translation that preserves security types from a minimal source language. The complete formal translation is given in the companion TR.

This source language is an imperative language with two security levels (`low` and `high`). An expression (E) is either a constant (`i`), a variable (`V`) or an addition ($\mathtt{E}_1 + \mathtt{E}_2$). A command (C) is either a no-op (`skip`), an assignment ($\mathtt{V} := \mathtt{E}$), a sequence ($\mathtt{C}_1; \mathtt{C}_2$), a conditional ($\mathtt{if}\ \mathtt{E}\ \mathtt{then}\ \mathtt{C}_1\ \mathtt{else}\ \mathtt{C}_2$), or a while-loop (`while E do C`). The type system maintains an environment ($\Phi$) specifying the security levels of variables. For example, the following typing rule says that a conditional ($\mathtt{if}\ \mathtt{E}\ \mathtt{then}\ \mathtt{C}_1\ \mathtt{else}\ \mathtt{C}_2$) is well-typed with respect to an environment ($\Phi$) and a PC type (pc) if, under the same environment

($\Phi$), the guard (E) and the branches ($C_1$ and $C_2$) are all well-typed with respect to the PC type (pc).

$$\frac{\Phi \vdash \mathtt{E} : \mathtt{pc} \quad \Phi; [\mathtt{pc}] \vdash \mathtt{C}_1 \quad \Phi; [\mathtt{pc}] \vdash \mathtt{C}_2}{\Phi; [\mathtt{pc}] \vdash \mathtt{if\ E\ then\ C_1\ else\ C_2}}$$

The low-high security hierarchy of this language defines a simple lattice consisting of two elements: $\bot$ and $\top$. We use $|\mathtt{t}|$ to denote the translation of source type t in $\mathrm{TAL}_C^+$: $|\mathtt{low}| \equiv \mathtt{int}_\bot$ and $|\mathtt{high}| \equiv \mathtt{int}_\top$.

We assume that the program translation starts in a heap $H_0$ and a heap type $\Psi_0$ which satisfy $\vdash H_0 : \Psi_0$ and contain entries for all the variables of the source program. For any source variable v that $\Phi(\mathtt{v}) = \mathtt{t}$, there exists a location $l_\mathtt{v}$ in the heap such that $\Psi(l_\mathtt{v}) = \langle|\mathtt{t}|\rangle_\bot$. We use $\Phi \sim \Psi$ to refer to this correspondence.

We define expression translation of the form $|\mathtt{E}| = \vec{\iota} \parallel r; t$. The instruction vector $\vec{\iota}$ computes the value of E, and the result is put in the register $r$. The time needed to complete $\vec{\iota}$ is $t$. For example, the translation rule for the addition expression is as follows:

$$[\text{TREadd}] \quad \frac{|\mathtt{E}| = \vec{\iota} \parallel r; t \qquad |\mathtt{E}'| = \vec{\iota'} \parallel r'; t' \qquad \vec{\iota'} \text{ does not use } r \qquad t'' = t + t' + |\mathtt{add}|}{|\mathtt{E} + \mathtt{E}'| = \vec{\iota}; \vec{\iota'}; \mathtt{add}\ r'', r, r' \parallel r''; t''}$$

We define command translation based on the structure of the typing derivation of the source program. Which translation rule to apply is determined by the last typing rule used to check the source command. We use TD to denote (possibly multiple) typing derivations. In particular, the command translation has the form:

$$\left| \frac{\mathtt{TD}}{[\mathtt{pc}] \vdash \mathtt{C}} \right| \begin{bmatrix} \Psi \\ H \\ l_{start}; l_{end} : t; \kappa \end{bmatrix} = \begin{bmatrix} \Psi' \\ H' \\ t' \end{bmatrix}.$$

The 6 arguments are: a code heap type $\Psi$, a code heap $H$, starting and ending labels $l_{start}$ and $l_{end}$ for the computation of C, the timing annotation $t$ of the code at the ending label $l_{end}$, and a security context $\kappa$. It generates the extended code heap type $\Psi'$ and code heap $H'$, and produces the timing annotation for the starting label $l_{start}$.

The command translation maintains the following invariants:

- $H$ is well-typed under $\Psi$; it contains entries for all source variables and procedures;
- $\Psi$ and $H$ contain the continuation code labeled $l_{end}$;
- The code at $l_{end}$ has the timing behavior $t$;
- The new code labeled $l_{start}$ will be put into $\Psi'$ and $H'$;
- The produced annotation $t'$ will reflect the timing behavior of the code at $l_{start}$;
- The security context $\kappa$ must match pc.

The rule for translating a conditional is given below. Suppose addition $+$ is extended in the expected way to work with $\infty$. This rule translates the guard expression E and the two branches $C_1$ and $C_2$, obtaining the timing information $t_0$, $t_1$ and $t_2$. It then pieces together the translation results in assembly code using a code block $l$. The final timing annotation obtained for $l$ takes into account the timing of the "longer" branch.

The companion TR contains the formal translation details and correctness lemmas.

$$\frac{\begin{array}{c}|\mathrm{E}| = \vec{\iota} \,\|\, r; t_0 \qquad l_1, l_2 \text{ are fresh} \qquad t' = t_0 + \max\{(t_1 + |\mathtt{bnz}|), (t_2 + |\mathtt{bnz}| + |\mathtt{jmp}|)\} \\ \left|\frac{\mathrm{TD}_1}{\Phi; [\mathsf{pc}] \vdash \mathrm{C}_1}\right| \begin{bmatrix}\Psi \\ H \\ l_1; l' : t; \kappa\end{bmatrix} = \begin{bmatrix}\Psi_1 \\ H_1 \\ t_1\end{bmatrix} \qquad \left|\frac{\mathrm{TD}_2}{\Phi; [\mathsf{pc}] \vdash \mathrm{C}_2}\right| \begin{bmatrix}\Psi_1 \\ H_1 \\ l_2; l' : t; \kappa\end{bmatrix} = \begin{bmatrix}\Psi_2 \\ H_2 \\ t_2\end{bmatrix}\end{array}}{\left|\frac{\Phi \vdash \mathrm{E} : \mathsf{pc} \quad \frac{\mathrm{TD}_1}{\Phi; [\mathsf{pc}] \vdash \mathrm{C}_1} \quad \frac{\mathrm{TD}_2}{\Phi; [\mathsf{pc}] \vdash \mathrm{C}_2}}{\Phi; [\mathsf{pc}] \vdash \mathtt{if}\ \mathrm{E}\ \mathtt{then}\ \mathrm{C}_1\ \mathtt{else}\ \mathrm{C}_2}\right| \begin{bmatrix}\Psi \\ H \\ l; l' : t; \kappa\end{bmatrix} = \begin{bmatrix}\Psi_2\{l : (\forall[].\langle\kappa; t'\rangle\,\{\})_\perp\} \\ H_2\{l \mapsto \mathtt{code}[]\langle\kappa; t'\rangle\{\}.\vec{\iota}; \mathtt{bnz}\ r, l_1; \mathtt{jmp}\ l_2\} \\ t'\end{bmatrix}}$$

## 5 Timing Channels

In this section, we extend the machine model to explicitly specify execution time $t$ and output actions $\mathtt{output}\ n$ [1], allowing the observation of more exact timing information of the program execution.

On top of TAL$_C$'s small-step state transition in the form of $P \longmapsto P'$, we further specify the action sequences produced along with the program execution in the form of $P \overset{as}{\longmapsto} P'$. This means that $P$ steps to $P'$ producing observable action sequence $as$, where $as$ is a mixed sequence of output numbers $n$ and execution times $t$.

$$(\textit{Action Sequences}) \qquad as ::= \epsilon \mid t\ as \mid n\ as$$

In the operational semantics, the value of $as$ would be determined by the current instruction. Consider the following sample case:

$$(H, R, \mathtt{mov}\ r_d, w; I)_\kappa \overset{t_{\mathtt{movi}}}{\longmapsto} (H, R\{r_d \mapsto w\}, I)_\kappa$$

This is the operational semantics case of executing a mov instruction on an immediate operand $w$. Besides the regular machine state update, the above also specifies the time $t_{\mathtt{movi}}$ needed for completing this instruction. We omit the straightforward definition of the operational semantics, and use $t_{comm}$ to represent the execution time of instruction *comm*. Following previous source-level techniques [1], we assume that a primitive operation (*i.e.*, an assembly instruction) should execute in constant time, regardless of the values given as arguments. The reflexive transitive closure of the step transition is extended accordingly.

This extended machine model exposes information leak through the timing channels. Take the following source-level program as an example:

```
if h then {time-consuming operation} else skip;
output n
```

If $\mathtt{h} \neq 0$, the program produces observable action sequence $t_{long}\ n$, where $t_{long}$ is the execution time of the "*time-consuming operation*." If $\mathtt{h} = 0$, the program produces

$t_{skip}\, n$, where $t_{skip}$ is the execution time of the `skip` command. Obviously, this presents information leak, even if no low data is updated in the program.

The approach of the previous sections for closing termination channels can be extended to account for such information leak through timing channels. Instead of recording an upper bound of execution steps till the end of a high region, we use timing annotations to record the exact observable action sequence $as$. Based on the same reasoning for disallowing low updates in a high region, we also disallow output actions in a high region. In essence, the extended timing annotations reflect execution time. In such an extended system, the typing rule for branching should check that the timing annotations of the two branches match.

$$\frac{comm \text{ is any instruction}}{|comm| = t_{comm}} \qquad \frac{}{\bot \vdash t \xrightarrow{t'} t''} \qquad \frac{t = t' + t''}{\theta \vdash t \xrightarrow{t'} t''}$$

$$\frac{}{\bot \vdash t} \qquad \frac{t \neq \infty}{\theta \vdash t} \qquad \frac{}{\bot \vdash t \sim t'} \qquad \frac{t = t'}{\theta \vdash t \sim t'}$$

**Fig. 7.** Timing rules on timing channels

The exact adaptation to $\mathrm{TAL}_C^+$ is given in Figure 7. By giving the timing judgments different definitions, we obtain a type system for closing timing channels, and the typing rules of Figures 5 and 6 remain the same. For time passage $\theta \vdash t \xrightarrow{t'} t''$ in a high context, $t$ must reflect the sum of $t'$ and $t''$ exactly. $\infty$ is still only allowed in low contexts. Finally, the matching of timing $\theta \vdash t \sim t'$ requires the equality of $t$ and $t'$ unless in a low context; recall that this is used when type-checking a branching instruction to make sure that the branches exhibit the same timing behavior in high contexts.

The correctness of this approach is intuitive. At the beginning of a high branch, based on the extended timing annotations, the branches will meet at the end of the high region in the same amount of time. In addition, there are no outputs or updates to low variables in a high region. On the technical side, the noninterference proof follows that of Section 4, with minor difference on how to perform the induction. The proof for the termination-based system sometimes (Lemma 2 in particular) conducts induction directly on the timing annotation, which happens to reflect an upper bound of the number of operation steps. For this timing-based system, the timing annotation is different. By introducing a notion of "operation steps" and conducting induction on it, the proof goes through in the same way as before.

In terms of expressiveness, this system has decidable typing and is more restrictive than previous work by Agat [1] where type checking is undecidable. In particular, Agat's type system allows some low updates in high branches, such as the following:

`if h then l := 1 else l := 1`

In general, Agat's type system allows a high conditional as long as the two branches have the same "externally observable behavior." This notion is supported with a typing rule based on $\Gamma$-bisimulation, which is undecidable. For practical use, Agat uses "padding" commands to equalize the execution times of the branches. For example, a padding command for $\mathtt{h} := 1$ would be a special skip-command `SkipAsn h 1`, which costs the same time but does not perform actual state update. Using these padding commands, Agat proposes a cross-copying transformation that generates $\Gamma$-bisimular conditionals. In this transformation, $\Gamma$-bisimulation is used conservatively—a command is $\Gamma$-bisimular to itself and a high command is also $\Gamma$-bisimular to its padding counterpart.

This transformation does not accept programs which update low variables in high branches. Therefore, the above example is no longer considered valid. In the companion TR, we show that $\mathrm{TAL}_C^+$ is expressive enough to support all such transformed programs: if a program P is accepted by the cross-copying transformation and transformed into P′, then a certifying compilation scheme will translate P′ into well-typed $\mathrm{TAL}_C^+$ code.

# 6 Multi-threading and Internal Timing

## 6.1 Possibilistic Noninterference

To consider the problem of information flow in a multi-threaded setting, we need to extend the notion of noninterference to account for the nondeterministic execution of threads. A straightforward generalization is to define the observable behavior of a program as the set of possible execution results.

The interaction between threads can be exploited as a channel of information flow. Even if an attacker cannot observe the external timing behaviors of a program, some internal timing behaviors may still result in illicit information flow, *e.g.*, by affecting the execution order of interacting threads. An example is given in the companion TR.

Smith and Volpano [23] proposed a source-level information-flow type system for multi-threaded programs, and showed that it guarantees possibilistic noninterference in the presence of nondeterministic thread scheduling. In this type system, every thread is checked separately to satisfy two requirements in addition to those enforced for noninterference in the sequential setting:

1. The guard of a while-loop must have type `low`;
2. The while-loop itself must also have type `low`.

It is curious that these conditions happen to be the same as those for closing termination channels. Essentially, loops can only happen under low PCs. This is convenient, because we can now reused the techniques described in Section 3. In particular, we enforce the absence of backward jumps in high regions with monotonically decreasing timing annotations. The introduction of multi-threading does not affect the treatment described earlier, because the type checking is carried out separately for each thread.

## 6.2 Probabilistic Noninterference

The generalization of noninterference in Section 6.1 considers the set of possible execution results. This is sometimes not strong enough to prevent certain exploits in practice. For example, the probability distribution of the possible results may serve as a channel of information flow. An example is given in the companion TR.

Such probabilistic attacks exploit the internal timing behaviors of programs. Therefore, it is natural to adapt the techniques for closing timing channels in Section 5 from addressing external timing to addressing internal timing. More specifically, instead of reflecting the external execution time of the program instructions, we let the timing annotations reflect the number of potential context switches—the "internal time" observable by threads. This internal time advances by one unit whenever there is a potential context switch. The analysis of Section 5 would be adapted accordingly, enforcing:

1. To disallow low assignments in high regions;
2. To disallow while-loops in high regions;
3. To allow a high conditional only if the two branches have matching internal timing.

This approach is inspired by Sabelfeld and Sands [20], who obtained the desired probabilistic noninterference result for a source language by connecting context switches with the probability distribution of program execution paths in the context of arbitrary schedulers. Similar to Agat's transformation system [1], the system of Sabelfeld and Sands uses "padding" instructions to equalize program branches. Focusing on internal timing, their system uses skip instructions and dummy forks instead of the "skip-commands" (*e.g.*, `SkipAsn`) used by Agat. Transformed programs of their system will have the same number of atomic commands in high branches. It is natural for $\mathrm{TAL}_C^+$ to support the certifying compilation of such transformed programs, as long as one takes care to implement atomic commands, skip instructions, and dummy forks correctly.

In related work, Volpano and Smith [27] proposed a system that requires high conditionals to be protected so that the branches execute atomically. This can be viewed as a special instance of the above idea, because the atomic branches exhibit the same internal timing behavior (*i.e.*, no context switch).

More recently, Smith [22] proposed a less restrictive system that allows a high variable to appear in the guard of a while-loop as long as no assignment to a low variable follows. The key idea is that a command may be given a type of the form $\mathtt{t}_1$ *cmd* $\mathtt{t}_2$, meaning that the command assigns only to variables of level $\mathtt{t}_1$ or higher, and has running time that depends only on variables of level $\mathtt{t}_2$ or lower. It is conceivable to adapted this idea for assembly code, since both security levels and running times have clear counterparts in $\mathrm{TAL}_C^+$. We leave the details of this as future work.

We have elided the support for thread synchronization in this paper. The secure support for semaphore-based synchronization at a source level has been studied by Sabelfeld [18], where semaphore variables are restricted to have type `low`.

## 7 Related and Future Work

$\mathrm{TAL}_C^+$ is motivated by the need of certifying compilation for information-flow security [19,10,21]. On the technical aspects, $\mathrm{TAL}_C^+$ is inspired mainly by two lines of work: language-based information-flow security [19] and typed assembly languages [13].

From the perspective of information-flow security, we are inspired by previous work on covert channels and concurrency in high-level languages. Volpano and Smith [25] studied termination-sensitive noninterference, and proposed a type system that closes termination channels by disallowing loops from occurring at sensitive program points. Agat [1] used program transformation to prevent timing leaks, where the execution times of high branches are equalized by cross-padding with appropriate dummy instructions. Smith and Volpano [23] established possibilistic noninterference for a multi-threaded language by, again, disallowing loops from occurring at sensitive program points. Sabelfeld and Sands [20] proved a probabilistic noninterference result with respect to a scheduler-independent security condition. These systems are closely related to our solutions and have been discussed in the main body of this paper to illustrate the expressiveness of $\mathrm{TAL}_C^+$.

From the perspective of typed assembly languages, there are some recent efforts toward enforcing information-flow security directly at the target-code level [33,9,4,12,31,5]. However, relatively little is done on addressing covert channels or concurrency. Kobayashi and Shirane [9] proposed a JVML-based type system for timing-sensitive noninterference. The system relies on the computation of control dependency for identifying sensitive regions, and closes timing channels in sequential code by inserting a delay linear with respect to the normal execution time. Hedin and Sands [8] proposed another JVML-based type system parameterized over an abstract timing model characterizing execution times of instructions and an algorithm enforcing low-observable equivalence. When given a proper timing model and a corresponding algorithm, the system guarantees timing-sensitive noninterference in sequential code. The system relies on the computation of the least merge points of branch instructions to address the lack of program structures in low-level code. Barth *et al.* [6] proposed a framework for enforcing secure information flow for multi-threaded low-level code. Special primitives for interacting with the scheduler are introduced during compilation to prevent internal timing leaks. The system assumes that the low-level code comes with a security environment produced by the compiler for describing the security levels of program points.

In general, the lack of a suitable target for certifying compilation, especially one that handles both covert channels and concurrency uniformly, presents difficulty when applying related solutions to the real world, where covert channels and concurrency are easily exploitable. In this paper, we introduced timing extensions to $\mathrm{TAL}_C$ applicable under various security assumptions. Only simple arithmetic manipulations on the timing annotations are required during type checking. Although the annotations are produced by a compiler, they are verified separately by the $\mathrm{TAL}_C^+$ type system, thus bad annotations will be caught. As a result, only the type checker is in the trusted computing base, and the system correctness will not be affected by (a buggy implementation of) the computation on dependence regions, least merge points, or security environments. Using the generic $\mathrm{TAL}_C^+$ framework, it is promising to build a common typed assembly language for "customized" noninterference (termination-sensitive, timing-sensitive, possibilistic, probabilistic, and plain). In addition, it is interesting to note that timing extensions of typed assembly languages also have applications beyond noninterference [16,24].

There are nonetheless still many aspects that deserve further research, especially on the practical implementation of the theoretical ideas. In particular, the interaction between security-type preserving compilation and optimization remains an open question. In this paper, we provided a compilation scheme that preserves security types, where we did not perform any optimizations. Conventional compilers perform sophisticated optimizations to produce efficient code. Some of these optimizations may invalidate the security guarantees established for source programs. A simple example is that an optimization might change the execution time of program branches, affecting timing-sensitive noninterference. Whereas there is likely a trade-off between security and efficiency, optimizations that preserve types and security are worth investigating.

There are also topics which have been studied for high-level languages, but not for low-level code. Some examples include related security policies [14,32,11,17], practical implementation and type inference [15,2], and abstraction-violating attacks [2].

## 8 Conclusion

We have presented a generic type system $TAL_C^+$ for information-flow security in assembly code under various practical settings. Since some useful abstractions (*e.g.*, program structures) are missing from assembly code, $TAL_C^+$ introduces various timing annotations to guide the information-flow analysis. When equipped with different timing annotations, $TAL_C^+$ can guarantee termination-sensitive, timing-sensitive, possibilistic and probabilistic noninterference. Besides proving the soundness of the type system, we also provide a certifying compilation scheme targeting $TAL_C^+$. We consider this as a useful step toward the practical use of security-type systems in assembly code.

## References


1. Agat, J.: Transforming out timing leaks. In: Proc. 27th ACM Symposium on Principles of Programming Languages, Boston, MA, pp. 40–53 (January 2000)
2. Agat, J.: Type-based techniques for covert channel elimination and register allocation. PhD thesis, Chalmers Univ. of Technology & Gothenburg Univ. Gothenburg, Sweden (December 2000)
3. Ball, T.: What's in a region? Or computing control dependence regions in near-linear time for reducible control flow. ACM Letters on Prog. Lang. & Syst. 2(1–4), 1–16 (1993)
4. Barthe, G., Basu, A., Rezk, T.: Security types preserving compilation. In: Steffen, B., Levi, G. (eds.) VMCAI 2004. LNCS, vol. 2937, pp. 2–15. Springer, Heidelberg (2004)
5. Barthe, G., Naumann, D., Rezk, T.: Deriving an information flow checker and certifying compiler for Java. In: Proc. 2006 IEEE Symposium on Security and Privacy, Oakland, CA, pp. 230–242 (May 2006)
6. Barthe, G., Rezk, T., Russo, A., Sabelfeld, A.: Security of multithreaded programs by compilation. In: ESORICS 2007. LNCS, vol. 4734, Springer, Heidelberg (2007)
7. Crary, K., Weirich, S.: Resource bound certification. In: Proc. 27th ACM symposium on Principles of programming languages, Boston, MA, USA, pp. 184–198 (January 2000)
8. Hedin, D., Sands, D.: Timing aware information flow security for a JavaCard-like bytecode. In: Proc. 1st Workshop on Bytecode Semantics, Verification, Analysis and Transformation, Edinburgh, Scotland, UK, pp. 163–182 (April 2005)
9. Kobayashi, N., Shirane, K.: Type-based information flow analysis for low-level languages. In: 3rd Asian Workshop on Prog. Lang. & Syst. Shanghai, China, pp. 302–316 (November 2002)
10. Kozen, D.: Language-based security. In: Kutyłowski, M., Wierzbicki, T., Pacholski, L. (eds.) MFCS 1999. LNCS, vol. 1672, pp. 284–298. Springer, Heidelberg (1999)

11. Laud, P.: Semantics and program analysis of computationally secure information flow. In: Proc. 10th European Symposium on Programming, Genova, Italy, pp. 77–91 (April, 2001)
12. Medel, R., Compagnoni, A., Bonelli, E.: A typed assembly language for non-interference. In: Proc. 9th ICTCS, Siena, Italy, pp. 360–374 (October 2005)
13. Morrisett, G., Walker, D., Crary, K., Glew, N.: From system F to typed assembly language. ACM Transactions on Programming Languages and Systems 21(3), 527–568 (1999)
14. Myers, A.C., Liskov, B.: Complete, safe information flow with decentralized labels. In: Proc. IEEE Symposium on Security and Privacy, Oakland, CA, pp. 186–197 (May 1998)
15. Myers, A.C., et al.: Jif: Java + information flow (2001), `http://www.cs.cornell.edu/jif/`
16. Necula, G.C., Lee, P.: Safe, untrusted agents using proof-carrying code. In: Vigna, G. (ed.) Mobile Agents and Security. LNCS, vol. 1419, pp. 61–91. Springer, Heidelberg (1998)
17. Pierro, A.D., Hankin, C., Wiklicky, H.: Approximate non-interference. In: Proc. 15th CSFW, Cape Breton, NS, Canada, pp. 1–17 (June 2002)
18. Sabelfeld, A.: The impact of synchronisation on secure information flow in concurrent programs. In: Bjørner, D., Broy, M., Zamulin, A.V. (eds.) PSI 2001. LNCS, vol. 2244, pp. 227–241. Springer, Heidelberg (2001)
19. Sabelfeld, A., Myers, A.C.: Language-based information-flow security. IEEE Journal on Selected Areas in Communications 21(1), 5–19 (2003)
20. Sabelfeld, A., Sands, D.: Probabilistic noninterference for multi-thread programs. In: CSFW, Cambridge, England, pp. 200–214 (July 2000)
21. Schneider, F.B., Morrisett, G., Harper, R.: A language-based approach to security. In: Wilhelm, R. (ed.) Informatics. LNCS, vol. 2000, pp. 86–101. Springer, Heidelberg (2001)
22. Smith, G.: A new type system for secure information flow. In: CSFW, Cape Breton, NS, Canada, pp. 115–125 (2001)
23. Smith, G., Volpano, D.: Secure information flow in a multi-threaded imperative language. In: POPL, San Diego, CA, pp. 355–364 (January 1998)
24. Vanderwaart, J.C., Crary, K.: Automated and certified conformance to responsiveness policies. In: TLDI, Long Beach, CA, pp. 79–90 (January 2005)
25. Volpano, D., Smith, G.: Eliminating covert flows with minimum typings. In: CSFW, Rockport, MA, pp. 156–169 (June 1997)
26. Volpano, D., Smith, G.: A type-based approach to program security. In: Bidoit, M., Dauchet, M. (eds.) CAAP 1997, FASE 1997, and TAPSOFT 1997. LNCS, vol. 1214, pp. 607–621. Springer, Heidelberg (1997)
27. Volpano, D., Smith, G.: Probabilistic noninterference in a concurrent language. In: CSFW, Rockport, MA, pp. 34–43 (June 1998)
28. Xi, H., Harper, R.: A dependently typed assembly language. In: Proc. 6th ACM International Conference on Functional Programming, Florence, Italy, pp. 169–180 (September 2001)
29. Yu, D.: More typed assembly languages for confidentiality. Technical Report DCL-TR-2006-0021, DoCoMo USA Labs, San Jose, CA (September 2006), `http://www.docomolabsresearchers-usa.com/~dyu/talcp-tr.pdf`
30. Yu, D., Islam, N.: A typed assembly language for confidentiality. Technical Report DCL-TR-2005-0002, DoCoMo USA Labs, San Jose, CA (March 2005), `http://www.docomolabsresearchers-usa.com/~dyu/talc-tr.pdf`
31. Yu, D., Islam, N.: A typed assembly language for confidentiality. In: Sestoft, P. (ed.) ESOP 2006 and ETAPS 2006. LNCS, vol. 3924, pp. 162–179. Springer, Heidelberg (2006)
32. Zdancewic, S., Myers, A.C.: Robust declassification. In: CSFW, Cape Breton, NS, Canada, pp. 15–23 (June 2001)
33. Zdancewic, S., Myers, A.C.: Secure information flow via linear continuations. Higher-Order and Symbolic Computation 15(2–3), 209–234 (2002)

# A Novel Test Case Generation Method for Prolog Programs Based on Call Patterns Semantics

Lingzhong Zhao[1,2], Tianlong Gu[1], Junyan Qian[1], and Guoyong Cai[1]

[1] School of Computer and Control, Guilin University of Electronic Technology, Guilin, 541004 China
[2] Electronic Engineering School, Xidian University, Xi'an, 710071 China
zhaolingzhong163@163.com

**Abstract.** A natural way to generate test cases for a Prolog program is to view the call patterns of the procedures in the program as an implicit representation of the control flow graph (CFG) of the program. This paper explores the idea by proposing a call patterns-based test case generation method, where a set of call patterns or computed answers is used to describe the paths in a CFG. With a constraint-based call patterns semantics, this method is formalized. Through the use of a proper constraints solver, we can generate test cases automatically from the sets of constraints. This method can be based on any approximation of the call patterns semantics. So compared with traditional CFG-based test case generation, the method is more flexible and can be easily adapted to meet the requirements of a tester expressed by the approximation of the call patterns semantics we use.

## 1 Introduction

Test case generation is a key issue in software testing for which mainly two approaches have been proposed in literature. With specification-based testing (black-box testing), test cases are generated from the specification of a program; and with implementation-based testing (white-box testing), test cases are produced by considering the code of a program. This paper is concerned with the latter.

In the testing of Prolog programs, both approaches have been applied. [12,14] studied category partitioning method (CPM) testing [3,18], where test cases for a Prolog procedure are generated from a set of user defined test frames, and [1,2,17] studied implementation-based testing for logic or Prolog programs, where test cases are generated by making use of a structure analysis or control flow based path analysis.

A ***call pattern*** of a goal in a program P is a procedure call that is selected during the SLD-resolution or execution of the goal in P. By definition the call patterns of a goal describe the control transfer in the execution of the goal. If we express the control transfer with a CFG, a subset of the set of call patterns of a goal in a program P will denote one or more paths in the CFG of P. In some sense the set of call patterns of a procedure call can be viewed as an implicit representation of the CFG for the procedure. Therefore it's very natural to use call patterns as the base for generating test cases that are supposed to cover certain paths in the CFG of a Prolog program. To what we have known no work has been done on this issue.

Z. Shao (Ed.): APLAS 2007, LNCS 4807, pp. 105–121, 2007.

This paper fills the gap by proposing a test case generation method based on a constraint-based *call patterns semantics* (*cp semantics* for short) of Prolog programs. A consistent set of constraints, denoting a set of call patterns or computed answers of a procedure call, is used to describe the path(s) in a CFG of a program. Through the use of a proper constraints solver, we can generate a test case from a consistent set of constraints. Moreover we can base this method on the approximation of the cp semantics used in this paper, which provides a way to meet the particular requirement of a tester and makes the proposed method very flexible.

The remainder of this paper is organized as follows. Section 2 introduces the constraint-based cp semantics we use in this paper. Section 3 describes the test case generation method. Section 4 presents an approximation of the cp semantics and gives an example to illustrate the application of the proposed method. Related work is presented in section 5, with the emphasis on the relationship between our method and CFG-based testing. Finally we conclude in section 6 by discussing the future work.

## 2 A Constraint-Based Call Patterns Semantics for Prolog

In this section we introduce a simplified version of the Spoto's call patterns semantics proposed in [20] by assuming that the Prolog programs under consideration do not contain cut operators. This semantics will serve as the base for our test case generation method. We note that the simplification of the original cp semantics has nothing to do with the applicability of our method, and is only for the convenience of presentation.

The reason for us to choose the Spoto's cp semantics is two-fold. Firstly, the semantics is goal-independent, which means that the denotation, i.e. the set of call patterns of any goal in a program can be achieved from the semantics of the program; in other words, the semantics of a program contains complete information that is necessary to describe the control flow transfer that may arise in any execution of the program. Secondly, the semantics uses as semantic domain the set of constraints sequences, which makes it possible for us to use a constraints solver to derive test cases for a procedure.

We assume the familiarity with the basic algebraic structures and Prolog language. The basic notations are used in the usual way. A sequence is an ordered collection of elements possibly with repetitions. The set of non-empty sequences of elements of E is denoted by $Seq^+(E)$. The symbol :: represents sequence concatenation. A sequence is denoted by a variable.

***Syntax of Prolog***

To simplify the design of semantic operators, Spoto's cp semantics uses an abstract syntax for Prolog programs. The basic idea is to look at Prolog as an instance of the general CLP scheme [13]. Since atom p(X,Y) can be represented as $\exists Z(Z=(X,Y)\wedge p(Z))$, without loss of generality all the predicates in Prolog programs are assumed to be unary. The clause has the form p(X):- $G_1$ or…or $G_n$ with $n\geqslant 1$, where $G_1,\ldots,G_n$ are goals defined by the grammar

$$G ::= c \mid p(X) \mid \text{exists X. } G \mid G \text{ and } G$$

where $c$ is a constraint, and X is a program variable. The expression $p$(X), where $p$ is a predicate symbol, is called a *procedure call.* A goal is called *divergent* if it contains a procedure call. A goal which is not divergent is said to be *convergent.* The constraint domain from which $c$ is taken is defined as a lattice $<\mathcal{B}, \leq, \vee, \wedge, true, false>$. It is assumed that $\mathcal{B}$ contains the element $\delta_{X,Z}$ for each pair of variables X and Z, which represents the constraint identifying the variables X and Z. Moreover, there is a family of monotonic operators $\exists X$ on the set of constraints, representing the restriction of a constraint obtained by hiding all the information related to the variable X. Operator $\exists X$ and $\delta_{X,Z}$ provide a simple way to avoid renaming problems. For example, instead of explicitly renaming variable X in expression T to a new variable $\alpha$, we can use the expression $\exists X(\delta_{X,\alpha} \wedge T)$ to model the effect. In the following sections the constraints in $\mathcal{B}$ are called *basic constraints.*

Standard Prolog program can be translated in a straightforward way. For example, the following Prolog program $P'$:

{ p(X):-q(X), r(X). p(X):-X=4. q(X):-X=5. r(X):- X=5, q(X).}

can be translated into $P$:

{ p(X):- q(X) and r(X) or X=4. q(X):- X=5. r(X):- X=5 and q(X).}.

***Semantic domain***

The main idea of Spoto's cp semantics is to make use of constraints to model the control of Prolog, as well as the computed answer substitutions (computed answers for short) and partially computed answer substitutions (partial answers for short) produced in the resolution of a goal. Basic constraints are adequate for the description of the partial answers associated with call patterns. For example, the substitution (X/2, Y/3) can simply be described as basic constraint ($X=2 \wedge Y=3$). For the purpose of modeling control of Prolog the concept of observability constraints is introduced.

**Definition 2.1.** The set $\mathcal{O}$ of observability constraints is defined as the minimal set containing $\mathcal{B}$ such that if $S \subseteq \mathcal{O}$ then $\sqcap S$ and $\sqcup S$ belong to $\mathcal{O}$ and such that if $o \in \mathcal{O}$ then its negation $-o \in \mathcal{O}$. We will often write $o_1 \sqcap \ldots \sqcap o_n$ for $\sqcap\{o_1,\ldots,o_n\}$ and $o_1 \sqcup \ldots \sqcup o_n$ for $\sqcup\{o_1,\ldots,o_n\}$. Moreover $true_{\mathcal{O}}$ and $false_{\mathcal{O}}$ are shorthands for $\sqcap\varnothing$ and $\sqcup\varnothing$, respectively.

**Definition 2.2.** The usual notion of satisfiability is defined on basic constraints. A basic constraint $b$ is satisfiable in a constraint store $S$ and in a structure interpretation $\mathcal{I}$, if and only if there exists an environment $\rho$ such that $\models_{\mathcal{I}}^{\rho} (S \wedge b)$. Satisfiability for observability constraints is different in that different environments can be used in different proofs.

1) $o \in \mathcal{B}$ is satisfiable in $S$ and $\mathcal{I}$, if and only if $o$ is satisfiable in $S$ and $\mathcal{I}$ as a basic constraint;
2) $o_1 \sqcap o_2$ is satisfiable in $S$ and $\mathcal{I}$ if and only if both $o_1$ and $o_2$ are satisfiable in $S$ and $\mathcal{I}$;
3) $o_1 \sqcup o_2$ is satisfiable in $S$ and $\mathcal{I}$, if and only if $o_1$ or $o_2$ is satisfiable in $S$ and $\mathcal{I}$;
4) $-o$ is satisfiable in $S$ and $\mathcal{I}$, if and only if $o$ is not satisfiable in $S$ and $\mathcal{I}$.

An observability constraint can be viewed as a set of basic constraints. The satisfiability of an observability constraint models the satisfiability of the individual component basic constraints. Let $o$=(X=4)⊓(X=2), S=∅, then $o$ is satisfiable in S because both (X=4) and (X=2) are satisfiable in S. It's obvious that under the satisfiability definition of definition 2.2, ⊓ is different from the greatest lower bound operator ∧ and ⊔ is different from least upper bound operator ∨.

Note that observability constraint $true_{\mathcal{O}}$ is satisfiable in a constraint store $S$ and in a structure interpretation $\mathcal{I}$ if and only if $S$ is satisfiable in $\mathcal{I}$, and $false_{\mathcal{O}}$ is not satisfiable in any given constraint store and structure interpretation. In this paper we assume that the satisfiability of a basic or observability constraint is decidable. For simplicity, we'll not explicitly mention the structure interpretation when we state the satisfiability of a basic or observability constraint in the following sections.

A unary operator ∝*obs* is defined on $\mathcal{B}$ which converts a basic constraint to an observability constraint. For simplicity we write $b$ for $b$∝*obs* when it does not make confusions. A bullet operator "•" is used to instantiate an observability constraint with a basic constraint and is defined as:

$b'\bullet(b\propto obs)=(b'\wedge b)\propto obs$; $b'\bullet\sqcap S=\sqcap\{b'\bullet o \mid o\in S\}$; $b'\bullet\sqcup S=\sqcup\{b'\bullet o\mid o\in S\}$; $b'\bullet(-o)=-(b'\bullet o)$.

The operation $\exists X(o)$ is used for changing the variable $X$ in $o$ to a bounded variable and is defined as

$$\exists X(b\propto obs)= (\exists X(b))\propto obs;\ \exists X(\sqcap S)= \sqcap\{\exists X(o)\mid o\in S\};$$
$$\exists X(\sqcup S)= \sqcup\{\exists X(o)\mid o\in S\};\ \exists X(-o)= -(\exists X(o)).$$

Roughly, basic constraints are used to describe computed answers and partial answers; observability constraints are used to tell how a call pattern or computed answer obtained at a certain step in the resolution of a goal is affected by divergent computation, and therefore it can be used to determine whether the call pattern or computed answer can actually be produced.

Based on the above definition the semantic domain $Seq^+(\mathbb{CP})$ for computed answer semantics is defined as $\mathbb{CP}=C^c\cup C^p\cup C^d$, where $C^c$ is the set of convergent constraints and $C^c = \{o+^c b \mid o\in\mathcal{O}, b\in\mathcal{B}\}$, $C^p$ is the set of call patterns constraints and $C^p=\{o+^p b, p \mid o\in\mathcal{O}, b\in\mathcal{B}$ and $p$ is a predicate$\}$, $C^d$ is the set of divergent constraints and $C^d = \{o+^d b \mid o\in\mathcal{O}, b\in\mathcal{B}\}$. A convergent constraint $(o+^c b)$ represents a computed answer described by $b$ such that it can actually be produced only if $o$ is satisfiable in a given constraint store. A call patterns constraint $(o+^p b, p)$ denotes a call pattern for p, where $b$ describes the partial answer obtained when the call pattern arises and $o$ describes the conditions for the call pattern to arise. A divergent constraint $(o+^d b)$ denotes a divergent computation, where $b$ describes the substitution when the divergence happens and $o$ describes the conditions for the divergence to happen. The order of the constraints in a constraint sequence $s\in Seq^+(\mathbb{CP})$ will reflect the order in which different constraints are obtained in the resolution of a goal.

**Example 2.3.** Given a Prolog program P: {p(X):-(X=4 and p(X)) or q(X). q(X):- X=3 or X=5.}, the resolution from the goal p(X) will produce a constraints sequence:

$$s=(true_{\mathcal{O}}+^p true, p) :: (true_{\mathcal{O}}+^p X=4, p) :: (true_{\mathcal{O}}+^d X=4) :: (-(X=4)+^p true, q)$$
$$:: (-(X=4)+^c X=3) :: (-(X=4)+^c X=5).$$

This sequence suggests that the resolution diverges after producing two call patterns (i.e. p(X) and p(4)) for p. By ($true_{\mathcal{O}}+^{d}$X=4) it is meant that the computation diverges when (X=4) is satisfiable. The observability constraint –(X=4) suggests that the computed answer X/3 and X/5 can be obtained only when (X=4) is not satisfied, otherwise the computation from p(4) will encounter an infinite resolution path which makes the above two computed answers not achievable.

**Definition 2.4.** The following maps describe the properties of a sequence of constraints.

$$\delta(s) = \sqcup\{o \sqcap b \propto obs \mid o+^{d}b \in s\};\quad \xi(s_1, s_2) = \sqcup\{o \sqcap (b \bullet \delta(s_2)) \mid o+^{c}b \in s_1\}.$$

Intuitively, if $\delta(s)$ is satisfiable divergence happens in $s$. $\xi(s_1, s_2)$ denotes the conditions for $s_1$ to have a solution which makes $s_2$ diverge.

***Call patterns semantics***

**Definition 2.5.** A call patterns interpretation $I$ is a map that associates to any predicate symbol $p$ in a program an element $I(p)$ of Seq$^{+}$(ℂℙ) which models the behavior, i.e. the collection of call patterns achieved in all possible resolutions of procedure call $p(\alpha)$ in the program, where $\alpha$ is a distinguished variable that is not allowed in the syntax of the clauses.

The immediate consequence operator $T_P$ of program $P$ is defined as

$$T_P\,(I)(p) = \exists_Y(\delta_{\,Y,\alpha} \circledcirc (\phi^{P}(\mathcal{J}_P[\![G_1]\!]I \oplus \ldots \oplus \mathcal{J}_P[\![G_n]\!]I)),$$

where $p(Y)$:-$G_1$ *or…or* $G_n$ is the definition of $p$ in $P$, $I$ is a call patterns interpretation representing the environment, i.e. the denotation of program $P$ computed so far, and $\mathcal{J}_P[\![G]\!]I$ is the denotation of goal $G$ computed from environment $I$ and is defined as:

$$\mathcal{J}_P[\![c]\!]I = true_{\mathcal{O}}+^{c}c;\ \mathcal{J}_P[\![p(\mathrm{X})]\!]I = I(p)[\mathrm{X}/\alpha];$$

$$\mathcal{J}_P[\![exists\ \mathrm{X}.G]\!]I = \exists\mathrm{X}(\mathcal{J}_P[\![G]\!]I);\ \mathcal{J}_P[\![G_1\ and\ G_2]\!]I = \mathcal{J}_P[\![G_1]\!]I \otimes \mathcal{J}_P[\![G_2]\!]I;$$

The operators present in the above definition are defined as follows.

**Definition 2.6**

(1) Given $b' \in \mathcal{B}$, the instantialization of a sequence $s$ with a basic constraint $b'$ is accomplished by operation $b' \circledcirc s$ and is defined as $b' \circledcirc (s_1 :: s_2) = b' \circledcirc s_1 :: b' \circledcirc s_2$, where $b' \circledcirc (o+^{p}b, p) = (b' \bullet o+^{p} b' \wedge b, p)$; $b' \circledcirc (o+^{c}b) = b' \bullet o+^{c} b' \wedge b$; $b' \circledcirc (o+^{d}b) = b' \bullet o+^{d} b' \wedge b$.

(2) Operation $\exists$X($s$) makes variable X in $s$ a bounded variable and is defined as $\exists\mathrm{X}(s_1 :: s_2) = \exists\mathrm{X}(s_1) :: \exists\mathrm{X}(s_2)$, where $\exists\mathrm{X}(o+^{p}b, p) = (\exists\mathrm{X}(o)+^{p} \exists\mathrm{X}(b), p)$; $\exists\mathrm{X}\,(o+^{c}b) = \exists\mathrm{X}(o)+^{c} \exists\mathrm{X}(b)$; $\exists\mathrm{X}(o+^{d}b) = \exists\mathrm{X}(o)+^{d} \exists\mathrm{X}(b)$.

(3) Given $o' \in \mathcal{O}$, the instantialization of a sequence $s$ with an observability constraint $o'$ is accomplished by operation $o' \odot s$ and is defined as $o' \odot (s_1 :: s_2) = o' \odot s_1 :: o' \odot s_2$, where $o' \odot (o+^{p}b, p) = (o' \sqcap o+^{p} b, p)$; $o' \odot (o+^{c}b) = o' \sqcap o+^{c} b$; $o' \odot (o+^{d}b) = o' \sqcap o+^{d}b$.

(4) Product operator $\otimes$ is defined as $(s_1 :: s_2) \otimes s = s_1 \otimes s :: -\xi(s_1, s) \odot (s_2 \otimes s)$, where $(o+^{p}b, p) \otimes s = (o+^{p}b, p)$; $(o+^{c}b) \otimes s = o \odot (b \circledcirc s)$; $(o+^{d}b) \otimes s = o+^{d}b$.

(5) Sum operator $\oplus$ is defined as $s_1 \oplus s_2 = s_1 :: -\delta(s_1) \odot s_2$.

(6) Expansion operator $\phi^P(s)$ and substitution operator $s[X/\alpha]$ are defined as $\phi^P(s)$= $(true_O+^P true, p)$:: $s$ and $s[X/\alpha]=\exists_\alpha(\delta_{X,\alpha} \circledcirc s)$, respectively.

On a properly defined ordering on the set of call patterns interpretations, the cp semantics of a program $P$ can be defined as the least fixpoint of $T_P$. The minimal interpretation $I_0$ is such that: $I_0(p)$= $(true_O+^P true, p)::(true_O+^d true)$ for every predicate $p$. The least fixpoint of $T_P$ is defined as: $lfp(T_P)=\text{lub}_{i\geq 0}((T_P)^i(I_0))$.

**Definition 2.7.** The cp semantics $\mathcal{F}_P$ of a program $P$ is defined as the least fixpoint of $T_P$: $\mathcal{F}_P = lfp(T_P)$.

## 3 Test Case Generation

Since call patterns are denoted by call patterns constraints in the semantics in section 2, a set of call patterns constraints possibly describes one or more control transfer paths in a CFG. In this section, we'll explore the idea by studying the consistency among call patterns constraints, divergent constraints and convergent constraints. Two types of consistent constraints subsets, *maximum consistent and divergent subset* and *maximum consistent and convergent subset*, will be proposed to describe the paths in a CFG, from which test cases for a procedure could be generated by a constraints solver.

**Definition 3.1.** A constraint set $C \subseteq C^c \cup C^p \cup C^d$ is called *consistent* if there exists a constraint store $S$ and a structure interpretation $I$ such that $\wedge\{b' \mid (o'+^P b', q) \in C \vee (o'+^d b') \in C \vee (o'+^c b') \in C\}$ is satisfiable in $S$ and $I$ and for each $(o+^P b, p)$, $(o+^d b)$ and $(o+^c b)$ of $C$ $o$ is satisfiable in $S \cup \{b' \mid (o'+^P b', q) \in C \vee (o'+^d b') \in C \vee (o'+^c b') \in C\}$ and $I$.

Since by definition the consistency of a set of call patterns, divergent and convergent constraints is deduced to the satisfiability of basic and observability constraints, it's possible to decide the consistency with a constraints solver. For example, the call patterns constraints set $\{(true_O+^P X=4, r), (-(X=4)+^P X=5, r)\}$ is not consistent because $X=4 \wedge X=5$ is not satisfiable under the same constraint store and structure interpretation. The constraints solver will be discussed later in this section.

**Definition 3.2.** Let $C \subseteq C^c \cup C^p \cup C^d$ be a set of constraints, $C'$ is called a *Maximum Consistent Subset (MCS) of* $C$ if $C'$ is consistent and for each element $r \in C - C'$, $\{r\} \cup C'$ is not consistent.

Let $C$ be a set of call patterns, divergent and convergent constraints, the following procedure *MCS_finder*($C$, $r$) computes a MCS of $C$ that contains $r$.

```
Set MCS_finder(C, r)
  { C_r :={r};
    For each element s of C,
    if {s}∪C_r is consistent, then C_r:= {s}∪C_r;
    Return(C_r); }
```

Note that there may exist more than one MCS of a set $C$ that contains $r$. Which MCS is produced by procedure *MCS_finder* depends on the order in which the elements of $C$ are considered.

For example, let $C$={($true_{\emptyset}+^{p}true$, p), ($true_{\emptyset}+^{p}true$, q), ($true_{\emptyset}+^{p}$X=4, r), $true_{\emptyset}+^{d}$X=4, (–(X=4)+$^{p}$X=5, r), (–(X=4)+$^{p}$X=5, q), –(X=4)+$^{d}$X=5}, we compute the MCS of $C$ containing ($true_{\emptyset}+^{p}true$, p). If we consider ($true_{\emptyset}+^{p}$X=4, r) and ($true_{\emptyset}+^{d}$X=4) before (–(X=4)+$^{p}$X=5, r), (–(X=4)+$^{p}$X=5, q) and (–(X=4)+$^{d}$X=5), the resultant MCS is

$C_1$={($true_{\emptyset}+^{p}true$, p), ($true_{\emptyset}+^{p}true$, q), ($true_{\emptyset}+^{p}$X=4, r), $true_{\emptyset}+^{d}$X=4};

Otherwise the resultant MCS will be

$C_2$={($true_{\emptyset}+^{p}true$, p), ($true_{\emptyset}+^{p}true$, q), (–(X=4)+$^{p}$X=5, r),
(–(X=4)+$^{p}$X=5, q), –(X=4)+$^{d}$X=5}.

In order to create test cases on which the executions of a procedure diverge we consider the divergent and call patterns constraints in the cp semantics of a program.

**Definition 3.3.** Let $C \subseteq C^d \cup C^p$ be a set of divergent and call patterns constraints, $C'$ is called a *Maximum Consistent and Divergent Subset (MCDS) of* $C$ if $C'$ is a MCS of $C$ and $C'$ contains at least one divergent constraint.

**Definition 3.4.** Let $C \subseteq C^d \cup C^p$ be a set of divergent and call patterns constraints, and $\Sigma=\{C_1,\ldots,C_m\}$ be a set of MCDSs of $C$, we say $\Sigma$ *covers* $C$ if for each divergent constraint $r \in C$ there exists $C_i \in \Sigma$ such that $r \in C_i$.
In the above example, both $C_1$ and $C_2$ are MCDSs of $C$, and $\{C_1, C_2\}$ obviously covers $C$. Next we present an algorithm *CoveringSet-1* for obtaining a set of MCDSs of $C$ that covers $C$.

*Input*: a set $C \subseteq C^d \cup C^p$;

*Output*: a set $\Sigma$ of MCDSs of $C$ that covers $C$;

```
CoveringSet-1(C)
  { R:={r| r∈C is a divergent constraint} ; Σ=∅;
   WHILE( R is not empty)
   {     Draw an element r of R and C' := MCS_finder(C, r);
         R:=R−C' ; Σ:=Σ∪{C'}; }
  }
```

Let P={$p_1$,..,$p_k$} denote a Prolog program, where $p_i$ ($i$=1,…,$k$) is a procedure. The domain of the interpretation is assumed to be the set D.

**Definition 3.5.** Let p be a procedure of P and $n$ be the input arity of p, an element of $D^n$ is called a *test case* for procedure p.

**Definition 3.6.** A test case $(d_1,\ldots,d_n)$ for procedure p *respects* a call patterns constraint $(o+^{p}b, q)$ if both $o$ and $b$ are satisfiable in the constraint store $\{\alpha=(d_1,\ldots,d_n)\}$;

and $(d_1,\ldots,d_n)$ *respects* a divergent constraint $(o{+}^d b)$ if both $o$ and $b$ are satisfiable in the same constraint store.

**Definition 3.7.** Let $C\subseteq C^d\cup C^p$ be a consistent set of constraints, and $(d_1,\ldots,d_n)$ be a test case for procedure p, $(d_1,\ldots,d_n)$ *respects* $C$ if $(d_1,\ldots,d_n)$ respects each element of $C$.

By the definitions of the satisfiability of basic and observability constraints, we have the following proposition.

**Proposition 3.8.** Let $C=\{o_{p1}+{}^p b_{p1}, \mathrm{p}_1,\ldots, o_{pw}+{}^p b_{pw}, \mathrm{p}_w, o_{c1}+{}^c b_{c1},\ldots, o_{cv}+{}^c b_{cv}\}$ be a consistent set of constraints and $(d_1,\ldots,d_n)$ be a test case for procedure p, $(d_1,\ldots,d_n)$ *respects* $C$ if both $(o_{p1}\sqcap\ldots\sqcap o_{pw}\sqcap o_{c1}\sqcap\ldots\sqcap o_{cv})$ and $(b_{p1}\wedge\ldots\wedge b_{pw}\wedge b_{c1}\wedge\ldots\wedge b_{cv})$ are satisfiable in the constraint store $\{\alpha=(d_1,\ldots,d_n)\}$.

In order to generate test cases respecting a set of divergent and call patterns constraints, constraints solvers could be applied. This viewpoint critically depends on one feature of the semantics in section 2, namely, Prolog is regarded as an instance of constraint logic programming (CLP) language [13], where $\mathcal{B}$ is the constraint domain. Recall that every implementation of CLP is parametric w.r.t. a constraint domain $D$ (such as the domain of linear arithmetic constraints, the domain of Boolean constraints) and contains a corresponding constraints solver, which given a set $C$ of constraints on $D$ judges the satisfiability of $C$, and in the case $C$ is satisfiable gives instances of the variables appearing in $C$. Given a goal made up of constraints and ordinary sub-goals, CLP engine will reduce the goal to a collection of constraints and solve the constraints by the constraints solver embedded in the engine.

For example, given a CLP program:

{ sumto(0, 0). sumto(N, S):- N>1, N<=S, sumto(N-1, S-N). }

The goal " S<=3, sumto(N, S)" will give rise to the answer (N=0, S=0), (N=1, S=1), (N=2, S=3) and terminates.

Let *sol* be a constraints solver on the set $\mathcal{B}$ of basic constraints. By the definition of observability constraints, *sol* can also be used for deciding the satisfiability of observability constraints. With this solver test cases respecting a set of divergent and call patterns constraints could be produced automatically. If $\mathcal{B}$ is the set of equations over terms, linear arithmetic constraints and Boolean constraints, *sol* is similar to the solvers used in CHIP [10] or Prolog III [4] systems. The details of the solver cannot be discussed here.

Based on the above definitions we can define the set of test cases for a procedure p on which the executions of p diverge.

**Definition 3.9.** Let $\mathcal{F}_P$ be the cp semantics of a program $P$, p be a procedure, $C$ be the set of divergent and call patterns constraints contained in $\mathcal{F}_P$(p) and $\Sigma=\{C_1,\ldots,C_m\}$ be a set of MCDSs of $C$ that covers $C$, the set $T$ of test cases for p respecting $\Sigma$ is defined as $T=\{d_1,\ldots,d_m\}$ where $d_i$ $(i=1,\ldots,m)$ is a test case for p that respects $C_i$.

By definition 3.9 and proposition 3.8 we can use the constraints solver *sol* to derive test cases for a procedure that respect a given set of MCDSs. Given a test case for a procedure p obtained according to definition 3.9, the call patterns that actually arise in the execution of p on the test case are determined as follows.

**Proposition 3.10.** Given a program P and a procedure p, let $C'$ be a MCDS of the set $C$ of divergent and call patterns constraints contained in $\mathcal{F}_P$(p), $d$ be the test case generated from $C'$, then the divergent computation and call patterns arising in the execution of p($d$) are described by the constraints set $C''=\{\ o''+^{p}b'',\ q\in C \mid d$ respects $(o''+^{p}b'',\ q)\}\cup\{\ o''+^{d}b''\in C \mid d$ respects $(o''+^{d}b'')\}$.

By the above proposition, we easily have $C'\subseteq C''$. Moreover we can show that $C'=C''$, since otherwise an element $r\in C''-C'$ will be such that $\{r\}\cup C'$ is consistent, i.e. $\{r\}\cup C'$ is satisfiable in the constraint store $\{\alpha=(d_1,\ldots,d_n)\}$, which contradicts the definition of MCDS.

Next we give a simple example to illustrate the test case generation for a procedure.

**Example 3.11.** Take the example 2.3 again, the denotations of $p$ and $q$ are initialized to $I_0(p)=true_{\emptyset}+^{P}true,\ p$ and $I_0(q)=true_{\emptyset}+^{P}true,\ q$.

The computation reaches a fixpoint at the second step with the resulting semantics as follows.

$$\mathcal{F}_P(p)=T_P^{\,2}(I_0)(p)=(true_{\emptyset}+^{P}true,\ p) :: (true_{\emptyset}+^{P}\alpha=4,\ p) :: true_{\emptyset}+^{d}\alpha=4$$
$$:: (-(\alpha=4)+^{P}true,\ q) :: -(\alpha=4)+^{c}\alpha=3 :: -(\alpha=4)+^{c}\alpha=5;$$
$$\mathcal{F}_P(q)=T_P^{\,2}(I_0)(q)=(true_{\emptyset}+^{P}true,\ q) :: true_{\emptyset}+^{c}\alpha=3 :: true_{\emptyset}+^{c}\alpha=5.$$

From $\mathcal{F}_P(p)$ we have the set $C$ of call patterns constrains and divergent constraints: $C=\{(true_{\emptyset}+^{P}true,\ p),\ (true_{\emptyset}+^{P}\alpha=4,\ p),\ (-(\alpha=4)+^{P}true,\ q),\ true_{\emptyset}+^{d}\alpha=4\}$, from which we get a MCDS of $C$:

$$C_1=\{(true_{\emptyset}+^{P}true,\ p),\ (true_{\emptyset}+^{P}\alpha=4,\ p),\ true_{\emptyset}+^{d}\alpha=4\}.$$

By definition 3.9 we get a test case $p(4)$ from $C_1$. The divergent computation and call patterns that arise in the execution of $p(4)$ are described exactly by $C_1$.

In order to create test cases that surely succeed we now consider the convergent constraints in the cp semantics of a program. In this case we need another specialization of the notion of MCSs.

**Definition 3.12.** Let $C\subseteq C^{c}\cup C^{p}$ be a set of convergent and call patterns constraints, $C'$ is called a *Maximum Consistent and Convergent Subset (MCCS) of C* if $C'$ is a MCS of $C$ and $C'$ contains at least one convergent constraint.

**Definition 3.13.** Let $C\subseteq C^{c}\cup C^{p}$ be a set of convergent and call patterns constraints, and $\Sigma=\{C_1,\ldots,C_m\}$ be a set of MCCSs of $C$, we say $\Sigma$ *covers* $C$ if for each convergent constraint $r\in C$ there exists $C_i\in\Sigma$ such that $r\in C_i$.

Given a set $C\subseteq C^{c}\cup C^{p}$, the algorithm *CoveringSet-2* for finding a set of MCCSs of $C$ that covers $C$ can be obtained from algorithm *CoveringSet-1* by changing "$R:=\{r \mid r\in C$ is a divergent constraint$\}$" to "$R:=\{r\mid r\in C$ is a convergent constraint$\}$".

A test case that respects a convergent constraint can be defined in the same way as definition 3.6. Definition 3.9 can easily be adapted for the case of MCCSs. So given the cp semantics $\mathcal{F}_P$ of a program $P$ we can generate test cases for a procedure p that respect a given set of MCCSs that covers the set $C$ of convergent and call patterns constraints contained in $\mathcal{F}_P$(p).

Similar to the case for MCDS, we have the following proposition.

**Proposition 3.14.** Given a program $P$ and a procedure p, let $C'$ be a MCCS of the set $C$ of convergent and call patterns constraints contained in $\mathcal{F}_P$(p) and $d$ be the test case that respects $C'$, then the set of computed answers obtained and the call patterns arising in the execution of p($d$) is described exactly by $C'$.

Next we consider the problem of generating test cases on which the executions of a procedure fail. Since the cp semantics we use does not explicitly describe the failure computation, an alternative way is to consider the computation that neither diverges nor succeeds. The following definition will serve this purpose.

**Definition 3.15.** Given a set $C \subseteq C^c \cup C^p \cup C^d$ of constraints, the failure condition $\Psi_C$ w.r.t. $C$ is defined as follows: $\Psi_C = (\sqcap\{-(o \sqcap b \propto obs) \mid o +^d b \in C\}) \sqcap (\sqcap\{-(o \sqcap b \propto obs) \mid o +^c b \in C\})$.

Given a set $C \subseteq C^c \cup C^p \cup C^d$, $\Psi_C$ can be used to generate test cases that make the executions of a procedure fail. A test case $d$ respects $\Psi_C$ if it belongs to the following set $F$:

$$F = \{d \mid \Psi_C \text{ is satisfiable in } \{\alpha = d\}.\}.$$

In example 3.11, by applying algorithm *CoveringSet-1* to set $C = \{(true_{\emptyset} +^p true, p), (true_{\emptyset} +^p \alpha=4, p), (-(\alpha=4) +^p true, q), true_{\emptyset} +^d \alpha=4\}$ we have obtained an MCDS $C_1$. Now by applying *CoveringSet-2* we find two MCCSs of $C' = \{(true_{\emptyset} +^p true, p), (true_{\emptyset} +^p \alpha=4, p), (-(\alpha=4) +^p true, q), -(\alpha=4) +^c \alpha=3, -(\alpha=4) +^c \alpha=5\}$, i.e.

$$C_2 = \{(true_{\emptyset} +^p true, p), (-(\alpha=4) +^p true, q), -(\alpha=4) +^c \alpha=3\} \text{ and}$$

$$C_3 = \{(true_{\emptyset} +^p true, p), (-(\alpha=4) +^p true, q), -(\alpha=4) +^c \alpha=5\}.$$

Let $C'' = \{(true_{\emptyset} +^p true, p), (true_{\emptyset} +^p \alpha=4, p), true_{\emptyset} +^d \alpha=4, (-(\alpha=4) +^p true, q), -(\alpha=4) +^c \alpha=3, -(\alpha=4) +^c \alpha=5\}$, the failure condition $\Psi_{C''}$ is:

$$\Psi_{C''} = -(\alpha=4) \sqcap (\alpha=4 \sqcup -(\alpha=3 \sqcup \alpha=5)).$$

From $C_2$ and $C_3$ we get two test cases, $p(3)$ and $p(5)$, and from $\Psi_{C''}$ we get one test case, say $p(7)$, that respects $\Psi_{C''}$. So in total we generate four test cases for procedure $p$, i.e. $p(4)$, $p(3)$, $p(5)$ and $p(7)$.

Finally we can define the set of test cases that are generated for a procedure of a program based on the cp semantics of the program.

**Definition 3.16.** Let $\mathcal{F}_P$ be the cp semantics of a program $P$, p be a procedure, $C_1$, $C_2$ and $C_3$ be the set of call patterns constraints, divergent constraints and convergent constraints contained in $\mathcal{F}_P(\mathrm{p})$, respectively, $\Sigma_d=\{C_{11},\ldots,C_{1m}\}$ be a set of MCDSs of $C_1\cup C_2$ that covers $C_1\cup C_2$ and $\Sigma_c=\{C_{21},\ldots,C_{2t}\}$ be a set of MCCSs of $C_1\cup C_3$ that covers $C_1\cup C_3$, the set $T$ of test cases for p is defined as $T=\{d_{11},\ldots,d_{1m}, d_{21},\ldots,d_{2t}\}\cup\{d_f\}$ where $d_{1i}$ ($i=1,\ldots, m$) is a test case for p that respects $C_{1i}$, $d_{2j}$ ($j=1,\ldots, t$) is a test case for p that respects $C_{2j}$, and $d_f$ is a test case that respects $\Psi_{C'}$, where $C'=C_1\cup C_2\cup C_3$ and $\Psi_{C'}$ is called the failure condition of $p$.

Recall that in Prolog program testing we have the notion of test cases selection criteria, such as the path coverage in CFG-based testing and clause coverage in PROTest II [17,1,2]. Definition 3.16 implies that the test case selection criteria used in our method is the MCDS/MCCS coverage and failure coverage, i.e. we require that: for each procedure p, 1) the MCDSs and MCCSs, from which test cases are produced, cover the set $C_1\cup C_2$ of call patterns and divergent constraints of $p$ and the set $C_1\cup C_3$ of call patterns and convergent constraints of $p$, respectively; and 2) there exist test cases that respect the failure condition of $p$.

## 4 Test Case Generation on an Approximation CP Semantics

The method in section 3 requires the existence of a finitely computable cp semantics of a program. Unfortunately, the cp semantics in section 2 is not generally computable. In order to apply our method to ordinary Prolog programs we can make use of existing semantics approximation techniques [7,8,15,21]. Two techniques in the framework of abstract interpretation can be used for this purpose [7]. One is to design widening/narrowing operators on infinite semantic domain to assure or speed up the convergence of the semantics computation process, the other is to follow the Galois connection approach to abstract interpretation to design a finite abstract semantic domain on which to build a finite abstraction of the cp semantics. Next we present a finite cp semantics using the second method.

We assume that testers are interested in the lists $[e_1, \ldots, e_w]$ containing no more than $k$ elements, i.e. $w\leq k$. If $e_i\in D$ ($i$=1, …, $w$) with $D$ being a finite set, the number of such lists must be finite. By requiring that in the computation of cp semantics any element $t_i$ ($i$=1, …, $m$) of a term ($t_1$, …, $t_m$) could only be a variable or a list having a maximum length of $k$, we could get a finite semantic domain. Formally, the length of a term is defined as follows.

**Definition 4.1.** Given a term T=($t_1$, …, $t_m$), the length |T| of T is defined as: |T|=MAX{$|t_1|$, …, $|t_m|$}, where $|t_i|$ is defined as:

$$|t_i| = \begin{cases} 1 & \text{if } t_i \text{ is a variable;} \\ 0 & \text{if } t_i = []; \\ 1+n & \text{if } t_i = [X|t_i'] \text{ and } |t_i'|=n. \end{cases}$$

Note that this is a partial definition on the set of Prolog terms, but is enough for our purpose. Now we can adapt the definition of the immediate consequence operator $T_P$ of program $P$ by adding a constraint $|\alpha|\leq k$:

$$T_P(I)(p)= (|\alpha|\leq k) \circledcirc \exists_Y(\delta_{Y,\alpha} \circledcirc (\phi^P(\mathcal{J}_P[\![G_1]\!]I \oplus \ldots \oplus \mathcal{J}_P[\![G_n]\!]I)).$$

The definitions of the semantic operators present in the above definition are kept unchanged. With this definition of cp semantics we can carry out the testing of some ordinary Prolog programs. Next we present an example to illustrate the application of our test case generation method based on the adapted semantics with $k$=2.

**Example 4.2.** Given a program $P'$:

{ insert (X, [Y|U], [Y|V]) :- Y<X, insert(X, U, V).
insert(X, [Y|U], [X,Y|U]) :- X⩽Y. insert(X,[],[X]). },

it can be translated into $P$:

{ insert(T):- exists X, Y, U, V, S. (T=(X, [Y|U], [Y|V]) and
(Y<X) and S=(X, U, V) and insert(S)) or
exists X, Y, U. (T=(X, [Y|U], [X,Y|U]) and X⩽Y) or
exists X. (T=(X, [], [X]). ).

Let $cond$=∃X, Y, U, V, S (α=(X, [Y|U], [Y|V]) ∧ (Y<X) ∧ S=(X, U, V)) and $cond'$=∃X', Y', U', V', S' (S=(X', [Y'|U'], [Y'|V']) ∧ (Y'<X') ∧ S'=(X',U',V')).

The computation of the approximation cp semantics of P reaches a fixpoint at the fourth step with the resulting semantics as follows. For simplicity, we write $\exists X_1, \ldots, X_n(T)$ as T in the following.

$\mathcal{F}_P$ (insert)= $true_{\emptyset}+^P true$, insert
:: $true_{\emptyset}+^P$ (α=(X, [Y|U], [Y|V]) ∧ (Y<X) ∧ |α|≤2), insert
:: $true_{\emptyset}+^P$ (α=(X, [Y, Y'|U'], [Y, Y'|V']) ∧ (Y<X)∧ (Y'<X) ∧|α|≤2), insert
:: −($cond$ ∧$cond'$) $+^c$ (α=(X, [Y], [Y, X]) ∧ Y<X∧ |α|≤2)
:: −$cond$ $+^c$ (α=(X, [Y|U], [X,Y|U]) ∧ X⩽Y∧ |α|≤2)
:: −$cond$ $+^c$ (α=(X, [], [X]) ∧ |α|≤2).

Let C={($true_{\emptyset}+^P true$, insert), ($true_{\emptyset}+^P$(α=(X, [Y|U], [Y|V])∧ (Y<X) ∧ |α|≤2), insert),
($true_{\emptyset}+^P$ (α=(X, [Y, Y'|U'], [Y, Y'|V']) ∧ (Y<X)∧ (Y'<X) ∧ |α|≤2), insert),
−($cond$ ∧$cond'$) $+^c$ (α=(X, [Y], [Y, X]) ∧ Y<X∧ |α|≤2),
−$cond$ $+^c$ (α=(X, [Y|U], [X,Y|U]) ∧ X⩽Y∧ |α|≤2),
−$cond$ $+^c$ (α=(X, [], [X]) ∧ |α|≤2)},

then we get the following set of MCCSs:

$C_1$={($true_{\emptyset}+^P true$, insert), ($true_{\emptyset}+^P$(α=(X, [Y|U], [Y|V])∧(Y<X)∧|α|≤2), insert), −($cond$ ∧$cond'$) $+^c$ (α=(X, [Y], [Y, X]) ∧ Y<X∧ |α|≤2)};
$C_2$={($true_{\emptyset}+^P true$, insert), −$cond$ $+^c$ (α=(X, [Y|U], [X,Y|U]) ∧ X⩽Y∧ |α|≤2)};
$C_3$={($true_{\emptyset}+^P true$, insert), −$cond$ $+^c$ (α=(X, [], [X]) ∧ |α|≤2)}.

The failure condition of insert is

$\Psi_C$ =(($cond$ ∧$cond'$) ⊔ −(α=(X, [Y], [Y, X]) ∧ Y<X∧ |α|≤2))⊓

$(cond \sqcup -(\alpha=(X, [Y|U], [X,Y|U]) \wedge X\leqslant Y \wedge |\alpha|\leq 2)) \sqcap$
$(cond \sqcup -(\alpha=(X, [], [X]) \wedge |\alpha|\leq 2))$.

From the above sets of constraints we get the following test cases for procedure insert:

- insert(5, [3], [3, 5]) respecting $C_1$,
- insert(1, [4, 9, 8], [1,4, 9, 8]) respecting $C_2$,
- insert(2, [], [2]) respecting $C_3$.
- insert(5, [2,3], [2, 3]) respecting $\Psi_C$.

## 5 Related Work

In this section we compare the test case generation method in this paper with the work proposed in literature. Generally, the effort in the testing of Prolog programs falls into two categories, i.e. specification-based testing and implementation-based testing. An example of specification-based testing is the CPM testing [3,18,12,14] that is implemented in the IDTS system–an environment for algorithmic debugging and specification-based testing of Prolog programs. The main purpose of the IDTS system is to make use of CPM testing to improve the efficiency of diagnosing Prolog programs. The test case generation is mainly produced from a user-defined set of test frames and is improved with the result of algorithmic diagnosis [19].

With implementation-based testing, the generation of test cases is usually guided by a formal analysis of the program under consideration. Our method and the works presented in [1,2,17] belong to this class.

The PROTest II system [1,2] is a Prolog test environment developed by Belli and Jack. In this system every program to be tested is augmented with declarative information about the types and modes of the arguments of a procedure. A structure checker is used to validate that a procedure is consistent with the types declarations for the procedure. The test cases are generated by structural induction using types declarations, and in this process modes declarations are used to partition the test cases. The advantage of our method is that beside types and modes information we can make use of more information about a program through the means of semantics approximation.

Yan [22] studied the declarative testing of logic programs using a reliable test set. A test set *T* is reliable for program *P* and specification $I_P$ if that *P* computes the same value as $I_P$ on each point of *T* implies that *P* computes the same value as $I_P$ on each point at which *P* is defined. If a finite set of reliable test set is available the testing will be efficient. Unfortunately it's shown that there is no effect procedure to generate reliable test data.

Considerable effort on logic program testing has been devoted to the work under the title abstract debugging, abstract interpretation based debugging and deductive debugging [5,6,9,11,16]. The main idea of this kind of work is to compare the formal specification *I* of a program *P* with the formal semantics *O*(*P*) of *P* that describes the interested behaviors of *P*. If $I\neq O(P)$, some fault must exist in the clauses of the program, and in this case a particularly designed method will be applied to find the fault.

The call patterns of a goal describe the control transfer in the execution of the goal in a program. From this viewpoint, the work that has close relation to our method is Luo's [17] control flow based testing of Prolog programs, where *P-flowgraph* (Prolog control flow graph) and *reduced global P-flowgraph* are used to describe the control flow of a Prolog program. The following constructs or events are represented as nodes of a P-flowgraph:

- The head of each clause of a procedure, whose corresponding node is called a *head node* in the following;
- Each sub-goal in the body of a clause, whose corresponding node is called a *sub-goal node* in the following;
- The successes of the unifications of all sub-goals in the body of a clause, whose corresponding node is called *T node*; and
- The failure of the execution of a procedure, whose corresponding node is called *F-node*.

T-node exists for each clause of a procedure, however, there is only one F-node for a P-flowgraph or a reduced global P-*flowgraph*. So in total there are four types of nodes in the control flow graph of a procedure. Directed edges (branches) are created to describe possible control transfer between each pair of nodes. By selecting an appropriate test selection criteria based on a P-flowgraph, such as the branch coverage and branch-to-branch coverage of a P-flowgraph, the test cases for a procedure in a Prolog program can be generated. As an example, branch coverage criteria requires that the running of the test cases generated for a procedure traverse every branch of the P-flowgraph of the procedure. Since the global P-flowgraph of a Prolog program is generally infinite, a reduced global P-flowgraph is adopted to describe a part of it. Similar criteria can also be defined on the reduced global P-*flowgraph*.

Next we show some correspondence between our method and P-flowgrph based method. Since the successes of a procedure call are represented as convergent constraints, a path ending with a T-node corresponds to a consistent constraint set containing convergent constraints; and a path ending with a F-node corresponds to a consistent constraint set that contains no convergent constraints.

Take example 2.3 again, the P-flowgraph of a procedure p is described in Fig.1(a). Note that we delete the branches between the head nodes for the same procedure and

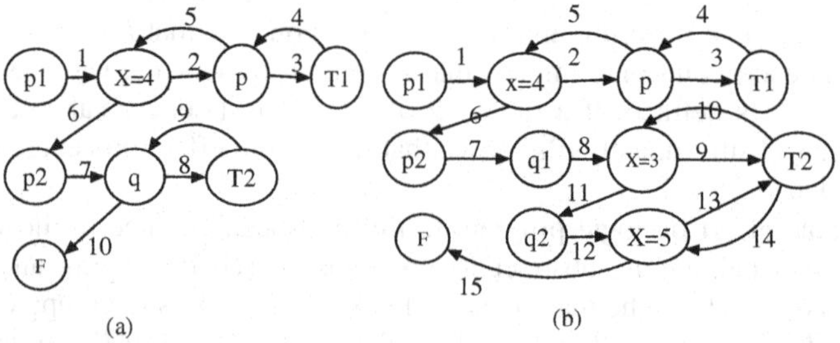


**Fig. 1.** (a) P-flowgraph of procedure p; and (b) part of global P-flowgraph of p

the branches between a head node and F-node to fit the abstract syntax in section 2, since these control transfer actually cannot happen according to the abstract syntax. The MCDS $C_1$={$(true_\emptyset+^p true,\ p)$, $(true_\emptyset+^p\alpha=4,\ p)$, $true_\emptyset+^d\alpha=4$} corresponds to an infinite path: 1-2-5-2-5-2-5-... in Fig.1(a).

Since the cp semantics of a procedure describes all possible call patterns that are directly or indirectly called in the procedure execution, a consistent sets of constraints also describe the paths of a reduced global P-flowgraph and global P-flowgraph. In this example, the reduced global P-flowgraph for p is the P-flowgraph itself. Fig.1(b) presents a part of the global P-flowgraph of p. The MCCS $C_2$={$(true_\emptyset+^p true,\ p)$, $(-(\alpha=4)+^p true,\ q)$, $-(\alpha=4)+^c\alpha=3$} corresponds to the path: 1-6-7-8-9-10 in the graph; and $C_3$={$(true_\emptyset+^p true,\ p)$, $(-(\alpha=4)+^p true,\ q)$, $-(\alpha=4)+^c\alpha=5$} corresponds to the path: 1-6-7-8-11-12-13-14. If we generate a test case p(7) from $\Psi_{C''}$, its execution will traverse the path: 1-6-7-8-11-12-15.

In practice, it's not uncommon for a tester to be interested only in some properties of a program expressed by means of approximation or abstraction. When taking this concern into consideration in the testing of a program, the main problem with the reduced global P-flowgraph lies in its flexibility, i.e. it provides only one reduced version of the global P-flowgraph, which cannot be adjusted according to the requirement of a tester. On the contrary, our method is very flexible. Our method is based a Prolog cp semantics whose approximation techniques have been studied extensively in literature [15,21]. By designing a widening/narrowing operator or a finite abstract semantic domain (and corresponding semantic operators on it), an approximation semantics of the cp semantics can be achieved. So we can generate test cases based on the approximation cp semantics of a program. In this way we achieve the effect of merging in a global P-flowgraph the paths that are equivalent in the view of a tester. This means that we can test a Prolog program according to testers' requirements expressed by means of approximations. So in summary the flexibility of our method comes from the ability that we can design multiple approximation semantics based on the cp semantics in section 2.

## 6 Conclusion and Future Work

It's a natural idea to generate test cases for a Prolog procedure based the call patterns of the procedure. This paper proposes a novel call patterns-based method for generating test cases for a Prolog program, which is based on a constraint-based call patterns semantics, where call patterns, divergent computation and computed answers are denoted by call patterns constraints, divergent constraints and convergent constraints, respectively. By studying the consistency among these constraints, we propose to use the maximum consistent and divergent subsets-MCDSs and maximum consistent and convergent subsets–MCCSs to describe the control flow path(s) of a program. Test cases respecting a set of MCDSs or MCCSs could be generated with a proper constraints solver. Moreover, failure condition of a procedure is used to generate test cases on which the executions of the procedure fail. Compared with traditional CFG-based test case generation method, our method is very flexible. By selecting a proper approximation of the call patterns semantics we use, test cases can be generated automatically according to the particular requirements of a tester. The applicability of our method is illustrated by examples in this paper.

The development of a testing tool for Prolog programs based on our method is now in progress. We plan to use them in the testing of non-trivial applications. The further work will integrate it with the existing program analysis tools.

## Acknowledgment

The authors are very grateful to the anonymous reviewers of this paper for their constructive comments. This work is supported by National Natural Science Foundation of China (No.60563005, No.60663005) and Guangxi Natural Science Foundation of China (0728093,0542036).

## References

1. Belli, F., Jack, O.: Implementation-based Analysis and Testing of Prolog Programs. In: Proceedings of the 1993 ACM SIGSOFT International Symposium on Software Testing and Analysis, pp. 70–80 (1993)
2. Belli, F., Jack, O.: PROTest II, Testing Logic Programs, Technical report, 1992/13, ADT (October 1992)
3. Chen, T.Y., Poon, P.-L., Tse, T.H.: A Choice Relation Framework for Supporting Category-Partition Test Case Generation. IEEE Transactions on Software Engineering 29(7), 577–593 (2003)
4. Colmerauer, A.: An Introduction to PROLOG-III. Communications of the ACM 33(7), 69–90 (1990)
5. Comini, M., Levi, G., Vitiello, G.: Abstract Debugging of Logic Program. In: META, pp. 440–450 (1994)
6. Comini, M., Levi, G., Vitiello, G.: Efficient Detection of Incompleteness Errors in the Abstract Debugging of Logic Programs. In: Proceedings of AADEBUG 1995, pp. 159–174 (1995)
7. Cousot, P., Cousot, R.: Abstract Interpretation and Applications to Logic Programs. Journal of Logic Programming 13(23), 103–179 (1992)
8. Cousot, P., Cousot, R.: Comparing the Galois connection and widening/narrowing approaches to abstract interpretation. In: Bruynooghe, M., Wirsing, M. (eds.) PLILP 1992. LNCS, vol. 631, pp. 269–295. Springer, Heidelberg (1992)
9. Dershowitz, N., Lee, Y.: Deductive Debugging. In: Proceedings of the Fourth IEEE Symposium on Logic Programming, pp. 298–306 (1987)
10. Dincbas, M., Van Hentenryck, P., Simonis, H., Aggoun, A.: The Constraint Logic Programming Language CHIP. In: Proceedings of the International Conference on Fifth Generation Computer Systems, pp. 693–702 (1988)
11. Hermenegildo, M., Puebla, G., Bueno, F., López-García, P.: Integrated Program Debugging, Verification, and Optimization Using Abstract Interpretation (and the Ciao system preprocessor). Science of Computer Programming. 58(1-2), 115–140 (2005)
12. Horváth, T., Gyimóthy, T., Alexin, Z., Kocsis, F.: Interactive Diagnosis and Testing of Logic Programs. In: Proceedings of the Third Finnish-Estonian-Hungarian Symposium on Programming Languages and Software Tools Kääriku, Estonia, pp. 34–46 (1993)

13. Jaffar, J., Maher, M.J.: Constraint Logic Programming: A survey. Journal of Logic Programming 19–20, 503–581 (1994)
14. Kókai, G., Harmath, L., Gyimóthy, T.: IDTS: a Tool for Debugging and Testing of Prolog Programs. In: Proceedings of LIRA 1997, The 8th Conference on Logic and Computer Science, Novi Sad, Yugoslavia, September 1-4, 1997 pp. 103–110 (1997)
15. Levi, G., Spoto, F.: Accurate Analysis of Prolog with Cut. In: Lucio, P., Martelli, M., Navarro, M. (eds.) Proceedings APPIA-GULP-PRODE 1996, pp. 481–492 (1996)
16. Lu, L., Greenfield, P.: Logic Program Testing Based on Abstract Interpretation. In: Pottosin, I.V., Bjorner, D., Broy, M. (eds.) Formal Methods in Programming and Their Applications. LNCS, vol. 735, pp. 170–180. Springer, Heidelberg (1993)
17. Luo, G., Bochmann, G., Sarikaya, B., Boyer, M.: Control Flow Based Testing of Prolog Programs. In: Proceedings of the 3rd International Symposium on Software Reliability Engineering, pp. 104–113 (1992)
18. Ostrand, T.J., Balcer, M.J.: The Category-Partition Method for Specifying and Generating Functional Tests. Communications of ACM 31(6), 676–686 (1988)
19. Shapiro, E.Y.: Algorithmic Program Diagnosis. In: POPL 1982, pp. 299–308 (1982)
20. Spoto, F.: Operational and Goal-independent Denotational Semantics for Prolog with Cut. The Journal of Logic Programming 42, 1–46 (2000)
21. Spoto, F., Levi, G.: Abstract Interpretation of Prolog Programs. In: Haeberer, A.M. (ed.) AMAST 1998. LNCS, vol. 1548, pp. 455–470. Springer, Heidelberg (1998)
22. Yan, S.Y.: Declarative Testing in Logic Programming. In: Proceedings of the Third Australian Software Engineering Conference, pp. 423–435 (1987)

# On a Tighter Integration of Functional and Logic Programming*

Bernd Braßel and Frank Huch

Institute of Computer Science
University of Kiel, 24098 Kiel, Germany
{bbr,fhu}@informatik.uni-kie.de

**Abstract.** The integration of functional and logic programming is a well developed field of research. We discuss that the integration could be improved significantly in two separate aspects: sharing computations across non-deterministic branching and the declarative encapsulation of logic search. We then present a formal approach which shows how these improvements can be realized and prove the soundness of our approach.

## 1 Introduction

There are two main streams in declarative programming: functional and logic programming. For several years now a third stream aims at combining the key advantages of these two paradigms. This third stream is often called "functional logic programming" but could also be simply denoted as "declarative programming". Declarative programming languages try to bridge the chasm between the deterministic world of (lazy) functional programming and the non-deterministic multiverse of logic programming. By now the theory is well developed and among the many approaches we name only three works we consider the main theoretic fundament: A denotational semantics was developed in [9] and extended in many subsequent publications. A formal base on narrowing was given in [3] and an operational semantics was introduced in [1].

There are, however, reasons to believe that the integration of both paradigms could be tighter, demonstrated by two examples in the functional logic language Curry:

*Example 1 (Sharing across Non-Determinism).* We consider parser combinators which can elegantly make use of the non-determinism of functional logic languages to implement the different rules of a grammar. A simple set of parser combinators, consisting of the always successful parser `succ`, a parser for a single character `sym` and the sequential composition of two parsers `(<*>)`, can be defined as follows:

```
type Parser a = String -> (String,a)

succ :: a -> Parser a
succ r cs = (cs,r)
```

* This work has been partially supported by DFG grant Ha 2457/5-1.

Z. Shao (Ed.): APLAS 2007, LNCS 4807, pp. 122–138, 2007.

```
sym :: Char -> Parser Char
sym c (c':cs) | c==c' = (cs,c)

(<*>)  :: Parser (a -> b) -> Parser a -> Parser b
(p1 <*> p2) str = case p1 str of
                    (str1,f) -> case p2 str1 of
                                  (str2,x) -> (str2,f x)
parse :: Parser a -> String -> a
parse p str = case p str of ("",r) -> r
```

As an example, we construct a non-deterministic parser for the inherent ambiguous language of palindromes without marked center $L = \{w\overleftarrow{w} \mid w \in \{a,b\}\}$[1], which, if parsing is possible, returns the word $w$ and fails otherwise:

```
pal :: Parser String
pal = succ (\ c str _ -> c:str) <*> sym 'a' <*> pal <*> sym 'a'
    ? succ (\ c str _ -> c:str) <*> sym 'b' <*> pal <*> sym 'b'
    ? succ ""
```

where `(?) :: a -> a -> a` induces non-deterministic branching and is defined by:

```
x ? _ = x
_ ? y = y
```

In all Curry implementations the parser `pal` analyses a `String` of length 100 within milliseconds. We call this time $t_{parse}$. Unfortunately, this program does not scale well with respect to the time it takes to compute the argument string, which we consider to be a list of expressions `[`$e_1, \ldots, e_{100}$`]` where each $e_i$ evaluates to a character taking an amount of time $t >> t_{parse}$ and constructing the string `[`$e_1, \ldots, e_{100}$`]` takes time $100 \cdot t$. Then one would expect the total time to compute `parse pal [`$e_1$`,...,`$e_{100}$`]` is $100 \cdot t + t_{parse} \approx 100 \cdot t$. But measurements for the Curry implementation PAKCS ([10]) show that, e.g., for $t = 0.131s$ it takes more than $5000 \cdot t$ to generate a solution for a palindrome `[`$e_1, \ldots, e_{100}$`]` and $9910 \cdot t$ to perform the whole search for all solutions. We obtain similar results for other implementations of lazy functional logic languages, like the Münster Curry Compiler [15].

The reason is that these systems do not provide sharing across non-determinism. For all non-deterministic branches in the parser the elements of the remaining list are computed again and again. Only values which are evaluated before non-determinism occurs are shared over the non-deterministic branches. This behavior is not only a minor implementation detail but poses problems concerning the fundamentals of declarative languages. These problems have never been treated at a formal level before.

The consequence of Example 1 is that programmers have to avoid using non-determinism for functions that might be applied to expensive computations. But in connection with *laziness* a programmer cannot know which arguments are already computed because evaluations are suspended until their value is demanded. Hence, the connection of laziness with logic search always threatens to perform with the considerable slowdown discussed above. Thus, sadly, when

[1] We restrict to this small alphabet for simplicity.

looking for possibilities to improve efficiency, the programmer in a lazy functional logic language is well advised to either try to eliminate the logic features he might have employed or to strictly evaluate expressions prior to each search. Both alternatives show that he still follows either the functional or the logic paradigm but cannot profit from a seamless integration of both.

A second important topic when connecting logic search with the lazy functional paradigm is *encapsulated search*. Encapsulated search is employed whenever different values of one expression have to be related in some way, e.g., to compute a list of all values or to find the minimal value and also to formulate a search strategy. But again we find that the connection of this feature with laziness is problematic as illustrated by the following example.

*Example 2 (Encapsulated Search).* Reconsider the notion of palindrome and the parser definitions of Example 1. We call a palindrome *prime*, if it does not contain a proper, non-empty prefix which is also a palindrome. For a given string `s` we can check this property by inspecting the result of applying our parser. `s` is a prime palindrome if `(pal s)` meets two conditions: 1) `s` is a palindrome, i.e., the parser succeeds consuming the whole input and 2) there are only two successful parses as the empty prefix is a palindrome by definition. Hence, we can use the operation `allValues`, which performs encapsulated search to yield a list containing all values of its argument, to count the number of successful parses and we define:

```
prime : (String,a) -> Success
prime r = fst r =:= "" & length (allValues r) =:= 2
```

To express the conditions, we use the strict equality operator `(=:=)`) which implements unification. The two conditions are expressed as constraints on the parse results connected by the operator `(&)`. `(&)` is called "concurrent conjunction" and is a primitive, i.e., an externally defined operator. The adjective "concurrent" suggests that the result should not depend on the order in which the constraints are evaluated. But if `allValues` is based on encapsulated search as available in PAKCS, the result of, e.g., `prime (pal "abba")` does indeed depend on the order of evaluation. If the constraint `fst r =:= ""` is solved first then PAKCS yields no solution and if the second constraint is preferred, the computation is successful. We will not explain how this behavior comes to pass and refer to [5] for a detailed discussion. Here, it is only important that this problem also stems from the connection of laziness with logic search and is caused by the sharing of `r` in both constraints.

In an alternative approach as implemented in the Münster Curry Compiler (MCC) [14] the result does not depend on the order in which the two constraints are evaluated. The evaluation of `(prime (pal "abba"))` fails in any case, again cf. [5] for details. Although the approach of [14] does not require any knowledge about the order of evaluation, detailed knowledge about the compiler and the executed optimizations are needed to successfully employ encapsulated search in the MCC. For instance, a program can yield different values if one writes `(\x -> x=:=(0 ? 1))` instead of `(=:=(0 ? 1))` although by the very definition of the language Curry [11] the latter expression is just an abbreviation of the former.

$$
\begin{array}{lll}
P & ::= D_1 \ldots D_m & \\
D & ::= f(x_1, \ldots, x_n) = e & \\
e & ::= x & \text{(variable)} \\
 & \mid\ c(x_1, \ldots, x_n) & \text{(constructor call)} \\
 & \mid\ f(x_1, \ldots, x_n) & \text{(function call)} \\
 & \mid\ \text{case } e \text{ of } \{p_1 \to e_1; \ldots; p_n \to e_n\} & \text{(rigid case)} \\
 & \mid\ \text{fcase } e \text{ of } \{p_1 \to e_1; \ldots; p_n \to e_n\} & \text{(flexible case)} \\
 & \mid\ e_1 \text{ or } e_2 & \text{(disjunction)} \\
 & \mid\ \text{let } x_1 = e_1, \ldots, x_n = e_n \text{ in } e & \text{(let binding)} \\
p & ::= c(x_1, \ldots, x_n) &
\end{array}
$$

where $P$ denotes a program, $D$ a function definition, $p$ a pattern and $e \in$ Expr an arbitrary expression.

**Fig. 1.** Syntax for Normalized Flat Curry Programs

Example 2 shows that encapsulated search is a second area on which the integration of functional and logic programming could be tighter. The work presented in this paper does not suffer from the illustrated problems: The time to parse a string which is expensive to construct is not multiplied by the number of non-deterministic branches and the evaluation of, e.g., `(prime (pal "abba"))` is successful regardless of the order of evaluation. In general, the use of encapsulated search does neither depend on evaluation order nor on the way the compiler transforms the programs. The approach has been successfully implemented in our Curry to Haskell Compiler, the Kiel Curry System (*KiCS*), available at `www-ps.informatik.uni-kiel.de/~bbr/download/kics_src.tgz`.

functions of arity 0. In the following sections we show that both problems, sharing across non-determinism and encapsulation, can be interleaved in such a way that a solution to one also solves the other. While we are not the first to present an approach to sharing across non-determinism, cf. Section 5, the seamless integration of both aspects, and especially the purity of encapsulation, is the contribution of the presented work. We propose a natural (big step) semantics for functional logic languages which features sharing across non-determinism. This semantics can be seen as an extension of the one presented in [1] and we formally relate our results to that work. The key idea of the extension is to treat non-deterministic branching as constructors, so called "or-nodes". This enables sharing beneath these nodes just as beneath any other constructor. As a consequence, however, an or-node is also in head normal form. As the semantics of a given expression in [1] is normally its head normal form, we need a further concept to yield values in the sense of [1]. Surprisingly, this additional concept is encapsulated search. Adding this feature, we can show a strong relationship between the values computed by our semantics and the one of [1].

The paper mainly consists of enhancing the semantics proposed in [1] stepwise. First, the semantics is substantially simplified and then extended to cover sharing across non-determinism and encapsulated search. We only sketch the ideas of the proofs. The complete proofs are presented in [7].

## 2 Preliminaries

For the syntax of functional logic programs we consider the first-order core language *Flat Curry*. Furthermore, we restrict to *normalized Flat Curry*, in which only variables are allowed as arguments of constructors and functions. The normalization of arbitrary Flat Curry programs is defined in [1]. This normalization is the key idea to express sharing, the main concept of laziness in the functional setting [13] and call-time choice in the functional logic setting. The syntax is presented in Figure 1. Free variables are introduced as circular *let* bindings of the form *let x=x in e*. To keep programs containing multiple ors more readable, we omit brackets for or expressions and assume that or binds left associatively. We also omit argument brackets for constructors and

The semantics is similarly defined to the semantics in [1], with the exception that a black hole detection (like present in [13]) is added in the rule (VarExp). Without this black hole detection, a non-deterministic choice might produce a proof tree in which the same variable is updated with different values in the heap. [7] presents such an undesired derivation. Hence, this slight modification can be seen as a correction of [1]. We refer to this semantics as $\Downarrow_0$ and will stepwise modify it. For lack of space, we cannot explain the ideas of the rules in this paper and refer to [1]. Nevertheless, we want to introduce some notations used in the semantics.

(VarCons) $\Gamma[x \mapsto t] : x \Downarrow_0 \Gamma[x \mapsto t] : t$ where $t$ is constructor-rooted

(VarExp) $\dfrac{\Gamma \setminus \{(x, \Gamma(x))\} : \Gamma(x) \Downarrow_0 \Delta : v}{\Gamma : x \Downarrow_0 \Delta[x \mapsto v] : v}$ where $\Gamma(x)$ is not constructor-rooted and $\Gamma(x) \neq x$

(Val) $\Gamma : v \Downarrow_0 \Gamma : v$ where $v$ is constructor-rooted or a variable with $\Gamma(v) = v$

(Fun) $\dfrac{\Gamma : \sigma(e) \Downarrow_0 \Delta : v}{\Gamma : f(\overline{x_n}) \Downarrow_0 \Delta : v}$ where $f(\overline{y_n}) = e \in P$ and $\sigma = \{\overline{y_n \mapsto x_n}\}$

(Let) $\dfrac{\Gamma[\overline{y_k \mapsto \sigma(e_k)}] : \sigma(e) \Downarrow_0 \Delta : v}{\Gamma : \text{let } \{\overline{x_k = e_k}\} \text{ in } e \Downarrow_0 \Delta : v}$ where $\sigma = \{\overline{x_k \mapsto y_k}\}$ and $\overline{y_k}$ are fresh variables

(Or) $\dfrac{\Gamma : e_i \Downarrow_0 \Delta : v}{\Gamma : e_1 \text{ or } e_2 \Downarrow_0 \Delta : v}$ where $i \in \{1, 2\}$

(Select) $\dfrac{\Gamma : e \Downarrow_0 \Delta : c(\overline{y_n}) \quad \Delta : \sigma(e_i) \Downarrow_0 \Theta : v}{\Gamma : (\text{f})\text{case } e \text{ of } \{\overline{p_k \to e_k}\} \Downarrow_0 \Theta : v}$ where $p_i = c(\overline{x_n})$ and $\sigma = \{\overline{x_n \mapsto y_n}\}$

(Guess) $\dfrac{\Gamma : e \Downarrow_0 \Delta : x \quad \Delta[x \mapsto \sigma(p_i), \overline{y_n \mapsto y_n}] : \sigma(e_i) \Downarrow_0 \Theta : v}{\Gamma : \text{fcase } e \text{ of } \{\overline{p_k \to e_k}\} \Downarrow_0 \Theta : v}$
where $p_i = c(\overline{x_n})$, $\sigma = \{\overline{x_n \mapsto y_n}\}$, and $\overline{y_n}$ are fresh variables

**Fig. 2.** Natural Semantics for Functional Logic Programs

**Definition 1 (Heap, Update $\Gamma[\mapsto]$).** *Let Var* $= \{x, y, z, \ldots\}$ *be a finite set of variables, Expr the set of expressions, as defined in Figure 1, and Heap* $\subset$ *Var*$\times$ *Expr a finite set, called* heap, *where each element* $x \in$ *Var appears at most once in a pair* $(x, e)$ *within the set, i.e. a heap represents a partial function from*

*Var to Expr. Heaps will be denoted with upper case greek letters (e.g.* $\Gamma, \Delta, \Theta$*) and we adopt the usual notation for functions to write* $\Gamma(x) = e$ *for* $(x, e) \in \Gamma$. *A* heap update $\Gamma[x \mapsto e]$ *is an abbreviation for* $(\Gamma \setminus \{(x, \Gamma(x))\}) \cup \{(x, e)\}$. *We will also make use of the usual notations Dom(*$\Gamma$*) and Rng(*$\Gamma$*) to denote the domain and range of a heap, respectively.*

Note that an updated heap is again a heap and that for all heaps $\Gamma$ the equation $\Gamma[x \mapsto e][x \mapsto e] = \Gamma[x \mapsto e]$ holds. Like in the rules (Let), (Select), and (Guess) of Figure 2, we often refer to a sequence of arguments, bindings, expressions, or similar objects. We usually write $\overline{o_n}$ as an abbreviation for a sequence of $n$ objects $o_1, \ldots, o_n$. Finally, in example programs, we will often use non-normalized programs and Curry-like notations in which we may use pattern matching instead of case expressions and write function and constructor application in curried form.

## 3 Simplifications of the Semantics

Before we extend the semantics, we apply some further simplifications.

### 3.1 Elimination of Free Variables

In [4], Antoy and Hanus presented the surprising result that under certain circumstances one can replace free variables by generator functions. Unfortunately, they prove their result only for a term-rewriting based semantics not considering sharing. A similar result was presented in [8] in the context of the *Constructor-based ReWriting Logic (CRWL)*, a different semantic framework for functional logic languages. Unfortunately, this result cannot be transfered to our framework so easily. Since, on the other hand, this technique is crucial for our semantics extensions, we transfer this result to the setting with sharing. To do this we change the setting from $\Downarrow_0$ as follows and refer to the new semantics as $\Downarrow_1$.

1. Replace in each heap and each expression program bindings of the form $x = x$ by $x =$ generate, cf. Definition 2 below.
2. Add to each program the definition of the special function generate:

$$\begin{aligned} \text{generate} = &\ (\text{let } \{\overline{x_{n_1} = \text{generate}}\} \text{ in } c_1(\overline{x_{n_1}})) \\ &\ \text{or } \ldots \\ &\ \text{or } (\text{let } \{\overline{x_{n_k} = \text{generate}}\} \text{ in } c_k(\overline{x_{n_k}})) \end{aligned}$$

where $\overline{c_k}$ are all program constructors and $c_i$ has arity $n_i$ for all $1 \leq i \leq k$.

Note that normally, the generator is type oriented, i.e., it generates only values of the correct type. This greatly prunes the search space and can be implemented by approaches analogous to those used for type classes.

Now all free variables in a program can be replaced by such generators.

**Definition 2 (Free Variable Eliminations $e^{\dagger}$ and $\Gamma^{\otimes}$).** *We eliminate free variables in expressions by replacing them with a call to the special function* generate.

$$\begin{aligned}
x^\dagger &= x\\
s(\overline{x_n})^\dagger &= s(\overline{x_n}) \quad \textit{s function or constructor}\\
(e_1 \text{ or } e_2)^\dagger &= e_1^\dagger \text{ or } e_2^\dagger\\
((\text{f})\text{case } e \text{ of } \{\overline{p_k \to e_k}\})^\dagger &= (\text{f})\text{case } e^\dagger \text{ of } \{\overline{p_k \to e_k^\dagger}\}\\
(\text{let } \{\overline{x_k = e_k}\} \text{ in } e)^\dagger &= \text{let } \{\overline{(x_k = e_k)^\ddagger}\} \text{ in } e^\dagger\\
(x = e)^\ddagger &= \begin{cases} x = \text{generate} , & \textit{if } e = x\\ x = e^\dagger & , \textit{otherwise}\end{cases}
\end{aligned}$$

*Likewise, we replace free variables in heaps by defining:*

$$\Gamma^\otimes = \{(x, e^\dagger) \mid (x,e) \in \Gamma \wedge x \neq e\} \cup \{(x, \text{generate}) \mid (x,x) \in \Gamma\}$$

*We also write $P^\dagger$ for the result of transforming all expressions in a program $P$ by means of $^\dagger$.*

Note that both $e^\dagger$ and $\Gamma^\otimes$ are unambiguously invertible.

The evaluation of the special function generate is a linear proof tree which non-deterministically chooses one of the constructors of the program as a value. In order to be able to refer to such a tree, we define:

**Definition 3 (Generator Tree $gT$).** *For an arbitrary heap $\Gamma$, a variable $x$ with $\Gamma(x) = x$ and an $n_i$-ary constructor $c_i$ the generator tree is defined as:*

$$(\Gamma, x) gT(\Theta, c_i(\overline{x_n})) = \dfrac{\dfrac{\dfrac{\Delta^\otimes := \Gamma'^\otimes[\overline{x_{n_i} \mapsto \text{generate}}] : c_i(\overline{x_n}) \Downarrow_1 \Delta^\otimes : c_i(\overline{x_n})}{\Gamma'^\otimes : e_i = \text{let } \{\overline{y_{n_i} = \text{generate}}\} \text{ in } c_i(\overline{y_n}) \Downarrow_1 \Delta^\otimes : c_i(\overline{x_{n_i}})} \quad \times_{j=1}^{i-1}\left(\dfrac{\Gamma'^\otimes : e_{j+1} \text{ or } \ldots \text{ or } e_k \Downarrow_1 \Delta^\otimes : c_i(\overline{x_n})}{\Gamma'^\otimes : e_j \text{ or } e_{j+1} \text{ or } \ldots \text{ or } e_k \Downarrow_1 \Delta^\otimes : c_i(\overline{x_n})}\right)}{\Gamma'^\otimes := \Gamma^\otimes \setminus \{(x, \text{generate})\} : \text{generate} \Downarrow_1 \Delta^\otimes : c_i(\overline{x_n})}}{\Gamma^\otimes : x \Downarrow_1 \Theta^\otimes := \Delta^\otimes[x \mapsto c_i(\overline{x_n})] : c_i(\overline{x_n})}$$

*where $e_j :=$ let $\{\overline{x_{n_j} = \text{generate}}\}$ in $c_j(\overline{x_{n_j}})$, $j \in \{1, \ldots, k\}$ and $\overline{c_k}$ are all constructors of the program. Note that, by construction, $\Theta = \Gamma[x \mapsto c_i(\overline{x_n}), \overline{x_n \mapsto x_n}]$*

Now we are ready to establish the link between $\Downarrow_0$ and $\Downarrow_1$.

**Theorem 1.** *Let $P$ be a program, $e$ an expression, and $C$ the set of all constructors used in $P$. Then the following properties hold:*

*If $\Gamma : e \Downarrow_0 \Delta : c(\overline{x_n})$ , then $\Gamma^\otimes : e^\dagger \Downarrow_1 \Delta^\otimes : c(\overline{x_n})$.*
*If $\Gamma : e \Downarrow_0 \Delta : x$ , then $\forall c \in C : \Gamma^\otimes : e^\dagger \Downarrow_1 \Delta_1^\otimes : c(\overline{x_n})$ and $\Delta_1 = \Delta[x \mapsto c(\overline{x_n}), \overline{x_n \mapsto x_n}]$.*
*If $\Gamma^\otimes : e^\dagger \Downarrow_1 \Delta_1^\otimes : c(\overline{x_n})$, then $\Gamma : e \Downarrow_0 \Delta_1 : c(\overline{x_n})$ or $\Gamma : e \Downarrow_0 \Delta : x$ and $\Delta_1 = \Delta[x \mapsto c(\overline{x_n}), \overline{x_n \mapsto x_n}]$.*

*Proof (Central Idea).* Whenever the intermediate result of a sub computation in $\Downarrow_0$ is a free variable, the corresponding application of (Val) $\Gamma : x \Downarrow_0 \Gamma : x$ is replaced by the generator tree $gT(\Gamma, x, \Gamma[x \mapsto c(\overline{x_n}), \overline{x_n \mapsto x_n}], c(\overline{x_n}))$. The differences between the resulting heaps is effectively eliminated when the rule (Guess) is applied for $\Downarrow_0$. The remaining proof is concerned with showing that the mappings $^\otimes$ and $^\dagger$ correctly replace free variables by calls to the generator function.

According to this theorem, we can eliminate the rule (Guess), the distinction between *case* and *fcase* and also all conditions concerned with free variables in the remaining rules. Note, however, that for each free variable used in the proof tree for $\Downarrow_0$ one generator tree is used in the proof tree for $\Downarrow_1$. I.e., variable elimination does not imply loss of efficiency. Furthermore, another simplification is possible, as the next section shows.

### 3.2 Elimination of (VarCons)

After eliminating variables from the semantics, the rule (VarCons) is not needed anymore, because now it is a simple short-cut for applying rules (VarExp) directly followed by (Val). We only have to omit the restrictions, when (Val) and (VarExp) can be applied. We replace (VarExp) by the similar rule (Lookup) and refer to this new semantics without (VarCons) as $\downarrow$:

$$\text{(Lookup)}\ \frac{\Gamma \setminus \{(x, \Gamma(x))\} : \Gamma(x) \downarrow \Delta : v}{\Gamma : x \downarrow \Delta[x \mapsto v] : v}$$

We obtain the following theorem, which can easily be proven by a direct derivation by rule (Lookup) and (Val).

**Theorem 2.** $\Gamma : e \Downarrow_1 \Delta : v$ *iff* $\Gamma : e \downarrow \Delta : v$

### 3.3 Summarization of the Simplified Semantics

In the semantics considered so far, it was not necessary to normalize the arguments of *or*. We want to introduce sharing over non-determinism, for which the main idea is to handle *or* as a kind of constructor. Hence, it is necessary to normalize *or* expressions as well and introduce variables by means of a *let* expression for *or*.

**Definition 4 (Stronger Normalization $e^\star$).** *Stronger normalization of an expression e flattens the arguments of "*or*" by means of the mapping $e^\star$ which is defined inductively as follows:*

$$\begin{aligned}
x^\star &= x \\
s(\overline{x_n})^\star &= s(\overline{x_n}) \\
(e_1 \text{ or } e_2)^\star &= \text{let } \{x_1 = e_1^\star, x_2 = e_2^\star\} \text{ in } (x_1 \text{ or } x_2) \\
(\text{(f)case } e \text{ of } \{\overline{p_k \to e_k}\})^\star &= \text{(f)case } e^\star \text{ of } \{\overline{p_k \to e_k^\star}\} \\
(\text{let } \{\overline{x_k = e_k}\} \text{ in } e)^\star &= \text{let } \{\overline{x_k = e_k^\star}\} \text{ in } e^\star
\end{aligned}$$

It is easy to see that the stronger normalization conserves all values of the semantics. With this last simplification we obtain a condensed semantics which we have shown to be equivalent to the one defined in [1]. Since this semantics is the basis for our extensions, we summarize its rules again in Figure 3 and refer to it as $\downarrow$.

## 4 Extending the Semantics

### 4.1 Constructors Representing Non-determinism

There have been several attempts to define libraries for logical features for lazy functional programming, e.g. [12]. All these approaches encode the non-deterministic search as a kind of lazily constructed data structure, e.g. a list

$$\text{(Lookup)} \quad \frac{\Gamma \setminus \{(x, \Gamma(x))\} : \Gamma(x) \downarrow \Delta : v}{\Gamma : x \downarrow \Delta[x \mapsto v] : v}$$

$$\text{(Val)} \quad \Gamma : v \downarrow \Gamma : v \qquad \text{where } v \text{ is constructor-rooted}$$

$$\text{(Fun)} \quad \frac{\Gamma : \sigma(e) \downarrow \Delta : v}{\Gamma : f(\overline{x_n}) \downarrow \Delta : v} \qquad \text{where } f(\overline{y_n}) = e \in P \text{ and } \sigma = \{\overline{y_n \mapsto x_n}\}$$

$$\text{(Let)} \quad \frac{\Gamma[\overline{y_k \mapsto \sigma(e_k)}] : \sigma(e) \downarrow \Delta : v}{\Gamma : \text{let } \{\overline{x_k = e_k}\} \text{ in } e \downarrow \Delta : v} \qquad \text{where } \sigma = \{\overline{x_k \mapsto y_k}\} \text{ and } \overline{y_k} \text{ are fresh variables}$$

$$\text{(Or)} \quad \frac{\Gamma : x_i \downarrow \Delta : v}{\Gamma : x_1 \text{ or } x_2 \downarrow \Delta : v} \qquad \text{where } i \in \{1, 2\}$$

$$\text{(Select)} \quad \frac{\Gamma : e \downarrow \Delta : c(\overline{y_n}) \quad \Delta : \sigma(e_i) \downarrow \Theta : v}{\Gamma : \text{case } e \text{ of } \{\overline{p_k \to e_k}\} \downarrow \Theta : v} \qquad \text{where } p_i = c(\overline{x_n}) \text{ and } \sigma = \{\overline{x_n \mapsto y_n}\}$$

**Fig. 3.** Simplified Natural Semantics for Functional Logic Programs

(embedded in some backtracking monad). The context demands elements from this list (requires their evaluation) which relates to searching solutions within non-deterministic computations in the logical setting.

Our idea is similar in the sense that we employ a data structure representing the values computed in all non-deterministic computations. Since non-deterministic branching may result in an infinite search-space, this data structure may by infinite which is no problem in a lazy language. We just need to ensure that it is built only if demanded by the surrounding computation.

But what is an appropriate structure to represent the non-determinism of our semantics? Since it has to reflect the branching of non-determinism, a tree is most appropriate. The nodes in this structure (labeled with `OR`) relate to the evaluation of or expressions. Since we use binary ors in Flat Curry, we obtain a binary tree as well.[2] The leafs in this tree contain either values or failed computations.

*Example 3.* We consider the following Flat Curry program (`Zero`, `One`, and `Two` are constructors):

```
coin = Zero or One
add x y = case x of { Zero -> y;
                      One  -> case y of { Zero -> One;
                                          One  -> Two } }
main = add coin coin
```

Computing the semantics of `coin` yields the tree `OR [Zero,One]`. Now in the computation of `main` the result of `coin` has to be combined twice. We obtain `OR [OR [Zero,One], OR [One,Two]]`. But consider the definition

```
main = let { c = coin } in add c c
```

In a call-time choice semantics, like $\Downarrow_0$ and $\downarrow$ as well, it is important that there are only two results for this computation: `Zero` and `Two`. But how can we guarantee call-time choice when we twice combine the OR tree representation of `c` in `add`?

[2] Note however, that we present more general or nodes with a list of branches. This becomes useful when considering the fairness of search strategies, cf. Section 4.3.

We identify each OR by a special reference. In the example with sharing, this is `OR` $r_1$ `[OR` $r_1$ `[Zero,One], OR` $r_1$ `[One,Two]]` with the same reference $r_1$ for every `OR` node. When later the value is presented to the user or consumed by the context we can consider which branching was chosen for which reference and choose exactly the same branching for this reference everywhere within the OR structure. Especially, in the example the result `One` is not reachable anymore.

### 4.2 Sharing Across Non-determinism

In the semantics we replace the non-deterministic *or* by introducing an *internal constructor* OR which may not appear in any Flat Curry program. Later, we will introduce another internal constructor FAIL. To distinguish internal constructors from other constructors, we write them with all upper case letters.

(OR) $\Gamma : x_1 \text{ or } x_2 \Downarrow \Gamma : \text{OR } r\ [x_1, x_2]$ where $r$ fresh

$$\text{(Lift)}\ \frac{\Gamma : e \Downarrow \Delta : \text{OR } r\ [\overline{x_n}]}{\Gamma : \text{case } e \text{ of } \{bs\} \Downarrow \Delta[\overline{y_n \mapsto \text{case } x_n \text{ of } \{bs\}}] : \text{OR } r\ [\overline{y_n}]} \quad \text{where } \overline{y_n} \text{ fresh}$$

By replacing the rule (Or) by the rule (OR), we obtain a deterministic semantics. Beside its children (the variables $x_1$ and $x_2$), the introduced OR constructor also contains a reference which identifies it in more complex OR structures and which is used to realize call-time choice. The rule (Lift) is used to push computations inside an OR-branching, i.e. lift the OR constructor one level up.

But, how does this modification relate to the original semantics $\Downarrow$? The original semantics $\downarrow$ computes the head-normal form of the expression on the control. The same holds for the new semantics $\Downarrow$, but now also OR expressions are constructor terms. Hence, the semantics stops whenever the original semantics branches non-deterministically. To retrieve values in the original sense, we have to add a special computation yielding head-normal forms underneath OR nodes for the new semantics. We extend the relation $\Downarrow$ as follows:

$$\text{(Hnf-Val)}\quad \frac{\Gamma : e \Downarrow \Delta : c(\overline{x_n})}{\Gamma : \text{hnf } \rho\ e \Downarrow \Delta : c(\overline{x_n})} \quad \text{where } c \neq OR$$

$$\text{(Hnf-Choose)}\ \frac{\Gamma : e \Downarrow \Delta : \text{OR } r\ [\overline{x_n}] \quad \Delta : \text{hnf } \rho\ x_{\rho(r)} \Downarrow \Theta : v}{\Gamma : \text{hnf } \rho\ e \Downarrow \Theta : v} \quad \text{if } r \in \text{Dom}(\rho)$$

The *branching information* $\rho$ is a partial function from OR references to branching positions, i.e. the natural numbers (for binary ors: $\{1, 2\}$). It expresses which branch is to be selected for which OR reference. Later, it will be computed by the surrounding computation. For the moment, it is chosen arbitrarily and corresponds exactly to one non-deterministic computation of $\downarrow$. When the branching information $\rho$ is given, it is straight forward to prune a heap constructed in a $\Downarrow$-proof to a simple heap constructed by the corresponding $\downarrow$-proof. Such a pruning is defined next.

**Definition 5 (Heap Pruning** $cut(\rho, \Gamma)$**)**

$$cut(\rho, \Gamma)(x) = \begin{cases} cut(\rho, \Gamma)(x_{\rho(r)}) & , \textit{if } \Gamma(x) = OR\ r\ [\overline{x_n}] \\ \Gamma(x) & , \textit{otherwise} \end{cases}$$

*cut* is not well defined for all possible arguments $\rho$ and $\Gamma$. However, this is not a problem since we only use the definition to prove the existence of a heap with certain properties. Hence, *cut* will only be applied to appropriate arguments.

**Theorem 3 (Completeness of $\Downarrow$)**
*If* $\Gamma : e \downarrow \Delta : v$ *then there exist a heap* $\Delta'$ *and a sequence* $s$ *of branching updates such that* $\Gamma : hnf\ \rho\ e \Downarrow \Delta' : v$ *and* $\Delta = cut(\rho, \Delta')$ *where* $\rho := \emptyset s$.

*Proof (Central Idea).* The main difference between $\downarrow$ and $\Downarrow$ is the treatment of expressions $(x_1$ or $x_2)$. In $\downarrow$ such an expression is derived from the value of one of the $x_i$ whereas in $\Downarrow$ the expression directly yields the value OR $r\ [x_1, x_2]$. The key idea to construct a corresponding proof tree in $\Downarrow$ from one in $\downarrow$ is to update $\rho$ with $[r \mapsto i]$ whenever $x_i$ is chosen in $\downarrow$. Furthermore, the rule (Lift) of $\Downarrow$ makes sure that each case is finally applied to a head normal form according to the choice represented by $\rho$. The rest of the proof consists of showing that cut correctly maps between corresponding heaps.

We achieve sharing across non-determinism as the following example shows.

*Example 4 (Sharing in action).* In Example 1 we showed the importance of sharing across. As a simpler example for sharing across non-determinism, we consider the function `ins` which non-deterministically inserts an element to arbitrary position in a list:

```
ins x ys = case ys of {[]       -> x:[];
                       (a:as) -> (x:a:as) or (a:ins x as)}
```

Similar to our parser example, the evaluation of the element added to the list would be performed in every non-deterministic computation in most functional logic languages. To demonstrate how our new semantics shares these evaluation, we consider the following simple expression (let $\{x = \texttt{long}\}$ in `ins(x,[x])`), which computes only two results non-deterministically. Usually, the demands for different results of `ins` come from the context `ins` is used in. Here, we somewhat artificially force the demand by the context (&&(hnf $\rho$ $h$, hnf $\tau$ $h$)) where $h$ denotes the application of the `head` function to the above expression and $\rho, \tau$ contain branching information such that $\rho(1) = 1, \tau(1) = 2$. This keeps the example manageable while proving the main point.

A linearization of the proof tree for this example is presented in Figure 4. For space constraints and sake of readability, the computation is somewhat abbreviated. Constructors are not normalized and sub computations are only introduced, if a look up in the heap occurs.

### 4.3 Encapsulated Search

The goal of this section is to provide a primitive function which computes the internal branching information and represents the search space as a *search tree* according to the definition (cf. [5]):

```
data SearchTree a = Value a | Or [SearchTree a] | Fail
```

$\emptyset :$ let $\{x = long, i = ins(x, x : []), h = head(i), n = \text{hnf } \rho\ h, m = \text{hnf } \tau\ h\}$ in $\&\&(n, m)$
$\Gamma := [x \mapsto long, i \mapsto ins(x, x : []), h \mapsto head(i), n \mapsto \text{hnf } \rho\ h, m \mapsto \text{hnf } \tau\ h] : \&\&(n, m)$
$\Gamma :$ case $n$ of $\{T \to m, F \to F\}$
- $\Gamma : n$
- $\Gamma :$ hnf $\rho\ h$
  - $\Gamma : h$
  - $\Gamma : head(i)$
  - $\Gamma :$ case $i$ of $\{z{:}zs \to z\}$
    - $\Gamma : i$
    - $\Gamma : ins(x, x : [])$
    - $\Gamma :$ case $x : []$ of $\{[] \to x : [], a : as \to \text{let } \{l = ins(x, as)\} \text{ in } (x : a : as) \text{ or } (a : l)\}$
    - $\Gamma :$ let $\{l = ins(x, [])\}$ in $(x : x : [])$ or $(x : l)$
    - $\Gamma' := \Gamma[l \mapsto ins(x, [])] : (x : x : [])$ or $(x : l)$
    - $\Gamma' :$ OR 1 $[x : x : [], x : l]$
    - $\Gamma'' := \Gamma'[i \mapsto \text{OR } 1\ [x : x : [], x : l]] :$ OR 1 $[x : x : [], x : l]$
  - $\Delta := \Gamma''[y_1 \mapsto$ case $x : x : []$ of $\{z : zs \to z\}$,
    $y_2 \mapsto$ case $x : l$ of $\{z : zs \to z\}]$: OR 1 $[y_1, y_2]$
  - $\Delta' := \Delta[h \mapsto \text{OR } 1\ [y_1, y_2]] :$ OR 1 $[y_1, y_2]$
- $\Delta' :$ hnf $\rho\ y_{\rho(1)}$
  - $\Delta' : y_1$
  - $\Delta' :$ case $x : x : []$ of $\{z : zs \to z\}$
    - $\Delta' : x$
    - $\Delta' : long$
    - $\ldots$ — here the long deterministic evaluation takes place
    - $\Delta' : T$
    - $\Theta := \Delta''[x \mapsto T] : T$
  - $\Theta' := \Theta[y_1 \mapsto T] : T$
- $\Theta'' := \Theta'[n \mapsto T] : T$
- $\Theta'' : m$
- $\Theta'' :$ hnf $\tau\ h$
  - $\Theta'' : h$
  - $\Theta'' :$ OR 1 $[y_1, y_2]$
- $\Theta'' :$ hnf $\tau\ y_{\tau(1)}$
  - $\Theta'' : y_2$
  - $\Theta'' :$ case $x : l$ of $\{z : zs \to z\}$
    - $\Theta'' : x$ — here the result of the long computation is looked up in the heap
    - $\Theta'' : T$
  - $\Omega := \Theta''[y_1 \mapsto T] : T$
- $\Omega[m \mapsto T] : T$

**Fig. 4.** Semantics of Example 4 – Proof Tree presented in Linearized Form

The programmer should be able to access the search tree of a given expression via the function `searchTree :: a -> SearchTree a`, which should provide the tree in a lazy manner (cf. [5]) such that different search strategies like breadth first and depth first search can easily be formulated just by matching the tree structure. Although we use the same definition for a search tree, in comparison to [5] the approach in this paper provides sharing across non-determinism and employs a much simpler mechanism with just a single heap.

Before we can reach our goal, we have to extend the setting by information about failure. To do this, we add the following rule:

$$(\mathsf{Fail})\ \frac{\Gamma : e \Downarrow \Delta : c(\overline{x_n})}{\Gamma : \text{case } e \text{ of } \{\overline{p_k \to e_k}\} \Downarrow \Delta : \text{FAIL}} \quad \text{where for all } i \text{ with } 1 \leq i \leq k \text{ holds: } p_i \neq c(\overline{y_n}).$$

Note, that especially, since FAIL is an internal constructor, it cannot be a pattern of any case expression. Furthermore, FAIL is a valid result of an application of rule (Hnf-Val), as defined above. By adding rule (Fail), we do neither introduce new results other than FAIL nor lose existing results:

**Theorem 4**

*a) If $\Gamma : e \Downarrow \Delta : FAIL$ then there exists no $\Delta', v \neq FAIL$ such that $\Gamma : e \Downarrow \Delta' : v$.*
*b) If $\Gamma : e \Downarrow \Delta : v$ with $v \neq FAIL$ then there exists no $\Delta'$ such that $\Gamma : e \Downarrow \Delta' : FAIL$.*

*Proof*

a) The internal constructor FAIL is only introduced by the rule (Fail). This rule is applicable only if no rule of $\Downarrow$ can be applied.
b) The only rule that changes the result of a derivation is (Select). Since FAIL is an internal constructor there can be no pattern matching it in any program. Thus, FAIL is the final result whenever it appears.

So far we have presented how a head normal form can be computed if the branching information $\rho$ is already given. The next step is to define how this information is introduced. This is the responsibility of *encapsulation.* The first thing to do is to define how the hnf function should behave if the reference of a computed OR node is not contained in the given branching information $\rho$. In this case the evaluation to head normal form should stop:

$$(\mathsf{Hnf\text{-}Stop})\ \frac{\Gamma : e \Downarrow \Delta : \text{OR } r\ [\overline{x_n}]}{\Gamma : \text{hnf } \rho\ e \Downarrow \Delta : \text{OR } r\ [\overline{x_n}]} \qquad \text{if } r \notin \text{Dom}(\rho)$$

We are now ready to define encapsulated search. We introduce the function st which mostly translates internal (untyped) OR and FAIL constructors with call-time choice references to the typed search trees without references, as defined at the beginning of this section. There is only one more thing, st does: the OR references are added to the branching information for hnf:

$$(\textsf{St-Val})\ \frac{\Gamma : \text{hnf}\ \rho\ x \Downarrow \Delta : c(\overline{x_n})}{\Gamma : \text{st}\ \rho\ x \Downarrow \Delta\,[y \mapsto c(\overline{x_n})] : \text{Value}(y)}\quad \text{where } c \notin \{\text{OR}, \text{FAIL}\} \text{ and } y \text{ fresh}$$

$$(\textsf{St-Fail})\ \frac{\Gamma : \text{hnf}\ \rho\ x \Downarrow \Delta : \text{FAIL}}{\Gamma : \text{st}\ \rho\ x \Downarrow \Delta : \text{Fail}}$$

$$(\textsf{St-Or})\ \frac{\Gamma : \text{hnf}\ \rho\ x \Downarrow \Delta : \text{OR}\ r\ [\overline{x_n}]}{\Gamma : \text{st}\ \rho\ x \Downarrow \Delta\left[\overline{y_n \mapsto \text{st}\ (\rho \cup \{(r,n)\})\ x_n}, y \mapsto (y_1 : \ldots : y_n : [\,])^\star\right] : \text{Or}(y)}\quad \text{where } y, \overline{y_n} \text{ fresh}$$

As mentioned above, we provide the function `searchTree` which can now be defined such that each expression of the form `(searchTree x)` is replaced by $(\text{st}\ \emptyset\ x)$. Our final theorem states that the programmer is thus provided with a *complete* representation of the search which he can traverse according to his needs.

**Theorem 5 (Completeness of Representation).** *If* $\Gamma : e \downarrow \Delta : v$ *then there exist a heap* $\Delta'$ *and a case expression* $c :=$ case $x$ of $\{bs\}$ *such that* $\Gamma$ : let $\{x = \text{st}\ \emptyset\ e\}$ in $c \Downarrow \Delta' : v$.

*Proof (Central Idea).* By Theorem 3 there exists a sequence of updates $s$ such that if $\Gamma : e \downarrow \Delta : v$ then $\Gamma : \text{hnf}\ (\emptyset s)\ e \Downarrow \Delta' : v$. As the function st invokes the function hnf systematically with all possible alternatives such that the $i$th element beneath an Or constructor contains the evaluation of hnf with the update $[r \mapsto i]$ we need only to construct a case expression which chooses that $i$th element beneath Or while also eliminating the Value constructor at the end of the evaluation.

There are various reasons to employ encapsulated search. One is to express properties about all possible non-deterministic branches (e.g., their number) as given in the introduction. Other reasons are pruning the search space like done in the branch and bound method, to encapsulate non-determinism for the integration of external functions, which normally are defined on ground terms only, or to ensure that I/O operations do not perform conflicting actions. This latter use, called *complete encapsulation*, requires that arguments of the encapsulation's `Value` constructor are solutions, i.e. do not contain the internal constructors OR or FAIL. This can only be ensured by an evaluation to normal form. We include a simple example for computing a normal form mainly because the importance of complete encapsulation was convincingly discussed in [5].

*Example 5 (Complete Encapsulation).* We restrict ourselves to the simplest form of a recursive data structure. The extension to more complex structures is straight forward.

```
data Nat = Z | S Nat
nf Z = Z
nf (S x) = case nf x of {Z -> S Z; S y -> S (S y)}
```

Now the expression `(searchTree (nf x))` will compute a complete encapsulation of `x`, i.e. a search tree where the arguments of the `Value` constructor are *solutions*, they do not contain any internal constructor OR or FAIL. Note that `nf` copies the given data structure regardlessly. There are of course ways to do this more cleverly by defining a suitable primitive function. Also it could be convenient to define a polymorphic function which ensures the required property for any data structure, maybe using an overloaded function, like possible with Haskells type classes, or use `=..`-like term deconstruction methods as in Prolog.

Whether or not the encapsulation is complete, an important point about the presented encapsulation is that the result of the function `searchTree` is *generated lazily*. This implies that different search strategies can easily be defined on the level of the source language. E.g., for Curry we can easily define depth-first and breadth-first search, from which we only present the more interesting breadth-first search:

```
allValuesB :: SearchTree a -> [a]
allValuesB t = all [t]
  where all ts | null ts = []
               | otherwise = [x | Val x <- ts] ++
                             all [t | Or ts' <- ts,  t <- ts']
```

Also, a *fair* search can be implemented by an *action* `fair :: SearchTree a -> IO [a]`, which forks a thread for each child of an `Or` node. As such a search essentially realizes a *committed choice* by computing the results in arbitrary order, it destroys the purity of the encapsulations presented so far. In consequence, we regard this function as an I/O-Operation.

## 5 Related Work

There has been only one other approach prior to this work to formalize sharing deterministic computations across non-deterministic branches which is called bubbling [2]. Bubbling is defined as a graph rewriting technique and the call-time choice semantics is realized by manipulating the graph globally. We, in contrast, do only the local manipulation of lifting or-nodes and realize call-time choice by storing branching information and comparing or-references later on. This definitely speeds up deterministic computations in comparison, putting the whole overhead on branching. Since the implementation of bubbling is not yet finished, it remains difficult to judge which approach performs better in practice. The amount of sharing, however, is the same.

Our previous work [6] exhaustively discussed all aspects of encapsulation, but did not solve it as elegantly as the work presented here. Furthermore, sharing across non-determinism was not covered. However, it formulates a "wish list" for implementations of encapsulation, which is fully met by the presented approach. The general considerations of [6] also show that bubbling prohibits to reach the level of purity achieved here, because it executes a fair search beneath or-nodes prior to induce the non-determinism globally. This can be expected to increase the efficiency of a certain class of programs. But it can not lead to deterministic encapsulation as fair search is essentially a committed choice.

## 6 Conclusion

We have presented a new operational semantics for functional logic languages, like Curry [11]. It covers in a clear and seamless way two main problems of the integration of functional and logic languages: encapsulated search and sharing across non-determinism. Both are in our opinion key issues for the applicability of functional logic languages in practice. The key idea is to handle non-determinism as a (lazily constructed) data structure. We obtain a deterministic semantics in which search strategies, like depth-first and breadth-first search, can easily be defined as pure functions on top of the resulting `SearchTree` by the user. The up to now unreached purity of encapsulation enables new programming methods like the delaying of non-deterministic choices.

At the moment we have two implementations based on this semantics. The first is an interpreter, exactly implementing the operational semantics $\Downarrow$. It is very useful for analyzing how the operational semantics works and for computing small examples. We also developed a compiler for this semantics. The key feature of the implementation is the representation of the search tree as a data structure in the heap, which is not provided by the existing Curry implementation and makes the extension of these systems very difficult. Hence, we implemented a new compiler which translates Curry to Haskell (the Kiel Curry System, *KiCS*). It implements Curry's non-determinism by means of extended Haskell data structures providing special constructors for representing the internal OR and FAIL constructors of our semantics. The implementation handles encapsulated search and sharing across non-determinism similar to the semantics presented in this paper. In many practical applications this compiler has proven that the presented approach is feasible for general use.

## References

1. Albert, E., Hanus, M., Huch, F., Oliver, J., Vidal, G.: Operational semantics for declarative multi-paradigm languages. Journal of Symbolic Computation 40(1), 795–829 (2005)
2. Antoy, S., Brown, D., Chiang, S.-H.: On the correctness of bubbling. In: Pfenning, F. (ed.) RTA 2006. LNCS, vol. 4098, pp. 35–49. Springer, Heidelberg (2006)
3. Antoy, S., Echahed, R., Hanus, M.: A needed narrowing strategy. Journal of the ACM 47(4), 776–822 (2000)
4. Antoy, S., Hanus, M.: Overlapping rules and logic variables in functional logic programs. In: Etalle, S., Truszczyński, M. (eds.) ICLP 2006. LNCS, vol. 4079, pp. 87–101. Springer, Heidelberg (2006)
5. Braßel, B., Hanus, M., Huch, F.: Encapsulating non-determinism in functional logic computations. Journal of Functional and Logic Programming 2004(6) (2004)
6. Braßel, B., Huch, F.: Translating Curry to Haskell. In: WCFLP 2005, pp. 60–65. ACM Press, New York (2005)
7. Braßel, B., Huch, F.: On the tighter integration of functional and logic programming. Technical Report 0710, Institute of Computer Science, CAU Kiel (2007)
8. Dios, J., López-Fraguas, F.J.: Elimination of extra variables from functional logic programs. In: Lucio, P., Orejas, F. (eds.) PROLE 2006, pp. 121–135 (2006)
9. González-Moreno, J.C., Hortalá-González, M.T., López-Fraguas, F.J., Rodríguez-Artalejo, M.: An approach to declarative programming based on a rewriting logic. Journal of Logic Programming 40, 47–87 (1999)

10. Hanus, M., Antoy, S., Braßel, B., Engelke, M., Höppner, K., Koj, J., Niederau, P., Sadre, R., Steiner, F.: PAKCS: The Portland Aachen Kiel Curry System (2006), Available at `http://www.informatik.uni-kiel.de/~pakcs/`
11. Hanus, M. (ed): Curry: An integrated functional logic language (vers. 0.8.2) (2006), Available at `http://www.informatik.uni-kiel.de/~curry`
12. Hinze, R.: Prolog's control constructs in a functional setting - axioms and implementation. International Journal of Foundations of Computer Science 12(2), 125–170 (2001)
13. Launchbury, J.: A natural semantics for lazy evaluation. In: POPL 1993, pp. 144–154. ACM Press, New York (1993)
14. Lux, W.: Implementing encapsulated search for a lazy functional logic language. In: Middeldorp, A. (ed.) FLOPS 1999. LNCS, vol. 1722, pp. 100–113. Springer, Heidelberg (1999)
15. Lux, W., Kuchen, H.: An efficient abstract machine for Curry. In: Beiersdörfer, K., Engels, G., Schäfer, W. (eds.) Informatik 1999 — Annual meeting of the German Computer Science Society (GI), pp. 390–399. Springer, Heidelberg (1999)

# Scalable Simulation of Cellular Signaling Networks

Vincent Danos[1,4,*], Jérôme Feret[3], Walter Fontana[1,2], and Jean Krivine[5]

[1] Plectix Biosystems
[2] CNRS, Université Denis Diderot
[3] Harvard Medical School
[4] École Normale Supérieure
[5] École Polytechnique

**Abstract.** Given the combinatorial nature of cellular signalling pathways, where biological agents can bind and modify each other in a large number of ways, concurrent or agent-based languages seem particularly suitable for their representation and simulation [1,2,3,4]. Graphical modelling languages such as $\kappa$ [5, 6, 7, 8], or the closely related BNG language [9,10,11,12,13,14], seem to afford particular ease of expression. It is unclear however how such models can be implemented.[1] Even a simple model of the EGF receptor signalling network can generate more than $10^{23}$ non-isomorphic species [5], and therefore no approach to simulation based on enumerating species (beforehand, or even on-the-fly) can handle such models without sampling down the number of potential generated species.

We present in this paper a radically different method which does not attempt to count species. The proposed algorothm uses a representation of the system together with a super-approximation of its 'event horizon' (all events that may happen next), and a specific correction scheme to obtain exact timings. Being completely local and not based on any kind of enumeration, this algorithm has a per event time cost which is independent of (i) the size of the set of generable species (which can even be infinite), and (ii) independent of the size of the system (ie, the number of agent instances). We show how to refine this algorithm, using concepts derived from the classical notion of causality, so that in addition to the above one also has that the even cost is depending (iii) only logarithmically on the size of the model (ie, the number of rules). Such complexity properties reflect in our implementation which, on a current computer, generates about $10^6$ events per minute in the case of the simple EGF receptor model mentioned above, using a system with $10^5$ agents.

---

* This research was partly supported by the NIH/NIGMS grant R43GM81319-01.

[1] Eg, from Ref. [15, p. 4]: "programs implementing these methods include StochSim, BioNetGen, and Moleculizer. However, at the present time only a part of the entire EGFR network can be analyzed using these programs".

Z. Shao (Ed.): APLAS 2007, LNCS 4807, pp. 139–157, 2007.

## 1 Introduction

An important thread of work in systems biology concerns the modelling of the intra-cellular signalling networks triggered by extra-cellular stimuli (such as hormones and growth factors). Such networks determine growth, differentiation, and other cell responses. Many pathological states and diseases are now traced down to subtle dysfunctions of components in those noteworks. Accordingly there is a increasing need for fine-grained, executable, and quantitative descriptions of those pathways [16].

Early on, Regev et al. [1, 2, 3] have proposed to describe those complex networks using $\pi$-calculus [17], a minimal language for concurrent systems. Variants emphasizing different types of biological processes have been put forward since [18,19,20,4,21,22]. While the syntactic choices differ, they share a same concern, namely to rescue the structure-less language of chemical reactions, and to convey the combinatorics of real biological networks in a natural and executable notation. We shall use here an agent-based language called $\kappa$ [8,7,6,5]. The agents we consider have internal states, accommodating protein post-translational modifications. They can also bind each other at certain specific sites called 'domains', allowing for a direct representation of protein assembly into so-called 'complexes'. This simple graph-rewriting framework naturally captures the domain level description of protein-protein interactions [23].

An example of a signalling model written in $\kappa$ is that of the EGF receptor signalling network presented in Ref. [5]. This simple model generates more than $10^{23}$ distinct species, and that places specific demands on a simulation algorithm. Any simulation method based on enumerating species beforehand, or on-the-fly, has to sample down the combinatorics of such models to make them amenable to species counting. This is the approach followed by the current implementations of the BNG language which attempts to generate species beforehand, as well as by the recent SPIM (an implementation of stochastic $\pi$-calculus) and beta-binders (another process language for representing biological systems) implementations which register species on-the-fly [24, 25]. It is also the route taken by differential models which ignore altogether the structure of agents and so don't have the advantage of a rule-based or contextual semantics in the first place.

We propose here a radically different method which does not attempt to count species, and works even if there is an infinite number of them. The obtained algorithm has a *per event cost* which does not depend on the number of distinct species, nor does it depend on the number of agent instances in the system. The next section gives a preliminary description of the algorithm. (Some of the relevant notions only find a complete definition later in the text.) We must hasten to say that our method is not unconditionally faster, and enumeration-based techniques, including differential equations, when they apply, that is to say when the combinatorial complexity is limited, will in general be more efficient. However for the particular application to signalling systems where the combinatorial complexity makes enumeration unfeasible, only such an approach can take the complexity upfront. The simulation algorithm was implemented and tested on the EGFR example model. Using $10^5$ initial agent instances of various types, it takes 30' to run that model for a total of $10^7$ events on an ordinary computer. Thus this methodological route, which can non doubt still be perfected, seems to make hitherto unfeasibly complex cellular signalling models amenable to simulation.

## 2 Preliminaries

We recall first the generic derivation of a continuous time Markov chain from a labelled transition system. In the particular case of flat chemical reactions (aka multiset rewriting, or equivalently Petri nets) this derivation has come to be known as Gillespie's algorithm [26, 27, 28]. This method is widely used to simulate the kinetics of coupled elementary chemical reactions. The idea is to assign to a reaction a probability which is proportional to the number of its instances (or matches), while the frequency at which events are produced is obtained from the total number of rule instances.

### 2.1 Exponential Distributions

We start with a few definitions relevant to exponential distributions, which we will need when considering the temporal aspects of the simulation algorithm.

For $a > 0$, $n \in \mathbb{N}$, $t \in \mathbb{R}^+$ define:

$$\exp_{a,n}(t) = ae^{-at}(at)^n/n! \tag{1}$$

**Lemma 1.** *For all $n \in \mathbb{N}$, $\exp_{a,n}$ is a probability density on $\mathbb{R}^+$ with complementary cumulative distribution function $H_{a,n}(t) := (\sum_0^n (at)^i/i!)e^{-at}$.*

*Proof.* $H_{a,n}$ is clearly decreasing and continuous in $t$; $H_{a,n}(0) = 1$, $H_{a,n}(\infty) = 0$; so $H_{a,n}$ is a complementary distribution function, and since $\exp_{a,n} = -\frac{d}{dt}H_{a,n}(t)$, $\exp_{a,n}$ is the density associated to $H_{a,n}$.

Since $H_{a,n}$ is increasing with $n$, the associated probability shifts to the right when $n$ increases (see Fig. 1).

**Lemma 2.** *Define inductively on $f$ in $\mathbb{N}^R$ (equipped with the product ordering):*

$$H_{a,f}(t) = \textstyle\sum_{r\in R} \frac{f(r)}{F} H_{a,f-\mathbf{1}_r}(t) + e^{-at}\frac{(at)^F}{F!}$$

*with $a > 0$, $\mathbf{1}_r \in \mathbb{N}^R$ the indicator function of $\{r\}$, and $F := \sum_{r\in R} f(r)$. (By convention all terms including an $f(r) < 0$ are supposed to be zero.)*

*One has $H_{a,f} = H_{a,F}$.*

*Proof.* The definition above is a well-formed inductive definition on the product ordering on $\mathbb{N}^R$ and therefore uniquely defines $H_{a,f}$. Now, defining $G_{a,f}(t) := H_{a,f}(t) - (\sum_0^F (at)^i/i!)e^{-at}$, it is easy to see that

$$G_{a,f}(t) = \textstyle\sum_{r\in R} \frac{f(r)}{F} G_{a,f-\mathbf{1}_r}(t)$$

and since $G_{a,f}(t) \equiv 0$ is a (unique) solution the conclusion follows. □

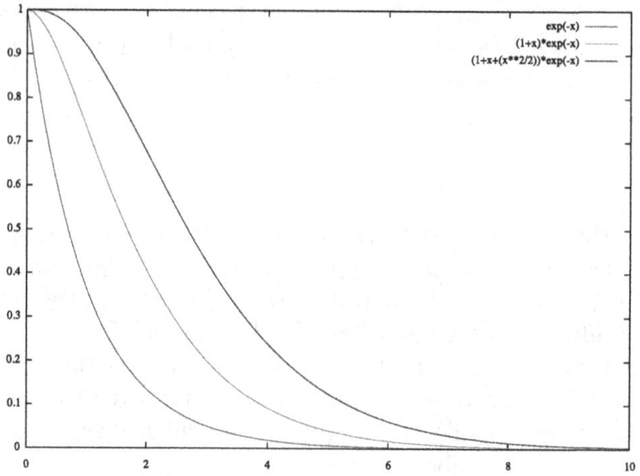


**Fig. 1.** Shifted exponential distributions: $H_{1,0}$, $H_{1,1}$, and $H_{1,2}$. The base curve $H_{1,0}$ is the usual exponential distribution with density $\exp_a(t) = ae^{-at} = \exp_{a,0}(t)$.

So $H_{a,f}$ is just a complicated way to write $H_{a,F}$; this will be used later where $f$ will map a reaction $s$ to $f(s)$ the number of clashes on an $s$ selection attempt as defined below ($F$ is then the total number of clashes).

## 2.2 The Basic CTMC Construction

Usually one sees a labelled transition system (LTS) as an $R$-indexed family of binary relations $\rightarrow_r$ on the state space $X$. But in a quantitative setting it is important to know in how many distinct ways one can go from a state $x$ to another one $x'$, since the more, the likelier.[2] We will therefore start with a slight variant of LTSs that represent events explicitly and allows for counting them.

Suppose given a state space $X$, a finite set of labels $R$, a rate map $\tau$ from $R$ to $\mathbb{R}^+$, and for each $r \in R$, and $x \in X$, a finite set of $r$-*events* $\mathcal{E}(x,r)$, and an *action* map $\_ \cdot x$ from $\mathcal{E}(x,r)$ to $X$. The action map specifies the effect of an event on the state $x$. We write $\mathcal{E}(x)$ for the (finite) disjoint sum $\sum_{r \in R} \mathcal{E}(x,r)$ which we will call the *event horizon.*

One can think of $r$ as a reaction or a rewrite rule, of $\tau(r)$ as a relative measure of the rule rate, and of an event $e \in \mathcal{E}(x,r)$ as a particular application of $r$.

Define the *activity* of $r$ at $x$ as the quantity $\mathbf{a}(x,r) := \tau(r)|\mathcal{E}(x,r)|$, and the *global activity* at $x$ as $\mathbf{a}(x) := \sum_{r \in R} \mathbf{a}(x,r) \geq 0$.

Supposing $\mathbf{a}(x) > 0$, the probability at $x$ that the next event is $e \in \mathcal{E}(x,r)$, and the subsequent time advance are given by:

$$p(x,e) := \tau(r)/\mathbf{a}(x) \tag{2}$$

[2] An example is $r_1 = A \rightarrow$, $r_2 = A, B \rightarrow A$, then $A, nB \rightarrow_{r_1} nB$ and $A, nB \rightarrow_{r_2} A, (n-1)B$, but the latter can happen in $n$ different ways, whereas the former can happen in only one way. As a consequence $A$ is protected from erasure by $r_1$ as long as there is a significant number of $B$s.

$$p(\delta t(x) > t) := e^{-\mathbf{a}(x)t} \tag{3}$$

The probability that the next event will be an $r$-event is $\mathbf{a}(x, r)/\mathbf{a}(x)$, which justifies calling $\mathbf{a}(x, r)$ the activity of $r$. The time advance $\delta t(x)$ is an exponential random variable with parameter $\mathbf{a}(x)$, ie has density $\exp_{\mathbf{a}(x)}$. Note that the time advance is independent from the actual event $e$ that took place and only depends on $x$. Therefore, the lower the activity, the slower the system, and in the limit where the activity is zero, ie $\mathbf{a}(x) = 0$, the time advance is infinite, which means that the system is deadlocked. This implies among other things that the right unit of measure for performance of a simulation algorithm is the cost of an event, not the cost of a unit of simulation time. Indeed how many events are needed for a time unit to pass depends on the activity.

The above data $(X, R, \mathcal{E}, \tau, \cdot)$ defines a continuous time Markov chain (CTMC) with values in $X$, where the time advance is as in (3) above and:

$$p(x \to x') = \sum_{r \in R} \sum_{\{e \in \mathcal{E}(x,r) | e \cdot x = x\}} p(x, e)$$

### 2.3 Implementation by Conditioning

Let us write $rand(A, f)$ for the random variable which returns an element of the set $A$ according to the unique probability on $A$ which has density $f$ wrt to the uniform one. That definition will only be used for sets $A$ with a canonical structure of measurable space that evidently carries a uniform distribution.

One gets a straightforward implementation $P(x)$ of the CTMC above as a random function that takes as an input $x$ the current state, and returns a selected event $e$ and a time advance $\delta t$:

$$\begin{aligned} r &:= rand(R, \lambda r.\mathbf{a}(x, r)/\mathbf{a}(x)); \\ e &:= rand(\mathcal{E}(x, r), 1); \\ \delta t &:= rand(\mathbb{R}^+, \exp_{\mathbf{a}(x)}) \end{aligned}$$

The question one wishes to address is how to implement this Markov chain efficiently when the underlying labelled transition system is generated by a $\kappa$ model. In that case $x$ stands for the current system of agents, including their bindings and internal states, and an event $x \to_r x'$ corresponds to the application of a graph-rewriting rule $r$ to $x$ (which kind of graph rewriting we are using is not important at this stage of the discussion). That brings additional structure to the transition system. Specifically each rule $r$ has a left hand side that decomposes as a multiset of connected components $C(r)$, and the set $\mathcal{E}(x, r)$, ie the set of the instances of $r$ in $x$, can be naturally seen as a subset of the Cartesian product $\times_{c \in C(r)}[c, x]$, where $[c, x]$ is the set of matches for $c$ in $x$. Depending on how a match is defined, $\mathcal{E}(x, r)$ may be a proper subset of the above product and therefore contain pseudo-events that do not correspond to the application of a rule.[3] Using this approximate decomposition of the event horizon $\mathcal{E}(x)$ makes it

[3] In our specific case one requires that two distinct connected components in $C(r)$ be matched to disjoint set of agents in $x$. For instance a rule $A, A \to B$ will mean that one must pick in $x$ two distinct $A$s in $x$. In categorical terms the 'disjoint sum' is only a weak sum in the category of graphs and graph embeddings we are considering.

possible to handle states and events locally, and at the same time preserves the CTMC semantics above as we will show now.

Suppose given for each $x$, and $r$ a finite $\mathcal{E}'(x,r) \supseteq \mathcal{E}(x,r)$ (and therefore $\mathbf{a}'(x,r) \geq \mathbf{a}(x,r)$). We can define an alternative implementation $Q(x)$:

$$\begin{aligned}
&[0]\ f := 0;\\
&[1]\ r := rand(R, \lambda r.\mathbf{a}'(x,r)/\mathbf{a}'(x));\\
&[2]\ e := rand(\mathcal{E}'(x,r), 1);\\
&[3]\ if(e \notin \mathcal{E}(x,r))(f := f+1; goto\ [1]);\\
&[4]\ \delta t := rand(\mathbb{R}^+, \exp_{\mathbf{a}(x),f})
\end{aligned}$$

Just as $P(x)$, $Q(x)$ defines a distribution on $\mathcal{E}(x,r)$ since pseudo-events are rejected at step [3]. We call such a rejection a *clash*. This new procedure also defines a time distribution at step [4], the choice of which depends on $f$ the number of successive clashes.

The probability to fail at step [3] given that $r$ was chosen at step [1] is given by $\epsilon_r(x) = |\mathcal{E}'(x,r) \setminus \mathcal{E}(x,r)|/|\mathcal{E}'(x,r)|$. Define $\epsilon(x) := \max_{s\in R} \epsilon_s(x)$. If $\epsilon(x) = 0$ then no clash can happen, and $P(x)$ and $Q(x)$ are clearly equivalent. In fact this is always true:

**Proposition 1.** *For all $x \in X$, $P(x)$ and $Q(x)$ generate the same probability distribution on $\mathcal{E}(x)$ (next event), and $\mathbb{R}^+$ (time advance). The expected number of clashes for $Q(x)$ is bounded by $\epsilon(x)/(1-\epsilon(x))^2$.*

*Proof.* The probability to draw a rule $s$ at step [4] and then fail at step [3] is $(\mathbf{a}'(x,s)/\mathbf{a}'(x))\epsilon_s(x)$. Therefore the probability to eventually obtain an event in $\mathcal{E}(x,r)$ is:[4]

$$\begin{aligned}
&(1-\epsilon_r(x))\frac{\mathbf{a}'(x,r)}{\mathbf{a}'(x)} \cdot \frac{1}{(1-\sum_{s\in R}(\mathbf{a}'(x,s)/\mathbf{a}'(x))\epsilon_s(x))}\\
&= \frac{(1-\epsilon_r(x))\mathbf{a}'(x,r)}{\mathbf{a}'(x) - \sum_{s\in R}\mathbf{a}'(x,s)\epsilon_s(x)} = \frac{(1-\epsilon_r(x))\mathbf{a}'(x,r)}{\sum_{s\in R}\mathbf{a}'(x,s)(1-\epsilon_s(x))}
\end{aligned}$$

and since $\mathbf{a}'(x,s)(1-\epsilon_s(x)) = \mathbf{a}(x,s)$, the above probability is $\mathbf{a}(x,r)/\mathbf{a}(x)$ which is the same as the one defined by $P(x)$.[5]

Hence the $Q(x)$ selection scheme is equivalent to that of $P(x)$ for the next event, whatever the values of $\epsilon_r$ are. Of course its expected time of convergence will depend on those values. The probability of converging after exactly $n$ clashes is:

---

[4] the left term represent the successful drawing of $r$ at step 1, and of an e in $\mathcal{E}(x,r)$ at step 2, and the right one includes all possible sequences of failures according to the usual formula $1/(1-x) = \sum x^n$.

[5] A limit case being when for all $s$, $\epsilon_s(x) = 1$, or equivalently $\mathbf{a}'(x) = \sum \mathbf{a}'(x,r)\epsilon_r(x)$ (which prevents the above computation to work, see second line above), or yet equivalently when the real activity $\mathbf{a}(x)$ is zero. In this case the protocol will loop forever never finding a legitimate event, since there is none. Concretely, one stops the simulation after a certain number of successive clashes, and it works well. Such precisions are necessary since this case will happen in practice.

$$(\sum_s \epsilon_s(x)\mathbf{a}'(x,s)/\mathbf{a}'(x))^n(\sum_s(1-\epsilon_s(x))\mathbf{a}'(x,s)/\mathbf{a}'(x)) \leq$$
$$\epsilon(x)^n(\sum_s(1-\epsilon_s(x))\mathbf{a}'(x,s)/\mathbf{a}'(x)) \leq \epsilon(x)^n$$

So the expected number of clashes is bounded by $\sum_n n\epsilon(x)^n = \epsilon(x)/(1-\epsilon(x))^2$.

To see that $Q(x)$ has also the time advance right, let us start with the case of a single reaction with clash probability $\epsilon$ in a given state. In this case the real activity at $x$ is $\mathbf{a}'(x)(1-\epsilon)$, so what we need to prove is:

$$\sum_n \epsilon^n(1-\epsilon)H_{\mathbf{a}\ (x),n}(t) = e^{-\mathbf{a}\ (x)t(1-\epsilon)}$$

or equivalently:

$$\begin{aligned} e^{\mathbf{a}\ (x)t}\sum_n \epsilon^n H_{\mathbf{a}\ (x),n}(t) &= e^{-\mathbf{a}\ (x)t\epsilon}/(1-\epsilon) \\ \sum_n \epsilon^n \sum_{0\leq i\leq n}(\mathbf{a}'(x)t)^i/i! &= e^{-\mathbf{a}\ (x)t\epsilon}/(1-\epsilon) \end{aligned}$$

Developing the right hand side as a power series of $\epsilon$ gives:

$$e^{-\mathbf{a}\ (x)t\epsilon}/(1-\epsilon) = (\sum_i \frac{(\mathbf{a}'(x)t)^i}{i!}\epsilon^i)(\sum_j \epsilon^j) = \sum_n(\sum_{0\leq i\leq n}\frac{(\mathbf{a}'(x)t)^i}{i!})\epsilon^n$$

So the time advance is correct. The case of many reactions follows easily from the same computation and Lemma 2. □

We have obtained a flexible scheme that we will use to 'pad' the event horizon and make random selections and updates of events feasible. We now turn to a definition of $\kappa$ including a description of its LTS semantics (from which the CTMC semantics follows as in the general case above); we will then proceed to the detailed definition of the simulation algorithm; and finish with a discussion of the complexity aspects of the algorithm.

## 3 $\kappa$

We have made a certain number of simplifications to the actual language to keep the notations and definitions simple.

### 3.1 Agents and Interfaces

Atomic elements of the calculus are called *agents* $(a, a', \ldots)$ and represent basic Lego pieces of the system. The grammar describing an agent is given Fig. ??. Each agent has a *name* and an *interface*, that is to say a set of *interaction sites* $(x, y, z, \ldots)$ where each site is equipped with an *internal state* $\iota$, and a *link state* $\lambda$. The former is used to denote post-translational modifications and sometimes cellular locations.

A site may have an unknown link state ($\lambda = ?$), or be connected to an undetermined site ($\lambda = \_$), or be connected via a particular edge ($\lambda = \alpha \in \mathcal{L}$), or be free ($\lambda = \epsilon$). The associated ordering is given Fig. ??.

Let *Site*$(a)$ denote the sites of the agent $a$, *Intf*$(a)$ its interface, and *Name*$(a)$ its name. We suppose given a *signature* function $\Sigma$ which maps an agent's name

$$
\begin{array}{lll}
a & ::= N(\sigma) & \text{(Agent)} \\
N & ::= A, B, \cdots \in \mathcal{N} & \text{(Name)} \\
\sigma & ::= \varnothing \mid x^{\iota,\lambda}, \sigma & \text{(Interface)} \\
\iota & ::= \epsilon & \text{(Any state)} \\
 & \mid m \in \mathcal{I} & \text{(Internal state)} \\
\lambda & ::= \epsilon & \text{(Free site)} \\
 & \mid ? & \text{(Bound or free site)} \\
 & \mid \_ & \text{(Semi link)} \\
 & \mid \alpha, \beta, \cdots \in \mathcal{L} & \text{(link)}
\end{array}
$$

**Fig. 2.** Syntax of agents, assuming 3 disjoint sets of agent names $\mathcal{N}$, link names $\mathcal{L}$, and internal states $\mathcal{I}$

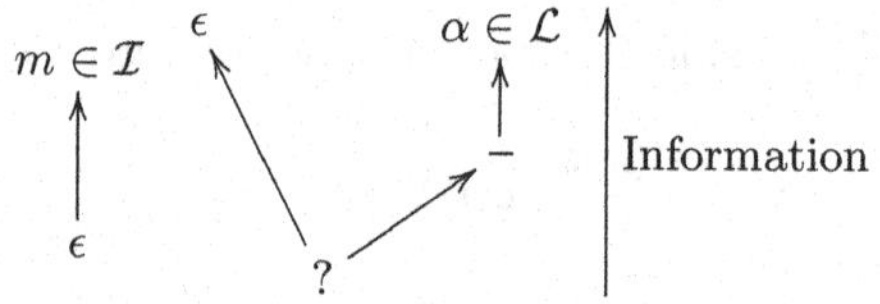


**Fig. 3.** Ordering internal and link state values

to the set of sites its interface may contain and we assume that $Site(a) \subseteq \Sigma(Name(a))$.

An agent $a$ is said *partial* if its interface is partial, ie:
- there exists $x^{\iota,\lambda} \in Intf(a)$ such that $\iota = \epsilon$ or $\lambda \in \{?, \_\}$.
- or $Site(a) \subset \Sigma(Name(a))$.

Note that the form $A(x^{\epsilon,?}, \sigma)$ is equivalent (in terms of potential interactions) to the simpler form $A(\sigma)$ since no information is required concerning the states of site $x$. We shall thus consider agents up to the following equivalence:

$$
\begin{array}{ll}
A(x^{\iota,\lambda}, y^{\iota',\lambda'}, \sigma) & \equiv A(y^{\iota',\lambda'}, x^{\iota,\lambda}, \sigma) \\
A(x^{\epsilon,?}, \sigma) & \equiv A(\sigma)
\end{array}
$$

for $x$, $y$ in $\Sigma(A)$.

### 3.2 Solutions and Embeddings

We use the chemical term *solution* to denote a syntactical term of the form:

$$S ::= \varnothing \mid a, S \text{ (Solution)}$$

Solutions are considered as multisets of agents and are thus taken up to congruence $a, S \equiv S, a$. In the following we will consider them as sets of occurrences of agents and by convention we use $a, b, \cdots \in S$ to denote occurrences of agents in a solution $S$. In particular $a \neq a'$ indicates different occurrences of agents even though $a$ may be syntactically equal to $a'$. We will write $(a, x) \in S$ to mean $a \in S$ with $x \in Intf(a)$.

Say a solution $S$ is *well formed* if each link name in $S$ occurs exactly twice. Say a well formed solution is *partial* if it contains partial agents, and *complete* otherwise.

Link names $\alpha$, $\beta$, ... are implicitly bound in all solutions, and we extend the equivalence on agents, and consider two solutions differing only in the names of their edges and in the position of their agents to be equivalent. As a result solutions may be seen as (site) graphs, and we shall use graph-theoretic terminology freely. We give Fig. 4 an example of the graphical notation we commonly use.

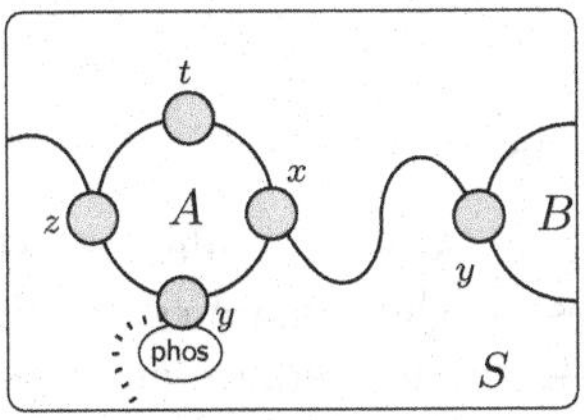


**Fig. 4.** Graphical representation of the solution $S = A(x^{\alpha}, y^{\mathsf{phos},?}, z^{-}, t), B(y^{\alpha})$. The dotted semi edge indicates that the link state of site $y$ is unknown, while the solid semi edge shows that site $z$ is bound in the context. Internal state phos denotes a phosphorylated site.

A map $\phi$ between solutions $S$ and $T$ is an *embedding* if for all $a, b \in S$:

$$\begin{array}{l} \phi(a) = \phi(b) \Rightarrow a = b \\ Name(a) = Name(\phi(a)) \\ Site(a) \subseteq Site(\phi(a)) \\ x^{\iota,\lambda} \in Intf(a) \Rightarrow x^{\iota\ ,\lambda} \in Intf(\phi(a)) \text{ with } \iota \leq \iota', \lambda \leq \lambda' \end{array}$$

where $\leq$ denotes the partial order induced by the semi lattices given Fig. ??.

Given a possibly partial map between solutions $S$ and $T$, we write $cod(\phi)$ for the sets of occurrences of sites in the image or codomain of $\phi$ in $T$, and $dom(\phi)$ for those in its domain.

We say an embedding $\phi$ is an *iso* if it is bijective on nodes, and $\phi^{-1}$ is also an embedding. Two embeddings $\phi_1$, $\phi_2$ between $S$ and $T$ are said to be equivalent if there is an iso $\psi$ from $S$ to $S$ such that $\phi_1 = \psi\phi_2$, and one writes $[\phi]$ for $\phi$'s equivalence class. Finally we write $[S, T]$ for all embedding of $S$ in $T$.

We give an example of an embedding Fig. 5. Contrary to the usual notion of graph morphism, one asks embeddings to 'reflect' edges, ie a free site can only be mapped to a free one. Another unusual fact is the following simple rigidity lemma which is key for the control of the simulation complexity:

**Lemma 3 (rigidity).** *If $S$ is connected, a non-empty partial map $\phi : S \to T$ extends to at most one embedding of $S$ into $T$.*

So if $S$ is connected, the number of embeddings of $S$ in $T$ is linear in $|T|$, and so is the cost of verifying the existence of an embedding, given a particular 'anchor' agent or site in $T$.

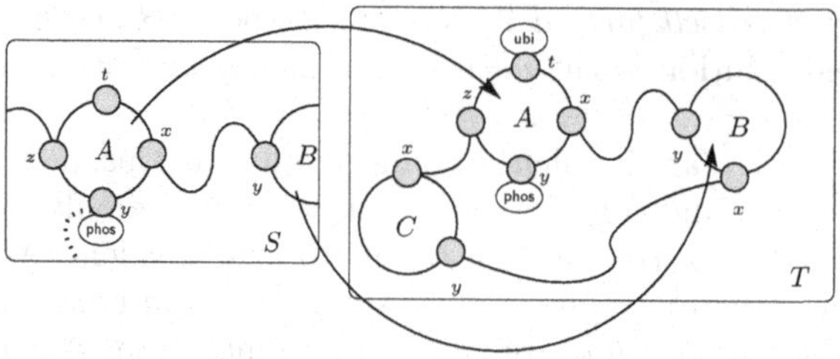


**Fig. 5.** Solution $S$ embeds into $T$: note that site $t$ on $A$ has to stay free in the codomain of the embedding

### 3.3 Rules and Transitions

In contrast with process algebras where rules are simple and behaviours are mostly encoded in the processes, the dynamics of solutions in $\kappa$ is expressed in rewriting rules. Rules can test the immediate environment of an agent, whereas in a process approach one would have to encode that exploration in the participating processes, (although a translation from $\kappa$ to $\pi$-calculus is possible [7, 6]).

One could use double push-out methods to describe our rewrite rules, but we have found more convenient to define a rule as a pair $\langle S, act\rangle$ where $S$ is a solution, and *act* is a map from agents in $S$ to sets of *actions* subject to certain conditions explained below.

The actions one may perform on agents are:[6]

- $\mathsf{set}(x, m)$ to set the internal state of site $x$ to $m \in \mathcal{I}$,
- $\mathsf{bnd}(x, \alpha)$ to set the link state of site $x$ to $\alpha$,
- and $\mathsf{brk}(x, \alpha)$ to set the link state of site $x$ to $\epsilon$.

Given a rule $r = \langle S, act\rangle$, one says:

- $(a, x) \in S$ is *ι-modified* by $r$ if $\mathsf{set}(x, m) \in act(a)$ for some $m$;
- $(a, x) \in S$ is *λ-modified* by $r$ if $\mathsf{bnd}(x, \alpha)$ or $\mathsf{brk}(x, \alpha) \in act(a)$ for some $\alpha$.

One says $(a, x) \in S$ is modified by $r$ if it is either $\iota$-modified, or $\lambda$-modified.

An action map *act* on $S$ is said to be *valid* if:

- every $(a, x) \in S$ is $\iota$-modified at most once and

$$\mathsf{set}(x, m) \in act(a) \Rightarrow x^{\iota,\lambda} \in \mathit{Intf}(a),\ \iota \neq \epsilon$$

- every $(a, x) \in S$ is $\lambda$-modified at most once and

$$\mathsf{bnd}(x, \alpha) \in act(a) \Rightarrow x^{\iota,\epsilon} \in \mathit{Intf}(a)\ ,\ \exists!(b, y) \in S : \mathsf{bnd}(y, \alpha) \in act(b)\ ,\ \alpha \notin S,\ a \neq b$$
$$\mathsf{brk}(x, \alpha) \in act(a) \ \Rightarrow x^{\iota,\alpha} \in \mathit{Intf}(a)\ ,\ \exists!(b, y) \in S : \mathsf{brk}(y, \alpha) \in act(b),\ a \neq b$$

Well formedness of solutions is evidently preserved by valid actions.

---

[6] The full language also allows the deletion and creation of agents, but that complicates the presentation of the operational semantics. Eg if one erases an agent then one has to erase all the links it shares with its neighbours. We have refrained from presenting the full set of actions since the simulation strategy can be discussed just as well in this simpler 'mass-preserving' fragment.

Whenever $act$ is an action map over $S$, we write $act \cdot S$ for the solution obtained by applying $act$ to agents of $S$, with the obvious definition. Given an embedding $\phi : S' \to S$, one writes $\phi(act) \cdot S$ for the result of $act$ on $S$ along $\phi$, again with the obvious definition.

**Definition 1 (Transition system).** *Let $R$ be a set of rules, $S$ a complete solution, $r = \langle S_r, act_r \rangle$ a rule in $R$, and $\phi : S_r \to S$ an embedding. One defines the transition relation over complete solutions associated to $R$ as:*

$$S \to^r_\phi \phi(act_r) \cdot S$$

That definition of the LTS of a rule set fits in the in the framework of the preceding section:
- the state space $X$ is the set of all complete solutions,
- the set $R$ is the set of rules of interest,
- the $r$-event horizon $\mathcal{E}(x, r)$ is $\{[\phi] \mid \phi \in [S_r, x]\}$ (instances of $r$),
- and $[\phi] \cdot x = \phi(act_r) \cdot x$.

Thus one obtains from any $\kappa$ rule set a CTMC as in Subsection 2.2.

### 3.4 Rule Activation and Inhibition

We need one last preparatory step pertaining to a well studied notion in concurrency theory namely causality [29,30,31]. In the particular framework of process algebra numerous notions of causality have been studied [32,33,34,35] and some were used to study dependencies among events in biological systems [36, 37]. Causality is a relation among computation *events*, and we wish to define here an analog notion between rules.

Consider for instance a solution composed of a thousand $A$s and a thousand $B$s together with two rules $r_1 = A \to B$, and $r_2 = B \to C$. Then it is always the case that the application of $r_1$ increases the probability to trigger $r_2$. Thus, we may say that $r_1$ *activates* $r_2$ although it is not always the case that an instance of $r_2$ will use a $B$ created by an instance of $r_1$ ($B$ could be created in another way). In Section 4, activation and inhibition will allow us to bound the cost of updating various data structures after the application of a given rule in the stochastic simulation, and obtain a neat statement of its complexity properties.

A rule $r_1 = \langle S_1, act_1 \rangle$ *activates* a rule $r_2 = \langle S_2, act_2 \rangle$, written $r_1 \prec r_2$ if there exists $S$, $\phi : act_1 \cdot S_1 \to S$, and $\psi : S_2 \to S$ such that $cod(\phi) \cap cod(\psi)$ contains at least one site modified by $r_1$.

Similarly, $r_1$ *inhibits* $r_2$, written $r_1 \# r_2$, if there exists $S$, $\phi : S_1 \to S$, and $\psi : S_2 \to S$ such that $cod(\phi) \cap cod(\psi)$ contains at least one site modified by $r_1$.

Note that neither inhibition nor activation is *a priori* a symmetric relation. Fig. 6 shows an example of an activation.

## 4 The Simulation Algorithm

There are three ingredients to the algorithm. The first is to introduce in the state of the simulation an explicit representation of the event horizon $\mathcal{E}(x)$.

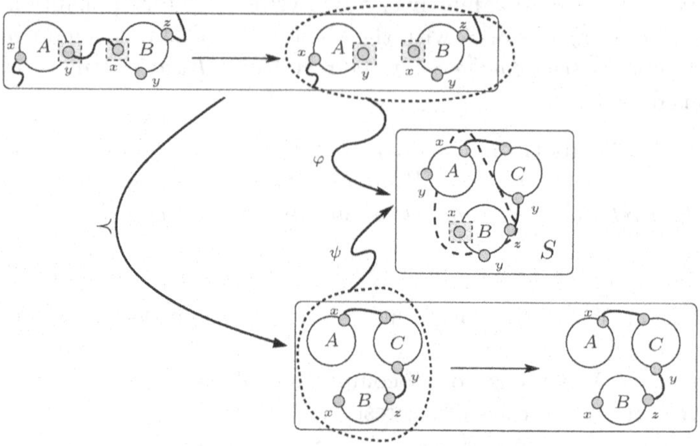

**Fig. 6.** Activation relation: the image by the upper embedding $\phi$ of $B$'s modified site $x$ is also in the image of the lower embedding $\psi$ in $S$; therefore the upper reaction activates the lower one

The second is to use a product approximation of $\mathcal{E}(x)$, and maintain separately a representation of the embeddings of each component of a given rule. The last ingredient is to correct for that approximation by using the time advance corrections introduced in Section 2.

### 4.1 The State

Given a fixed set of rules $R$, the *simulation state* consists in:
- a complete solution $S$
- a *matching map* which associates a connected component $c$ of a rule $r$ to the set of its possible embeddings in $S$:

$$\Phi(r, c) := [c, S]$$

- an *(overestimated) activity map*, with $aut(S_r)$ is the set of automorphisms of the left hand side of rule $r$:[7]

$$\mathbf{a}'(r) = \tau(r)/|aut(S_r)| \cdot \times_{c \in C(r)} |\Phi(r, c)|$$

- a *lift map* which maps $(a, x) \in S$ to the set of embeddings in $\Phi(r, c)$ that have $(a, x)$ in their codomain, for some $r$, and $c \in C(r)$:

$$\ell(a, x) := \{\langle r, c, \phi_c \rangle \mid \phi_c \in \Phi(r, c),\ (a, x) \in cod(\phi_c)\}$$

The maps $\Phi$ and $\mathbf{a}'$ track all rule applications and their activities. Both are computed once during an initialization phase and then updated with local cost at

[7] Recall from the preceding section that an event is isomorphism class of embeddings; the term $aut(S_r)$ makes sure that one is counting events and not embeddings.

each simulation step. The associated data structure has a size which is controlled as follows:

**Proposition 2.** *The size of the matching map is linear in the size of $S$ and bounded by $a_{max}(R) \cdot |R| \cdot |S|$ where $a_{max}(R)$ is the maximum arity in $R$.*

Proof. By Lemma 3, each component in $\Phi(r, c)$ is uniquely defined by the image of any agent of $c$ in $S$. Therefore, $|\Phi(r, c)| \leq |S|$, and the size of the injection map is bounded by $a_{max}(R) \cdot |R| \cdot |S|$ □

## 4.2 The Event Loop

The event generating loop naturally decomposes into a *drawing phase* and an *update phase* described below (See Fig 7).

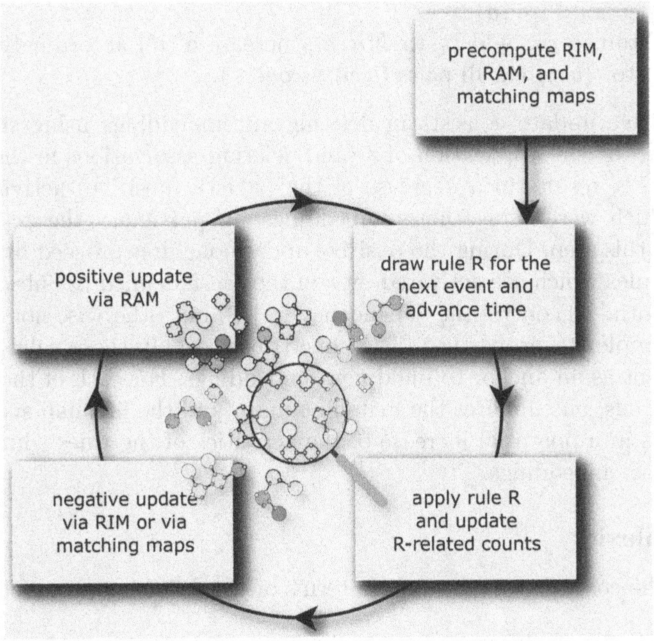


**Fig. 7.** The event generating loop; the RIM is the rule inhibition map, the RAM is the rule activation map

*The drawing phase:*

1. set $clash := 0$
2. draw some $r$ with probability $\mathbf{a}'(r)/\mathbf{a}'(R)$
3. for $c \in C(r)$ draw uniformly $\phi_c \in \Phi(r, c)$
4. if $\sum_{C(r)} \phi_c$ is not injective increment $clash$ and go to 2
5. draw time advance $\delta t$ with $H_{\mathbf{a}(S), clash}$ and increase global time
6. do $S \rightarrow^r_\phi S'$ with $\phi := \langle \phi_c; c \in C(r) \rangle$

The drawing phase is a straightforward specialisation of the protocol $Q(x)$ of Section 2 and is therefore correct. Note that the criterion for a clash is the lack of joint injectivity of the component embeddings $\phi_c$. It remains now to see how to perform the updates to the event horizon that the application of the selected event made necessary.

*The negative update phase:*
for all pairs $(a, x) \in S$ modified by $r$, $\phi$ and $\langle r', c, \phi_c \rangle \in \ell(a, x)$ do:

1. remove $\phi_c$ from $\Phi(r', c)$ and decrease $\mathbf{a}'(r')$ accordingly
2. for all pairs $(b, y) \in cod(\phi_c)$ remove $\langle r', c, \phi_c \rangle$ from $\ell(b, y)$
3. set $\ell(a, x) := \varnothing$

*The positive update phase:*
for all pairs $(a, x) \in S$ modified by $r$, $\phi$ and $r'$ such that $r \prec r'$ do:

1. for every $c \in C(r')$ try to find a (unique) embedding extension $\phi_c \in [c, S']$ of the injection $c \mapsto \{a\}$
2. for all obtained $\phi_c$s add $\phi_c$ to $\Phi(r', c)$, increase $\mathbf{a}'(r')$ accordingly, and add $\langle r', c, \phi_c \rangle$ to $\ell(b, y)$ for all pairs $(b, y) \in cod(\phi_c)$.

The negative update consists in deleting all embeddings using sites which were modified by the application of $r$ (and deleting associations in the lift map accordingly). It results in a decrease of the (strictly positive) activities of all the rules which were using those embeddings. In particular the activity of $r$ decreases at this step. During the positive update one first proceed by "waking-up" all the rules which are activated by $r$ in the sense defined in Subsection 3.4. (This is essential to control the dependency in $|R|$, but otherwise not related to the other complexity properties). Then one tries to apply those rules using the modified agent as an anchor to build new embeddings. For each of the obtained new embeddings, one updates the matching map (and the lift map accordingly) which results in a potential increase of the activities of the rules which in turn may use those embeddings.

### 4.3 Complexity

We bound the cost of an event loop in terms of the following parameters of the rule set:
- $s_{max}(R)$ the maximal number of sites modified by a rule,
- $c_{max}(R)$ the maximal size of a rule connected component, and
- $a_{max}(R)$ for the maximal rule arity (usually 2).
- $\delta_{\prec}(R)$ (resp. $\delta_{\#}(R)$) the maximum out-degree of the activation (resp. inhibition) map (see Subsection 3.4).

We neglect the cost induced by clashes as they only have an impact on small solutions which are not the target of our algorithm. Indeed the simulation of the EGFR example [5] for $10^6$ events, with a total of 3000 agents produced only 4 clashes. The algorithm uses extensible arrays whose size is bound according to Prop. 2, so that the deletion (negative update) and insertion (positive update) or uniform selection of a component in the matching map takes a constant time.

**Proposition 3.** *For any rule set $R$, there exists constants $C_1$ and $C_2$ such that the event loop cost is bounded above by:*

$$C_1 \cdot \log(|R|) + C_2 \cdot a_{max}(R) \cdot c_{max}(R) \cdot s_{max}(R) \cdot (\delta_{\#}(R) + \delta_{\prec}(R))$$

Proof. The dominant cost in the drawing phase is step 2 which can be done in $C_1 \cdot \log(|R|)$ for some constant $C_1$ using an appropriate tree representation.[8] Applying $r$ at step 6 is linear in $s_{max}(R)$ since rules perform at most one modification per site. The complexity of the negative update is the following: the number of pairs $(a, x)$ in $S$ modified by $r$ is bounded by $s_{max}(R)$ and for any such pair $(a, x)$, the number of triple $\langle r', c, \phi_c \rangle$ in $\ell(a, x)$ is bounded by $a_{max}(R) \cdot \delta_{\#}(R)$. Indeed suppose $(a, x)$ is modified by $r$, $\phi$. Then if there is $\psi \neq \phi$ such that $\langle r', c, \psi \rangle \in \ell(a, x)$, by definition $r \# r'$. And for any rule $r'$ there are at most $a_{max}(R)$ embeddings having $(a, x)$ in their codomain. Steps 1 and 3 are performed in negligible time and step 2 takes a time at most proportional to $c_{max}(R)$. Hence the overall cost of the negative update is proportional to $a_{max}(R) \cdot c_{max}(R) \cdot s_{max}(R) \cdot \delta_{\#}(R)$.

The cost of the positive update is straightforward. The number of pairs $(a, x)$ modified by $r$ is bounded by $s_{max}(R)$ and the number of rules to wake up is bounded by $\delta_{\prec}(R)$. For each of these rules one has to look for $a_{max}(R)$ new injections each of them being constructed in a time proportional to $c_{max}(R)$. So the overall positive update phase takes a time proportional to $a_{max}(R) \cdot c_{max}(R) \cdot s_{max}(R) \cdot \delta_{\prec}(R)$, and the overall time of the update phase is proportional to $a_{max}(R) \cdot c_{max}(R) \cdot s_{max}(R) \cdot (\delta_{\#}(R) + \delta_{\prec}(\mathcal{R}))$. □

Note that the rule inhibition map is not used in the algorithm above, but is used in giving an upper bound on the per event cost.

## 5 Conclusion

We have presented a low event cost stochastic simulation algorithm for $\kappa$. This algorithm generalises the Gillespie algorithm. The key insight is to keep a representation of the next events which is linear in the size of the state, and does not present unfeasible space requirements, while being locally updatable. Although this representation introduces event clashes, it can be made to coincide with the intended stochastic semantics, by skewing the next reaction and time advance distributions in a suitable way.

In practice, as one would expect from the complexity analysis, the algorithm indeed scales well. We were able to run simulations involving a million agents,

[8] The rule set can be represented as a tree of size $|R|$ whose nodes are triples $\langle r_i, \mathbf{a}'(r_i), \mathbf{a}'(sub_i) \rangle$ where $\mathbf{a}'(sub_i)$ is the sum of the activities of the rules contained in the left and right subtrees. Drawing a random rule according to its activity consists in generating a random number $0 < n \leq \mathbf{a}'(R)$ and, at node $i$, either returning $r_i$ if $n < \mathbf{a}'(r_i)$ or doing one of the following alternatives: either going to the left subtree $j$ whenever $n < sub_j$ or to the right subtree $k$ and it that case set $n := n - sub_j$. This drawing scheme is in logarithmic time.

with about 50 rules, and about 10000 non-isomorphic reachable configurations, resulting in a simulation time of about 15 minutes for a million events. So even in conditions where agents far exceed in number the possible combinations, which are a priori not the best for our dimension-insensitive method, the algorithm still works. It also scales well with respect to the number of rules, because it is using a static approximate causality structure to determine whether a rule should be activated, and we ran simulations on (machine-generated) systems comprising thousands of rules, with no detectable impact on event costs.

Previous simulation methods include the traditional species-sensitive procedures, working on a ground rewriting system where every configuration is identified beforehand. This is the way the current BNG implementation works, although it is rule-based (hence the name biological network generator). The simulation then boils down to the simulation of stochastic Petri nets, and a natural implementation is to partition events into the ground reactions they correspond to, and count each class, which is an efficient thing to do for small dimensions. The fact is that all such methods have to sample the dimensionality of the rule set (since the generated network could be infinite), either explicitly, as in the current BNG implementation, or implicitly as in traditional ODE modelling, whereas as said above, the method we present here does not.

An intermediate approach one might think is worth pursuing, as in the recent betaWB implementation [25] of an extension of the beta-binders language to enable the description of complexes [38], or the latest SPIM implementation [24], is that of computing the species produced during a single trajectory on-the-fly. This will certainly fare better than a prior enumeration as in the current BNG implementation, however it is still showing a dependency in the size of that increasing set of species, because one has to scan it at each step to identify (up to isomorphism) the species just produced. In signalling systems where the set of on-the-fly species becomes large, this dependency could slow down the simulation.

The StochSim [39] simulation is based on a different agent-centric scheme, whereby one picks two agents $A$, $B$ (supposing all rule are binary to simplify), and apply a reaction if any does. It shares an interesting feature with ours, namely that it behaves well with respect to the number of reactions $|R|$, an effect obtained in our case by resorting to the activation relation. However, it generates as many unproductive steps on average as there are non-reacting pairs of agents, and that number is typically $O(N^2)$ where $N$ is the number of distinct species. This can be efficient only if the number of reactions $|R| \gg N$, ie if the reaction network is dense, which is not the expected case for signalling. Specifically, the probability of success, meaning of picking two reacting agents, is about $d_m/N$ where $d_m$ is the mean number of co-reactants; so the mean time for success will be $N/d_m$, which is increasingly bad if $d_m$ is constant or logarithmic in $N$ (a reasonable assumption for signalling). So the Stochsim method cost may be independent of $|R|$, but it is getting slower linearly in $N$ (supposing $d_m$ to be constant in $N$) the dimension of the system, so is highly species sensitive.

There are various attempts at general simulation engines for grammars of various sorts. An interesting one is in Ref. [40], where the authors develop a formal semantics in terms of operator algebras; another is MGS [41]. Those generic engines address a much more general situation than we have done in this paper. It should be instructive however to see to which extent the event horizon methods we have developed here apply.

## References


1. Regev, A., Silverman, W., Shapiro, E.: Representation and simulation of biochemical processes using the $\pi$-calculus process algebra. In: Altman, R.B., Dunker, A.K., Hunter, L., Klein, T.E. (eds.) Pacific Symposium on Biocomputing, vol. 6, pp. 459–470. World Scientific Press, Singapore (2001)
2. Priami, C., Regev, A., Shapiro, E., Silverman, W.: Application of a stochastic name-passing calculus to representation and simulation of molecular processes. Information Processing Letters (2001)
3. Regev, A., Shapiro, E.: Cells as computation. Nature 419 (2002)
4. Regev, A., Panina, E., Silverman, W., Cardelli, L., Shapiro, E.: BioAmbients: an abstraction for biological compartments. Theoretical Computer Science 325(1), 141–167 (2004)
5. Danos, V., Feret, J., Fontana, W., Harmer, R., Krivine, J.: Rule-based modelling of cellular signalling. In: Caires, L., Vasconcelos, V. (eds.) CONCUR 2007. LNCS, vol. 4703, Springer, Heidelberg (2007)
6. Curien, P.L., Danos, V., Krivine, J., Zhang, M.: Computational self-assembly (submitted, 2007)
7. Danos, V., Laneve, C.: Formal molecular biology. Theoretical Computer Science 325, 69–110 (2004)
8. Danos, V., Laneve, C.: Core formal molecular biology. In: Degano, P. (ed.) ESOP 2003 and ETAPS 2003. LNCS, vol. 2618, pp. 302–318. Springer, Heidelberg (2003)
9. Faeder, J., Blinov, M., Hlavacek, W.: Graphical rule-based representation of signal-transduction networks. In: Proc. ACM Symp. Appl. Computing, pp. 133–140 (2005)
10. Faeder, J., Blinov, M.B.G., Hlavacek, W.: BioNetGen: software for rule-based modeling of signal transduction based on the interactions of molecular domains. Complexity 10, 22–41 (2005)
11. Blinov, M., Yang, J., Faeder, J., Hlavacek, W.: Graph theory for rule-based modeling of biochemical networks. In: BioCONCUR 2005 (2005)
12. Faeder, J.R., Blinov, M.L., Goldstein, B., Hlavacek, W.S.: Combinatorial complexity and dynamical restriction of network flows in signal transduction. Systems Biology 2(1), 5–15 (2005)
13. Blinov, M.L., Faeder, J.R., Goldstein, B., Hlavacek, W.S.: A network model of early events in epidermal growth factor receptor signaling that accounts for combinatorial complexity. BioSystems 83, 136–151 (2006)
14. Hlavacek, W., Faeder, J., Blinov, M., Posner, R., Hucka, M., Fontana, W.: Rules for Modeling Signal-Transduction Systems. Science's STKE 2006(344) (2006)
15. Kiyatkin, A., Aksamitiene, E., Markevich, N., Borisov, N., Hoek, J., Kholodenko, B.: Scaffolding Protein Grb2-associated Binder 1 Sustains Epidermal Growth Factor-induced Mitogenic and Survival Signaling by Multiple Positive Feedback Loops. Journal of Biological Chemistry 281(29) (2006)

16. Aldridge, B., Burke, J., Lauffenburger, D., Sorger, P.: Physicochemical modelling of cell signalling pathways. Nat. Cell. Biol. 8, 1195–1203 (2006)
17. Milner, R.: Communicating and mobile systems: the $\pi$-calculus. Cambridge University Press, Cambridge (1999)
18. Eker, S., Knapp, M., Laderoute, K., Lincoln, P., Meseguer, J., Sonmez, K.: Pathway logic: Symbolic analysis of biological signaling. In: Proceedings of the Pacific Symposium on Biocomputing, pp. 400–412 (2002)
19. Priami, C., Quaglia, P.: Beta binders for biological interactions. In: Danos, V., Schachter, V. (eds.) CMSB 2004. LNCS (LNBI), vol. 3082, pp. 20–33. Springer, Heidelberg (2005)
20. Danos, V., Krivine, J.: Formal molecular biology done in CCS. In: Proceedings of BIO-CONCUR 2003, Marseille, France. Electronic Notes in Theoretical Computer Science, vol. 180, pp. 31–49. Elsevier, Amsterdam (2003)
21. Cardelli, L.: Brane calculi. In: BIO-CONCUR 2003, Marseille, France. Electronic Notes in Theoretical Computer Science, vol. 180, Elsevier, Amsterdam (2003)
22. Calder, M., Gilmore, S., Hillston, J.: Modelling the influence of RKIP on the ERK signalling pathway using the stochastic process algebra PEPA. In: Priami, C., Ingólfsdóttir, A., Mishra, B., Nielson, H.R. (eds.) Transactions on Computational Systems Biology VII. LNCS (LNBI), vol. 4230, pp. 1–23. Springer, Heidelberg (2006)
23. Pawson, T., Nash, P.: Assembly of Cell Regulatory Systems Through Protein Interaction Domains. Science 300, 445–452 (2003)
24. Phillips, A., Cardelli, L.: Efficient, correct simulation of biological processes in the stochastic pi-calculus. In: Proceedings of CMSB 2007. LNCS(LNBI), vol. 4695, Springer, Heidelberg (2007)
25. Degano, P., Prandi, D., Priami, C., Quaglia, P.: Beta-binders for biological quantitative experiments. In: Proceedings of QAPL. ENTCS, vol. 164, pp. 101–117 (2006)
26. Bortz, A.B., Kalos, M.H., Lebowitz, J.L.: A new algorithm for Monte Carlo simulation of Ising spin systems. J. Comp. Phys. 17, 10–18 (1975)
27. Gillespie, D.T.: Exact stochastic simulation of coupled chemical reactions. J. Phys. Chem 81, 2340–2361 (1977)
28. Gillespie, D.T.: A general method for numerically simulating the stochastic time evolution of coupled chemical reactions. J. Comp. Phys. 22, 403–434 (1976)
29. Berry, G., Lévy, J.J.: Minimal and optimal computation of recursive programs. JACM 26, 148–175 (1979)
30. Nielsen, M., Plotkin, G., Winskel, G.: Petri nets, event structures and domains. Theoretical Computer Science 13, 85–108 (1981)
31. Darondeau, P., Degano, P.: Causal trees. In: Ronchi Della Rocca, S., Ausiello, G., Dezani-Ciancaglini, M. (eds.) Automata, Languages and Programming. LNCS, vol. 372, pp. 234–248. Springer, Heidelberg (1989)
32. Winskel, G.: Event structure semantics for CCS and related languages. In: Nielsen, M., Schmidt, E.M. (eds.) Automata, Languages, and Programming. LNCS, vol. 140, pp. 561–576. Springer, Heidelberg (1982)
33. Boudol, G., Castellani, I.: Permutation of transitions: An event structure semantics for CCS and SCCS. In: de Bakker, J.W., de Roever, W.-P., Rozenberg, G. (eds.) Linear Time, Branching Time and Partial Order in Logics and Models for Concurrency. LNCS, vol. 354, pp. 411–427. Springer, Heidelberg (1989)
34. Boreale, M., Sangiorgi, D.: A fully abstract semantics for causality in the $\pi$-calculus. Acta Inf. 35, 353–400 (1998)

35. Degano, P., Priami, C.: Non-interleaving semantics for mobile processes. Theoretical Computer Science 216(1-2), 237–270 (1999)
36. Baldi, C., Degano, P., Priami, C.: Causal $\pi$-calculus for biochemical modeling. In: Proceedings of the AI*IA Workshop on BioInformatics 2002, pp. 69–72 (2002)
37. Curti, M., Degano, P., Priami, C., Baldari, C.T.: Modelling biochemical pathways through enhanced $\pi$-calculus. Theor. Comp. Sci. 325, 111–140 (2004)
38. Priami, C., Quaglia, P.: Beta binders for biological interactions. In: Danos, V., Schachter, V. (eds.) CMSB 2004. LNCS (LNBI), vol. 3082, pp. 20–33. Springer, Heidelberg (2005)
39. Morton-Firth, C.J.: Stochastic simulation of cell signalling pathways. PhD thesis, Cambridge (1998)
40. Mjolsness, E., Yosiphon, G.: Stochastic process semantics for dynamical grammars. Annals of Mathematics and Artificial Intelligence (2007)
41. Giavitto, J.L., Michel, O.: MGS: a programming language for the transformations of topological collections. Technical Report 61-2001, LaMI (2001)

# Timed, Distributed, Probabilistic, Typed Processes

Martin Berger and Nobuko Yoshida

Department of Computing, Imperial College London

**Abstract.** This paper studies types and probabilistic bisimulations for a timed $\pi$-calculus as an effective tool for a compositional analysis of probabilistic distributed behaviour. The types clarify the role of timers as interface between non-terminating and terminating communication for guaranteeing distributed liveness. We add message-loss probabilities to the calculus, and introduce a notion of approximate bisimulation that discards transitions below a certain specified probability threshold. We prove this bisimulation to be a congruence, and use it for deriving quantitative bounds for practical protocols in distributed systems, including timer-driven message-loss recovery and the Two-Phase Commit protocol.

## 1 Introduction

Designing formalisms for the development and verification of distributed systems (DS), understood as computation in the presence of partial failures and malevolent adversaries [26], is challenging: DS are often written in semantically rich high-level languages with expressive typing systems. Failures in DS (e.g. message-loss) are typically detected by timing. Hence programming environments for DS feature sophisticated timer mechanisms. State explosion, the key problem in verification, is worse in DS because timing and partial failures increase dramatically the space of possible system behaviour. Finally, although DS operate in adversarial environments, the behaviour of adversaries and the occurrences of failures is nevertheless structured: for example message-loss in the Internet can be assumed to occur only rarely, and cryptography is based on similar frequentist suppositions about attackers guessing passwords correctly. Such structural assumptions are usually phrased in probabilistic terms. We propose a type-based analysis for DS that addresses these points using a distributed, timed and probabilistic $\pi$-calculus: our formalism is not intended as an ultimate model for all issues pertaining to DS, but a good starting point for further investigations, capturing the above central elements in DS.

Following [3], we turn the $\pi$-calculus into a model for DS by adding locations and allowing messages travelling between locations (but not within a location) to be lost. This notion of failure exhibits a key feature of DS (as timers usually are provided to handle message-loss), and is a stepping stone towards more advanced forms of failure. As timed computation is not known to be reducible to untimed computation, we introduce (discrete) timing directly into our model via timers.

To allow compositional verification, to reduce the state space of checking distributed process behaviour and to aid programming DS, we use *types*. Types constrain processes and their contexts, leading to a marked reduction of possible behaviour. In this paper, we focus on the *linear type discipline* studied and extended for various purposes

Z. Shao (Ed.): APLAS 2007, LNCS 4807, pp. 158–174, 2007.

since [18,23]. One of the key concepts of this discipline is to distinguish terminating and (potentially) non-terminating communication channels [19] (often called deadlock-freedom [20, 22]). This distinction is highly useful in DS, where exchanges on (potentially) non-terminating channels correspond to remote communication, while termination is restricted to local interaction. For example loss of liveness due to failure is counteracted in DS by aborting distributed invocations that do not respond within some expected time. We model this situation with typing rules for timers such that a timer is a *converter* from (potential) non-terminating to terminating channels. Timers thus offer channel-based distributed liveness where an output at a certain channel can eventually happen, despite failures, thus guaranteeing transparency between remote and local invocations in the presence of message-loss. In addition, the linear type discipline has the capability to model DS with failures and timers where applications written in typed high-level languages run inside distributed locations, without losing expressivity and usability. For example it can be extended to type-based programming analyses such as secure information flow [19,21], it embeds various higher-order programming languages fully abstractly [6,19,32] and models distributed Java [1] and web services [8]. The main contribution of this paper is to show that the linear type discipline generalises smoothly to distributed computation: no new types have to be invented and all existing typing rules stay unchanged.

To demonstrate the stability and applicability of our types, we add message-loss probabilities to reason about fine-grained behaviour of distributed processes. We use probabilistic automata [28] so non-determinism and probabilities can coexist. We define a new form of approximate bisimulation that expresses that two processes are equivalent, except that some of their transitions are allowed not to be matched, as long the probability of those unmatched transitions is below some factor $\varepsilon \in [0,1]$. Because the typing system works for non-deterministic message loss, it is also sound when message-loss is governed by probabilities, justifying our typing system. We prove our approximate bisimulation to be a *congruence*, allowing compositional reasoning for DS. We then use this approximate bisimulation to analyse message failure recovery mechanisms. An RPC protocol (similar to a concurrent alternating bit protocol in [2], but extended with timers and message forwarding), distributed leases [16] and the Two-Phase Commit protocol (2PCP) with probabilistic message-loss are specified in our timed $\pi$-calculus and reasoned about with the approximate bisimulation. Types and their liveness property reduce the number of transitions to be compared in proofs for DS. Omitted definitions and proofs are in [7]. We close with a summary of our results.

- We present the first typing for timers as a smooth generalisation of the linear type disciplines. This clarifies the behavioural status of timers as a converter from non-terminating to terminating behaviour. As a simple instance, we use the linear/affine typing system from [19] where linear and affine stand for termination and (potential) non-termination, respectively. This extension is achieved without additional types. All existing typing rules are unchanged on processes. The usefulness of the typing system is demonstrated by examples.
- We introduce approximate bisimulation for the distributed $\pi$-calculus and prove congruency. As far as we know, this is the first congruency result for probabilistic bisimulations of the $\pi$-calculus.

- We offer convenient verification of quantitative bounds for probabilistic processes. We reason about some distributed protocols, and demonstrate the use of types for reducing the burden of checking for bisimilarity of probabilistic processes.

## 2 Distributed Timed Processes

The syntax of *processes* $(P, Q, ...)$ and *networks* $(M, N, ...)$ is given by the following grammar where $a, b, x, y, v, ...$ range over a countably infinite set of names.

$$P ::= 0 \mid \overline{a}\langle\tilde{v}\rangle \mid a(\tilde{x}).P \mid !a(\tilde{x}).P \mid P|Q \mid (\nu a)P \mid \mathsf{timer}^t\langle a(\tilde{x}).P,\ Q\rangle$$
$$M ::= 0 \mid [P] \mid M \mid N \mid (\nu a)M$$

In applications we also communicate values in outputs, e.g. $\overline{x}\langle 3\rangle$. We abbreviate $\overline{x}\langle\rangle$ to $\overline{x}$, $x().P$ to $x.P$ and write $\overline{x}(\tilde{c})P$ for $(\nu\tilde{c})(\overline{x}\langle\tilde{c}\rangle|P)$ when $x \notin \tilde{c}$. Free names $\mathsf{fn}(\cdot)$ are standard, except that $\mathsf{fn}(\mathsf{timer}^t\langle a(\tilde{x}).P,\ Q\rangle) = \mathsf{fn}(a(\tilde{x}).P) \cup \mathsf{fn}(Q)$ and $\mathsf{fn}([P]) \stackrel{\text{def}}{=} \mathsf{fn}(P)$. The structural congruence $\equiv$ is defined as usual, but over our extended syntax: for example, we have $[(\nu a)P] \equiv (\nu a)[P]$. The *timer* construct $\mathsf{timer}^t\langle a(\tilde{x}).P,\ Q\rangle$, with $t > 0$ being an integer, supports two operations: (1) *timeout* which means that after $t$ steps it turns into $Q$, unless (2) it has been *stopped*, i.e. that a message has been received by the timer at $a$. It is easy to modify timers so they can be stopped at multiple channels.

$$\textsc{Stop}\ \frac{}{\mathsf{timer}^{t+1}\langle a(\tilde{x}).P,\ Q\rangle \mid \overline{a}\langle\tilde{v}\rangle \to P\{\tilde{v}/\tilde{x}\}}$$

The flow of time is communicated at each step in the computation by a *timestepper function* $\phi$, which acts on processes. It models the implicit broadcast of time passing. The main two rules are:

$$\phi(\mathsf{timer}^{t+1}\langle P,\ Q\rangle) = \mathsf{timer}^t\langle P,\ Q\rangle \qquad\qquad \phi(\mathsf{timer}^1\langle P,\ Q\rangle) = Q$$

The others are: $\phi(P \mid Q) = \phi(P) \mid \phi(Q)$, $\phi((\nu a)P) = (\nu a)\phi(P)$ and otherwise $\phi(P) = P$. The remaining reduction rules for processes are given as follows:

$$\textsc{Par}\ \frac{P \to Q}{P|R \to Q|\phi(R)} \quad \textsc{Com}\ \frac{}{\overline{a}\langle\tilde{v}\rangle|a(\tilde{x}).P \to P\{\tilde{v}/\tilde{x}\}} \quad \textsc{Rep}\ \frac{}{\overline{a}\langle\tilde{v}\rangle|!a(\tilde{x}).P \to P\{\tilde{v}/\tilde{x}\}|!a(\tilde{x}).P}$$

$$\textsc{Res}\ \frac{P \to Q}{(\nu a)P \to (\nu a)Q} \quad \textsc{Idle}\ \frac{}{P \to \phi(P)} \quad \textsc{Cong}\ \frac{P \equiv P' \to Q' \equiv Q}{P \to Q}$$

Note that we have $\phi(R)$ in the conclusion of [Par]: this ensures that each *active timer*, that is any timer not under a prefix, is ticked one unit at each interaction. [Idle] prevents the flow of time from ever being halted by deadlocked processes. The reduction relation of the networks, $\longrightarrow$, is defined as:

$$\textsc{Intra}\ \frac{P \to Q}{[P] \longrightarrow [Q]} \quad \textsc{Par}\ \frac{M \longrightarrow N}{M|L \longrightarrow N|L} \quad \textsc{Res}\ \frac{M \longrightarrow N}{(\nu a)M \longrightarrow (\nu a)N} \quad \textsc{Cong}\ \frac{M \equiv M' \longrightarrow N' \equiv N}{M \longrightarrow N}$$

$$\textsc{Loss}\ \frac{}{[P|\overline{a}\langle\tilde{v}\rangle] \mid [Q|a(\tilde{y}).R] \longrightarrow [\phi(P)] \mid [Q|a(\tilde{y}).R]} \quad \textsc{Com}\ \frac{}{[P|\overline{a}\langle\tilde{v}\rangle]|[Q|a(\tilde{y}).R] \longrightarrow [\phi(P)]|[\phi(Q)|R\{\tilde{v}/\tilde{y}\}]}$$

Rules for replicated input or timer input corresponding to [Loss, Com] have been omitted. We define: $\twoheadrightarrow \stackrel{\text{def}}{=} (\equiv \cup \longrightarrow)^*$. [Par] at the network level prevents the synchronisation of clocks between sites: this models that over the Internet, clock-synchronisation better than about 100 milliseconds (which is several orders of magnitude coarser than the temporal resolution available within CPU) is not currently achievable [25].

*Example 1.* The *remote invoker* $\overline{a}\langle\tilde{v}\rangle;\,(\tilde{x}).P \rhd^t Q$ sends a message on $a$ to a remote site and awaits a reply for $t$ ticks on a private channel.

$$\overline{a}\langle\tilde{v}\rangle;\,(\tilde{x}).P \rhd^t Q \stackrel{\text{def}}{=} (\nu r)(\overline{a}\langle\tilde{v}r\rangle \mid \mathsf{timer}^t\langle r(\tilde{x}).P,\ (r(\tilde{x}).0 \mid Q)\rangle)$$

(Note that $r(\tilde{x}).0$ in the timeout continuation is necessary only for the typing to be introduced in §3.) While the remote invoker can be used locally, its intended use can be seen in the network $M \stackrel{\text{def}}{=} [!a(\tilde{y}r).\overline{r}\langle\tilde{b}\rangle] \mid [\overline{a}\langle\tilde{v}\rangle;\,(\tilde{x}).P \rhd^t Q]$ which has two reductions:

$$M \twoheadrightarrow [!a(\tilde{y}r).\overline{r}\langle\tilde{b}\rangle] \mid [P\{\tilde{b}/\tilde{x}\}] \qquad\qquad M \twoheadrightarrow [!a(\tilde{y}r).\overline{r}\langle\tilde{b}\rangle] \mid [Q \mid (\nu r)r(\tilde{x}).0]$$

Often such invocations are iterated: if the server does not reply within time $t$, we assume message-loss to have occurred and resend the invocation a bounded number of times $n$ before giving up. This recovery mechanism can be defined inductively.

$$\overline{a}\langle\tilde{v}\rangle^n;\,(\tilde{x}).P \rhd^t Q \stackrel{\text{def}}{=} \overline{a}\langle\tilde{v}\rangle;\,(\tilde{x}).P \rhd^t Q_{n-1} \text{ with } Q_0 \stackrel{\text{def}}{=} Q,\ Q_{k+1} \stackrel{\text{def}}{=} \overline{a}\langle\tilde{v}\rangle;\,(\tilde{x}).P \rhd^t Q_k$$

For example, we can model a remote arithmetic operation (using an extended syntax with numbers and their operations).

$$[!a(yr).\overline{r}\langle y\times 3\rangle] \mid [(\nu b)(\overline{a}\langle 10\rangle^{100};\,(\tilde{x}).\overline{b}\langle x+7\rangle \rhd^5 \overline{b}\langle 0\rangle \mid b(z).R)] \qquad (1)$$

This remote invoker tries to get $3\times 10$ evaluated remotely and if there is no reply within 5 timesteps, it re-sends a request again. This routine is repeated until success or until 100 tries have been fruitless, when the invoker gives up and emits an exception (here in form of a value 0): this is in essence what real DS do to deal with message failure.

## 3 A Typing System for Distribution and Timer

Our typing system is based on the *linear/affine typing* of [19] but without a sequentiality constraint (i.e. multiple threads of control are permitted) and augmented for timers and message-loss. This system is a proper generalisation of [5,6,19] and a simple instance of various linearity-based typing systems which ensure that interactions at certain channels will eventually succeed. [32] is the most accessible introduction to the key ideas behind linear typing. Our aim is for the extension to DS to preserve the ability to embed high-level sequential and concurrent multi-threaded languages [6, 19, 32].

### 3.1 Linear/Affine Typing System: Basic Idea

The linear/affine typing system introduced in [19] assigns types to free channels, which constrain the direction of information flow, the kind of information that flows on a channel, and how often a channel may be used: linear (exactly once), affine (at most once) or replicated (an unlimited number of times, including not at all).

This is achieved with the following basic constraints: first, each channel is classified as either linear, affine, replicated-linear or replicated-affine; orthogonally, each channel is either input or output. *Affinity* denotes possibly diverging behaviour in which a question is given an answer at most once. *Linearity* means terminating behaviour in which a question is always given an answer precisely once. Replicated-linear channels stand for servers that are guaranteed to return an answer, while replicated-affine channels are for servers that may exhibit divergence. Syntactically, typing enforces the following constraints:

1. For each replicated name there is a unique replicator with zero or more outputs
2. For each linear or affine name there is a unique input with a unique output
3. Linear channels have no circular dependency
4. Affine input channels cannot prefix linear channels
5. Replicators cannot prefix linear or affine channels

Under (1) above, $P_1 \stackrel{\text{def}}{=} !b.\overline{a} \mid !b.\overline{c}$ is not typable because $b$ is associated with two replicators, but $P_2 \stackrel{\text{def}}{=} !b.\overline{a} \mid \overline{b} \mid !c.\overline{b}$ is typable since, while the output at $b$ appears twice, there is just one replicator at $b$. As an example for (2), $P_3 \stackrel{\text{def}}{=} b.\overline{a} \mid c.\overline{a}$ is untypable with $a$ being linear, as $a$ appears twice as output. $P_4 \stackrel{\text{def}}{=} b.\overline{a} \mid c.\overline{b} \mid a.(\overline{c} \mid \overline{e})$ is typable since each channel appears at most once as input and output. By (3), we can ensure *termination* behaviour over linear channels. For example, $P_5 \stackrel{\text{def}}{=} !b.\overline{a} \mid !a.\overline{b}$ is untypable under this constraint: if we compose it with $\overline{a}$, then the computation does not terminate. $P_4$ is also untypable under (3). As given above, "linearity" means more than just termination: it indicates *a process always returns an answer if it is asked for*, which we call *liveness*. (4) ensures liveness at linear channels in the presence of termination: $P_6 = a.\overline{b}$ where $a$ is affine and $\overline{b}$ is linear should be untypable since we do not know the input $a$ surely happens. (5) is a standard constraint for affinity/linearity, by which $!a.\overline{b}$ where $b$ is either linear or affine output is untypable.

**Linear and Affine Types.** We outline the formal definitions of types and the typing system, introducing the minimum definitions needed. *Action modes* (ranged over $p, p', ...$) [5, 32] prescribe different modes of interaction at each channel. The L-modes correspond to linear [32] while the A-modes to affine [5]. The last line denotes the grammar of types.

| | | | |
|---|---|---|---|
| $\downarrow_{\text{L}}$ Linear input | $\uparrow_{\text{L}}$ Linear output | $\downarrow_{\text{A}}$ Affine input | $\uparrow_{\text{A}}$ Affine output |
| $!_{\text{L}}$ Linear server | $?_{\text{L}}$ Client request to $!_{\text{L}}$ | $!_{\text{A}}$ Affine server | $?_{\text{A}}$ Client request to $!_{\text{A}}$ |

$$\tau ::= (\tilde{\tau})^p \mid \updownarrow$$

The modes in the first and third columns are *input* while the second and forth are *output*. The input and output modes in each row are *dual* to each other, writing $\overline{p}$ for the dual of $p$. In types, $\tilde{\tau}$ is a vector of types. $\updownarrow$ indicates that a channel is no longer available for *further* composition with the outside; for example, if $x.0$ has a $\downarrow_{\text{L}}$-mode and $\overline{x}$ has a $\uparrow_{\text{L}}$-mode, then $x.0 \mid \overline{x}$ has $\updownarrow$-mode at $x$. The $\updownarrow$-mode at $x$ indicates that the process $x.0 \mid \overline{x}$ cannot be composed with any process that has $x$ as a free name. $\updownarrow$'s mode is $\updownarrow$. We assume a replicated affine input does not carry linear output (and dually). This condition ensures an invocation at linear replication will eventually terminate, firing an associated linear output [19]. We write $\mathsf{md}(\tau)$ for the outermost mode of $\tau$; $\tau^p$ also indicates that $p$ is the (outermost) mode of $\tau$. The *dual of* $\tau$, written $\overline{\tau}$, is the result of dualising all action modes. Then the least commutative partial operation, $\odot$, which controls the composition of channels is defined as:

$$\text{(a)}\ \tau \odot \tau = \tau \text{ and } \tau \odot \overline{\tau} = \overline{\tau} \text{ with } \mathsf{md}(\tau) = ? \qquad \text{(b)}\ \tau \odot \overline{\tau} = \updownarrow \text{ with } \mathsf{md}(\tau) = \uparrow$$

(a) and (b) ensure the two constraints (1) and (2) in the list of § 3.1.
An *action type*, denoted $A, B, \ldots$, is a finite directed graph with nodes of the form $x\!:\!\tau$, such that no names occur twice; and *causality edges* $x\!:\!\tau \to y\!:\!\tau'$ is of the form: from a linear input $\downarrow_{\mathrm{L}}$ to a linear output $\uparrow_{\mathrm{L}}$; or from a linear replication $!_{\mathrm{L}}$ to a linear client $?_{\mathrm{L}}$. $\overline{A}$ dualises all types in $A$. We write $A(x)$ for the channel type assigned to $x$ occurring in $A$. The partial operator $A \odot B$ is defined iff channel types with common names compose and the adjoined graph does not have a cycle. This avoids divergence on linear channels. For example, $a\!:\!\tau_1 \to b\!:\!\tau_2$ and $b\!:\!\overline{\tau_2} \to a\!:\!\overline{\tau_1}$ are not composable, hence a process such as $P_5 \stackrel{\text{def}}{=} !a.\overline{b} \mid !b.\overline{a}$ is untypable. We write $A_1 \asymp A_2$ when such composition is possible, while the result of composition is written $A_1 \odot A_2$ (see [7] for details). By this operation, we can guarantee the condition (3) in § 3.1 for the linear channels. Non-circular causality between linear channels guarantees liveness at linear output channels, resulting in the distributed liveness theorem below.

### 3.2 Typing Systems for Message-Loss and Timers

The typing judgements for processes forms $P \vdash A$ (a process $P$ has an action type $A$) and networks forms $N \vdash A$ (a network $N$ has an action type $A$). We list the selected rules below. Types and rules for non-distributed processes identical with those in [19].

$$\textsc{Loc}\ \frac{P \vdash A \quad A \text{ distributable}}{[P] \vdash A} \qquad \textsc{Timer}\ \frac{x(\tilde{y}).P \vdash A \quad Q \vdash A}{\mathsf{timer}^t\langle x(\tilde{y}).P,\ Q\rangle \vdash A} \qquad \textsc{Timer}_c\ \frac{x(\tilde{y}).P \vdash (x\!:\!(\tilde{\tau})^{\downarrow_{\mathrm{L}}} \to A), B \quad Q \vdash x\!:\!(\tilde{\tau})^{\downarrow_{\mathrm{A}}}, A, B}{\mathsf{timer}^t\langle x(\tilde{y}).P,\ Q\rangle \vdash x\!:\!(\tilde{\tau})^{\downarrow_{\mathrm{A}}}, A, B}$$

**Typing Networks.** The key difficulty in typing networks is that messages can get lost, but we must ensure that linear inputs and outputs do not get lost, i.e. linear names must never be sent to remote sites. We achieve this by imposing that free names observable at the network level cannot be linear input or linear output, and cannot carry such names recursively: we say type $\tau$ is *distributable* if $\tau$ does not contain either linear input or linear output in its subexpressions. For example, neither $()^{\uparrow_{\mathrm{L}}}$ nor $(()^{\downarrow_{\mathrm{L}}})^{?_{\mathrm{L}}}$ is distributable. We say $A$ is *distributable* if $A(x)$ is distributable for all $x$. Then by [Loc], we transfer a process $P$ which has a distributable type to the network level as $[P]$. Note that linear names can also exist hidden by a restriction or bound by prefixes. But because by construction distributable types cannot carry linear names, no hidden linear name can escape to the network, thus preserving linearity.

**Typing Timers.** Timers can be seen as a form of mixed choice (ignoring timing, $\mathsf{timer}^t\langle x(\tilde{v}).P,\ Q\rangle$ can be translated as $x(\tilde{v}).P + \tau.Q$) where one branch is chosen by the environment while the other can be triggered internally. Hence, if both branches can be given the same type $A$, then the timer also has type $A$, thus explaining [Timer].

While natural, this rule is not expressive enough: the most important use of timers, detection of message-loss is not typable. To see why, consider

$$[!x(vr).P] \mid [(\nu r)(\overline{x}\langle ar\rangle \mid \mathsf{timer}^t\langle r(\tilde{v}).Q,\ R\rangle|...)]$$

a simplified version of the remote invoker from Example 1 where the timer triggers some recovery action in $R$ if the remote action does not reply in time. For this process to be typable, $x$ must not carry linear names, hence $r$ must be affine. (4) in §3.1 does not allow to suppress linear names under an affine input, hence $r(\tilde{v}).Q$ would not have any linear (liveness) behaviour. Timers are used to make liveness guarantees so that a computation does not hang forever, even if messages get lost or servers do not reply.

To overcome this lack of expressivity, we introduce [TIMER$_c$] that allows to suppress linear names under an affine output without breaking the typing system. We can then use timers to ensure distributed liveness, but refining the concept of liveness from "the result of an invocation will always eventually be returned" to "*either* a result *or* an indication of error will be returned". Formally, [TIMER$_c$] first types $x(\tilde{v}).P$ assuming $x$ is a linear input $x:(\tilde{\tau})^{\downarrow_{\mathrm{L}}}$, hence permitting to suppress linear outputs $A$ (here $x:(\tilde{\tau})^{\downarrow_{\mathrm{L}}} \rightarrow A$ is a type which is obtained by adding edges from $x:(\tilde{\tau})^{\downarrow_{\mathrm{L}}}$ to $A$). Notice that we *cannot* apply the same method for $Q$ since after $t$-ticks, when $Q$ is launched, it may wait forever on $x$ (see Example 2 below). Hence, the second premise assumes that $x$ is an affine input, and no linear names can depend causally on $x$, i.e. linear names must be available without external interaction, and are hence guaranteed to fire eventually. This means $Q$ will be of the form $(\nu\tilde{z})(R|x(\tilde{v}).Q'), x \notin \tilde{z}$, with all free linear names being in $R$. [TIMER$_c$] then gives the timer the type of its timeout continuation. Note that the typing rules for timers do not depend on the concrete details of the timing model (e.g. discrete or continuous), but rather apply to all.

**Theorem 1.** *If $P \vdash A$ and $P \rightarrow Q$ then $Q \vdash A$, and likewise for networks.*

Next we formulate a distributed liveness property which states that linear local outputs always fire (under the usual implicit fairness assumptions that each process that is not deadlocked or terminated will eventually be scheduled [7]). Write $P \Downarrow_a$ if there exist $\tilde{b}, R, \tilde{v}$ s.t. $P \twoheadrightarrow (\nu\tilde{b})(R \mid \overline{a}\langle\tilde{v}\rangle)$ with $a \notin \{\tilde{b}\}$.

**Definition 1.**
1. *(local liveness) We say $A$ is* closed *if* $\mathsf{md}(A) \in \{!_{\mathrm{A}}, !_{L}, \updownarrow\}$. *Suppose $P \vdash A, a:\tau$ with $A$ closed and* $\mathsf{md}(\tau) = \uparrow_L$. *Then we say $P$ satisfies* liveness at *$a$ if whenever $P \twoheadrightarrow P'$, $P' \Downarrow_a$.*
2. *(distributed liveness) We say network $N$ satisfies* distributed liveness, *if, for all $P$ such that $N \equiv (\nu\tilde{a})([P \mid Q] \mid M)$ which is derived from $P \vdash A, a:\tau$ with $A$ closed and* $\mathsf{md}(\tau) = \uparrow_L$, *$P$ has a local liveness at $a$.*

The following is proved from Theorem 1 as stated in [19].

**Theorem 2.** *For all $N$ such that $N \vdash A$, $N$ satisfies distributed liveness.*

*Example 2.* Suppose that $a, b$ are linear names and $c, u$ are affine.

1. $a.\overline{b}$, $b.\overline{c}$ and $c.0 \mid \overline{b}$ are typable as $a.\overline{b} \vdash a:()^{\downarrow_{\mathrm{L}}} \rightarrow b:()^{\uparrow_{\mathrm{L}}}$, $b.\overline{c} \vdash b:()^{\downarrow_{\mathrm{L}}}, c:()^{\uparrow_{\mathrm{A}}}$ and $c.0 \mid \overline{b} \vdash c:()^{\downarrow_{\mathrm{A}}}, b:()^{\uparrow_{\mathrm{L}}}$, respectively. But $c.\overline{b}$ is not typable.

2. Let $\Omega_u \stackrel{\text{def}}{=} (\nu y)(\mathsf{fw}_{uy}|\mathsf{fw}_{yu})$ with $\mathsf{fw}_{xy} \stackrel{\text{def}}{=} !x(z).\overline{y}\langle z\rangle$. $\mathsf{fw}_{xy}$ is called a *forwarder*, while $\Omega_u$ is an *omega* which diverges with a message as: $\Omega_u|\overline{u}\langle e\rangle \rightarrow \Omega_u|\overline{u}\langle e\rangle \rightarrow ....$ It is typed as $\Omega_u \vdash u : ((\,)^{\uparrow_{\mathrm{A}}})^{?_{\mathrm{A}}}$.
3. $\mathsf{timer}^5\langle a.\overline{b},\ a.\overline{b}\rangle$, $\mathsf{timer}^5\langle c.0,\ c.0\rangle$ and $P \stackrel{\text{def}}{=} \mathsf{timer}^5\langle c.\overline{b},\ (c.0 \mid \overline{b})\rangle$ are typable but $Q \stackrel{\text{def}}{=} \mathsf{timer}^5\langle c.\overline{b},\ c.\overline{b}\rangle$ is not typable. The first two are by [TIMER], and $P$ is by [TIMER$_c$]. We shall see how the liveness at $b$ is guaranteed in $P$ by dividing into the two cases. The first case is when $c$ is returned within the time limit 5 because the call between the first and second processes terminates.
$$!e(y).\overline{y} \mid (\nu x)(\overline{e}\langle x\rangle \mid x.\overline{c}) \mid P \rightarrow\rightarrow !e(y).\overline{y} \mid \overline{c} \mid \phi^2(P) \rightarrow !e(y).\overline{y} \mid \overline{b}$$
The second case is a time-out due to non-termination of the call.
$$\Omega_u \mid (\nu x)(\overline{e}\langle x\rangle \mid x.\overline{c}) \mid P \rightarrow^5 \Omega_u \mid (\nu x)(\overline{e}\langle x\rangle \mid x.\overline{c}) \mid \phi^5(P) \equiv \Omega_u \mid (\nu x)(\overline{e}\langle x\rangle \mid x.\overline{c}) \mid c.0 \mid \overline{b}$$
This shows if we replace $P$ by $Q$, we cannot guarantee the liveness at $b$.
4. We show typing of the remote invoker from (1) in Example 1. First we type the server as: $[!a(yr).\overline{r}\langle y \times 3\rangle] \vdash a\!:\!\tau$ with $\tau = (\mathtt{nat}(\mathtt{nat})^{\uparrow_{\mathrm{A}}})^{!_{\mathrm{A}}}$ Then the remote invoker has type $\overline{a}\langle 10\rangle^{100}; (\tilde{x}).\overline{b}\langle x+7\rangle \rhd^5 \overline{b}\langle 0\rangle \vdash a\!:\!\overline{\tau}, b\!:\!(\mathtt{nat})^{\uparrow_{\mathrm{L}}}$. Here we assume $\mathtt{nat}$ is the type of natural numbers. Note that $b$ has a linear output, hence ensuring liveness. By hiding $b$, the client location can also have a distributable type.

## 4 Probabilistic Distributed Timed Processes and Bisimulation

We refine our model by replacing non-deterministic message-loss with a probability $r \in [0,1]$ which structures all message-loss globally and independently (i.e. the message-loss probability does not change throughout the course of a computation, and the events that two different messages get lost are independent). More general forms of probability like having different message-loss probabilities for different channels, or having probabilities change over time, are easily expressible in our framework, but have been omitted for brevity. Our approach to adding probabilities, inspired by [11, 12], is classical in that we use probabilistic automata [28].

**Definition 2.** Let $A$ be a discrete set (i.e. finite or countably infinite). A *formal quantity* over $A$ is a relation $\mathcal{R} \subseteq A \times \mathbb{R}^+$, where $\mathbb{R}^+$ denotes the non-negative real numbers. The *support* of $\mathcal{R}$ is $\mathsf{support}(\mathcal{R}) \stackrel{\text{def}}{=} \{a \in A \mid (a,r) \in \mathcal{R}, r > 0\}$. We often omit $A$. We can add formal quantities, and multiply them with scalars: if $r \in \mathbb{R}^+$ then $r \cdot \mathcal{R} \stackrel{\text{def}}{=} \{(a, r \cdot a) \mid (a,r) \in \mathcal{R}\}$. Likewise $\Sigma_{i \in I}\mathcal{R}_i \stackrel{\text{def}}{=} \bigcup_{i \in I}\mathcal{R}_i$. We often write $\Sigma_{(a,r)\in\mathcal{R}} r \cdot \overline{a}$ for $\mathcal{R}$. If $\mathcal{R}$ is a function, we call $\mathcal{R}$ a *quantity* over $A$. An important example of a quantity over $A$ is $\overline{a} \stackrel{\text{def}}{=} \{(a,1)\} \cup \{(a',0) \mid a' \neq a\}$. We call $\overline{a}$ the *Dirac-distribution for a* (in $A$), and often write simple $a$ for $\overline{a}$. Many formal quantities $\mathcal{R}$ can be *flattened* into a quantity $\flat(\mathcal{R})$ which is the map $a \mapsto \Sigma_{(a,r)\in\mathcal{R}} r$, assuming that the sum in this expression converges for every $a$. Hence $\flat(\cdot)$ is a partial operation. Scalar multiplication of quantities is that of formal quantities, whereas summation on quantities is given by $\Sigma_{i\in I} f_i \stackrel{\text{def}}{=} \flat(\bigcup_{i\in I} f_i)$, which is only defined where $\flat(\cdot)$ is defined.

A *subprobability distribution*, ranged over by $\Delta, ...$, over a discrete set $A$ is a quantity over $A$ such $\Delta : A \to [0,1]$ such that $\Sigma_{a\in A}\Delta(a) \leq 1$. We often call subprobability distributions just distributions. A subprobability distribution $\Delta$ is a *probability distribution* if $\Sigma_{a\in A}\Delta(a) = 1$. We write $\Delta_1|\Delta_2$ for the distribution $\Delta$ such that $\Delta(M) = \Delta_1(N)\cdot\Delta_2(L)$, provided that $M = N|L$, and $\Delta(M) = 0$ otherwise. $\Delta|M$ is short for $\Delta|\overline{M}$. Similarly, $(\nu x)\Delta$ is the distribution $\Delta'$ such that $\Delta'(N)$ is $\Delta(M)$ if $N = (\nu x)M$ and 0 otherwise. If $\mathsf{support}(\Delta) = \{M_1,...,M_n\}$ and $\Delta(M_i) = p_i$, we also write $(M_1 : p_1,...,M_n : p_n)$ or just $\tilde{M} : \tilde{p}$ for $\Delta$. We write $()$ for the subprobability distribution that is 0 everywhere, and often do not specify 0 probabilities. We call a formal quantity $\mathcal{R}$ such that $\flat(\mathcal{R})$ is a subprobability distribution a *formal subprobability distribution*. We write $\Delta_1 \equiv \Delta_2$ provided $\Delta_i = (M^i_1 : p_1,...,M^i_n : p_n)$ for $i = 1,2$ and for all $j$: $M^1_j \equiv M^2_j$. If $\mathcal{R}$ is a relation on networks, its *lifting* to subprobability distributions is: $\flat(\tilde{M} : \tilde{r})\,\mathcal{R}\,\flat(\tilde{N} : \tilde{r})$ iff for all $i$: $M_i\,\mathcal{R}\,N_i$. By $\sim$ we denote the usual *probabilistic strong bisimilarity* and also its lifting.

**Reductions and Transitions.** We define probabilistic reductions on networks by the rules below. Reductions are of the form $M \to \Delta$ where $\Delta$ is a probability distribution over networks. $\Delta(N)$ expresses the probability that $M$ can evolve into $N$ in one step. Probabilistic choices are made only about loosing messages in remote communication. All other choices relating are resolved non-deterministically.

$$\textsc{Intra}\ \frac{P \to Q}{[P] \to_1 [Q]} \qquad \textsc{Par}\ \frac{M \to \Delta}{M|N \to \Delta|N} \qquad \textsc{Res}\ \frac{M \to \Delta}{(\nu a)M \to (\nu a)\Delta} \qquad \textsc{Cong}\ \frac{M \equiv M' \to \Delta' \equiv \Delta}{M \to \Delta}$$

$$\textsc{Com}\ \frac{}{[P|\overline{x}\langle\tilde{y}\rangle] \mid [Q|x(\tilde{v}).R] \to \left\{\begin{array}{ll}[\phi(P)]|[Q|x(\tilde{v}).R] & : r\\ {[\phi(P)]|[\phi(Q)|R\{\tilde{y}/\tilde{v}\}]} & : 1-r\end{array}\right\}}$$

$$\textsc{Rep}\ \frac{}{[P|\overline{x}\langle\tilde{y}\rangle] \mid [Q|!x(\tilde{v}).R] \to \left\{\begin{array}{ll}[\phi(P)]|[Q|!x(\tilde{v}).R] & : r\\ {[\phi(P)]|[\phi(Q)|R\{\tilde{y}/\tilde{v}\}|!x(\tilde{v}).R]} & : 1-r\end{array}\right\}}$$

Here $r \in [0,1]$ is the aforementioned message-loss probability. The corresponding reductions for replicated input and timed input are omitted. Reductions on processes are unchanged. We write $M \to_1 N$ to mean $M \to \overline{N}$. *Network transitions* are of the form $P \xrightarrow{l} \Delta$ where $\Delta$ is a probability distribution, and $l$ is a *label* generated as usual by $l ::= \tau \mid x(\tilde{y}) \mid \overline{x}\langle(\nu\tilde{y})\tilde{z}\rangle$. The process transitions are standard [4], non-probabilistic and listed in [7]. We write $M \xrightarrow{l}_1 N$ for $M \xrightarrow{l} \overline{N}$. The transition system is given by the rules:

$$\frac{P \xrightarrow{l} Q}{[P] \xrightarrow{l}_1 [Q]}\ \textsc{Loc} \qquad \frac{M \xrightarrow{l} \Delta \quad \mathsf{fn}(N)\cap\mathsf{bn}(l) = \emptyset}{M|N \xrightarrow{l} \Delta|N}\ \textsc{Par} \qquad \frac{M \xrightarrow{l} \Delta \quad x \notin \mathsf{n}(l)}{(\nu x)M \xrightarrow{l} (\nu x)\Delta}\ \textsc{Res}$$

$$\frac{M \xrightarrow{\overline{x}\langle(\nu\tilde{y})\tilde{z}\rangle} \Delta_1 \quad N \xrightarrow{x(\tilde{z})} \Delta_2 \quad \tilde{y}\cap\mathsf{fn}(N) = \emptyset}{M|N \xrightarrow{\tau} r\cdot(\nu\tilde{y})(\Delta_1|\overline{N}) + (1-r)(\nu\tilde{y})(\Delta_1|\Delta_2)}\ \textsc{Com}$$

$$\frac{M \xrightarrow{\overline{x}\langle(\nu\tilde{y})\tilde{z}\rangle} \Delta \quad a \in \tilde{z}\setminus(\tilde{y}\cup\{x\})}{(\nu a)M \xrightarrow{\overline{x}\langle(\nu a\tilde{y})\tilde{z}\rangle} \Delta}\ \textsc{Open} \qquad \frac{M \equiv_\alpha M' \quad M' \xrightarrow{l} \Delta}{M \xrightarrow{l} \Delta}\ \textsc{Alpha}$$

It is easy to show that $M \rightarrow \Delta$ iff $M' \equiv M \xrightarrow{\tau} \Delta' \equiv \Delta$. Clearly, whenever $M \xrightarrow{l} \Delta$ then $|\mathsf{support}(\Delta)| < 3$ and $\Delta$ is a probability distribution. Next we prepare for defining our notion of bisimilarity. For this we need to abstract from $\tau$-transitions with transitions $M \xrightarrow{\hat{l}} \Delta$ and define $\Delta \stackrel{\hat{l}}{\Longrightarrow} \Delta'$ where $\Delta$ and $\Delta'$ are *sub*probability distributions. The need for subprobability distributions is explained below.

**Definition 3.** *The* auxiliary transitions $\stackrel{l}{\rightsquigarrow}$ *are defined by: (1)* $M \xrightarrow{l} \Delta$ *implies* $M \stackrel{l}{\rightsquigarrow} \Delta$ *and (2)* $M \stackrel{l}{\rightsquigarrow} ()$. *Now* weak transitions $M \xrightarrow{\hat{l}} \Delta$ *are defined if (1)* $M \stackrel{l}{\rightsquigarrow} \Delta$ *or (2)* $l = \tau$ *and* $\Delta = \overline{M}$. *This is extended to distributions as follows. We write* $\Delta \xrightarrow{\hat{l}} \Delta'$ *provided: (1)* $\Delta = \Sigma_{i \in I} p_i \cdot \overline{M_i}$, *(2) for all* $i \in I$ *with* $p_i > 0$: $M_i \xrightarrow{\hat{l}} \Delta_i$, *(3)* $\Delta' = \Sigma_{i \in I} p_i \cdot \Delta_i$. *Now we set* $\Delta \stackrel{\hat{\tau}}{\Longrightarrow} \Delta'$ *whenever* $\Delta (\xrightarrow{\hat{\tau}})^* \Delta'$. *We define* $\Delta \stackrel{\hat{l}}{\Longrightarrow} \Delta'$ *when* $\Delta \stackrel{\hat{\tau}}{\Longrightarrow} \xrightarrow{l} \stackrel{\hat{\tau}}{\Longrightarrow} \Delta'$. *Similarly, for* $l \neq \tau$, *we also write* $\Delta \stackrel{\hat{l}}{\Longrightarrow} \Delta'$ *for* $\Delta \stackrel{l}{\Longrightarrow} \Delta'$. $M \stackrel{\hat{l}}{\Longrightarrow} \Delta$ *stands for* $\overline{M} \stackrel{\hat{l}}{\Longrightarrow} \Delta$.

*Example 3.* Let $M \stackrel{\text{def}}{=} [\overline{x}\langle y\rangle] | [x(v).\overline{v}], \Delta = ([0] | [x(v).\overline{v}] : r, [0] | [\overline{y}] : 1-r), \Delta' \stackrel{\text{def}}{=} ([0] | [x(v).\overline{v}] : 0, [0] | [0] : 1-r)$. Note that $\Delta'$ is a subprobability distribution. Then $M$'s (auxiliary/weak) transitions and reductions include:

$$M \rightarrow \Delta \qquad M \stackrel{\tau}{\rightsquigarrow} \Delta \qquad M \stackrel{\hat{\tau}}{\rightsquigarrow} \overline{M} \qquad M \stackrel{\hat{\tau}}{\rightsquigarrow} \Delta \qquad M \stackrel{\hat{\overline{y}}}{\Longrightarrow} \Delta'$$

Weak transitions have a proper subprobability distribution as target. It is inferred as $M \stackrel{\hat{\tau}}{\rightsquigarrow} \Delta \stackrel{\hat{\overline{y}}}{\Longrightarrow} \Delta'$. Then $\Delta \stackrel{\hat{\overline{y}}}{\Longrightarrow} \Delta'$ is inferred as the combination of $[0] | [\overline{y}] \stackrel{\hat{\overline{y}}}{\rightsquigarrow} \overline{[0] | [0]}$ and $[0] | [x(v).\overline{v}] \stackrel{\hat{\overline{y}}}{\rightsquigarrow} ()$. Note that this last transition uses $()$ only to specify that $[0] | [x(v).\overline{v}]$ does not in fact have a transition labelled $\overline{y}$. Presenting the absence of a transition this way simplifies defining bisimulations.

### 4.1 Approximate Bisimulation

We introduce probabilistic approximate bisimulations. They are useful in the study of DS where we often want to give erroneous behaviour a different status from normal operation. To explain the issue, consider:

$$M \stackrel{\text{def}}{=} (\nu x)([\overline{x}\langle y\rangle] \mid [x(v).P]) \qquad\qquad N \stackrel{\text{def}}{=} [P\{y/v\}]$$

Assuming $x \notin \mathsf{fn}(P)$ and no message-loss, we expect $M \approx N$, where $\approx$ is a chosen notion of weak equivalence. However, if $r > 0$ is the global message-loss probability, such an equality can no longer hold, *irrespective of how negligible r may be*. This often stands in the way of reasoning, because we want to abstract away from negligible probabilities. Now consider

$$M^n \stackrel{\text{def}}{=} (\nu x)([\Pi_{i=1}^n \overline{x}\langle y\rangle] \mid [x(v).P]) \qquad\qquad (n > 0)$$

In general, with $x \notin \mathsf{fn}(P)$, $M^n$ can only be distinguished from $N$ if that all $n$ outputs $\overline{x}\langle y\rangle$ get lost. The probability of this happening is $r^n$. We would like to have a notion of equality $\approx^{\varepsilon}$ such that $M^n \approx^{r^n} N$, i.e. $\varepsilon \in [0,1]$ gives a quantitative bound on how much the processes compared by $\approx^{\varepsilon}$ are allowed to mismatch. Approximate notions of equality are of prime importance in cryptography where one usually demonstrates the safety of a cryptographic protocol by showing that the probability that it can be broken vanishes exponentially quickly in a chosen system parameter (like password length). Approximate bisimulations are intended to generalise this style of verification and connect it with standard methods in concurrency theory.

**Definition 4.** *An* approximate bisimulation *is a family* $\{\mathcal{R}^{\varepsilon}\}_{\varepsilon \in B}$ *where* $B \subseteq [0,1]$ *of relations on networks such that* $M \mathcal{R}^{\varepsilon} N$ *implies: whenever* $M \xrightarrow{l} \Delta$ *then also* $N \xRightarrow{\hat{l}} \Delta'$ *for some* $\Delta'$ *with* $\Delta \mathcal{R}^{\varepsilon} \Delta'$*, and vice versa. Here* $\Delta \mathcal{R}^{\varepsilon} \Delta'$ *means that we can find two formal subprobability distributions* $\tilde{M} : \tilde{r}, \tilde{M}' : \tilde{s}$ *and* $\tilde{N} : \tilde{r}, \tilde{N}' : \tilde{t}$ *such that: (1)* $\Delta = \flat(\tilde{M} : \tilde{r}, \tilde{M}' : \tilde{s})$*; (2)* $\Delta' = \flat(\tilde{N} : \tilde{r}, \tilde{N}' : \tilde{t})$*; (3)* $1 - \Sigma_i r_i \leq \varepsilon$*; (4) for all i:* $M_i \mathcal{R}^{\varepsilon'_i} N_i$ *for some* $\varepsilon'_i \leq \frac{\varepsilon}{r_i}$*. We call* $\varepsilon$ *the* discount *of* $\mathcal{R}^{\varepsilon}$ *and* $\mathcal{R}^{\varepsilon}$ *on distributions the* $\varepsilon$-lift. Strong approx. bisimulations *are defined similarly.*

This definition refines [15] by weighting discounts through clause (4). Similar techniques can be used to produce approx. forms of other equivalence (e.g. traces). Without refinement, one cannot prove, e.g. $M^n \approx^{r^n} N$, only the weaker $M^n \approx^{r} N$.

**Lemma 1.** *1.* $\{\equiv^0\}$ *is an approx. bisimulation.*

2. $\{\mathcal{R}^1\}$ *is an approx. bisimulation for every* $\mathcal{R}$*.*
3. *If* $\{\mathcal{R}^{\varepsilon_i}\}_{i \in I}$ *is an approx. bisimulation and* $\varepsilon_i \leq \varepsilon'_i$ *for all i then* $\{\mathcal{R}^{\varepsilon'_i}\}_{i \in I}$ *is an approx. bisimulation.*
4. *If* $\{\mathcal{R}_j^{\varepsilon}\}_{\varepsilon \in B_j}$ *is an approx. bisimulation for each j then so is* $\{\mathcal{S}^{\varepsilon} \mid \varepsilon \in \bigcup_j B_j\}$ *where* $\mathcal{S}^{\varepsilon} \stackrel{def}{=} \{(M,N) \mid \exists j.(M,N) \in \mathcal{R}_j^{\varepsilon}\}$.
5. $\{\mathcal{R}^0\}$ *is an approx. bisimulation, where* $\mathcal{R} \stackrel{def}{=} \{([P],[Q]) \mid P \approx Q\}$ *with* $\approx$ *being the usual bisimulation on processes [19, 4].*

Lemma 1.5 transfers the chosen equivalence on processes to networks.

**Definition 5.** *M and N are* $\varepsilon$-bisimilar *if* $M \mathcal{R}^{\varepsilon} N$ *for some approx. bisimulation* $\{\mathcal{R}^{\varepsilon_i}\}_i$*. In this case we also write* $M \approx^{\varepsilon} N$*.*

To aid reasoning about approx. bisimulations one can use up-to techniques.

**Definition 6.** $\{\mathcal{R}^{\varepsilon_i}\}_i$ *is an approx. bisimulation* up to $\sim$ (resp. up to restriction) *if* $M \mathcal{R}^{\varepsilon} N$ *implies that whenever* $M \xrightarrow{l} \Delta$ *there is* $N \xRightarrow{\hat{l}} \Delta'$ *such that* $\Delta\, (\sim \circ \mathcal{R}^{\varepsilon} \circ \sim)\, \Delta'$ *(resp.* $\Delta_0\ \mathcal{R}^{\varepsilon}\ \Delta'_0$ *with* $\Delta = (\nu\tilde{x})\Delta_0, \Delta' = (\nu\tilde{x})\Delta'$*), and vice versa.*

The main result follows.

**Theorem 3 (congruency).** $\approx^{\varepsilon}$ *is a congruence.*

The following theorem offers compositional and tractable verification tools for approx. bisimulations.

**Theorem 4.** *1. If* $\{\mathcal{R}^{\varepsilon}\}_{\varepsilon \in B}$ *is an* $\varepsilon$*-bisimulation up to* $\sim$ *or up to restriction then* $\mathcal{R}^{\varepsilon} \subseteq \approx^{\varepsilon}$ *for all* $\varepsilon \in B$*.*

2. *If* $M \approx^r N$ *and* $N \approx^s L$ *then* $M \approx^{\min(r+s,1)} L$.
3. *With r being the global message-loss probability,* $(\nu\tilde{x})([P|Q]) \approx^r (\nu\tilde{x})([P]\|[Q])$ *for all* $\tilde{x}$ *and all timer-free* $P, Q$.

The restriction to timer-free processes in (3) is vital because the relative timing between $P$ and $Q$ is very different if these processes run in a single location rather than in two.

We can now motivate subprobability distributions and the shape of auxiliary transitions: consider $(\nu x)M$ with $M$ as in Example 3. If we want to show that $(\nu x)M \approx^r [\overline{y}]$, we need to match $[\overline{y}] \xrightarrow{\overline{y}} [0]$. But $(\nu x)M$ can do an output on $y$ only if the internal message on $x$ is not lost. This is expressed by the subprobability appearing in the matching weak transition $(\nu x)M \xrightarrow{\hat{\tau}} (\nu x)\Delta \xRightarrow{\hat{\overline{y}}} (\nu x)\Delta'$. Without this definition of weak transitions, the definition of approx. bisimulation would be more complicated.

**Typed Approximate Bisimulations.** We now show how types lead to more efficient approximate reasoning. The key point [5] is that some transitions cannot be observed in a typed setting because no well-typed observer can interact with it. E.g. $P \stackrel{\text{def}}{=} \overline{x}\langle v\rangle|x(y).Q$ has transitions at $x$, but if $P \vdash x : \updownarrow, A$ then $x$ is not available for further composition. Hence we need not consider transitions at $x$ when comparing $P$ with another process of the same type. Similarly from $\overline{x}\langle v\rangle|!x(y).Q$, we cannot observe the output at $x$ since it should be consumed in the unique replicator. This intuition is formalised as follows: let $A$ be an action type and $l$ an action. The predicate $A \vdash l$ is defined if (1) $l = \overline{x}\langle(\nu\tilde{y})\tilde{z}\rangle$ implies $\mathsf{md}(A(x)) \in \{\uparrow_{\mathrm{L}}, \uparrow_{\mathrm{A}}, ?_{\mathrm{L}}, ?_{\mathrm{A}}\}$; or (2) $l = x(\tilde{y})$ implies $A(x) \in \{\downarrow_{\mathrm{L}}, \downarrow_{\mathrm{A}}, !_{\mathrm{L}}, !_{\mathrm{A}}\}$; or (3) $l = \tau$. A (sub)probability distribution has *type A* if $\Delta(M) > 0$ implies $M \vdash A$. *Typed labelled transitions* $P \xrightarrow{l} Q \vdash A$ are defined if $P \vdash A$, $A \vdash l$ and $P \xrightarrow{l} Q$. For networks we have $M \xrightarrow{l} \Delta \vdash A$ provided $M \vdash A$, $A \vdash l$ and $M \xrightarrow{l} \Delta$.

**Definition 7.** *A* typed approximate bisimulation *is a family* $\{\mathcal{R}^\varepsilon\}_{\varepsilon\in B}$ *where* $B \subseteq [0,1]$ *of binary relations on typed networks, relating only terms of the same type, such that* $M\,\mathcal{R}^\varepsilon N$ *implies that whenever* $M \xrightarrow{l} \Delta \vdash A$ *then also* $N \xRightarrow{\hat{l}} \Delta'$ *for some* $\Delta'$ *with* $\Delta\,\mathcal{R}^\varepsilon\,\Delta'$*, and vice versa. The definition of* $\Delta\,\mathcal{R}^\varepsilon\,\Delta'$ *is similarly adapted.*

We note that Theorems 3 and 4 also hold for the typed bisimilarity.

## 4.2 Examples of Distributed Protocols

**Verifying an RPC Protocol with Message Recovery.** We show how to use approx. bisimulations to reason about remote procedure calls (RPCs), an important distributed algorithm that uses timers to increase the reliability of remote communication. In this subsection, we assume that [IDLE] is only used when no other rules apply. This standard assumption is called *maximal progress* in the literature and prevents the timer aborting by itself even when communication is possible. Consider:

$$P \stackrel{\text{def}}{=} !x(mv).\overline{v}\langle m+2\rangle \qquad\qquad Q \stackrel{\text{def}}{=} (\nu y)(\overline{x}\langle 5y\rangle|y(m).\overline{a}\langle m+1\rangle)$$

We type: $P|Q \vdash A$ with $A \stackrel{\text{def}}{=} x : (\mathtt{nat}(\mathtt{nat})^{\uparrow_{\mathrm{A}}})^{!_{\mathrm{A}}}, a : (\mathtt{nat})^{\uparrow_{\mathrm{L}}}$. It is easy to show that $P|Q \approx P|\overline{a}\langle 8\rangle$ (where $\approx$ is the typed bisimilarity on processes [19]), hence by Theorem 4 and Lemma 1, we have:

$$[P|\overline{a}\langle 8\rangle|a(z).R] \quad \approx^0 \quad [P|Q|a(z).R] \quad \approx^r \quad [P] \mid [Q|a(z).R]$$

Theorem 4 is thus useful because it gives a straightforward upper bound on how different (untimed) processes can be when distributed. But since it does so without assumptions on $P$ and $Q$, the bounds are weak. To improve on the right bound, we can use the remote invoker from Example 1:

$$Q^n \stackrel{\text{def}}{=} \overline{x}\langle 5\rangle^n;(m).\overline{a}\langle m+1\rangle \rhd^t \overline{a}\langle 0\rangle$$

The timer is used to amplify the reliability of communication over an unreliable channel $x$. It uses a hidden name, generated at the client, to get the acknowledgement. The timer re-sends the invocation repeatedly, if the acknowledgement is not received within time $t$. The receiver $a(z).R$ at the server side knows whether it was correctly delivered a datum or whether a timeout happened, because $\overline{a}\langle 0\rangle$ signals $n$-ary timeout, which can be taken as indicating failure. Assuming that $r$ is the global message-loss probability, we want to establish that

$$[P] \mid [Q^n \mid a(z).R] \quad \approx^{r^n} \quad [P] \mid [\overline{a}\langle 8\rangle \mid a(z).R] \tag{2}$$

provided $t > 1$ and $x \notin \mathsf{fn}(R)$. Note that $a$ in (2) has type $x :\updownarrow$. Establishing (2) is straightforward by induction. The base case is trivial. For the inductive step note that $[P]|[\overline{a}\langle 8\rangle \mid a(z).R] \xrightarrow{\hat{\tau}}_1 [P]|[0 \mid R\{8/z\}]$. This can be matched in several ways: either the first invocation attempt already succeeds with probability $1-r$, or the first fails but the second succeeds (probability $r\cdot(1-r)$) and so on, giving the weak transition $[P]|[Q^n \mid a(z).R] \stackrel{\hat{\tau}}{\Longrightarrow} ([P]|[0 \mid R\{8/z\}] : 1-r^n)$. The other remaining transitions can be matched exactly since linear liveness at $a$ guarantees that the interaction with $a(z).R$ will always happen. Due to typing, we do not need to consider output transitions of $Q^n$ because no typable observer can interact with them. This way, typing reduces the number of transitions to be matched in approx. bisimulations. Overall we easily establish (2) which means that $n$-ary remote invokers are an effective error recovery technique, reducing the possibility of message failures exponentially quickly in the parameter $n$.

Next we show that conversely, the more a DS relies on networked communication, the more error-prone it becomes. To this end, define

$$M^{n+1} \stackrel{\text{def}}{=} (\nu\tilde{x})([\overline{x_1}\langle v\rangle] \mid \Pi_{i=1}^{n-1}[x_i(y).\overline{x_{i+1}}\langle y\rangle] \mid [x_n(y).\overline{y}]) \qquad M^0 \stackrel{\text{def}}{=} [\overline{v}]$$

As in the previous examples one can then show that $M^n \approx^{1-(1-r)^n} [\overline{v}]$. This says that the chance of $M^n$ behaving like $[\overline{v}]$ diminishes exponentially quickly.

**Leases.** Another important example for fault-tolerant DS are *leases* [16] which allow clients to access a remote service for a limited amount of time. Once that time has expired without the client renewing the lease, access is denied to the client, and the server holding the service is free to close it, to make it available to others, or to withdraw it completely. In our setting, leases are naturally expressed using *typed, timed forwarders*. A timed forwarder $\mathsf{tfw}_{xy}^{t\cdot P}$ does the same, but only for $t$ units of time, and after expiry of the lease executes the 'clean-up process' $P$.

$$\mathsf{tfw}_{xy}^{0\cdot P} \stackrel{\text{def}}{=} P|x(\tilde{v}).0 \qquad \mathsf{tfw}_{xy}^{t+1\cdot P} \stackrel{\text{def}}{=} \mathsf{timer}^1\langle x(\tilde{v}).(\overline{y}\langle v\rangle \mid \mathsf{tfw}_{xy}^{t\cdot 0}),\ \mathsf{tfw}_{xy}^{t\cdot P}\rangle$$

where $x, y$ are affine input and output. This is vital for consistent usage of the clean-up process $P$. Timed forwarders can be typed in two easy ways: (1) with the tailor-made rules below, or (2) in the system that replaces replication with general recursion, given in [7].

$$\text{IGN}\ \frac{a(\tilde{x}).P \vdash a : (\tilde{\tau})^{\downarrow_A}, A^{-a}}{a(\tilde{x}).(P \mid !a(\tilde{x}).0) \vdash a : (\tilde{\tau})^{!_A}, A} \qquad \text{TFW}_0\ \frac{P \vdash A^{-xy}}{\mathsf{tfw}_{xy}^{0 \cdot P} \vdash x : (\tilde{\tau})^{\downarrow_A}, y : (\overline{\tilde{\tau}})^{\uparrow_A}, A} \qquad \text{TFW}_t\ \frac{\mathsf{tfw}_{xy}^{t+1 \cdot P} \vdash A}{\mathsf{tfw}_{xy}^{t+2 \cdot P} \vdash A}$$

Now $\mathsf{tfw}_{xy}^{t \cdot P}$ is typable as $\mathsf{tfw}_{xy}^{t \cdot P} \vdash x : \tau, y : \overline{\tau}, A$ assuming $\tau$ is an distributable affine output, $A$ is a type of $P$, and $x, y$ do not occur in $A$. We now consider a simple use of leases. Let the resource in question be $y.\overline{a}$: all we can do with it is to close it by sending a message to the affine name $y$. Clearly $(\nu y)[y.\overline{a} \mid \overline{y}] \approx^0 [\overline{a}]$. When we access the resource over the net, message loss may leave the resource unclosed: $(\nu y)([y.\overline{a}] \mid [\overline{y}]) \rightarrow (\nu y)[y.\overline{a}]$. Now we employ a lease $P \stackrel{\text{def}}{=} !b(r).\overline{r}(x)\mathsf{tfw}_{xy}^{t \cdot \overline{y}}$ to ensure that the resource gets closed automatically if the leaseholder does not close it explicitly.

$$M \stackrel{\text{def}}{=} (\nu y b)([P | y.\overline{a}] \mid [\overline{b}(r) r(x).\overline{x}])$$

Then we show that message-loss does not affect closing the resource: $M \approx^0 [\overline{a}]$.

**Verifying the 2PCP.** The Two-Phase Commit protocol (2PCP) is a ubiquitous distributed algorithm [3]. It is a network of the form

$$\mathsf{2PCP} \stackrel{\text{def}}{=} (\nu \tilde{d} \tilde{v})([P_1] \mid \ldots \mid [P_n] \mid [C])$$

It has a coordinator $C$ and $n$ participants $P_i$, all of which can decide to commit or abort. If all processes decide to commit and the coordinator receives all the votes towards commitment in time, then every participant will commit, otherwise they will all abort. We shall verify this property using our formalism. The protocol is described as follows:

$$P_i \stackrel{\text{def}}{=} P_i^a \oplus P_i^c \quad P_i^a \stackrel{\text{def}}{=} \overline{v_i}^k\langle \mathsf{true} \rangle | \overline{a_i} | !d_i(b).0 \qquad P_i^c \stackrel{\text{def}}{=} \overline{v_i}^k\langle \mathsf{false} \rangle \mid !d_i(b).\mathsf{if}\ b\ \mathsf{then}\ \overline{a_i}\ \mathsf{else}\ \overline{c_i}$$

$$C \stackrel{\text{def}}{=} (\nu a \tilde{e})(C_{\mathsf{wait}} | C_{\mathsf{and}} | C_{\mathsf{ab}}) \qquad C_{\mathsf{wait}} \stackrel{\text{def}}{=} \Pi_i v_i(b).\mathsf{if}\ b\ \mathsf{then}\ \overline{e_i}\langle \tilde{d} \rangle\ \mathsf{else}\ \overline{a}\langle \tilde{d} \rangle$$

$$C_{\mathsf{and}} \stackrel{\text{def}}{=} e_1(\tilde{d}). \ldots e_n(\tilde{d}).\Pi_i \overline{d_i}^k\langle \mathsf{false} \rangle \qquad C_{\mathsf{ab}} \stackrel{\text{def}}{=} a(\tilde{d}).(\Pi_i \overline{d_i}^k\langle \mathsf{true} \rangle \mid !a(\tilde{d}).0)$$

Here we use standard extended syntax $P \oplus Q$ (internal choice) and if-branch (see [7] for their straightforward typing rules). $P_i$ makes a non-deterministic choice between aborting ($P_i^a$) and committing ($P_i^c$). $P_i^a$ does two things: it signals its decision to abort to the outside world by sending an $a_i$. At the same time, the coordinator is informed of its choice, by sending a vote $\overline{v_i}\langle \mathsf{true} \rangle$ on the internal voting channel $v_i$. $P_i^c$ is similar in that it sends its vote to the coordinator, but it externalises its decision only after having received back the overall decision from the coordinator. The coordinator has a subprocess $C_{\mathsf{wait}}$ that awaits the votes from all participants. Communication between participants and the coordinator happens on $v_i$, where the votes are cast, and $d_i$ where the coordinator returns its decision back to the participants. This protocol guarantees that either all participants will commit or all participants will abort, assuming that eventually all sent messages will be delivered with high probability. In $P_i$, $\overline{x}^k\langle \tilde{y} \rangle$ with $k > 0$ is a simpler version of the remote invoker in Example 1 with the following semantics: $\phi(\overline{x}^k\langle\tilde{y}\rangle) = \overline{x}^k\langle\tilde{y}\rangle$ and, writing $\overline{x}^0\langle\tilde{y}\rangle$ for 0,

$$[P|\overline{x}^k\langle\tilde{y}\rangle] \mid [x(\tilde{v}).Q|R] \rightarrow \left\{ \begin{array}{ll} [\phi(P)|\overline{x}^{k-1}\langle\tilde{y}\rangle] \mid [x(\tilde{v}).Q|R] & : r \\ [\phi(P)] \mid [Q\{\tilde{y}/\tilde{v}\}|R] & : 1-r \end{array} \right\}.$$

Here $x$ is of affine type $(\tilde{\tau})^{\uparrow_{\mathsf{A}}}$ with $y_i$ typed by $\tau_i$. The detailed types of this protocol, including the choice and if-branch are given in [7].

Next we state the main result of this subsection that the probability this protocol fails vanishes exponentially quickly in the parameter $k$.

**Theorem 5.** *Recall that r is the global message-loss probability. Then:*

$$\mathsf{2PCP} \approx^{e(k)} (\Pi_i[\overline{a_i}]) \oplus (\Pi_i[\overline{c_i}]) \qquad \textit{with } e(k) \stackrel{def}{=} 1-(1-r^k \cdot n)^n$$

*Here* $\approx^{e(k)}$ *is the typed approx. bisimulation.*

This theorem states that the probability that the protocol does not reach a consensus is negligible in $k$. This result improves on [3] in that precise quantities for failure of the protocol are derived. The types are also useful in compositional and quick reasoning about this 2PCP. First the protocol is typed as $\mathsf{2PCP} \vdash \tilde{a}:()^{?_{\mathsf{A}}}, \tilde{c}:()^{?_{\mathsf{A}}}$ where $\tilde{c}:\tau$ means $c_1:\tau,..,c_n:\tau$. Then, for example when considering $C$ we use the fact that $C \vdash \tilde{v}:(\mathtt{bool})^{\downarrow_{\mathsf{A}}}, \tilde{d}:(\mathtt{bool})^{?_{\mathsf{A}}}, \tilde{e}:\updownarrow$. This means we do not have to consider input or output actions happening on $a$ or $e_i$ in the external environment. Likewise, we do not observe non-$\tau$ actions from $[P_1] \mid ... \mid [P_n] \mid [C]$ by types. This significantly reduces a number of transitions needed to be considered in reasoning.

## 5 Conclusion and Related Work

We introduced a convenient typing system for a timed, distributed $\pi$-calculus that generalises the existing linear/affine typing discipline [19] for the asynchronous $\pi$-calculus. We refined some of the non-determinism in our calculus into probabilities and proposed a notion of typed approximate bisimulation to discard behaviour under a probability threshold. The timed calculus was originally introduced in [3,4]; [27,10] propose different timed $\pi$-calculi without distribution. Neither alternative considers typing or probabilities. Probabilistic $\pi$-calculi are investigated in [9,11,12,17,30]. None of these works considers types, timing or distribution, except that [30] uses the affine typing system [5] to prove a correspondence between probabilistic automata, confusion-free event structures and a typed probabilistic $\pi$-calculus. The notions of equivalence studied in these works are not directly applicable to our setting because they are not approximate (i.e. they do not allow to quantify parts of the computation that is discarded when considering equality), hence it is not possible to verify the examples in § 4.2.

Our work can be extended in several dimensions. One topic is to investigate our approximate bisimulation, for example by asking how to axiomatise it. We believe the techniques developed for axiomatising weak bisimilarity in [32] to be applicable to the present probabilistic extension, leading to a tractable transformation for reasoning about liveness at each location. It would also be fruitful to use probabilities for constraining other forms of non-determinism. A starting point would be the [IDLE] rule: rather than requiring maximal progress, we could have probabilistic idling. More ambitiously, timer behaviour could be guided by a probability distribution: the key technical challenge here is to find a tractable way of expressing the correlations between *different* probabilistic timers running in parallel.

The paper proposes a general way to integrate the timer with linearity, offering extensibility of various type-based analyses of processes [1, 5, 6, 8, 20, 22, 32] to timing and distribution. First, the secure information flow analysis (SIF) from [19, 21] can be adapted to study timing attacks [24] in distribution. Following [20, 22] an extension of types that accounts of usage numbers of linear channels can lead to more precise type-based SIF analysis in the presence of timers. Secondly, more complicated forms of failure can be considered, like message duplication, correlations between message failures (e.g. if a channel looses a message, the probability of subsequent message-losses increases), site failure [3] or byzantine message corruption [31]. It would also be fruitful to use probabilities for constraining other forms of non-determinism such as the permissible amount of idling. Finally, there is much recent work on (pseudo-)metrics for probabilistic automata [13, 14, 29]. These works do not feature distribution or types, but forging connections with the present approach would be very interesting.

**Acknowledgements.** We thank anonymous reviewers for their helpful comments. This work is partially supported by EPSRC GR/T04724, GR/T03208 and IST-2005-015905 MOBIUS.

## References

1. Ahern, A., Yoshida, N.: Formalising Java RMI with Explicit Code Mobility. In: Proc. OOPSLA 2005, ACM Press, New York (2005) A full version will appear in TCS
2. Andova, S., Baeten, J.C.M., Willemse, T.A.C.: A complete axiomatisation of branching bisimulation for probabilistic systems with an application in protocol verification. In: Baier, C., Hermanns, H. (eds.) CONCUR 2006. LNCS, vol. 4137, pp. 327–342. Springer, Heidelberg (2006)
3. Berger, M.: Towards Abstractions for Distributed Systems. PhD thesis, Imperial College, London (2002)
4. Berger, M.: Basic Theory of Reduction Congruence for Two Timed Asynchronous $\pi$-Calculi. In: Gardner, P., Yoshida, N. (eds.) CONCUR 2004. LNCS, vol. 3170, pp. 115–130. Springer, Heidelberg (2004)
5. Berger, M., Honda, K., Yoshida, N.: Sequentiality and the $\pi$-calculus. In: Abramsky, S. (ed.) TLCA 2001. LNCS, vol. 2044, pp. 29–45. Springer, Heidelberg (2001)
6. Berger, M., Honda, K., Yoshida, N.: Genericity and the $\pi$-calculus. Acta Inf. 42(2-3), 83–141 (2005)
7. Berger, M., Yoshida, N.: Timed, distributed, probabilistic, typed processes. Long version of the present paper, draft (2007)
8. Carbone, M., Honda, K., Yoshida, N.: Structured Communication-Centred Programming for Web Services. In: ESOP 2007. LNCS, vol. 4421, Springer, Heidelberg (2007)
9. Chatzikokolakis, K., Palamidessi, C.: A Framework to Analyze Probabilistic Protocols and its Application to the Partial Secrets Exchange. TCS (to appear)

10. Chen, J.: A timed mobile calculus. In: Proc. Nordic Workshop on Programming Theory, pp. 65–67 (2004)
11. Deng, Y., Du, W.: Probabilistic Barbed Congruence. In: Proc. QAPL (to appear, 2007)
12. Deng, Y., Palamidessi, C.: Axiomatizations for probabilistic finite-state behaviors. TCS 373(1-2), 92–114 (2007)
13. Desharnais, J., Gupta, V., Jagadeesan, R., Panangaden, P.: Metrics for Labelled Markov Processes. TCS 318(3), 354–413 (2004)
14. Desharnais, J., Jagadeesan, R., Gupta, V., Panangaden, P.: The metric analogue of weak bisimulation for probabilistic processes. In: Proc. LICS, pp. 413–422 (2002)
15. Giacalone, A., Jou, C.-C., Smolka, S.A.: Algebraic reasoning for probabilistic concurrent systems. In: Proc. Conf. on Programming Concepts and Methods, pp. 443–458 (1990)
16. Gray, C.G., Cheriton, D.R.: Leases: an efficient fault-tolerant mechanism for distributed file cache consistency. Technical Report CS-TR-90-1298, Stanford University (1990)
17. Herescu, O.M., Palamidessi, C.: Probabilistic asynchronous π-calculus. In: Tiuryn, J. (ed.) ETAPS 2000 and FOSSACS 2000. LNCS, vol. 1784, pp. 146–160. Springer, Heidelberg (2000)
18. Honda, K.: Composing Processes. In: POPL 1996, pp. 344–357. ACM Press, New York (1996)
19. Honda, K., Yoshida, N.: A uniform type structure for secure information flow. In: POPL 2002, pp. 81–92. ACM Press, New York (2002) Full version to appear in ACM TOPLAS
20. Igarashi, A., Kobayashi, N.: A generic type system for the pi-calculus. Theoretical Computer Science 311(1-3), 121–163 (2004)
21. Kobayashi, N.: Type-based information flow analysis for the pi-calculus. Acta Inf. 42(4-5), 291–347 (2005)
22. Kobayashi, N.: A new type system for deadlock-free processes. In: Baier, C., Hermanns, H. (eds.) CONCUR 2006. LNCS, vol. 4137, pp. 233–247. Springer, Heidelberg (2006)
23. Kobayashi, N., Pierce, B.C., Turner, D.N.: Linearity and the Pi-Calculus. ACM TOPLAS 21(5), 914–947 (1999)
24. Kocher, P.C.: Timing Attacks on Implementations of Diffie-Hellman, RSA, DSS, and Other Systems. In: McCurley, K.S., Ziegler, C.D. (eds.) Advances in Cryptology 1981 - 1997. LNCS, vol. 1440, pp. 104–113. Springer, Heidelberg (1999)
25. Mills, D.L.: The network computer as precision timekeeper. In: PTTI, pp. 96–108 (1996)
26. Mullender, S. (ed.): Distributed Systems. Addison-Wesley, Reading (1993)
27. Rounds, W.C., Song, H.: The Phi-Calculus: A Language for Distributed Control of Reconfigurable Embedded Systems. In: Proc. HSCC, pp. 435–449 (2003)
28. Segala, R.: Probability and Nondeterminism in Operational Models of Concurrency. In: Baier, C., Hermanns, H. (eds.) CONCUR 2006. LNCS, vol. 4137, pp. 64–78. Springer, Heidelberg (2006)
29. van Breugel, F., Worrell, J.: A Behavioural Pseudometric for Probabilistic Transition Systems. TCS 331(1), 115–142 (2005)
30. Varacca, D., Yoshida, N.: Probabilistic π-Calculus and Event Structures. In: Proc. QAPL, ENTCS (to appear, 2007)
31. Ying, M.: π-calculus with noisy channels. Acta Informatica 41(9), 525–593 (2005)
32. Yoshida, N., Berger, M., Honda, K.: Strong Normalisation in the π-Calculus. Inf. & Comp. 191(2004), 145–202 (2004)

# A Probabilistic Applied Pi–Calculus*

Jean Goubault-Larrecq[1], Catuscia Palamidessi[2], and Angelo Troina[1,2]

[1] LSV - ENS Cachan
61 Avenue du Président Wilson, 94235 Cachan - France
{goubault,troina}@lsv.ens-cachan.fr
[2] LIX - École Polytechnique
Rue de Saclay, 91128 Palaiseau - France
{catuscia,troina}@lix.polytechnique.fr

**Abstract.** We propose an extension of the Applied Pi–calculus by introducing nondeterministic and probabilistic choice operators. The semantics of the resulting model, in which probability and nondeterminism are combined, is given by Segala's Probabilistic Automata driven by schedulers which resolve the nondeterministic choice among the probability distributions over target states. Notions of static and observational equivalence are given for the enriched calculus. In order to model the possible interaction of a process with its surrounding environment a labeled semantics is given together with a notion of weak bisimulation which is shown to coincide with the observational equivalence. Finally, we prove that results in the probabilistic framework are preserved in a purely nondeterministic setting.

## 1 Introduction

Security protocols are a critical element of the infrastructures needed for secure communication and processing information. Most security protocols are quite simple if only their length is considered. However, the properties they are supposed to ensure are extremely subtle, hence it is hard to get protocols correct just by informal reasoning. The history of cryptography and security protocols has a lot of examples where weaknesses of supposedly correct algorithms or protocols were discovered even years later. Thus, security protocols are excellent candidates for rigorous formal analysis. They are critical components of distributed security, are very easy to express and very difficult to evaluate by hand.

The use of formal methods for modeling and analyzing cryptographic protocols is now well-established. After the seminal paper by Dolev and Yao [11], which introduced a simple and intuitive description for cryptographic protocols, many alternative definitions have been proposed on the basis of several approaches, ranging from modal logics to process algebras (see the calculi in [15,25,2]).

Probabilistic models are nowadays widely used in the design and verification of complex systems in order to quantify unreliable or unpredictable behaviour in security, performance and reliability analysis. Probability is taken into account

* This work has been partially supported by the INRIA/ARC project ProNoBiS.

Z. Shao (Ed.): APLAS 2007, LNCS 4807, pp. 175–190, 2007.

when analyzing quantitative security properties (measuring, in a sense, the security level of the protocol) or when dealing with probabilistic protocols. Probabilistic frameworks applied to security analysis are, just as an example, [3,10,20]). In particular, in [20] Mitchell et al. introduce a variant of CCS allowing probabilistic polynomial-time expressions in messages and boolean tests. The semantics of the calculus schedules probabilistically the exchanged messages. The authors also define a form of asymptotic protocol equivalence that allows security properties to be expressed using observational equivalence.

In [1], Abadi and Fournet introduce the Applied Pi–calculus, an extension of the Pi–calculus [18] with functions and equations allowing to treat messages not only as atomic names, but also as more complex terms constructed from names and functions. Such an extension gives rise to an important interaction between the *new* construct and value–passing communication allowing to model unforgeable capabilities. Applications to security are immediate. Moreover, the Applied Pi–calculus permits a general and systematic development of syntax, operational semantics, equivalences and proof techniques.

It has been remarked that the Applied Pi–calculus, thanks to its explicit substitutions, is similar to Concurrent Constraint calculi like CCP [24], the $\rho$–calculus [21] and the CC–pi calculus [5].

Bisimulation relations [17] are well–established behavioural equivalences and are now widely used for the verification of properties of computer systems. Actually, a property can be verified by assessing the bisimilarity of the considered system with a specification one knows to enjoy the property. Moreover, bisimulations can sometimes be verified automatically thanks to successful implementations of verification tools like, e.g., the Concurrency Workbench [7] or the Mobility Workbench [28]. It is also extremely important for bisimulations to be congruences in order to account on compositional behavioural equivalences.

## Contribution

In this paper we introduce an extension of the Applied Pi–calculus, called Probabilistic Applied Pi–calculus (PAPi for short), where both nondeterministic and probabilistic choices are taken into account. The semantics of the resulting model is given by Segala's Probabilistic Automata [26] driven by schedulers which resolve the nondeterministic choice among the probability distributions over target states (see [27]).

For the enriched calculus, we propose a notion of static equivalence (inherited from the Applied Pi–calculus) and a notion of probabilistic observational congruence. We also give a labeled semantics for modeling the interaction of a process with its surrounding environment. We derive a notion of weak bisimulation and show that it is a congruence relation coinciding with the observational equivalence defined for the unlabeled semantics. Finally, abstracting away from probabilities, we prove that results holding in the probabilistic version of the calculus are preserved within a purely nondeterministic framework.

As an application, we use PAPi to model and analyze the 1-out-of-2 oblivious transfer protocol given in [12]. Such a protocol makes use of cryptographic operations and randomization to achieve fairness in information exchange.

## 2 Preliminaries

In this section we recall some preliminary notions about terms, equational theories and probability distributions.

**Terms.** A signature $\Sigma = \{(f_1, a_1), \ldots, (f_n, a_n)\}$ consists of a finite set of function symbols $f_i$ each with an arity $a_i$. A function with arity 0 denotes a constant symbol. Given a signature $\Sigma$, and infinite set of names and variables, the set of *terms* is defined by the grammar:

$$M, N \ ::= \ a, b, c, \ldots \quad | \quad x, y, z, \ldots \quad | \quad f(M_1, \ldots, M_l)$$

where $M, N$ are terms, $a, b, c$ are names, $x, y, z$ are variables and $f(M_1, \ldots, M_l)$ denotes function application with $(f, l) \in \Sigma$. With $\mathcal{T}$ we denote the set of terms. A term is called *ground* when it does not contain free variables and we use $\mathcal{T}_G$ to denote the set of ground terms. Metavariables $u, v$ range over both names and variables. Tuples $u_1, \ldots, u_l$ and $M_1, \ldots, M_l$ are abbreviated to $\tilde{u}$ and $\tilde{M}$, respectively.

As in [1], we rely on a sort system for terms. It may include a set of base types, such as $\mathsf{Integer}$, $\mathsf{Key}$, etc., or simply a universal base type $\mathsf{Data}$. In addition, if $\mathcal{S}$ is a sort, then $\mathsf{Channel}(\mathcal{S})$ is the sort of those channels that convey messages of sort $\mathcal{S}$. Variables and names can have any sort. We would use $a$, and $c$ as channel names, $s$ and $k$ as names of some base type, and $m$ and $n$ as names of any sort. For simplicity, function symbols take arguments and produce results of base types only. In the following of the paper we always assume that terms are well-sorted and that substitutions preserve sorts.

**Equational Theories.** Given a signature $\Sigma$, we equip it with an *equational theory E*. An equational theory is a congruence over terms closed under substitutions of terms for variables (see [19,9,13]). We require this equational theory to be also closed under one-to-one substitutions on names. We use the standard notation $\Sigma \vdash M =_E N$ when the equation $M = N$ is in the theory $E$ of $\Sigma$, and $\Sigma \not\vdash M =_E N$ for the negation of $\Sigma \vdash M =_E N$.

In [1] one may find several examples of equational theories for the modeling of different kinds of cryptographic applications such as pairing, symmetric and asymmetric encryption, hashing, probabilistic encryption (modeled in a nondeterministic sense), signatures and XOR. We recall just some of them.

Algebraic data types such as pairs and lists could be defined by equipping a signature $\Sigma$ with the binary function symbol $\mathsf{pair}$ and the unary function symbols $\mathsf{fst}$ and $\mathsf{snd}$, with equations $\mathsf{fst}(\mathsf{pair}(x, y)) = x$ and $\mathsf{snd}(\mathsf{pair}(x, y)) = y$.

Now, the equational theory for algebraic data types consists of these equations and all the ones obtained by reflexivity, symmetry and transitivity and by substituting terms for variables. The sort system should enforce that fst and snd are applied only to pairs (alternatively a boolean function recognizing pairs may be added). Equations can be added to describe particular behaviours. For example, a constant symbol wrong can be considered such that $\mathsf{fst}(M) = \mathsf{snd}(M) = \mathsf{wrong}$ for appropriate ground terms $M$ which are not pairs. In the following we use the abbreviations $(M, N)$ for $\mathsf{pair}(M, N)$ and $(L, M, N)$ for $\mathsf{pair}(\mathsf{pair}(L, M), N)$.

A one-way hash function can be represented as a unary function symbol h with no equations. The one-wayness of h is modeled by the absence of an inverse while the fact that h is collision-free results from $\mathsf{h}(M) = \mathsf{h}(N)$ only for $M = N$.

Symmetric cryptography (shared-key cryptography), is modeled via binary function symbols enc and dec for encryption and decryption with equation $\mathsf{dec}(\mathsf{enc}(x, y), y) = x$, where $x$ represents the plaintext and $y$ the key.

Asymmetric encryption can be modeled introducing two unary function symbols pk and sk for generating the public and the secret keys from a seed with the equation $\mathsf{dec}(\mathsf{enc}(x, \mathsf{pk}(y)), \mathsf{sk}(y)) = x$.

Sometimes, it may be useful to assume that encrypted messages come with sufficient redundancy such that decryption with a wrong key is evident. We may incorporate this property by adding equations $\mathsf{dec}(M, N) = \mathsf{wrong}$ for all ground terms $M$ and $N$ such that $M \neq \mathsf{enc}(L, N)$ for all $L$.

**Probability Measures.** A *discrete probability measure* over a countable set $X$ is a function $\mu : 2^X \to [0, 1]$ such that $\mu(X) = 1$ and for each countable family $\{X_i\}$ of pairwise disjoint elements of $2^X$, $\mu(\cup_i X_i) = \sum_i \mu(X_i)$. We adopt the convenient abuse of notation $\mu(x)$ for $\mu(\{x\})$. Let us denote by $D(X)$ the set of discrete probability measures over $X$. Given an element $x \in X$, we denote by $\delta_x$ the *Dirac measure* on $x$, namely, the probability measure $\mu$ such that $\mu(x) = 1$.

Given two probability measures $\mu_1, \mu_2$ and a real number $p \in [0, 1]$, we define the *convex combination* $\mu_1 +_p \mu_2$ to be the probability measure $\mu$ such that for each set $Y \in 2^X$, $\mu(Y) = p \cdot \mu_1(Y) + (1 - p) \cdot \mu_2(Y)$.

Recall that any discrete probability measure is the countable linear combination $\sum_{x.\mu(x)\neq 0} \mu(x) \cdot \delta_x$.

## 3 The Probabilistic Applied Pi–Calculus

In this section we introduce the Probabilistic Applied Pi–calculus (PAPi).

### 3.1 Syntax

The grammar of PAPi processes is obtained by extending the one for the Applied Pi–calculus with a nondeterministic $(+)$ and a probabilistic $(\oplus_p)$ choice operator:

$$\begin{array}{rl} P, Q ::= \mathbf{0} \mid \overline{u}\langle M\rangle.P \mid u(x).P \mid P{+}Q \mid P{\oplus_p}Q \mid \\ P \mid Q \mid\ !P \mid \nu n.P \mid \text{if } M = N \text{ then } P \text{ else } Q \end{array}$$

The null process $\mathbf{0}$ does nothing; $\overline{u}\langle M\rangle.P$ outputs the term $M$ on channel $u$ and then behaves like $P$; $u(x).P$ is ready to perform an input on channel $u$, then to behave like $P$ with the actual received message replacing the formal parameter $x$; $P+Q$ denotes a process which may behave either like $P$ or $Q$; $P \oplus_p Q$ behaves like $P$ with probability $p$, like $Q$ with probability $1-p$; $P \mid Q$ is the parallel composition of $P$ and $Q$; the replication $!P$ behaves as an infinite number of copies of $P$ running in parallel; $\nu n.P$ generates a fresh private name $n$ and then behaves like $P$; if $M = N$ then $P$ else $Q$ is the usual conditional process, it behaves like $P$ if $M = N$ and like $Q$ otherwise. Note that $M = N$ represents equality (i.e. with respect to some equational theory) rather than syntactic identity. We may omit a process when it is equal to $\mathbf{0}$.

As was done for the Applied Pi–calculus, we extend plain processes with *active substitutions*:

$$A, B ::= P \quad | \quad \nu n.A \quad | \quad \nu x.A \quad | \quad A \mid B \quad | \quad \{M/x\}$$

where $P$ is a plain process. We denote with $\mathcal{A}$ the set of extended processes. We write $\{M/x\}$ for the active substitution that replaces the variable $x$ with the term $M$. The substitution $\{M/x\}$ is like *let* $x = M$ *in*..., with the ability to *float* and to apply to any process that comes in contact with it. By applying a restriction $\nu x.(\{M/x\} \mid P)$ we obtain exactly *let* $x = M$ *in* $P$. Intuitively, a substitution $\{M/x\}$ denotes either a static public information known to every participant of the protocol, or it may appear when the term $M$ has been sent to the environment, and the environment may not contain the atomic names appearing in $M$; in this situation, the variable $x$ is just a way to refer to $M$. We write $\{M_1/x_1, \ldots, M_l/x_l\}$ for the parallel substitutions $\{M_1/x_1\} \mid \ldots \mid \{M_l/x_l\}$. We denote substitutions by $\sigma$, the image of a variable $x$ according to $\sigma$ as $x\sigma$ and the result of applying $\sigma$ to the free variables of a term $T$ as $T\sigma$. In the following we identify the empty frame and the null process $\mathbf{0}$.

Extending the sort system for terms, we rely on a sort system for extended processes. This should enforce that $M$ and $N$ are of the same sort in the conditional expression, that $u$ has sort $\mathsf{Channel}(\mathcal{S})$ for some $\mathcal{S}$ in the input and output expressions, and that $x$ and $M$ have the corresponding sort $\mathcal{S}$ in those expressions. As done before, we omit the details of the sort system, and we just assume that extended processes are well-sorted.

Names and variables have scopes which are delimited by restrictions and by inputs. As usual, we denote with $fv(A)$ and $fn(A)$ the *free* variables and names of $A$ which do not occur within the scope of any binder $\nu u$ and $v(u)$. With $bv(A)$ and $bn(A)$ we denote the *bound* variables and names of $A$, respectively.

An extended process is *closed* when every variable is either bound or defined by an active substitution. With $\mathcal{A}_C$ we denote the set of closed extended processes. We may use the abbreviation $\nu\tilde{u}$ for the (possibly empty) series of pairwise-distinct binders $\nu u_1.\nu u_2 \ldots \nu u_l$.

Intuitively, we may see extended processes as plain processes extended with a context for the interpretation of their variables. As usual, an *evaluation context* is an expression (an extended process) with a hole. Formally, an evaluation context $C[\_]$ is defined by the following grammar:

$$C[\_] ::= \Box \;\big|\; \nu n.C[\_] \;\big|\; \nu x.C[\_] \;\big|\; A \,|\, C[\_] \;\big|\; C[\_] \,|\, A$$

where $A \in \mathcal{A}$ is an extended process. A context $C[\_]$ *closes* $A$ when $C[A]$ is closed.

A *frame* is an extended process built up from $\mathbf{0}$ and active substitutions by parallel composition and restriction. The domain $dom(\varphi)$ of a frame $\varphi$ is the set of variables that $\varphi$ exports (those variables $x$ for which $\varphi$ has an active substitution $\{M/x\}$ not under a restriction on $x$). We assume all substitutions in a frame to be cycle-free, and that there is at most one substitution for each variable (and exactly one when the variable is restricted).

A frame can be viewed as an approximation of an extended process $A$ that accounts for the static knowledge exposed by $A$ to its environment, but not for $A$'s dynamic behaviour. Given a probabilistic extended process $A$, with $\varphi(A)$ we denote the frame obtained from $A$ by replacing every plain process embedded in $A$ with $\mathbf{0}$. For example, given the process $A = (P \oplus_p Q) \,|\, \{M/x\} \,|\, \{N/x\}$, we have that $\varphi(A) = \mathbf{0} \,|\, \{M/x\} \,|\, \{N/x\}$. The domain $dom(A)$ of $A$ is the domain of its frame $\varphi(A)$; namely, $dom(A) = dom(\varphi(A))$.

### 3.2 Semantics

*Structural congruence* ($\equiv$) is the smallest equivalence relation on extended processes that is closed (i) by $\alpha$-conversion on both names and variables, (ii) by application of evaluation contexts, and such that:

$$\begin{array}{c}
(\textsc{Par-}\mathbf{0}) \quad A \equiv A \,|\, \mathbf{0} \qquad (\textsc{Par-C}) \quad A \,|\, B \equiv B \,|\, A \\
(\textsc{Par-A}) \quad A \,|\, (B \,|\, C) \equiv (A \,|\, B) \,|\, C \qquad (\textsc{Repl}) \quad !P \equiv P \,|\, !P \\
(\textsc{New-}\mathbf{0}) \quad \nu n.\mathbf{0} \equiv \mathbf{0} \qquad (\textsc{New-C}) \quad \nu u.\nu v.A \equiv \nu v.\nu u.A \\
(\textsc{New-Par}) \quad A \,|\, \nu u.B \equiv \nu u.(A \,|\, B) \text{ if } u \notin fv(A) \cup fn(A) \\
(\textsc{Alias}) \quad \nu x.\{M/x\} \equiv \mathbf{0} \qquad (\textsc{Subst}) \quad \{M/x\} \,|\, A \equiv \{M/x\} \,|\, A\{M/x\} \\
(\textsc{Rewrite}) \quad \{M/x\} \equiv \{N/x\} \text{ if } \Sigma \vdash M =_E N
\end{array}$$

Rules for parallel composition and restriction are standard. Alias enables the introduction of an arbitrary active substitution, Subst describes the application of an active substitution to a process in contact with it, and Rewrite deals with equational term rewriting. As pointed out in [1], Alias and Subst yield $A\{M/x\} \equiv \nu x.(\{M/x\} \,|\, A)$ for $x \notin fv(M)$.

We let $\mu$ range over distributions over the classes of extended processes defined by the structural congruence relation. Namely, $\mu : 2^{\mathcal{A}/\equiv} \to [0,1]$. In the following we abbreviate $\mu([B])$ with $\mu(B)$, where $[B]$ is the equivalence class of $B$ up to structural congruence $\equiv$.

The *internal probabilistic reduction* $A \to \mu$, which describes a transition that leaves from $A$ and leads to a probability distribution $\mu$, is the smallest relation satisfying the following axioms:

$$(\text{Id})\quad P \to \delta_P \qquad (\text{Comm})\quad \overline{a}\langle x\rangle.P \mid a(x).Q \to \delta_{P\,|\,Q}$$

$$(\text{NdBran})\quad \frac{P \to \mu}{P{+}Q \to \mu} \qquad (\text{NdBran'})\quad \frac{Q \to \mu}{P{+}Q \to \mu}$$

$$(\text{PrBran})\quad \frac{P \to \mu_1 \quad Q \to \mu_2}{P \oplus_p Q \to \mu_1 +_p \mu_2} \qquad (\text{Then})\quad \text{if } M = M \text{ then } P \text{ else } Q \to \delta_P$$

$$(\text{Else})\quad \text{if } M = N \text{ then } P \text{ else } Q \to \delta_Q \qquad \text{for } M, N \in \mathcal{T}_G \text{ s.t.} \Sigma \not\vdash M =_E N$$

$$(\text{EvCon})\quad \frac{A \to \mu}{C[A] \to \mu_C}$$

A stuttering reduction (Id) is needed to deal with $+$ and $\oplus_p$ (see Example 1). Communication (Comm) is kept simple considering as a variable the message sent. There is no loss of generality since Alias and Subst can introduce a variable to stand for a term (see [1]). Nondeterministic branching (NdBran) is as usual. Probabilistic branching (PrBran) results from the convex combination of probability measures. Comparisons (Then and Else) rely on the underlying equational theory $E$; using Else may sometimes require to apply active substitutions in the context in order to get ground terms $M$ and $N$. Note that the only rule that gives rise to a probabilistic choice is PrBran, the other ones just return a Dirac measure.

Since reduction rules should be closed under application of evaluation contexts, we need to define extensions of the distributions $\mu$ such that given $A \to \mu$ we could define $\mu_C$ such that $C[A] \to \mu_C$. Formally, given an evaluation context $C[\_]$ and a distribution $\mu$, we define the unique distribution $\mu_C$ such that for any extended process $A$, $\mu_C(C[A]) = \mu(A)$. For example, with $\mu_{\square\,|\,B}$ we denote the distribution $\mu'$ such that $\mu'(A \mid B) = \mu(A)$, with $\mu_{\nu_u.\square}$ we denote the distribution $\mu'$ such that $\mu'(\nu u.A) = \mu(A)$.

*Example 1.* Consider the process $A = (\overline{a}\langle M\rangle + \overline{b}\langle M\rangle) \oplus_p \overline{c}\langle M\rangle$. We have $A \to \mu$ and $A \to \mu'$, where $\mu = \delta_{\overline{a}\langle M\rangle} +_p \delta_{\overline{c}\langle M\rangle}$ and $\mu' = \delta_{\overline{b}\langle M\rangle} +_p \delta_{\overline{c}\langle M\rangle}$. Moreover, we have $A \mid B \to \mu_{\square\,|\,B}$ and $A \mid B \to \mu'_{\square\,|\,B}$ for any process $B$.

There is a step from a process $A$ to a process $B$ through the distribution $\mu$ (denoted $A \to_\mu B$) if $A \to \mu$ and $\mu([B]) > 0$.

An *execution* of $A$ is a finite (or infinite) sequence of steps $e = A \to_{\mu_1} A_1 \to_{\mu_2} \ldots \to_{\mu_k} A_k$, where $A_0, \ldots, A_k \in \mathcal{A}$ and $\mu_i \in D(\mathcal{A}/_\equiv)$. With $Exec_A$ we denote the set of executions starting from $A$. For the finite execution $e = A \to_{\mu_1} A_1 \to_{\mu_2} \ldots \to_{\mu_k} A_k$ we define $last(e) = A_k$ and $|e| = k$. For any $j \le |e|$, with $e^j$ we define the sequence of steps $A \to_{\mu_1} A_1 \to_{\mu_2} \ldots \to_{\mu_j} A_j$.

Finally, with $e\uparrow$ we denote the set of executions $e'$ such that $e \le_{prefix} e'$, where $\le_{prefix}$ is the usual prefix relation over sequences.

*Example 2.* Consider again process $A$ of Example 1, and process $B = a(x)$. We have $A \mid B \to_{\mu_{\square\,|\,B}} \overline{a}\langle M\rangle \mid a(x) \to_{\delta_0} \mathbf{0}$, with $\mu = \delta_{\overline{a}\langle M\rangle} +_p \delta_{\overline{c}\langle M\rangle}$ and $\overline{a}\langle M\rangle \mid a(x) \equiv \nu x.(\overline{a}\langle x\rangle \mid a(x) \mid \{M/x\})$. Note that we also have $A \mid B \to_{\mu_{\square\,|\,B}} \overline{c}\langle M\rangle \mid a(x)$.

Since we allow nondeterministic choices, an extended process may behave in several different ways. Intuitively, the nondeterministic choice is among the possible probability distributions that a process may follow. Given a process $A$, we denote with *behave*$(A)$ the set of the possible behaviours of $A$, i.e., $behave(A) = \{\mu \mid A \rightarrow \mu\}$. Hence, each possible probabilistic transition $A \rightarrow_\mu$ can be seen as arising from a *scheduler* resolving the nondeterminism in $A$ (see [27]). A *scheduler* is a total function $F$ assigning to a finite execution $e$ a distribution $\mu \in behave(last(e))$. Given a scheduler $F$ and a process $A$, we define $Exec_A^F$ as the set of executions starting from $A$ and driven by $F$, namely the set of executions $\{e = A \rightarrow_{\mu_1} A_1 \rightarrow_{\mu_2} A_2 \rightarrow_{\mu_3} \dots \mid \forall i, \mu_i(A_i) > 0 \text{ where } \mu_i = F(e^{i-1})\}$. Given the finite execution $e = A \rightarrow_{\mu_1} A_1 \rightarrow_{\mu_2} \dots \rightarrow_{\mu_k} A_k \in Exec_A^F$, we define $P_A^F(e) = \mu_1(A_1) \cdot \ldots \cdot \mu_k(A_k)$.

We define the probability space on the executions starting from a given process $A \in \mathcal{A}$, as follows. Given a scheduler $F$, $\sigma Field_A^F$ is the smallest sigma field on $Exec_A^F$ that contains the basic cylinders $e\uparrow$, where $e \in Exec_A^F$. The probability measure $Prob_A^F$ is the unique measure on $\sigma Field_A^F$ such that $Prob_A^F(e\uparrow) = P_A^F(e)$.

*Example 3.* Consider again the process $A$ of Example 1, and the scheduler $F$ such that $F(A) = \mu = \delta_{\overline{a}\langle M\rangle} +_p \delta_{\overline{c}\langle M\rangle}$. We have that the executions $e = A \rightarrow_\mu \overline{a}\langle M\rangle$ and $e' = A \rightarrow_\mu \overline{c}\langle M\rangle$ are in $Exec_A^F$ with $P_A^F(e) = p$ and $P_A^F(e') = 1 - p$. Note that with the chosen $F$, action $\overline{b}\langle M\rangle$ is never performed.

Given a scheduler $F$, a process $A$ and a measurable set of processes $H \subseteq \mathcal{A}$, with $Exec_A^F(H)$ we denote the set of executions starting from $A$ that cross a process in the set $H$. Namely, $Exec_A^F(H) = \{e \in Exec_A^F \mid last(e^i) \in H, \text{ for some } i\}$.

We define the probability of reaching a process in $H$ starting from $A$ according to the policy given by $F$ as $Prob_A^F(H) = Prob_A^F(Exec_A^F(H))$.

# 4 Equivalences

In this section we recall the definition of *static equivalence* for frames introduced in [1]. We also introduce a notion of *observational congruence* allowing to argue when PAPi extended processes cannot be distinguished by any context. Contexts can be used to represent active attackers and observational congruence may capture security properties. For example, secrecy and authentication properties have been defined in this way in [2] for the Spi–calculus.

## 4.1 Static Equivalence

Two frames should be considered equivalent when they behave equivalently when applied to terms obeying a certain equational theory $E$. We denote this equivalence (also called *static equivalence*) with $\approx_E$. As pointed out in [1], defining a static equivalence in presence of the $\nu$ construct becomes somehow delicate. Consider, for instance, the three frames:

$$\varphi_0 = \nu k.\{k/x\} \mid \nu s.\{s/y\} \quad \varphi_1 = \nu k.\,\{\mathsf{f}(k)/x, \mathsf{g}(k)/y\} \quad \varphi_2 = \nu k.\,\{k/x, \mathsf{f}(k)/y\}$$

where $\mathsf{f}$ and $\mathsf{g}$ are unary functions with no equations (two independent one-way hash functions). In $\varphi_0$, since $k$ and $s$ are new, variables $x$ and $y$ are mapped to unrelated values different from any value a context may build. This also holds for $\varphi_1$ (even if $\mathsf{f}(k)$ and $\mathsf{g}(k)$ are based on the same fresh value, they look unrelated). Thus, a context obtaining values for $x$ and $y$ cannot distinguish between $\varphi_0$ and $\varphi_1$. However, a context may discriminate $\varphi_2$ by checking the predicate $\mathsf{f}(x) = y$. Hence, static equivalence is defined so that $\varphi_0 \approx_E \varphi_1 \not\approx_E \varphi_2$.

**Definition 1.** *Given an equational theory $E$, two terms $M$ and $N$ are equal in the frame $\varphi \equiv \nu\tilde{n}.\sigma$ (written $(M =_E N)\varphi$), if and only if $M\sigma =_E N\sigma$ and $\{\tilde{n}\} \cap (fn(M) \cup fn(N)) = \emptyset$.*

Hence, for the previous example, we have $(\mathsf{f}(x) = y)\varphi_2$ but not $(\mathsf{f}(x) = y)\varphi_0$.

**Definition 2.** *Given an equational theory $E$, two closed frames $\varphi$ and $\psi$ are statically equivalent (written $\varphi \approx_E \psi$) when $dom(\varphi) = dom(\psi)$ and for all terms $M$ and $N$, $(M =_E N)\varphi$ iff $(M =_E N)\psi$.*

*We say that two closed extended processes $A$ and $B$ are statically equivalent (written $A \approx_E B$) iff $\varphi(A) \approx_E \varphi(B)$.*

Note that deciding static equivalence can be quite hard to check (it depends on $E$ and $\Sigma$) [8]. The next lemma, proved in [1], states a basic property of $\approx_E$.

**Lemma 1.** *Static equivalence is closed by structural congruence, by reduction, and by application of closing evaluation contexts.*

## 4.2 Observational Congruence

We write $A \Downarrow_p^F a$ (a *probabilistic barb*) when $A$ can send a message on $a$ with probability $p$ according to the scheduler $F$, namely, when $Prob_A^F(H) = p$ where $A' \in H$ if and only if $A' = C[\overline{a}\langle x\rangle.P]$ for some evaluation context $C[\_]$ that does not bind $a$. Notice that the set of executions starting from $A$ and crossing a process in $H$ is measurable since it can be seen as the countable union of measurable sets $\bigcup_{C,P,x,e.e\in Exec_A^F \wedge last(e)=C[\overline{a}\langle x\rangle.P]} e\!\uparrow$.

**Definition 3.** Observational congruence *$(\approx)$ is the largest symmetric relation $\mathcal{R}$ between closed extended processes with the same domain such that $A\mathcal{R}B$ implies:*

1. *for all schedulers $F$ such that $A \Downarrow_p^F a$, there exists a scheduler $F'$ such that $B \Downarrow_p^{F'} a$;*
2. *for all schedulers $F$ there exists a scheduler $F'$ such that for all classes $\mathcal{C} \in \mathcal{A}_C/_\mathcal{R}$, $Prob_A^F(\mathcal{C}) = Prob_B^{F'}(\mathcal{C})$;*
3. *$C[A]\mathcal{R}C[B]$ for all closing evaluation contexts $C[\_]$.*

The quantification on the schedulers means, intuitively, that given $A \approx B$, for any possible behaviour (scheduler) of $A$ there exists an analogous behaviour of $B$ and viceversa.

As pointed out in [1], if $A \approx B$, then, for any test $C$ of the form if $M = N$ then $\overline{a}\langle s\rangle$ else $\mathbf{0}$, where $a$ does not occur in $A$ or $B$, $A \mid C$ and $B \mid C$ should have the same barbs, thus implying static equivalence for $A$ and $B$. As a consequence, the following lemma holds, stating that observational congruence is finer than static equivalence.

**Lemma 2.** *Given $A, B \in \mathcal{A}$, $A \approx B$ implies $A \approx_E B$.*

### 4.3 Labeled Semantics and Weak Bisimulation

In process calculi theory, a labeled semantics usually allows describing the potential interactions of a process with other ones that could occur in its environment. Such interactions are modeled by allowing the process to perform as many transitions as its active actions are. Each transition has the corresponding action as label and leads to a new process which corresponds to the result of the execution of that action. Moreover, a labeled semantics may include silent (or internal) transitions, usually labeled with $\tau$, which describe the internal activity of the process, namely the interactions occurring between internal components of the system. Furthermore, the actions performed may include parameters. As an example, since the action of sending or receiving a message on a channel may require the transmitted message as parameter, one should explicitly show the parameter within the transition label.

Thus, to model the interaction of PAPi processes with the environment, a labeled operational semantics can be provided which defines a relation $A \xrightarrow{\alpha} \mu$, where $\alpha$ is a label of one of the following forms:

- the symbol $\tau$ (corresponding to an internal reduction);
- a label $a(M)$, where $M$ may contain names and variables (corresponding to an input of $M$ on $a$);
- a label $\overline{a}\langle u\rangle$ or $\nu u.\overline{a}\langle u\rangle$, where $u$ is either a channel name or a variable of base type (corresponding to an output of $u$ on $a$).

In addition to the structural congruence rules and the internal reduction semantics of Section 3.2 (where each reduction rule should be equipped with the label $\tau$), we adopt the following rules:

$$(\textsc{In})\quad a(x).P \xrightarrow{a(M)} \delta_{P\{M/x\}} \qquad (\textsc{Out-Atom})\quad \overline{a}\langle u\rangle.P \xrightarrow{\overline{a}\langle u\rangle} \delta_P$$

$$(\textsc{Open-Atom})\ \frac{A \xrightarrow{\overline{a}\langle u\rangle} \mu \quad u \neq a}{\nu u.A \xrightarrow{\nu u.\overline{a}\langle u\rangle} \mu} \qquad (\textsc{Scope})\ \frac{A \xrightarrow{\alpha} \mu \quad u \text{ does not occur in } \alpha}{\nu u.A \xrightarrow{\alpha} \mu_{\nu_u.\square}}$$

$$(\textsc{Par})\ \frac{A \xrightarrow{\alpha} \mu \quad bv(\alpha) \cap fv(B) = bn(\alpha) \cap fn(B) = \emptyset}{A \,|\, B \xrightarrow{\alpha} \mu_{\square \,|\, B}}$$

$$(\textsc{Struct})\ \frac{A \equiv B \quad B \xrightarrow{\alpha} \mu}{A \xrightarrow{\alpha} \mu}$$

There is a step from a process $A$ to a process $B$ through the distribution $\mu$ with label $\alpha$ (denoted $A \xrightarrow{\alpha}_{\mu} B$) if $A \xrightarrow{\alpha} \mu$ and $\mu(B) > 0$. Given a process $A$, different reaction rules $A \xrightarrow{\alpha} \mu$ may be applied according to $\alpha$ and $\mu$. As a consequence, we redefine the set of possible behaviours of $A$ as $behave_l(A) = \{(\alpha, \mu) \mid A \xrightarrow{\alpha} \mu\}$.

A *labeled execution* of $A$ is a finite (or infinite) sequence of steps $e = A \xrightarrow{\alpha_1}_{\mu_1} A_1 \xrightarrow{\alpha_2}_{\mu_2} \dots \xrightarrow{\alpha_k}_{\mu_k} A_k$, where $A_0, \dots, A_k \in \mathcal{A}$ and $\mu_i \in D(\mathcal{A}/_\equiv)$. With abuse of notation, we define $Exec_A$, $last(e) = A_k$, $|e|$, $e^j$ and $e\uparrow$ as for unlabeled executions.

Executions arise by resolving the nondeterminism on both $\alpha$ and $\mu$. As a consequence, a scheduler for the labeled semantics is a function $F$ assigning to a finite labeled execution $e$ a pair $(\alpha, \mu) \in behave_l(last(e))$.

Given a scheduler $F$ and a process $A$, we define $Exec_A^F$ as the set of executions starting from $A$ and driven by $F$, namely the set of executions $\{e = A \xrightarrow{\alpha_1}_{\mu_1} A_1 \xrightarrow{\alpha_2}_{\mu_2} A_2 \xrightarrow{\alpha_3}_{\mu_3} \dots \mid \forall i, \mu_i(A_i) > 0 \text{ where } (\alpha_i, \mu_i) = F(e^{i-1})\}$. Given the finite execution $e = A \xrightarrow{\alpha_1}_{\mu_1} A_1 \xrightarrow{\alpha_2}_{\mu_2} \dots \xrightarrow{\alpha_k}_{\mu_k} A_k \in Exec_A^F$, we define $P_A^F(e) = \mu_1(A_1) \cdot \dots \cdot \mu_k(A_k)$.

*Example 4.* Consider the process $A$ of Example 1 and the scheduler $F$ such that $F(A) = (\tau, \mu)$, with $\mu$ defined as in Example 1, and, trivially, $F(A \xrightarrow{\tau}_\mu \overline{a}\langle M\rangle) = (\overline{a}\langle M\rangle, \delta_0)$ and $F(A \xrightarrow{\tau}_\mu \overline{c}\langle M\rangle) = (\overline{c}\langle M\rangle, \delta_0)$. We have $e = A \xrightarrow{\tau}_\mu \overline{a}\langle M\rangle \xrightarrow{\overline{a}\langle M\rangle}_{\delta_0} \mathbf{0}$ and $e' = A \xrightarrow{\tau}_\mu \overline{c}\langle M\rangle \xrightarrow{\overline{c}\langle M\rangle}_{\delta_0} \mathbf{0}$ with $P_A^F(e) = p$ and $P_A^F(e') = 1 - p$. Note, again, that with such a scheduler the label $\overline{b}\langle M\rangle$ does never appear. Also note that the process $\nu c.A$ may reach with probability $(1-p)$ the process $\nu c.\overline{c}\langle M\rangle$ from which it cannot perform any other step.

Again, given a scheduler $F$, a finite execution $e$ and a measurable set $H$, $Prob_A^F(e\uparrow)$, $Exec_A^F(H)$ and $Prob_A^F(H)$ are defined analogously as for the unlabeled case. Let $Exec_A^F(\tau^*\alpha\tau^*, H)$ be the set of executions that, starting from $A$, lead to a process in $H$ via an execution performing an $\alpha$ action preceded and followed by an arbitrary number of $\tau$ steps. We define the probability $Prob_A^F(\tau^*\alpha\tau^*, H) = Prob_A^F(Exec_A^F(\tau^*\alpha\tau^*, H))$.

**Definition 4.** Weak bisimulation $(\approx_l)$ *is the largest symmetric relation $\mathcal{R}$ between closed extended processes with the same domain such that $A\mathcal{R}B$ implies:*

1. *$A \approx_E B$;*
2. *for all schedulers $F$ there exists a scheduler $F'$ such that for all classes $\mathcal{C} \in \mathcal{A}_C/_\mathcal{R}$, $Prob_A^F(\mathcal{C}) = Prob_B^{F'}(\mathcal{C})$;*
3. *for all schedulers $F$ there exists a scheduler $F'$ such that $Prob_A^F(\alpha, \mathcal{C}) = Prob_B^{F'}(\tau^*\alpha\tau^*, \mathcal{C})$, for all classes $\mathcal{C} \in \mathcal{A}_C/_\mathcal{R}$ and for all $\alpha \neq \tau$ with $fv(\alpha) \subseteq dom(A)$ and $bn(\alpha) \cap fn(B) = \emptyset$.*

The following lemma states that given $A \approx_l B$ and a closing evaluation context $C[\_]$, $C[A] \approx_l C[B]$ holds.

**Lemma 3.** *$\approx_l$ is closed under application of closing evaluation contexts.*

The next theorem derives immediately from the previous lemma.

**Theorem 1.** *$\approx_l$ is a congruence.*

We can also show that $\approx_l$ and $\approx$ coincide. Even if the notion of weak bisimulation does not include an explicit condition about contexts, it is still closed under application of evaluation contexts. As a consequence, $\approx_l$ is simpler than the notion of observational congruence given in Definition 3. The following theorem holds.

**Theorem 2.** *$A \approx_l B$ if and only if $A \approx B$.*

## 5 An Application

We give an implementation of the *1-out-of-2-oblivious transfer* protocol ($\mathrm{OT}_2^1$) in PAPi. The notion of oblivious transfer (OT) was first introduced by Rabin [22] in a number theoretic context and then generalized by Even, Goldreich and Lampel [12] with the $\mathrm{OT}_2^1$ notion. Intuitively, $\mathrm{OT}_2^1$ allows one party ($S$) to transfer exactly one secret, out of two different recognizable secrets ($M_0, M_1$), to his counterpart ($R$). Each secret is received with probability one half and the sender is completely ignorant of which secret has been received. Intuitively, $\mathrm{OT}_2^1(S, R, M_0, M_1)$ is a protocol that should satisfy the following axioms: (A) $R$ can read exactly one message: either $M_0$ or $M_1$, the probability of each to be read is one half; (B) if $R$ does not read $M_i$ he gains no useful information about $M_i$ by the execution of $\mathrm{OT}_2^1$; (C) for $S$, the a posteriori probability that $R$ got $M_0$ ($M_1$) remains one half. Oblivious transfer is widely used in protocols for secure multiparty computation and has been shown to be rather efficient.

In order to describe $\mathrm{OT}_2^1$ in PAPi, and recalling the notation in [12], we should extend the equational theory for asymmetric encryption with two binary functions $\boxplus$ and $\boxminus$ such that $(x \boxplus y) \boxminus y = x$ and the mappings $x \mapsto x \boxplus y$ and $y \mapsto x \boxplus y$ are permutations on the set of terms. Intuitively, when using RSA [23], $x \boxplus y$ is implemented as reduction modulo $N$ (the RSA modulus) of $x + y$, while $x \boxminus y$ is the reduction modulo $N$ of $x - y$. The full list of equations is:

$$
\begin{array}{llll}
(1) & \mathsf{fst}(\mathsf{pair}(x, y)) = x & (2) & \mathsf{snd}(\mathsf{pair}(x, y)) = y \\
(3) & \mathsf{dec}(\mathsf{enc}(x, \mathsf{pk}(y)), \mathsf{sk}(y)) = x & (4) & \mathsf{enc}(\mathsf{dec}(x, \mathsf{sk}(y)), \mathsf{pk}(y)) = x \\
(5) & (x \boxplus y) \boxminus y = x & (6) & x \boxplus (y \boxminus x) = y \\
(7) & x \boxplus y = y \boxplus x & &
\end{array}
$$

We are now ready to implement $\mathrm{OT}_2^1$ in PAPi in the following way:

$$
\begin{array}{l}
\mathrm{OT}_2^1(S, R, M_0, M_1) ::= S(M_0, M_1) \mid R \qquad \text{where:} \\
S(M_0, M_1) ::= \nu e.\nu m_0.\nu m_1.\left(\bar{c}\langle \mathsf{pk}(e), m_0, m_1\rangle.c(y).(\bar{c}\langle T_{00}, T_{11}, 0\rangle \oplus_{\frac{1}{2}} \bar{c}\langle T_{01}, T_{10}, 1\rangle)\right) \\
\text{with} \quad T_{ij} = M_i \boxplus \mathsf{dec}(y \boxminus m_j, \mathsf{sk}(e)) \quad \text{and:} \\
R ::= \nu l.\left(c(z, x_0, x_1).(\bar{c}\langle \mathsf{enc}(l, z) \boxplus x_0\rangle.P_0 \oplus_{\frac{1}{2}} \bar{c}\langle \mathsf{enc}(l, z) \boxplus x_1\rangle.P_1)\right) \\
\text{with, for } i \in \{0, 1\} \quad P_i ::= c(y_0, y_1, y_2).\,(\text{if } y_2 =_E 0 \text{ then } \bar{a}\langle y_i \boxminus l\rangle \text{ else } \bar{a}\langle y_{1-i} \boxminus l\rangle)\,.
\end{array}
$$

For simplicity we write input actions with multiple variables (this can be easily encoded with pair, fst and snd). $S$ picks two fresh messages $m_0$ and $m_1$ and transmits them to $R$, together with the public key of the fresh secret $e$. The receiver $R$ receives this triple and randomly (with probability $\frac{1}{2}$) sends back to $S$ the term $T = \mathsf{enc}(l, \mathsf{pk}(e)) \boxplus m_i$, for $i \in \{0, 1\}$. Since $S$ does not know the secret value $l$, it cannot tell whether $T$ has been obtained from $m_0$ or $m_1$. $S$ generates the messages $T_{ij}$ obtained by combining $M_i$ and $m_j$ and with probability $\frac{1}{2}$ sends to $R$ the $M_i$ combined with the right $m_j$ used by $R$. The flag 0 (1, resp.) is used to indicate that $S$ used $m_0$ ($m_1$, resp.) for the first part of the message. The receiver can now compute the secret ($M_0$ or $M_1$) from the right $T_{ij}$ and $l$. At the final step, $R$ sends the value of the received secret on channel $a$.

Note that we do not consider equations of the form $\mathsf{dec}(M, \mathsf{sk}(e)) = \mathsf{wrong}$ when $M$ is not encrypted with $\mathsf{sk}(e)$. Otherwise, $S$ may be able to know which $m_j$ was used by $R$ through the test $\mathsf{dec}(\mathsf{enc}(l, \mathsf{pk}(e)) \boxplus m_i \boxminus m_j, \mathsf{sk}(e)) = \mathsf{wrong}$. Such a test is true only if $i \neq j$. In the case of $i = j$, $S$ is able to compute the secret $l$ as $\mathsf{dec}(\mathsf{enc}(l, \mathsf{pk}(e)) \boxplus m_i \boxminus m_j, \mathsf{sk}(e))$. This problem is avoided by using an asymmetric cipher (e.g., RSA), obtained with equations (4) and (5) such that $\mathsf{enc}$ and $\mathsf{dec}$ commute. In this way, the test never returns the value $\mathsf{wrong}$ and $S$ cannot tell whether the result of $\mathsf{dec}(\mathsf{enc}(l, \mathsf{pk}(e)) \boxplus m_i \boxminus m_j, \mathsf{sk}(e))$ is $l$ or just a random decryption.

By means of our notion of weak bisimulation we can show that the protocol implementation in PAPi, given the well–behaving sender $S(M_0, M_1)$ and receiver $R$, satisfies the $\mathrm{OT}^1_2$ axioms. In particular, we can show that the receiver $R$ receives $M_0$ or $M_1$ with probability $\frac{1}{2}$ by checking the weak bisimulation of the protocol implementation with the process that simply outputs $M_0$ or $M_1$ on a channel $a$ with probability $\frac{1}{2}$. Such a system, which captures axioms (A), (B) and (C) required by $\mathrm{OT}^1_2$, may be seen as the correct behaviour of the protocol. Namely, imposing a restriction on channel $c$, thus forcing synchronization among $S$ and $R$, it holds that:

$$\nu c.\mathrm{OT}^1_2(S, R, M_0, M_1) \approx_l \bar{a}\langle M_0\rangle \oplus_{\frac{1}{2}} \bar{a}\langle M_1\rangle.$$

This can be proved easily, since $\nu c.\mathrm{OT}^1_2(S, R, M_0, M_1)$ performs only internal reductions labeled with $\tau$ before performing the output of $M_0$ or $M_1$ (with probability $\frac{1}{2}$, resp.) on channel $a$. The two bisimilar labeled probabilistic automata modeling the behaviour of $\nu c.\mathrm{OT}^1_2(S, R, M_0, M_1)$ and $\bar{a}\langle M_0\rangle \oplus_{\frac{1}{2}} \bar{a}\langle M_1\rangle$ are shown in Figure 1 (probabilities equal to 1 are omitted). Notice that at each step there is just a probability distribution that a scheduler can choose (the only nondeterministic choices are among blocking schedulers).

## 6 A Conservative Extension

Many process algebraic approaches are non–probabilistic and, in general, probabilistic choice can be approximated by suitable nondeterministic mechanisms. Using probabilistic features, however, provides stronger safety and security guarantees. We give formal substance to this claim (Proposition 1 below), by showing that $\approx$ is a conservative extension of an appropriate notion of observational

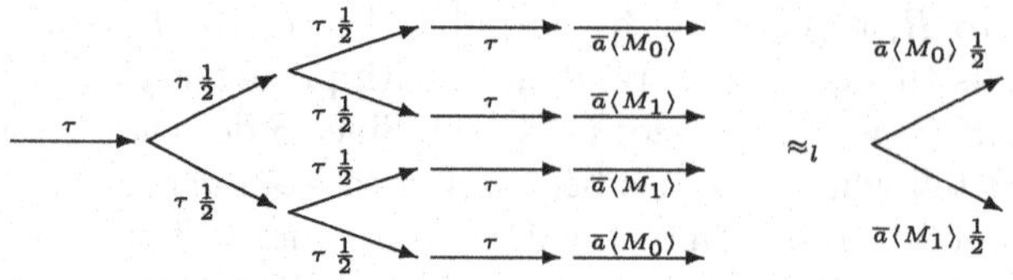

**Fig. 1.** $\nu c.\mathrm{OT}_2^1(S,R,M_0,M_1) \approx_l \overline{a}\langle M_0\rangle \oplus_{\frac{1}{2}} \overline{a}\langle M_1\rangle$

congruence for the purely Nondeterministic Applied Pi–calculus (NAPi), obtained by removing the probabilistic choice operators from the syntax of plain processes.

With $\mathcal{A}_{NP}$ we denote the set of extended processes in NAPi. The *internal reduction* $A \rightarrow A'$, becomes now the smallest relation on $\mathcal{A}_{NP}$ closed by structural congruence and application of evaluation contexts such that:

$$\overline{a}\langle x\rangle.P \mid a(x).Q \rightarrow P \mid Q \qquad \frac{P \rightarrow P'}{P{+}Q \rightarrow P'} \qquad \frac{Q \rightarrow Q'}{P{+}Q \rightarrow Q'}$$

$$\text{if } M = M \text{ then } P \text{ else } Q \rightarrow P$$

$$\text{if } M = N \text{ then } P \text{ else } Q \rightarrow Q \quad \text{for } M, N \in \mathcal{T}_G \text{ s.t.} \Sigma \not\vdash M =_E N$$

Given a process $A \in \mathcal{A}$ we define the plain process $A_{NP} \in \mathcal{A}_{NP}$ obtained by replacing each probabilistic choice operator appearing in $A$ with a purely nondeterministic choice operator.

As an example, given $A = (P \oplus_p Q) \mid \{M/x\}$, we get $A_{NP} = (P{+}Q) \mid \{M/x\}$.

Note that NAPi essentially results in the Applied Pi–calculus given in [1] enriched with a nondeterministic choice operator. Actually, the lack of an explicit nondeterministic choice operator in [1] is not a real limitation since it can be derived by means of restriction and parallel composition in the standard way.

The notion of observational congruence introduced in the probabilistic framework (see Definition 3) can be rewritten for the purely nondeterministic case.

For $A \in \mathcal{A}_{NP}$, we write $A \Downarrow a$ when $A$ can send a message on $a$, namely when $A \rightarrow^* C[\overline{a}\langle x\rangle.P]$ for some evaluation context $C[\_]$ that does not bind $a$.

**Definition 5.** Nondeterministic observational congruence *($\approx_{NP}$) is the largest symmetric relation $\mathcal{R}$ between closed extended processes in $\mathcal{A}_{NP}$ with the same domain such that $A\mathcal{R}B$ implies:*

1. *if $A \Downarrow a$, then $B \Downarrow a$;*
2. *if $A \rightarrow^* A'$, then $B \rightarrow^* B'$ and $A'\mathcal{R}B'$ for some $B'$;*
3. *$C[A]\mathcal{R}C[B]$ for all closing evaluation contexts $C[\_]$.*

The following proposition states that removing probabilities from two observationally equivalent probabilistic extended processes the equivalence is preserved in the purely nondeterministic setting.

**Proposition 1.** *Given $A, B \in \mathcal{A}$ such that $A \approx B$, then $A_{NP} \approx_{NP} B_{NP}$.*

Hence, if a system satisfies an observational equivalence property in the probabilistic setting, its nondeterministic counterpart does still satisfy the property in the nondeterministic setting. The converse implication does, in general, not hold, since systems satisfying a property in the nondeterministic setting may turn out to lose the property in the more expressive probabilistic framework.

*Example 5.* Consider the process $A = \nu c.\mathrm{OT}_2^1(S, R, M_0, M_1)$ introduced in Section 5 and the family of processes $B = \overline{a}\langle M_0\rangle \oplus_p \overline{a}\langle M_1\rangle$. It is easy to see that $A_{NP} \approx_{NP} B_{NP}$ (both processes have just a barb on channel $a$). However, it is not true that $A \approx B$ for all $p$. Actually, the equivalence holds just for $p = \frac{1}{2}$.

## 7 Conclusions

In this paper we have introduced the Probabilistic Applied Pi–calculus (PAPi), an extension of the Applied Pi–calculus ([1]) for dealing with probability, nondeterminism and equations (which are shown to be rich enough for modeling the most common cryptographic operations). We have given a labeled operational semantics and a labeled weak bisimulation, which we have then shown to be a congruence. As one expects, the results given in the probabilistic framework are preserved with respect to the results given in the non-probabilistic one.

As an application, we have shown how PAPi applies to the $\mathrm{OT}_2^1$ protocol where probability and cryptographic operations play an important role. While we just prove the correct execution of the protocol for two given parties, it would be quite natural to develop a framework for the analysis of security properties (as, for example, in [2]) in order to prove more general properties.

As another possible future application, we mention, just as an example, sensor networks, for which: (a) environmental distributed sensing can be modeled with a nondeterministic choice among input channels waiting for external stimuli; (b) randomization is crucial (see the probabilistic routing policies introduced in [4], or the randomized sleeping architecture proposed in [6]); (c) cryptography is fundamental when dealing with secure wireless communication. Notice, moreover, that thanks to the generality of equational theories, PAPi can also be applied to domains different from security.

## References

1. Abadi, M., Fournet, C.: Mobile Values, New Names, and Secure Communication. In: POPL 2001, pp. 104–115. ACM Press, New York (2001)
2. Abadi, M., Gordon, A.D.: A Calculus for Cryptographic Protocols: The Spi Calculus. Information and Computation 148(1), 1–70 (1999)
3. Aldini, A., Bravetti, M., Gorrieri, R.: A Process-algebraic Approach for the Analysis of Probabilistic Non Interference. Journal of Computer Security 12, 191–245 (2004)
4. Barrett, C.L., Eidenbenz, S.J., Kroc, L., Marathe, M., Smith, J.P.: Parametric Probabilistic Sensor Network Routing. In: WSNA 2003, pp. 122–131. ACM Press, New York (2003)
5. Buscemi, M.G., Montanari, U.: CC–pi: A Constraint–based Language for Specifying Service Level Agreements. In: ESOP 2007. LNCS, vol. 4421, pp. 19–32. Springer, Heidelberg (2007)
6. Cao, Q., Abdelzaher, T., He, T., Stankovic, J.: Towards Optimal Sleep Scheduling in Sensor Networks for Rare-event Detection. In: IPSN 2005, pp. 20–27. IEEE Computer Society Press, Los Alamitos (2005)

7. Cleaveland, R., Parrow, J., Steffen, B.: The concurrency workbench: a semantics-based tool for the verification of concurrent systems. ACM Trans. Program. Lang. Syst. 15(1), 36–72 (1993)
8. Cortier, V., Abadi, M.: Deciding Knowledge in Security Protocols under Equational Theories. Theoretical Computer Science 367(1–2), 2–32 (2006)
9. Dershowitz, N., Jouannaud, J.-P.: Rewrite Systems. Handbook of Theoretical Computer Science. Formal Models and Sematics (B) B, 243–320 (1990)
10. Di Pierro, A., Hankin, C., Wiklicky, H.: Approximate Non-Interference. Journal of Computer Security 12, 37–82 (2004)
11. Dolev, D., Yao, A.C.: On the Security of Public Key Protocols. IEEE Transactions on Information Theory 29(12), 198–208 (1983)
12. Even, S., Goldreich, O., Lempel, A.: A Randomized protocol for Signing Contracts. Communications of the ACM 28(6), 637–647 (1985)
13. Goguen, J.A., Thatcher, J.W., Wagner, E.G., Wright, J.B.: Initial Algebra Semantics and Continuous Algebras. Journal of the ACM 24(1), 68–95 (1977)
14. Jung, A., Tix, R.: The Troublesome Probabilistic Powerdomain. In: Proc. of Workshop on Computation and Approximation. ENTCS, vol. 13, Elsevier, Amsterdam (1998)
15. Lowe, G.: Casper: A compiler for the analysis of security protocols. Journal of Computer Security 6, 53–84 (1998)
16. Mislove, M.W., Ouakine, J., Worrell, J.: Axioms for Probability and Nondeterminism. In: EXPRESS 2003, 96th edn. ENTCS, pp. 7–28. Elsevier, Amsterdam (2004)
17. Milner, R.: Communication and Concurrency. Prentice Hall, Englewood Cliffs (1989)
18. Milner, R.: Communicating and Mobile Systems: the $\pi$–Calculus. Cambridge University Press, Cambridge (1999)
19. Mitchell, J.C.: Foundations for Programming Languages. MIT Press, Cambridge (1996)
20. Mitchell, J.C., Ramanathan, A., Scedrov, A., Teague, V.: Polynomial-time Process Calculus for the Analysis of Cryptographic Protocols. Theoretical Computer Science 353(1–3), 118–164 (2006)
21. Niehren, J., Mueller, M.: Constraints for Free in Concurrent Computation. In: Kanchanasut, K., Levy, J.-J. (eds.) ACSC. LNCS, vol. 1023, pp. 171–186. Springer, Heidelberg (1995)
22. Rabin, M.O.: How to Exchange Secrets by Oblivious Transfer. Unpublished manuscript (1981)
23. Rivest, R., Shamir, A., Adleman, L.: A Method for Obtaining Digital Signatures and Public-Key Cryptosystems. Communications of the ACM 21(2), 120–126 (1978) Previously released as an MIT "Technical Memo" in April 1977
24. Saraswat, V.A., Rinard, M.C., Panangaden, P.: Semantic Foundations of Concurrent Constraint Programming. In: POPL 1991, pp. 333–352. ACM Press, New York (1991)
25. Schneider, S.: Security properties and CSP. In: Proc. of the IEEE Symposium on Security and Privacy (1996)
26. Segala, R.: Modeling and Verification of Randomized Distributed Real-Time Systems. PhD thesis, MIT, Laboratory for Computer Science (1995)
27. Segala, R., Lynch, N.: Probabilistic Simulations for Probabilistic Processes. Nordic Journal of Computing 2(2), 250–273 (1995)
28. Victor, B., Moller, F.: The Mobility Workbench - A Tool for the pi-Calculus. In: Dill, D.L. (ed.) CAV 1994. LNCS, vol. 818, pp. 428–440. Springer, Heidelberg (1994)

# Type-Based Verification of Correspondence Assertions for Communication Protocols

Daisuke Kikuchi and Naoki Kobayashi

Graduate School of Information Sciences, Tohoku University
{kikuchi,koba}@kb.ecei.tohoku.ac.jp

**Abstract.** Gordon and Jeffrey developed a type system for checking correspondence assertions. The correspondence assertions, proposed by Woo and Lam, state that when a certain event (called an "end" event) happens, the corresponding "begin" event must have occurred before. They can be used for checking authenticity in communication protocols. In this paper, we refine Gordon and Jeffrey's type system and develop a polynomial-time type inference algorithm, so that correspondence assertions can be verified fully automatically, without any type annotations. The main key idea that enables polynomial-time type inference is to introduce fractional effects; Without the fractional effects, the type inference problem is NP-hard.

## 1 Introduction

Woo and Lam [11] introduced the notion of *correspondence assertions* for stating expected authenticity properties formally. The correspondence assertions consist of *begin*-assertions and *end*-assertions, and assert that whenever an end-event occurs, the corresponding begin-event must have occurred before. For example, consider a simple transmit-acknowledgment-handshake protocol, where a process $A$ sends a message to $B$ and waits for an acknowledgment. Let the event that $B$ receives a message from $A$ be a begin-event, and the event that $A$ receives an acknowledgment be an end-event. By checking that the begin event always precedes the end-event, one can verify that whenever $A$ believes that the message has been received by $B$, the message has indeed been delivered to $B$.

Gordon and Jeffrey [7] introduced an extension of the $\pi$-calculus with correspondence assertions, and proposed a type-and-effect system for checking correspondence assertions. Since well-typed processes satisfy correspondence assertions, the problem of checking correspondence assertions is reduced to the type-checking problem. They further extended the type system to deal with cryptographic primitives [4, 6, 5].

In this paper, we refine Gordon and Jeffrey's type system for correspondence assertions and develop a polynomial-time type inference algorithm, so that correspondence assertions can be verified fully automatically without any type annotations (which were necessary for Gordon and Jeffrey's type checking algorithm [7]). The key idea to enable type inference is to introduce *fractional* effects, which are mappings from events to rational numbers; In Gordon and Jeffrey's

Z. Shao (Ed.): APLAS 2007, LNCS 4807, pp. 191–205, 2007.

type system, effects are multisets of events, or mappings from events to natural numbers. We show that with fractional effects (and with the assumptions that the size of simple types is polynomial in the size of untyped programs and that the size of events is bound by a constant), type inference can be performed in polynomial time, while without fractional effects, the type inference problem is NP-hard (even with the assumption that both the size of simple types and the size of events are bound by a constant).

The rest of this paper is structured as follows. Section 2 introduces $\pi^{\mathbf{CA}}$, Gordon and Jeffrey's calculus *without* type-and-effect annotations. Section 3 introduces a type system with fractional effects. Section 4 describes a polynomial-time type inference algorithm, and also shows that the type inference problem is NP-hard without fractional effects. Section 5 discusses related work and Section 6 concludes.

## 2 $\pi^{\mathbf{CA}}$: $\pi$-Calculus with Correspondence Assertions

In this section, we introduce the language $\pi^{\mathbf{CA}}$, the $\pi$-calculus extended with correspondence assertions. The language is essentially the same as Gordon and Jeffrey's calculus [7], except that there are no type annotations in our language.

### 2.1 Syntax

**Definition 1 (processes).** The set of processes, ranged over by $P$, is given by:

$$\begin{array}{rcl} P \text{ (Processes)} & ::= & \mathbf{0} \mid x![\tilde{y}] \mid x?[\tilde{y}].P \mid (P_1 \mid P_2) \mid *P \mid (\nu x)P \\ & & \mid \mathbf{if}\ x = y\ \mathbf{then}\ P\ \mathbf{else}\ Q \mid \mathbf{begin}\ L.P \mid \mathbf{end}\ L.P \\ L \text{ (Event labels)} & ::= & \langle x_1, \ldots, x_n \rangle \end{array}$$

Here, $\tilde{y}$ abbreviates a sequence of names $y_1, \ldots, y_n$. The meta-variables $x_i$ and $y_j$ range over the set $\mathcal{N}$ of names.

The processes **begin** $L.P$ and **end** $L.P$ are special processes for declaring correspondence assertions; **begin** $L.P$ raises a "**begin** $L$" event and then behaves like $P$, while **end** $L.P$ raises an "**end** $L$" event and then behaves like $P$. An event label $L$ is a sequence of names.

The remaining processes are those of the standard polyadic, asynchronous $\pi$-calculus. The process $\mathbf{0}$ is an inaction. The process $x![\tilde{y}]$ sends a tuple of names $\tilde{y}$ on channel $x$. The process $x?[\tilde{y}].P$ waits to receive a tuple of names on channel $x$, binds $\tilde{y}$ to them, and then behaves like $P$. $P_1 \mid P_2$ runs $P_1$ and $P_2$ in parallel, while $*P$ runs infinitely many copies of $P$ in parallel. The process $(\nu x)P$ creates a fresh name, binds $x$ to it, and behaves like $P$. The process **if** $x = y$ **then** $P$ **else** $Q$ behaves like $P$ if $x$ and $y$ are the same name, and behaves like $Q$ otherwise.

The prefixes $x?[\tilde{y}]$ and $(\nu x)$ bind $\tilde{y}$ and $x$ respectively. We identify processes up to $\alpha$-conversion. We assume that $\alpha$-conversion is implicitly applied so that bound variables are always different from each other and free variables. We often omit trailing $\mathbf{0}$, and write **end** $L$ for **end** $L.\mathbf{0}$.

*Example 1.* The transmit-acknowledgment-handshake protocol mentioned in Section 1 can be expressed as follows [7]:

$$(\nu c)(\mathit{Sender}(a,b,c) \mid \mathit{Receiver}(a,b,c)),$$

where $\mathit{Sender}(a,b,c)$ and $\mathit{Receiver}(a,b,c)$ are:

$$\mathit{Sender}(a,b,c) \triangleq (\nu \mathit{msg})(\nu \mathit{ack})(c![\mathit{msg},\mathit{ack}] \mid \mathit{ack}?[\,].\mathbf{end}\ \langle a,b,\mathit{msg}\rangle)$$

$$\mathit{Receiver}(a,b,c) \triangleq c?[m,r].\mathbf{begin}\ \langle a,b,m\rangle.r![\,]$$

$\mathit{Sender}(a,b,c)$ creates a fresh message $\mathit{msg}$, creates a new channel for receiving an acknowledgment, and sends a pair consisting of them on channel $c$. It then waits for an acknowledgment and raises the "**end** $\langle a,b,\mathit{msg}\rangle$"-event. $\mathit{Receiver}(a,b,c)$ waits to receive a pair $[m,r]$ on channel $c$, raises a "**begin** $\langle a,b,m\rangle$"-event (where $m$ is bound to $\mathit{msg}$), and then sends an acknowledgment on $r$.

As explained in Section 1, the property "whenever *Sender* receives an acknowledgment for $\mathit{msg}$, *Receiver* has received it" can be captured by the property that whenever an "**end** $\langle a,b,\mathit{msg}\rangle$"-event occurs, a "**begin** $\langle a,b,\mathit{msg}\rangle$"-event must have occurred before.

### 2.2 Semantics

We give below the operational semantics of $\pi^{\mathbf{CA}}$ and then define the safety of a process, meaning that whenever an end-event occurs, the corresponding begin-event must have occurred before. Note that the semantics is essentially the same as that of Gordon and Jeffrey's calculus.

The operational semantics is defined via the reduction relation $\langle \Psi, E, N\rangle \longrightarrow \langle \Psi', E', N'\rangle$, where $\Psi$ is a multiset of processes, $N$ is a set of names, and $E$ is a multiset consisting of event labels $L$ such that the event **begin** $L$ has been raised but **end** $L$ has not. The reduction relation is defined by the rules in Figure 1.

$$\begin{array}{c}
\langle \Psi \uplus \{x?[\tilde{y}].P, x![\tilde{z}]\}, E, N\rangle \longrightarrow \langle \Psi \uplus \{[\tilde{z}/\tilde{y}]P\}, E, N\rangle \\
\langle \Psi \uplus \{P \,|\, Q\}, E, N\rangle \longrightarrow \langle \Psi \uplus \{P, Q\}, E, N\rangle \\
\langle \Psi \uplus \{*P\}, E, N\rangle \longrightarrow \langle \Psi \uplus \{*P, P\}, E, N\rangle \\
\langle \Psi \uplus \{(\nu x)P\}, E, N\rangle \longrightarrow \langle \Psi \uplus \{[y/x]P\}, E, N \cup \{y\}\rangle\ (y \notin N) \\
\langle \Psi \uplus \{\mathbf{if}\ x = y\ \mathbf{then}\ P\ \mathbf{else}\ Q\}, E, N\rangle \longrightarrow \langle \Psi \uplus \{P\}, E, N\rangle\ (\text{if } x = y) \\
\langle \Psi \uplus \{\mathbf{if}\ x = y\ \mathbf{then}\ P\ \mathbf{else}\ Q\}, E, N\rangle \longrightarrow \langle \Psi \uplus \{Q\}, E, N\rangle\ (\text{if } x \neq y) \\
\langle \Psi \uplus \{\mathbf{begin}\ L.P\}, E, N\rangle \longrightarrow \langle \Psi \uplus \{P\}, E \uplus \{L\}, N\rangle \\
\langle \Psi \uplus \{\mathbf{end}\ L.P\}, E \uplus \{L\}, N\rangle \longrightarrow \langle \Psi \uplus \{P\}, E, N\rangle
\end{array}$$

**Fig. 1.** Operational Semantics

We write $\langle \Psi, E, N\rangle \longrightarrow \mathbf{Error}$ if $\mathbf{end}\ L.P \in \Psi$ but $L \notin E$. We write $\longrightarrow^*$ for the reflexive and transitive closure of $\longrightarrow$. The safety of a process is defined as follows.

**Definition 2 (safety).** A process $P$ is *safe* if $\langle \{P\}, \emptyset, N\rangle \not\longrightarrow^* \mathbf{Error}$, where $N$ is the set of free names in $P$.

# 3 Type System

In this section, we introduce a type-and-effect system for checking the safety of a process. The main differences between our type system and Gordon and Jeffrey's type system [7] (GJ type system, in short) are (i) an effect in our type system is a mapping from event labels to *rational numbers* whereas an effect in GJ type system is a mapping from event labels to natural numbers, and (ii) processes are implicitly-typed in our type system.

## 3.1 Types and Effects

We first introduce the syntax of types and effects.

**Definition 3 (effects).** The sets of *types* and *effects*, ranged over by $T$ and $e$, are given by:

$$\begin{array}{rcl} T \text{ (Types)} & ::= & \mathbf{Name} \mid \mathbf{Ch}(T_1,\ldots,T_n)e \\ e \text{ (Effects)} & ::= & [L_1 \mapsto t_1,\ldots,L_n \mapsto t_n] \\ L \text{ (extended event labels)} & ::= & \langle \alpha_1,\ldots,\alpha_k\rangle \\ \alpha \text{ (extended names)} & ::= & x \mid \iota \\ \iota \text{ (indices)} & ::= & \uparrow\iota \mid 1 \mid 2 \mid \cdots \end{array}$$

Here, $t_1,\ldots,t_n$ ranges over the set of non-negative rational numbers.

Note that an event label has been extended to a sequence of *extended names*. An extended name is either a name (ranged over by $x, y, \ldots$), or an index $\iota$ of the form $\uparrow\cdots\uparrow n$.

An effect $[L_1 \mapsto t_1,\ldots,L_n \mapsto t_n]$ denotes the mapping $f$ from the set of events to the set of rational numbers such that $f(L_i) = t_i$ for $i \in \{1,\ldots,n\}$ and $f(L) = 0$ for $L \notin \{L_1,\ldots,L_n\}$.

A type is either the type **Name** of pure names (which are not used as a channel), or a channel type of the form $\mathbf{Ch}(T_1,\ldots,T_n)e$. Here, $\mathbf{Ch}(T_1,\ldots,T_n)e$ is the type of channels that can be used for transmitting tuples consisting of values of types $T_1,\ldots,T_n$ with a *latent effect* $e$. The latent effect $e$ describes capabilities for raising end-events that are passed from a sender to a receiver through the channel. For example, if $x$ has type $\mathbf{Ch}(\mathbf{Name})[\langle y\rangle \mapsto 2, \langle z,w\rangle \mapsto 1]$, then $x$ can be used for passing one name, and when a communication on $x$ occurs, the capabilities to raise "**end** $\langle y\rangle$" events twice and an "**end** $\langle z,w\rangle$" event once are passed from the sender to the receiver (so that $x?[u].\mathbf{end}\ \langle y\rangle.\mathbf{end}\ \langle z,w\rangle.\mathbf{end}\ \langle y\rangle$ is a valid process). Note that we allow fractional effects. For example, if $x$ has type $\mathbf{Ch}(\,)[\langle y\rangle \mapsto 0.5]$, then a *half* of the capability to raise an **end** $\langle y\rangle$ event is passed each time $x$ is used for communication. The process $x?[\,].\mathbf{end}\ \langle y\rangle$ is therefore invalid, but $x?[\,].x?[\,].\mathbf{end}\ \langle y\rangle$ is valid. Dependencies of a latent effect on transmitted names are expressed by using indices. The type $\mathbf{Ch}(\mathbf{Name},\mathbf{Name})[\langle 1,2\rangle \mapsto$

1], which corresponds to the type $\mathbf{Ch}(x:\mathbf{Name}, y:\mathbf{Name})\langle x,y\rangle$ in GJ type system, describes a channel such that when a pair of names $x$ and $y$ are passed through the channel, a capability to raise an $\mathbf{end}\ \langle x,y\rangle$ event is passed. The index constructor $\uparrow$ is used to refer to the name occurring in an outer position. For example, $\uparrow 1$ in the type $\mathbf{Ch}(\mathbf{Name}, \mathbf{Ch}(\,)[\langle\uparrow 1\rangle \mapsto 1])\langle 1,2\rangle$ refers to the name passed as the first argument (of type $\mathbf{Name}$). Note that the type corresponds to $\mathbf{Ch}(x:\mathbf{Name}, y:\mathbf{Ch}(\,)\langle x\rangle)\langle x,y\rangle$ in GJ type system. Thanks to this canonical representation of types, renaming is unnecessary for unification or matching of two types; That is convenient for the type inference algorithm described in Section 4.

A substitution $[x_1/\iota_1,\ldots,x_k/\iota_k]$, denoted by meta-variable $\theta$, is a mapping from indices to names, The substitution, summation, least upper-bound, and order $\leq$ on effects are defined by:

$$\begin{array}{l}(\theta e)(L) = \Sigma\{e(L') \mid \theta L' = L\}\\ (e_1 + e_2)(L) = e_1(L) + e_2(L)\\ (e_1 \vee e_2)(L) = \mathbf{max}(e_1(L), e_2(L))\\ e \leq e' \Leftrightarrow \forall L.e(L) \leq e'(L)\end{array}$$

The substitution $\theta T$ on types is defined by:

$$\begin{array}{l}\theta\mathbf{Name} = \mathbf{Name}\\ \theta\mathbf{Ch}(T_1,\ldots,T_n)e = \mathbf{Ch}((\uparrow\theta)T_1,\ldots,(\uparrow\theta)T_n)\theta e\end{array}$$

Here, $\uparrow[x_1/\iota_1,\ldots,x_k/\iota_k]$ denotes $[x_1/\uparrow\iota_1,\ldots,x_k/\uparrow\iota_k]$.

### 3.2 Typing Rules

We introduce three judgment forms: $\Gamma \vdash \diamond$, meaning that the type environment $\Gamma$ is well-formed; $N \vdash T$, meaning that the type $T$ is well-formed under the set $N$ of names; and $\Gamma \vdash P : e$, meaning that $P$ has effect $e$ under the type environment $\Gamma$. The judgment $N \vdash T$ is used to exclude ill-formed types like $\mathbf{Ch}(\mathbf{Name})[\langle 2\rangle \mapsto 1]$ (which refers to a non-existent index 2). The judgment $\Gamma \vdash P : e$ intuitively means that $P$ may raise end-events described by $e$ that are not preceded by begin-events. In other words, $P$ is a good process on the assumption that $P$ is given the capabilities to raise end-events described by $e$. For example, $x:\mathbf{Name}, y:\mathbf{Name} \vdash \mathbf{begin}\ \langle x\rangle.\mathbf{end}\ \langle x,y\rangle.\mathbf{end}\ \langle x\rangle : [\langle x,y\rangle \mapsto 1]$ and $x:\mathbf{Ch}(\mathbf{Name})[\langle 1\rangle \mapsto 2] \vdash x?[y].\mathbf{end}\ \langle y\rangle.\mathbf{end}\ \langle y\rangle : [\,]$ are valid judgments. The latter process receives a capability to raise two "$\mathbf{end}\ \langle y\rangle$" events through $x$. On the other hand, $x:\mathbf{Name} \vdash \mathbf{begin}\ \langle x\rangle.\mathbf{end}\ \langle x\rangle.\mathbf{end}\ \langle x\rangle : [\,]$ is an invalid judgment.

The relations $\Gamma \vdash \diamond$, $N \vdash T$, and $\Gamma \vdash P{:}e$ are defined by the rules in Figure 2. In the figure, $\theta_{y_1,\ldots,y_k}$ denotes the substitution $[y_1/1,\ldots,y_k/k]$. $\mathbf{N}(e)$ denotes the set $\bigcup\{\mathbf{N}(L) \mid e(L) > 0\}$, where $\mathbf{N}(L)$ is the set of extended names occuring in $L$. For example, $\mathbf{N}([\langle x,y\rangle \mapsto 0.5, \langle y,z\rangle \mapsto 0]) = \{x,y\}$. The typing rules are basically the same as those of Gordon and Jeffrey's type system [7], except that the syntax of types has been changed and effects have been replaced by mappings from names to rational numbers. In rule WT-CHAN, $\uparrow N$ denotes the set $\{\uparrow \iota \mid \iota \in N\} \cup (N \cap \mathcal{N})$. For example, $\uparrow\{x, 1, \uparrow 2\} = \{x, \uparrow 1, \uparrow\uparrow 2\}$. In T-IF, $[y/x]\Gamma$ is defined as follows.

$$\begin{array}{l}[y/x]\Gamma = [y/x](x_1 : T_1, \ldots, x_n : T_n) = \\ \quad ([y/x]x_1) : ([y/x]T_1); \ldots ; ([y/x]x_n) : ([y/x]T_n) \\ \quad\quad \text{where } \Gamma; x : T \text{ is } \Gamma \text{ if } x \in \mathbf{dom}(\Gamma), \text{ and is } \Gamma, x : T \text{ otherwise}\end{array}$$

*Example 2.* The process *Receiver*$(a, b, c)$ in Example 1 is typed as follows.

$$\dfrac{\dfrac{\Gamma_0, m : \mathbf{Name}, r : T_2 \vdash r![\,] : [\langle a, b, m\rangle \mapsto 1]}{\Gamma_0, m : \mathbf{Name}, r : T_2 \vdash \mathbf{begin}\ \langle a, b, m\rangle.r![\,] : [\,]}}{\Gamma_0 \vdash \mathit{Receiver}(a, b, c) : [\,]}$$

Here, $\Gamma_0 = a : \mathbf{Name}, b : \mathbf{Name}, c : \mathbf{Ch}(\mathbf{Name}, \mathbf{Ch}(\,)[\langle a, b, \uparrow 1\rangle \mapsto 1])[\,]$ and $T_2 = \mathbf{Ch}(\,)[\langle a, b, m\rangle \mapsto 1]$.

Similarly, *Sender*$(a, b, c)$ is typed as follows.

$$\dfrac{\dfrac{\dfrac{\Gamma_2 \vdash c![\mathit{msg}, \mathit{ack}] : [\,] \qquad \dfrac{\Gamma_2 \vdash \mathbf{end}\ \langle a, b, \mathit{msg}\rangle : [\langle a, b, \mathit{msg}\rangle \mapsto 1]}{\Gamma_2 \vdash \mathit{ack}?[\,].\mathbf{end}\ \langle a, b, \mathit{msg}\rangle : [\,]}}{\Gamma_2 \vdash c![\mathit{msg}, \mathit{ack}] \mid \mathit{ack}?[\,].\mathbf{end}\ \langle a, b, \mathit{msg}\rangle : [\,]}}{\Gamma_1 \vdash (\nu \mathit{ack})(c![\mathit{msg}, \mathit{ack}] \mid \mathit{ack}?[\,].\mathbf{end}\ \langle a, b, \mathit{msg}\rangle) : [\,]}}{\Gamma_0 \vdash \mathit{Sender}(a, b, c) : [\,]}$$

Here, $\Gamma_1 = \Gamma_0, \mathit{msg} : \mathbf{Name}$ and $\Gamma_2 = \Gamma_1, \mathit{ack} : \mathbf{Ch}(\,)[\langle a, b, \mathit{msg}\rangle \mapsto 1]$. By using T-PAR, we obtain:

$$\Gamma_0 \vdash \mathit{Sender}(a, b, c) \mid \mathit{Receiver}(a, b, c) : [\,].$$

### 3.3 Type Soundness

The following theorem states that a process is safe if it is well-typed and has an empty effect.

**Theorem 1 (type soundness).** *If $\Gamma \vdash P : [\,]$, then $P$ is safe.*

The proof is essentially the same as that of the type sound theorem for GJ type system [7].

### 3.4 Comparison with GJ Type System

Our type system is *strictly* more expressive than GJ type system [7]. Note that the only difference between our type system and GJ type system is that an effect is a mapping from names to *rational numbers* in our type system, while it is a mapping from names to *natural numbers* in GJ type system. Therefore, it should be trivial that any process well-typed in GJ type system is also well-typed in

$$\frac{}{\emptyset \vdash \diamond} \quad \text{(TE-Empty)}$$

$$\frac{\mathbf{dom}(\Gamma) \vdash T \qquad x \notin \mathbf{dom}(\Gamma)}{\Gamma, x : T \vdash \diamond} \quad \text{(TE-Ext)}$$

$$\frac{}{N \vdash \mathbf{Name}} \quad \text{(WT-Name)}$$

$$\frac{\begin{array}{c}\uparrow(N \cup \{1, \ldots, i-1\}) \vdash T_i \text{ (for each } i \in \{1, \ldots, n\})\\ \mathbf{N}(e) \subseteq N \cup \{1, \ldots, n\}\end{array}}{N \vdash \mathbf{Ch}(T_1, \ldots, T_n)e} \quad \text{(WT-Chan)}$$

$$\frac{\Gamma \vdash P : e \qquad e \leq e' \qquad \mathbf{N}(e') \subseteq \mathbf{dom}(\Gamma)}{\Gamma \vdash P : e'} \quad \text{(T-Subsum)}$$

$$\frac{\Gamma \vdash \diamond}{\Gamma \vdash \mathbf{0} : [\,]} \quad \text{(T-Zero)}$$

$$\frac{\begin{array}{c}\Gamma \vdash x : \mathbf{Ch}(T_1, \ldots, T_n)e\\ \Gamma \vdash y_i : (\uparrow \theta_{y_1, \ldots, y_{i-1}})T_i \text{ (for each } i \in \{1, \ldots, n\})\end{array}}{\Gamma \vdash x![y_1, \ldots, y_n] : \theta_{y_1, \ldots, y_n} e} \quad \text{(T-Out)}$$

$$\frac{\begin{array}{c}\Gamma \vdash x : \mathbf{Ch}(T_1, \ldots, T_n)e_1 \qquad \Gamma, y_1 : T'_1, \ldots, y_n : T'_n \vdash P : e_2\\ T'_i = (\uparrow \theta_{y_1, \ldots, y_{i-1}})T_i \text{ (for each } i \in \{1, \ldots, n\})\\ e_2 \leq \theta_{y_1, \ldots, y_n} e_1 + e \qquad (\mathbf{N}(e) \cup \mathbf{N}(e_1)) \cap \{y_1, \ldots, y_n\} = \emptyset\end{array}}{\Gamma \vdash x?[y_1, \ldots, y_n].P : e} \quad \text{(T-In)}$$

$$\frac{\Gamma \vdash P_1 : e_1 \qquad \Gamma \vdash P_2 : e_2}{\Gamma \vdash P_1 \,|\, P_2 : e_1 + e_2} \quad \text{(T-Par)}$$

$$\frac{\Gamma \vdash P : [\,]}{\Gamma \vdash *P : [\,]} \quad \text{(T-Rep)}$$

$$\frac{\Gamma, x : T \vdash P : e \qquad x \notin \mathbf{N}(e)}{\Gamma \vdash (\nu x)P : e} \quad \text{(T-Res)}$$

$$\frac{\Gamma \vdash x : T \qquad \Gamma \vdash y : T \qquad [y/x]\Gamma \vdash [y/x]P : [y/x]e_P \qquad \Gamma \vdash Q : e_Q}{\Gamma \vdash \mathbf{if}\ x = y\ \mathbf{then}\ P\ \mathbf{else}\ Q : e_P \vee e_Q} \quad \text{(T-Cond)}$$

$$\frac{\Gamma \vdash P : e + [L \mapsto 1] \qquad \mathbf{N}(L) \subseteq \mathbf{dom}(\Gamma)}{\Gamma \vdash \mathbf{begin}\ L.P : e} \quad \text{(T-Begin)}$$

$$\frac{\Gamma \vdash P : e \qquad \mathbf{N}(L) \subseteq \mathbf{dom}(\Gamma)}{\Gamma \vdash \mathbf{end}\ L.P : e + [L \mapsto 1]} \quad \text{(T-End)}$$

**Fig. 2.** Typing Rules

our type system. On the other hand, there is a process that is typable in our type system but *not* in GJ type system. Consider the following process:[1]

$$\mathbf{begin}\ \langle a \rangle.(c![\,] \,|\, c![\,]) \,|\, c?[\,].c?[\,].\mathbf{end}\ \langle a \rangle.$$

[1] The example was suggested by Tachio Terauchi.

The process on the lefthand side first raises a begin-event, and then sends a capability to raise an end-event on channel $c$, while the process on the righthand side receives the capability from channel $c$, and raises the end-event.

In our type system, the process is typed under the type environment: $a : \mathbf{Name}, c : \mathbf{Ch}(\mathbf{Name})[\langle a \rangle \mapsto 0.5]$. Note that $c$ carries a *half* of the capability to raise the end-event. Since two messages are sent on $c$, $0.5 + 0.5 = 1$ capability is passed from the left process to the right process.

To see why the above process is not typable in GJ type system, let the type of $c$ be $\mathbf{Ch}(\,)e$ where $e(\langle a \rangle) = n$. In order for the left process to be typable, it must be the case that $n + n \leq 1$. On the other hand, for the right process to be typable, it must be the case that $n + n \geq 1$. There is no natural number $n$ that satisfies both the constraints.

## 4 Type Checking Algorithm

This section describes an algorithm which, given a process $P$, judges whether there exists a type environment $\Gamma$ such that $\Gamma \vdash P : [\,]$.

The algorithm consists of the following steps.

- Step 1: Generate constraints on effects based on the typing rules.
- Step 2: Reduce the constraints on effects into linear inequalities on rational numbers.
- Step 3: Check whether the linear inequalities have a solution.

We first explain the first and second steps below. We then show in Subsection 4.4 that the algorithm runs in time polynomial in the size of the process (provided that the size of the simple type of each name is polynomial in the size of the process and that the size of each begin/end-event is bound by a constant). In Subsection 4.5, we show that without fractional effects, the type inference problem is NP-hard.

### 4.1 Step 1: Generating Constraints on Effects

Figure 3 gives an algorithm *Inf*, which takes a closed process $P$ as an input, and generates a set $C$ of constraints. $C$ expresses a necessary and sufficient condition for $\Gamma \vdash P : [\,]$ where all the effects in $\Gamma$ are empty.

*Inf* calls a sub-procedure *inf*, which takes a type environment and a process, and generates a pair $(e, C)$ where $C$ is a necessary and sufficient condition for $\Gamma \vdash P : e$. We assume that the simple type of each name has been already inferred by the standard type inference algorithm,[2] and that $\mathbf{typeof}(x)$ decorates the simple type of $x$ with fresh effect variables and returns it. For example, if the simple type of $x$ is $\mathbf{Ch}(\mathbf{Ch}(\mathbf{Name}))$, $\mathbf{typeof}(x)$ returns $\mathbf{Ch}(\mathbf{Ch}(\mathbf{Name})\rho_1)\rho_2$ where $\rho_1$ and $\rho_2$ are fresh. In the definition of *inf* (the clauses for input and output processes), $\mathbf{Ch}(T_1, \ldots, T_n)e = \Gamma(x)$ expresses a matching of $\Gamma(x)$ against the pattern $\mathbf{Ch}(T_1, \ldots, T_n)e$. For example, if $n = 1$ and $\Gamma(x) = \mathbf{Ch}(\mathbf{Ch}(\mathbf{Name})\rho_1)\rho_2$,

[2] If there is an undetermined type, let it be **Name**.

then $T_1$ and $e$ are instantiated to $\mathbf{Ch}(\mathbf{Name})\rho_1$ and $\rho_2$ respectively. In the clauses for input and output processes, a substitution $\theta$ works as an *operation* for types but as an *constructor* for effects. For example, let $\theta = [a/x, b/1]$. Then $\theta\mathbf{Ch}(\mathbf{Ch}(\mathbf{Name})\rho_1)\rho_2$ is $\mathbf{Ch}(\mathbf{Ch}(\mathbf{Name})[a/x, b/\uparrow 1]\rho_1)[a/x, b/1]\rho_2$. $teq(T_1, T_2)$ matches $T_1$ and $T_2$, and generates equality constraints on effects. For example, $teq(\mathbf{Ch}(\mathbf{Ch}(\mathbf{Name})e_1)e_2, \mathbf{Ch}(\mathbf{Ch}(\mathbf{Name})e_1')e_2')$ generates $\{e_1 = e_1', e_2 = e_2'\}$. Note that the number of equality constraints generated by $teq(T_1, T_2)$ is linear in the size of $T_1$ and $T_2$. Note also that the matching of types never fails because of the assumption that type inference for the simple type system has been already performed. The substitution operation $\theta T$ can be performed in time $O(mn)$, where $m$ is the size of $T$ and $n$ is the size of $\theta$. $wf(N, T)$ generates the conditions for $T$ being well-formed under the names $N$.

*Inf* generates constraints of the following forms:

- inequalities on effects $e_1 \geq e_2$, where $e_1$ and $e_2$ are expressions constructed from effect constants ($[L \mapsto 1]$), effect variables, substitutions, and summation (+).
- equalities on effects $e_1 = e_2$, where $e_1$ and $e_2$ are either $[\,]$ or of the form $\theta_1 \cdots \theta_k \rho$.
- $\mathbf{notin}(x, e)$, where $e$ is $[\,]$ or an effect variable.
- $\mathbf{N}(e) \subseteq N$, where $e$ is of the form $\theta_1 \cdots \theta_k \rho$.

The algorithm *Inf* is sound and complete with respect to the type system in Section 3 in the following sense.

**Lemma 1.** *$Inf(P)$ is satisfiable if and only if $\Gamma \vdash P : [\,]$ holds for a type environment $\Gamma$ such that all the effects in $\Gamma$ are empty.*

*Remark 1.* The reason why we require that all the effects in $\Gamma$ are empty is that $P$ may be executed in parallel with an untrusted process $Q$. The condition that the effects in $\Gamma$ are empty ensures that $P$ does not expect to receive any capability (to raise end-events) from $Q$. Thus, even in the presence of the untrusted process $Q$, the correspondence assertions in $P$ hold. (Since $Q$ may not be simply-typed, execution of $P \,|\, Q$ may get stuck, however.)

### 4.2 Step 2: Reducing Constraints on Effects

Let $\mathcal{N}_1$ be the set of all the names occurring in $P$ (including bound names), and let $\mathcal{N}_2$ be the set of indices of the form $\uparrow^k l$. Here, $k$ is less than or equal to the maximum *depth* of the type of a channel occurring in $P$, and $l$ is less than or equal to the maximum *width* of the type of a channel occurring in $P$ (in other words, the maximum size of tuples sent along channels). Let $w$ be the maximal size of the begin/end-events occurring in $P$. (Here, the size of $\langle x_1, \ldots, x_k \rangle$ is $k$.) Then, we need to consider only events in the following set $\mathcal{L}$:

$$\{\langle \alpha_1, \ldots, \alpha_k \rangle \mid k \leq w, \alpha_1, \ldots, \alpha_k \in \mathcal{N}_1 \cup \mathcal{N}_2\}.$$

Note that the size of $\mathcal{N}_1 \cup \mathcal{N}_2$ is polynomial in the size of $P$, since both the maximum depth and the maximum width of simple types are polynomial in the

$$\begin{array}{l}
\mathit{Inf}(P) = \\
\quad \textbf{let} \\
\qquad \Gamma = \{x : \textbf{typeof}(x) \mid x \in \mathbf{N}(P)\} \\
\qquad (e, C_1) = \mathit{inf}(\Gamma, P) \\
\qquad C_2 = \{e = [\,]\} \\
\qquad\qquad \cup\{e_1 = [\,] \mid e_1 \text{ appears in } \Gamma\} \\
\quad \textbf{in } C_1 \cup C_2
\end{array}$$

$$\mathit{inf}(\Gamma, \mathbf{0}) = ([\,], \emptyset)$$

$$\begin{array}{l}
\mathit{inf}(\Gamma, x![y_1, \ldots, y_n]) = \\
\textbf{let} \\
\quad \mathbf{Ch}(T_1, \ldots, T_n)e = \Gamma(x) \\
\quad C = \{\mathit{teq}(\Gamma(y_i), (\uparrow \theta_{y_1,\ldots,y_{i-1}})T_i) \\
\qquad\qquad \mid i \in \{1, \ldots, n\}\} \\
\textbf{in } (\rho, C \cup \{\rho \geq \theta_{y_1,\ldots,y_n} e\}) \\
\qquad \text{where } \rho \text{ is fresh}
\end{array}$$

$$\begin{array}{l}
\mathit{inf}(\Gamma, x?[y_1, \ldots, y_n].P) = \\
\textbf{let} \\
\quad \Gamma' = \Gamma, \tilde{y} : \textbf{typeof}(\tilde{y}) \\
\quad (e_P, C_P) = \mathit{inf}(\Gamma', P) \\
\quad \mathbf{Ch}(T_1, \ldots, T_n)e = \Gamma(x) \\
\quad C_1 = \{\mathit{teq}(\Gamma'(y_i), (\uparrow \theta_{y_1,\ldots,y_{i-1}})T_i) \\
\qquad\qquad \mid i \in \{1, \ldots, n\}\} \\
\quad C_2 = \{\mathbf{notin}(y_i, \rho) \mid i \in \{1, \ldots, n\}\} \\
\quad C_3 = \{\rho + \theta_{y_1,\ldots,y_n} e \geq e_P\} \\
\quad C_4 = \bigcup_{1 \leq i \leq n} \mathit{wf}(\uparrow(\{y_1, \ldots, y_{i-1}\} \\
\qquad\qquad\qquad \cup \mathbf{dom}(\Gamma)), \Gamma(y_i)) \\
\textbf{in } (\rho, C_P \cup C_1 \cup C_2 \cup C_3 \cup C_4) \\
\qquad \text{where } \rho \text{ is fresh}
\end{array}$$

$$\begin{array}{l}
\mathit{inf}(\Gamma, P \,|\, Q) = \\
\textbf{let} \\
\quad (e_P, C_P) = \mathit{inf}(\Gamma, P) \\
\quad (e_Q, C_Q) = \mathit{inf}(\Gamma, Q) \\
\textbf{in } (\rho, C_P \cup C_Q \cup \{\rho \geq e_P + e_Q\}) \\
\qquad \text{where } \rho \text{ is fresh}
\end{array}$$

$$\begin{array}{l}
\mathit{inf}(\Gamma, *P) = \\
\textbf{let } (e_P, C_P) = \mathit{inf}(\Gamma, P) \\
\textbf{in } ([\,], C_P \cup \{e_P = [\,]\})
\end{array}$$

$$\begin{array}{l}
\mathit{inf}(\Gamma, (\nu x)P) = \\
\textbf{let } T = \textbf{typeof}(x) \\
\quad (e_P, C_P) = \mathit{inf}((\Gamma, x : T), P) \\
\textbf{in } (\rho, C_P \cup \{\rho \geq e_P\} \cup \{\mathbf{notin}(x, e_P)\} \\
\qquad\qquad \cup \mathit{wf}(\mathbf{dom}(\Gamma), T)) \\
\qquad \text{where } \rho \text{ is fresh}
\end{array}$$

$$\begin{array}{l}
\mathit{inf}(\Gamma, \textbf{if } x = y \textbf{ then } P \textbf{ else } Q) = \\
\textbf{let} \\
\quad (e_P, C_P) = \mathit{inf}([y/x]\Gamma, [y/x]P) \\
\quad (e_Q, C_Q) = \mathit{inf}(\Gamma, Q) \\
\quad C_1 = \{[y/x]\rho \geq e_P, \rho \geq e_Q\} \\
\textbf{in } (\rho, C_P \cup C_Q \cup C_1 \cup \{\mathit{teq}(\Gamma(x), \Gamma(y))\}) \\
\qquad \text{where } \rho \text{ is fresh}
\end{array}$$

$$\begin{array}{l}
\mathit{inf}(\Gamma, \textbf{begin } L.P) = \\
\textbf{let } (e_P, C_P) = \mathit{inf}(\Gamma, P) \\
\textbf{in } (\rho, C_P \cup \{\rho + [L \mapsto 1] \geq e_P\}) \\
\qquad \text{where } \rho \text{ is fresh and } \mathbf{N}(L) \subseteq \mathbf{dom}(\Gamma)
\end{array}$$

$$\begin{array}{l}
\mathit{inf}(\Gamma, \textbf{end } L.P) = \\
\textbf{let } (e_P, C_P) = \mathit{inf}(\Gamma, P) \\
\textbf{in } (\rho, C_P \cup \{\rho \geq e_P + [L \mapsto 1]\}) \\
\qquad \text{where } \rho \text{ is fresh and } \mathbf{N}(L) \subseteq \mathbf{dom}(\Gamma)
\end{array}$$

$$\mathit{teq}(T, T) = \emptyset$$

$$\begin{array}{l}
\mathit{teq}(\mathbf{Ch}(\tilde{T})e_1, \mathbf{Ch}(\tilde{T}')e_2) = \\
\quad \{e_1 = e_2\} \cup \mathit{teq}(\tilde{T}, \tilde{T}')
\end{array}$$

$$\mathit{wf}(N, \mathbf{Name}) = \emptyset$$

$$\begin{array}{l}
\mathit{wf}(N, \mathbf{Ch}(T_1, \ldots, T_n)e) \\
\quad = (\bigcup_{1 \leq i \leq n} \mathit{wf}(\uparrow(N \cup \{1, \ldots, i-1\}), T_i)) \\
\qquad \cup \{\mathbf{N}(e) \subseteq N \cup \{1, \ldots, n\}\}
\end{array}$$

**Fig. 3.** Constraint Generation Algorithm

size of $P$. On the assumption that the maximum size of events is bound by a constant, therefore, the size $N$ of $\mathcal{L}$ is polynomial in the size of $P$.

Let $\mathcal{L} = \{L_1, \ldots, L_N\}$. For each effect variable $\rho$ in $C$, prepare $N$ variables $\xi_{\rho,L_1}, \ldots, \xi_{\rho,L_N}$, ranging over rational numbers. Then, the constraints $C$ on effect variables are replaced with constraints on $\xi_{\rho,L}$ as follows.

$$\begin{aligned}
\mathbf{cconv}(e_1 \geq e_2) &= \{\mathbf{econv}(e_1)(L) \geq \mathbf{econv}(e_2)(L) \mid L \in \mathcal{L}\}\\
\mathbf{cconv}(e_1 = e_2) &= \{\mathbf{econv}(e_1)(L) = \mathbf{econv}(e_2)(L) \mid L \in \mathcal{L}\}\\
\mathbf{cconv}(\mathbf{notin}(x, e)) &= \{\mathbf{econv}(e)(L) = 0 \mid L \in \mathcal{L} \wedge x \in \mathbf{N}(L)\}\\
\mathbf{cconv}(\mathbf{N}(e) \subseteq N) &= \{\mathbf{econv}(e)(L) = 0 \mid L \in \mathcal{L} \wedge \mathbf{N}(L) \not\subseteq N\}\\
\mathbf{econv}(\rho) &= \{L_1 \mapsto \xi_{\rho,L_1}, \ldots, L_N \mapsto \xi_{\rho,L_N}\}\\
\mathbf{econv}(e_1 + e_2) &= \{L_1 \mapsto \mathbf{econv}(e_1)(L_1) + \mathbf{econv}(e_2)(L_1), \ldots,\\
&\qquad L_n \mapsto \mathbf{econv}(e_1)(L_N) + \mathbf{econv}(e_2)(L_N)\}\\
\mathbf{econv}(\theta e) &= \{L_1 \mapsto \Sigma\{\mathbf{econv}(e)(L) \mid \theta L = L_1\}, \ldots,\\
&\qquad L_N \mapsto \Sigma\{\mathbf{econv}(e)(L) \mid \theta L = L_N\}\}
\end{aligned}$$

### 4.3 Example

Recall the process in Example 1. By the standard type inference, the following types are assigned to names:

$$\begin{aligned}
&a : \mathbf{Name}, b : \mathbf{Name}, c : \mathbf{Ch}(\mathbf{Name}, \mathbf{Ch}(\,)\rho_0)\rho_c, \mathit{msg} : \mathbf{Name},\\
&\mathit{ack} : \mathbf{Ch}(\,)\rho_{ack}, m : \mathbf{Name}, r : \mathbf{Ch}(\,)\rho_r
\end{aligned}$$

Here, $\rho_0, \rho_c, \rho_{ack}$ are effect variables to express unknown effects.

By running the constraint generation algorithm for $\mathit{Sender}(a, b, c)$, we obtain the following constraints.

$$\begin{aligned}
&\rho_{c!} \geq [\mathit{msg}/1, \mathit{ack}/2]\rho_c, \quad \rho_{ack?} + \rho_{ack} \geq [\langle a, b, \mathit{msg}\rangle \mapsto 1]\\
&\rho_s \geq \rho_{c!} + \rho_{ack?}, \quad \rho_{ack} = [\mathit{msg}/\uparrow 1]\rho_0, \mathbf{notin}(\mathit{msg}, \rho_s), \mathbf{notin}(\mathit{ack}, \rho_s)\\
&\mathbf{N}(\rho_0) \subseteq \{a, b, \uparrow 1\}, \quad \mathbf{N}(\rho_c) \subseteq \{a, b, 1, 2\}, \quad \mathbf{N}(\rho_{ack}) \subseteq \{a, b, c, \mathit{msg}\}
\end{aligned}$$

Here, $\rho_s$, $\rho_{c!}$, and $\rho_{ack?}$ are effects of the processes $\mathit{Sender}(a, b, c)$, $c![\mathit{msg}, \mathit{ack}]$, and $\mathit{ack}?[\,].\cdots$ respectively. The constraints on the first line come from the output and input processes, and those on the second line come from the parallel composition and $\nu$-prefixes. Those on the third line come from the well-formedness conditions (*wf* in the algorithm).

Similarly, we obtain the following constraints from $\mathit{Receiver}(a, b, c)$:

$$\begin{aligned}
&\rho_{bg} + [\langle a, b, m\rangle \mapsto 1] \geq \rho_r, \quad \rho_{rec} + [m/1, r/2]\rho_c \geq \rho_{bg}, \quad \rho_r = [m/\uparrow 1]\rho_0\\
&\mathbf{notin}(m, \rho_{rec}), \mathbf{notin}(r, \rho_{rec}), \mathbf{N}(\rho_r) \subseteq \{a, b, c, m\}
\end{aligned}$$

From the entire process $(\nu c)(\mathit{Sender}(a, b, c) \mid \mathit{Receiver}(a, b, c))$, we also obtain:

$$\rho_{sys} \geq \rho_s + \rho_{rec}, \quad \rho_{sys} = [\,]$$

The next step is to reduce the above constraints into linear inequalities. The set $\mathcal{L}$ of relevant events is:

$$\{\langle x_1, x_2, x_3\rangle \mid x_1, x_2, x_3 \in \{a, b, c, \mathit{msg}, \mathit{ack}, m, r, 1, 2, \uparrow 1\}\}$$

We prepare a variable $\xi_{i,L}$ for each effect variable $\rho_i$ and event $L$. (In practice, we can reduce the number of variables by looking at the substitutions and events occurring in the effect constraints.)

We show only inequalities relevant to $\langle a, b, msg\rangle$:

$$\begin{array}{l}
\xi_{c!,\langle a,b,msg\rangle} \geq \xi_{c,\langle a,b,\uparrow 1\rangle}, \quad \xi_{ack?,\langle a,b,msg\rangle} + \xi_{ack,\langle a,b,msg\rangle} \geq 1 \\
\xi_{s,\langle a,b,msg\rangle} \geq \xi_{c!,\langle a,b,msg\rangle} + \xi_{ack?,\langle a,b,msg\rangle}, \quad \xi_{ack,\langle a,b,msg\rangle} = \xi_{0,\langle a,b,\uparrow 1\rangle} \\
\xi_{s,\langle a,b,msg\rangle} = 0 \\
\xi_{bg,\langle a,b,m\rangle} + 1 \geq \xi_{r,\langle a,b,m\rangle}, \quad \xi_{c,\langle a,b,1\rangle} \geq \xi_{bg,\langle a,b,m\rangle}, \quad \xi_{r,\langle a,b,m\rangle} = \xi_{0,\langle a,b,\uparrow 1\rangle} \\
\xi_{sys,\langle a,b,msg\rangle} \geq \xi_{s,\langle a,b,msg\rangle} + \xi_{rec,\langle a,b,msg\rangle}, \quad \xi_{sys,\langle a,b,msg\rangle} = 0
\end{array}$$

Additionally, we have the inequality $\xi_{i,L} \geq 0$ for every variable.

The above inequalities have the following solution:

$$\begin{array}{l}
\xi_{ack,\langle a,b,msg\rangle} = \xi_{r,\langle a,b,m\rangle} = \xi_{0,\langle a,b,\uparrow 1\rangle} = 1, \\
\xi_{c!,\langle a,b,msg\rangle} = \xi_{c,\langle a,b,msg\rangle} = \xi_{c,\langle a,b,1\rangle} = \xi_{ack?,\langle a,b,msg\rangle} = \xi_{bg,\langle a,b,m\rangle} \\
\quad = \xi_{rec,\langle a,b,msg\rangle} = \xi_{s,\langle a,b,msg\rangle} = \xi_{sys,\langle a,b,msg\rangle} = 0.
\end{array}$$

Thus, we obtain the following type for each name:

$$\begin{array}{l}
a : \mathbf{Name}, b : \mathbf{Name}, c : \mathbf{Ch}(\mathbf{Name}, \mathbf{Ch}(\,)[\langle a, b, \uparrow 1\rangle \mapsto 1])[\,], msg : \mathbf{Name}, \\
ack : \mathbf{Ch}(\,)[\langle a, b, msg\rangle \mapsto 1], m : \mathbf{Name}, r : \mathbf{Ch}(\,)[\langle a, b, m\rangle \mapsto 1],
\end{array}$$

### 4.4 Efficiency of the Algorithm

Let $|P|$ be the size of the input $P$ of the algorithm *Inf*. We show that, if the size of simple types is polynomial in $|P|$, and the size of begin/end-events is bounded by a constant, then our algorithm runs in time polynomial in $|P|$. First, the number of the constraints generated by $Inf(P)$ is polynomial in $|P|$. Note here that by the assumption on the size of simple types, the size of $teq(T_1, T_2)$ is also polynomial in $|P|$: the number of effect equalities generated by $teq(T_1, T_2)$ is linear in the size of $T_1$, and the size of effect expressions occurring in each equality is also polynomial in $|P|$. Since the size of the event set $\mathcal{L}$ is polynomial in the size of the process, the second step runs in time polynomial in $|P|$ and generates linear inequalities of size polynomial in $|P|$. Since linear inequalities can be solved in polynomial time, the third step can also be performed in polynomial time.

*Remark 2.* Note that in general, the size of simple types (expressed as terms instead of graphs) can be *exponential* in the size of $|P|$. For example consider the following process:

$$x_0![x_1, x_1] \mid x_1![x_2, x_2] \mid \cdots \mid x_n![x_{n+1}, x_{n+1}]$$

The size of the type of $x_0$ is exponential in $n$. We believe, however, that in practice, the maximum size of types depends on what data structures and communication protocols are used in the program, and it is generally independent of the size of the program itself. If the assumption on the size of simple types is not met or if there are recursive types, we can use graph representation of simple types and assign the same effect to the same type node. Then, our algorithm still runs in time polynomial in the size of the program, although the completeness of the inference algorithm would be lost.

### 4.5 Complexity of GJ Type System

Next, we show that the typability in GJ type system [7] is NP-hard without type annotations (in other words, if fractional effects in our type system are replaced by multisets of events as in GJ type system).

Since the 3-SAT problem is NP-complete, in order to prove NP-hardness, it suffices to show that any instance $q$ of 3-SAT problem can be encoded into a process $\mathit{SAT2P}(q)$ so that the size of $\mathit{SAT2P}(q)$ is polynomial in the size of $q$, and so that $q$ is satisfiable if and only if $\emptyset \vdash \mathit{SAT2P}(q) : [\,]$ is typable.

Let a 3-SAT problem $q$ be $d_1 \wedge \cdots \wedge d_n$ where $d_i$ is $A_{i1} \vee A_{i2} \vee A_{i3}$ and $A_{ij}$ is either a variable $X_k$ or its negation $\overline{X}_k$. By representing the truth value by 1 and 0 (and assuming that each variable ranges over $\{0, 1\}$), we can encode each disjunction $d_i$ into an integer constraint $\mathit{f2ic}(d_i)$, which is one of the following forms:

$$X + Y + Z \geq 1 \qquad X \leq Y + Z \quad X + Y \leq Z + 1 \quad X + Y + Z \leq 2$$

For example, $X_1 \vee \overline{X_2} \vee X_3$ is expressed by $X_1 + (1 - X_2) + X_3 \geq 1$, which is equivalent to $X_2 \leq X_1 + X_3$.

For each of the above inequalities, define the following processes:

$$\begin{aligned}
P_{X+Y+Z\geq 1} &= c_X?[x].c_Y?[y].c_Z?[z].\\
&\qquad \textbf{if } x = y \textbf{ then if } y = z \textbf{ then end } \langle x \rangle \textbf{ else } \mathbf{0} \textbf{ else } \mathbf{0}\\
P_{X \leq Y+Z} &= c_Y?[y].c_Z?[z].\textbf{if } y = z \textbf{ then } c_X![y] \textbf{ else } \mathbf{0}\\
P_{X+Y \leq Z+1} &= c_Z?[z].\textbf{begin } \langle z \rangle.(c_X![z] \mid c_Y![z])\\
P_{X+Y+Z \leq 2} &= (\nu a)\textbf{begin } \langle a \rangle.\textbf{begin } \langle a \rangle.(c_X![a] \mid c_Y![a] \mid c_Z![a])
\end{aligned}$$

Then, for each inequality $\beta$, $\beta$ holds if and only if

$$\begin{aligned}
c_X : \mathbf{Ch}(\mathbf{Name})[\langle 1 \rangle \mapsto X], c_Y : \mathbf{Ch}(\mathbf{Name})[\langle 1 \rangle \mapsto Y],&\\
c_Z : \mathbf{Ch}(\mathbf{Name})[\langle 1 \rangle \mapsto Z] \vdash P_\beta : [\,]&
\end{aligned}$$

holds.

For each variable $X$, let $Q_X$ be the process $(\nu a)\textbf{begin } \langle a \rangle.c_X![a]$. Then, $0 \leq X \leq 1$ if and only if $c_X : \mathbf{Ch}(\mathbf{Name})[\langle 1 \rangle \mapsto X] \vdash Q_X$.

For an instance of 3-SAT problem $q = d_1 \wedge \cdots \wedge d_n$, define $\mathit{SAT2P}(q)$ by:

$$\begin{aligned}
&\mathit{SAT2P}(d_1 \wedge \cdots \wedge d_n) =\\
&\quad (\nu c_{X_1}) \cdots (\nu c_{X_m})(Q_{X_1} \mid \cdots \mid Q_{X_m} \mid P_{\mathit{f2ic}(d_1)} \mid \cdots \mid P_{\mathit{f2ic}(d_n)}).
\end{aligned}$$

Here, $X_1, \ldots, X_m$ are the variables in $q$. Then, $q$ is satisfiable if and only if $\emptyset \vdash \mathit{SAT2P}(q) : [\,]$ holds. Since the size of $\mathit{SAT2P}(q)$ is linear in the size of $q$ and the 3-SAT problem is NP-complete, the typability (i.e., the problem of judging whether there exists $\Gamma$ such that $\Gamma \vdash P : [\,]$ holds) is NP-hard.

*Remark 3.* Note that the above encoding uses only events of the form $\langle a \rangle$ and types of the form **Ch**(**Name**)$e$ and **Name**. Thus, the type inference problem is NP-hard even on the assumption that the sizes of simple types and events are bound by a constant.

## 5 Related Work

As already mentioned, this work is based on Gordon and Jeffrey's type system for correspondence assertions [7]. We have extended effects to *fractional effects* and removed explicit type annotations. The resulting type system is more expressive than their type system, and is more suitable for automatic type inference. Gordon and Jeffrey [4, 6, 5] have extended their type system to verify authenticity of security protocols using cryptographic primitives. It is left for future work to check whether type inference algorithms for those type systems can be constructed in a similar manner.

Blanchet [1, 2] studied completely different techniques for checking correspondence assertions in cryptographic security protocols, and implemented protocol verification systems. Like in our type system (and unlike in Gordon and Jeffrey's type systems [7,4,6,5]), his systems do not require any annotations (except for correspondence assertions). It is difficult to make fair comparison between our work and his techniques because we have not yet extended the type system to deal with cryptographic primitives. A possible advantage of our type-based approach is that our algorithm runs in polynomial time. On the other hand, there seem to be no guarantee that his systems terminate [1]. A clear advantage of his recent work [2] over the type-based methods is that it can guarantee soundness in the computational model (rather than in the formal model with the perfect encryption assumption).

The idea of using rational numbers in type systems have been proposed by Boyland [3] and Terauchi and Aiken [9,10]. They used rational numbers (ranging over $[0, 1]$, rather than $[0, \infty)$ in our type system) to prevent interference of read/write operations on reference cells or channels. Terauchi and Aiken [10] observed that type inference can be performed in polynomial time thanks to the use of rational numbers. A main difference between their system and ours is that effects are mapping from *channel handles* to rational numbers in their system [10], while effects are mapping from *names* to rational numbers in ours. Because of the name-dependent feature of GJ type system, reduction of the typability to linear programming was less trivial.

Gordon and Jeffrey's type system for checking correspondence assertions [7] can be regarded as an instance of the generic type system for the $\pi$-calculus [8]. Thus, it would be interesting to extend the idea of this paper to develop a type inference algorithm for the generic type system.

## 6 Conclusion

We have extended Gordon and Jeffrey's type system by introducing fractional effects, and developed a polynomial-time type inference algorithm. Future work includes implementation of the type inference algorithm and extension of the type system to deal with cryptographic primitives.

## Acknowledgment

We would like to thank Tachio Terauchi for discussions on this work. We would also like to thank anonymous referees for useful comments.

## References

1. Blanchet, B.: From Secrecy to Authenticity in Security Protocols. In: Hermenegildo, M.V., Puebla, G. (eds.) SAS 2002. LNCS, vol. 2477, pp. 342–359. Springer, Heidelberg (2002)
2. Blanchet, B.: Computationally sound mechanized proofs of correspondence assertions. In: CSF 2007, pp. 97–111. IEEE Computer Society Press, Los Alamitos (2007)
3. Boyland, J.: Checking interference with fractional permissions. In: Cousot, R. (ed.) SAS 2003. LNCS, vol. 2694, pp. 55–72. Springer, Heidelberg (2003)
4. Gordon, A.D., Jeffrey, A.: Authenticity by typing for security protocols. In: CSFW 2001, pp. 145–159. IEEE Computer Society Press, Los Alamitos (2001)
5. Gordon, A.D., Jeffrey, A.: Types and effects for asymmetric cryptographic protocols. In: CSFW-15, pp. 77–91. IEEE Computer Society Press, Los Alamitos (2002)
6. Gordon, A.D., Jeffrey, A.: Typing one-to-one and one-to-many correspondences in security protocols. In: Okada, M., Pierce, B.C., Scedrov, A., Tokuda, H., Yonezawa, A. (eds.) ISSS 2002. LNCS, vol. 2609, pp. 263–282. Springer, Heidelberg (2003)
7. Gordon, A.D., Jeffrey, A.: Typing correspondence assertions for communication protocols. Theoretical Computer Science 300, 379–409 (2003)
8. Igarashi, A., Kobayashi, N.: A generic type system for the pi-calculus. Theoretical Computer Science 311(1-3), 121–163 (2004)
9. Terauchi, T., Aiken, A.: Witnessing side-effects. In: Proceedings of International Conference on Functional Programming, pp. 105–115. ACM Press, New York (2005)
10. Terauchi, T., Aiken, A.: A capability calculus for concurrency and determinism. In: Baier, C., Hermanns, H. (eds.) CONCUR 2006. LNCS, vol. 4137, pp. 218–232. Springer, Heidelberg (2006)
11. Woo, T.Y., Lam, S.S.: A semantic model for authentication protocols. In: RSP: IEEE Computer Society Symposium on Research in Security and Privacy, pp. 178–193 (1993)

# Deriving Compilers and Virtual Machines for a Multi-level Language*

Atsushi Igarashi[1] and Masashi Iwaki[2]

[1] Kyoto University, Japan
igarashi@kuis.kyoto-u.ac.jp
[2] Hitachi, Ltd., Japan
masashi.iwaki.ew@hitachi.com

**Abstract.** We develop virtual machines and compilers for a multi-level language, which supports multi-stage specialization by composing program fragments with quotation mechanisms. We consider two styles of virtual machines—ones equipped with special instructions for code generation and ones without—and show that the latter kind can deal with, more easily, low-level code generation, which avoids the overhead of (run-time) compilation by manipulating instruction sequences, rather than source-level terms, as data. The virtual machines and accompanying compilers are derived by program transformation, which extends Ager et al.'s derivation of virtual machines from evaluators.

## 1 Introduction

Multi-level (or multi-stage) languages are designed to support manipulation of program fragments as data and execution of generated code, often by the mechanism of quasi-quotation and eval as in Lisp. Most of those languages are considered extensions of the two-level λ-calculus [1] to an arbitrary number of levels, which has been proposed and studied by Glück and Jørgensen [2].

In the last decade, designs, semantics, and type systems of multi-level languages have been studied fairly extensively by many people [3,4,5,6,7,8,9,10,11]. On the other hand, implementation issues have been discussed mostly in the context of *two-level* systems [12,13,14,15], in which generated code itself does not generate code. As is pointed out by Wickline et al. [4], implementation of two-level languages does not extend straightforwardly to multi-level, especially when one wants a program to generate low-level machine code directly, since there is possible code-size blow-up in generating instructions that themselves generate instructions.

Wickline et al. [4] have addressed this problem by developing an extension of the Categorical Abstract Machine (CAM) [16] with a facility for run-time code generation and a compilation scheme for a multi-level extension of ML called $ML^{\square}$. Unfortunately, however, the design of the extended CAM is rather ad-hoc and it is not clear how their technique can be applied to different settings.

* Supported in part by Grant-in-Aid for Scientific Research No. 19300007 from MEXT of Japan.

Z. Shao (Ed.): APLAS 2007, LNCS 4807, pp. 206–221, 2007.

*Our Approach and Contributions.* We develop virtual machines (VMs) and compilers for multi-level languages as systematically as possible, by extending Ager et al.'s technique [17,18] to derive from evaluators, by a sequence of well-known program transformations, abstract machines (which take a source term as an input) or VMs (which take an instruction sequence) with compilers. Although this technique has been shown to be applicable to various evaluation strategies including call-by-value, call-by-name, call-by-need, and even strong reduction [19], application to multi-level languages is new (at least, to our knowledge).

We also identify the following two aspects of compilation schemes and how they appear in the derivation of VMs.

- One aspect is whether a VM generates low-level code or source-level code. It would be desirable that a VM support low-level code generation since the overhead of compilation of the generated code can be reduced.
- The other is whether or not a VM is equipped with instructions *dedicated* for emitting instructions. At first, it may sound counter-intuitive that a VM supports code generation without such instructions. It is, however, possible by introducing two execution modes to a VM: in one mode, an instruction is executed as usual, and in the other, the same instruction emits some code. Correspondingly, a compiler will generate the same instruction for the same source language construct, however deep it appears under quotation. We call this scheme *uniform compilation*, while we call the other scheme, using a dedicated instruction set for code generation, *non-uniform compilation.*

Interestingly, the choice between uniform or non-uniform compilation naturally arises during the derivation process. We also find out that deriving VMs supporting low-level code generation fails when non-uniform compilation is chosen; we discuss why it is difficult from the viewpoint of our derivation scheme.

Our main technical contributions can be summarized as follows:

- Derivation of compilers and VMs for a foundational typed calculus $\lambda^{\bigcirc}$ by Davies [3] for multi-level languages; and
- Identification of the two compilation schemes of uniform and non-uniform compilation, which, in fact, arise naturally during derivation.

Although we omit it from this paper for brevity, we have also succeeded to apply the same derivation scheme to another calculus $\lambda^{\Box}$ [8] of multi-level languages.

*The Rest of the Paper.* We start with reviewing $\lambda^{\bigcirc}$ in Section 2. Then, we first describe the uniform compilation scheme and a VM that generates low-level code in Section 3 and then the non-uniform compilation, which fails at low-level code generation, in Section 4. After discussing related work in Section 5, we conclude in Section 6. The concrete OCaml code of the derivation is available at `http://www.sato.kuis.kyoto-u.ac.jp/~igarashi/papers/VMcircle.html`.

## 2 $\lambda^{\bigcirc}$

$\lambda^{\bigcirc}$ [3] is a typed $\lambda$-calculus, which corresponds to linear-time temporal logic with the temporal operator $\bigcirc$ ("next") by the Curry-Howard isomorphism. A

$\lambda^{\bigcirc}$-term is considered a multi-level generating extension, which repeatedly takes part of the input of a program and yields a residual program, which is a specialized generating extension; and its type system can be considered that for a multi-level binding-time analysis [2,3]. The term syntax includes **next** and **prev**, which roughly correspond to backquote and unquote in Lisp, respectively. So, in addition to the usual $\beta$-reduction, $\lambda^{\bigcirc}$ has reduction to cancel **next** by **prev**: $\textbf{prev}(\textbf{next}\, t) \longrightarrow t$. Unlike Lisp, however, all variables are statically bound and substitution is capture-avoiding, or "hygienic" [20]. For example, the term $(\lambda x.\ \textbf{next}(\lambda y.\ \textbf{prev}\, x))\ (\textbf{next}\, y)$ reduces to $\textbf{next}(\lambda z.\, y)$ in two steps—notice that the bound variable $y$ has been renamed to a fresh one to avoid variable capture. It is a common practice to generate fresh names in implementations where variables have named representation. In this paper, we adopt de Bruijn indices to represent variable binding with a low-level, nameless implementation in mind. So, index shifting will be used to avoid variable capture, instead of renaming bound variables.

### 2.1 Syntax and Operational Semantics

We first give the syntax and a big-step semantics of a variant of $\lambda^{\bigcirc}$, in which variables are represented by de Bruijn indices. The definitions of terms $t$, values $v$, and environments $E$, are given by the following grammar:

$$t ::= n \mid \lambda t \mid t_0\, t_1 \mid \textbf{next}\, t \mid \textbf{prev}\, t \qquad v ::= \langle E, t \rangle \mid \ulcorner t \urcorner \qquad E ::= \cdot \mid v :: E$$

The *level* of a (sub)term is the number of **next**s minus the number of **prev**s to reach the (sub)term. A variable $n$ refers to the $n$-th $\lambda$-binder *at the same level.* For example, $\lambda y.\ \textbf{next}(\lambda x.\, x(\textbf{prev}\, y))$ will be represented by $\lambda\, \textbf{next}(\lambda 0(\textbf{prev}\, 0))$, not $\lambda\, \textbf{next}(\lambda 0(\textbf{prev}\, 1))$, since $x$ appears at level 1 but $y$ at level 0. This indexing scheme is required because an environment is a list of bindings of level-0 variables and variables at higher levels are treated like constants—so, in order for indices to correctly work, binders at higher levels have to be ignored in computing indices. A value is either a function closure $\langle E, t \rangle$ or a quotation $\ulcorner t \urcorner$[1]. An environment $E$ is a list of values. We focus on a minimal set of language features in this paper but our derivation works when recursion or integers are added.

These definitions can be easily represented by datatype definitions in OCaml, which we use as a meta language in this paper.

```
type term = Var of int | Abs of term | App of term * term
          | Next of term | Prev of term
type value = Clos of env * term | Quot of term  and env = value list
```

As we have mentioned evaluation in $\lambda^{\bigcirc}$ can go under $\lambda$-binders. To deal with it, we need "shift" operations to adjust indices. The expression $t \uparrow^{\ell}_{j}$ denotes a term obtained by incrementing the indices of free level-$\ell$ variables by 1. The

[1] In Davies [3], **next** is used for $\ulcorner \cdot \urcorner$. Our intention here is to distinguish an *operator* for quotation and the result of applying it. Also, we do not stratify values by levels as in [3] since it is not really necessary—the type system does the stratification.

auxiliary argument $j$ counts the number of $\lambda$-binders encountered, in order to avoid incrementing the indices of bound variables.

$$n \uparrow^\ell_j = \begin{cases} n+1 & (\text{if } n \geq j \text{ and } \ell = 0) \\ n & (\text{otherwise}) \end{cases} \qquad (t_0\, t_1) \uparrow^\ell_j = (t_0 \uparrow^\ell_j)\,(t_1 \uparrow^\ell_j)$$

$$(\lambda t) \uparrow^\ell_j = \lambda(t \uparrow^\ell_{j+1}) \qquad (\mathbf{next}\, t) \uparrow^\ell_j = \mathbf{next}(t \uparrow^{\ell-1}_j) \qquad (\mathbf{prev}\, t) \uparrow^\ell_j = \mathbf{prev}(t \uparrow^{\ell+1}_j)$$

Notice that $\ell$ is adjusted when **next** or **prev** is encountered. Shifting $E \uparrow^\ell$ of environments is defined as a pointwise extension of term shifting; we omit the definition. We implement these functions as `shift` and `shiftE`, respectively, whose straightforward definitions are also omitted.

Now, we define the call-by-value, big-step operational semantics of $\lambda^{\bigcirc}$ with the judgment $E \vdash t \Downarrow^\ell r$ where $r$ is either a value $v$ (when $\ell = 0$) or a term $t'$ (otherwise), read "level-$\ell$ term $t$ evaluates to $r$ under environment $E$". The inference rules for this judgment are given in Fig. 1, in which $E(n)$ stands for the $n$-th element of $E$. As usual, bottom-up reading gives how to evaluate an expression, given an environment and a level. The rules for the case $\ell = 0$ are straightforward extensions of those for the $\lambda$-calculus. The rules Eq-— mean that, when $\ell \geq 1$ (i.e., the term is under **next**), the result of evaluation is *almost* the input term; only subterms inside **prev** at level 1 is evaluated, as is shown in E-Prev, in which the quotation of the value is canceled. To avoid variable capture, indices of quoted terms in the environment have to be shifted (by $E \uparrow^\ell$), when evaluation goes under $\lambda$-bindings (Eq-Abs).[2] Fig. 2 shows the derivation for the evaluation of $\mathbf{next}(\lambda\, \mathbf{prev}(\lambda\, \mathbf{next}(\lambda\, \mathbf{prev}\, 0))\, (\mathbf{next}\, 0))$, which could be written `` `(lambda (x),((lambda (y) `(lambda (z) ,y)) `x)) `` in Scheme.

The type system, which we omit mainly for brevity, guarantees the absence of type errors and that a term of a quotation type evaluates to a quoted term $\ulcorner t \urcorner$, where $t$ is well typed at level 0 and does not contain subterms at a negative level. Our evaluator simply discards type information and types do not play important roles in our development. We assume every term is well typed.

## 2.2 Environment-Passing, Continuation-Passing Evaluator for $\lambda^{\bigcirc}$

Once an operational semantics is defined, it is a straightforward task to write an environment-passing, continuation-passing evaluator. It takes not only a term, an environment, and a continuation, but also a level of the input term; hence, the evaluator has type `term * int * env * (value -> value) -> value` (the return type of continuations is fixed to `value`).

```
type cont = value -> value
(* eval0 : term * int * env * cont -> value *)
let rec eval0 (t, l, e, k) = match t, l with
  Var n, 0 -> k (List.nth e n)
```

[2] In the implementation below, shifting is applied to values in an environment eagerly, but it can be delayed to reduce overhead, until the values are referred to by a corresponding variable.

$\boxed{E \vdash t \Downarrow^0 v}$

$$\frac{(E(n) = v)}{E \vdash n \Downarrow^0 v} \quad \text{(E-VAR)}$$

$$\frac{}{E \vdash \lambda t \Downarrow^0 \langle E, t \rangle} \quad \text{(E-ABS)}$$

$$\frac{E \vdash t_0 \Downarrow^0 \langle E', t \rangle \qquad E \vdash t_1 \Downarrow^0 v \qquad v :: E' \vdash t \Downarrow^0 v'}{E \vdash t_0\, t_1 \Downarrow^0 v'} \quad \text{(E-APP)}$$

$$\frac{E \vdash t \Downarrow^1 t'}{E \vdash \mathsf{next}\, t \Downarrow^0 \ulcorner t' \urcorner} \quad \text{(E-NEXT)}$$

$\boxed{E \vdash t \Downarrow^\ell t' \quad (\ell \geq 1)}$

$$\frac{E \vdash t \Downarrow^0 \ulcorner t' \urcorner}{E \vdash \mathsf{prev}\, t \Downarrow^1 t'} \quad \text{(E-PREV)}$$

$$\frac{}{E \vdash n \Downarrow^\ell n} \quad \text{(EQ-VAR)}$$

$$\frac{E \uparrow^\ell \vdash t \Downarrow^\ell t'}{E \vdash \lambda t \Downarrow^\ell \lambda t'} \quad \text{(EQ-ABS)}$$

$$\frac{E \vdash t_0 \Downarrow^\ell t_0' \qquad E \vdash t_1 \Downarrow^\ell t_1'}{E \vdash t_0\, t_1 \Downarrow^\ell t_0'\, t_1'} \quad \text{(EQ-APP)}$$

$$\frac{E \vdash t \Downarrow^{\ell+1} t'}{E \vdash \mathsf{next}\, t \Downarrow^\ell \mathsf{next}\, t'} \quad \text{(EQ-NEXT)}$$

$$\frac{E \vdash t \Downarrow^\ell t'}{E \vdash \mathsf{prev}\, t \Downarrow^{\ell+1} \mathsf{prev}\, t'} \quad \text{(EQ-PREV)}$$

**Fig. 1.** The operational semantics of $\lambda^{\bigcirc}$

$$\mathcal{D} \equiv \dfrac{\dfrac{\dfrac{\dfrac{}{\ulcorner 1 \urcorner :: \cdot \vdash 0 \Downarrow^0 \ulcorner 1 \urcorner}\ \text{E-VAR}}{\ulcorner 1 \urcorner :: \cdot \vdash \mathsf{prev}\, 0 \Downarrow^1 1}\ \text{E-PREV}}{\ulcorner 0 \urcorner :: \cdot \vdash \lambda\, \mathsf{prev}\, 0 \Downarrow^1 \lambda 1}\ \text{EQ-ABS}}{\ulcorner 0 \urcorner :: \cdot \vdash \mathsf{next}(\lambda\, \mathsf{prev}\, 0) \Downarrow^0 \ulcorner \lambda 1 \urcorner}\ \text{E-NEXT}$$

$$\dfrac{\dfrac{\dfrac{\dfrac{\dfrac{}{\cdot \vdash \lambda\, \mathsf{next}(\lambda\, \mathsf{prev}\, 0) \Downarrow^0 \langle \cdot, \mathsf{next}(\lambda\, \mathsf{prev}\, 0) \rangle}\ \text{E-ABS} \qquad \dfrac{\dfrac{}{\cdot \vdash 0 \Downarrow^1 0}\ \text{EQ-VAR}}{\cdot \vdash \mathsf{next}\, 0 \Downarrow^0 \ulcorner 0 \urcorner}\ \text{E-NEXT} \qquad \begin{matrix}\vdots \\ \mathcal{D}\end{matrix}}{\cdot \vdash (\lambda\, \mathsf{next}(\lambda\, \mathsf{prev}\, 0))\ \mathsf{next}\, 0 \Downarrow^0 \ulcorner \lambda 1 \urcorner}\ \text{E-APP}}{\cdot \vdash \mathsf{prev}((\lambda\, \mathsf{next}(\lambda\, \mathsf{prev}\, 0))\ \mathsf{next}\, 0) \Downarrow^1 \lambda 1}\ \text{E-PREV}}{\cdot \vdash \lambda\, \mathsf{prev}((\lambda\, \mathsf{next}(\lambda\, \mathsf{prev}\, 0))\ \mathsf{next}\, 0) \Downarrow^1 \lambda\lambda 1}\ \text{EQ-ABS}}{\cdot \vdash \mathsf{next}(\lambda\, \mathsf{prev}((\lambda\, \mathsf{next}(\lambda\, \mathsf{prev}\, 0))\ \mathsf{next}\, 0)) \Downarrow^0 \ulcorner \lambda\lambda 1 \urcorner}\ \text{E-NEXT}$$

**Fig. 2.** The derivation of $\cdot \vdash \mathsf{next}(\lambda\, \mathsf{prev}((\lambda\, \mathsf{next}(\lambda\, \mathsf{prev}\, 0))\ \mathsf{next}\, 0)) \Downarrow^0 \ulcorner \lambda\lambda 1 \urcorner$

```
| Abs t0, 0 -> k (Clos (e, t0))
| App(t0, t1), 0 -> eval0 (t0, 0, e, fun1 (Clos(e',t')) ->
                    eval0 (t1, 0, e, fun2 v -> eval0 (t', v::e', k)))
| Next t0, 0 -> eval0 (t0, 1, e, fun3 (Quot t) -> k (Quot t))
| Prev t0, 1 -> eval0 (t0, 0, e, fun4 (Quot t) -> k (Quot t))
| Var n, l -> k (Quot (Var n))
| Abs t0, l -> eval0 (t0, l, shiftE (e, l), fun5 (Quot t) ->
               k (Quot (Abs t)))
| App(t0, t1), l -> eval0 (t0, l, e, fun6 (Quot t2) ->
                    eval0 (t1, l, e, fun7 (Quot t3) ->
                     k (Quot (App(t2, t3)))))
| Next t0, l -> eval0 (t0, l+1, e, fun8 (Quot t) -> k (Quot (Next t)))
| Prev t0, l -> eval0 (t0, l-1, e, fun9 (Quot t) -> k (Quot (Prev t)))
(* main0 : term -> value *)
let main0 t = eval0 (t, 0, [], fun0 v -> v)
```

Underlines with subscripts are not part of the program—they will be used to identify function abstractions in the next section. We use a constructor `Quot` of `value` to represent both quoted values $\ulcorner t \urcorner$ and terms returned when `l > 0`. So, the continuations in the fourth and fifth branches (corresponding to E-NEXT and E-PREV) are (essentially) the identity function (except for checking the constructor). Note that, in the last five branches, which correspond to the rules EQ-—, a term is constructed by using the same constructor as the input.

## 3 Deriving a Uniform Compiler and VM with Low-Level Code Generation

We first give a very brief review of Ager et al.'s functional derivation of a compiler and a VM [17,18]. A derivation from a continuation-passing evaluator consists of the following steps:

1. defunctionalization [21] to represent continuations by first-order data;
2. currying transformation to split compile- and run-time computation; and
3. defunctionalization to represent run-time computation by first-order data.

The first step makes a tail-recursive, first-order evaluator, which can be viewed as an abstract machine.[3] The succeeding steps decompose the abstract machine into two functions: the first function that takes a $\lambda$-term and generates an intermediate datum is a compiler and the second function that interprets intermediate data is a VM—the intermediate data, obtained by the the third step of defunctionalization, are VM instructions.

We will follow these steps mostly but claim, however, that it is not just an exercise. We will see an interesting issue of the distinction between uniform and non-uniform compilation naturally arises from how the abstract machine can be curried. Also, a VM with low-level code generation cannot be obtained solely

[3] According to Ager et al.'s terminology, an abstract machine takes a $\lambda$-term as an input whereas a VM takes an instruction sequence obtained by compiling a term.

by following this scheme: since these derivation steps preserve the behavior of the original evaluator, the resulting VM would yield quoted *source terms* even when VM instructions are introduced. So, we have to devise an additional step to derive a new VM for low-level code generation.

The following commuting diagram illustrates our derivation scheme:

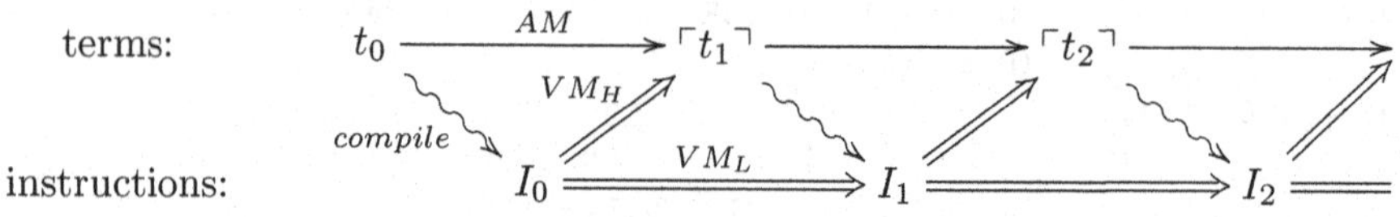


The solid arrows on top represent executions of an abstract machine, which is extensionally equal to the initial evaluator; since $\lambda^{\bigcirc}$-terms are multi-level generating extensions, a residual program $t_1$ (possibly with further inputs) obtained by executing $t_0$ will be executed again. We decompose $\longrightarrow$ into a compiler $\rightsquigarrow$ and a VM $\overset{VM_H}{\Longrightarrow}$; and then derive a VM $\overset{VM_L}{\Longrightarrow}$ with low-level code generation, which commutes with $\overset{VM_H}{\Longrightarrow}$ followed by compilation. So, once $t_0$ is compiled, the run-time system (that is, $\overset{VM_L}{\Longrightarrow}$) can forget about source-level terms.

The following subsections describe each step of the derivation in detail.

### 3.1 Defunctionalizing Continuations

The first step is defunctionalization of continuations. The basic idea of defunctionalization [21] is to represent functional values by datatype constructors and to replace function applications by calls to an "apply" function. This function executes the function body corresponding to the given constructor, which also carries the value of free variables in the original function abstraction. In the definition of the evaluator in the last section, there are ten function abstractions of type `value -> value`: one in `main0` and nine in `eval0`. So, the datatype `cont` is given ten constructors.

The resulting code is as follows (throughout the paper, shaded part represents main changes from the previous version):

```
type cont = Cont0 | Cont1 of term * env * cont | ... | Cont9 of cont
(* eval1 : term * int * env * cont -> value *)
let rec eval1 (t, l, e, k) = match t, l with
  Var n, 0 -> appK1 (k, List.nth e n )
| App (t0, t1), 0 -> eval1 (t0, 0, e, Cont1 (t1, e, k) )
| Var n, 1 -> appK1 (k, Quot (Var n) )
| App (t0, t1), 1 -> eval1 (t0, 1, e, Cont6 (t1, 1, e, k) )   ...
(* appK1 : cont * value -> value *)
and appK1 (k, v) = match k, v with
  Cont0, v -> v
| Cont1 (t1, e, k), v -> eval1 (t1, e, Cont2 (v, k))
| Cont2 (Clos (e', t'), k), v -> eval1 (t', v::e', k)
```

```
| Cont5 k, Quot t -> appK1 (k, Quot (Abs t))
| Cont6 (t1, l, e, k), Quot t2 -> eval1 (t1, l, e, Cont7 (t2, k))
| Cont7 (t2, k), Quot t3 -> appK1 (k, Quot (App (t2, t3)))
...
(* main1 : term -> value *)
let main1 t = eval1 (t, 0, [], Cont0)
```

The occurrences of $\underline{\texttt{fun}}_i$ have been replaced with constructors Cont*i*, applied to free variables in the function body. The bodies of those functions are moved to branches of the apply function appK1. For example, the initial continuation is represented by Cont0 (without arguments) and the corresponding branch in appK1 just returns the input v.

The derived evaluator can be viewed as a CEK-style abstract machine [22] for $\lambda^{\bigcirc}$. Indeed, for the pure $\lambda$-calculus fragment, this evaluator behaves exactly like the CEK-machine [18].

### 3.2 Currying and Primitive Recursive Evaluator

Now, we decompose eval1 above into two functions for compilation and execution. For this purpose, we first curry eval1 so that it takes compile-time entities such as terms as arguments and returns a "run-time computation," i.e., a function, which takes run-time entities such as environments and continuations as arguments and returns a value. Also, the evaluator is transformed into a primitive recursive form in such a way that closures carry run-time computation, instead of terms. This transformation removes the dependency of run-time entities on compile-time entities.

Actually, at this point, we have two choices about how it is curried: one choice is to curry to `term * int -> env * cont -> value` and the other is to `term -> int * env * cont -> value`. The former choice amounts to regarding a level as compile-time information, so the resulting compiler can generate different instructions from the same term, depending on its levels; it leads to non-uniform compilation, which will be discussed in Section 4. In this section, we proceed with the latter choice, in which the resulting compiler will depend only on the input term, so it necessarily generates the same instruction from the same term, regardless of its levels.

The currying transformation yields the following code:

```
type value = Clos of env * compt | Quot of term  and env = ...
and compt = int * env * cont -> value
and cont = Cont0 | Cont1 of compt * env * cont | ...
| Cont6 of compt * int * env * cont | Cont7 of term * cont | ...
(* appK2 : cont * value -> value *)
let rec appK2 (k, v) = match k, v with
  Cont0, v -> v
| Cont1 (c1, e, k), v -> c1 ( 0, e, Cont2 (v, k) )
| Cont6 (c1, l, e, k), Quot t2 -> c1 ( l, e, Cont7 (t2, k) )
```

```
| Cont7 (t2, k), Quot t3 -> appK2 (k, Quot (App (t2, t3)))
...
(* eval2 : term -> compt *)
let rec eval2 t = match t with
  Var n -> (fun0 (l, e, k) -> if l = 0 then appK2 (k, List.nth e n)
                                        else appK2 (k, Quot (Var n)))
| Abs t0 -> let c0 = eval t0 in
    (fun1 (l, e, k) -> if l = 0 then appK2 (k, Clos (e, c0))
                                 else c0 (l, shiftE (e, l), Cont5 k))
| App(t0,t1) -> let c0 = eval2 t0 and c1 = eval2 t1 in
    (fun2 (l, e, k) -> if l = 0 then c0 (0, e, Cont1 (c1, e, k))
                                 else c0 (l, e, Cont6 (c1, l, e, k))) ...
(* main2 : term -> value *)
let main2 t = eval2 t (0, [], Cont0)
```

Case branching in eval2 is now in two steps and the second branching on levels is under function abstractions, which represent run-time computation. Some occurrences of term in cont have been replaced with compt, but arguments to Cont7 (as well as Quot) remains the same because it records the *result* of evaluation of the function part of an application at a level greater than 0.

Note that the definitions of value, env and cont are now independent of that of term, indicating the separation of compile- and run-time. Also, unlike the previous version, functions appK2 and eval2 are not mutually recursive. The function eval2 becomes primitive recursive and also higher-order (it returns a functional value); we get rid of funs by another defunctionalization.

### 3.3 Defunctionalizing Run-Time Computation

The next step is to make compt first-order data by applying defunctionalization. Here, the datatype for compt will be represented by using lists:

```
type compt = inst list
and inst = Compt0 of int | Compt1 of compt | Compt2 of compt | ...
```

rather than

```
type compt = Compt0' of int | Compt1' of compt
           | Compt2' of compt * compt | ...
```

which would be obtained by straightforward defunctionalization. In fact, the latter can be embedded into the former—Compt0' n and Compt2'(c0,c1) are represented by [Compt0 n] and [Compt2 c1; c0], respectively. This scheme allows defunctionalized run-time computation to be represented by a linear data structure, that is, a sequence of instructions. Indeed, as its name suggests, inst can be viewed as machine instructions. The resulting evaluator eval3, which generates a value of type compt from a term, is a compiler; a new apply function appC3, which interprets compt, together with appK3 is a VM. In the following code, constructors of inst are given mnemonic names.

```
type value = ... and env = ... and cont = ... and compt = inst list
and inst = Access of int | Close of compt | Push of compt | Enter | Leave
(* eval3 : term -> compt *)
let rec eval3 t = match t with
  Var n -> [Access n]  | Abs t0 -> [Close (eval3 t0)]
| App (t0, t1) -> Push (eval3 t1) :: (eval3 t0)
| Next t0 -> Enter :: eval3 t0  | Prev t0 -> Leave :: eval3 t0
(* appK3 : cont * value -> value *)
let rec appK3 (k, v) = match k, v with ...
| Cont1 (c1, e, k), v -> appC3 (c1, 0, e, Cont2 (v,k) )
| Cont6 (c1, l, e, k), Quot t2 -> appC3 (c1, l, e, Cont7(t2, k) )
...
(* appC3 : compt * int * env * cont -> value *)
and appC3 (c, l, e, k) = match c, l with
  [Access n], 0 -> appK3 (k, List.nth e n)
| [Access n], l -> appK3 (k, Quot (Var n))
| [Close c0], 0 -> appK3 (k, Clos (e, c0))
| [Close c0], l -> appC3 (c0, l, shiftE (e, l), Cont5 k)
| Push c1::c0, 0 -> appC3 (c0, 0, e, Cont1 (c1, e, k))
| Push c1::c0, l -> appC3 (c0, l, e, Cont6 (c1, l, e, k))
...
(* main3 : term -> value *)
let main3 t = appC3 (eval3 t, 0, [], Cont0)
```

The compiler `eval3` is uniform since it generates the same instruction regardless of the levels of subterms and the VM interprets the same instruction differently, according to the level.

### 3.4 Virtual Machine for Low-Level Code Generation

Code generation in the VM derived above is still high-level: as shown in the branch for `Cont7` of `appK3` (or `appK2`), terms, not instructions, are generated during execution. The final step is to derive a VM that generates instructions. This is, in fact, rather easy—everywhere a term constructor appears, we apply the compiler by hand (but leave variables unchanged): for example, the branch

```
| [Access n], l -> appK3 (k, Quot (Var n))
```

in `appC3` becomes

```
| [Access n], l -> appK3 (k, Quot [Access n ]))
```

Other changes include replacement of type `term` with `compt` in `value` or `cont` and new definitions to shift indices in an instruction list.

Here is the final code:

```
type value = ... | Quot of compt  and compt = ...  and inst = ...
and cont = ... | Cont7 of compt * cont | ...  and env = ...
```

```
let rec shift_inst (i, l, j) = ... and shift_compt (c, l, j) = ...
let rec shiftE (e, l) = ...

(* eval4 : term -> compt *)
let rec eval4 t = ... (* the same as eval3 *)

(* appK4 : cont * value -> value *)
and appK4 (k, v) = match k, v with ...
| Cont7 (c2, k), Quot c3 -> appK4 (k, Quot (Push c3::c2))
...
(* appC4 : compt * int * env * cont -> value *)
and appC4 (c, l, e, k) = match (c, l) with
| [Access n], l -> appK4 (k, Quot [Access n])
...
(* main4 : term -> value *)
let main4 t = appC4 (eval4 t, 0, [], Cont0)
```

The definitions of code blocks $c$, instructions $I$, continuations $k$, the compiler $[\![t]\!]$, and the transition $\Longrightarrow$ of the VM states are summarized in Fig. 3 (in which the names of continuation constructors are also renamed). An (intermediate) state is of the form $\langle c, \ell, E, k\rangle$ (corresponding to an input to appC4), $\langle k, v\rangle$, or $\langle k, c\rangle$ (corresponding to an input to appK4). A VM instruction is executed differently according to $\ell$. For example, **close**$(c)$ creates a function closure and passes it to the current continuation when $\ell = 0$, whereas the same instruction generates code to build a closure when $\ell > 0$, by first pushing QAbs onto the continuation stack and executing the body—when this execution finished, the VM reaches the state $\langle$QAbs$(k)$, $c\rangle$, in which $c$ is the generated function body; finally the VM returns an instruction to build a closure (that is, **close**).

## 4 Non-uniform Compilation and Failure of Low-level Code Generation

In this section, we briefly describe the derivation of a non-uniform compiler with a VM and see how and why low-level code generation fails. As we already mentioned, currying the evaluation function as `term * int -> env * cont -> value`, by regarding levels as compile-time information, leads us to a non-uniform compiler, which generates special instructions for code generation if the given level is greater than 0. We skip the intermediate steps and show only the resulting non-uniform compiler and VM for high-level code generation, obtained after defunctionalizing `compt`, which is first defined to be `env * cont -> value`.

```
type value = ... and env = ... and cont = ... and compt = inst list
and inst = Access of int | ... | Leave | QVar of int | PushQAbs of int
        | PushQApp of compt | PushQNext | PushQPrev
(* eval3' : term * int -> inst list *)
```

**Instructions, values, and continuations:**

$$\begin{aligned}
I &::= \textbf{access}\ n \mid \textbf{close}(c) \mid \textbf{push}(c) \mid \textbf{enter} \mid \textbf{leave}\\
c &::= I_0; \cdots ; I_n\\
v &::= \langle E, c\rangle \mid \ulcorner c \urcorner\\
k &::= \texttt{Halt} \mid \texttt{EvArg}(c, E, k) \mid \texttt{EvBody}(v, k) \mid \texttt{Quote}(k) \mid \texttt{Unquote}(k)\\
&\mid\ \texttt{QAbs}(k) \mid \texttt{QApp'}(c, \ell, E, k) \mid \texttt{QApp}(c, k) \mid \texttt{QNext}(k) \mid \texttt{QPrev}(k)
\end{aligned}$$

**Compilation:**

$$\begin{aligned}
[\![n]\!] &= \textbf{access}\ n & [\![\textbf{next}\ t]\!] &= \textbf{enter}; [\![t]\!]\\
[\![\lambda t]\!] &= \textbf{close}([\![t]\!]) & [\![\textbf{prev}\ t]\!] &= \textbf{leave}; [\![t]\!]\\
[\![t_0\ t_1]\!] &= \textbf{push}([\![t_1]\!]); [\![t_0]\!] & &
\end{aligned}$$

**VM transition:**

$$\begin{aligned}
c &\Longrightarrow \langle c,\ 0,\ \cdot,\ \texttt{Halt}\rangle\\
\langle \textbf{access}\ n,\ 0,\ E,\ k\rangle &\Longrightarrow \langle k,\ E(n)\rangle\\
\langle \textbf{close}(c),\ 0,\ E,\ k\rangle &\Longrightarrow \langle k,\ \langle E, c\rangle\rangle\\
\langle \textbf{push}(c'); c,\ 0,\ E,\ k\rangle &\Longrightarrow \langle c,\ 0,\ E,\ \texttt{EvArg}(c', E, k)\rangle\\
\langle \textbf{enter}; c,\ 0,\ E,\ k\rangle &\Longrightarrow \langle c,\ 1,\ E,\ \texttt{Quote}(k)\rangle\\
\langle \textbf{leave}; c,\ 1,\ E,\ k\rangle &\Longrightarrow \langle c,\ 0,\ E,\ \texttt{Unquote}(k)\rangle\\
\langle \textbf{access}\ n,\ \ell,\ E,\ k\rangle &\Longrightarrow \langle k,\ \textbf{access}\ n\rangle & (\ell \geq 1)\\
\langle \textbf{close}(c),\ \ell,\ E,\ k\rangle &\Longrightarrow \langle c,\ \ell,\ E\uparrow^{\ell},\ \texttt{QAbs}(k)\rangle & (\ell \geq 1)\\
\langle \textbf{push}(c'); c,\ \ell,\ E,\ k\rangle &\Longrightarrow \langle c,\ \ell,\ E,\ \texttt{QApp'}(c', \ell, E, k)\rangle & (\ell \geq 1)\\
\langle \textbf{enter}; c,\ \ell,\ E,\ k\rangle &\Longrightarrow \langle c,\ \ell+1,\ E,\ \texttt{QNext}(k)\rangle & (\ell \geq 1)\\
\langle \textbf{leave}; c,\ \ell+1,\ E,\ k\rangle &\Longrightarrow \langle c,\ \ell,\ E,\ \texttt{QPrev}(k)\rangle & (\ell \geq 1)
\end{aligned}$$

$$\begin{aligned}
\langle \texttt{EvArg}(c, E, k),\ v\rangle &\Longrightarrow \langle c,\ 0,\ E,\ \texttt{EvBody}(v, k)\rangle\\
\langle \texttt{EvBody}(\langle E, c\rangle, k),\ v\rangle &\Longrightarrow \langle c,\ 0,\ v :: E,\ k\rangle\\
\langle \texttt{Quote}(k),\ c\rangle &\Longrightarrow \langle k,\ \ulcorner c \urcorner\rangle\\
\langle \texttt{Unquote}(k),\ \ulcorner c \urcorner\rangle &\Longrightarrow \langle k,\ c\rangle\\
\langle \texttt{QAbs}(k),\ c\rangle &\Longrightarrow \langle k,\ \textbf{close}(c)\rangle\\
\langle \texttt{QApp'}(c', \ell, E, k),\ c\rangle &\Longrightarrow \langle c',\ \ell,\ E,\ \texttt{QApp}(c, k)\rangle\\
\langle \texttt{QApp}(c, k),\ c'\rangle &\Longrightarrow \langle k,\ \textbf{push}(c'); c\rangle\\
\langle \texttt{QNext}(k),\ c\rangle &\Longrightarrow \langle k,\ \textbf{enter}; c\rangle\\
\langle \texttt{QPrev}(k),\ c\rangle &\Longrightarrow \langle k,\ \textbf{leave}; c\rangle\\
\langle \texttt{Halt},\ v\rangle &\Longrightarrow v
\end{aligned}$$

**Fig. 3.** The derived uniform compiler and VM with low-level code generation

```
let rec eval3' (t, l) = match t, l with
  Var n, 0 -> [Access n]  | Var n, 1 -> [QVar n]
| App (t0, t1), 0 -> Push (eval3' (t1, 0)) :: eval3' (t0, 0)
| App (t0, t1), 1 -> PushQApp (eval3' (t1, 1)) :: eval3' (t0, 1)
...
(* appK3' : cont * value -> value *)
let rec appK3' (k, v) = (* the same as appK2 *) ...
| Cont7 (t2, k), Quot t3 -> appK3' (k, Quot (App (t2, t3)))
...
```

```
(* appC3' : compt * env * cont -> value *)
and appC3' (c, e, k) = match c with
  [Access n] -> appK3' (k, List.nth e n)
| [QVar n] -> appK3' (k, Quot (Var n))
| Push c1::c0 -> appC3' (c0, e, Cont1 (c1, e, k))
| PushQApp c1::c0 -> appC3' (c0, e, Cont6 (c1, e, k))
...
(* main3' : term -> value *)
let main3' t = appC3' (eval3' (t, 0), [], Cont0)
```

The resulting instruction set is twice as large as that for uniform compilation. Instructions PushQXXX push onto a continuation stack a marker that represents the corresponding term constructor; the marker is eventually consumed by appK3' to attach a term constructor to the current result: for example, Cont6 and Cont7 are markers for application.

Unfortunately, we fail to derive a VM for low-level code generation. This is simply because the compiler now takes a *pair* of a term and a level but a level is missing around term constructors in appK3' or appC3'!

We think that this failure is inherent in multi-level languages. In a multi-level language, one language construct has different meanings, depending on where it appears: for example, in $\lambda^{\bigcirc}$, a $\lambda$-abstraction at level 0 evaluates to a function closure, whereas one at level $\ell > 0$ evaluates to quoted $\lambda$-abstraction at level $\ell - 1$. Now, notice that the compiler derived here is still uniform at levels greater than 0 (one term constructor is always compiled to the same instruction, regardless of its level). So, it would not be possible for a VM to emit different instructions without level information, which, however, has been compiled away. If the number of possible levels is bounded, "true" non-uniform compilation would be possible but would require different instructions for *each* level, which would be unrealistic. We conjecture that this problem can be solved by a hybrid of uniform and non-uniform compilation, which is left for future work.

## 5 Related Work

*Implementation of Multi-Level Languages.* A most closely related piece of work is Wickline et al. [4], who have developed a compiler of $ML^{\Box}$, which is an extension of ML with the constructs of $\lambda^{\Box}$ [8], and the target virtual machine CCAM, an extension of the Categorical Abstract Machine [16]. The CCAM is equipped with, among others, a set of special (pseudo) instructions **emit** $I$, which emit the single instruction $I$ to a code block and are used to implement generating extensions. The instruction **emit**, however, is not allowed to be nested because such nested emits would be represented by real instructions whose size is exponential in the depth of nesting. They developed a strategy for compiling nested quotation by exploiting another special instruction **lift** to transform a value into a code generator that generates the value and the fact that environments are first-class values in the CAM. In short, their work supports both non-uniform compilation and low-level code generation in one system. Unfortunately, the design of the abstract machine is fairly ad hoc and it is not clear how the proposed compilation scheme can be exported to other combinations of programming languages and VMs. Our method solves the exponential blow-up problem above simply because a compound instruction **emit** $I$ is represented by a single VM instruction $I$. Although our method does not support non-uniform compilation with low-level code generation, it would be possible to derive a compiler and a VM for one's favorite multi-level language in a fairly systematic manner. It might be interesting future work to incorporate their ideas into our framework to realize non-uniform compilation with low-level code generation.

MetaOCaml[4] is a multi-level extension of Objective Caml[5]. Calcagno et al. [23] have reported its implementation by translation to a high-level language with datatypes for ASTs, gensyms, and run-time compilation but do not take direct low-level code generation into account. We believe our method is applicable to MetaOCaml, too.

As mentioned in Section 1, there are several practical systems that are capable of run-time low-level (native or VM) code generation. Tempo [14] is a compile-time and run-time specialization system for the C language; DyC [15] is also a run-time specialization system for C; 'C [12] is an extension of C, where programmers can explicitly manipulate, compile, and run code fragments as first-class values with (non-nested) backquote and unquote; Fabius [24] is a run-time specialization system for a subset of ML. They are basically two-level systems but Tempo supports multi-level specialization by incremental self-application [2,25]. The code-size blowup problem is solved by the template filling technique [14,26], which amounts to allowing the operand to the emit instruction to be (a pointer to) a *block* of instructions.

*Functional Derivation of Abstract and Virtual Machines.* Ager et al. describe derivations of abstract and virtual machines from evaluation functions by program transformation [18,17] and have shown that the Krivine machine [27] is derived from a call-by-name evaluator and that the CEK machine [22] indeed corresponds to a call-by-value evaluator. They also applied the same technique to call-by-need [28], monadic evaluators [29], or strong reduction [19,17]. However, they mainly focus on different evaluation strategy or side-effects and have not attempted to apply their technique to multi-level languages.

## 6 Conclusions

In this paper, we have shown derivations of compilers and VMs for a foundational multi-level language $\lambda^{\bigcirc}$. We have investigated the two compilation schemes of uniform compilation, which compiles a term constructor to the same instruction regardless of the level at which the term appears, and non-uniform compilation, which generates different instructions from the same term according to its level, and have shown that the former is more suitable for low-level code generation. Our derivation is fairly systematic and would be applicable to one's

[4] `http://www.metaocaml.org/`

[5] `http://caml.inria.fr/ocaml/`

favorite multi-level language. In fact, although omitted from this paper, we have successfully derived a compiler and a VM for another calculus $\lambda^{\Box}$ [8].

The final derivation step for low-level code generation may appear informal and ad hoc. We are developing a formal translation based on function fusion.

Although it would not be easy to implement our machines for uniform compilation *directly* by the current, real processor architecture, we think they still can be implemented fairly efficiently as a VM. Our future work includes implementation of a uniform compiler and a corresponding VM by extending an existing VM, such as the ZINC abstract machine [30]. We believe our method is applicable to VMs with different architectures, which correspond to different evaluation semantics of the $\lambda$-calculus, and is useful to see how they can be extended for multi-level languages.

*Acknowledgments.* We thank anonymous reviewers for providing useful comments and for pointing out missing related work.

## References

1. Nielson, F., Nielson, H.R.: Two-Level Functional Languages. Cambridge University Press, Cambridge (1992)
2. Glück, R., Jørgensen, J.: Efficient multi-level generating extensions for program specialization. In: Swierstra, S.D. (ed.) PLILP 1995. LNCS, vol. 982, pp. 259–278. Springer, Heidelberg (1995)
3. Davies, R.: A temporal-logic approach to binding-time analysis. In: Proc. of IEEE LICS, pp. 184–195 (July 1996)
4. Wickline, P., Lee, P., Pfenning, F.: Run-time code generation and Modal-ML. In: Proc. of ACM PLDI, pp. 224–235 (1998)
5. Taha, W., Benaissa, Z.E.A., Sheard, T.: Multi-stage programming: Axiomatization and type-safety. In: Larsen, K.G., Skyum, S., Winskel, G. (eds.) ICALP 1998. LNCS, vol. 1443, pp. 918–929. Springer, Heidelberg (1998)
6. Moggi, E., Taha, W., Benaissa, Z.E.A., Sheard, T.: An idealized MetaML: Simpler, and more expressive. In: Swierstra, S.D. (ed.) ESOP 1999 and ETAPS 1999. LNCS, vol. 1576, pp. 193–207. Springer, Heidelberg (1999)
7. Taha, W., Sheard, T.: MetaML and multi-stage programming with explicit annotations. Theoretical Computer Science 248, 211–242 (2000)
8. Davies, R., Pfenning, F.: A modal analysis of staged computation. Journal of the ACM 48(3), 555–604 (2001)
9. Taha, W., Nielsen, M.F.: Environment classifiers. In: Proc. of ACM POPL, pp. 26–37 (2003)
10. Calcagno, C., Moggi, E., Taha, W.: ML-like inference for classifiers. In: Schmidt, D. (ed.) ESOP 2004. LNCS, vol. 2986, pp. 79–93. Springer, Heidelberg (2004)
11. Yuse, Y., Igarashi, A.: A modal type system for multi-level generating extensions with persistent code. In: Proc. of ACM PPDP, pp. 201–212. ACM Press, New York (2006)
12. Poletto, M., Hsieh, W.C., Engler, D.R., Kaashoek, M.F.: 'C and tcc: A language and compiler for dynamic code generation. ACM Transactions on Programming Languages and Systems 21(2), 324–369 (1999)

13. Masuhara, H., Yonezawa, A.: Run-time bytecode specialization: A portable approach to generating optimized specialized code. In: Danvy, O., Filinski, A. (eds.) PADO 2001. LNCS, vol. 2053, pp. 138–154. Springer, Heidelberg (2001)
14. Consel, C., Lawall, J.L., Meur, A.F.L.: A tour of Tempo: A program specializer for the C language. Science of Computer Programming 52(1–3), 341–370 (2004)
15. Grant, B., Mock, M., Philipose, M., Chambers, C., Eggers, S.J.: DyC: An expressive annotation-directed dynamic compiler for C. Theoretical Computer Science 248(1–2), 147–199 (2000)
16. Cousineau, G., Curien, P.L., Mauny, M.: The categorical abstract machine. Science of Computer Programming 8(2), 173–202 (1987)
17. Ager, M.S., Biernacki, D., Danvy, O., Midtgaard, J.: From interpreter to compiler and virtual machine: A functional derivation. Technical Report RS-03-14, BRICS (March 2003)
18. Ager, M.S., Biernacki, D., Danvy, O., Midtgaard, J.: A functional correspondence between evaluators and abstract machines. In: Proc. of ACM PPDP, pp. 8–19 (2003)
19. Grégoire, B., Leroy, X.: A compiled implementation of strong reduction. In: Proc. of ACM ICFP, pp. 235–246 (2002)
20. Kohlbecker, E., Friedman, D.P., Felleisen, M., Duba, B.: Hygienic macro expansion. In: Proc. of ACM LFP, pp. 151–161 (1986)
21. Reynolds, J.C.: Definitional interpreters for higher-order programming languages. Higher-Order Symbolic Computation 11(4), 363–397 (1998)
22. Felleisen, M., Friedman, D.P.: Control operators, the SECD machine, and the $\lambda$-calculus. In: Proc. Formal Description of Prog. Concepts III, pp. 193–217 (1986)
23. Calcagno, C., Taha, W., Huang, L., Leroy, X.: Implementing multi-stage languages using ASTs, gensym, and reflection. In: Pfenning, F., Smaragdakis, Y. (eds.) GPCE 2003. LNCS, vol. 2830, pp. 57–76. Springer, Heidelberg (2003)
24. Leone, M., Lee, P.: Optimizing ML with run-time code generation. In: Proc. of ACM PLDI, pp. 137–148 (1996)
25. Marlet, R., Consel, C., Boinot, P.: Efficient incremental run-time specialization for free. In: Proc. of ACM PLDI, pp. 281–292 (1999)
26. Consel, C., Noël, F.: A general approach for run-time specialization and its application to C. In: Proc. of ACM POPL, pp. 145–156 (1996)
27. Krivine, J.L.: A call-by-name lambda-calculus machine. Available online, from `http://www.pps.jussieu.fr/~krivine`
28. Ager, M.S., Danvy, O., Midtgaard, J.: A functional correspondence between call-by-need evaluators and lazy abstract machines. Information Processing Letters 90(5), 223–232 (2004)
29. Ager, M.S., Danvy, O., Midtgaard, J.: A functional correspondence between monadic evaluators and abstract machines for languages with computational effects. Theoretical Computer Science 342(1), 149–172 (2005)
30. Leroy, X.: The ZINC experiment: An economical implementation of the ML language. Technical Report 117, INRIA (1990)

# Finally Tagless, Partially Evaluated*
## Tagless Staged Interpreters for Simpler Typed Languages

Jacques Carette[1], Oleg Kiselyov[2], and Chung-chieh Shan[3]

[1] McMaster University
carette@mcmaster.edu
[2] FNMOC
oleg@pobox.com
[3] Rutgers University
ccshan@rutgers.edu

**Abstract.** We have built the first family of tagless interpretations for a higher-order typed object language in a typed metalanguage (Haskell or ML) that require no dependent types, generalized algebraic data types, or postprocessing to eliminate tags. The statically type-preserving interpretations include an evaluator, a compiler (or staged evaluator), a partial evaluator, and call-by-name and call-by-value CPS transformers.

Our main idea is to encode HOAS using cogen functions rather than data constructors. In other words, we represent object terms not in an initial algebra but using the coalgebraic structure of the $\lambda$-calculus. Our representation also simulates inductive maps from types to types, which are required for typed partial evaluation and CPS transformations.

Our encoding of an object term abstracts over the various ways to interpret it, yet statically assures that the interpreters never get stuck. To achieve self-interpretation and show Jones-optimality, we relate this exemplar of higher-rank and higher-kind polymorphism to plugging a term into a context of let-polymorphic bindings.

It should also be possible to define languages with a highly refined syntactic type structure. Ideally, such a treatment should be metacircular, in the sense that the type structure used in the defined language should be adequate for the defining language. John Reynolds [28]

## 1 Introduction

A popular way to define and implement a language is to embed it in another [28]. Embedding means to represent terms and values of the *object language* as terms and values in the *metalanguage*. Embedding is especially appropriate for domain-specific object languages because it supports rapid prototyping and integration with the host environment [16]. If the metalanguage supports *staging*, then the

* We thank Martin Sulzmann and Walid Taha for helpful discussions. Sam Staton, Pieter Hofstra, and Bart Jacobs kindly provided some useful references. We thank anonymous reviewers for pointers to related work.

Z. Shao (Ed.): APLAS 2007, LNCS 4807, pp. 222–238, 2007.

$$\frac{\begin{array}{c}[x:t_1]\\ \vdots\\ e:t_2\end{array}}{\lambda x.\, e:t_1\to t_2} \qquad \frac{\begin{array}{c}[f:t_1\to t_2]\\ \vdots\\ e:t_1\to t_2\end{array}}{\mathrm{fix}\, f.\, e:t_1\to t_2} \qquad \frac{e_1:t_1\to t_2 \quad e_2:t_1}{e_1e_2:t_2} \qquad \frac{n \text{ is an integer}}{n:\mathbb{Z}}$$

$$\frac{b \text{ is a boolean}}{b:\mathbb{B}} \qquad \frac{e:\mathbb{B} \quad e_1:t \quad e_2:t}{\text{if } e \text{ then } e_1 \text{ else } e_2:t} \qquad \frac{e_1:\mathbb{Z} \quad e_2:\mathbb{Z}}{e_1+e_2:\mathbb{Z}} \qquad \frac{e_1:\mathbb{Z} \quad e_2:\mathbb{Z}}{e_1\times e_2:\mathbb{Z}} \qquad \frac{e_1:\mathbb{Z} \quad e_2:\mathbb{Z}}{e_1\le e_2:\mathbb{B}}$$

**Fig. 1.** Our typed object language

embedding can compile object programs to the metalanguage and avoid the overhead of interpreting them on the fly [23]. A staged definitional interpreter is thus a promising way to build a domain-specific language (DSL).

We focus on embedding a *typed* object language into a *typed* metalanguage. The benefit of types in this setting is to rule out meaningless object terms, thus enabling faster interpretation and assuring that our interpreters do not get stuck. To be concrete, we use the typed object language in Figure 1 throughout this paper. We aim not just for evaluation of object programs but also for compilation, partial evaluation, and other processing.

Pašalić et al. [23] and Xi et al. [37] motivated interpreting a typed object language in a typed metalanguage as an interesting problem. The common solutions to this problem store object terms and values in the metalanguage in a universal type, a generalized algebraic data type (GADT), or a dependent type. In the remainder of this section, we discuss these solutions, identify their drawbacks, then summarize our proposal and contributions. We leave aside the solved problem of writing a parser/type-checker, for embedding object language objects into the metalanguage (whether using dependent types [23] or not [2]), and just enter them by hand.

### 1.1 The Tag Problem

It is straightforward to create an algebraic data type, say in OCaml, Fig. 2(a), to represent object terms such as those in Figure 1. For brevity, we elide treating integers, conditionals, and fixpoint in this section. We represent each variable using a unary de Bruijn index.[1] For example, we represent the object term $(\lambda x.\, x)$ true as `let test1 = A (L (V VZ), B true)`.

Following [23], we try to implement an interpreter function `eval0`, Fig. 2(b). It takes an object term such as `test1` above and gives us its value. The first argument to `eval0` is the environment, initially empty, which is the list of values bound to free variables in the interpreted code. If our OCaml-like metalanguage were untyped, the code above would be acceptable. The `L e` line exhibits interpretive overhead: `eval0` traverses the function body `e` every time (the result of evaluating) `L e` is applied. Staging can be used to remove this interpretive overhead [23, §1.1–2].

[1] We use de Bruijn indices to simplify the comparison with Pašalić et al.'s work [23].

(a)
```
type var = VZ | VS of var
type exp = V of var | B of bool | L of exp | A of exp * exp
```
(b)
```
let rec lookup (x::env) = function VZ -> x | VS v -> lookup env v
let rec eval0 env = function
| V v        -> lookup env v
| B b        -> b
| L e        -> fun x -> eval0 (x::env) e
| A (e1,e2) -> (eval0 env e1) (eval0 env e2)
```
(c)
```
type u = UB of bool | UA of (u -> u)
```
(d)
```
let rec eval env = function
| V v        -> lookup env v
| B b        -> UB b
| L e        -> UA (fun x -> eval (x::env) e)
| A (e1,e2) -> match eval env e1 with UA f -> f (eval env e2)
```

**Fig. 2.** OCaml code illustrating the tag problem

However, the function `eval0` is ill-typed if we use OCaml or some other typed language as the metalanguage. The line `B b` says that `eval0` returns a boolean, whereas the next line `L e` says the result is a function, but all branches of a pattern-match form must yield values of the same type. A related problem is the type of the environment `env`: a regular OCaml list cannot hold both boolean and function values.

The usual solution is to introduce a universal type [23, §1.3] containing both booleans and functions, Fig. 2(c). We can then write a typed interpreter, Fig. 2(d), whose inferred type is `u list -> exp -> u`. Now we can evaluate `eval [] test1` obtaining `UB true`. The unfortunate tag `UB` in the result reflects that `eval` is a partial function. First, the pattern match `with UA f` in the line `A (e1,e2)` is not exhaustive, so `eval` can fail if we apply a boolean, as in the ill-typed term `A (B true, B false)`. Second, the `lookup` function assumes a nonempty environment, so `eval` can fail if we evaluate an open term `A (L (V (VS VZ)), B true)`. After all, the type `exp` represents object terms both well-typed and ill-typed, both open and closed.

If we evaluate only closed terms that have been type-checked, then `eval` would never fail. Alas, this soundness is not obvious to the metalanguage, whose type system we must still appease with the nonexhaustive pattern matching in `lookup` and `eval` and the tags `UB` and `UA` [23, §1.4]. In other words, the algebraic data types above fail to express in the metalanguage that the object program is well-typed. This failure necessitates tagging and nonexhaustive pattern-matching operations that incur a performance penalty in interpretation [23] and impair optimality in partial evaluation [33]. In short, the universal-type solution is unsatisfactory because it does not preserve typing.

It is commonly thought that to interpret a typed object language in a typed metalanguage while preserving types is difficult and requires GADTs or dependent types [33]. In fact, this problem motivated much work on GADTs [24, 37] and on dependent types [11, 23]. Yet other type systems have been proposed to distinguish closed terms like `test1` from open terms [9, 21, 34], so that `lookup` never receives an empty environment. We discuss these proposals further in §5.

## 1.2 Our Final Proposal

We represent object programs using ordinary functions rather than data constructors. These functions comprise the entire interpreter, shown below.

```
let varZ env     = fst env              let b (bv:bool) env = bv
let varS vp env = vp (snd env)     let lam e env       = fun x -> e (x,env)
let app e1 e2 env    = (e1 env) (e2 env)
```

We now represent our sample term $(\lambda x.\,x)$true as `let testf1 = app (lam varZ) (b true)`. This representation is almost the same as in §1.1, only written with lowercase identifiers. To evaluate an object term is to apply its representation to the empty environment, `testf1 ()`, obtaining `true`. The result has no tags: the interpreter patently uses no tags and no pattern matching. The term `b true` evaluates to a boolean and the term `lam varZ` evaluates to a function, both untagged. The `app` function applies `lam varZ` without pattern matching. What is more, evaluating an open term such as `app (lam (varS varZ)) (b true)` gives a type error rather than a run-time error. The type error correctly complains that the initial environment should be a tuple rather than `()`. In other words, the term is open.

In sum, by Church-encoding terms using ordinary functions, we achieve a tagless evaluator for a typed object language in a metalanguage with a simple Hindley-Milner type system. In this *final* rather than *initial* approach, both kinds of run-time errors in §1.1 (applying a nonfunction and evaluating an open term) are reported at compile time. Because the new interpreter uses no universal type or pattern matching, it never results in a run-time error, and is in fact total. Because this safety is obvious not just to us but also to the metalanguage implementation, we avoid the serious performance penalty [23] of error checking. Glück [12] explains deeper technical reasons that inevitably lead to these performance penalties.

Our solution is *not* Church-encoding the universal type. The Church encoding of the type `u` in §1.1 requires two continuations; the function `app` in the interpreter above would have to provide both to the encoding of `e1`. The continuation corresponding to the `UB` case of `u` must either raise an error or loop. For a well-typed object term, that error continuation is never invoked, yet it must be supplied. In contrast, our interpreter has no error continuation at all.

The evaluator above is wired directly into the functions `b`, `lam`, `app`, and so on. We explain how to abstract the interpreter so as to process the *same* term in many other ways: compilation, partial evaluation, CPS conversion, and so forth.

## 1.3 Contributions

The term "constructor" functions `b`, `lam`, `app`, and so on appear free in the encoding of an object term such as `testf1` above. Defining these functions differently gives rise to different interpreters, that is, different folds on object programs. Given the same term representation but varying the interpreter, we can

- evaluate the term to a value in the metalanguage;
- measure the size or depth of the term;
- compile the term, with staging support such as in MetaOCaml;
- partially evaluate the term, online; and
- transform the term to continuation-passing style (CPS), even call-by-name (CBN) CPS, so as to isolate the evaluation order of the object language from that of the metalanguage.[2]

We have programmed our interpreters in OCaml (and, for staging, MetaOCaml [19]) and standard Haskell. The complete code is available at `http://okmij.org/ftp/packages/tagless-final.tar.gz` to supplement the paper. For simplicity, main examples in the paper will be in MetaOCaml; all examples have also been implemented in Haskell.

We attack the problem of tagless (staged) typed-preserving interpretation exactly as it was posed by Pašalić et al. [23] and Xi et al. [37]. We use their running examples and achieve the result they call desirable. Our contributions are as follows.

1. We build interpreters that evaluate (§2), compile (or evaluate with staging) (§3), and partially evaluate (§4) a typed higher-order object language in a typed metalanguage, in direct and continuation-passing styles.
2. All these interpreters use no type tags, patently never get stuck, and need no advanced type-system features such as GADTs, dependent types, or intentional type analysis.
3. The partial evaluator avoids polymorphic lift and delays binding-time analysis. It bakes a type-to-type map into the interpreter interface to eliminate the need for GADTs and thus remain portable across Haskell 98 and ML.
4. We use the type system of the metalanguage to check statically that an object program is well-typed and closed.
5. We show clean, comparable implementations in MetaOCaml and Haskell.
6. We specify a functor signature that encompasses all our interpreters, from evaluation and compilation (§2) to partial evaluation (§4).
7. We point a clear way to extend the object language with more features such as state.[3]
8. We describe an approach to self-interpretation compatible with the above. Self-interpretation turned out to be harder than expected.[3]

Our code is surprisingly simple and obvious in hindsight, but it has been cited as a difficult problem ([32] notwithstanding) to interpret a typed object language in a typed metalanguage without tagging or type-system extensions. For example, Taha et al. [33] say that "expressing such an interpreter in a statically typed

[2] Due to serious lack of space, we refer the reader to the accompanying code for this.
[3] Again, please see our code.

programming language is a rather subtle matter. In fact, it is only recently that some work on programming type-indexed values in ML [38] has given a hint of how such a function can be expressed." We discuss related work in §5.

To reiterate, we do *not* propose any new language feature or new technique. We use features already present in mainstream functional languages—Hindley-Milner type system with either an inference-preserving module system or constructor classes, as realized in ML and Haskell 98—and techniques which have all appeared in the literature (in particular, [32, 38]), to solve a problem that was stated in the published record as unsolved and likely unsolvable in ML or Haskell 98 without extensions. The simplicity of our solution and its use of only mainstream features make it more practical to build typed, embedded DSLs.

## 2 The Object Language and Its Tagless Interpreters

Figure 1 shows our object language, a simply-typed $\lambda$-calculus with fixpoint, integers, booleans, and comparison. The language is close to Xi et al.'s [37], without their polymorphic lift but with more constants so as to more conveniently express Fibonacci, factorial, and power. In contrast to §1, we encode binding using higher-order abstract syntax (HOAS) [20, 25] rather than de Bruijn indices. This makes the encoding convenient and ensures that our object programs are closed.

### 2.1 How to Make Encoding Flexible: Abstract the Interpreter

We embed our language in (Meta)OCaml and Haskell. In Haskell, the functions that construct object terms are methods in a type class `Symantics` (with a parameter `repr` of kind `* -> *`), Fig. 3(a). The class is so named because its interface gives the syntax of the object language and its instances give the semantics. For example, we encode the term `test1`, or $(\lambda x.\, x)$ true, from §1.1 above as `app (lam (\x -> x)) (bool True)`, whose inferred type is `Symantics repr => repr Bool`. For another example, the classical *power* function is in Fig. 3(b) and the partial application $\lambda x.\, power\ x\ 7$ is in Fig. 3(c). The dummy argument `()` above is to avoid the monomorphism restriction, to keep the type of `testpowfix` and `testpowfix7` polymorphic in `repr`. The methods `add`, `mul`, and `leq` are quite similar, and so are `int` and `bool`. Therefore, we often show only one method of each group and elide the rest. The accompanying code has the complete implementations.

Comparing `Symantics` with Fig. 1 shows how to represent *every* typed, closed object term in the metalanguage. Moreover, the representation preserves types.

**Proposition 1.** *If an object term has the object type t, then its representation in the metalanguage has the type* `forall repr. Symantics repr => repr t`.

Conversely, the type system of the metalanguage statically checks that the represented object term is well-typed and closed. If we err, say replace `int 7` with `bool True` in `testpowfix7`, Haskell will complain there that the expected type `Int` does not match the inferred `Bool`. Similarly, the object term $\lambda x.\, xx$ and

(a)
```
class Symantics repr where
  int :: Int  -> repr Int;        bool :: Bool -> repr Bool
  lam :: (repr a -> repr b) -> repr (a -> b)
  app :: repr (a -> b) -> repr a -> repr b
  fix :: (repr a -> repr a) -> repr a

  add :: repr Int -> repr Int -> repr Int
  mul :: repr Int -> repr Int -> repr Int
  leq :: repr Int -> repr Int -> repr Bool
  if_ :: repr Bool -> repr a -> repr a -> repr a
```
(b)
```
testpowfix () = lam (\x -> fix (\self -> lam (\n ->
                  if_ (leq n (int 0)) (int 1)
                      (mul x (app self (add n (int (-1))))))))
```
(c)
```
testpowfix7 () = lam (\x -> app (app (testpowfix ()) x) (int 7))
```

**Fig. 3.** Symantics in Haskell

its encoding `lam (\x -> app x x)` both fail occurs-checks in type checking. Haskell's type checker also flags syntactically invalid object terms, such as if we forget `app` somewhere above.

To embed the same object language in (Meta)OCaml, we replace the type class `Symantics` and its instances by a module signature `Symantics` and its implementations. Figure 4 shows a simple signature that suffices until §4. The two differences are: the additional type parameter `'c`, an *environment classifier* [34] required by MetaOCaml for code generation in §3; and the $\eta$-expanded type for `fix` and thunk types in `if_` since OCaml is a call-by-value language.

The functor `EX` in Fig. 4 encodes our running examples `test1` and the *power* function (`testpowfix`). The dummy argument to `test1` and `testpowfix` is an artifact of MetaOCaml, related to monomorphism: in order for us to run a piece of generated code, it must be polymorphic in its environment classifier (the type variable `'c` in Figure 4). The value restriction dictates that the definitions of our object terms must look syntactically like values. (Alternatively, we could have used the rank-2 record types of OCaml to maintain the necessary polymorphism.) Thus, we represent an object expression in OCaml as a functor from `Symantics` to an appropriate semantic domain. This is essentially the same as the constraint `Symantics repr =>` in the Haskell embedding.

### 2.2 Two Tagless Interpreters

Having abstracted our term representation over the interpreter, we are now ready to present a series of interpreters. Each interpreter is an instance of the `Symantics` class in Haskell and a module implementing the `Symantics` signature in MetaOCaml.

The first interpreter evaluates an object term to its value in the metalanguage. The module below interprets each object-language operation as the corresponding metalanguage operation.

```
module type Symantics = sig type ('c, 'dv) repr
  val int : int  -> ('c, int) repr
  val bool: bool -> ('c, bool) repr

  val lam : (('c, 'da) repr -> ('c, 'db) repr) -> ('c, 'da -> 'db) repr
  val app : ('c, 'da -> 'db) repr -> ('c, 'da) repr -> ('c, 'db) repr
  val fix : ('x -> 'x) -> (('c, 'da -> 'db) repr as 'x)

  val add : ('c, int) repr -> ('c, int) repr -> ('c, int) repr
  val mul : ('c, int) repr -> ('c, int) repr -> ('c, int) repr
  val leq : ('c, int) repr -> ('c, int) repr -> ('c, bool) repr
  val if_ : ('c, bool) repr
          -> (unit -> 'x) -> (unit -> 'x) -> (('c, 'da) repr as 'x)
end
module EX(S: Symantics) = struct open S
  let test1 () = app (lam (fun x -> x)) (bool true)
  let testpowfix () =
       lam (fun x -> fix (fun self -> lam (fun n ->
        if_ (leq n (int 0)) (fun () -> int 1)
            (fun () -> mul x (app self (add n (int (-1))))))))
  let testpowfix7 = lam (fun x -> app (app (testpowfix ()) x) (int 7))
end
```

**Fig. 4.** A simple (Meta)OCaml embedding of our object language, and examples

```
module R = struct type ('c,'dv) repr = 'dv (* no wrappers *)
  let int  (x:int)   = x          let bool (b:bool) = b
  let lam  f         = f          let app  e1 e2    = e1 e2
  let fix  f         = let rec self n = f self n in self
  let add  e1 e2     = e1 + e2    let mul  e1 e2    = e1 * e2
  let leq  x y       = x <= y
  let if_  eb et ee = if eb then et () else ee () end
```

As in §1.2, this interpreter is patently tagless, using neither a universal type nor any pattern matching: the operation `add` is really OCaml's addition, and `app` is OCaml's application. To run our examples, we instantiate the `EX` functor from §2.1 with `R`: `module EXR = EX(R)`. Thus, `EXR.test1 ()` evaluates to the untagged boolean value `true`. It is obvious to the compiler that pattern matching cannot fail, because there is no pattern matching. Evaluation can only fail to yield a value due to interpreting `fix`. (The source code shows a total interpreter `L` that measures the size of each object term.) We can also generalize from `R` to all interpreters; these propositions follow immediately from the soundness of the metalanguage's type system.

**Proposition 2.** *If an object term e encoded in the metalanguage has type t, then evaluating e in the interpreter* `R` *either continues indefinitely or terminates with a value of the same type t.*

(a)
```
module C = struct type ('c,'dv) repr = ('c,'dv) code
  let int (x:int)   = .<x>.             let bool (b:bool) = .<b>.
  let lam f         = .<fun x -> .~(f .<x>.)>.
  let app e1 e2     = .<.~e1 .~e2>.
  let fix f =  .<let rec self n = .~(f .<self>.) n in self>.
  let add e1 e2     = .<.~e1 + .~e2>.  let mul e1 e2 = .<.~e1 * .~e2>.
  let leq x y       = .<.~x <= .~y>.
  let if_ eb et ee = .<if .~eb then .~(et ()) else .~(ee ())>. end
```
(b)
```
let module E = EX(C) in E.test1 ()
```
(c)
```
let module E = EX(C) in E.testpowfix7
```
(d)
```
.<fun x_1 -> (fun x_2 -> let rec self_3 = fun n_4 ->
   (fun x_5 -> if x_5 <= 0 then 1 else x_2 * self_3 (x_5 + (-1)))
   n_4 in self_3) x_1 7>.
```

**Fig. 5.** The tagless staged interpreter `C`

**Proposition 3.** *If an implementation of* `Symantics` *never gets stuck, then the type system of the object language is sound with respect to the dynamic semantics defined by that implementation.*

## 3 A Tagless Compiler (or, a staged interpreter)

Besides immediate evaluation, we can compile our object language into OCaml code using MetaOCaml's staging facilities. MetaOCaml represents future-stage expressions of type $t$ as values of type `('c,` $t$`) code`, where `'c` is the environment classifier [6, 34]. Code values are created by a *bracket* form `.<`$e$`>.`, which quotes the expression $e$ for evaluation at a future stage. The *escape* `.~`$e$ must occur within a bracket and specifies that the expression $e$ must be evaluated at the current stage; its result, which must be a code value, is spliced into the code being built by the enclosing bracket. The *run* form `.!`$e$ evaluates the future-stage code value $e$ by compiling and linking it at run time. Bracket, escape, and run are akin to quasi-quotation, unquotation, and `eval` of Lisp.

Inserting brackets and escapes appropriately into the evaluator `R` above yields the simple compiler `C` in Fig. 5(a). This is a straightforward staging of `module R`. This compiler produces unoptimized code. For example, interpreting our `test1` with Fig. 5(b) gives the code value `.<(fun x_6 -> x_6) true>.` of inferred type `('c, bool) C.repr`. Interpreting `testpowfix7` with Fig. 5(c) gives a code value with many apparent $\beta$- and $\eta$-redexes, Fig. 5(d). This compiler does not incur any interpretive overhead: the code produced for $\lambda x.\, x$ is simply `fun x_6 -> x_6`. The resulting code obviously contains no tags and no pattern matching. The environment classifiers here, like the tuple types in §1.2, make it a type error to run an open expression. The accompanying code shows the Haskell implementation.

# 4 A Tagless Partial Evaluator

Surprisingly, we can write a partial evaluator using the idea above, namely to build object terms using ordinary functions rather than data constructors. We present this partial evaluator in a sequence of three attempts. It uses no universal type and no tags for object types. We then discuss residualization and binding-time analysis. Our partial evaluator is a modular extension of the evaluator in §2.2 and the compiler in §3, in that it uses the former to reduce static terms and the latter to build dynamic terms.

## 4.1 Avoiding Polymorphic Lift

Roughly, a partial evaluator interprets each object term to yield either a static (present-stage) term (using `R`) or a dynamic (future-stage) term (using `C`). To distinguish between static and dynamic terms, we might try to define `repr` in the partial evaluator as `type ('c,'dv) repr = S0 of ('c,'dv) R.repr | E0 of ('c,'dv) C.repr`. Integer and boolean literals are immediate, present-stage values. Addition yields a static term (using `R.add`) if and only if both operands are static; otherwise we extract the dynamic terms from the operands and add them using `C.add`. We use `C.int` to convert from the static term `('c,int) R.repr`, which is just `int`, to the dynamic term.

Whereas `mul` and `leq` are as easy to define as `add`, we encounter a problem with `if_`. Suppose that the first argument to `if_` is a dynamic term (of type `('c,bool) C.repr`), the second a static term (of type `('c,'a) R.repr`), and the third a dynamic term (of type `('c,'a) C.repr`). We then need to convert the static term to dynamic, but there is no polymorphic "lift" function, of type `'a -> ('c,'a) C.repr`, to send a value to the future stage [34, 37].

Our `Symantics` only includes separate lifting methods `bool` and `int`, not a parametrically polymorphic lifting method, for good reason: When compiling to a first-order target language such as machine code, booleans, integers, and functions may well be represented differently. Thus, compiling polymorphic lift requires intensional type analysis. To avoid needing polymorphic lift, we turn to Asai's technique [1, 32]: build a dynamic term alongside every static term.

## 4.2 Delaying Binding-Time Analysis

We switch to the data type `type ('c,'dv) repr = P1 of ('c,'dv) R.repr option * ('c,'dv) C.repr` so that a partially evaluated term always contains a dynamic component and sometimes contains a static component. By distributivity, the two alternative constructors of an `option` value, `Some` and `None`, tag each partially evaluated term with a phase: either present or future. This tag is not an object type tag: all pattern matching below is exhaustive. Because the future-stage component is always present, we can now define the polymorphic function `let abstr1 (P1 (_,dyn)) = dyn` of type `('c,'dv) repr -> ('c,'dv) C.repr` to extract it without requiring polymorphic lift into `C`. We then try to define the interpreter `P1`—and get as far as the first-order constructs of our object language, including `if_`.

```
module P1 : Symantics = struct
  let int (x:int) = P1 (Some (R.int x), C.int x)
  let add e1 e2 = match (e1,e2) with
    | (P1 (Some n1,_),P1 (Some n2,_)) -> int (R.add n1 n2)
    | _ -> P1 (None,(C.add (abstr1 e1) (abstr1 e2)))
  let if_ = function
    | P1 (Some s,_) -> fun et ee -> if s then et () else ee ()
    | eb -> fun et ee -> P1 (None, C.if_ (abstr1 eb)
                                      (fun () -> abstr1 (et ()))
                                      (fun () -> abstr1 (ee ())))
```

However, we stumble on functions. According to our definition of `P1`, a partially evaluated object function, such as the identity $\lambda x.\, x$ embedded in OCaml as `lam (fun x -> x) : ('c,'a->'a) P1.repr`, consists of a dynamic part (type `('c,'a->'a) C.repr`) and maybe a static part (type `('c,'a->'a) R.repr`). The dynamic part is useful when this function is passed to another function that is only dynamically known, as in $\lambda k.\, k(\lambda x.\, x)$. The static part is useful when this function is applied to a static argument, as in $(\lambda x.\, x)\,\mathrm{true}$. Neither part, however, lets us *partially* evaluate the function, that is, compute as much as possible statically when it is applied to a mix of static and dynamic inputs. For example, the partial evaluator should turn $\lambda n.\, (\lambda x.\, x)n$ into $\lambda n.\, n$ by substituting $n$ for $x$ in the body of $\lambda x.\, x$ even though $n$ is not statically known. The same static function, applied to different static arguments, can give both static and dynamic results: we want to simplify $(\lambda y.\, x \times y)0$ to 0 but $(\lambda y.\, x \times y)1$ to $x$.

To enable these simplifications, we delay binding-time analysis for a static function until it is applied, that is, until `lam f` appears as the argument of `app`. To do so, we have to incorporate `f` as it is into the `P1.repr` data structure: the representation for a function type `'a->'b` should be one of

```
S1 of ('c,'a) repr -> ('c,'b) repr | E1 of ('c,'a->'b) C.repr
P1 of (('c,'a) repr -> ('c,'b) repr) option * ('c,'a->'b) C.repr
```

unlike `P1.repr` of `int` or `bool`. That is, we need a nonparametric data type, something akin to type-indexed functions and type-indexed types, which Oliveira and Gibbons [22] dub the *typecase* design pattern. Thus, typed partial evaluation, like typed CPS transformation, inductively defines a map from source types to target types that performs case distinction on the source type. In Haskell, typecase can be equivalently implemented either with GADTs or with type-class functional dependencies [22]. The accompanying code shows both approaches, neither portable to OCaml. In addition, the problem of nonexhaustive pattern-matching reappears in the GADT approach because GHC 6.6.1 cannot see that a particular type of a GADT value precludes certain constructors. Thus GADTs fail to make it *syntactically* apparent that pattern matching is exhaustive.

### 4.3 The "Final" Solution

Let us re-examine the problem in §4.2. What we would ideally like is to write `type ('c,'dv) repr = P1 of (repr_pe ('c,'dv)) R.repr option * ('c,'dv) C.repr` where `repr_pe` is the type function defined by

```
repr_pe ('c,int) = ('c,int); repr_pe ('c,bool) = ('c,bool)
repr_pe ('c,'a->'b) = ('c,'a) repr -> ('c,'b) repr
```

Although we can use type classes to define this type function in Haskell, that is not portable to MetaOCaml. However, these three typecase alternatives are already present in existing methods of `Symantics`. A simple and portable solution thus emerges: we bake `repr_pe` into the signature `Symantics`. We recall from Figure 4 in §2.1 that the `repr` type constructor took two arguments `'c` and `'dv`. We add an argument `'sv` for the result of applying `repr_pe` to `'dv`. Figure 6 shows the new signature.

```
module type Symantics = sig type ('c,'sv,'dv) repr
  val int : int -> ('c,int,int) repr
  val lam : (('c,'sa,'da) repr -> ('c,'sb,'db) repr as 'x)
            -> ('c,'x,'da -> 'db) repr
  val app : ('c,'x,'da -> 'db) repr
            -> (('c,'sa,'da) repr -> ('c,'sb,'db) repr as 'x)
  val fix : ('x -> 'x) -> (('c, ('c,'sa,'da) repr -> ('c,'sb,'db) repr,
                                 'da -> 'db) repr as 'x)
  val add : ('c,int,int) repr -> ('c,int,int) repr -> ('c,int,int) repr
  val if_ : ('c,bool,bool) repr
            -> (unit->'x) -> (unit->'x) -> (('c,'sa,'da) repr as 'x) end
```

**Fig. 6.** A (Meta)OCaml embedding of our object language that supports partial evaluation (`bool`, `mul`, `leq` are elided)

The interpreters `R`, `L` and `C` above only use the old type arguments `'c` and `'dv`, which are treated by the new signature in the same way. Hence, all that needs to change in these interpreters to match the new signature is to add a phantom type argument `'sv` to `repr`. For example, the compiler `C` now begins `module C = struct type ('c,'sv,'dv) repr = ('c,'dv) code` with the rest the same. In contrast, the partial evaluator `P` relies on the type argument `'sv`.

Figure 7 shows the partial evaluator `P`. Its type `repr` literally expresses the type equation for `repr_pe` above. The function `abstr` extracts a future-stage code value from the result of partial evaluation. Conversely, the function `pdyn` injects a code value into the `repr` type. As in §4.2, we build dynamic terms alongside any static ones to avoid polymorphic lift.

The static portion of the interpretation of `lam f` is `Some f`, which just wraps the HOAS function `f`. The interpretation of `app ef ea` checks to see if `ef` is such a wrapped HOAS function. If it is, we apply `f` to the concrete argument `ea`, giving us a chance to perform static computations (see the example below). If `ef` has only a dynamic part, we residualize.

To illustrate how to add optimizations, we improve `add` (and `mul`, elided) to simplify the generated code using the monoid (and ring) structure of `int`: not only is addition performed statically (using `R`) when both operands are statically known, but it is eliminated when one operand is statically 0; similarly for

```
module P = struct
  type ('c,'sv,'dv) repr = {st: 'sv option; dy: ('c,'dv) code}
  let abstr {dy = x} = x    let pdyn x = {st = None; dy = x}

  let int  (x:int)  = {st = Some (R.int x);  dy = C.int x}
  let add e1 e2 = match e1, e2 with
  | {st = Some 0}, e | e, {st = Some 0} -> e
  | {st = Some m}, {st = Some n} -> int (R.add m n)
  | _ -> pdyn (C.add (abstr e1) (abstr e2))
  let if_ eb et ee = match eb with
  | {st = Some b} -> if b then et () else ee ()
  | _ -> pdyn (C.if_ (abstr eb) (fun () -> abstr (et ()))
                                (fun () -> abstr (ee ())))
  let lam f = {st = Some f; dy = C.lam (fun x -> abstr (f (pdyn x)))}
  let app ef ea = match ef with {st = Some f} -> f ea
                  | _ -> pdyn (C.app (abstr ef) (abstr ea)) end
```

**Fig. 7.** Our partial evaluator (`bool`, `mul`, `leq` and `fix` are elided)

multiplication by 0 or 1. Such optimizations can be quite effective in a large language with more base types and primitive operations.

Any partial evaluator must decide how much to unfold recursion. Our code naïvely unfolds `fix` whenever the argument is static. In the accompanying source code is a conservative alternative `P.fix` that unfolds recursion only once, then residualizes. Many sophisticated approaches have been developed to decide how much to unfold [17], but this issue is orthogonal to our presentation.

Given this implementation of `P`, our running example `let module E=EX(P) in E.test1 ()` evaluates to `{P.st = Some true; P.dy = .<true>.}` of type `('a, bool, bool) P.repr`. Unlike with `C` in §3, a $\beta$-reduction has been statically performed to yield `true`. More interestingly, whereas `testpowfix7` compiles to a code value with many $\beta$-redexes in §3, the partial evaluation `let module E = EX(P) in E.testpowfix7` gives the desired result

```
  {P.st = Some <fun>;
   P.dy = .<fun x -> x * (x * (x * (x * (x * (x * x)))))>.}
```

All pattern-matching in `P` is *syntactically* exhaustive, so it is patent to the metalanguage implementation that `P` never gets stuck. Further, all pattern-matching occurs during partial evaluation, only to check if a value is known statically, never what type it has. In other words, our partial evaluator tags phases (with `Some` and `None`) but not object types.

## 5 Related Work

Our initial motivation came from several papers [23, 24, 33, 37] that use embedded interpreters to justify advanced type systems, in particular GADTs. We admire all this technical machinery, but these motivating examples do not need it. Although GADTs may indeed be simpler and more flexible, they are unavailable in mainstream ML, and their implementation in GHC 6.6.1 fails to detect exhaustive pattern matching. We also wanted to find the minimal set of widespread language features needed for tagless type-preserving interpretation.

Even a simply typed λ-calculus obviously supports self-interpretation, provided we use universal types [33]. The ensuing tagging overhead motivated Taha et al. [33] to propose tag elimination, which however does not statically guarantee that all tags will be removed [23].

Pašalić et al. [23], Taha et al. [33], Xi et al. [37], and Peyton Jones et al. [24] seem to argue as follows that a self-interpreter of a typed language cannot be tagless or Jones-optimal: (1) One needs to encode a typed language in a typed language based on a sum type (at some level of the hierarchy); (2) A *direct* interpreter for such an encoding of a typed language in a typed language requires either advanced types or tagging overhead; (3) Thus, an indirect interpreter is necessary, which needs a universal type and hence tagging. While the logic is sound, we (following Yang [38]) showed that the first step's premise is not valid.

Danvy and López [8] discuss Jones optimality at length and apply HOAS to typed self-interpretation. However, their source language is untyped. Therefore, their object-term encoding has tags, and their interpreter can raise run-time errors. Nevertheless, HOAS lets the partial evaluator remove all the tags. In contrast, our object encoding and interpreters do not have tags to start with and obviously cannot raise run-time errors.

Our partial evaluator establishes a bijection `repr_pe` between static and dynamic types (the valid values of `'sv` and `'dv`), and between static and dynamic terms. It is customary to implement such a bijection using an injection-projection pair, as done for interpreters [4, 27], partial evaluation [7], and type-level functions [22]. As explained in §4.3, we avoid injection and projection at the type level by adding an argument to `repr`. Our solution could have been even more straightforward if MetaOCaml provided total type-level functions such as `repr_pe` in §4.3—simple type-level computations ought to become mainstream.

At the term level, we also avoid converting between static and dynamic terms by building them in parallel, using Asai's method [1]. This method type-checks in Hindley-Milner once we deforest the object term representation. Put another way, we manual apply type-level partial evaluation to our type functions (see §4.3) to obtain simpler types acceptable to MetaOCaml.

Sumii and Kobayashi [32] also use Asai's method, to combine online and offline partial evaluation. They predate us in deforesting the object term representation to enable tagless partial evaluation. We strive for modularity by reusing interpreters for individual stages [31]: our partial evaluator `P` reuses our tagless evaluator `R` and tagless compiler `C`, so it is patent that the *output* of `P` never gets stuck. It would be interesting to try to derive a *cogen* [35] in the same manner.

It is common to implement an embedded DSL by providing multiple interpretations of host-language pervasives such as addition and application. It is also common to use phantom types to rule out ill-typed object terms, as done in Lava [5] and by Rhiger [29]. However, these approaches are not tagless because they still use universal types, such as Lava's `Bit` and `NumSig`, and Rhiger's `Raw` (his Fig. 2.2) and `Term` (his Chap. 3), which incur the attendant overhead of pattern matching. The universal type also greatly complicates the soundness and completeness proofs of embedding [29], whereas our proofs are trivial. Rhiger's approach does not support typed CPS transformation (his §3.3.4).

We are not the first to implement a typed interpreter for a typed language. Läufer and Odersky [18] use type classes to implement a metacircular interpreter (rather than a self-interpreter) of a typed version of the SK language, which is quite different from our object language. Their interpreter appears to be tagless, but they could not have implemented a compiler or partial evaluator in the same way, since they rely heavily on injection-projection pairs.

Fiore [10] and Balat et al. [3] also build a tagless partial evaluator, using delimited control operators. It is type-directed, so the user must represent, as a term, the type of every term to be partially evaluated. We shift this work to the type checker of the metalanguage. By avoiding term-level type representations, our approach makes it easier to perform algebraic simplifications (as in §4.3).

We encode terms in elimination form, as a coalgebraic structure. Pfenning and Lee [26] first described this basic idea and applied it to metacircular interpretation. Our approach, however, can be implemented in mainstream ML and supports type inference, typed CPS transformation and partial evaluation. In contrast, Pfenning and Lee conclude that partial evaluation and program transformations "do not seem to be expressible" even using their extension to $F_\omega$, perhaps because their avoidance of general recursive types compels them to include the polymorphic lift that we avoid in §4.1.

Our encoding of the type function `repr_pe` in §4.3 emulates type-indexed types and is related to intensional type analysis [13, 14]. However, our object language and running examples in HOAS include `fix`, which intensional type analysis cannot handle [37]. Our final approach seems related to Washburn and Weirich's approach to HOAS using catamorphisms and anamorphisms [36].

We could not find work that establishes that the *typed* λ-calculus has a final coalgebra structure. (See Honsell and Lenisa [15] for the untyped case.)

We observe that higher-rank and higher-kind polymorphism lets us type-check and compile object terms separately from interpreters. This is consistent with the role of polymorphism in the separate compilation of modules [30].

## 6 Conclusions

We solve the problem of embedding a typed object language in a typed metalanguage without using GADTs, dependent types, or a universal type. Our family of interpreters include an evaluator, a compiler, a partial evaluator, and CPS transformers. It is patent that they never get stuck, because we represent object types as metalanguage types. This work makes it safer and more efficient to embed DSLs in practical metalanguages such as Haskell and ML.

Our main idea is to represent object programs not in an initial algebra but using the existing coalgebraic structure of the λ-calculus. More generally, to squeeze more invariants out of a type system as simple as Hindley-Milner, we shift the burden of representation and computation from consumers to producers:

encoding object terms as calls to metalanguage functions (§1.2); build dynamic terms alongside static ones (§4.1); simulating type functions for partial evaluation (§4.3) and CPS transformation. This shift also underlies fusion, functionalization, and amortized complexity analysis.

Our representation of object terms in elimination form encodes primitive recursive folds over the terms. We still have to understand if and how non-primitively recursive operations can be supported.

## References


[1] Asai, K.: Binding-time analysis for both static and dynamic expressions. New Generation Computing 20(1), 27–52 (2001)

[2] Baars, A.I., Swierstra, S.D.: Typing dynamic typing. In: ICFP, pp. 157–166 (2002)

[3] Balat, V., Di Cosmo, R., Fiore, M.P.: Extensional normalisation and type-directed partial evaluation for typed lambda calculus with sums. In: POPL, pp. 64–76 (2004)

[4] Benton, P.N.: Embedded interpreters. JFP 15(4), 503–542 (2005)

[5] Bjesse, P., Claessen, K., Sheeran, M., Singh, S.: Lava: Hardware design in Haskell. In: ICFP, pp. 174–184 (1998)

[6] Calcagno, C., Moggi, E., Taha, W.: ML-like inference for classifiers. In: Schmidt, D. (ed.) ESOP 2004. LNCS, vol. 2986, pp. 79–93. Springer, Heidelberg (2004)

[7] Danvy, O.: Type-directed partial evaluation. In: POPL, pp. 242–257 (1996)

[8] Danvy, O., López, P.E.M.: Tagging, encoding, and Jones optimality. In: Degano, P. (ed.) ESOP 2003 and ETAPS 2003. LNCS, vol. 2618, pp. 335–347. Springer, Heidelberg (2003)

[9] Davies, R., Pfenning, F.: A modal analysis of staged computation. J. ACM 48(3), 555–604 (2001)

[10] Fiore, M.P.: Semantic analysis of normalisation by evaluation for typed lambda calculus. In: PPDP, pp. 26–37 (2002)

[11] Fogarty, S., Pasalic, E., Siek, J., Taha, W.: Concoqtion: Indexed types now! In: PEPM (2007)

[12] Glück, R.: Jones optimality, binding-time improvements, and the strength of program specializers. In: ASIA-PEPM, pp. 9–19 (2002)

[13] Harper, R., Morrisett, J.G.: Compiling polymorphism using intensional type analysis. In: POPL, pp. 130–141 (1995)

[14] Hinze, R., Jeuring, J., Löh, A.: Type-indexed data types. Science of Computer Programming 51(1–2), 117–151 (2004)

[15] Honsell, F., Lenisa, M.: Coinductive characterizations of applicative structures. Math. Structures in Comp. Sci. 9(4), 403–435 (1999)

[16] Hudak, P.: Building domain-specific embedded languages. ACM Comp. Surv. 28(4es), 196 (1996)

[17] Jones, N.D., Gomard, C.K., Sestoft, P.: Partial Evaluation and Automatic Program Generation. Prentice Hall, Englewood Cliffs (1993)

[18] Läufer, K., Odersky, M.: Self-interpretation and reflection in a statically typed language. In: OOPSLA/ECOOP Workshop on Object-Oriented Reflection and Metalevel Architectures (1993)

[19] MetaOCaml `http://www.metaocaml.org`

[20] Miller, D., Nadathur, G.: A logic programming approach to manipulating formulas and programs. In: IEEE Symp. on Logic Programming, pp. 379–388 (1987)

[21] Nanevski, A., Pfenning, F.: Staged computation with names and necessity. JFP 15(6), 893–939 (2005)

[22] Oliveira, B.C.d.S., Gibbons, J.: TypeCase: A design pattern for type-indexed functions. In: Haskell Workshop, pp. 98–109 (2005)

[23] Pašalić, E., Taha, W., Sheard, T.: Tagless staged interpreters for typed languages. In: ICFP, pp. 157–166 (2002)

[24] Peyton Jones, S.L., Vytiniotis, D., Weirich, S., Washburn, G.: Simple unification-based type inference for GADTs. In: ICFP, pp. 50–61 (2006)

[25] Pfenning, F., Elliott, C.: Higher-order abstract syntax. In: PLDI, pp. 199–208 (1988)

[26] Pfenning, F., Lee, P.: Metacircularity in the polymorphic λ-calculus. Theor. Comp. Sci. 89(1), 137–159 (1991)

[27] Ramsey, N.: ML module mania: A type-safe, separately compiled, extensible interpreter. In: ML Workshop (2005)

[28] Reynolds, J.C.: Definitional interpreters for higher-order programming languages. In: Proc. ACM Natl. Conf. vol. 2, 717–740 Repr. with a foreword in HOSC 11(4) 363–397 (1972)

[29] Rhiger, M.: Higher-Order Program Generation. PhD thesis, BRICS, Denmark (2001)

[30] Shao, Z.: Typed cross-module compilation. In: ICFP, pp. 141–152 (1998)

[31] Sperber, M., Thiemann, P.: Two for the price of one: Composing partial evaluation and compilation. In: PLDI, pp. 215–225 (1997)

[32] Sumii, E., Kobayashi, N.: A hybrid approach to online and offline partial evaluation. HOSC 14(2–3), 101–142 (2001)

[33] Taha, W., Makholm, H., Hughes, J.: Tag elimination and Jones-optimality. In: Danvy, O., Filinski, A. (eds.) PADO 2001. LNCS, vol. 2053, pp. 257–275. Springer, Heidelberg (2001)

[34] Taha, W., Nielsen, M.F.: Environment classifiers. In: POPL, pp. 26–37 (2003)

[35] Thiemann, P.: Cogen in six lines. In: ICFP, pp. 180–189 (1996)

[36] Washburn, G., Weirich, S.: Boxes go bananas: Encoding higher-order abstract syntax with parametric polymorphism. In: ICFP, pp. 249–262 (2003)

[37] Xi, H., Chen, C., Chen, G.: Guarded recursive datatype constructors. In: POPL, pp. 224–235 (2003)

[38] Yang, Z.: Encoding types in ML-like languages. In: ICFP, pp. 289–300 (1998)

# Polymorphic Delimited Continuations

Kenichi Asai[1] and Yukiyoshi Kameyama[2]

[1] Department of Information Science, Ochanomizu University
asai@is.ocha.ac.jp
[2] Department of Computer Science, University of Tsukuba
kameyama@acm.org

**Abstract.** This paper presents a polymorphic type system for a language with delimited control operators, shift and reset. Based on the monomorphic type system by Danvy and Filinski, the proposed type system allows pure expressions to be polymorphic. Thanks to the explicit presence of answer types, our type system satisfies various important properties, including strong type soundness, existence of principal types and an inference algorithm, and strong normalization. Relationship to CPS translation as well as extensions to impredicative polymorphism are also discussed. These technical results establish the foundation of polymorphic delimited continuations.

**Keywords:** Type System, Delimited Continuation, Control Operator, CPS Translation, Predicative/Impredicative Polymorphism.

## 1 Introduction

Delimited continuation operators enable us to manipulate control of programs in a concise manner without transforming them into continuation-passing style (CPS). In particular, shift and reset, introduced by Danvy and Filinski [6], have strong connection to CPS, and thus most of the control effects compatible with CPS can be expressed using shift and reset [8]. They have been used, for example, to program backtracking [6], A-normalization in direct style [1], let-insertion in partial evaluation [1], and type-safe "printf" in direct style [2].

Despite the increasing interest in the use of delimited continuations in typed programming languages, there has been little work that investigates their basic properties without sacrificing their expressive power. The original type system for shift and reset by Danvy and Filinski [5] is the only type system that allows modification of answer types but is restricted to monomorphic types. Polymorphism in the presence of `call/cc` has been discussed in the context of ML [11] but strong type soundness [21] does not hold for their type system. Gunter, Rémy, and Riecke [10] proposed typed `cupto` operator with strong type soundness theorem as well as various properties, but their type system is restricted to a fixed answer type for each prompt. As such, none of the above type systems can type check, for instance, the "printf" program written with shift and reset.

To establish the basic properties of shift and reset without sacrificing their expressive power, we present in this paper a polymorphic type system, an extension of the monomorphic type system by Danvy and Filinski, and show that

Z. Shao (Ed.): APLAS 2007, LNCS 4807, pp. 239–254, 2007.

it satisfies a number of basic properties needed to use them in ordinary programming languages. In particular, we show strong type soundness, existence of principal types and an efficient type inference algorithm, and strong normalization among others. The polymorphism does not break the semantic foundation of the original monomorphic type system: CPS translation is naturally defined for our polymorphic calculus and preserves types and equivalence. Because of its natural connection to CPS, our framework can be extended to a calculus with impredicative polymorphism [9].

Unrestricted polymorphism in the presence of control operators leads to an unsound type system [11]. We introduce and employ a new criteria called "purity" restriction instead of more restrictive value restriction. An expression is said to be pure if it has no control-effects [18]. By allowing pure expressions to be polymorphic, an interesting non-value term can be given a polymorphic type.

Based on these results, we have implemented a prototypical type inference algorithm, and applied it to many interesting programs to obtain their principal types.

The rest of this paper is organized as follows: Section 2 illustrates a few programming examples to give intuition about the type structure for shift and reset. In Section 3, we formalize a predicatively polymorphic calculus for shift and reset, and prove its properties such as type soundness. We then study a CPS translation for our calculus in Section 4. In Section 5, we extend our study to cover impredicative polymorphism under two evaluation strategies. In Section 6, we compare our work with related work and give conclusion. Proofs of theorems in this paper can be found in the extended version of this paper [3].

## 2 Programming Examples

Polymorphism is inevitable in programming [17]. A simple example of polymorphism is found in list manipulating functions: a reverse function works for a list of elements of any type. In this section, we introduce the control operators, `shift` and `reset`, and show examples of polymorphism that involves control operators.

### 2.1 List Append: Answer Type Modification

Consider the following program [5] written in OCaml syntax:

```
let rec append lst = match lst with
    [] -> shift (fun k -> k)
  | a :: rest -> a :: append rest
```

This program is a curried version of list append, written with control operators. Here, `shift` captures its current continuation and passes it to its argument (typically a one-argument function `fun k -> ...`) in the empty context. Unlike `callcc`, however, continuations are captured only up to its enclosing `reset` (hence called *delimited* continuations).

When append is invoked in a delimited context as follows:

```
let append123 = reset (fun () -> append [1; 2; 3])
```

append recursively stores each element of its argument into the control stack. When all the elements are stacked, the control stack could be thought of as a term with a hole: $1 :: 2 :: 3 :: \bullet$, waiting for the value for the [] case. Then, shift (fun k -> k) captures it, turns it into an ordinary function $\lambda x.1 :: 2 :: 3 :: x$, and returns it. The returned continuation append123 is the partially applied append function: given a list, it appends 1, 2, and 3 to it in the reversed order.

When shift is used in a program, it typically has an impact on the answer type of its enclosing context. Before shift (fun k -> k) is executed, the context $1 :: 2 :: 3 :: \bullet$ was supposed to return a list (given a list for $\bullet$). In other words, the answer type of this context was a list. After shift (fun k -> k) is executed, however, what is returned is the captured continuation $\lambda x.1 :: 2 :: 3 :: x$ of type int list -> int list. In other words, execution of shift (fun k -> k) modifies the answer type from 'a list to 'a list -> 'a list, where 'a is the type of the elements of the list.

To accommodate this behavior, Danvy and Filinski used a function type of the form S / A -> T / B [5]. It is the type of a function from S to T, but modifies the answer type from A to B when applied. Using this notation, append has the type 'a list / 'a list -> 'a list / ('a list -> 'a list) for all 'a: given a list of type 'a list, append returns a list of type 'a list to its immediate context; during this process, however, the answer type of the context is modified from 'a list to 'a list -> 'a list.

Gunter, Rémy, and Riecke mention the type of context (prompt) in their type system [10]. However, they fix the answer type and do not take the answer type modification into account, limiting the use of control operators. To characterize the full expressive power of shift and reset, it is necessary to cope with *two* answer types together with polymorphism.

### 2.2 List Prefix: Answer Type Polymorphism

Once answer types are included in a function type, polymorphism becomes more important in programming. First of all, the conventional function type S -> T is regarded as polymorphic in the answer type [18]: S / 'a -> T / 'a for a new type variable 'a. This indicates that even a simple, apparently monomorphic, function like:

```
let add1 x = x + 1
```

has to be treated as polymorphic in the answer type. Otherwise, it cannot be used in different contexts as in:

```
reset (fun () -> add1 2; ()); reset (fun () -> add1 3; true)
```

The first occurrence of add1 is used at type int / unit -> int / unit whereas the second one at type int / bool -> int / bool. To unify them, add1 has to be given a polymorphic type: int / 'a -> int / 'a.

Answer type polymorphism plays an important role in captured continuations, too. Consider the following program [4]:

```
let rec visit lst = match lst with
    [] -> shift (fun h -> [])
  | a :: rest -> a :: shift (fun k ->
                                    (k []) :: reset (k (visit rest)))
let rec prefix lst = reset (visit lst)
```

When applied to a list, e.g., `[1; 2 3]`, `prefix` returns a list of its prefixes: `[[1]; [1; 2]; [1; 2; 3]]`. In this example, there are two occurrences of `shift`. Intuitively, the continuation captured by the second `shift` represents consing of elements read so far. It is applied twice: once to an empty list to construct a current prefix and once to construct a list of longer prefixes. Finally, the first occurrence of `shift` initiates the construction of prefixes by returning an empty list of type `'a list list`, discarding the current continuation.

It is important that the captured continuation `k` is polymorphic in its answer type. A closer look at the function reveals that `k` is used in two different contexts: the first occurrence of `k` has type `'a list / 'a list list -> 'a list / 'a list list` whereas the second one has type `'a list / 'a list -> 'a list / 'a list`. This demonstrates that without answer type polymorphism in the captured continuations, the above program does not type check.

### 2.3 Printf

Finally, we present a type-safe printf program written in direct style with `shift` and `reset` (detailed in [2]). Given a representation of types:

```
let int x = string_of_int x
let str (x : string) = x
```

the following program achieves the behavior of printf in a type-safe manner:

```
let % to_str = shift (fun k -> fun x -> k (to_str x))
let sprintf p = reset p
```

Namely, the following programs are all well-typed:

```
sprintf (fun () -> "Hello world!")
sprintf (fun () -> "Hello " ^ % str ^ "!") "world"
sprintf (fun () -> "The value of " ^ % str ^ " is " ^ % int) "x" 3
```

and give `"Hello World!"` for the first two and `"The value of x is 3"` for the last. Depending on `%` appearing in the formatting text, `sprintf` returns a different type of values.

The dependent behavior of `sprintf` is well understood by examining its type: `(unit / string -> string / 'a) -> 'a`. The formatting text is represented as a thunk that modifies the final answer type into `'a` according to the occurrence of `%`. Then, the type of the return value of `sprintf` is polymorphic to this `'a`. The dependent behavior of `sprintf` is only achievable through the support of both the answer type modification and polymorphism.

$$
\begin{array}{rll}
v & ::= c \mid x \mid \lambda x.e \mid \texttt{fix}\ f.x.e & \text{value} \\
e & ::= v \mid e_1 e_2 \mid \mathcal{S}k.e \mid \langle e \rangle \mid \texttt{let}\ x = e_1\ \texttt{in}\ e_2 & \\
 & \mid \texttt{if}\ e_1\ \texttt{then}\ e_2\ \texttt{else}\ e_3 & \text{expression} \\
\alpha, \beta, \gamma, \delta & ::= t \mid b \mid (\alpha/\gamma \to \beta/\delta) & \text{monomorphic type} \\
A & ::= \alpha \mid \forall t.A & \text{polymorphic type}
\end{array}
$$

**Fig. 1.** Syntax of $\lambda_{let}^{s/r}$

## 3 Predicative Polymorphism with Shift/Reset

We now introduce polymorphic typed calculi for shift and reset, and study their properties such as type soundness. Following the literature, we distinguish two versions of polymorphism: *predicative* polymorphism (let-polymorphism) found in ML and *impredicative* polymorphism which is based on the second order lambda calculus (Girard's System F [9]). In this section, we give the predicative version $\lambda_{let}^{s/r}$. The impredicative version will be given in later sections.

### 3.1 Syntax and Operational Semantics

We assume that the sets of constants (denoted by $c$), variables (denoted by $x, y, k, f$), type variables (denoted by $t$), and basic types (denoted by $b$) are mutually disjoint, and that each constant is associated with a basic type. We assume `bool` is a basic type which has constants `true` and `false`.

The syntax of $\lambda_{let}^{s/r}$ is given by BNF in Figure 1. A value is either a constant, a variable, a lambda abstraction, or a fixpoint expression $\texttt{fix}\ f.x.e$ which represents a recursive function defined by the equation $f(x) = e$. The variables $f$ and $x$ are bound in $\texttt{fix}\ f.x.e$. An expression is either a value, an application, a shift expression, a reset expression, a let expression, or a conditional. The expressions $\mathcal{S}k.e$ and $\langle e \rangle$, resp., correspond to OCaml expressions `shift (fun k -> e)` and `reset (fun () -> e)`, resp. Types are similar to those in ML except that the function type is now annotated with answer types as $(\alpha/\gamma \to \beta/\delta)$. Free and bound variables (type variables, resp.) in expressions (types, resp.) are defined as usual, and $\texttt{FTV}(\alpha)$ denotes the set of free type variables in $\alpha$.

We give call-by-value operational semantics for $\lambda_{let}^{s/r}$. First we define evaluation contexts (abbreviated as e-contexts), pure e-contexts, and redexes as follows:

$$
\begin{array}{ll}
E ::= [\,] \mid vE \mid Ee \mid \langle E \rangle \mid \texttt{let}\ x = E\ \texttt{in}\ e \mid \texttt{if}\ E\ \texttt{then}\ e\ \texttt{else}\ e & \text{e-context} \\
F ::= [\,] \mid vF \mid Fe \mid \texttt{let}\ x = F\ \texttt{in}\ e \mid \texttt{if}\ F\ \texttt{then}\ e\ \texttt{else}\ e & \text{pure e-context} \\
R ::= (\lambda x.e)v \mid \langle v \rangle \mid \langle F[\mathcal{S}k.e] \rangle \mid \texttt{let}\ x = v\ \texttt{in}\ e & \\
\quad \mid \texttt{if true then}\ e_1\ \texttt{else}\ e_2 \mid \texttt{if false then}\ e_1\ \texttt{else}\ e_2 & \\
\quad \mid (\texttt{fix}\ f.x.e)v & \text{redex}
\end{array}
$$

$$
\begin{aligned}
(\lambda x.e)v &\rightsquigarrow e[v/x] \\
(\texttt{fix}\ f.x.e)v &\rightsquigarrow e[\texttt{fix}\ f.x.e/f][v/x] \\
\langle v\rangle &\rightsquigarrow v \\
\langle F[\mathcal{S}k.e]\rangle &\rightsquigarrow \langle \texttt{let}\ k = \lambda x.\langle F[x]\rangle\ \texttt{in}\ e\rangle \\
\texttt{let}\ x = v\ \texttt{in}\ e &\rightsquigarrow e[v/x] \\
\texttt{if true then}\ e_1\ \texttt{else}\ e_2 &\rightsquigarrow e_1 \\
\texttt{if false then}\ e_1\ \texttt{else}\ e_2 &\rightsquigarrow e_2
\end{aligned}
$$

**Fig. 2.** Reduction rules for $\lambda^{s/r}_{let}$

A pure e-context $F$ is an evaluation context such that no reset encloses the hole. Therefore, in the redex $\langle F[\mathcal{S}k.e]\rangle$, the outermost reset is guaranteed to be the one corresponding to this shift, i.e., no reset exists inbetween.

A one-step *evaluation* in $\lambda^{s/r}_{let}$ is $E[R] \rightsquigarrow E[e]$ where $R \rightsquigarrow e$ is an instance of reductions in Figure 2 where $e[v/x]$ denotes the ordinary capture-avoiding substitution. For example, `prefix [1; 2]` is reduced as follows. (We use `fix` implicitly through recursion, and assume that lists and other constructs are available in the language).

$$
\begin{aligned}
& \texttt{prefix [1; 2]} \\
\rightsquigarrow\ & \langle 1 :: \mathcal{S}k.(k\,\texttt{[]} :: \langle k\,(\texttt{visit [2]})\rangle)\rangle \\
\rightsquigarrow\ & \langle \texttt{let}\ k = \lambda x.\langle 1 :: x\rangle\ \texttt{in}\ k\,\texttt{[]} :: \langle k\,(\texttt{visit [2]})\rangle\rangle \\
\rightsquigarrow\ & \langle(\lambda x.\langle 1 :: x\rangle)\,\texttt{[]} :: \langle(\lambda x.\langle 1 :: x\rangle)(\texttt{visit [2]})\rangle\rangle \\
\rightsquigarrow^+\ & \langle \texttt{[1]} :: \langle(\lambda x.\langle 1 :: x\rangle)(2 :: \mathcal{S}k.(k\,\texttt{[]} :: \langle k\,(\texttt{visit []})\rangle))\rangle\rangle \\
\rightsquigarrow\ & \langle \texttt{[1]} :: \langle \texttt{let}\ k = \lambda x.\langle(\lambda x.\langle 1 :: x\rangle)(2 :: x)\rangle\ \texttt{in}\ k\,\texttt{[]} :: \langle k\,(\texttt{visit []})\rangle\rangle\rangle \\
\rightsquigarrow\ & \langle \texttt{[1]} :: \langle(\lambda x.\langle(\lambda x.\langle 1 :: x\rangle)(2 :: x)\rangle)\,\texttt{[]} :: \langle(\lambda x.\langle(\lambda x.\langle 1 :: x\rangle)(2 :: x)\rangle)(\texttt{visit []})\rangle\rangle\rangle \\
\rightsquigarrow^+\ & \langle \texttt{[1]} :: \langle \texttt{[1; 2]} :: \langle(\lambda x.\langle(\lambda x.\langle 1 :: x\rangle)(2 :: x)\rangle)(\mathcal{S}h.\texttt{[]})\rangle\rangle\rangle \\
\rightsquigarrow\ & \langle \texttt{[1]} :: \langle \texttt{[1; 2]} :: \texttt{let}\ h = \lambda x.\langle(\lambda x.\langle(\lambda x.\langle 1 :: x\rangle)(2 :: x)\rangle)x\rangle\ \texttt{in}\ \texttt{[]}\rangle\rangle \\
\rightsquigarrow\ & \langle \texttt{[1]} :: \langle \texttt{[1; 2]} :: \texttt{[]}\rangle\rangle \rightsquigarrow^+ \texttt{[[1]; [1; 2]]}
\end{aligned}
$$

The notion of *reduction* $\rightsquigarrow$ is defined as the compatible closure[1] of those in Figure 2, and $\rightsquigarrow^*$ (and $\rightsquigarrow^+$, resp.) denotes the reflexive-transitive (transitive, resp.) closure of $\rightsquigarrow$.

### 3.2 Type System

We begin with Danvy and Filinski's monomorphic type system for shift and reset [5]. Since the evaluation of an expression with shift and reset may modify answer types, a type judgment in their type system involves not only a type of an expression being typed, but also answer types before and after evaluation. Symbolically, a judgment takes the form:

[1] A binary relation is compatible if it is closed under term-formation, for instance, whenever $e_1$ and $e_2$ are related by this relation, $\lambda x.e_1$ and $\lambda x.e_2$ are related.

$$\Gamma;\ \alpha \vdash e : \tau;\ \beta$$

which means that, under the type context $\Gamma$, the expression $e$ has type $\tau$ and the evaluation of $e$ changes the answer type from $\alpha$ to $\beta$. A rationale behind this formulation is that, the CPS counterpart of $e$ has type $(\tau^* \to \alpha^*) \to \beta^*$ under the type context $\Gamma^*$ in the simply typed lambda calculus, where $(\_)^*$ is the CPS translation for types and type contexts defined in the next section.

Introducing polymorphism into their type system is, however, not straightforward since the subject reduction property fails for the system with unrestricted uses of let-polymorphism and side effects such as references and control effects. In the literature, there are many proposals to solve this problem by restricting the let-expression $\texttt{let}\ x = e_1\ \texttt{in}\ e_2$ or by changing its operational semantics, some of which are:

- Value restriction [20]: $e_1$ must be a value.
- Weak type variables [19]: the type variable in the type of $e_1$ can be generalized only when it is not related to side effects.
- Polymorphism by name [15]: the evaluation of $e_1$ is postponed until $x$ is actually used in $e_2$, thus enforcing the call-by-name evaluation to $e_1$.

We take an alternative approach: we restrict that $e_1$ in $\texttt{let}\ x = e_1\ \texttt{in}\ e_2$ must be free from control effects, that is, *pure*. Intuitively, an expression is pure when it is polymorphic in answer types.[2] In Danvy and Filinski's type system, we can define that $e$ is pure if the judgment $\Gamma;\ \alpha \vdash e : \tau;\ \alpha$ is derivable for any type $\alpha$. Typical examples of pure expressions are values but the expression $\langle e \rangle$ is also pure, since all control effects in $e$ are delimited by reset. To represent purity of expressions, we introduce a new judgment form $\Gamma \vdash_p e : \tau$.

Now let us formally define the type system of $\lambda_{let}^{s/r}$. A *type context* (denoted by $\Gamma$) is a finite list of the form $x_1 : A_1, \cdots, x_n : A_n$ where the variables $x_1, \cdots, x_n$ are mutually distinct, and $A_1, \cdots, A_n$ are (polymorphic) types. *Judgments* are either one of the following forms:

$$\begin{array}{rl} \Gamma \vdash_p e : \tau & \text{judgment for pure expression} \\ \Gamma;\ \alpha \vdash e : \tau;\ \beta & \text{judgment for general expression} \end{array}$$

Figure 3 lists the type inference rules of $\lambda_{let}^{s/r}$ where $\tau \le A$ in the rule (var) means the instantiation of type variables by monomorphic types. Namely, if $A \equiv \forall t_1. \cdots \forall t_n.\rho$ for some monomorphic type $\rho$, then $\tau \equiv \rho[\sigma_1, \cdots, \sigma_n/t_1, \cdots, t_n]$ for some monomorphic types $\sigma_1, \cdots, \sigma_n$. The type $\texttt{Gen}(\sigma; \Gamma)$ in the rule (let) is defined by $\forall t_1. \cdots \forall t_n.\sigma$ where $\{t_1, \cdots, t_n\} = \texttt{FTV}(\sigma) - \texttt{FTV}(\Gamma)$.

The type inference rules are a natural extension of the monomorphic type system by Danvy and Filinski [5]. Pure expressions are defined by one of the

---

[2] Thielecke studied the relationship between answer type polymorphism and the absence of control in depth [18].

$$\frac{(x : A \in \Gamma \text{ and } \tau \leq A)}{\Gamma \vdash_p x : \tau}\ \text{var} \qquad \frac{(c \text{ is a constant of basic type } b)}{\Gamma \vdash_p c : b}\ \text{const}$$

$$\frac{\Gamma, f : (\sigma/\alpha \to \tau/\beta), x : \sigma;\ \alpha \vdash e : \tau;\ \beta}{\Gamma \vdash_p \mathtt{fix}\ f.x.e : (\sigma/\alpha \to \tau/\beta)}\ \text{fix} \qquad \frac{\Gamma, x : \sigma;\ \alpha \vdash e : \tau;\ \beta}{\Gamma \vdash_p \lambda x.e : (\sigma/\alpha \to \tau/\beta)}\ \text{fun}$$

$$\frac{\Gamma;\ \gamma \vdash e_1 : (\sigma/\alpha \to \tau/\beta);\ \delta \quad \Gamma;\ \beta \vdash e_2 : \sigma;\ \gamma}{\Gamma;\ \alpha \vdash e_1 e_2 : \tau;\ \delta}\ \text{app} \qquad \frac{\Gamma \vdash_p e : \tau}{\Gamma;\ \alpha \vdash e : \tau;\ \alpha}\ \text{exp}$$

$$\frac{\Gamma, k : \forall t.(\tau/t \to \alpha/t);\ \sigma \vdash e : \sigma;\ \beta}{\Gamma;\ \alpha \vdash \mathcal{S}k.e : \tau;\ \beta}\ \text{shift} \qquad \frac{\Gamma; \sigma \vdash e : \sigma;\ \tau}{\Gamma \vdash_p \langle e \rangle : \tau}\ \text{reset}$$

$$\frac{\Gamma \vdash_p e_1 : \sigma \quad \Gamma, x : \mathtt{Gen}(\sigma; \Gamma);\ \alpha \vdash e_2 : \tau;\ \beta}{\Gamma;\ \alpha \vdash \mathtt{let}\ x = e_1\ \mathtt{in}\ e_2 : \tau;\ \beta}\ \text{let}$$

$$\frac{\Gamma;\ \sigma \vdash e_1 : \mathtt{bool};\ \beta \quad \Gamma;\ \alpha \vdash e_2 : \tau;\ \sigma \quad \Gamma;\ \alpha \vdash e_3 : \tau;\ \sigma}{\Gamma;\ \alpha \vdash \mathtt{if}\ e_1\ \mathtt{then}\ e_2\ \mathtt{else}\ e_3 : \tau;\ \beta}\ \text{if}$$

**Fig. 3.** Type Inference Rules of $\lambda_{let}^{s/r}$

rules (fix), (fun), or (reset).[3] They can be freely turned into general expressions through the rule (exp). Pure expressions can be used polymorphically through the rule (let). It generalizes the standard let-polymorphism found in ML. We can allow a let expression $\mathtt{let}\ x = e_1\ \mathtt{in}\ e_2$ even when $e_1$ is not pure, in which case it is macro-expanded to $(\lambda x.e_2)e_1$ where $e_1$ is treated monomorphically. Finally, the rule (shift) is extended to cope with the answer type polymorphism of captured continuations: $k$ is given a polymorphic type $\forall t.(\tau/t \to \alpha/t)$.

*Examples.* We show the principal types for the examples shown in Section 2.

Using the type inference rules (augmented with rules for lists, etc.), we can deduce that `append` (rewritten with `fix`) has type `'a list / 'b -> 'a list / ('a list -> 'b)`,[4] where `'a list -> 'b` is a shorthand for `'a list / 'c -> 'b / 'c` for a new type variable `'c`. Given this type, the type of `append123`, i.e., `reset (fun () -> append [1; 2; 3])`, becomes `int list -> int list` (or `int list / 'c -> int list / 'c`). Since it is pure, `append123` can be given a polymorphic type in its answer type `'c`. Notice that `append123` is not bound to a value but an effectful expression enclosed by reset. If we employed value restriction, `append123` could not be polymorphic, and thus could only be used in a context with a fixed answer type.

[3] We could have introduced a more general rule such as: if $\Gamma;\ t \vdash e : \tau;\ t$ is derivable for $t \notin \mathtt{FTV}(\Gamma, \tau)$, then $\Gamma \vdash_p e : \tau$. It would then allow expressions that are not syntactically values nor reset expressions but in fact pure, such as $\mathcal{S}k.k3$. We did not take this approach, because we can always insert reset around pure expressions to make them syntactically pure.

[4] This is the principal type for `append`. In the typical case where the call to `append` is immediately enclosed by `reset` as is the case for `append123`, `'b` is instantiated to `'a list`.

Next, the principal type for `visit` is `'a list / 'b -> 'a list / 'b list`.[5] To deduce this type, we need to use the rule (shift) to give `k` a polymorphic type in its answer type. Then, the type of `prefix` becomes `'a list -> 'a list list`. In other words, it accepts a list of any type `'a`. Since it is pure (that is, answer type polymorphic), it can be used in any context.

Finally, the principal type for `%` is somewhat complicated:

```
('a / 'p -> 's / 'q) / 't -> 's / ('a / 'p -> 't / 'q)
```

In the typical case where `to_str` is pure (`'p='q`) and has type `'a -> string`, and the output `'t` is `string`, the above type becomes:

```
('a -> string) / string -> string / ('a -> string)
```

This type describes the behavior of `%`: given a representation of a type (of type `'a -> string`), it changes the answer type from `string` to a function that receives a value of the specified type `'a`. Then, `sprintf` returns a function of this final answer type, thus accepting an argument depending on the occurrence of `%`.

### 3.3 Properties

We have introduced the polymorphic calculus $\lambda_{let}^{s/r}$ with shift and reset. We claim that our calculus provides a good foundation for studying the interaction between polymorphism and delimited continuations. To support this claim, we prove the following properties:

- Subject reduction (type preservation).
- Progress and unique decomposition.
- Principal types and existence of a type inference algorithm.
- Preservation of types and equality through CPS translation.
- Confluence.
- Strong normalization for the subcalculus without `fix`.

We first show type soundness, i.e., subject reduction and progress.

**Theorem 1 (Subject Reduction).** *If $\Gamma;\ \alpha \vdash e_1 : \tau;\ \beta$ is derivable and $e_1 \rightsquigarrow^* e_2$, then $\Gamma;\ \alpha \vdash e_2 : \tau;\ \beta$ is derivable. Similarly, if $\Gamma \vdash_p e_1 : \tau$ is derivable and $e_1 \rightsquigarrow^* e_2$, then $\Gamma \vdash_p e_2 : \tau$ is derivable.*

The above theorem not only assures that a well-typed program does not go wrong (so-called *weak* type soundness [21]) but also guarantees that the evaluated term has the same type as the original term (*strong* type soundness [21]). This is the consequence of having answer types explicitly in our type system. We need three lemmas to prove this theorem.

**Lemma 1 (Weakening of Type Context).** *Suppose $\Gamma_1 \subset \Gamma_2$ and $\Gamma_2$ is a valid type context. If $\Gamma_1;\ \alpha \vdash e : \sigma;\ \beta$ is derivable, then $\Gamma_2;\ \alpha \vdash e : \sigma;\ \beta$ is derivable. Similarly for $\Gamma_1 \vdash_p e : \sigma$.*

[5] Again, `'b` is typically instantiated to `'a list`.

**Lemma 2 (Substitution for Monomorphic Variables).** *Suppose $\Gamma_1 \subset \Gamma_2$, $\Gamma_2$ is a valid type context, and $\Gamma_1 \vdash_p v : \sigma$ is derivable.*

*If $\Gamma_2, x : \sigma;\ \alpha \vdash e : \tau;\ \beta$ is derivable, then $\Gamma_2;\ \alpha \vdash e[v/x] : \tau;\ \beta$ is derivable. Similarly, if $\Gamma_2, x : \sigma \vdash_p e : \tau$ is derivable, then $\Gamma_2 \vdash_p e[v/x] : \tau$ is derivable.*

**Lemma 3 (Substitution for Polymorphic Variables).** *Suppose $\Gamma_1 \subset \Gamma_2$, $\Gamma_2$ is a valid type context, and $\Gamma_1 \vdash_p v : \sigma$ is derivable.*

*If $\Gamma_2, x : \mathit{Gen}(\sigma; \Gamma_1);\ \alpha \vdash e : \tau;\ \beta$ is derivable, then $\Gamma_2;\ \alpha \vdash e[v/x] : \tau;\ \beta$ is derivable. Similarly for $\Gamma_2, x : \mathit{Gen}(\sigma; \Gamma_1) \vdash_p e : \tau$.*

We next prove the progress property, which states that evaluation of a program does not get stuck. Although a program is usually defined as an expression with no free variables, we need to refine it, since, for instance, $Sk.k3$ cannot be reduced further due to the absence of an enclosing reset. Here, we define a program to be an expression with a toplevel reset of the form $\langle e \rangle$ which has no free variables.

**Theorem 2 (Progress and Unique Decomposition).** *If $\vdash_p \langle e \rangle : \tau$ is derivable, then either $e$ is a value, or $\langle e \rangle$ can be uniquely decomposed into the form $E[R]$ where $E$ is an evaluation context and $R$ is a redex.*

By Theorems 1 and 2, we can conclude that our type system is sound (Type Soundness).

Although our type system may look rather complex, we can smoothly extend Hindley-Milner type inference algorithm $W$ to accommodate $\lambda^{s/r}_{let}$. The extended algorithm $W'$ takes two arguments as its inputs: $\Gamma$ (for a valid context) and $e$ (for a raw expression) such that all free variables in $e$ are contained in $\Gamma$. Then, $W'$ either fails or returns a tuple $(\theta;\ \alpha, \tau, \beta)$ where $\theta$ is a substitution for type variables, and $\alpha$, $\tau$, and $\beta$ are types.

**Theorem 3 (Principal Type and Type Inference).** *We can construct a type inference algorithm $W'$ for $\lambda^{s/r}_{let}$ such that:*

1. *$W'$ always terminates.*
2. *if $W'$ returns $(\theta;\ \alpha, \tau, \beta)$, then $\Gamma\theta;\ \alpha \vdash e : \tau;\ \beta$ is derivable. Moreover, for any $(\theta';\ \alpha', \tau', \beta')$ such that $\Gamma\theta';\ \alpha' \vdash e : \tau';\ \beta'$ is derivable, $(\Gamma\theta', \alpha', \tau', \beta') \equiv (\Gamma\theta, \alpha, \tau, \beta)\phi$ for some substitution $\phi$.*
3. *if $W'$ fails, then $\Gamma\theta;\ \alpha \vdash e : \tau;\ \beta$ is not derivable for any $(\theta;\ \alpha, \tau, \beta)$.*

We have implemented a prototypical type inference algorithm system for our language based on this theorem. The principal types shown in Section 3.2 are all inferred by it.

Finally, we can show confluence for $\lambda^{s/r}_{let}$, and strong normalization for the subcalculus without `fix`. This is in contrast to `cupto` operator, where strong normalization does not hold.[6]

**Theorem 4 (Confluence and Strong Normalization)**

1. *The reduction $\rightsquigarrow$ in $\lambda^{s/r}_{let}$ is confluent.*
2. *The reduction $\rightsquigarrow$ in $\lambda^{s/r}_{let}$ without $\mathit{fix}$ is strongly normalizing.*

[6] See `http://okmij.org/ftp/Computation/Continuations.html#cupto-nontermination`.

$$
\begin{aligned}
b^* &= b \quad \text{for a basic type } b\\
t^* &= t \quad \text{for a type variable } t\\
((\alpha/\gamma \to \beta/\delta))^* &= \alpha^* \to (\beta^* \to \gamma^*) \to \delta^*\\
(\forall t.A)^* &= \forall t.A^*\\
(\Gamma, x : A)^* &= \Gamma^*, x : A^*
\end{aligned}
$$

**Fig. 4.** CPS translation for types and type contexts

$$
\begin{aligned}
c^* &= c\\
v^* &= v\\
(\lambda x.e)^* &= \lambda x.[e]\\
(\mathtt{fix}\ f.x.e)^* &= \mathtt{fix}\ f.x.[e]\\
[v] &= \lambda\kappa.\kappa v^*\\
[e_1 e_2] &= \lambda\kappa.[e_1](\lambda m.[e_2](\lambda n.mn\kappa))\\
[\mathcal{S}k.e] &= \lambda\kappa.\mathtt{let}\ k = \lambda n\kappa'.\kappa'(\kappa n)\ \mathtt{in}\ [e](\lambda m.m)\\
[\langle e\rangle] &= \lambda\kappa.\kappa([e](\lambda m.m))\\
[\mathtt{let}\ x = e_1\ \mathtt{in}\ e_2] &= \lambda\kappa.\mathtt{let}\ x = [e_1](\lambda m.m)\ \mathtt{in}\ [e_2]\kappa\\
[\mathtt{if}\ e_1\ \mathtt{then}\ e_2\ \mathtt{else}\ e_3] &= \lambda\kappa.[e_1](\lambda m.\mathtt{if}\ m\ \mathtt{then}\ [e_2]\kappa\ \mathtt{else}\ [e_3]\kappa)
\end{aligned}
$$

**Fig. 5.** CPS translation for values and expressions

## 4 CPS Translation of $\lambda_{let}^{s/r}$

The semantics of control operators have often been given through a CPS translation. In their first proposal, Danvy and Filinski gave the precise semantics of shift and reset in terms of a CPS translation [6,7]. In this section, we show that it can be naturally extended to polymorphic setting.

Harper and Lillibridge [12] were the first to systematically study CPS translations in polymorphic language with control operators. They introduced CPS translations from $F\omega$+`call/cc` to $F\omega$, and proved that, under a condition similar to the value restriction, a call-by-value CPS translation preserves types and semantics (equality). We follow Harper and Lillibridge to give a type-and-equality preserving CPS translation for polymorphic calculi with shift and reset.

The CPS translation for $\lambda_{let}^{s/r}$ is a Plotkin-style, call-by-value translation, and is defined in Figures 4 and 5, where the variables $\kappa$, $m$ and $n$ are fresh. The target calculus (the image) of the translation is $\lambda_{let}$, the minimum lambda calculus with let-polymorphism and conditional expressions.[7]

[7] $\lambda_{let}$ may be obtained from $\lambda_{let}^{s/r}$ by eliminating shift, reset, and answer types $\alpha$ and $\beta$ in $\Gamma$; $\alpha \vdash e : \tau$; $\beta$ and $(\sigma/\alpha \to \tau/\beta)$. Since all expressions are pure in $\lambda_{let}$, we do not distinguish two kinds of judgments.

The type $(\alpha/\gamma \to \beta/\delta)$ is translated to the type of a function which, given a parameter of type $\alpha^*$ and a continuation of type $\beta^* \to \gamma^*$ returns a value of type $\delta^*$. For instance, the type of the `visit` function (in the `prefix` example) `'a list / 'b -> 'a list / 'b list` is CPS translated to `'a list -> ('a list -> 'b) -> 'b list`.

The translation of reset is the same as that in Danvy and Filinski's. For shift, we use a let-expression rather than substitution, so that the captured continuation $\lambda n\kappa'.\kappa'(\kappa n)$ may be used polymorphically in the body $[\![e]\!](\lambda m.m)$. This is essential to retain enough polymorphism for delimited continuations.

The translation of the let expression `let` $x = e_1$ `in` $e_2$ needs care to take polymorphism into account. We use a let-expression to express the polymorphism in the source term, and supply the identity continuation $\lambda m.m$ to the CPS transform $[\![e_1]\!]$. This is typable in the target calculus, since a pure expression is translated to an expression of type $\forall t.((\tau \to t) \to t)$.

We can prove that the CPS translation preserves types and equality:

**Theorem 5 (Preservation of Types).** *If* $\Gamma;\ \alpha \vdash e : \tau;\ \beta$ *is derivable in* $\lambda_{let}^{s/r}$*, then* $\Gamma^* \vdash [\![e]\!] : (\tau^* \to \alpha^*) \to \beta^*$ *is derivable in* $\lambda_{let}$*.*

*If* $\Gamma \vdash_p e : \tau$ *is derivable in* $\lambda_{let}^{s/r}$*, then,* $\Gamma^* \vdash [\![e]\!] : (\tau^* \to \gamma) \to \gamma$ *is derivable for an arbitrary type* $\gamma$ *in* $\lambda_{let}$*.*

**Theorem 6 (Preservation of Equality).** *If* $\Gamma;\ \alpha \vdash e_1 : \tau;\ \beta$ *is derivable and* $e_1 \leadsto^* e_2$ *in* $\lambda_{let}^{s/r}$*, then* $[\![e_1]\!] = [\![e_2]\!]$ *in* $\lambda_{let}$ *where* $=$ *is the least congruence relation which contains* $\leadsto$ *in* $\lambda_{let}$*.*[8]

## 5 Impredicative Polymorphism with Shift and Reset

The second order lambda calculus (Girard's System F) is a solid foundation for advanced concepts in programming languages, since its *impredicative polymorphism* is strictly more expressive than the predicative one. In this section, we study an extension of (call-by-value version of) System F with shift and reset. It is an *explicitly typed* calculus rather than an implicitly typed calculus like $\lambda_{let}^{s/r}$. Hence, we add two constructs to the expressions: $\Lambda t.e$ for type-abstraction and $e\{\alpha\}$ for type-application. Following Harper and Lillibridge [12], we consider two calculi with impredicative polymorphism that differ in evaluation strategies. The first calculus, $\lambda_2^{s/r,Std}$, adopts the "standard" strategy: $\Lambda t.e$ is treated as a value, and hence we do not evaluate under $\Lambda$. The second one, $\lambda_2^{s/r,ML}$, adopts the "ML-like" strategy: $\Lambda t.e$ is a value only when $e$ is a value, and hence we evaluate under $\Lambda$.

The syntax of $\lambda_2^{s/r,Std}$ and $\lambda_2^{s/r,ML}$ extends that of $\lambda_{let}^{s/r}$ with the new constructs listed in Figure 6. We annotate bound variables with types, for instance, $\lambda x : \alpha.\ e$. We eliminate let expressions, since they can be macro-defined: for instance, the expression `let` $f = \lambda x.x$ `in` $(ff)0$ in $\lambda_{let}^{s/r}$ is represented[9] as

[8] The reduction $\leadsto$ in $\lambda_{let}$ is the reduction $\leadsto$ restricted to the expressions in $\lambda_{let}$.

[9] We assume that 0 is a constant of type `int`.

| | | |
|---|---|---|
| $\alpha, \beta, \gamma, \delta ::= \cdots \mid \forall t.\alpha$ | $::= \cdots \mid \forall t.\alpha$ | type |
| $v ::= \cdots \mid \Lambda t.e$ | $::= \cdots \mid \Lambda t.v$ | value |
| $e ::= \cdots \mid e\{\alpha\}$ | $::= \cdots \mid \Lambda t.e \mid e\{\alpha\}$ | expression |
| $\lambda_2^{s/r,Std}$(standard) | $\lambda_2^{s/r,ML}$(ML-like) | |

**Fig. 6.** Syntax of $\lambda_2^{s/r,Std}$ and $\lambda_2^{s/r,ML}$

$$\frac{\Gamma \vdash_p e : \tau}{\Gamma \vdash_p \Lambda t.e : \forall t.\tau}\ \text{tabs}, t \notin \texttt{FTV}(\Gamma) \qquad \frac{\Gamma;\ \alpha \vdash e : \forall t.\tau;\ \beta}{\Gamma;\ \alpha \vdash e\{\sigma\} : \tau[\sigma/t];\ \beta}\ \text{tapp}$$

**Fig. 7.** Type inference rules for new constructs

$(\lambda f : \forall t.(t \to t).\ f\{\texttt{int} \to \texttt{int}\}(f\{\texttt{int}\})0)(\Lambda t.\lambda x : t.\ x)$. Monomorphic and polymorphic types are merged, since the type quantifier $\forall$ may occur at any place in types. The definitions for values and expressions reflect the difference between the two calculi.

The type inference rules for new constructs are common to $\lambda_2^{s/r,Std}$ and $\lambda_2^{s/r,ML}$, and are given in Figure 7. As can be seen by the rule (tabs), the body $e$ in $\Lambda t.e$ is restricted to a pure expression. For $\lambda_2^{s/r,ML}$, this restriction is necessary[10] to ensure the type soundness due to a similar reason as Harper and Lillibridge [12] who proposed to put a kind of value restriction when abstracting types. Unfortunately, their calculus under the value restriction is not very interesting, since the standard and ML-like strategies completely agree on the restricted calculus. We relax the restriction so that $e$ in $\Lambda t.e$ may be an arbitrary pure expression, which makes the two strategies differ on some expressions.

Operational semantics is defined in Figure 8 with a new reduction rule:

$$(\Lambda t.e)\{\alpha\} \leadsto e[\alpha/t]$$

where $e[\alpha/t]$ denotes the capture-avoiding substitution for types. For $\lambda_2^{s/r,ML}$, the subexpression $e$ in the reduction rule is restricted to a value.

Polymorphism in $\lambda_2^{s/r,Std}$ is a generalization of Leroy's "polymorphism by name" [15]: consider the expression $\texttt{let}\ f = \langle e \rangle\ \texttt{in}\ (ff)0$ for an expression $e$ of type $t \to t$ and a constant 0 of type $\texttt{int}$. It is represented by $(\lambda f : \forall t.(t \to t).(f\{\texttt{int} \to \texttt{int}\})(f\{\texttt{int}\})0)(\Lambda t.\langle e \rangle)$ in $\lambda_2^{s/r,Std}$, and it is easy to see that the evaluation of $e$ is postponed until a type is applied to $\Lambda t.\langle e \rangle$.

Polymorphism in $\lambda_2^{s/r,ML}$ is a generalization of that for ML. Taking the same example, the outermost $\beta$-redex is computed only after $\langle e \rangle$ is computed and returns a value. Then, the variable $f$ is substituted for the value of $\Lambda t.\langle e \rangle$, and the body $f\{\texttt{int} \to \texttt{int}\})(f\{\texttt{int}\})0$ is computed.

We can show type soundness for $\lambda_2^{s/r,Std}$ and $\lambda_2^{s/r,ML}$.

[10] For $\lambda_2^{s/r,Std}$, the restriction is not necessary, and we could have defined a more liberal type system. In the present paper, however, we choose a uniform, simpler syntax.

| | | |
|---|---|---|
| $E ::= \cdots \mid E\{\alpha\}$ | $::= \cdots \mid E\{\alpha\} \mid \Lambda t.E$ | e-context |
| $F ::= \cdots \mid F\{\alpha\}$ | $::= \cdots \mid F\{\alpha\}$ | pure e-context |
| $R ::= \cdots \mid (\Lambda t.e)\{\alpha\}$ | $::= \cdots \mid (\Lambda t.v)\{\alpha\}$ | redex |
| $\lambda_2^{s/r,Std}$ | $\lambda_2^{s/r,ML}$ | |

**Fig. 8.** Evaluation Contexts and Redexes

$$(\forall t.\tau)^* = \forall t.\forall s.((\tau^* \to s) \to s) \text{ for a fresh type variable } s$$
$$[\![\Lambda t.e]\!]_{\alpha,\forall t.\tau,\alpha} = \lambda\kappa : ((\forall t.\tau)^* \to \alpha).\kappa(\Lambda t.\Lambda s.[\![e]\!]_{s,\tau,s})$$
$$[\![e\{\sigma\}]\!]_{\alpha,\tau[\sigma/t],\beta} = \lambda\kappa : ((\tau[\sigma/t])^* \to \alpha^*).[\![e]\!]_{\alpha,\forall t.\tau,\beta}(\lambda u : (\forall t.\tau)^*.u\{\sigma^*\}\{\alpha^*\}\kappa)$$

**Fig. 9.** CPS translation for $\lambda_2^{s/r,Std}$

$$(\forall t.\tau)^* = \forall t.\tau^*$$
$$[\![\Lambda t.e]\!]_{\alpha,\forall t.\tau,\alpha} = \lambda\kappa : ((\forall t.\tau^*) \to \alpha).\kappa(\Lambda t.[\![e]\!]_{\tau,\tau,\tau}(\lambda m : \tau^*.m))$$
$$[\![e\{\sigma\}]\!]_{\alpha,\tau[\sigma/t],\beta} = \lambda\kappa : ((\tau[\sigma/t])^* \to \alpha^*).\ [\![e]\!]_{\alpha,\forall t.\tau,\beta}(\lambda u : \forall t.\tau^*.\kappa(u\{\sigma^*\}))$$

**Fig. 10.** CPS translation for $\lambda_2^{s/r,ML}$

**Theorem 7 (Type Soundness).** *Subject reduction property and progress property hold for* $\lambda_2^{s/r,Std}$ *and* $\lambda_2^{s/r,ML}$.

We define a CPS transformation for $\lambda_2^{s/r,Std}$ and $\lambda_2^{s/r,ML}$ in Figures 9 and 10. The target calculus of the translation is System F augmented with basic types, constants, `fix` and conditionals. Equality of the target calculus is the least congruence relation which includes call-by-value $\beta\eta$-equaltiy, $\beta$-equaltiy for types ($(\Lambda t.e)\{\alpha\} = e[\alpha/t]$), and equality for `fix` and conditionals. Since the target calculus is explicitly typed, the CPS translation for expressions is annotated by types as $[\![e]\!]_{\alpha,\tau,\beta}$, which is well-defined when $\Gamma;\ \alpha \vdash e : \tau;\ \beta$ is derivable for some $\Gamma$. It is interesting to see how the difference of evaluation strategies affect the difference of CPS translations in Figures 9 and 10.

Note that the CPS translation for $\lambda_2^{s/r,ML}$ is a natural extension of that for $\lambda_{let}^{s/r}$: for instance, $[\![\texttt{let}\ f = \langle e\rangle\ \texttt{in}\ (ff)0]\!]$ in $\lambda_{let}^{s/r}$ is equal (up to the call-by-value $\beta\eta$-equality) to $[\![(\lambda f : \forall t.(t \to t).(f\{\texttt{int} \to \texttt{int}\})(f\{\texttt{int}\})0)(\Lambda t.\langle e\rangle)]\!]$ in $\lambda_2^{s/r,Std}$.

We can show that the CPS transformations for the two calculi preserve types and equality. Let $T$ be $\lambda_2^{s/r,Std}$ or $\lambda_2^{s/r,ML}$.

**Theorem 8 (Preservation of Types and Equality)**

1. *If* $\Gamma;\ \alpha \vdash e : \tau;\ \beta$ *is derivable in* $T$, *then* $\Gamma^* \vdash [\![e]\!]_{\alpha,\tau,\beta} : (\tau^* \to \alpha^*) \to \beta^*$ *is derivable in the target calculus.*

2. *If* $\Gamma \vdash_p e : \tau$ *is derivable in* $T$*, then* $\Gamma^* \vdash [\![e]\!]_{s,\tau,s} : (\tau^* \to s) \to s$ *is derivable for any type variable* $s$ *in the target calculus.*
3. *If* $\Gamma;\ \alpha \vdash e : \tau;\ \beta$ *is derivable in* $T$*, and* $e \rightsquigarrow^* e'$*, then* $[\![e]\!]_{\alpha,\tau,\beta} = [\![e']\!]_{\alpha,\tau,\beta}$ *under the equality of the target calculus.*

## 6 Conclusion

We have introduced predicative and impredicative polymorphic typed calculi for shift and reset, and investigated their properties such as type soundness and relationship to CPS translations. We have extended Danvy and Filinski's monomorphic type system for shift and reset to polymorphic one, and have shown that a number of pleasant properties hold for the polymorphic calculi. We have shown that our calculi have a natural representation for the "purity" of expressions, and that the purity restriction suffices for the type systems to be sound, thus generalizing value restriction used in Standard ML and OCaml.

In the literature, a number of authors have tackled the unsoundness problem of polymorphism and effects [19,15,20,12]. We have proposed a simple solution based on the notion of "purity", which is, in the presence of the reset operator, less restrictive than the notion of "syntactic values" in ML. We have also investigated two evaluation strategies for impredicative calculi, each of which generalizes ML's and Leroy's solutions for the unsoundness problem.

Several authors have studied polymorphic calculi with control operators for delimited continuations. Introducing polymorphism into a calculus with shift and reset has been implicit by Danvy who gave many programming examples (see, for instance, [4]). In fact, his interesting examples encouraged us to formulate the calculi in the present paper. Filinski [8] implemented shift and reset in SML/NJ, thus enabling one to write polymorphic functions with shift and reset. However, the expressivity of his system is limited since the answer type is fixed once and for all. The same goes for the calculus with `cupto` by Gunter et al. [10]. Kiselyov et al. [14] have implemented shift and reset in OCaml, and their examples made use of let-polymorphism. However, their paper did not give formal accounts for polymorphism. As far as we know, the present paper is the first to provide a systematic study on the interaction of polymorphism and control operators for delimited continuations.

Although we believe that our calculus serves as a good foundation for studying polymorphic delimited continuations calculi, this is only the first step; we need deeper understanding and better theories. The first author of the present paper has studied logical relations based on Danvy and Filinski's monomorphic type system [1], but it is not apparent if his result extends to the polymorphic case. Hasegawa [13] studied parametricity principle for the second order, call-by-name $\lambda\mu$-calculus (similar to System F + `call/cc`), and obtained the notion of "focal parametricity". Although he works in call-by-name, we hope to find some connection between our work and his results in the future. A recent work by Mogelberg and Simpson [16] treats a similar notion in call-by-value.

**Acknowledgments.** We would like to thank Olivier Danvy and Masahito Hasegawa for helpful comments and suggestions. This work was partly supported by JSPS Grant-in-Aid for Scientific Research (C) 18500005 and 16500004.

## References

1. Asai, K.: Logical Relations for Call-by-value Delimited Continuations. Trends in Functional Programming 6, 63–78 (2007)
2. Asai, K.: On Typing Delimited Continuations: Three New Solutions to the Printf Problem. See `http://pllab.is.ocha.ac.jp/~asai/papers/` (submitted, 2007)
3. Asai, K., Kameyama, Y.: Polymorphic Delimited Continuations. Technical Report CS-TR-07-10, Dept. of Computer Science, University of Tsukuba (September 2007)
4. Danvy, O.: An Analytical Approach to Program as Data Objects. DSc thesis, Department of Computer Science, University of Aarhus, Aarhus, Denmark (2006)
5. Danvy, O., Filinski, A.: A Functional Abstraction of Typed Contexts. Technical Report 89/12, DIKU, University of Copenhagen (July 1989)
6. Danvy, O., Filinski, A.: Abstracting Control. In: Proc. 1990 ACM Conference on Lisp and Functional Programming, pp. 151–160 (1990)
7. Danvy, O., Filinski, A.: Representing Control: a Study of the CPS Transformation. Mathematical Structures in Computer Science 2(4), 361–391 (1992)
8. Filinski, A.: Representing Monads. In: POPL, pp. 446–457 (1994)
9. Girard, J.-Y., Lafont, Y., Taylor, P.: Proofs and Types. Cambridge Tracts in Theoretical Computer Science, vol. 7. Cambridge University Press, Cambridge (1989)
10. Gunter, C.A., Remy, D., Riecke, J.G.: A Generalization of Exceptions and Control in ML-Like Languages. In: FPCA, pp. 12–23 (1995)
11. Harper, R., Duba, B.F., MacQueen, D.: Typing First-Class Continuations in ML. J. Funct. Program. 3(4), 465–484 (1993)
12. Harper, R., Lillibridge, M.: Explicit polymorphism and CPS conversion. In: POPL, pp. 206–219 (1993)
13. Hasegawa, M.: Relational parametricity and control. Logical Methods in Computer Science 2(3) (2006)
14. Kiselyov, O., Shan, C.-c., Sabry, A.: Delimited dynamic binding. In: ICFP, pp. 26–37 (2006)
15. Leroy, X.: Polymorphism by name for references and continuations. In: POPL, pp. 220–231 (1993)
16. Mogelberg, R.E., Simpson, A.: Relational parametricity for computational effects. In: LICS (2007)
17. Strachey, C.: Fundamental concepts in programming languages. International Summer School in Computer Programming, Copenhagen, Denmark (August 1967)
18. Thielecke, H.: From Control Effects to Typed Continuation Passing. In: POPL, pp. 139–149. ACM Press, New York (2003)
19. Tofte, M.: Type inference for polymorphic references. Inf. Comput. 89(1), 1–34 (1990)
20. Wright, A.K.: Simple imperative polymorphism. Lisp and Symbolic Computation 8(4), 343–355 (1995)
21. Wright, A.K., Felleisen, M.: A syntactic approach to type soundness. Inf. Comput. 115(1), 38–94 (1994)

# Adjunct Elimination in Context Logic for Trees

Cristiano Calcagno, Thomas Dinsdale-Young, and Philippa Gardner

Department of Computing
Imperial College London
London, UK
{ccris,td202,pg}@doc.ic.ac.uk

**Abstract.** We study adjunct-elimination results for Context Logic applied to trees, following previous results by Lozes for Separation Logic and Ambient Logic. In fact, it is not possible to prove such elimination results for the original single-holed formulation of Context Logic. Instead, we prove our results for multi-holed Context Logic.

## 1 Introduction

Separation Logic [1,2,3] and Ambient Logic [4] are related theories for reasoning, respectively, about local heap update and static trees. Inspired by this work, Calcagno, Gardner and Zarfaty invented Context Logic [5] for reasoning about structured resource, extending the general theory of Bunched Logic [6] for reasoning about unstructured resource. In particular, we use Context Logic applied to trees to reason about tree update, following the local reasoning style of Separation Logic; such reasoning is not possible using Ambient Logic [7].

These logics extend the standard propositional connectives with a structural (separating) composition for reasoning about disjoint subdata and the corresponding structural adjoint(s) for expressing properties such as weakest pre-conditions and safety conditions. For Separation Logic and Ambient Logic, Lozes [8] and then Dawar, Gardner and Ghelli [9] showed that the structural adjoints provide no additional expressive power on closed formulae. This result is interesting, as the adjunct connectives introduce quantification over potentially infinite sets whereas the structural composition only requires quantification over finite substructures. Following this work, Calcagno, Gardner and Zarfaty proved adjunct elimination for Context Logic applied to sequences, and showed the correspondence with the $*$-free regular languages [10,7]. We expected an analogous result for Context Logic applied to trees, but instead found a counter-example (first reported in Dinsdale-Young's Masters thesis [11]). Instead, we prove an adjunct-elimination result for *multi-holed* Context Logic applied to trees.

The original Context Logic was introduced to establish local Hoare reasoning about tree update. For this application, it was enough to work with single-holed contexts, although we always understood that there were other forms of contexts requiring study. Our counter-example to the adjunct-elimination result for single-holed Context Logic motivates our exploration of these other context structures. In our original presentation, the data formula $K(P)$ expresses that

Z. Shao (Ed.): APLAS 2007, LNCS 4807, pp. 255–270, 2007.

the given tree is the result of applying a single-holed context satisfying context formula $K$ to a tree satisfying data formula $P$. The adjunct context formula $P \triangleright Q$ expresses that, whenever a tree satisfying property $P$ is put in the context hole, then the resulting tree satisfies $Q$. Consider the single-holed context formula $0 \triangleright (True(u[0]))$ expressing that, when the empty tree 0 is put in the context hole, then somewhere there is a subtree of the form $u[0]$ with top node labelled $u$ and empty subtree. This formula cannot be expressed without the separating adjoint connective '$\triangleright$'. For example, consider contexts of the form $v^n[u[\_]]$, denoting a vertical line of $n$ nodes labelled $v$, followed by one node labelled $u$ and then the context hole. These contexts all satisfy the formula $0 \triangleright (True(u[0]))$, whereas the contexts $v^n[\_]$ do not. There is no adjoint-free context formula that can distinguish between these sets of contexts because, in our original presentation of Context Logic, trees can be split arbitrarily into contexts and trees, but contexts cannot be split. Our counter-example shows that such splitting is necessary for adjunct elimination to hold.

Context Logic can be extended with context composition, for analysing the splitting of contexts, and its adjoints. However, we currently do not know if adjunct elimination holds for this extension. We do know that current techniques for proving such results cannot be immediately adapted. Instead, we prove adjunct elimination for multi-holed Context Logic with context composition. Our proof, adapting the technique for proving adjunct elimination using model-checking games [9], naturally requires the extension to multi-holed contexts. To illustrate this, consider the tree $t = c_1(t_1)$ which denotes the application of context $c_1$ to tree $t_1$. An application move in a game will split $t$ into $c_2(t_2)$, leading to a case analysis relating $c_1$ and $t_1$ with $c_2$ and $t_2$ involving multi-holed contexts. For example, when $t_2$ is a subtree of $c_1$, this case is simply expressed using a two-holed context $d(\_,\_)$ with $d(t_2,\_) = c_1$ and $d(\_,t_1) = c_2$. Using multi-holed Context Logic, we are thus able to provide an adjunct-elimination result which conforms with the analogous results for Separation Logic and Ambient Logic. In addition, we believe multi-holed Context Logic presented here will play an important role in our future development of Context Logic since, although analysing multi-holed contexts was not necessary for our preliminary work on tree update, they do seem to be fundamental for other applications such as reasoning about concurrent tree update.

## 2 Multi-holed Context Logic for Trees

We work with finite, ordered, unranked trees (strictly speaking, forests) and contexts, with nodes labelled from a node alphabet $\Sigma$ ranged over by $u, v, w$. Our contexts are simply trees with some of the leaves — the context holes — uniquely labelled from a hole alphabet $X$, ranged over by $x, y, z$. We view trees as contexts without context holes.

**Definition 1 (Multi-holed Tree Contexts).** *We define the set of multi-holed tree contexts, $C_{\Sigma,X}$, ranged over by $c, d$, by the grammar*

$$c ::= \varepsilon \;\big|\; u[c] \;\big|\; c_1 \,|\, c_2 \;\big|\; x$$

*with the restriction that each hole label,* $x \in X$*, occurs* at most once *in the context* $c$*, and subject to the* $|$ *operator being associative and having identity* $\varepsilon$*. We denote the set of hole labels that occur in* $c$ *by* $fn(c)$*. We use* $u$ *as an abbreviation of* $u[\varepsilon]$*.*

**Definition 2 (Context Application).** *We define* context application *(or* context composition*) as a set of partial functions identified with the hole labels,* $ap_x : C_{\Sigma,X} \times C_{\Sigma,X} \rightharpoonup C_{\Sigma,X}$.

$$ap_x(c_1, c_2) = \begin{cases} c_1[c_2/x] & \textit{if } x \in fn(c_1) \textit{ and } fn(c_1) \cap fn(c_2) \subseteq \{x\} \\ \text{undefined} & \textit{otherwise} \end{cases}$$

*We abbreviate* $ap_x(c_1, c_2)$ *by* $c_1 \; ⓧ \; c_2$*.*

This definition of multi-holed context, also studied in [12], seems to be the most appropriate for our reasoning style, since it allows contexts to be separated easily. An alternative formulation is to order the holes, rather than uniquely name them, but this approach does not sit so naturally with separating contexts.

*Example 1.* The context $c_1 = u[u[v] \mid u[u \mid v]] \mid v$ is a tree with no hole labels. It may be expressed as the application of a single-holed context to another tree, e.g. $c_1 = u[x \mid u[u \mid v]] \mid v \; ⓧ \; u[v]$. It may also be expressed as a two-holed context applied to two trees, e.g. $c_1 = (u[x \mid u[u \mid y]] \mid v \; ⓨ \; v) \; ⓧ \; u[v]$. Recall that the context holes are labelled uniquely by $x$ and $y$, with the first application $u[x \mid u[u \mid y]] \mid v \; ⓨ \; v$ declaring that the argument $v$ should be placed in the hole labelled $y$. Note that $u[x \mid u[u \mid x]] \mid v$ does not fit our definition of a context since the hole label $x$ occurs more than once.

**Lemma 1.** *If* $y = x$ *or* $y \notin fn(c_1)$*, then* $c_1 \; ⓧ \; (c_2 \; ⓨ \; c_3) = (c_1 \; ⓧ \; c_2) \; ⓨ \; c_3$*, where defined.*

**Lemma 2.** *If* $y \neq x$*,* $x, y \in fn(c_1)$*,* $y \notin fn(c_2)$*,* $x \notin fn(c_3)$*, then*

$$(c_1 \; ⓧ \; c_2) \; ⓨ \; c_3 = (c_1 \; ⓨ \; c_3) \; ⓧ \; c_2.$$

We define multi-holed Context Logic for trees, denoted $CL^m_{Tree}$. For those who are familiar with Separation Logic and Ambient Logic, this follows the familiar pattern of extending the propositional connectives of classical logic with structural connectives for analysing the structure of multi-holed contexts, and specific connectives for analysing the particular data structure under consideration (in this case, trees).

**Definition 3 (Formulae of $CL^m_{Tree}$).** *Let* $\Theta$ *be an alphabet of hole variables ranged over by* $\alpha, \beta, \gamma$*. Multi-holed Context Logic formulae,* $K_1, K_2, \ldots$*, are defined by the grammar:*

$$\begin{aligned} K ::= \; & 0 \mid u[K] \mid K_1 \mid K_2 \\ & \alpha \mid K_1 \circ_\alpha K_2 \mid K_1 \circ\!\!-_\alpha K_2 \mid K_1 -\!\!\circ_\alpha K_2 \mid \exists \alpha. K \\ & \mathit{False} \mid K_1 \Rightarrow K_2. \end{aligned}$$

We use the Boolean connectives '*False*' and '$\Rightarrow$'. The specific connectives '0', '$u[]$' and '$|$' express basic structural properties of our tree contexts: a tree context is empty, has top node labelled $u$, or is the concatenation of two contexts respectively. The structural connectives '$\alpha$', '$\circ_\alpha$', '$\circ\!-_\alpha$' and '$-\!\circ_\alpha$' describe fundamental properties of multi-holed contexts. The connective '$\alpha$' expresses that a context is a hole whose label is the value of the variable $\alpha$. The '$\circ_\alpha$' specifies that a context is a composition of two contexts where the hole being filled is the value of $\alpha$. The '$\circ\!-_\alpha$' and '$-\!\circ_\alpha$' are the adjoints of composition: $K_1 \circ\!-_\alpha K_2$ expresses that, whenever a context satisfying $K_1$ is $\alpha$-composed *on the left* with the given context, the result satisfies $K_2$; while $K_1 -\!\circ_\alpha K_2$ expresses that, whenever a context satisfying $K_1$ is $\alpha$-composed *on the right* with the given context, the result satisfies $K_2$. In addition, we have existential quantification over hole labels, which allows us to specify context composition without specific reference to the hole name.

**Definition 4 (Satisfaction relation of $CL^m_{Tree}$).** *An environment is a finite partial function $\sigma : \Theta \rightharpoonup X$ which assigns hole labels to variables. We denote the empty environment by $\emptyset$, and the extension of $\sigma$ with a new domain element $\alpha$ with value $y$ by $\sigma[\alpha \mapsto y]$. The satisfaction relation for $CL^m_{Tree}$ is given with respect to an environment as follows, where $x = \sigma\alpha$:*

$$
\begin{aligned}
c, \sigma &\models 0 & &\Longleftrightarrow & c &= \varepsilon \\
c, \sigma &\models u[K] & &\Longleftrightarrow & &\exists c'. \, c = u[c'] \wedge c', \sigma \models K \\
c, \sigma &\models K_1 \mid K_2 & &\Longleftrightarrow & &\exists c_1, c_2. \, c = c_1 \mid c_2 \wedge c_1, \sigma \models K_1 \wedge c_2, \sigma \models K_2 \\
c, \sigma &\models \alpha & &\Longleftrightarrow & c &= x \\
c, \sigma &\models K_1 \circ_\alpha K_2 & &\Longleftrightarrow & &\exists c_1, c_2. \, c = c_1 \, \textcircled{x} \, c_2 \wedge c_1, \sigma \models K_1 \wedge c_2, \sigma \models K_2 \\
c, \sigma &\models K_1 \circ\!-_\alpha K_2 & &\Longleftrightarrow & &\forall c_1, c_2. \, c_2 = c_1 \, \textcircled{x} \, c \wedge c_1, \sigma \models K_1 \implies c_2, \sigma \models K_2 \\
c, \sigma &\models K_1 -\!\circ_\alpha K_2 & &\Longleftrightarrow & &\forall c_1, c_2. \, c_2 = c \, \textcircled{x} \, c_1 \wedge c_1, \sigma \models K_1 \implies c_2, \sigma \models K_2 \\
c, \sigma &\models \exists \alpha. \, K & &\Longleftrightarrow & &\exists y. \, c, \sigma[\alpha \mapsto y] \models K \\
c, \sigma &\not\models False & & & & \\
c, \sigma &\models K_1 \Rightarrow K_2 & &\Longleftrightarrow & c, \sigma &\models K_1 \implies c, \sigma \models K_2.
\end{aligned}
$$

We use two conventions for convenience. Firstly, we adopt Barendregt's convention and assume that bound variable names differ from free variable names, and furthermore differ from elements of the domain of any environment under consideration; if that is not the case, the bound variables may and are assumed to be renamed. Secondly, we only ever consider satisfaction of a formula when all of its free variables are assigned values by the environment. We also make use of standard derived connectives, where appropriate: *True*, $\neg, \wedge, \vee, \forall$. We assume the following binding order among the connectives: $\neg, \mid, \circ_\alpha, \wedge, \vee, \{\circ\!-_\alpha, -\!\circ_\alpha\}, \Rightarrow, \exists, \forall$, with no precedence between $\circ\!-_\alpha$ and $-\!\circ_\alpha$.

*Example 2.* We present a few example formulae

1. The formula $u[0]$ expresses that a tree consists of a single node labelled $u$.

**Table 1.** Ranks of Selected Formulae

| Formula | Rank |
|---|---|
| $u[0] \mid (u[0] \mid u[0]) \vee \neg 0$ | $(4, 0, \{u\})$ |
| $\exists\alpha.\, (\neg u[v[0] \mid \mathit{True}]) \circ_\alpha \beta$ | $(6, 0, \{u, v\})$ |
| $u[v[\alpha] \multimap_\alpha (w[0] \circ\!\!-_\beta v[u[w[0]]])]$ | $(5, 2, \{u, v, w\})$ |

2. The formula $\exists\alpha.\, (\mathit{True} \circ_\alpha u[0])$ expresses that a context contains tree $u[0]$.
3. The formula $(\mathit{True} \circ_\alpha \alpha)$ expresses that the value of $\alpha$ must be in the context.
4. The formula $\exists\alpha.\, (\mathit{True} \circ_\alpha \alpha) \wedge (0 \multimap_\alpha (\exists\beta.\, \mathit{True} \circ_\beta u[0]))$ expresses that the empty tree may be placed into some context hole such that the resulting tree has some leaf node labelled $u$.

As in the original Context Logic, we can derive the adjoints of the specific formulae: the adjoint of $u[-]$ is $\forall\alpha.\, (u[\alpha] \circ\!\!-_\alpha -)$; that of $- \mid K$ is $\forall\alpha.\, ((\alpha \mid K) \circ\!\!-_\alpha -)$; and that of $K \mid -$ is $\forall\alpha.\, ((K \mid \alpha) \circ\!\!-_\alpha -)$.

# 3 Games

We define Ehrenfeucht-Fraïssé style games for $CL^m_{\mathit{Tree}}$. The games are useful for our results because they are sound and complete with respect to the logic: two contexts can be distinguished by a logical formula if and only if Spoiler has a winning strategy for a corresponding game. Our presentation is similar to that of [9]. However, we use a more relaxed definition of rank, which simply distinguishes between the adjunct and non-adjunct moves. The proofs of the lemmata in this section will appear in the full version of this paper.

We first define the rank of a logical formula, a concept which is also used to parametrise games. Some examples are given in Table 1.

**Definition 5 (Rank).** *The* rank *of a formula is a tuple $r = (n, s, \mathcal{L})$ where:*

- *$n$ is the greatest nesting depth of the non-adjunct, non-Boolean connectives, i.e. $0, u[K], K_1 \mid K_2, \alpha, K_1 \circ_\alpha K_2, \exists\alpha.K$;*
- *$s$ is the greatest nesting depth of the adjunct, non-Boolean connectives, i.e. $K_1 \circ\!\!-_\alpha K_2, K_1 \multimap_\alpha K_2$; and*
- *$\mathcal{L}$ is the subset of $\Sigma$ consisting of the node labels that occur in the formula.*

**Lemma 3.** *For each rank $r$ and finite set of variables $\mathcal{V} \subset \Theta$, there are finitely many non-equivalent formulae of rank $r$ whose free variables are in $\mathcal{V}$.*

**Lemma 4.** *Let $\mathcal{T}$ be a set of context-environment pairs such that, for any $\mathcal{T}$-discriminated pair[1] $((c,\sigma),(c',\sigma'))$ there exists a formula $K_{(c,\sigma),(c',\sigma')}$ of rank $r$ and free variables in finite set $\mathcal{V}$ such that $c, \sigma \models K_{(c,\sigma),(c',\sigma')}$ and $c', \sigma' \not\models K_{(c,\sigma),(c',\sigma')}$. Then $\mathcal{T}$ can be defined by a rank-$r$ formula $K$ with free variables in $\mathcal{V}$.*

[1] A $\mathcal{T}$-discriminated pair is a pair $(a, b)$ with $a \in \mathcal{T}$ and $b \notin \mathcal{T}$, or $a \notin \mathcal{T}$ and $b \in \mathcal{T}$.

We now define the Ehrenfeucht-Fraïssé-style games that we shall use in our main result. A game state is a tuple, $((c, \sigma), (c', \sigma'), r)$, where $c$ and $c'$ are contexts, $\sigma$ and $\sigma'$ are environments with coincident domains, and $r = (n, s, \mathcal{L})$ is a rank. The game is played between two players, Spoiler and Duplicator. At each step, Spoiler selects a move to play, and the two players make choices according to the rules for that move. After a move is played out, either Spoiler will have won the game or the game will continue with a new state that has a reduced rank (either $n$ or $s$ will be reduced by one, depending on the move). If the rank reaches $(0, 0, \mathcal{L})$, Duplicator wins.

Each move in the game $((c, \sigma), (c', \sigma'), (n, s, \mathcal{L}))$ begins by Spoiler selecting one of the pairs $(c, \sigma)$ or $(c', \sigma')$. We shall call Spoiler's selection $(d, \rho)$ and the other $(d', \rho')$. Spoiler may only play a particular move when the rank allows it. A move is also prohibited when Spoiler cannot make the choice stipulated by the move. The moves are defined as follows:

Moves playable when $n > 0$ (the *non-adjunct moves*):

**EMP move.** Spoiler's choice is such that $d = \varepsilon$ and $d' \neq \varepsilon$. Spoiler wins.

**VAR move.** Spoiler chooses $\alpha \in \Theta$ with $d = \rho\alpha$ and $d' \neq \rho'\alpha$. Spoiler wins.

**LAB move.** Spoiler chooses some $u \in \mathcal{L}$ and $d_1 \in \mathcal{C}$ such that $d = u[d_1]$. If $d' = u[d'_1]$ for some $d'_1 \in \mathcal{C}$, the game continues with $((d_1, \rho), (d'_1, \rho'), (n-1, s, \mathcal{L}))$. Otherwise, Spoiler wins.

**PAR move.** Spoiler chooses some $d_1, d_2 \in \mathcal{C}$ such that $d = d_1 \mid d_2$. Duplicator chooses some $d'_1, d'_2 \in \mathcal{C}$ such that $d' = d'_1 \mid d'_2$. Spoiler decides whether the game continues with $((d_1, \rho), (d'_1, \rho'), (n-1, s, \mathcal{L}))$ or $((d_2, \rho), (d'_2, \rho'), (n-1, s, \mathcal{L}))$.

**CMP move.** Spoiler chooses $x = \rho\alpha$ for some $\alpha$, and $d_1, d_2 \in \mathcal{C}$ such that $d = d_1 \circledx d_2$. Duplicator then chooses $d'_1, d'_2 \in \mathcal{C}$ such that $d' = d'_1 \circled{\acute{x}} d'_2$ for $\acute{x} = \rho'\alpha$. Spoiler decides whether the game will continue with $((d_1, \rho), (d'_1, \rho'), (n-1, s, \mathcal{L}))$ or $((d_2, \rho), (d'_2, \rho'), (n-1, s, \mathcal{L}))$.

**EXS move.** Let $\alpha \in \Theta$ be some new hole variable (i.e. $\sigma\alpha$, and equivalently $\sigma'\alpha$, are undefined). Spoiler chooses some $x \in X$. Duplicator chooses an answering $\acute{x} \in X$. The game then continues with $((d, \rho[\alpha \mapsto x]), (d', \rho'[\alpha \mapsto \acute{x}]), (n-1, s, \mathcal{L}))$.

Moves playable when $s > 0$ (the *adjunct moves*):

**LEF move.** Spoiler chooses $x = \rho\alpha$ for some $\alpha$, and $d_1, d_2 \in \mathcal{C}$ such that $d_2 = d_1 \circledx d$. Duplicator then chooses $d'_1, d'_2 \in \mathcal{C}$ such that $d'_2 = d'_1 \circled{\acute{x}} d'$ for $\acute{x} = \rho'\alpha$. Spoiler decides whether the game will continue with $((d_1, \rho), (d'_1, \rho'), (n, s-1, \mathcal{L}))$ or $((d_2, \rho), (d'_2, \rho'), (n, s-1, \mathcal{L}))$.

**RIG move.** Spoiler chooses $x = \rho\alpha$ for some $\alpha$, and $d_1, d_2 \in \mathcal{C}$ such that $d_2 = d \circledx d_1$. Duplicator then chooses $d'_1, d'_2 \in \mathcal{C}$ such that $d'_2 = d' \circled{\acute{x}} d'_1$ for $\acute{x} = \rho'\alpha$. If Duplicator cannot make such a choice, Spoiler wins. Otherwise, Spoiler decides whether the game will continue with $((d_1, \rho), (d'_1, \rho'), (n, s-1, \mathcal{L}))$ or $((d_2, \rho), (d'_2, \rho'), (n, s-1, \mathcal{L}))$.

Of more interest than the outcome of an individual run of a game is the question of which player has a winning strategy for that game: Spoiler or Duplicator is capable of ensuring his or her victory regardless of how the other plays. If Spoiler has a winning strategy, we say $((c, \sigma), (c', \sigma'), r) \in SW$. Otherwise, we say $((c,\sigma),(c',\sigma'),r) \in DW$. The following useful properties are direct consequences of the definitions.

**Proposition 1 (Downward Closure).** *If* $((c,\sigma),(c',\sigma'),(n,s,\mathcal{L})) \in DW$ *then* $((c,\sigma),(c',\sigma'),(n',s',\mathcal{L}')) \in DW$ *for any* $n' \leq n$, $s' \leq s$ *and* $\mathcal{L}' \subseteq \mathcal{L}$.

**Proposition 2 (Downward Closure for Environments).** *If* $((c,\sigma[\alpha \mapsto x]), (c',\sigma'[\alpha \mapsto \acute{x}]),r) \in DW$ *then* $((c,\sigma),(c',\sigma'),r) \in DW$.

At each stage, Spoiler is trying to show that the two contexts are different, while Duplicator is trying to show that they are similar enough that Spoiler cannot identify a difference. The game moves correspond closely with the (non-Boolean) connectives of the logic. For instance, the RIG move corresponds to $\multimap_\alpha$ connective: it speaks of applying the given context to a new one and then reasoning about the result or the new context. If Spoiler wins on playing that move, it means that the two (current) trees are differentiated by the formula *True* $\multimap_\alpha$ *False* — one tree has a $\alpha$-labelled hole (so the formula is not satisfied) while the other does not (so the formula is satisfied trivially).

The reason for this correspondence is that formulae, of rank $r$, which distinguish between two contexts, will correspond to winning strategies for Spoiler for the game of rank $r$ on those two contexts. This is formalised in the soundness and completeness results which we state.

**Lemma 5 (Game Soundness).** *For* $c, c' \in \mathcal{C}$ *and domain-coincident environments* $\sigma, \sigma'$, *if there is a formula* $K$ *of rank* $r$ *such that* $c,\sigma \models K$ *and* $c',\sigma' \not\models K$, *then Spoiler has a winning strategy for the game* $((c,\sigma),(c',\sigma'),r)$.

**Lemma 6 (Game Completeness).** *If Spoiler has a winning strategy for the game* $((c,\sigma),(c',\sigma'),r)$ *then there exists a formula,* $K$, *of rank at most* $r$ *such that* $c,\sigma \models K$ *and* $c',\sigma' \not\models K$.

The following two lemmata are useful for checking structural properties. The first establishes a relationship between the hole labels in two contexts, which provides a convenient way of checking that composition is well defined. The second establishes a structural similarity through games. Both are proven by showing how Spoiler would have a winning strategy for the game in a certain number of moves (hence the bounds on $n$) if the desired property did not hold.

**Lemma 7.** *If* $((c,\sigma),(c',\sigma'),(n,s,\mathcal{L})) \in DW$ *with* $n \geq 2$, *then, for* $x = \sigma\alpha$, $\acute{x} = \sigma'\alpha$,

$$x \in fn(c) \iff \acute{x} \in fn(c')$$

**Lemma 8.** *Suppose that* $((c,\sigma),(c',\sigma'),(n,s,\mathcal{L})) \in DW$ *with* $n \geq 2$. *Then if* $c = \bar{c} \mid x$ *for* $x = \sigma\alpha$, $\bar{c} \in \mathcal{C}$ *then* $c' = \bar{c}' \mid \acute{x}$ *for* $\acute{x} = \sigma'\alpha$ *and some* $\bar{c}' \in \mathcal{C}$. *Similarly, if* $c = x \mid \bar{c}$ *then* $c' = \acute{x} \mid \bar{c}'$.

The next lemma essentially gives two sufficient conditions on Duplicator's response to the EXS move in order for it to give a winning strategy for her. The key part is that if Spoiler introduces a fresh hole label, Duplicator may respond by introducing *any* fresh hole label. The restriction on $n$ is used to establish freshness for the second of the cases.

**Lemma 9 (Interchangablity of Fresh Labels).** *If* $((c,\sigma),(c',\sigma'),(n,s,\mathcal{L})) \in DW$ *with* $n \geq 3$, *then* $((c,\sigma[\alpha \mapsto x]),(c',\sigma'[\alpha \mapsto \acute{x}]),(n-1,s,\mathcal{L})) \in DW$ *if either* $x = \sigma\beta$ *and* $\acute{x} = \sigma'\beta$, *or* $x \notin fn(c) \cup range(\sigma)$ *and* $\acute{x} \notin fn(c') \cup range(\sigma')$.

## 4 Adjunct Elimination

We now have the background required to prove adjunct elimination for $CL^m_{Tree}$. Proposition 3 is the key, most complicated result. It states that, with no adjunct moves, a winning strategy for the composition of contexts follows from winning strategies for its components. A consequence is that if Duplicator has a winning strategy with adjunct moves, then she has a winning strategy without adjunct moves, since adjunct moves simply perform context composition. The final theorem then translates this move elimination result into an adjunct elimination result for the formulae of the logic.

**Proposition 3 (One-step move elimination).** *For all ranks of the form* $r = (n, 0, \mathcal{L})$, *for all* $c_1, c_1', c_2, c_2' \in C$, *for all domain-coincident environments* $\sigma, \sigma'$, *if*

$$((c_1,\sigma),(c_1',\sigma'),(3n,0,\mathcal{L})) \in DW \tag{1}$$

$$((c_2,\sigma),(c_2',\sigma'),(3n,0,\mathcal{L})) \in DW \tag{2}$$

*then for all* $\alpha \in dom(\sigma)$ *with* $x = \sigma\alpha$, $\acute{x} = \sigma'\alpha$: *if* $c = c_1 \circledast_x c_2$ *and* $c' = c_1' \circledast_{\acute{x}} c_2'$ *are defined then*

$$((c,\sigma),(c',\sigma'),r) \in DW. \tag{3}$$

*Proof.* The proof is by induction on $n$ and by cases on Spoiler's choice of move in the game of (3). The base case, $n = 0$, is trivial, since Spoiler can never win a game of such a rank. We assume as the inductive hypothesis that the proposition holds for lesser values of $n$. Assume without loss of generality that Spoiler selects $(c, \sigma)$ for his move.

Throughout the proof, we consider strategies that Spoiler might adopt in the games of (1) and (2). Knowing that Duplicator has a winning strategy in these games, we are able to establish properties, usually concerning the structure of $c_1'$ and $c_2'$, based on her strategy, and, often using the inductive hypothesis, use these to construct a winning response for Duplicator to Spoiler's move on (3).

**EMP move.** In order for Spoiler to be able to play this move, it must be the case that $c = \varepsilon$ and $c' \neq \varepsilon$. Thus $c_1 = x$ and $c_2 = \varepsilon$. Hence $c_1' = \acute{x}$ and $c_2' = \varepsilon$, so $c' = \varepsilon$. Therefore, Spoiler cannot play this move after all.

**LAB move.** Suppose that Spoiler plays this move picking $u \in \mathcal{L}$ and $d \in C$ with $c = u[d]$. Then there are three cases of the possible structure of $c_1$ and $c_2$: 1. $c_1 = u[d_1]$ and $d = d_1 \circledast_x c_2$; 2. $c_1 = u[d] \mid x$ and $c_2 = \varepsilon$; 3. $c_1 = x \mid u[d]$ and $c_2 = \varepsilon$.

In the first of these cases, Spoiler could play the LAB move on the game of (1), with label $u$ and context $d_1$. Hence, by (1), $c_1' = u[d_1']$ with

$$((d_1,\sigma),(d_1',\sigma'),(3n-1,0,\mathcal{L})) \in DW. \tag{4}$$

By downward closure and the inductive hypothesis, noting that $d'_1 \textcircled{\scriptsize $\acute{x}$} c'_2$ is defined, since $fn(d'_1) = fn(c'_1)$ and $c'_1 \textcircled{\scriptsize $\acute{x}$} c'_2$ is defined, it follows that

$$((d_1 \textcircled{\scriptsize $x$} c_2, \sigma), (d'_1 \textcircled{\scriptsize $\acute{x}$} c'_2, \sigma'), (n-1, 0, \mathcal{L})) \in DW. \tag{5}$$

By structural considerations, $c' = u[d']$ where $d' = d'_1 \textcircled{\scriptsize $\acute{x}$} c'_2$. Thus Duplicator has a winning strategy when Spoiler plays this way.

In the second of the cases, $c'_2 = \varepsilon$ by (2). Further, Spoiler could play the PAR move on (1) so we have $c'_1 = d'_1 \mid d'_2$ with

$$((u[d], \sigma), (d'_1, \sigma'), (3n-1, 0, \mathcal{L})) \in DW \tag{6}$$
$$((x, \sigma), (d'_2, \sigma'), (3n-1, 0, \mathcal{L})) \in DW. \tag{7}$$

Since $3n - 1 \geq 1$, by (7) we know $d'_2 = \acute{x}$. Spoiler could play the LAB move on the former, using $u$ as the label, so that we must have $d'_1 = u[d']$ with

$$((d, \sigma), (d', \sigma'), (3n-2, 0, \mathcal{L})) \in DW. \tag{8}$$

We now have $c' = (u[d'] \mid \acute{x}) \textcircled{\scriptsize $\acute{x}$} \varepsilon = u[d']$. Hence, Duplicator can respond and the game continues as $((d, \sigma), (d', \sigma'), (n-1, 0, \mathcal{L}))$ and, by downward closure on (8), Duplicator has a winning strategy. The third case is essentially the same as this.

In each of the three cases, Duplicator has a winning strategy, so she has a winning strategy if Spoiler plays the LAB move.

**PAR move.** In this move, Spoiler splits $c = d_1 \mid d_2$ in one of three ways:

1. Spoiler splits in $c_1$ to the left of the $x$. That is, $c_1 = d_1 \mid d_3$, $d_2 = d_3 \textcircled{\scriptsize $x$} c_2$.
2. Spoiler splits in $c_1$ to the right of the $x$. This case is essentially the same as the first, so we shall not consider it.
3. Spoiler splits in $c_2$. In order for this case to be applicable, the $x$ must occur at the top level of $c_1$, so $c_1 = \bar{d}_3 \mid x \mid \bar{d}_4$, $d_1 = \bar{d}_3 \mid d_5$ and $d_2 = d_6 \mid \bar{d}_4$ with

$$c_1 \textcircled{\scriptsize $x$} c_2 = d_1 \mid d_2 = (d_3 \textcircled{\scriptsize $x$} d_5) \mid (d_4 \textcircled{\scriptsize $x$} d_6)$$
$$d_3 = \bar{d}_3 \mid x \qquad d_4 = x \mid \bar{d}_4$$
$$c_1 = d_3 \textcircled{\scriptsize $x$} d_4 = (\bar{d}_3 \mid x) \textcircled{\scriptsize $x$} (x \mid \bar{d}_4) \qquad c_2 = d_5 \mid d_6.$$

In the first case, $c_1 \textcircled{\scriptsize $x$} c_2 = (d_1 \mid d_3) \textcircled{\scriptsize $x$} c_2 = d_1 \mid (d_3 \textcircled{\scriptsize $x$} c_2)$. As Spoiler could play the PAR move in the game in (1), we know that $c'_1 = d'_1 \mid d'_3$ such that

$$((d_1, \sigma), (d'_1, \sigma'), (3n-1, 0, \mathcal{L})) \in DW \tag{9}$$
$$((d_3, \sigma), (d'_3, \sigma'), (3n-1, 0, \mathcal{L})) \in DW. \tag{10}$$

Note that $fn(d'_3) \subseteq fn(c'_1)$ and $\acute{x} \in fn(d'_3)$ by Lemma 7 (since $x \in fn(d_3)$), so $d'_2 = d'_3 \textcircled{\scriptsize $\acute{x}$} c'_2$ is defined. By downward closure on (10) and (2) and by the inductive hypothesis,

$$((d_3 \textcircled{\scriptsize $x$} c_2, \sigma), (d'_3 \textcircled{\scriptsize $\acute{x}$} c'_2, \sigma'), (n-1, 0, \mathcal{L})) \in DW. \tag{11}$$

Observe that $c' = c'_1 \textcircled{\acute{x}} c'_2 = (d'_1 \mid d'_3) \textcircled{\acute{x}} c'_2 = d'_1 \mid (d'_3 \textcircled{\acute{x}} c'_2) = d'_1 \mid d'_2$. Thus responding with $d'_1$ and $d'_2$ gives Duplicator a winning strategy in this case, by downward closure on (9) and by (11).

In the third case, Spoiler could play the CMP move on the game in (1), so $c'_1 = d'_3 \textcircled{\acute{x}} d'_4$ with

$$((d_3, \sigma), (d'_3, \sigma'), (3n-1, 0, \mathcal{L})) \in DW \tag{12}$$
$$((d_4, \sigma), (d'_4, \sigma'), (3n-1, 0, \mathcal{L})) \in DW. \tag{13}$$

Also, Spoiler could play the PAR move on the game in (2), so $c'_2 = d'_5 \mid d'_6$ with

$$((d_5, \sigma), (d'_5, \sigma'), (3n-1, 0, \mathcal{L})) \in DW \tag{14}$$
$$((d_6, \sigma), (d'_6, \sigma'), (3n-1, 0, \mathcal{L})) \in DW. \tag{15}$$

Since $c'_1 = d'_3 \textcircled{\acute{x}} d'_4$ and $c'_2 = d'_5 \mid d'_6$, it follows that that $\acute{x} \in fn(d'_3) \subseteq fn(c'_1)$, $\acute{x} \in fn(d'_4) \subseteq fn(c'_1)$, $fn(d'_5) \subseteq fn(c'_2)$ and $fn(d'_6) \subseteq fn(c'_2)$. Hence $d'_1 = d'_3 \textcircled{\acute{x}} d'_5$ and $d'_2 = d'_4 \textcircled{\acute{x}} d'_6$ are well defined. By downward closure and the inductive hypothesis on (12) and (14), and on (13) and (15), we get

$$((d_3 \textcircled{x} d_5, \sigma), (d'_3 \textcircled{\acute{x}} d'_5, \sigma'), (n-1, 0, \mathcal{L})) \in DW \tag{16}$$
$$((d_4 \textcircled{x} d_6, \sigma), (d'_4 \textcircled{\acute{x}} d'_6, \sigma'), (n-1, 0, \mathcal{L})) \in DW. \tag{17}$$

It remains to show that $c' = d'_1 \mid d'_2$. For this to be the case, it is sufficient that $d'_3 = \bar{d}'_3 \mid \acute{x}$ and $d'_4 = \acute{x} \mid \bar{d}'_4$, which both hold by applying Lemma 8 to (12) and (13). Thus, by structural considerations, $c' = c'_1 \textcircled{\acute{x}} c'_2 = (d'_3 \textcircled{\acute{x}} d'_4) \textcircled{\acute{x}} (d'_5 \mid d'_6) = ((\bar{d}'_3 \mid \acute{x}) \textcircled{\acute{x}} (\acute{x} \mid \bar{d}'_4)) \textcircled{\acute{x}} (d'_5 \mid d'_6) = \bar{d}'_3 \mid d'_5 \mid d'_6 \mid \bar{d}'_4 = (d'_3 \textcircled{\acute{x}} d'_5) \mid (d'_4 \textcircled{\acute{x}} d'_6) = d'_1 \mid d'_2$. Hence, by (16) and (17), Duplicator has a winning strategy if she responds by splitting $c'$ as $d'_1 \mid d'_2$.

Thus, Duplicator has a winning strategy whenever Spoiler plays the PAR move.

**CMP move.** In this move, Spoiler chooses $y = \sigma\beta$ (let $\acute{y} = \sigma'\beta$), and splits $c_1 \textcircled{x} c_2$ as $d_1 \textcircled{y} d_2$. Note that Spoiler cannot play the CMP move as the final move of a winning strategy, so we may therefore assume that $n \geq 2$. (If $n = 1$, Duplicator would have a winning strategy by splitting $c' = \acute{y} \textcircled{\acute{y}} c'$, for instance.)

There are four cases for how Spoiler can make the splitting $c = d_1 \textcircled{y} d_2$. We shall consider each in turn.

*Case 1:* Spoiler splits inside $c_2$, as

$$c_1 \textcircled{x} c_2 = c_1 \textcircled{x} (d_3 \textcircled{y} d_2) = (c_1 \textcircled{x} d_3) \textcircled{y} d_2 = d_1 \textcircled{y} d_2$$
$$c_2 = d_3 \textcircled{y} d_2 \qquad d_1 = c_1 \textcircled{x} d_3.$$

Spoiler would be able to play the CMP move on the game in (2), so Duplicator must be able to split $c'_2$ as $d'_3 \textcircled{\acute{y}} d'_2$ such that

$$((d_3, \sigma), (d'_3, \sigma'), (3n-1, 0, \mathcal{L})) \in DW \tag{18}$$
$$((d_2, \sigma), (d'_2, \sigma'), (3n-1, 0, \mathcal{L})) \in DW. \tag{19}$$

Note that $fn(d'_3) \subseteq fn(c'_2) \cup \{\acute{y}\}$. Also, by Lemma 7, $\acute{y} \notin fn(c'_1)$ since $y \notin fn(c_1)$. Hence $d'_1 = c'_1 \textcircled{\acute{x}} d'_3$ is well defined. By downward closure on (1) and (18) and by the inductive hypothesis,

$$((c_1 \textcircled{x} d_3, \sigma), (c'_2 \textcircled{\acute{x}} d'_3, \sigma'), (n-1, 0, \mathcal{L})) \in DW. \tag{20}$$

By Lemma 1, since $\acute{y} \notin fn(c'_1)$, $c'_1 \textcircled{\acute{x}} c'_2 = c'_1 \textcircled{\acute{x}} (d'_3 \textcircled{\acute{y}} d'_2) = (c'_1 \textcircled{\acute{x}} d'_3) \textcircled{\acute{y}} d'_2 = d'_1 \textcircled{\acute{y}} d'_2$. Hence, by (20) and by downward closure on (19), Duplicator has a winning strategy if she splits $c'$ as $d'_1 \textcircled{\acute{y}} d'_2$.

*Case 2:* Spoiler splits outside $c_2$, including all of $c_2$ itself:

$$c_1 \textcircled{x} c_2 = (d_1 \textcircled{y} d_3) \textcircled{x} c_2 = d_1 \textcircled{y} (d_3 \textcircled{x} c_2) = d_1 \textcircled{y} d_2$$
$$c_1 = d_1 \textcircled{y} d_3 \qquad d_2 = d_3 \textcircled{x} c_2.$$

Spoiler would be able to play the CMP move on the game in (1), so Duplicator must be able to split $c'_1$ as $d'_1 \textcircled{\acute{y}} d'_3$ such that

$$((d_1, \sigma), (d'_1, \sigma'), (3n-1, 0, \mathcal{L})) \in DW \tag{21}$$
$$((d_3, \sigma), (d'_3, \sigma'), (3n-1, 0, \mathcal{L})) \in DW. \tag{22}$$

Note that $fn(d'_3) \subseteq fn(c'_1)$ and that, by Lemma 7, $\acute{x} \in fn(d'_3)$ since $x \in fn(d_3)$. Thus $d'_2 = d'_3 \textcircled{\acute{x}} c'_2$ is well defined. By downward closure on (22) and (1) and by the inductive hypothesis,

$$((d_3 \textcircled{x} c_2, \sigma), (d'_3 \textcircled{\acute{x}} c'_2, \sigma'), (n-1, 0, \mathcal{L})) \in DW. \tag{23}$$

By Lemma 1, since $\acute{x} \notin fn(d'_1)$ (since $\acute{x} \in fn(d'_3)$ and $c'_1 = d'_1 \textcircled{\acute{y}} d'_3$), $c'_1 \textcircled{\acute{x}} c'_2 = (d'_1 \textcircled{\acute{y}} d'_3) \textcircled{\acute{x}} c'_2 = d'_1 \textcircled{\acute{y}} (d'_3 \textcircled{\acute{x}} c'_2) = d'_1 \textcircled{\acute{y}} d'_2$. Hence, by downward closure on (21) and by (23), Duplicator has a winning strategy if she splits $c'$ as $d'_1 \textcircled{\acute{y}} d'_2$.

*Case 3:* Spoiler splits part of $c_1$ and part of $c_2$:

$$c_1 = d_3 \textcircled{x} d_4 \qquad c_2 = d_5 \textcircled{y} d_6 \qquad d_1 = d_3 \textcircled{x} d_5 \qquad d_2 = d_4 \textcircled{x} d_6$$

with either: $d_4 = \bar{d}_4 \mid x$ and $d_5 = y \mid \bar{d}_5$; or $d_4 = x \mid \bar{d}_4$ and $d_5 = \bar{d}_5 \mid y$. In the former, for instance, we have

$$\begin{aligned} c_1 \textcircled{x} c_2 &= (d_3 \textcircled{x} d_4) \textcircled{x} (d_5 \textcircled{y} d_6) = (d_3 \textcircled{x} (\bar{d}_4 \mid x)) \textcircled{x} ((y \mid \bar{d}_5) \textcircled{y} d_6) \\ &= d_3 \textcircled{x} (\bar{d}_4 \mid d_6 \mid \bar{d}_5) = (d_3 \textcircled{x} (y \mid \bar{d}_5)) \textcircled{y} ((\bar{d}_4 \mid x) \textcircled{x} d_6) \\ &= (d_3 \textcircled{x} d_5) \textcircled{y} (d_4 \textcircled{x} d_6) = d_1 \textcircled{y} d_2. \end{aligned}$$

Spoiler could play the CMP move on (1), so $c'_1 = d'_3 \textcircled{\acute{x}} d'_4$ such that

$$((d_3, \sigma), (d'_3, \sigma'), (3n-1, 0, \mathcal{L})) \in DW \tag{24}$$
$$((d_4, \sigma), (d'_4, \sigma'), (3n-1, 0, \mathcal{L})) \in DW. \tag{25}$$

Similarly, from (2), we have that $c'_2 = d'_5 \textcircled{\acute{y}} d'_6$ such that

$$((d_5, \sigma), (d'_5, \sigma'), (3n-1, 0, \mathcal{L})) \in DW \tag{26}$$
$$((d_6, \sigma), (d'_6, \sigma'), (3n-1, 0, \mathcal{L})) \in DW. \tag{27}$$

Note that $\acute{x} \in fn(d'_3) \subseteq fn(c'_1)$ and $fn(d'_5) \subseteq fn(c'_2) \cup \{\acute{y}\}$. Furthermore, by Lemma 7, $\acute{y} \notin fn(d'_3)$, since $y \notin fn(d_3)$. Thus $d'_1 = d'_3 \textcircled{\acute{x}} d'_5$ is well defined. Similarly, $\acute{x} \in fn(d'_4) \subseteq fn(c'_1)$ and $fn(d'_6) \subseteq fn(c'_2)$, so $d'_2 = d'_4 \textcircled{\acute{x}} d'_6$ is well defined. Hence, by downward closure on (24), (26), (25) and (27), and by the inductive hypothesis, we have

$$((d_3 \textcircled{x} d_5, \sigma), (d'_3 \textcircled{\acute{x}} d'_5, \sigma'), (n-1, 0, \mathcal{L})) \in DW \tag{28}$$

$$((d_4 \textcircled{x} d_6, \sigma), (d'_4 \textcircled{\acute{x}} d'_6, \sigma'), (n-1, 0, \mathcal{L})) \in DW. \tag{29}$$

It remains to show that $c'_1 \textcircled{\acute{x}} c'_2 = d'_1 \textcircled{\acute{y}} d'_2$. By Lemma 1, $c'_1 \textcircled{\acute{x}} c'_2 = (d'_3 \textcircled{\acute{x}} d'_4) \textcircled{\acute{x}} (d'_5 \textcircled{\acute{y}} d'_6) = d'_3 \textcircled{\acute{x}} (d'_4 \textcircled{\acute{x}} (d'_5 \textcircled{\acute{y}} d'_6))$. Now suppose that $d_4 = \bar{d}_4 \mid x$ and $d_5 = y \mid \bar{d}_5$. By Lemma 8, we must have that $d'_4 = \bar{d}'_4 \mid \acute{x}$ and $d'_5 = \acute{y} \mid \bar{d}'_5$. Thus, $d'_4 \textcircled{\acute{x}} (d'_5 \textcircled{\acute{y}} d'_6) = \bar{d}'_4 \mid d'_6 \mid \bar{d}'_5 = d'_5 \textcircled{\acute{y}} (d'_4 \textcircled{\acute{x}} d'_6)$. In the alternative case (where $d_4 = x \mid \bar{d}_4$ and $d_5 = \bar{d}_5 \mid y$) the analogous result can be deduced. Hence, and by Lemma 1 (recalling that $\acute{y} \notin fn(d'_3)$), $c'_1 \textcircled{\acute{x}} c'_2 = d'_3 \textcircled{\acute{x}} (d'_5 \textcircled{\acute{y}} (d'_4 \textcircled{\acute{x}} d'_6)) = (d'_3 \textcircled{\acute{x}} d'_5) \textcircled{\acute{y}} (d'_4 \textcircled{\acute{x}} d'_6) = d'_1 \textcircled{\acute{y}} d'_2$, as required. We can see that Duplicator could respond to Spoiler's move by splitting $c'$ as $d'_1 \textcircled{\acute{y}} d'_2$ and that, by (28) and (29), this gives her a winning strategy.

*Case 4*: Spoiler splits part of $c_1$ disjoint from $c_2$. There are two subcases on Spoiler's choice of $y$ that we shall consider separately: (a) $y \neq x$ and (b) $y = x$.

*(a) $y \neq x$:*

$$c_1 \textcircled{x} c_2 = (d_3 \textcircled{y} d_2) \textcircled{x} c_2 = (d_3 \textcircled{x} c_2) \textcircled{y} d_2 = d_1 \textcircled{y} d_2$$
$$c_1 = d_3 \textcircled{y} d_2 \qquad d_1 = d_3 \textcircled{x} c_2$$

Spoiler would be able to play the CMP move on the game in (1), so we know that $c'_1 = d'_3 \textcircled{\acute{y}} d'_2$ for some $d'_3, d'_2$ such that

$$((d_3, \sigma), (d'_3, \sigma'), (3n-1, 0, \mathcal{L})) \in DW \tag{30}$$

$$((d_2, \sigma), (d'_2, \sigma'), (3n-1, 0, \mathcal{L})) \in DW. \tag{31}$$

Note that $fn(d'_3) \subseteq fn(c'_1) \cup \{\acute{y}\}$. Also, by Lemma 7, $\acute{x} \in fn(d'_3)$ and $\acute{y} \notin fn(c'_2)$. Thus $d'_1 = d'_3 \textcircled{\acute{x}} c'_2$ is well defined. By downward closure on (30) and (2), and by the inductive hypothesis,

$$((d_3 \textcircled{x} c_2, \sigma), (d'_3 \textcircled{\acute{x}} c'_2, \sigma'), (n-1, 0, \mathcal{L})) \in DW. \tag{32}$$

By Lemma 2, since $\acute{x} \in fn(d'_3)$ and $\acute{y} \notin fn(c'_2)$, $(d'_3 \textcircled{\acute{y}} d'_2) \textcircled{\acute{x}} c'_2 = (d'_3 \textcircled{\acute{x}} c'_2) \textcircled{\acute{y}} d'_2$. Hence, by (32) and downward closure on (31), we know that Duplicator has a winning strategy by splitting $c'$ as $d'_1 \textcircled{\acute{y}} d'_2$.

*(b) $y = x$*: For some $z \notin fn(c_1) \cup fn(c_2) \cup range(\sigma)$,

$$c = ((d_3 \textcircled{x} d_2) \textcircled{z} x) \textcircled{x} c_2 = (d_3 \textcircled{x} d_2) \textcircled{z} c_2 = (d_3 \textcircled{z} c_2) \textcircled{x} d_2 = d_1 \textcircled{x} d_2$$
$$c_1 = \bar{c}_1 \textcircled{z} x \qquad \bar{c}_1 = d_3 \textcircled{x} d_2 \qquad d_1 = d_3 \textcircled{z} c_2.$$

By Lemma 9, for some $\acute{z} \notin fn(c'_1) \cup fn(c'_2) \cup range(\sigma')$,

$$((c_1, \sigma[\gamma \mapsto z]), (c'_1, \sigma'[\gamma \mapsto \acute{z}]), (3n-1, 0, \mathcal{L})) \in DW \tag{33}$$

$$((c_2, \sigma[\gamma \mapsto z]), (c'_2, \sigma'[\gamma \mapsto \acute{z}]), (3n-1, 0, \mathcal{L})) \in DW. \tag{34}$$

Spoiler could play the CMP move on the game in (33), splitting $c_1$ as $\bar{c}_1 \textcircled{z} x$, so $c'_1 = \bar{c}'_1 \textcircled{\acute{z}} \hat{c}'_1$ such that

$$((\bar{c}_1, \sigma[\gamma \mapsto z]), (\bar{c}'_1, \sigma'[\gamma \mapsto \acute{z}]), (3n-2, 0, \mathcal{L})) \in DW \tag{35}$$
$$((x, \sigma[\gamma \mapsto z]), (\hat{c}'_1, \sigma'[\gamma \mapsto \acute{z}]), (3n-2, 0, \mathcal{L})) \in DW. \tag{36}$$

Since $3n - 2 \geq 1$, (36) implies that $\hat{c}'_1 = \acute{x}$. Spoiler could then play the CMP move on the game in (35), splitting $\bar{c}_1$ as $d_3 \textcircled{x} d_2$, so $\bar{c}'_1 = d'_3 \textcircled{\acute{x}} d'_2$ such that

$$((d_3, \sigma[\gamma \mapsto z]), (d'_3, \sigma'[\gamma \mapsto \acute{z}]), (3n-3, 0, \mathcal{L})) \in DW \tag{37}$$
$$((d_2, \sigma[\gamma \mapsto z]), (d'_2, \sigma'[\gamma \mapsto \acute{z}]), (3n-3, 0, \mathcal{L})) \in DW. \tag{38}$$

By construction and by Lemma 7 (recalling that $n \geq 2$), $\{\acute{x}, \acute{z}\} \subseteq fn(d'_3) \subseteq (fn(c') \setminus fn(c'_2)) \cup \{\acute{x}, \acute{z}\}$. Further, by Lemma 7 and by definition, neither $\acute{x}$ nor $\acute{z}$ occurs in $c'_2$. Hence $d'_1 = d'_3 \textcircled{\acute{z}} c'_2$ is well defined. Now we may apply the inductive hypothesis, using (37) and downward closure on (34), to obtain

$$((d_3 \textcircled{z} c_2, \sigma[\gamma \mapsto z]), (d'_3 \textcircled{\acute{z}} c'_2, \sigma[\gamma \mapsto \acute{z}]), (n-1, 0, \mathcal{L})) \in DW. \tag{39}$$

By (environment) downward closure on (39) and (38), we have

$$((d_1, \sigma), (d'_1, \sigma'), (n-1, 0, \mathcal{L})) \in DW \tag{40}$$
$$((d_2, \sigma), (d'_2, \sigma'), (n-1, 0, \mathcal{L})) \in DW. \tag{41}$$

Note that, by construction and by Lemma 7, $\acute{x}, \acute{z} \notin fn(d'_2)$ and $\acute{x} \notin fn(c'_2)$. Thus, by structural considerations and Lemma 2, $c' = ((d'_3 \textcircled{\acute{x}} d'_2) \textcircled{\acute{z}} \acute{x}) \textcircled{\acute{x}} c'_2 = (d'_3 \textcircled{\acute{x}} d'_2) \textcircled{\acute{z}} c'_2 = (d'_3 \textcircled{\acute{z}} c'_2) \textcircled{\acute{x}} d'_2 = d'_1 \textcircled{\acute{x}} d'_2$. Hence Duplicator could respond by splitting $c'$ as $d'_1 \textcircled{\acute{x}} d'_2$ and by (40) and (41) that gives her a winning strategy.

We have considered all of the possible cases for how Spoiler could play CMP move, and shown that Duplicator has a winning response in each. Therefore, Duplicator has a winning strategy if Spoiler plays the CMP move.

**EXS move.** In playing this move, Spoiler chooses to instantiate $\beta$ as $y$, say. If $n = 1$, any choice gives Duplicator a winning strategy, so assume $n \geq 2$. We consider four mutually exclusive cases for Spoiler's choice: 1. $y \in range(\sigma)$; 2. $y \in fn(c_1)$ but $y \notin range(\sigma)$; 3. $y \in fn(c_2)$ but $y \notin range(\sigma)$; and 4. $y$ is fresh ($y \notin fn(c_1) \cup fn(c_2) \cup range(\sigma)$).

In case 1, $y = \sigma\alpha$ for some $\alpha$, and Duplicator can respond with $\acute{y} = \sigma'\alpha$. By the first case of Lemma 9, we know

$$((c_1, \sigma[\beta \mapsto y]), (c'_1, \sigma'[\beta \mapsto \acute{y}]), (3n-1, 0, \mathcal{L})) \in DW \tag{42}$$
$$((c_2, \sigma[\beta \mapsto y]), (c'_2, \sigma'[\beta \mapsto \acute{y}]), (3n-1, 0, \mathcal{L})) \in DW \tag{43}$$

and so, by downward closure and the inductive hypothesis,

$$((c, \sigma[\beta \mapsto y]), (c', \sigma'[\beta \mapsto \acute{y}]), (n-1, 0, \mathcal{L})) \in DW. \tag{44}$$

Hence choosing $\acute{y}$ gives Duplicator a winning strategy in this case.

In case 2, note that Spoiler could play the EXS move on the game in (1). Let $\acute{y}$ be Duplicator's response for her winning strategy:

$$((c_1, \sigma[\beta \mapsto y]), (c_1', \sigma'[\beta \mapsto \acute{y}]), (3n-1, 0, \mathcal{L})) \in DW. \tag{45}$$

Since $y \notin range(\sigma)$ and $3n - 2 \geq 2$, $\acute{y} \notin range(\sigma')$.[2] Also, since $y \in fn(c_1)$ and $3n - 2 \geq 2$, $\acute{y} \in fn(c_1')$ by Lemma 7. Thus, $y \notin fn(c_2) \cup range(\sigma)$ and $\acute{y} \notin fn(c_2') \cup range(\sigma')$, and hence, by the second case of Lemma 9,

$$((c_2, \sigma[\beta \mapsto y]), (c_2', \sigma'[\beta \mapsto \acute{y}]), (3n-1, 0, \mathcal{L})) \in DW. \tag{46}$$

So by downward closure and the inductive hypothesis we have

$$((c, \sigma[\beta \mapsto y]), (c, \sigma'[\beta \mapsto \acute{y}]), (n-1, 0, \mathcal{L})) \in DW. \tag{47}$$

Hence choosing $\acute{y}$ gives Duplicator a winning strategy in this case.

Case 3 is essentially the same as case 2, except that Duplicator's choice, $\acute{y}$ is derived from her winning response for the game in (2). Case 4 admits the same proof as case 2 (or indeed case 3). Having examined each case, we see that Duplicator has a winning response to Spoiler playing the EXS move.

Since we have now examined each possible move Spoiler could make in the game of (3) and concluded that Duplicator has a winning strategy in each case, we have shown that (3) holds. □

**Corollary 1 (Multi-step Move Elimination).** *For all ranks* $r = (n, s, \mathcal{L})$, *for all* $c, c' \in C$ *and for all domain-coincident environments* $\sigma, \sigma'$, *if*

$$((c, \sigma), (c', \sigma'), (3^s(n+1), 0, \mathcal{L})) \in DW \tag{48}$$

*then*

$$((c, \sigma), (c', \sigma'), (n, s, \mathcal{L})) \in DW. \tag{49}$$

*Proof (Sketch[3]).* The proof is by induction on the number of adjunct moves, $s$. We suppose that Spoiler is trying to find a winning strategy for the game in (49) and see that the moves he makes in that game can be replicated on the game in (48) until he first plays one of the adjunct moves. When he plays his first adjunct move, he introduces a new context to either apply around one of the contexts in the current state, or to apply the current context to.

We find a response for Duplicator by renaming the holes of Spoiler's choice so that the application is defined for her side of the game and so that she has a winning strategy if Spoiler chooses to continue with these newly introduced contexts. Proposition 3 shows that Duplicator has a winning strategy for the composed pair with an adjunct-free rank. Now, we can use the inductive hypothesis to deduce that Duplicator has a winning strategy for the game with $s-1$ adjunct moves, as required. □

[2] To see this, suppose that Spoiler plays the CMP move and splits $c_1 = y ⓨ c_1$ (having played the EXS move as described). Duplicator could not have a winning strategy since there is some $\gamma$ with $\acute{y} = \sigma'\gamma$ but $y \neq \sigma\gamma$.

[3] The full proof will appear in the full version of this paper.

These game results are now translated to results in the logic in the following theorem. The proof is not difficult (it depends on Lemma 4), and will appear in the full version of this paper.

**Theorem 1 (Adjunct Elimination).** *If* $r = (n, s, \mathcal{L})$ *and* $r' = (3^s(n+1), 0, \mathcal{L})$ *then, for any formula of rank* $r$*, there exists an equivalent formula of rank* $r'$*.*

## 5 Conclusions

We have introduced multi-holed Context Logic for trees ($CL^m_{Tree}$) and proved adjunct elimination. Our initial motivation was simply to understand if Lozes' results for Separation Logic and Ambient Logic extended to the original formulation of Context Logic. When we observed that this was not the case, this work turned from being a routine adaptation of previous results into a fundamental investigation of a natural version of Context Logic in which the adjoints could be eliminated.

Many open problems remain. We studied multi-holed Context Logic initially because we were unable to prove adjunct elimination for single-holed Context Logic with composition. We believe the result also holds for the single-holed case, but have not been able to prove it with current techniques. A further question, which would imply this result, is whether, in the absence of adjoints, multi-holed and and single-holed Context Logic with composition have equally expressive satisfaction relations on closed formulae for analysing trees (contexts without holes). This result appears to be difficult to prove.

Such results about expressivity on closed formulae form an important part of our investigation into the true nature of Context Logic for trees, not only because they provide a test on what is a natural formulation of Context Logic but also because they allow us to link our analysis of structured data (in this case trees) with traditional results about regular languages. For example, Heuter [12] has shown that a regular expression language, similar to multi-holed Context logic applied to *ranked* trees and without structural adjoints, is as expressive as First-order Logic (FOL) on ranked trees. Recently, Bojańczyk [13] has proved that a language equivalent to single-holed Context Logic for unranked trees, with composition but no adjoints, corresponds to FOL on forests. These results make use of the rich theory of formal languages, such as automata theory, which we hope to apply to $CL^m_{Tree}$ to obtain a complete understanding of its place in the study of forest-regular languages.

An intriguing question (for which we thank one of the anonymous referees) is to what extent the adjoints permit properties of trees to be expressed succinctly. The results in this paper give an upper bound: given a formula with adjoints, a corresponding adjunct-free formula has maximum nesting depth of non-Boolean connectives that is exponential in the number of adjoint connectives of the original formula. The total number of connectives might still be large, although by Lemma 3 we know it is bounded. By refining our methods and studying examples, we expect to find closer bounds. It is not clear whether this will lead to tight bounds on how much more succinct formulae with adjoints can be.

Finally, we should mention Calcagno, Gardner and Zarfaty's recent work on *parametric* expressivity [7], which compares logics on *open* formulae containing propositional variables. Despite our expressivity results on *closed* formulae in this paper, stating that the adjoints can be eliminated, we intuitively know that adjunct connectives are important for expressing weakest preconditions for local Hoare reasoning using Separation Logic and Context Logic, and for expressing security properties in Ambient Logic. This intuition is formally captured in [7] where it is shown that the adjoints cannot be eliminated on open formulae. For our style of logical reasoning, both types of expressivity result seem to be important: the expressivity on open formulae captures our intuition that the structural connectives are important for modular reasoning; and the expressivity on closed formulae allows us to compare our reasoning about structured data with the literature on regular languages.

## References

1. Ishtiaq, S.S., O'Hearn, P.W.: BI as an assertion language for mutable data structures. In: POPL 2001, ACM Press, New York (2001)
2. Reynolds, J.C.: Separation Logic: a logic for shared mutable data structures. In: LICS 2002, IEEE Computer Society, Los Alamitos (2002)
3. Yang, H., O'Hearn, P.W.: A semantic basis for local reasoning. In: Nielsen, M., Engberg, U. (eds.) ETAPS 2002 and FOSSACS 2002. LNCS, vol. 2303, Springer, Heidelberg (2002)
4. Cardelli, L., Gordon, A.D.: Anytime, anywhere: modal logics for mobile ambients. In: POPL 2000, ACM Press, New York (2000)
5. Calcagno, C., Gardner, P., Zarfaty, U.: Context Logic and tree update. In: POPL 2005, ACM Press, New York (2005)
6. O'Hearn, P., Pym, D.: Logic of bunched implications. Bulletin of Symbolic Logic 5(2), 215–244 (1999)
7. Calcagno, C., Gardner, P., Zarfaty, U.: Context logic as modal logic: completeness and parametric inexpressivity. In: POPL 2007, ACM Press, New York (2007)
8. Lozes, E.: Adjuncts elimination in the static Ambient Logic. In: Corradini, F., Nestmann, U. (eds.) EXPRESS 2003. ENTCS, vol. 96, Elsevier, Amsterdam (2003)
9. Dawar, A., Gardner, P., Ghelli, G.: Adjunct elimination through games in static Ambient Logic. In: Lodaya, K., Mahajan, M. (eds.) FSTTCS 2004. LNCS, vol. 3328, Springer, Heidelberg (2004)
10. Calcagno, C., Gardner, P., Zarfaty, U.: Separation Logic, Ambient Logic and Context Logic: parametric inexpressivity results (Unpublished, 2006)
11. Dinsdale-Young, T.: Adjunct elimination in Context Logic. Master's thesis, Imperial College London (2006)
12. Heuter, U.: First-order properties of trees, star-free expressions, and aperiodicity. Informatique théorique et applications 25(2), 125–145 (1991)
13. Bojańczyk, M.: Forest expressions. In: Duparc, J., Henzinger, T.A. (eds.) CSL 2007. LNCS, vol. 4646, Springer, Heidelberg (2007)

# Positive Arithmetic Without Exchange Is a Subclassical Logic

Stefano Berardi[1] and Makoto Tatsuta[2]

[1] Department of Computer Science
University of Turin
corso Svizzera 185, 10149 Torino, Italy
stefano@di.unito.it

[2] National Institute of Informatics
2-1-2 Hitotsubashi, Tokyo 101-8430, Japan
tatsuta@nii.ac.jp

**Abstract.** This paper shows the equivalence for provability between two infinitary systems with the $\omega$-rule. One system is the positive one-sided fragment of Peano arithmetic without Exchange rules. The other system is two-sided Heyting Arithmetic plus the law of Excluded Middle for $\Sigma_1^0$-formulas, and it includes Exchange. Thus, the logic underlying positive Arithmetic without Exchange, a substructural logic, is shown to be a logic intermediate between Intuitionism and Classical Logic, hence a subclassical logic. As a corollary, the authors derive the equivalence for positive formulas among provability in those two systems and validity in two apparently unrelated semantics: Limit Computable Mathematics, and Game Semantics with 1-backtracking.

## 1 Introduction

Formal systems based on substructural logics have been intensively studied and many interesting results have been achieved. However, the interplay between classical logic without Exchange rules and arithmetic has not been fully studied yet. Let $\mathrm{PA}^+_{\mathrm{inf}} - \mathrm{Exch}$ be the one-sided Peano Arithmetic with the $\omega$-rule, without implication and without right-Exchange. $\mathrm{PA}^+_{\mathrm{inf}} - \mathrm{Exch}$ is an arithmetical system whose underlying logic is a substructural logic. $\mathrm{PA}^+_{\mathrm{inf}} - \mathrm{Exch}$ is interesting of its own right, because it has a nice effective interpretation in term of games (§2). What we already know about $\mathrm{PA}^+_{\mathrm{inf}} - \mathrm{Exch}$ is that it has a sound and complete interpretation in term of Tarski games with 1-backtracking [4].

Let $\mathrm{EM}_1$ be the law of excluded middle for $\Sigma_1^0$-formulas. The main result of this paper is the equivalence of provability between $\mathrm{PA}^+_{\mathrm{inf}} - \mathrm{Exch}$ and $\mathrm{HA}_{\mathrm{inf}} + \mathrm{EM}_1$. This latter is Heyting arithmetic $\mathrm{HA}_{\mathrm{inf}}$ extended with $\mathrm{EM}_1$. Note that $\mathrm{HA}_{\mathrm{inf}}$ includes left-Exchange rule, which is part of intuitionistic logic. Thus, the logic underlying $\mathrm{PA}^+_{\mathrm{inf}} - \mathrm{Exch}$ is a subclassical logic in which, because of the equivalence with $\mathrm{HA}_{\mathrm{inf}} + \mathrm{EM}_1$, all usual intuitionistic rules are conditionally derivable, including, for instance, the commutativity rule for disjunction. Derivability of the commutativity rule is a bit surprising, because in $\mathrm{PA}^+_{\mathrm{inf}} - \mathrm{Exch}$ we dropped right-Exchange, the only Exchange rule we can have in a one-sided sequent calculus.

Z. Shao (Ed.): APLAS 2007, LNCS 4807, pp. 271–285, 2007.

We now discuss the motivations for our paper. The first motivation is rooted in the study of the computational content of proofs. This content was discovered in logic by the Realizability interpretation [11], and first translated into computer science by Curry-Howard isomorphism in [10]. This result showed that a proof in intuitionistic logic has a recursive function as its computational content. Later this relationship was extended to classical logic by Gödel's double negation interpretation, and it was shown that a proof in classical logic contains a program in lambda-calculus with continuation [7].

It is not simple, however, to characterize the computational content for *all* proofs of classical arithmetic. The papers [12,1,3] obtained, instead, nice characterizations for proofs which use only weak classical principles like $\mathrm{EM}_1$. One of our aims is to study of the computational content of classical proofs including $\mathrm{EM}_1$ as only classical principle. Therefore we are interested in finding a sequent calculus exactly formalizing the set of proofs of $\mathrm{HA}_{\mathrm{inf}} + \mathrm{EM}_1$. This paper solves this problem by showing that $\mathrm{PA}^+_{\mathrm{inf}} - \mathrm{Exch}$ is equivalent to $\mathrm{HA}_{\mathrm{inf}} + \mathrm{EM}_1$. The interest of $\mathrm{PA}^+_{\mathrm{inf}} - \mathrm{Exch}$ is that we can interpret the constructive content of its proofs through a game interpretation (§2) which simplifies Game Semantics of Coquand for Classical Arithmetic [6].

Another motivation for our paper comes from the study of Limit Computable Mathematics (from now on, LCM) by Hayashi and Nakata ([8], §6). LCM is a Realizability model with $\Delta^0_2$-partial functions as realizers. It is defined in the same way as Kleene's Realizability model with partial recursive functions, except that LCM has $\Delta^0_2$-partial functions as realizers, while Kleene's model has partial recursive functions as realizers. LCM gives a model of the notion of incremental learning [9]. Our goal is to describe the logical principles underlying LCM, in order to better understand the notion of learning in the limit. This is no easy task, because we know that LCM validates not only $\mathrm{EM}_1$, but also the 2-Markov principle, i.e. the subclassical principle $\forall x.\neg\neg P(x) \to P(x)$, for any $\Sigma^0_2$-predicate $P$. This principle was proved stronger than $\mathrm{EM}_1$ in [1]. Another puzzling fact is that LCM validates a principle in contradiction with classical arithmetic, such as $\Delta^0_2$-choice. This latter principle says that if $\forall x.\exists y.Q(x,y)$, then $\forall x.Q(x,f(x))$ for some integer $f$ coding some $\Delta^0_2$-map. Classical arithmetic, instead, proves that there a true statement $\forall x.\exists y.Q(x,y)$ such that $\forall x.Q(x,f(x))$ does not hold for any integer coding $f$ of some $\Delta^0_2$-map.

Our idea is to restrict the study of LCM to positive (i.e., implication-free) formulas, as a preliminary step. Positive formulas are already an expressive fragment for LCM. Indeed, for any $\Sigma^0_1$-formulas $A, B$, if $A^\perp(x)$ is the de Morgan's dual of $A(x)$, then $\mathrm{EM}_1$ implies $(A \to B) \leftrightarrow (A^\perp(x) \vee B)$. Therefore in LCM we can express the implication for $\Sigma^0_1$-formulas using only positive formulas. We could expect that LCM validates more positive formulas than $\mathrm{EM}_1$, because LCM includes 2-Markov and $\Delta^0_2$-choice, two principles which are underivable from $\mathrm{EM}_1$ in the language with implication. However, this is not the case. A corollary of our main result is that positive formulas valid in LCM are exactly the positive formulas derivable in $\mathrm{HA}_{\mathrm{inf}} + \mathrm{EM}_1$. This is the first logical characterization known for a non-trivial subset of LCM.

The last motivation for our paper comes from Game Theory. Several papers have intensively studied relationship between game semantics and logical systems [6,5]. [5] discussed a sound and complete game semantics for $HA_{inf}$. Another corollary of our main result is the equivalence between the set of positive formulas valid in game semantic with 1-backtracking, and the set of positive formulas provable in $HA_{inf} + EM_1$.

To prove the direction of our main result from $PA^+_{inf} - Exch$ to $HA_{inf} + EM_1$, we will use an idea of flag formulas (§4). A flag formula $S_i$ is a $\Pi^0_1$ formula assigned to each formula $A_i$ in a sequent $A_1, \ldots, A_n$ in $PA^+_{inf} - Exch$. $S_i$ means that the sequent $A_1, \ldots, A_n$ is derivable in $PA^+_{inf} - Exch$ by using only sequents of length equal to or greater than $i$.

To achieve the other direction, from $HA_{inf} + EM_1$ to $PA^+_{inf} - Exch$, we first will give a proof of validity of $HA_{inf} + EM_1$ in LCM. Then we remark that validity of positive formulas in LCM is equivalent to validity in game semantics with 1-backtracking [2]. The latter is equivalent to provability in $PA^+_{inf} - Exch$ [4]. We conclude the direction from $HA_{inf} + EM_1$ to $PA^+_{inf} - Exch$.

This is the plan of the paper. §2 defines the positive fragment $PA^+_{inf} - Exch$ of Peano arithmetic without right-Exchange rules, sketches an interpretation of the constructive content of proofs of $PA^+_{inf} - Exch$ using games, and includes an example of a proof in $PA^+_{inf} - Exch$. §3 gives an informal interpretation of $PA^+_{inf} - Exch$. §4 gives Heyting arithmetic $HA_{inf}$ with $\omega$-rules, and the law $EM_1$ of excluded middle for $\Sigma^0_1$ formulas. §5 proves the direction from $PA^+_{inf} - Exch$ to $HA_{inf} + EM_1$. The other direction is proved in §6. §7 shows the results we claimed about LCM and 1-backtracking games.

## 2 $PA^+_{inf} - Exch$, the Positive Fragment of Peano Arithmetic Without Exchange

We define the positive fragment $PA^+_{inf} - Exch$ of Peano arithmetic PA with the $\omega$-rule. This system is obtained from PA by
(1) replacing the induction principles by the use of the infinitary $\omega$-rule and recursive proof-trees,
(2) prohibiting implication and negation in formulas,
(3) removing the right-Exchange rules.

**Definition 2.1 (The language of $PA^+_{inf} - Exch$)**
This language is a first-order language generated from the following symbols.

We have variables $x, y, z, \ldots$.

Constants are numerals $0, 1, 2, \ldots$, denoted by $n, m, i, j, \ldots$.

Function symbols are denoted by $f, g, \ldots$. We assume that there is a function symbol for each primitive recursive function, and that all function symbols denote recursive functions.

Terms are denoted by $s, t, \ldots$.

Predicate symbols are denoted by $P, Q, \ldots$. We assume that there is a predicate symbol for each primitive recursive predicate, and that all predicate symbols denote recursive predicates. For a predicate symbol $P$, we use $P^{\perp}$ to denote the predicate symbol which means the negation of $P$.

Atomic formulas are denoted by $a, b, \ldots$. They are called atoms for short. Atomic formulas include `true` and `false`, which means the truth and the falsity respectively.

Formulas are defined by $A, B, C, \ldots ::= a|A \wedge B|A \vee B|\forall x A|\exists x A$.

A sentence is a closed formula. A sequent is a sequence of sentences and is denoted by $\Gamma, \Delta, \Pi, \ldots$. Note that we respect order of sentences in a sequent.

Substitution $A[t/x]$ is obtained from $A$ by replacing every free occurrence of $x$ by $t$. The formulas of $\mathrm{PA}^+_{\mathrm{inf}}$ – Exch do not have implication nor negation. The negation of a formula is represented in $\mathrm{PA}^+_{\mathrm{inf}}$ – Exch by de Morgan's dual of the formula, which is equivalent to negation of the formula in the standard model. We will say that the formulas in a first-order language without implication nor negation is positive. $\omega$ is the set of numerals.

**Definition 2.2 (Inference rules of $\mathbf{PA}^+_{\mathbf{inf}}$ – Exch).** Let $a$ be any atom true in the standard model, and $t$ be any closed term. Let $A, A_1, A_2, \exists x.B, \forall x.B$ be any closed formulas.

$$\frac{}{\Delta, a}\ (Ax) \quad \text{where } a \text{ is a true closed atom.} \qquad \frac{\Delta}{\Delta, A}\ (Weak)$$

$$\frac{\Delta, A_1 \quad \Delta, A_2}{\Delta, A_1 \wedge A_2}\ (\wedge) \qquad \frac{\Delta, B[n/x] \ \text{ for all } n \in \omega}{\Delta, \forall x.B}\ (\forall)$$

$$\frac{\Delta, A_1 \vee A_2, A_1}{\Delta, A_1 \vee A_2}\ (\vee 1) \qquad \frac{\Delta, A_1 \vee A_2, A_2}{\Delta, A_1 \vee A_2}\ (\vee 2) \qquad \frac{\Delta, \exists x.B, B[t/x]}{\Delta, \exists x.B}\ (\exists t)$$

The rule $(Ax)$ says that the sequent $\Delta, a$ is provable if $a$ is a true closed atom. The rule $(\wedge)$ says that the sequent $\Delta, A_1 \wedge A_2$ is provable if the sequents $\Delta, A_1$ and $\Delta, A_2$ are provable. The rule $(\forall)$ says that the sequent $\Delta, \forall x.B$ is provable if the sequent $\Delta, B[n/x]$ is provable for all $n \in \omega$. The rule $(\vee)$ says that that the sequent $\Delta, A_1 \vee A_2$ is provable if the sequent $\Delta, A_1 \vee A_2, A_i$ is provable for some $i$. The rule $(\exists)$ says that that the sequent $\Delta, \exists x.B$ is provable if the sequent $\Delta, \exists x.B, B[t/x]$ is provable for some $t$. There is another way of proving any sequent $\Gamma, A$, by the Weakening rule, from a proof of $\Gamma$.

All predicate symbols and function symbols denote recursive predicates and recursive functions in the standard model, and therefore the truth value of an atom in the standard model is computable. Rules are syntax-directed: if we know the name of the rule and the conclusion $\Gamma$ of the rule, we can compute the list $\Gamma_1, \Gamma_2, \ldots$ of assumptions of the rule. A proof in this system is any well-founded *recursive* tree built according to inference rules. Since we consider only recursive proof-trees, the rule $(\forall)$ requires that we can derive $\Delta, \forall x A$ from a recursive function $f$ such that $f(n)$ is the code of a proof of $A[n/x]$. We use $\lceil \cdot \rceil$ to denote a standard coding function so that $\lceil e \rceil$ denotes a code of a syntactical object $e$. A proof is defined as its integer code in this system. Formally, a proof is defined inductively as follows:

(1) $(\lceil Ax \rceil, \lceil \Gamma, a \rceil)$ is a proof if $a$ is a true atom.

(2) $(\lceil L \rceil, \lceil \Gamma \rceil, \lceil \Gamma_1 \rceil)$ is a proof if there exists an instance of the inference rule $L = (\vee 1), (\vee 2), (\exists t), (W)$ such that $\Gamma$ is its conclusion, and $\Gamma_1$ is its assumption.

(3) $(\lceil (\wedge) \rceil, \lceil \Gamma \rceil, \lceil \Gamma_1 \rceil, \lceil \Gamma_2 \rceil)$ is a proof if there is an instance of the rule $(\wedge)$ such that $\Gamma$ is its conclusion, and $\Gamma_1$ and $\Gamma_2$ are its assumptions.

(4) $(\lceil (\forall) \rceil, \lceil \Gamma \rceil, f)$ is a proof if $f$ is a code for a *recursive* function and there is an instance of the rule $(\forall)$ such that $\Gamma$ is its conclusion and $f(n)$ gives the proof of its $n$-th assumption.

## 2.1 An Effective Game Theoretical Interpretation of $\mathbf{PA}^+_{\mathbf{inf}}$ – Exch

We sketch an effective game theoretical interpretation of $\mathrm{PA}^+_{\mathrm{inf}}$–Exch, taken from [4], which can be used to give a constructive content to proofs of $\mathrm{PA}^+_{\mathrm{inf}}$–Exch. We use Tarski games with 1-backtracking. A formula $B$ is interpreted as a game, which is a debate between two players, Eloise, claiming that $B$ is true, and Abelard, claiming that $B$ is false.

When $B$ is $A_1 \vee A_2$ or $\exists x.A$, then Eloise moves, choosing some immediate subformula $A_i$ or $A[t/x]$ of $B$. The intuition is that Eloise argue in favor of the truth of $B$ by arguing in favor of the truth of some $A_i$, or some $A[t/x]$. When $B$ is $A_1 \wedge A_2$ or $\forall x.A$, then Abelard moves, choosing some immediate subformula $A_i$ or $A[n/x]$ of $B$. The intuition is that Abelard argue in favor of the falsity of $B$ by arguing in favor of the falsity of some $A_i$, or some $A[n/x]$. When $B$ is some atom $a$, if a is true then Eloise wins, and if $a$ is false then Abelard wins.

Eloise has a special move not available for Abelard: she can retract a move she did from some formula $C$, and all the moves she did after it, and then she can move again from $C$. Retracted moves cannot be recovered. Retraction is called 1-backtracking in [4]. Abelard wins if the play, because of infinitely many retractions by Eloise, continues forever.

A proof of $B$ in $\mathrm{PA}^+_{\mathrm{inf}}$ – Exch can be interpreted as a winning strategy for Eloise in the 1-backtracking game for $B$, as follows. A sequent in the proof of $B$ can be interpreted as the list of all the moves of the play that Eloise has not retracted. The rule $(Weak)$ is the act of retracting one move, and the upper sequent is the position of the play produced by this retraction. We can have many consecutive retractions of one move each. The rule $(\vee i)$ corresponds to Eloise's move from $A_1 \vee A_2$ to $A_i$. The rule $(\wedge)$ corresponds to the two possible moves $A_1$ and $A_2$ by Abelard from $A_1 \wedge A_2$. Eloise considers both possibilities, in order to be ready to reply in both cases. The interpretation for the rules $(\exists t)$ and $(\forall)$ is similar. The rule $(Ax)$ corresponds to the end of the play with Eloise's victory.

The strategy outlined is a winning strategy for Eloise, because each play in which Eloise follows this strategy corresponds to some branch in the proof-tree ending in an axiom, and therefore is a finite play won by Eloise.

## 2.2 A Proof of $\mathbf{EM}_1$ in $\mathbf{PA}^+_{\mathbf{inf}}$ – Exch

Suppose $P$ is a predicate symbol. Let $A(x) = \exists y P(x,y)$ and $A^\perp(x) = \forall y P^\perp(x,y)$. The following is a proof in $\mathrm{PA}^+_{\mathrm{inf}}$ – Exch. It proves Excluded Middle $\mathrm{EM}_1$ for a $\Sigma^0_1$-formula.

$$\dfrac{\dfrac{\dfrac{\overset{\vdots\ \pi_m}{A(n)\vee A^{\perp}(n),\ P^{\perp}(n,m)\quad \text{for all } m}}{A(n)\vee A^{\perp}(n),\ A^{\perp}(n)}\ \forall}{A(n)\vee A^{\perp}(n)}\ \vee 2 \qquad \text{for all } n}{\forall x(A(x)\vee A^{\perp}(x))}\ \forall$$

If $P(n,m)$ is false, then $P^{\perp}(n,m)$ is true and the proof $\pi_m$ is an axiom. If $P(n,m)$ is true, the proof $\pi_m$ is:

$$\dfrac{\dfrac{\dfrac{\dfrac{}{A(n)\vee A^{\perp}(n),\ A(n),\ P(n,m)}\ Ax}{A(n)\vee A^{\perp}(n),\ A(n)}\ \exists m}{A(n)\vee A^{\perp}(n)}\ \vee 1}{A(n)\vee A^{\perp}(n),\ P^{\perp}(n,m)}\ Weak$$

## 2.3 A True Sentence Not Provable in $\mathbf{PA}^{+}_{\mathbf{inf}}$ – Exch

$PA^{+}_{inf}$ – Exch does not have right-Exchange rules, and for this reason it cannot prove all classically true sentences. Suppose $P$ is a predicate symbol. Let $B(z) = \forall x.\exists y.P(x,y,z)$ and $B^{\perp}(z) = \exists x.\forall y.P^{\perp}(x,y,z)$. We call the set of formulas $\forall z.B(z)\vee B^{\perp}(z)$ the scheme $EM_2$, Excluded Middle for $\Sigma^0_2$ formulas. $EM_2$ is a larger fragment of the Excluded Middle axiom than $EM_1$ [1]. If we had right-Exchange rules, the following would be a proof of $\forall z.B(z)\vee B^{\perp}(z)$ where the use of the right-Exchange rule is marked with Exch:

$$\dfrac{\dfrac{\dfrac{\dfrac{\dfrac{\dfrac{\dfrac{\overset{\vdots\ \pi_m}{\exists y.P(n,y,l),\ B(l)\vee B^{\perp}(l),\ B^{\perp}(l),\ P^{\perp}(n,m,l)\quad (\forall m\in\omega)}}{\exists y.P(n,y,l),\ B(l)\vee B^{\perp}(l),\ B^{\perp}(l),\ \forall y.P^{\perp}(n,y,l)}\ \forall}{\exists y.P(n,y,l),\ B(l)\vee B^{\perp}(l),\ B^{\perp}(l)}\ \exists n}{\exists y.P(n,y,l),\ B(l)\vee B^{\perp}(l)}\ \vee 2}{B(l)\vee B^{\perp}(l),\ \exists y.P(n,y,l)}\ \mathbf{Exch}\qquad (\forall n\in\omega)}{B(l)\vee B^{\perp}(l),\ B(l)}\ \forall}{B(l)\vee B^{\perp}(l)}\ \vee 1\qquad (\forall l\in\omega)}{\forall z.B(z)\vee B^{\perp}(z)}\ \forall$$

where $\pi_m$ is an axiom if $P(n,m,l)$ is false, and is

$$\dfrac{\dfrac{\dfrac{\dfrac{\dfrac{}{\exists y.P(n,y,l),\ P(n,m,l)}\ Ax}{\exists y.P(n,y,l)}\ \exists m}{\exists y.P(n,y,l),\ B(l)\vee B^{\perp}(l)}\ Weak}{\exists y.P(n,y,l),\ B(l)\vee B^{\perp}(l),\ B^{\perp}(l)}\ Weak}{\exists y.P(n,y,l),\ B(l)\vee B^{\perp}(l),\ B^{\perp}(l),\ P^{\perp}(n,m,l)}\ Weak$$

if $P(n,m,l)$ is true. Indeed, this formula cannot be proved in $\mathrm{PA}^+_{\mathrm{inf}}-\mathrm{Exch}$ because of lack of right-Exchange rules. This underivability result is proved by combining the clause 3 in Lemma 10 in [2] and Theorem 1 in [4]. This shows that some classical principle does not hold in this system. On the other hand, the previous example shows $\mathrm{EM}_1$ is still provable in this system. Therefore $\mathrm{PA}^+_{\mathrm{inf}} - \mathrm{Exch}$ is strictly stronger than $\mathrm{HA}_{\mathrm{inf}}$, and strictly weaker than $\mathrm{PA}_{\mathrm{inf}}$. In §7 we will prove more, namely that the set of theorem of $\mathrm{PA}^+_{\mathrm{inf}}-\mathrm{Exch}$ is exactly the set of positive theorems of $\mathrm{HA}_{\mathrm{inf}} + \mathrm{EM}_1$.

### 2.4 Uniformly Admissible Rules of $\mathrm{PA}^+_{\mathrm{inf}} - \mathrm{Exch}$

In this subsection we define what is a uniformly admissible rule.

**Definition 2.3 (Uniformly Provable and Uniformly Admissible)**

1. A sequent schema $\Gamma$ with metavariables is defined to be uniformly provable in $\mathrm{PA}^+_{\mathrm{inf}} - \mathrm{Exch}$ if there is a recursive function such that the following holds. For any sequent $\Gamma'$ that is an instance of $\Gamma$, the function computes the code of a proof of the sequent $\Gamma'$ in $\mathrm{PA}^+_{\mathrm{inf}} - \mathrm{Exch}$ from the code of the sequent $\Gamma'$.
2. An inference rule schema $R$ with metavariables is defined to be uniformly admissible if there is a recursive function such that the following holds. For any rule $R'$ that is an instance of $R$, the function computes the code of a proof of the conclusion of $R'$ in $\mathrm{PA}^+_{\mathrm{inf}} - \mathrm{Exch}$ from the code of the conclusion of $R'$ and the codes of proofs for the premises of $R'$.

If a rule schema $R$ is uniformly admissible, the set of formulas provable in $\mathrm{PA}^+_{\mathrm{inf}} - \mathrm{Exch}$ is the same as the set of formulas provable in $\mathrm{PA}^+_{\mathrm{inf}} - \mathrm{Exch}$ plus $R$.

Some structural rules are restricted in $\mathrm{PA}^+_{\mathrm{inf}} - \mathrm{Exch}$, but the contraction rule can be proved to be uniformly admissible.

**Proposition 2.4.** *Define $B > A$ by $A \wedge B > A$, $A \wedge B > B$, and $\forall x A > A[n/x]$. Define the relation $>^*$ as the reflexive transitive closure of the relation $>$.*

*(1) If $B >^* A$ holds, then the rule* $\dfrac{\Gamma, B}{\Gamma, A}$ *is uniformly admissible.*

*(2) If $B >^* A$ holds, then the rule* $\dfrac{\Gamma_1, B, A, \Gamma_2}{\Gamma_1, A, \Gamma_2}$ *is uniformly admissible.*

*(3) The contraction rule* $\dfrac{\Gamma_1, A, A, \Gamma_2}{\Gamma_1, A, \Gamma_2}$ *is uniformly admissible.*

## 3 Sketching an Interpretation of $\mathrm{PA}^+_{\mathrm{inf}} - \mathrm{Exch}$ in $\mathrm{HA}_{\mathrm{inf}} + \mathrm{EM}_1$

Let $\pi$ be a proof of $\Gamma = A_1, \ldots, A_n$ in $\mathrm{PA}^+_{\mathrm{inf}} - \mathrm{Exch}$. In this section we sketch an interpretation of $\pi$ by a statement which implies $\Gamma$. In §5, starting from this interpretation we will define a formal embedding of $\mathrm{PA}^+_{\mathrm{inf}} - \mathrm{Exch}$ in $\mathrm{HA}_{\mathrm{inf}} + \mathrm{EM}_1$. This section is only intended to motivate §5, and is purely informal, with no proofs included.

We sketch now our interpretation of $\pi$. For each $i \in \omega$ we introduce a flag formula $S_i$. $S_i$ means that all sequents decorating the nodes of $\pi$ have at least $i$ formulas. Therefore $S_i \wedge \neg S_{i+1}$ means that the minimum length of a sequent in $\pi$ is $i$. $S_1$ is true, because each sequent of $\pi$ is the conclusion of some rule of $PA^+_{inf}$ – Exch, and therefore it includes at least one formula. Each $S_i$ implies $S_j$ for all $j < i$, because if all sequents in $\pi$ have at least $i$ formulas, then all sequents in $\pi$ have at least $j$ formulas. For all $i > n$, each $S_i$ is false, because the conclusion $\Gamma$ of $\pi$ has less than $i$ formulas. By combining the two remarks and by classical logic, we deduce that for some $1 \leq i \leq n$ we have $S_i \wedge \neg S_{i+1}$. Such an $i$ is unique because $S_i$ implies $S_{i-1}, \ldots, S_1$. We say that $\pi$ *succeeds in proving* $A_i$ if $S_i \wedge \neg S_{i+1}$ holds. If $i = n$, then we know that $S_{n+1}$ is false, therefore $\pi$ *succeeds in proving* $A_n$ if $S_n$ holds. We interpret each proof $\pi$ of $\Gamma$ by the following statement: *for all* $1 \leq i \leq n$, *if* $\pi$ *succeeds in proving* $A_i$, *then* $A_i$ *holds*. Since $S_i \wedge \neg S_{i+1}$ holds for some $i$, if this interpretation holds, then we deduce $A_i$ for some $i$, that is, $\Gamma$ holds. We claim that for all proofs $\pi$, this interpretation of $\pi$ is true. We informally explain why.

Let $\pi'$ be the tree obtained by taking each sequent $\Delta$ decorating $\pi$, and removing the first $n-1$ formulas from $\Delta$. We remove all formulas from $\Delta$ if $\Delta$ has less than $n$ formulas. If $S_n$ is true, then by induction on $\pi$ we can prove that $\pi'$ is a proof of $A_n$. If $S_n$ is false, then by induction on $\pi$ we can prove that $\pi$ includes some subproof $\pi_1$ of $A_1, \ldots, A_{n-1}$. We skip the proofs of these results, because they are not essential for our discussion, and because they are implicitly included in the proofs of §5.

If $S_n$ holds, then $\pi'$ proves $A_n$. If $\neg S_n$ holds, and if $S_{n-1}$ holds, then we can remove the first $n-2$ formulas from each sequent decorating $\pi_1$, obtaining some proof $\pi'_1$ of $A_{n-1}$. If $\neg S_{n-1}$ holds, then we can prove that $\pi_1$ includes some subproof $\pi'_1$ of $A_{n-2}$. If we continue in this way, since $S_1$ holds, eventually we find the unique $1 \leq i \leq n$ such that $S_i \wedge \neg S_{i+1}$, and together some $\pi'_i$ which is a proof of $A_i$. This implies that the interpretation of $\pi$ is true.

Our interpretation of $PA^+_{inf}$ – Exch requires only the classical axioms $S_i \vee \neg S_i$ and $\neg S_i \rightarrow S_i^{\perp}$. In §5, we will be able to formalize $S_i$ by means of $\Pi^0_1$ statements, and we will formalize the interpretation using only Excluded Middle for $\Sigma^0_1$ statements.

This interpretation is not fully effective, because to know whether $\pi$ succeeds in proving $A_n$ requires to know whether $S_n$ is true, and that if $S_n$ is false, then we have to provide some subproofs whose conclusion has $< n$ formulas. That is, this interpretation requires the classical principles $S_n \vee \neg S_n$ and $\neg S_i \rightarrow S_i^{\perp}$. We can check that $S_n$ is a $\Pi^0_1$-statement, and therefore the classical principle we need to define this interpretation is $EM_1$. In §5, we will develop this idea into a formal interpretation of $PA^+_{inf}$ – Exch into $HA_{inf} + EM_1$.

## 4 The System $HA_{inf} + EM_1$

We define the system $HA_{inf}$, which we will use to characterize $PA^+_{inf}$ – Exch. We do *not* remove Left-exchange, the intuitionistic version of Exchange rule, from

$\mathrm{HA}_{\mathrm{inf}}$. $\mathrm{HA}_{\mathrm{inf}}$ is Heyting arithmetic HA except that it is based on infinitary logic and recursive proof-trees, the inference rules $(\forall R)$ and $(\exists L)$ are replaced by $\omega$-rules with countably many assumptions, and it does not have induction rules. In fact, the induction principles are derivable. The language is the same as that of $\mathrm{PA}^+_{\mathrm{inf}}$ – Exch except that the formulas have implication.

**Definition 4.1 (The language of $\mathbf{HA}_{\mathrm{inf}}$)**
The language is a first-order language. Variables, constants, function symbols, predicate symbols, and atomic formulas are defined as those of $\mathrm{PA}^+_{\mathrm{inf}}$ – Exch. Let $\langle\cdot,\cdot\rangle$ be a function symbol for a primitive recursive surjective paring.

Formulas are defined by: $A, B, C, R, S, \ldots ::= a | A \wedge B | A \vee B | A \rightarrow B | \forall x A | \exists x A$.

$\neg A$ is an abbreviation of $A \rightarrow \mathtt{false}$. A closed formula is called a sentence. $\Gamma$, $\Delta$, and $\Pi$ denote a sequence $A_1, \ldots, A_n$ of sentences. A sequent is $A_1, \ldots, A_n \vdash B$ or $A_1, \ldots, A_n \vdash$ where $n \geq 0$ and $A_1, \ldots, A_n, B$ are sentences.

$\omega$ denotes the set of numerals. A formula $A$ is called a $\Pi^0_1$ formula if $A$ is $\forall x P(x)$ for some predicate symbol $P$.

**Definition 4.2 (The inference rules of $\mathbf{HA}_{\mathrm{inf}}$).** In the rules (Ax R) and (Ax L), true and false refer to the truth value in the standard model. $\Delta$ is empty or a formula. $t$ is a closed term.

$(Ax\ L)\quad \Gamma_1, a, \Gamma_2 \vdash \Delta \qquad$ if $a$ is a false closed atom

$(Ax\ R)\quad \Gamma \vdash a \qquad$ if $a$ is a true closed atom

$$\frac{\Gamma \vdash A_1 \quad \Gamma \vdash A_2}{\Gamma \vdash A_1 \wedge A_2}(\wedge R) \qquad \frac{\Gamma, A_1 \vdash \Delta}{\Gamma, A_1 \wedge A_2 \vdash \Delta}(\wedge L1) \qquad \frac{\Gamma, A_2 \vdash \Delta}{\Gamma, A_1 \wedge A_2 \vdash \Delta}(\wedge L2)$$

$$\frac{\Gamma \vdash A_1}{\Gamma \vdash A_1 \vee A_2}(\vee R1) \qquad \frac{\Gamma \vdash A_2}{\Gamma \vdash A_1 \vee A_2}(\vee R2) \qquad \frac{\Gamma, A_1 \vdash \Delta \quad \Gamma, A_2 \vdash \Delta}{\Gamma, A_1 \vee A_2 \vdash \Delta}(\vee L)$$

$$\frac{\Gamma, A \vdash B}{\Gamma \vdash A \rightarrow B}(\rightarrow R) \qquad \frac{\Gamma \vdash A \quad \Gamma, B \vdash \Delta}{\Gamma, A \rightarrow B \vdash \Delta}(\rightarrow L)$$

$$\frac{\Gamma \vdash A[m/x] \quad (\text{for all } m \in \omega)}{\Gamma \vdash \forall x A}(\forall R) \qquad \frac{\Gamma, A[t/x] \vdash \Delta}{\Gamma, \forall x A \vdash \Delta}(\forall L)$$

$$\frac{\Gamma \vdash A[t/x]}{\Gamma \vdash \exists x A}(\exists R) \qquad \frac{\Gamma, A[m/x] \vdash \Delta \quad (\text{for all } m \in \omega)}{\Gamma, \exists x A \vdash \Delta}(\exists L)$$

$$\frac{\Gamma \vdash}{\Gamma \vdash A}(WR) \qquad \frac{\Gamma \vdash \Delta}{\Gamma, A \vdash \Delta}(WL) \qquad \frac{\Gamma, A, A \vdash \Delta}{\Gamma, A \vdash \Delta}(ContrL)$$

$$\frac{\Gamma_1, B, A, \Gamma_2 \vdash \Delta}{\Gamma_1, A, B, \Gamma_2 \vdash \Delta}(ExchL) \qquad \frac{\Gamma \vdash A \quad \Pi, A \vdash \Delta}{\Gamma, \Pi \vdash \Delta}(Cut)$$

A proof in this system is defined as a well-founded *recursive* tree in a similar way to $\mathrm{PA}^+_{\mathrm{inf}}$ – Exch. Since all proofs are recursive trees, the rules $(\forall R)$ and $(\exists L)$

require the existence of some recursive function $f$ such that $f(m)$ is the code of a proof of $\Gamma \vdash A[m/x]$ and $\Gamma, A[m/x] \vdash \Delta$ respectively. "Uniformly provable" and "uniformly admissible" are defined in the same way as Definition 2.3.

The law $\mathrm{EM}_1$ of excluded middle for $\Sigma^0_1$ formulas is defined as the axiom schema $\vdash \forall x(\exists y P(x,y) \vee \neg \exists y P(x,y))$ for any predicate symbol $P$. $\mathrm{EM}_1$ is a weaker version of the law of excluded middle. The proofs of $\mathrm{HA}_{\mathrm{inf}} + \mathrm{EM}_1$ are defined as the proofs of $\mathrm{HA}_{\mathrm{inf}}$, except that an axiom of $\mathrm{HA}_{\mathrm{inf}} + \mathrm{EM}_1$ can also be an instance of $\mathrm{EM}_1$. $\mathrm{HA}_{\mathrm{inf}} + \mathrm{EM}_1$ strictly includes $\mathrm{HA}_{\mathrm{inf}}$ and is strictly included in $\mathrm{PA}_{\mathrm{inf}}$. Note that $\mathrm{EM}_1$ proves $A \vee \neg A$ for any $\Pi^0_1$ sentence $A$, since both $\neg \exists y P^{\perp}(x,y) \rightarrow \forall y P(x,y)$ and $\exists y P^{\perp}(x,y) \rightarrow \neg \forall y P(x,y)$ hold in intuitionistic logic.

We list below several basic properties for $\mathrm{HA}_{\mathrm{inf}} + \mathrm{EM}_1$. $A[n_1, \ldots, n_k/x_1, \ldots, x_k]$ is a simultaneous substitution and is defined by the formula obtained from $A$ by replacing every free occurrence of $x_1, \ldots, x_k$ by $n_1, \ldots, n_k$ simultaneously. We use vector notation to denote a sequence so that $\vec{x}$ denotes a sequence $x_1, \ldots, x_n$.

**Proposition 4.3.** *(Basic properties of $HA_{inf} + EM_1$) (1) The identity rule $A \vdash A$ is uniformly provable.*

*(2) $\forall \vec{x} A \vdash \forall \vec{y} B$ is uniformly provable if $A$ and $B$ are atoms and $A[\vec{m}/\vec{x}] \rightarrow B[\vec{n}/\vec{y}]$ is true for all $\vec{m}, \vec{n}$.*

*(3) $\forall \vec{x} A, \forall \vec{y} B \vdash \forall \vec{z} C$ is uniformly provable if $A$, $B$ and $C$ are atoms and $A[\vec{m}/\vec{x}] \rightarrow B[\vec{n}/\vec{y}] \rightarrow C[\vec{l}/\vec{z}]$ is true for all $\vec{m}, \vec{n}, \vec{l}$.*

*(4) $\forall \vec{x}(\exists \vec{y} A \vee \neg \exists \vec{y} A)$ is uniformly provable for any quantifier-free formula $A$.*

The next lemma includes the classical principles we will use in §5 in order to interpret $\mathrm{HA}_{\mathrm{inf}} + \mathrm{EM}_1$ into $\mathrm{PA}^+_{\mathrm{inf}} - \mathrm{Exch}$.

**Lemma 4.4.** *(1) For $\Pi^0_1$ sentences $S$ and $R$, $HA_{inf} + EM_1$ uniformly proves $\neg(S \wedge R) \vdash \neg S \vee \neg R$.*

*(2) For a predicate symbol $P$, $HA_{inf} + EM_1$ uniformly proves $\neg \forall x P(x) \vdash \exists x \neg P(x)$.*

Proof. (1) $\neg S, R, \neg(S \wedge R) \vdash \neg S$ trivially holds by the identity rule, so by $(\vee R1)$ we have $\neg S, R, \neg(S \wedge R) \vdash \neg S \vee \neg R$. Similarly by the identity rule and $(\vee R2)$ we have $\neg R, \neg(S \wedge R) \vdash \neg S \vee \neg R$. $S, R, \neg(S \wedge R) \vdash$ trivially holds, so by $(WR)$ we have $S, R, \neg(S \wedge R) \vdash \neg S \vee \neg R$. Hence by $(\vee L)$ we have $S \vee \neg S, R, \neg(S \wedge R) \vdash \neg S \vee \neg R$, which derives $R, \neg(S \wedge R) \vdash \neg S \vee \neg R$ by the cut rule with $\vdash S \vee \neg S$ by $\mathrm{EM}_1$. Therefore by $(\vee L)$ we have $R \vee \neg R, \neg(S \wedge R) \vdash \neg S \vee \neg R$, which derives the claim by the cut rule with $\vdash R \vee \neg R$ by $\mathrm{EM}_1$.

(2) First we consider cases according to $\exists x \neg P(x)$.

Case 1. $\exists x \neg P(x), \neg \forall x P(x) \vdash \exists x \neg P(x)$ trivially holds by the identity rule.

Case 2. We will show $\neg \exists x \neg P(x), \neg \forall x P(x) \vdash \exists x \neg P(x)$.

$\neg \exists x \neg P(x) \vdash P(m)$ holds when $P(m)$ is true by the axiom. $\neg \exists x \neg P(x) \vdash$ holds also when $P(m)$ is false, since the axiom gives $\vdash \neg P(m)$, which derives $\vdash \exists x \neg P(x)$ by $(\exists R)$ and $\neg \exists x \neg P(x) \vdash$ by $(\rightarrow L)$. Hence we have $\neg \exists x \neg P(x) \vdash P(m)$ for each $m$ by $(WR)$. By $(\forall R)$ we have $\neg \exists x \neg P(x) \vdash \forall x P(x)$, which derives $\neg \exists x \neg P(x), \neg \forall x P(x) \vdash$ by $(\rightarrow L)$. By $(WR)$, we have $\neg \exists x \neg P(x), \neg \forall x P(x) \vdash \exists x \neg P(x)$.

Hence by $(\vee L)$ we have $\exists x \neg P(x) \vee \neg \exists x \neg P(x), \neg \forall x P(x) \vdash \exists x \neg P(x)$. By the cut rule with $\vdash \exists x \neg P(x) \vee \neg \exists x \neg P(x)$ by $\mathrm{EM}_1$, we have the claim.□

## 5 From $PA^+_{inf}$ – Exch to $HA_{inf} + EM_1$

This section will show that if a positive sentence is provable in $PA^+_{inf}$ – Exch then it is provable in $HA_{inf} + EM_1$.

To prove it, we use the idea of flag formulas again. We recall that a flag formula $S_i$ is a $\Pi^0_1$ formula assigned to a proof $\pi$ of conclusion $A_1, \ldots, A_n$ in $PA^+_{inf}$ – Exch. $S_i$ means that the sequent is derived in $\pi$ without any sequent of length less than $i$. If $i > n$, then $S_i$ is trivially false, because the conclusion $\Gamma$ of $\pi$ has less than $i$ formulas. We will now prove what we informally claimed in §4, which states that for all $1 \leq i \leq n$, if $\pi$ "succeeds in proving $A_i$", that is, if we assume $S_i \wedge \neg S_{i+1}$, then $A_i$ follows. The proof is in $HA_{inf} + EM_1$.

**Theorem 5.1.** *There exists a recursive function $\phi$ such that if $\pi$ is a proof in $PA^+_{inf}$ – Exch of the sequent $A_1, ..., A_n$ $(n \geq 1)$, then $\phi(\pi)$ computes the codes of $\Pi^0_1$ formulas $S_1, \ldots, S_n$ and the codes of proofs of*
*(1)* $\vdash S_1$,
*(2)* $S_i, \neg S_{i+1} \vdash A_i$ $(1 \leq i < n)$,
*(3)* $S_n \vdash A_n$.

Proof. The recursive function $\phi$ is defined by simultaneous induction on the proof, using Kleene fixed point Theorem. All cases will be considered according to the last rule.

We will define $S_i$ for $i = 1, \ldots, n$ and for the conclusion of each rule by using the flag formulas $S^m_i$ for the $m$-th assumption of the rule. For the rules $(\vee 1)$, $(\vee 2)$, and $(\exists)$, $S_i$ is defined by $S_i = S^1_i$. For the rule $(\wedge)$, $S_i$ is defined by $S_i = \forall x P_i(x)$ where $S^1_i$ is $\forall x P^1_i(x)$ and $S^2_i$ is $\forall x P^2_i(x)$ for some predicate symbols $P^1_i$ and $P^2_i$, and $P_i$ is a predicate symbol such that $P_i(\langle n, m\rangle) \leftrightarrow P^1_i(n) \wedge P^2_i(m)$ is true for all $n, m$. Then $S_i \vdash S^1_i$ and $S_i \vdash S^2_i$ are uniformly provable by Proposition 4.3 (2). $S^1_i \wedge S^2_i \vdash S_i$ is also uniformly provable since $S^1_i, S^2_i \vdash S_i$ is uniformly provable by Proposition 4.3 (3).

For the rule $(\forall)$, $S_i$ is defined by $S_i = \forall x P_i(x)$ as follows. $S^m_i$ is $\forall x P^m_i(x)$ with some predicate symbol $P^m_i$ for each $m$. We suppose every recursive function and predicate is provided with a $\Pi^0_1$ formula that defines it. $P^m_i$ is recursive in $m$, so we have a predicate symbol $Q_i$ such that $\forall z Q_i(m, n, z) \leftrightarrow P^m_i(n)$ is true. Then we have a predicate symbol $P_i$ such that $P_i(\langle\langle n, m\rangle, l\rangle) \leftrightarrow Q_i(n, m, l)$ is true for all $n, m, l$. We define $S_i$ as $\forall x P_i(x)$. Then $S_i \vdash S^m_i$ is uniformly provable for each $m$ by Proposition 4.3 (2).

Case (Ax). We define $S_i = \texttt{true}$. The claims (1), (2), and (3) trivially hold.

Case (Weak). Let $\Delta = A_1, \ldots, A_{n-1}$. We define $S_i = S^1_i$ $(1 \leq i < n)$ and $S_n = \texttt{false}$. The claims (1), (2), and (3) trivially hold from induction hypothesis.

In the other cases, the claim (1) trivially holds. So we will show only the claims (2) and (3).

Case $(\wedge)$. Let $\Delta$ be $B_1, \ldots, B_{n-1}$.

(2) We will show $S_i, \neg S_{i+1} \vdash B_i$. We have $S_i, \neg S^1_{i+1} \vdash B_i$ by induction hypothesis $S^1_i, \neg S^1_{i+1} \vdash B_i$ and the cut rule with $S_i \vdash S^1_i$. Similarly we have $S_i, \neg S^2_{i+1} \vdash B_i$ by replacing 1 by 2. By the rule $(\vee L)$, we have $S_i, \neg S^1_{i+1} \vee \neg S^2_{i+1} \vdash B_i$. By Lemma

4.4 (1), we uniformly prove $\neg(S^1_{i+1} \wedge S^2_{i+1}) \vdash \neg S^1_{i+1} \vee \neg S^2_{i+1}$. By the cut rule with this and $\neg S_{i+1} \vdash \neg(S^1_{i+1} \wedge S^2_{i+1})$, we have the claim.

(3) We will show $S_n \vdash A_1 \wedge A_2$. We have $S^1_n \vdash A_1$ and $S^2_n \vdash A_2$ by induction hypothesis. Hence we have $S_n \vdash A_1$ and $S_n \vdash A_2$ by the cut rule with $S_n \vdash S^1_n$ and $S_n \vdash S^2_n$. By $(\wedge R)$, we have the claim.

Case $(\vee 1)$. Let $\Delta$ be $B_1, \ldots, B_{n-1}$.

(2) The claim is the same as the induction hypothesis since $S_i$ was defined as $S^1_i$.

(3) We will show $S_n \vdash A_1 \vee A_2$.

We have $S_n, S^1_{n+1} \vdash A_1 \vee A_2$ from induction hypothesis $S^1_{n+1} \vdash A_1$, $(WL)$, and $(\vee 1)$. We have $S_n, \neg S^1_{n+1} \vdash A_1 \vee A_2$ from induction hypothesis $S^1_n, \neg S^1_{n+1} \vdash A_1 \vee A_2$ and $S^1_n = S_n$. By the rule $(\vee L)$, we have $S_n, S^1_{n+1} \vee \neg S^1_{n+1} \vdash A_1 \vee A_2$. By the cut rule with $\vdash S^1_{n+1} \vee \neg S^1_{n+1}$ by $\mathrm{EM}_1$, we have the claim.

Case $(\forall)$. Let $\Delta$ be $B_1, \ldots, B_{n-1}$.

(2) We will show $S_i, \neg S_{i+1} \vdash B_i$. Induction hypothesis gives $S^m_i, \neg S^m_{i+1} \vdash B_i$ for each $m$. Hence we have $S_i, \neg S^m_{i+1} \vdash B_i$ for each $m$ by the cut rule with $S_i \vdash S^m_i$. We have $\neg \forall xz P_{i+1}(\langle\langle m, x\rangle, z\rangle) \vdash \neg S^m_{i+1}$ since $S^m_{i+1} \vdash \forall xz P_{i+1}(\langle\langle m, x\rangle, z\rangle)$ holds by Proposition 4.3 (2). By the cut rule with these two, we have $S_i, \neg \forall xz P_{i+1}(\langle\langle m, x\rangle, z\rangle) \vdash B_i$ for all $m$. By $(\exists L)$, we have (a) $S_i, \exists y \neg \forall xz P_{i+1}(\langle\langle y, x\rangle, z\rangle) \vdash B_i$.

Intuitionistic logic proves (b) $\exists yxz \neg P_{i+1}(\langle\langle y, x\rangle, z\rangle) \vdash \exists y \neg \forall xz P_{i+1}(\langle\langle y, x\rangle, z\rangle)$. We have (c) $\exists x \neg P_{i+1}(x) \vdash \exists yxz \neg P_{i+1}(\langle\langle y, x\rangle, z\rangle)$ by the rules $(\exists L)$ and $(\exists R)$, and $\neg P_{i+1}(w) \vdash \neg P_{i+1}(\langle\langle m, n\rangle, l\rangle)$ for all $w$ and some $m, n, l$, which is derived from the axiom $P_{i+1}(\langle\langle m, n\rangle, l\rangle) \vdash P_{i+1}(w)$ where $w = \langle\langle m, n\rangle, l\rangle$. We also have (d) $\neg \forall x P_{i+1}(x) \vdash \exists x \neg P_{i+1}(x)$ by Lemma 4.4 (2).

By the cut rule with (a) to (d), we have the claim.

(3) We will show $S_n \vdash \forall x A$. Induction hypothesis gives $S^m_n \vdash A[m/x]$ for each $m$. Hence we have $S_n \vdash A[m/x]$ for each $m$ by the cut rule with $S_n \vdash S^m_n$. By $(\forall R)$, we have the claim.

Case $(\exists)$. Let $\Delta$ be $B_1, \ldots, B_{n-1}$.

(2) The claim is the same as the induction hypothesis since $S_i$ was defined as $S^1_i$.

(3) We will show $S_n \vdash \exists x A$. Induction hypothesis gives $S^1_n, \neg S^1_{n+1} \vdash \exists x A$ and $S^1_{n+1} \vdash A[t/x]$, which derives $S^1_n, S^1_{n+1} \vdash \exists x A$ by $(\exists R)$ and $(WL)$. Hence we have $S_n, \neg S^1_{n+1} \vee S^1_{n+1} \vdash \exists x A$ by $(\vee L)$ and $S_n = S^1_n$. By using the cut rule with $\vdash \neg S^1_{n+1} \vee S^1_{n+1}$ by $\mathrm{EM}_1$, we have the claim.□

**Theorem 5.2.** *If $PA^+_{inf} - Exch$ proves the sequent $A$, then $HA_{inf} + EM_1$ proves $\vdash A$.*

Proof. By Theorem 5.1 with $n = 1$, there exists the $\Pi^0_1$ formula $S_1$ such that $\mathrm{HA}_{\mathrm{inf}} + \mathrm{EM}_1$ proves $\vdash S_1$ and $S_1 \vdash A$. By the cut rule, we have the claim.□

## 6 From $\mathbf{HA}_{\mathrm{inf}} + \mathbf{EM}_1$ to $\mathbf{PA}^+_{\mathrm{inf}} - \mathbf{Exch}$

This section will show that if a positive sentence is provable in $\mathrm{HA}_{\mathrm{inf}} + \mathrm{EM}_1$, then it is proved in $\mathrm{PA}^+_{\mathrm{inf}} - \mathrm{Exch}$. To prove this, we will use Limit Computable Mathematics and 1-backtracking Tarski games.

Limit computable mathematics, called LCM, is a realizability model [8]. It is defined in the same way as Kleene's realizability model except that LCM has $\Delta_2^0$-partial functions as realizers, and on the other hand Kleene's model has partial recursive functions as realizers. The set LCM of sentences is defined as the set of sentences which are realizable with realizers in the set of $\Delta_2^0$-partial functions.

We briefly introduce the theory of LCM. Fix any recursive enumeration of the set $\Delta_2^0$ of partial recursive maps in an oracle for the Halting Problem. $\{n\}'(m)$ denotes the result of the application of the $n$-th map to $m \in N$. $\{n\}'(m)$ may be undefined since $\{n\}'(\cdot)$ is a partial map. Let $\langle \cdot, \cdot \rangle$ be a primitive recursive pairing function, and $\pi_1, \pi_2$ be the inverse maps such that $\pi_i(\langle n_1, n_2 \rangle) = n_i$ for all $n_1, n_2 \in N$.

**Definition 6.1 (Realizability Relation of LCM).** For any arithmetical formula $A$ and any fresh variable $e$, we define a formula $e$ **r** $A$ in a language extended with $\{\cdot\}'(\cdot)$. We read $e$ **r** $A$ as "$e$ realizes $A$." This is defined by induction on $A$.

1. $e \mathbf{~r~} a \equiv e = 0 \wedge a$ if $a$ is an atom,
2. $e \mathbf{~r~} A \wedge B \equiv (\pi_1(e) \mathbf{~r~} A) \wedge (\pi_2(e) \mathbf{~r~} B)$,
3. $e \mathbf{~r~} A \vee B \equiv (\pi_1(e) = 0 \wedge (\pi_2(e) \mathbf{~r~} A)) \vee (\pi_1(e) = 1 \wedge (\pi_2(e) \mathbf{~r~} B))$,
4. $e \mathbf{~r~} A \rightarrow B \equiv \forall x.((x \mathbf{~r~} A) \rightarrow (\{e\}'(x) \mathbf{~r~} B))$,
5. $e \mathbf{~r~} \forall x.A \equiv \forall x.(\{e\}'(x) \mathbf{~r~} A)$,
6. $e \mathbf{~r~} \exists x.A \equiv \pi_2(e) \mathbf{~r~} A[\pi_1(e)/x]$.

We interpret the equality $s = t$ of two expressions $s$ and $t$ including $\{\cdot\}'(\cdot)$ by "$s$ and $t$ are both undefined, or both defined and equal." In this way we assign a truth value to each formula $n$ **r** $A$, for any closed $A$ and any constant $n \in N$. LCM is the set of closed arithmetical formulas $A$ such that $\exists e.(e \mathbf{~r~} A)$ is true in the standard model. The difference with the standard realizability interpretation is that we consider an enumeration of $\Delta_2^0$ partial maps, instead of partial recursive maps. The name of Limit Computable Mathematics comes from the fact that each map in $\Delta_2^0$ is the recursive limit of recursive maps.

First we show the next proposition stating that the system $\mathrm{HA_{inf}} + \mathrm{EM_1}$ is valid in LCM.

$\Gamma \rightarrow \Delta$ ($n \geq 0$) is defined as $B_1 \rightarrow \ldots \rightarrow B_n \rightarrow A$ when $\Gamma$ is $B_1, \ldots, B_n$ and $\Delta$ is $A$, and is defined as $B_1 \rightarrow \ldots \rightarrow B_n \rightarrow \mathtt{false}$ when $\Gamma$ is $B_1, \ldots, B_n$ and $\Delta$ is empty.

**Proposition 6.2 (Validity of $\mathbf{HA_{inf}} + \mathbf{EM_1}$ in LCM).** *There exists a recursive function $f$ such that from the code of a proof of $\Gamma \vdash \Delta$ in $HA_{inf} + EM_1$, $f$ computes a number $e$ such that $e$ **r** $\Gamma \rightarrow \Delta$ is true.*

Proof. The claim is proved by induction on the proof of $\Gamma \vdash \Delta$ in $\mathrm{HA_{inf}} + \mathrm{EM_1}$.□

The clause 4 of Corollary 1 in [2] showed the next theorem.

**Theorem 6.3 ([2]).** *For an implication-free sentence $A$, $A$ is valid in LCM if and only if $A$ has a recursive winning strategy in the Tarski game for $A$ with 1-backtracking.*

Theorem 11 in [4] showed the next theorem.

**Theorem 6.4** **([4]).** *For an implication-free sentence A, A has a recursive winning strategy in the Tarski game for A with 1-backtracking if and only if the sequent A is provable in* $PA^{+}_{inf} - Exch$.

**Proposition 6.5.** *For an implication-free sentence A, if* $HA_{inf} + EM_1$ *proves* $\vdash A$, *then* $PA^{+}_{inf} - Exch$ *proves the sequent A.*

Proof. Suppose $\vdash A$ is provable in $\mathrm{HA_{inf}} + \mathrm{EM}_1$. By Proposition 6.2, $A$ is valid in LCM. By Theorem 6.3, $A$ has a recursive winning strategy in the Tarski game for $A$ with 1-backtracking. By Theorem 6.4, the sequent $A$ is provable in $\mathrm{PA^{+}_{inf}} - \mathrm{Exch}$.□

## 7 Equivalence of $\mathbf{PA^{+}_{inf}} - \mathbf{Exch}$ and $\mathbf{HA_{inf}} + \mathbf{EM_1}$

Combining Theorem 5.2 and Proposition 6.5, we have our main result.

**Theorem 7.1 (Equivalence of $\mathbf{PA^{+}_{inf}} - \mathbf{Exch}$ and $\mathbf{HA_{inf}} + \mathbf{EM_1}$).** *For an implication-free sentence A,* $HA_{inf} + EM_1$ *proves* $\vdash A$ *if and only if* $PA^{+}_{inf} - Exch$ *proves the sequent A.*

We will now discuss a corollary of our main result for related topics.

Our main result gives us a characterization of the set of implication-free sentences in LCM.

As we explained in Section 2, a 1-backtracking game is a game where one player can retract some past move and all the moves after it, but he cannot recover a retracted move [2]. Our main result also gives us a characterization of 1-backtracking Tarski games.

**Theorem 7.2.** *The following four properties are equivalent for an implication-free sentence A:*

*(1) A is provable in* $PA^{+}_{inf} - Exch$,
*(2) A is provable in* $HA_{inf} + EM_1$,
*(3) A is in LCM,*
*(4) A has a recursive winning strategy in the 1-backtracking Tarski game for A.*

Proof. The direction from (1) to (2) is proved by Theorem 5.2. The direction from (2) to (3) is prove by Proposition 6.2. The equivalence between (3) and (4) is proved by Theorem 6.3. The equivalence between (4) and (1) is proved by Theorem 6.4.□

## References

1. Akama, Y., Berardi, S., Hayashi, S., Kohlenbach, U.: An Arithmetical Hierarchy of the Law of Excluded Middle and Related Principles. In: Proceedings of Nineteenth Annual IEEE Symposium on Logic in Computer Science, pp. 192–201 (2004)
2. Berardi, S., Coquand, T., Hayashi, S.: Games with 1-backtracking. In: Proceedings of Games for Logic and Programming Languages (2005, also submitted to APAL)

3. Berardi, S.: Some intuitionistic equivalents of classical principles for degree 2 formulas. Annals of Pure and Applied Logic 139, 185–200 (2006)
4. Berardi, S., Yamagata, Y.: A sequent calculus for Limit Computable Mathematics. Annals of Pure and Applied Logic (to appear)
5. Berardi, S.: Semantics for Intuitionistic Arithmetic based on Tarski Games with retractable moves. In: Proceedings of TLCA, LNCS, vol. 4583 (2007)
6. Coquand, T.: A Semantics of Evidence for Classical Arithmetic. Journal of Symbolic Logic 60(1), 325–337 (1995)
7. Griffin, T.G.: A formulae-as-types notion of control. In: Proceedings of Seventeenth Annual ACM Symposium on Principles of Programming languages, pp. 47–58 (1990)
8. Hayashi, S., Nakata, M.: Towards Limit Computable Mathematics. In: Callaghan, P., Luo, Z., McKinna, J., Pollack, R. (eds.) TYPES 2000. LNCS, vol. 2277, pp. 125–144. Springer, Heidelberg (2002)
9. Hayashi, S.: Can Proofs be animated by games? Fundamenta Informaticae 77, 1–13 (2007)
10. Howard, W.A.: The Formulae-as-types Notion of Constructions. In: To H.B. Curry: Essays on Combinatory Logic, Lambda Calculus and Formalism, pp. 479–490. Academic Press, London (1980)
11. Kleene, S.C.: Introduction to Metamathematics. North-Holland, Amsterdam (1967)
12. Kohlenbach, U.: Relative Constructivity. Journal of Symbolic Logic 63(4), 1218–1238 (1998)

# Mixed Inductive/Coinductive Types and Strong Normalization

Andreas Abel*

Department of Computer Science, University of Munich
Oettingenstr. 67, D-80538 München, Germany
andreas.abel@ifi.lmu.de

**Abstract.** We introduce the concept of *guarded* saturated sets, saturated sets of strongly normalizing terms closed under folding of corecursive functions. Using this tool, we can model equi-inductive and equi-coinductive types with terminating recursion and corecursion principles. Two type systems are presented: Mendler (co)iteration and sized types. As an application we show that we can directly represent the mixed inductive/coinductive type of stream processors with associated recursive operations.

## 1 Introduction

Symbolic evaluation, aka evaluation of terms with free variables, is used, amongst others, for optimization through partial evaluation in compilers and for checking term equivalence in languages based on dependent types—such as the theorem provers Agda, Coq, Epigram, and LEGO, founded on intensional type theory. In these applications, symbolic evaluation is required to terminate. My long term research goal is to develop expressive type systems that guarantee termination, and these type system shall include inductive and coinductive types.

Most research on inductive types has focused on the *iso*-style, i. e., there are explicit operations $\mathsf{in} : F(\mu F) \to \mu F$ and $\mathsf{out} : \mu F \to F(\mu F)$ for wrapping and unwrapping inductive types. In contrast, *equi*-inductive types come with the type equation $\mu F = F(\mu F)$, so wrapping and unwrapping is silent on the term level. Recently [4], I have put forth a type system for strongly normalizing terms with *equi*-(co)inductive types, but it behaves badly for so-called mixed inductive/coinductive types.

However, mixed inductive/coinductive types are important in the context of intensional type theory. Ghani, Hancock, and Pattinson [10] show how the type $\nu X.\,\mu Y.\,(B \times X) + (A \to Y)$ of stream processors is inhabited by codes of functions from streams over $A$ to streams over $B$. They define *eating*, a function which takes a stream processor and an input stream and produces an output stream; *eating* executes the code of a stream processor. Swierstra [17] demonstrated how a small modification of stream processors could be used to model I/O in a dependently typed programming language.

* Research partially supported by the EU coordination action *TYPES* (510996).

Z. Shao (Ed.): APLAS 2007, LNCS 4807, pp. 286–301, 2007.

In this article, I present a concept which paves the way to a satisfactory treatment of mixed equi-(co)inductive types: *guarded type expressions.* The term *guardedness* has been used as a criterion whether corecursive programs denote well-defined functions. A corecursive call is guarded if it appears under a constructor of the coinductive type. In the same sense, a type expression is guarded if it is headed by a proper type constructor, like function space, cartesian product, disjoint sum, or a primitive type. Using the guardedness criterion, we can avoid coinductive types which contain no weak head values, and the remaining coinductive types have the pleasant property that they already contain a corecursive value if they contain its unfolding. This property gives rise to the new concept of *guarded saturated set*, on which we base our normalization proof.

*Related Work.* There is a rich body of work on type systems for termination of recursion, starting with Mendler [12], with contributions by Amadio and Coupet-Grimal [6], a group around Giménez and Barthe [7,8], and Blanqui and Riba [9]. All of these works are concerned with *iso*-(co)inductive types. Parigot [13] introduces equi-inductive and coinductive types in second-order functional arithmetic, an extension of System F. [15] provides Mendler iteration and coiteration schemes for these types and proves that all well-typed terms are hereditarily solvable, if the involved types satisfy a certain *strictness* condition. We require a condition only on coinductive types. Hughes, Pareto, and Sabry [11] present sized types in the equi-style, yet they consider only finitely branching data types and explicitly exclude a type of stream processors. In my previous attempt at equi-(co)inductive types [4] I constructed a semantics based on biorthogonals, which are due to Girard and have been successfully applied at interpreting languages based on classical logic (see, e. g., Parigot [14]). However, I had to consider a recursive function applied to a corecursive value blocked, preventing the use of mixed inductive/coinductive types. In this article, this flaw is overcome by a semantics based on saturated sets.

*Overview.* In Sec. 2, we will see a $\lambda$-calculus with recursion and corecursion and a saturated-set semantics of strongly normalizing terms. On this semantics, we base first a type system with Mendler (co)iteration (Sec. 3), and then a more flexible one with sized types (Sec. 4).

## 2 Untyped Language and Semantics

As an idealized purely functional programming language, we consider the $\lambda$-calculus with pairs and projections, injections and case analysis, and recursion and corecursion. In this section, we define semantical types as sets of strongly normalizing terms and prove formation, introduction and elimination rules for these semantical types. Especially interesting will be the principles for terminating recursion and corecursion which will be derived from the construction of inductive and coinductive types by ordinal iteration.

In all expressions throughout this article a dot "." denotes an opening parenthesis closing as far to the right as syntactically meaningful. $[M/x]N$ denotes the capture avoiding substitution of $M$ for $x$ in $N$. Let $x$ range over a countably infinite set $\mathsf{Var}$ of variables. We define our language as the lambda calculus equipped with constants $c$. The values $v$ are $\lambda$-abstractions, pairs, injections, and not fully applied constants (including recursive functions and corecursive values).

$$
\begin{array}{lll}
c & ::= () \mid \mathsf{pair} \mid \mathsf{fst} \mid \mathsf{snd} \mid \mathsf{inl} \mid \mathsf{inr} \mid \mathsf{case} & \\
 & \quad \mid \mathsf{fix}^{\mu} \mid \mathsf{fix}^{\nu}_{n} \qquad (n \in \mathbb{N}) & \text{constants} \\
r, s, t & ::= c \mid x \mid \lambda x t \mid r\, s & \text{terms} \\
v, w & ::= c \mid \lambda x t \mid \mathsf{pair}\, r \mid \mathsf{pair}\, r\, s \mid \mathsf{inl}\, r \mid \mathsf{inr}\, r & \\
 & \quad \mid \mathsf{fix}^{\mu}\, s \mid \mathsf{fix}^{\nu}_{n} s\, \boldsymbol{t} \quad (|\boldsymbol{t}| \leq n) & \text{(weak-head) values} \\
e^{-}(\_) & ::= \_\, s \mid \mathsf{fst}\, \_ \mid \mathsf{snd}\, \_ \mid \mathsf{case}\, \_\, s\, t & \text{non-recursive evaluation frames} \\
e(\_) & ::= e^{-}(\_) \mid \mathsf{fix}^{\mu}\, s\, \_ & \text{evaluation frames} \\
E(\_) & ::= \_ \mid E(e(\_)) & \text{evaluation contexts.}
\end{array}
$$

We distinguish between possibly recursive $e(\_)$ and non-recursive $e^{-}(\_)$ evaluation frames. An evaluation context is $E(\_)$ is a stack of evaluation frames. Corecursive functions are only unfolded in a non-recursive evaluation frame

*Reduction.* Computation is modeled as small-step reduction relation. These are the axioms of $\beta$-contraction $e(v) \rightarrowtail t$.

$$
\begin{array}{llll}
(\lambda x t)\, s & \rightarrowtail [s/x]t & \mathsf{fst}\,(\mathsf{pair}\, r\, s) & \rightarrowtail r \\
\mathsf{fix}^{\mu}\, s\, v & \rightarrowtail s\,(\mathsf{fix}^{\mu}\, s)\, v & \mathsf{snd}\,(\mathsf{pair}\, r\, s) & \rightarrowtail s \\
e^{-}(\mathsf{fix}^{\nu}_{n}\, s\, t_{1..n}) & \rightarrowtail e^{-}(s\,(\mathsf{fix}^{\nu}_{n}\, s)\, t_{1..n}) & \mathsf{case}\,(\mathsf{inl}\, r)\, s\, t & \rightarrowtail s\, r \\
 & & \mathsf{case}\,(\mathsf{inr}\, r)\, s\, t & \rightarrowtail t\, r
\end{array}
$$

One-step reduction $\longrightarrow$ is the closure of $\rightarrowtail$ under all term constructors, multi-step reduction $\longrightarrow^{+}$ its transitive closure and $\longrightarrow^{*}$ its reflexive-transitive closure. Weak head reduction is defined by $E(t) \longrightarrow_{\mathsf{w}} E(t') \iff t \rightarrowtail t'$.

By only unfolding corecursive values in non-recursive evaluation frames, we avoid critical pairs. This does not lead to stuck terms, since in such a case the recursive function constituting the frame can be unfolded instead. In previous work [4], we considered a corecursive value in a recursive frame as stuck, leading to an unsatisfactory treatment of mixed induction/coinduction. The present work overcomes this flaw.

*Strong normalization and saturated sets.* A term $t$ is *strongly normalizing* (s.n.), written $t \in \mathsf{SN}$, if all reduction sequences starting with $t$ are finite. Note that subterms and reducts of s.n. terms are also s.n. Terms $E(x) \in \mathsf{SN}$ are called s.n. and neutral and their collection is denoted by $\mathsf{SNe}$.

A set of terms $\mathcal{A}$ is a *semantical type*, written $\mathcal{A} \in \mathsf{SAT}_{\mathsf{u}}$, if

1. $\mathsf{SNe} \subseteq \mathcal{A} \subseteq \mathsf{SN}$,
2. each term in $\mathcal{A}$ weak-head reduces either to a value or a neutral term,
3. $\mathcal{A}$ is closed under weak head expansion that does not introduce diverging terms.

The first condition ensures that each semantical type contains all variables, such that we can construct an open s.n. term model of our calculus. The second condition is used to justify recursive functions $\mathsf{fix}^\mu\, s$, which reduce under call-by-(weak-head)-value (see Lemma 3). The third condition ensures that a redex like $(\lambda x t)\, s$ inhabits a semantical type if its reduct (here $[s/x]t$) does so. This is needed, for instance, to establish that $\lambda x t$ is in the semantical function space, and similarly for $\mathsf{pair}\, r\, s$, case distinctions and recursive functions.

The third condition can be made precise by defining *safe weak head reduction*, $\rhd$, by the following rules:

$$\begin{array}{lll}
(\lambda x t)\, s & \rhd [s/x]t & \text{if } s \in \mathsf{SN} \\
\mathsf{fix}^\mu\, s\, v & \rhd s\,(\mathsf{fix}^\mu\, s)\, v & \\
\mathsf{e}^-(\mathsf{fix}^\nu_n\, s\, t_{1..n}) & \rhd \mathsf{e}^-(s\,(\mathsf{fix}^\nu_n\, s)\, t_{1..n}) & \\
E(t) & \rhd E(t') & \text{if } t \rhd t'
\end{array}
\qquad
\begin{array}{lll}
\mathsf{fst}\,(\mathsf{pair}\, r\, s) & \rhd r & \text{if } s \in \mathsf{SN} \\
\mathsf{snd}\,(\mathsf{pair}\, r\, s) & \rhd s & \text{if } r \in \mathsf{SN} \\
\mathsf{case}\,(\mathsf{inl}\, r)\, s\, t & \rhd s\, r & \text{if } t \in \mathsf{SN} \\
\mathsf{case}\,(\mathsf{inr}\, r)\, s\, t & \rhd t\, r & \text{if } s \in \mathsf{SN}
\end{array}$$

We define $\rhd$ as the reflexive-transitive closure of the above rules. Now if $t \rhd t' \in \mathsf{SN}$, then $t \in \mathsf{SN}$. For a reduction relation $R$, let ${}^R\mathcal{A} := \{t \mid t\ R\ t' \in \mathcal{A}\}$ and $\mathcal{A}^R := \{t' \mid \mathcal{A} \ni t\ R\ t'\}$. Condition 3 of semantical types can then be written as ${}^{\rhd}\mathcal{A} \subseteq \mathcal{A}$.

The greatest semantical type is called $\mathcal{S}$, it contains all s.n. terms except those whose weak-head reduction gets stuck, like $\mathsf{fst}\,(\lambda x x)$. The least semantical type is $\mathcal{N} := {}^{\rhd}\mathsf{SNe}$, and it is closed under s.n. evaluation contexts: if $r \in \mathcal{N}$ and $E(x) \in \mathsf{SNe}$ then $E(r) \in \mathcal{N}$.

*Guarded semantical types.* A semantical type $\mathcal{A}$ is *guarded*, written $\mathcal{A} \in \mathsf{SAT_g}$, if $s\,(\mathsf{fix}^\nu_n\, s)\, t_{1..n} \in \mathcal{A}$ implies $\mathsf{fix}^\nu_n\, s\, t_{1..n} \in \mathcal{A}$. Let $\blacktriangleright \supseteq \rhd$ be the reflexive-transitive closure of safe weak head reduction plus the axiom

$$\mathsf{fix}^\nu_n\, s\, t_{1..n} \blacktriangleright s\,(\mathsf{fix}^\nu_n\, s)\, t_{1..n}.$$

Note that $r \blacktriangleright r'$ implies $\mathsf{e}^-(r) \rhd \mathsf{e}^-(r')$.

A semantical type $\mathcal{A}$ is guarded iff ${}^{\blacktriangleright}\mathcal{A} \subseteq \mathcal{A}$. The premier example of a non-guarded type is $\mathcal{N}$. Note that $\mathcal{S}$ is closed under $\blacktriangleright$-expansion, since $\mathsf{fix}^\nu_n\, s\, t_{1..n}$ is a strongly normalizing value if $s, t_{1..n} \in \mathsf{SN}$. Thus, $\mathcal{S}$ is guarded.

*Constructions on semantical types.* The following constructions produce guarded semantical types, even for unguarded $\mathcal{A}, \mathcal{B} \in \mathsf{SAT_u}$.

$$\begin{array}{ll}
\mathcal{A} \to \mathcal{B} & := \{r \mid r\, s \in \mathcal{B} \text{ for all } s \in \mathcal{A}\} \\
\mathcal{A} \times \mathcal{B} & := \{r \mid \mathsf{fst}\, r \in \mathcal{A} \text{ and } \mathsf{snd}\, r \in \mathcal{B}\} \\
\mathcal{A} + \mathcal{B} & := {}^{\blacktriangleright}(\mathsf{inl}(\mathcal{A}) \cup \mathsf{inl}(\mathcal{B}) \cup \mathsf{SNe}) \\
1 & := {}^{\blacktriangleright}(\{()\} \cup \mathsf{SNe})
\end{array}$$

Note that $\mathsf{SAT_g}$ and $\mathsf{SAT_u}$ are closed under arbitrary intersections and *unions*. The last property is the advantage of saturated-sets semantics, it does not always hold for candidates of reducibility or biorthogonals, and even when it holds the proof is non-trivial [16].

If $\mathcal{F}$ is a monotone operator on sets of terms, and $\alpha$ an ordinal, we define the term sets $\mu^\alpha \mathcal{F}$ and $\nu^\alpha \mathcal{F}$ by iteration on $\alpha$ as follows.

$$\begin{array}{llll} \mu^0 & \mathcal{F} := \mathcal{N} & \nu^0 & \mathcal{F} := \mathcal{S} \\ \mu^{\alpha+1} & \mathcal{F} := \mathcal{F}(\mu^\alpha \mathcal{F}) & \nu^{\alpha+1} & \mathcal{F} := \mathcal{F}(\nu^\alpha \mathcal{F}) \\ \mu^\lambda & \mathcal{F} := \bigcup_{\alpha<\lambda} \mu^\alpha \mathcal{F} & \nu^\lambda & \mathcal{F} := \bigcap_{\alpha<\lambda} \nu^\alpha \mathcal{F} \end{array}$$

Herein, $\lambda$ denotes limit ordinals $> 0$. Let $\infty$ denote the ordinal at which, for any $\mathcal{F}$, iteration from below reaches the least fixed-point $\mu^\infty \mathcal{F} = \mathcal{F}(\mu^\infty \mathcal{F})$, and iteration from above reaches the greatest fixed-point $\nu^\infty \mathcal{F} = \mathcal{F}(\nu^\infty \mathcal{F})$. Since term sets are countable, $\infty$ is at most the first uncountable ordinal.

Now if $\mathcal{F}(\mathcal{A})$ is guarded for any $\mathcal{A} \in \mathsf{SAT}_\mathsf{u}$, then $\mu^\alpha \mathcal{F}$ will be guarded for $\alpha \geq 1$. If $\mathcal{F}(\mathcal{A})$ is guarded for any *guarded* $\mathcal{A}$, then $\nu^\alpha \mathcal{F}$ is guarded for all $\alpha$.

**Lemma 1 (Semantical formation).** *The following implications, written as rules, hold:*

$$\frac{\mathcal{A}, \mathcal{B} \in \mathsf{SAT}_\mathsf{u}}{\mathcal{A} \star \mathcal{B} \in \mathsf{SAT}_\mathsf{g}} \star \in \{\to, \times, +\} \qquad \frac{}{1 \in \mathsf{SAT}_\mathsf{g}} \qquad \frac{}{\mathcal{N} \in \mathsf{SAT}_\mathsf{u}} \qquad \frac{}{\mathcal{S} \in \mathsf{SAT}_\mathsf{g}}$$

$$\frac{\mathcal{F} \in \mathsf{SAT}_\mathsf{u} \to \mathsf{SAT}_\mathfrak{b}}{\mu^\infty \mathcal{F} \in \mathsf{SAT}_\mathfrak{b}} \; \mathfrak{b} \in \{\mathsf{u}, \mathsf{g}\} \qquad \frac{\mathcal{F} \in \mathsf{SAT}_\mathsf{g} \to \mathsf{SAT}_\mathfrak{b}}{\nu^\infty \mathcal{F} \in \mathsf{SAT}_\mathfrak{b}} \; \mathfrak{b} \in \{\mathsf{u}, \mathsf{g}\}$$

*Proof.* We show the first implication, $\mathcal{A} \to \mathcal{B} \in \mathsf{SAT}_\mathsf{g}$. It is sufficient to assume $\{x\} \subseteq \mathcal{A} \subseteq \mathsf{SN}$ and $\mathcal{B} \in \mathsf{SAT}_\mathsf{u}$. Let $r \in \mathcal{A} \to \mathcal{B}$. First, $r\,x \in \mathcal{B} \subseteq \mathsf{SN}$ by assumption, hence $r \in \mathsf{SN}$. Second, we know that $r\,x$ weak-head reduces to either a neutral term or a value. Hence, either $r$ weak-head reduces to a neutral term, or to a $\lambda$-abstraction, which is a value. Third, let $r' \blacktriangleright r$. Then for any $s \in \mathcal{A}$ we have $r'\,s \rhd r\,s$ which, since $\mathcal{B} \in \mathsf{SAT}_\mathsf{u}$, implies $r'\,s \in \mathcal{B}$. This entails $r' \in \mathcal{A}$.

**Lemma 2 (Semantical typing).** *The following implications hold:*

$$\frac{[s/x]t \in \mathcal{B} \textit{ for all } s \in \mathcal{A}}{\lambda x t \in \mathcal{A} \to \mathcal{B}} \qquad \frac{r \in \mathcal{A} \to \mathcal{B} \qquad s \in \mathcal{A}}{r\,s \in \mathcal{B}}$$

$$\frac{r \in \mathcal{A} \qquad s \in \mathcal{B}}{\mathsf{pair}\,r\,s \in \mathcal{A} \times \mathcal{B}} \qquad \frac{r \in \mathcal{A} \times \mathcal{B}}{\mathsf{fst}\,r \in \mathcal{A}} \qquad \frac{r \in \mathcal{A} \times \mathcal{B}}{\mathsf{snd}\,r \in \mathcal{B}} \qquad \frac{}{() \in 1}$$

$$\frac{t \in \mathcal{A}}{\mathsf{inl}\,t \in \mathcal{A} + \mathcal{B}} \qquad \frac{t \in \mathcal{B}}{\mathsf{inr}\,t \in \mathcal{A} + \mathcal{B}} \qquad \frac{r \in \mathcal{A} + \mathcal{B} \qquad s \in \mathcal{A} \to \mathcal{C} \qquad t \in \mathcal{B} \to \mathcal{C}}{\mathsf{case}\,r\,s\,t \in \mathcal{C}}$$

*Proof.* The rules for $\lambda$, pair, and case are proven by closure of saturated sets under safe weak head expansion. (The remaining rules hold already by definition.) We show the last implication. Assume $r \in \mathcal{A}{+}\mathcal{B}$, then $r \blacktriangleright r'$ where $r'$ is either neutral or a left or right injection. We observe that $\mathsf{case}\,r\,s\,t \rhd \mathsf{case}\,r'\,s\,t$ and distinguish the three cases: In the first case $\mathsf{case}\,r'\,s\,t \in \mathsf{SNe}$, hence, $\mathsf{case}\,r\,s\,t \in \mathcal{N} \subseteq \mathcal{C}$. In the second case, $r' = \mathsf{inl}\,r''$ with $r'' \in \mathcal{A}$, thus, $\mathsf{case}\,r\,s\,t \rhd s\,r'' \in \mathcal{C}$. The third case is analogous to the second.

The following semantical typing for recursion is the foundation of type-based termination à la Mendler [12], Amadio et al. [6] and Barthe et al. [7]. In a typical application of the following lemma, $\mathcal{I}(\alpha)$ will be some inductive type $\mu^\alpha \mathcal{F}$; then $\mathcal{I}(0) = \mathcal{N}$.

**Lemma 3 (Recursion).** *For all ordinals $\alpha \leq \infty$ let $\mathcal{I}(\alpha), \mathcal{C}(\alpha) \in \mathsf{SAT_u}$ with $\mathcal{I}(0) \subseteq \mathcal{N}$. Set $\mathcal{A}(\alpha) := \mathcal{I}(\alpha) \to \mathcal{C}(\alpha)$ and stipulate continuity: $\bigcap_{\alpha<\lambda} \mathcal{A}(\alpha) \subseteq \mathcal{A}(\lambda)$ for all limit ordinals $\lambda > 0$. Then the following implication holds for all $\beta \leq \infty$:*

$$\frac{s \in \bigcap_{\alpha<\infty} \mathcal{A}(\alpha) \to \mathcal{A}(\alpha+1)}{\mathsf{fix}^\mu\, s \in \mathcal{A}(\beta)}.$$

*Proof.* By transfinite induction on $\beta$. The limit case is handled by the continuity condition on $\mathcal{A}$. For the other cases, assume $r \in \mathcal{I}(\beta)$ and show $\mathsf{fix}^\mu\, s\, r \in \mathcal{C}(\beta)$. If $r \in \mathcal{N}$ then $\mathsf{fix}^\mu\, s\, r \in \mathcal{N} \subseteq \mathcal{C}(\beta)$; since $\mathcal{I}(0) \subseteq \mathcal{N}$, this handles the case $\beta = 0$. Otherwise $r \rhd v$ and $\beta = \alpha + 1$ for some $\alpha$. It is sufficient to show that the weak head reduct $s\,(\mathsf{fix}^\mu\, s)\, v$ of $\mathsf{fix}^\mu\, s\, r$ is in $\mathcal{C}(\alpha+1)$, but this follows from the induction hypothesis $\mathsf{fix}^\mu s \in \mathcal{A}(\alpha)$ by the assumption $s \in \mathcal{A}(\alpha) \to \mathcal{A}(\alpha+1)$.

The proof for $\beta = 0$ needs $\mathcal{N}$ to be closed under evaluation contexts, $\mathsf{fix}^\mu s\ \_$ in our case. If $\mathcal{N}$ was also guarded, then $\mathsf{fix}^\nu_0 \lambda\_x \in \mathcal{N}$ and $\mathsf{fix}^\mu(\lambda f f)(\mathsf{fix}^\nu_0 \lambda\_x) \in \mathcal{N}$, a diverging term. Thus, the least type needs to be classified as unguarded.

*Remark 1 (Continuity).* Let $\mathcal{N}at^\alpha = \mu^\alpha(\mathcal{X} \mapsto 1 + \mathcal{X})$ be the semantical type corresponding to the set of natural numbers $< \alpha$. The function $\mathcal{A}(\alpha) = (\mathcal{N}at^\omega \to \mathcal{N}at^\alpha) \to 1$ violates the continuity condition: one can implement a test $p(f)$ in our calculus that halts whenever it has found numbers $n, m$ with $f(n) = f(m)$. The test will halt for bounded functions $f \in \mathcal{N}at^\omega \to \mathcal{N}at^\alpha$ for $\alpha < \omega$, but diverges on, for example, any strictly monotone unbounded function $f \in \mathcal{N}at^\omega \to \mathcal{N}at^\omega$. This justifies the necessity of the continuity condition for the soundness of our semantics [2].

The following lemma dualizes Lemma 3; it is tailored for guarded $\mathcal{C}(\alpha) = \nu^\alpha \mathcal{F}$. To prove it, we have introduced the concept of guardedness in the first place.

**Lemma 4 (Corecursion).** *For $\alpha \leq \infty$ let $\mathcal{B}_1(\alpha), \ldots, \mathcal{B}_n(\alpha) \in \mathsf{SAT_u}$ and $\mathcal{C}(\alpha) \in \mathsf{SAT_g}$ such that $\mathcal{S} \subseteq \mathcal{C}(0)$. Set $\mathcal{A}(\alpha) := \mathcal{B}_1(\alpha) \to \cdots \to \mathcal{B}_n(\alpha) \to \mathcal{C}(\alpha)$ and stipulate $\bigcap_{\alpha<\lambda} \mathcal{A}(\alpha) \subseteq \mathcal{A}(\lambda)$ for limits $\lambda$. Then for all $\beta \leq \infty$,*

$$\frac{s \in \bigcap_{\alpha<\infty} \mathcal{A}(\alpha) \to \mathcal{A}(\alpha+1)}{\mathsf{fix}^\nu_n\, s \in \mathcal{A}(\beta)}.$$

*Proof.* By transfinite induction on $\beta$, limits again handled by continuity of $\mathcal{A}$. Assume $t_i \in \mathcal{B}_i(\beta)$ for $i = 1..n$ and show $r := \mathsf{fix}^\nu_n\, s\, t_{1..n} \in \mathcal{C}(\beta)$. In case $\beta = 0$ it is sufficient to show $r \in \mathcal{S}$, but this holds since $r$ is a value and its direct subterms are all s.n. In case $\beta = \alpha+1$, observe that $r \blacktriangleright s\,(\mathsf{fix}^\nu_n\, s)\, t_{1..n} \in \mathcal{C}(\alpha+1)$ by induction hypothesis $\mathsf{fix}^\nu_n\, s \in \mathcal{A}(\alpha)$ and assumption $s \in \mathcal{A}(\alpha) \to \mathcal{A}(\alpha+1)$. Since $\mathcal{C}(\alpha+1)$ is guarded, we are done.

We have identified semantically sound principles for recursion and corecursion. In the next sections, we implement two type systems on this basis.

## 3 A Basic Type System: Mendler (Co)Iteration

In this section, we consider a type system for iteration over equi-inductive types and coiteration over equi-coinductive types in the style of Mendler [12]. Mendler-iteration, like conventional iteration coming from initial algebra semantics, is usually formulated for iso-inductive types, with an explicit constructor $\mathsf{in} : F(\mu F) \to \mu F$. Our developments in the last section paved the way for equi-style formulations.

*Types* are given by the following grammar

$$\begin{array}{ll} \star & ::= \to \mid \times \mid + \\ A, B, C & ::= X \mid 1 \mid A \star B \mid \forall X A \mid \mu X A \mid \nu X A. \end{array}$$

The type constructors $\forall$, $\mu$, and $\nu$ bind variable $X$ in $A$. The type $\mu X X$ is an empty, unguarded type; we especially need to avoid unguarded coinductive types like $\nu Y \mu X X$. To this end, we present a kinding judgement with two base kinds: $*_{\mathsf{g}}$, guarded types, and $*_{\mathsf{u}}$, unguarded types.

Let $\theta$ be a map from type variables to semantical types. We define the semantics $[\![A]\!]_\theta$ of type $A$ by recursion on $A$ as follows:

$$\begin{array}{llll} [\![X]\!]_\theta & = \theta(X) & [\![\forall X A]\!]_\theta & = \bigcap_{\mathcal{X} \in \mathsf{SAT}_\mathsf{u}} [\![A]\!]_{\theta[X \mapsto \mathcal{X}]} \\ [\![A \star B]\!]_\theta & = [\![A]\!]_\theta \star [\![B]\!]_\theta & [\![\mu X A]\!]_\theta & = \mu^\infty(\mathcal{X} \in \mathsf{SAT}_\mathsf{u} \mapsto [\![A]\!]_{\theta[X \mapsto \mathcal{X}]}) \\ [\![1]\!]_\theta & = 1 & [\![\nu X A]\!]_\theta & = \nu^\infty(\mathcal{X} \in \mathsf{SAT}_\mathsf{g} \mapsto [\![A]\!]_{\theta[X \mapsto \mathcal{X}]}) \end{array}$$

*Kinding.* Let $\Delta$ be a finite map from type variables to base kinds. We write $\Delta, X : \kappa$ for the updated map $\Delta'$ with $\Delta'(X) = \kappa$ and $\Delta'(Y) = \Delta(Y)$ in case $Y \neq X$. In the update operation, we presuppose $X \notin \mathsf{dom}(\Delta)$. The judgment $\Delta \vdash A : \kappa$ is inductively given by the following rules (where $b \in \{\mathsf{u}, \mathsf{g}\}$).

$$\frac{}{\Delta \vdash X : \Delta(X)} \qquad \frac{}{\Delta \vdash 1 : *_\mathsf{g}} \qquad \frac{\Delta \vdash A : *_\mathsf{g}}{\Delta \vdash A : *_\mathsf{u}} \qquad \frac{\Delta \vdash A : *_\mathsf{u} \qquad \Delta \vdash B : *_\mathsf{u}}{\Delta \vdash A \star B : *_\mathsf{g}}$$

$$\frac{\Delta, X{:}*_\mathsf{u} \vdash A : *_b}{\Delta \vdash \forall X A : *_b} \qquad \frac{\Delta, X{:}*_\mathsf{u} \vdash A : *_b}{\Delta \vdash \mu X A : *_b}\ pos \qquad \frac{\Delta, X{:}*_\mathsf{g} \vdash A : *_\mathsf{g}}{\Delta \vdash \nu X A : *_\mathsf{g}}\ pos$$

In the formation rules for (co)inductive types we require (*pos*) that $X$ appears only positively in $A$ (otherwise, the denoted fixed-points might not exist).

The soundness of kinding is immediate. Let $\theta \in [\![\Delta]\!]$ iff $\Delta(X) = *_b$ implies $\theta(X) \in \mathsf{SAT}_b$ for all $X$.

**Theorem 1 (Soundness of kinding).** *If* $\Delta \vdash A : *_b$ *and* $\theta \in [\![\Delta]\!]$ *then* $[\![A]\!]_\theta \in \mathsf{SAT}_b$.

*Type equality.* Let $\Delta \vdash A = A'$ be the least congruence over the two axioms

$$\frac{\Delta \vdash \mu X A : *_\mathsf{u}}{\Delta \vdash \mu X A = [\mu X A / X] A} \qquad \frac{\Delta \vdash \nu X A : *_\mathsf{g}}{\Delta \vdash \nu X A = [\nu X A / X] A}.$$

**Lemma 5 (Soundness of type substitution and equality)**

1. $[\![B/X]A]\!]_\theta = [\![A]\!]_{\theta[X\mapsto[\![B]\!]_\theta]}$.
2. *If* $\Delta \vdash A = A'$ *and* $\theta \in [\![\Delta]\!]$ *then* $[\![A]\!]_\theta = [\![A']\!]_\theta$.

*Typing.* Let $\Gamma$ be a finite map from type variables to kinds and term variables to types, with additional update operation $\Gamma, x\!:\!A$. Each $\Gamma$ can be viewed as a $\Delta$, by ignoring the term variable bindings. The typing judgement $\Gamma \vdash t : A$ is inductively given by the following rules:

$$\frac{\Gamma \vdash \Gamma(x) : *_{\mathsf{u}}}{\Gamma \vdash x : \Gamma(x)} \qquad \frac{\Gamma, x\!:\!A \vdash t : B}{\Gamma \vdash \lambda x t : A \to B} \qquad \frac{\Gamma \vdash r : A \to B \qquad \Gamma \vdash s : A}{\Gamma \vdash r\, s : B}$$

$$\frac{\Gamma, X\!:\!*_{\mathsf{u}} \vdash t : A}{\Gamma \vdash t : \forall X A} \qquad \frac{\Gamma \vdash t : \forall X A \qquad \Gamma \vdash B : *_{\mathsf{u}}}{\Gamma \vdash t : [B/X]A} \qquad \frac{\Gamma \vdash t : A \qquad \Gamma \vdash A = B}{\Gamma \vdash t : B}$$

$$\frac{}{\Gamma \vdash c : \Sigma(c)} \qquad \frac{\Gamma \vdash \mu X A : *_{\mathsf{u}} \qquad \Gamma \vdash C : *_{\mathsf{u}}}{\Gamma \vdash \mathsf{fix}^\mu : (\forall X.\, (X \to C) \to A \to C) \to \mu X A \to C}$$

$$\frac{\Gamma \vdash \nu X A : *_{\mathsf{g}} \qquad \Gamma \vdash B_i : *_{\mathsf{u}} \text{ for } i = 1..n}{\Gamma \vdash \mathsf{fix}^\nu_n : (\forall X.\, (B_{1..n} \to X) \to B_{1..n} \to A) \to B_{1..n} \to \nu X A}$$

Herein, the signature $\Sigma$ assigns the following types to constants $c$:

$$\begin{array}{ll} \mathsf{pair} : \forall A \forall B.\, A \to B \to A \times B & \mathsf{inl} \;\; : \forall A \forall B.\, A \to A + B \\ \mathsf{fst} \;\; : \forall A \forall B.\, A \times B \to A & \mathsf{inr} \;\; : \forall A \forall B.\, B \to A + B \\ \mathsf{snd} \;\, : \forall A \forall B.\, A \times B \to B & \mathsf{case} : \forall A \forall B \forall C.\, A + B \to \\ () \quad\; : 1 & \qquad\qquad (A \to C) \to (B \to C) \to C \end{array}$$

*Example 1.* If we drop the guardedness condition in the corecursion rule, then the diverging term $\mathsf{fix}^\mu(\lambda f f)\,(\mathsf{fix}^\nu_0 \lambda\_x)$ can be typed. First observe that $\mathsf{fix}^\mu \lambda f f : \mu X X \to C$ for any $C$. In the context $x : \mu X X$ we have $\lambda\_x : \forall Y.\, Y \to \mu X X$, hence, $\mathsf{fix}^\nu_0 \lambda\_x : \nu Y \mu X X$. With $\nu Y \mu X X = \mu X X$ we get the typing $x\!:\!\mu X X \vdash \mathsf{fix}^\mu(\lambda f f)\,(\mathsf{fix}^\nu_0 \lambda\_x) : C$. This demonstrates that guardedness is vital for the termination of open expressions when mixing recursion and corecursion. Non-emptiness is not necessary, however; an analogous term constructed with the empty, but guarded type $\nu Y.\, 1 \to \mu X X$ is not diverging.

Let $\theta$ now be a finite map from type variables to semantical types and from term variables to terms. We write $\theta \in [\![\Gamma]\!]$ if additionally to the condition on type variables $\theta(x) \in [\![\Gamma(x)]\!]_\theta$ for all term variables $x \in \mathsf{dom}(\Gamma)$. Let $t\theta$ denote the simultaneous (capture-avoiding) substitution of all $x \in \mathsf{FV}(t)$ by $\theta(x)$.

**Theorem 2 (Soundness of typing).** *If* $\Gamma \vdash t : A$ *and* $\theta \in [\![\Gamma]\!]$ *then* $t\theta \in [\![A]\!]_\theta$.

*Proof.* By induction on the typing derivation, using the result of the last section.
In case of $\mathsf{fix}^\mu$, assume $s \in \bigcap_{\mathcal{X} \in \mathsf{SAT}_{\mathsf{u}}} [\![(X \to C) \to A \to C]\!]_{\theta[X\mapsto\mathcal{X}]}$ and show $\mathsf{fix}^\mu\, s \in [\![\mu X A \to C]\!]_\theta$. Lemma 3 (recursion) is applicable with types $\mathcal{I}(\alpha) =$

$\mu^\alpha(\mathcal{X} \mapsto [A]_{\theta[X \mapsto \mathcal{X}]})$ and $\mathcal{C}(\alpha) = [C]_\theta$. Since $r \in \mathcal{I}(\lambda) = \bigcup_{\alpha<\lambda} \mathcal{I}(\alpha)$ implies $r \in \mathcal{I}(\alpha)$ for some $\alpha < \lambda$ and $\mathcal{C}$ does not depend on its ordinal argument, the continuity condition is trivially satisfied for $\mathcal{A}(\alpha) = \mathcal{I}(\alpha) \to \mathcal{C}(\alpha)$. For all $\alpha$, the typing $s \in \mathcal{A}(\alpha) \to \mathcal{A}(\alpha+1)$ requested by the lemma is an instance of the given typing with $\mathcal{X} = \mathcal{I}(\alpha)$, since $[A]_{\theta[X \mapsto \mathcal{I}(\alpha)]} = \mathcal{I}(\alpha+1)$.

In case of $\mathsf{fix}^\nu$, Lemma 4 is applicable, analogously to the case of $\mathsf{fix}^\mu$. The kinding ensures that $\mathcal{C}(\alpha) := \nu^\alpha(\mathcal{X} \mapsto [A]_{\theta[X \mapsto \mathcal{X}]})$ is guarded for all $\alpha \leq \infty$. The continuity condition is again trivially satisfied.

**Corollary 1 (Strong normalization and consistency).** *Each typable term is strongly normalizing. Each closed well-typed term weak-head reduces to a value. No closed term inhabits* $\forall X X$.

*Proof.* By soundness of typing, letting $\theta(X) = \mathcal{N}$ for all type variables $X$ and $\theta(x) = x$ for all term variables $x$. Consistency, the last statement, follows since there are no closed terms in $\mathcal{N}$.

## Example: Stream Eating with Mendler (Co)Iteration

We first allow ourselves some syntactic sugar: we write $(r, s)$ for $\mathsf{pair}\, r\, s$ and use matching abstraction $\lambda(x, y).t$ as a shorthand for $\lambda z.\,[\mathsf{fst}\, z/x][\mathsf{snd}\, z/y]t$. ML-style pattern matching $\mathsf{match}\ t\ \mathsf{with}\ p_i \mapsto t_i$ for patterns $p_i$ composed from variables, $()$, $\mathsf{pair}$, $\mathsf{inl}$, and $\mathsf{inr}$, can also be defined easily [5, Sec. 2.4].

To provide some help for type-checking (by the reader and by the machine), we sometimes will use Church-style syntax and allow type-annotations $t : A$ in the example programs:

$$\frac{\Gamma \vdash t : A}{\Gamma \vdash (t : A) : A} \qquad \frac{\Gamma, x{:}A \vdash t : B}{\Gamma \vdash \lambda x{:}A.\, t : A \to B}$$

$$\frac{\Gamma, X{:}*_{\mathsf{u}} \vdash t : A}{\Gamma \vdash \Lambda X t : \forall X A} \qquad \frac{\Gamma \vdash t : \forall X A \qquad \Gamma \vdash B : *_b}{\Gamma \vdash t[B] : [B/X]A}$$

Streams $\mathsf{Stream}\, A := \nu X.\, A \times X$ can be constructed by $\mathsf{pair} : \forall A. A \to \mathsf{Stream}\, A \to \mathsf{Stream}\, A$ and destructed by $\mathsf{fst} : \forall A.\, \mathsf{Stream}\, A \to A$ and $\mathsf{snd} : \forall A.\, \mathsf{Stream}\, A \to \mathsf{Stream}\, A$. In Haskell, stream processors are defined as a data type and the code of the mapping function is generally recursive.

```
data SP a b where
  get :: (a -> SP a b) -> SP a b
  put :: b -> SP a b -> SP a b

map :: (a -> b) -> SP a b
map f = get (\ a -> put (f a) (map f))
```

In our system, we define the type of codes for stream processing functions [10] as a interleaved coinductive-inductive type.

$$\mathsf{SP}\, A\, B := \nu X \mu Y. B \times X + (A \to Y)$$

The equi-style enables a direct representation of the constructors:

$$\mathsf{put} := \mathsf{inl} : \forall A \forall B.\, B \times \mathsf{SP}\, A\, B \to \mathsf{SP}\, A\, B$$
$$\mathsf{get} := \mathsf{inr} : \forall A \forall B.\, (A \to \mathsf{SP}\, A\, B) \to \mathsf{SP}\, A\, B$$

The code of the stream-mapping function can be defined by Mendler coiteration as follows:

$$\begin{aligned}\mathsf{map} :&\ \ \forall A \forall B.\, (A \to B) \to \mathsf{SP}\, A\, B\\ \mathsf{map} :=&\ \Lambda A \Lambda B \lambda f{:}A \to B.\\ &\ \mathsf{fix}^{\nu}_{0}\, \Lambda X \lambda \mathit{map} : X.\, \mathsf{inr}\, (\lambda a{:}A.\, \mathsf{inl}\, (f\, a,\ \mathit{map}) : \mu Y.\, B \times X + (A \to Y))\end{aligned}$$

*Stream eating* executes the code of a stream processor, consuming an input stream and producing an output stream. In Haskell it is again defined by general recursion:

```
eat :: SP a b -> [a] -> [b]
eat (get f) (a:as) = eat (f a) as
eat (put b t)  as  = b : eat t as
```

We define eating by an outer Mendler coiteration on the output stream and an inner Mendler iteration on the stream processor.

$$\begin{aligned}\mathsf{eat} :&\ \ \mathsf{SP}\, A\, B \to \mathsf{Stream} A \to \mathsf{Stream} B\\ \mathsf{eat} :=&\ \mathsf{fix}^{\nu}_{2}\, \Lambda X \lambda \mathit{eat}^{\nu} : \mathsf{SP}\, A\, B \to \mathsf{Stream}\, A \to X\\ &\quad \mathsf{fix}^{\mu}\, \Lambda Y \lambda \mathit{eat}^{\mu} : Y \to \mathsf{Stream} A \to B \times X\\ &\quad\ \lambda t{:}B \times \mathsf{SP}\, A\, B + (A \to Y).\, \lambda(a, \mathit{as}).\, \mathsf{match}\ t\ \mathsf{with}\\ &\qquad \mathsf{put}\, (b, t') \mapsto (b,\ \mathit{eat}^{\nu}\, t'\, (a, \mathit{as})) : B \times X\\ &\qquad \mathsf{get}\, f \qquad \mapsto \mathit{eat}^{\mu}\, (f\, a : Y)\ \mathit{as}\end{aligned}$$

Some interesting functions, like composition of stream processors, are not (co)iterative, hence cannot be defined directly in the present type systems. Therefore, we introduce a more expressive system of sized types in the next section.

## 4 A Fancy Type System: Sized Types

Sized types allow a greater flexibility in defining recursive and corecursive functions by mapping the semantics more directly into the syntax of types. In the following, we describe an extension of the type system $\mathsf{F}^{\omega}$ that makes the following features of semantics available in syntax:

1. Ordinals $a$ and approximations $\mu^a F$ and $\nu^a F$ of inductive and coinductive types. The syntax of ordinals will be restricted to variables, successor and $\infty$. There is no need to provide notation for limit ordinals.
2. Distinction between guarded ($*_{\mathsf{g}}$) and unguarded types ($*_{\mathsf{u}}$). This feature is new in comparison to previous works [2,8,9].
3. Monotonicity information (polarity) of type constructors. For instance, the function space constructor is antitone in its first argument and monotone in its second argument, thus, it receives kind $*_{\mathsf{u}} \xrightarrow{-} *_{\mathsf{u}} \xrightarrow{+} *_{\mathsf{g}}$. Using polarities, the positivity test for (co)inductive types scales to higher-orders [1].

*Kinds* classify type constructors. Besides $*_\mathsf{g}$ and $*_\mathsf{u}$ we introduce a kind $\mathsf{ord_u}$ of ordinals and a subkind $\mathsf{ord_g} \leq \mathsf{ord_u}$ of non-zero ordinals. Function kinds are annotated with a polarity $p$.

| | |
|---|---|
| $p, q ::= \circ$ | mixed-variant (no monotonicity information) |
| $\mid +$ | covariant (monotone) |
| $\mid -$ | contravariant (antitone) |
| $\mid \top$ | constant (both mono- and antitone) |
| $\kappa \ ::= *_\mathsf{u} \mid *_\mathsf{g} \mid \mathsf{ord_u} \mid \mathsf{ord_g}$ | base kind |
| $\mid \kappa \xrightarrow{p} \kappa'$ | function kind |

Subkinding $\kappa \leq \kappa'$ is defined inductively by the following rules:

$$\frac{}{*_\mathsf{g} \leq *_\mathsf{u}} \qquad \frac{}{\mathsf{ord_g} \leq \mathsf{ord_u}} \qquad \frac{\kappa_1' \leq \kappa_1 \qquad p' \leq p \qquad \kappa_2 \leq \kappa_2'}{\kappa_1 \xrightarrow{p} \kappa_2 \leq \kappa_1' \xrightarrow{p'} \kappa_2'}$$

Herein, the order on polarities is the reflexive-transitive closure of the axioms $\circ \leq p$ and $p \leq \top$. If one composes a function in $\kappa_1 \xrightarrow{p} \kappa_2$ with a function in $\kappa_2 \xrightarrow{q} \kappa_3$ one obtains a function in $\kappa_1 \xrightarrow{pq} \kappa_3$. For the associative and commutative polarity composition $pq$ we have the laws $\top p = \top$, $\circ p = \circ$ (for $p \neq \top$), $+p = p$, and $-- = +$. Inverse application $p^{-1}q$ of a polarity $p$ to a polarity $q$ is defined as the solution of

$$\forall q, q'.\ p^{-1}q \leq q' \iff q \leq pq'.$$

*Type constructors* $F$ are type-level $\lambda$-terms over constants $C$:

$$\begin{array}{ll} C & ::= \to \mid \times \mid + \mid 1 \mid \forall_\kappa \mid \mu \mid \nu \mid 0 \mid \mathsf{s} \mid \infty \\ A, B, F, G & ::= C \mid X \mid \lambda XF \mid FG \end{array}$$

We use $\to$, $\times$, $+$ infix and write $\forall X\!:\!\kappa.A$ for $\forall_\kappa \lambda XA$. If $\kappa$ is $*_\mathsf{u}$, it can be dropped. We write the ordinal argument $a$ to $\mu$ and $\nu$ superscript, e.g., $\mu^a F$.

Let $\Delta$ denote a finite map from type (constructor) variables $X$ to pairs $p\kappa$ of a polarity $p$ and a kind $\kappa$. Inverse application $p^{-1}\Delta$ of a polarity $p$ to $\Delta$ is defined by $\Delta(X) = q\kappa \implies (p^{-1}\Delta)(X) = (p^{-1}q)\kappa$. The following kinding rules [1] and kind assignments to constants handle polarities properly:

$$\frac{C : \kappa}{\Delta \vdash C : \kappa} \qquad \frac{\Delta(X) = p\kappa \qquad p \leq +}{\Delta \vdash X : \kappa} \qquad \frac{\Delta, X\!:\!p\kappa \vdash F : \kappa'}{\Delta \vdash \lambda XF : \kappa \xrightarrow{p} \kappa'}$$

$$\frac{\Delta \vdash F : \kappa \xrightarrow{p} \kappa' \qquad p^{-1}\Delta \vdash G : \kappa}{\Delta \vdash FG : \kappa'} \qquad \frac{\Delta \vdash F : \kappa \qquad \kappa \leq \kappa'}{\Delta \vdash F : \kappa'}$$

$$\begin{array}{lll}
0 \ : \mathsf{ord_u} & \to : *_\mathsf{u} \xrightarrow{-} *_\mathsf{u} \xrightarrow{+} *_\mathsf{g} & \forall_\kappa : (\kappa \xrightarrow{\circ} *_b) \xrightarrow{+} *_b \\
\mathsf{s} \ : \mathsf{ord_u} \xrightarrow{+} \mathsf{ord_g} & \times : *_\mathsf{u} \xrightarrow{+} *_\mathsf{u} \xrightarrow{+} *_\mathsf{g} & \mu \ : \mathsf{ord}_b \xrightarrow{+} (*_\mathsf{u} \xrightarrow{+} *_b) \xrightarrow{+} *_b \\
\infty : \mathsf{ord_g} & + : *_\mathsf{u} \xrightarrow{+} *_\mathsf{u} \xrightarrow{+} *_\mathsf{g} & \nu \ : \mathsf{ord_u} \xrightarrow{-} (*_\mathsf{g} \xrightarrow{+} *_\mathsf{g}) \xrightarrow{+} *_\mathsf{g} \\
 & 1 \ : *_\mathsf{g} & 
\end{array}$$

These kindings express, for instance, that successor ordinals $\mathsf{s}\,a$ and the closure ordinal $\infty$ are "guarded" (i.e., non-zero), each of the proper constructions $\to$, $\times$, $+$, and 1 produces guarded types, a universal type $\forall_\kappa \lambda X A$ is guarded if its body $A$ is. Interesting is the kinding of inductive types: $\mu^a F$ is guarded if $a$ is non-zero and $F\,X$ is guarded even for unguarded $X$. For example, $\mu^0 F$ and $\mu^a \lambda X X$ are always unguarded, $\mu^{\mathsf{s}\,a} \lambda X.\, 1 + X$ is always guarded. Finally, coinductive types $\nu^a F$ are always guarded, but they are only well-kinded if $F$ maps guarded types to guarded types. Hence, the type $\nu^\infty \lambda X X$, which contains only the inhabitant $\mathsf{fix}_0^\nu \lambda x x$, is allowed, but $\nu^a \lambda X. \mu^\infty \lambda Y Y$ is prohibited, and so is $\nu^a \lambda X.\, \mu^0 F$.

*Type equality and subtyping.* The judgement $\Delta \vdash F = F' : \kappa$ is the least congruence over the following axioms [1], including a subsumption rule:

$$\frac{\Delta, X\!:\!p\kappa \vdash F : \kappa' \qquad p^{-1}\Delta \vdash G : \kappa}{\Delta \vdash (\lambda X F)\, G = [G/X]F : \kappa'} \qquad \frac{\Delta \vdash F : p\kappa \to \kappa'}{\Delta \vdash \lambda X.\, F\, X = F : p\kappa \to \kappa'}\; X \notin \mathsf{FV}(F)$$

$$\frac{\Delta \vdash F : \top\kappa \to \kappa' \qquad \Delta \vdash G : \kappa \qquad \Delta \vdash G' : \kappa}{\Delta \vdash F\, G = F\, G' : \kappa'}$$

$$\frac{}{\Delta \vdash \mathsf{s}\,\infty = \infty : \mathsf{ord}_\mathsf{g}} \qquad \frac{\Delta \vdash a : \mathsf{ord}_\mathsf{u} \qquad b \in \{\mathsf{u}, \mathsf{g}\}}{\Delta \vdash \mu^{\mathsf{s}a} = \lambda F.\, F\,(\mu^a\, F) : (*_\mathsf{u} \xrightarrow{+} *_b) \xrightarrow{+} *_b}$$

$$\frac{\Delta \vdash a : \mathsf{ord}_\mathsf{u}}{\Delta \vdash \nu^{\mathsf{s}a} = \lambda F.\, F\,(\nu^a\, F) : (*_\mathsf{g} \xrightarrow{+} *_\mathsf{g}) \xrightarrow{+} *_\mathsf{g}}$$

Subtyping $\Delta \vdash F \le F' : \kappa$ is induced by axioms expressing relations between ordinals and equipped with congruence rules that respect polarities.

$$\frac{\Delta \vdash a : \mathsf{ord}_\mathsf{u}}{\Delta \vdash 0 \le a : \mathsf{ord}_\mathsf{u}} \qquad \frac{\Delta \vdash a : \mathsf{ord}_b}{\Delta \vdash a \le \mathsf{s}\,a : \mathsf{ord}_b} \qquad \frac{\Delta \vdash a : \mathsf{ord}_b}{\Delta \vdash a \le \infty : \mathsf{ord}_b}$$

$$\frac{\Delta \vdash F \le F' : \kappa \xrightarrow{p} \kappa' \qquad p^{-1}\Delta \vdash G : \kappa}{\Delta \vdash F\, G \le F'\, G : \kappa'}$$

$$\frac{\Delta \vdash F : \kappa \xrightarrow{+} \kappa' \qquad \Delta \vdash G \le G' : \kappa}{\Delta \vdash F\, G \le F\, G' : \kappa'} \qquad \frac{\Delta \vdash F : \kappa \xrightarrow{-} \kappa' \qquad \Delta \vdash G' \le G : \kappa}{\Delta \vdash F\, G \le F\, G' : \kappa'}$$

Additionally, we have a congruence rule for $\lambda$-abstraction and rules for reflexivity, transitivity, antisymmetry, and subsumption. Typically, we will use subtyping to derive $\mu^a F \le \mu^{\mathsf{s}\,a} F \le \mu^\infty F$ and $\nu^\infty F \le \nu^{\mathsf{s}\,a} F \le \nu^a F$.

*Kind interpretation.* Kinds are interpreted as expected: $[\![*_\mathsf{u}]\!] = \mathsf{SAT}_\mathsf{u}$, $[\![*_\mathsf{g}]\!] = \mathsf{SAT}_\mathsf{g}$, $[\![\mathsf{ord}_\mathsf{u}]\!] = \{\alpha \mid 0 \le \alpha \le \infty\}$, $[\![\mathsf{ord}_\mathsf{g}]\!] = \{\alpha \mid 0 < \alpha \le \infty\}$, and $[\![\kappa \xrightarrow{p} \kappa']\!]$ is the space of $p$-variant operators from $[\![\kappa]\!]$ to $[\![\kappa']\!]$. For base kinds $\kappa_0$ let $\mathcal{A} \sqsubseteq_{\kappa 0} \mathcal{A}'$ hold iff $\mathcal{A} \subseteq \mathcal{A}'$. For higher kinds, let $\mathcal{F} \sqsubseteq_{\kappa \xrightarrow{p} \kappa'} \mathcal{F}'$ iff $\mathcal{F}(\mathcal{G}) \sqsubseteq_{\kappa'} \mathcal{F}'(\mathcal{G})$ for all $\mathcal{G} \in [\![\kappa]\!]$. With these definitions, we can set

$$[\![\kappa \xrightarrow{p} \kappa']\!] = \{\mathcal{F} \in [\![\kappa]\!] \to [\![\kappa']\!] \mid \mathcal{F}(\mathcal{G}) \sqsubseteq \mathcal{F}(\mathcal{G}') \text{ for all } \mathcal{G} \sqsubseteq^p \mathcal{G}' \in [\![\kappa]\!]\}.$$

Herein, $\sqsubseteq^+$ denotes $\sqsubseteq$, $\sqsubseteq^-$ denotes $\sqsupseteq$, $\sqsubseteq^\circ$ denotes equality, and $\mathcal{G} \sqsubseteq^\top \mathcal{G}'$ always holds.

**Lemma 6 (Soundness of subkinding).** *If $\kappa \le \kappa'$ then $[\kappa] \subseteq [\kappa']$.*

*Type interpretation.* We interpret the type constants $C$ as follows:

$$\begin{array}{ll} [0] = 0 & [\forall_\kappa](\mathcal{F}) = \bigcap_{\mathcal{G}\in[\![\kappa]\!]} \mathcal{F}(\mathcal{G}) \\ [\mathsf{s}](\infty) = \infty & [C] = C \qquad \text{for } C \in \{\to, \times, +, 1, \mu, \nu\} \\ [\mathsf{s}](\alpha < \infty) = \alpha + 1 & \\ [\infty] = \infty & \end{array}$$

This interpretation can be lifted to an interpretation $[F]_\theta$ of well-kinded constructors $F$. We let $\theta \sqsubseteq \theta' \in [\Delta]$ if $\theta(X) \sqsubseteq^p \theta'(X) \in [\kappa]$ for all $(X : p\kappa) \in \Delta$.

**Theorem 3 (Soundness of kinding, equality, and subtyping).** *Let $\theta \sqsubseteq \theta' \in [\Delta]$.*

1. *If $\Delta \vdash F : \kappa$ then $[F]_\theta \sqsubseteq [F]_{\theta'} \in [\kappa]$.*
2. *If $\Delta \vdash F = F' : \kappa$ then $[F]_\theta \sqsubseteq [F']_{\theta'} \in [\kappa]$.*
3. *If $\Delta \vdash F \le F' : \kappa$ then $[F]_\theta \sqsubseteq [F']_{\theta'} \in [\kappa]$.*

*Typing.* The rules for $\lambda$-abstraction, application, basic constants $c$ remain in place. The type conversion rule is replaced by a subsumption rule, and the generalization and instantiation rules for universal types are now higher-kinded.

$$\frac{\Gamma \vdash \Gamma(x) : *_\mathsf{u}}{\Gamma \vdash x : \Gamma(x)} \qquad \frac{\Gamma \vdash t : A \qquad \Gamma \vdash A \le B : *_\mathsf{u}}{\Gamma \vdash t : B}$$

$$\frac{\Gamma, X{:}\kappa \vdash t : F\,X}{\Gamma \vdash t : \forall_\kappa F}\ X \notin \mathsf{FV}(F) \qquad \frac{\Gamma \vdash t : \forall_\kappa F \qquad \Gamma \vdash G : \kappa}{\Gamma \vdash t : F\,G}$$

$$\frac{\Gamma \vdash F : *_\mathsf{u} \xrightarrow{+} *_\mathsf{u} \qquad \Gamma \vdash G : \mathsf{ord}_\mathsf{u} \xrightarrow{\circ} *_\mathsf{u} \qquad \Gamma \vdash a : \mathsf{ord}_\mathsf{u}}{\Gamma \vdash \mathsf{fix}^\mu : (\forall \imath{:}\mathsf{ord}_\mathsf{u}.\,(\mu^\imath F \to G\,\imath) \to \mu^{\mathsf{s}\,\imath} F \to G(\mathsf{s}\,\imath)) \to \mu^a F \to G\,a}\ adm^\mu$$

$$\frac{\Gamma \vdash F : *_\mathsf{g} \xrightarrow{+} *_\mathsf{g} \qquad \Gamma \vdash G_i : \mathsf{ord}_\mathsf{u} \xrightarrow{\circ} *_\mathsf{g} \text{ for } i = 1..n \qquad \Gamma \vdash a : \mathsf{ord}_\mathsf{u}}{\Gamma \vdash \mathsf{fix}^\nu_n : (\forall \imath{:}\mathsf{ord}_\mathsf{u}.\,(G_{1..n}\,\imath \to \nu^\imath F) \to G_{1..n}\,(\mathsf{s}\,\imath) \to \nu^{\mathsf{s}\,\imath} F) \to G_{1..n}\,a \to \nu^a F}\ adm^\nu$$

In the recursion rule, the side condition $adm^\mu$ needs to ensure that the type $\lambda\imath.\,\mu^\imath F \to G\,\imath$ is continuous in the sense of Lemma 3. Systematic criteria have been developed based on a saturated-set semantics in the context of iso-(co)inductive types [2], and these criteria are directly applicable for the equi-setting described in this article. Due to space restrictions, we only give a sound approximation here: There must be an $n \ge 0$, $\Gamma \vdash F_i : *_\mathsf{u} \xrightarrow{+} *_\mathsf{u}$ for $i = 1..n$ and $\Gamma \vdash B : \mathsf{ord}_\mathsf{u} \xrightarrow{+} *_\mathsf{u}$ such that $\Gamma \vdash G\,\imath = \mu^\imath F_1 \to \cdots \to \mu^\imath F_n \to B\,\imath : *_\mathsf{u}$.

For the criterion $adm^\nu$ we give the following sound approximation: For each $j = 1..n$, either $\Gamma \vdash G_j : \mathsf{ord}_\mathsf{u} \xrightarrow{-} *_\mathsf{u}$, or there exists $\Gamma \vdash F_j : *_\mathsf{u} \xrightarrow{+} *_\mathsf{u}$ such that $\Gamma \vdash G_j\,\imath = \mu^\imath F_j : *_\mathsf{u}$.

**Theorem 4 (Soundness of typing).** *If $\Gamma \vdash t : A$ and $\theta \in [\Gamma]$ then $t\theta \in [A]_\theta$.*

*Proof.* By induction on the typing derivation. The connection of the typing rules for recursion and corecursion to lemmata 3 and 4 is now immediate.

**Corollary 2 (Strong normalization and consistency).** *Each typable term is strongly normalizing. Each closed well-typed term weak-head reduces to a value. No closed term inhabits $\forall X X$.*

## Example: Composition of Stream Processors

The sized type system encompasses a number of recursion schemes: primitive recursion, Mendler (co)recursion, course-of-value recursion, and indirect recursion (where the recursive arguments are obtained via another function, like the filtering function in case of quicksort). In the following, we implement composition comp of stream processors such that $\mathsf{eat}\,(\mathsf{comp}\; t_1\, t_2) = \mathsf{eat}\, t_2 \circ \mathsf{eat}\, t_1$. There are two possible implementations for the case that $t_1$ wants to read an element and $t_2$ wants to output one. We give the latter priority and arrive at the following Haskell code:

```
comp :: SP a b -> SP b c -> SP a c
comp  t1        (put c t2) = put c (comp t1 t2)
comp (put b t1) (get f2)   = comp t1 (f2 b)
comp (get f1)         t2   = get (\ a -> comp (f1 a) t2)
```

We express SP through sized types and define two useful approximations of this type.

$$
\begin{array}{lll}
\mathsf{SP}\,A\,B & := \nu^{\infty}\lambda X.\,\mu^{\infty}\lambda Y.\,B \times X + (A \to Y) \\[4pt]
\mathsf{SP}^{\imath}\,A\,B & := \nu^{\imath}\lambda X.\,\mu^{\infty}\lambda Y.\,B \times X + (A \to Y) \\
\mathsf{SP}^{\mathsf{s}\,\imath}\,A\,B & = B \times \mathsf{SP}^{\imath}\,A\,B + (A \to \mathsf{SP}^{\mathsf{s}\,\imath}\,A\,B) \\
\mathsf{put} & : \;\; B \times \mathsf{SP}^{\imath}\,A\,B \to \mathsf{SP}^{\mathsf{s}\,\imath}\,A\,B \\
\mathsf{get} & : \;\; (A \to \mathsf{SP}^{\mathsf{s}\,\imath}\,A\,B) \to \mathsf{SP}^{\mathsf{s}\,\imath}\,A\,B \\[4pt]
\mathsf{SP}_{\jmath}\,A\,B & := \mu^{\jmath}\lambda Y.\,B \times \mathsf{SP}\,A\,B + (A \to Y) \\
\mathsf{SP}_{\mathsf{s}\,\jmath}\,A\,B & = B \times \mathsf{SP}\,A\,B + (A \to \mathsf{SP}_{\jmath}\,A\,B) \\
\mathsf{get} & : \;\; (A \to \mathsf{SP}_{\jmath}\,A\,B) \to \mathsf{SP}_{\mathsf{s}\,\jmath}\,A\,B \\
\mathsf{put} & : \;\; B \times \mathsf{SP}_{\infty}\,A\,B \to \mathsf{SP}_{\mathsf{s}\,\jmath}\,A\,B
\end{array}
$$

We will use the derived types of the constructors put and get below. Note the asymmetry between $\mathsf{SP}^{\imath}$ and $\mathsf{SP}_{\jmath}$, which shows in the last type of put.

In our analysis, $\mathsf{comp}\, t_1\, t_2$ is defined by corecursion into $\mathsf{SP}\,A\,C$ using a lexicographic recursion on $(t_2, t_1)$. It is conveniently coded with a generalized recursor $\mathsf{fix}^{\mu}_{n}$, which recurses on the $n+1$st argument and is definable from $\mathsf{fix}^{\mu}$ [3].

$$
\begin{array}{l}
\mathsf{comp} \\
\quad : \;\; \mathsf{SP}\,A\,B \to \mathsf{SP}\,B\,C \to \mathsf{SP}\,A\,C \\
\quad := \mathsf{fix}^{\nu}_{2}\Lambda\imath.\,\lambda comp^{\nu} : \mathsf{SP}\,A\,B \to \mathsf{SP}\,B\,C \to \mathsf{SP}^{\imath}\,A\,C. \\
\qquad\quad \mathsf{fix}^{\mu}_{1}\Lambda\jmath.\,\lambda comp^{\mu}_{1} : \mathsf{SP}\,A\,B \to \mathsf{SP}_{\jmath}\,B\,C \to \mathsf{SP}^{\mathsf{s}\,\imath} A\,C. \\
\qquad\qquad \mathsf{fix}^{\mu}_{0}\Lambda k.\,\lambda comp^{\mu}_{2} : \mathsf{SP}_{k}\,A\,B \to \mathsf{SP}_{\mathsf{s}\,\jmath}\,B\,C \to \mathsf{SP}^{\mathsf{s}\,\imath} A\,C.
\end{array}
$$

$$
\begin{array}{l}
\lambda t_1 : \mathsf{SP}_{\mathsf{s}\,k}\, A\, B.\ \lambda t_2 : \mathsf{SP}_{\mathsf{s}\,\jmath}\, B\, C.\ \mathsf{match}\ t_2\ \mathsf{with} \\
\quad \mathsf{put}\,(c,\ t_2' : \mathsf{SP}\, B\, C) \qquad\quad \mapsto \mathsf{put}\,(c,\ \mathit{comp}^{\nu}\, t_1\, t_2') : \mathsf{SP}^{\mathsf{s}\,\imath}\, A\, C \\
\quad \mathsf{get}\,(f_2 : B \to \mathsf{SP}_{\jmath}\, B\, C) \mapsto \mathsf{match}\ t_1\ \mathsf{with} \\
\qquad \mathsf{put}\,(b,\ t_1' : \mathsf{SP}\, A\, B) \qquad \mapsto \mathit{comp}_1^{\mu}\, t_1'\, (f_2\, b) : \mathsf{SP}^{\mathsf{s}\,\imath}\, A\, C \\
\qquad \mathsf{get}\,(f_1 : A \to \mathsf{SP}_k\, A\, B) \mapsto \mathsf{get}\,(\lambda a.\ \mathit{comp}_2^{\mu}\, (f_1\, a)\, t_2) : \mathsf{SP}^{\mathsf{s}\,\imath}\, A\, C
\end{array}
$$

In the corecursive call to $\mathit{comp}^{\nu}$, the first argument is casted from $\mathsf{SP}_{\mathsf{s}\,k}\, A\, B$ to $\mathsf{SP}_{\infty}\, A\, B$ using subtyping of inductive types. Such a cast is not available in Mendler iteration, but could be simulated with Mendler recursion. Hence, comp is a mixed coiterative/recursive/recursive function.

## 5 Conclusions

We have presented a construction of saturated sets for equi-inductive and coinductive types and derived two type systems which guarantee termination of recursion and corecursion under lazy unfolding. In contrast to candidates of reducibility or biorthogonals, saturated sets are closed under unions, hence, the continuity criteria for sized iso-(co)inductive types developed in previous work [2] are directly transferable to the equi-setting.

We have given two type systems for terminating (co)recursion in the presence of equi-(co)inductive types and showed by some examples that they handle mixed inductive/coinductive types properly. The system of sized types is ready for extension to higher-kinded (co)inductive types.

Although the operational semantics of corecursive values in the equi-setting suggests a semantics using biorthogonals, we have succeeded to apply a modification of the saturated sets approach. This substantiated the conjecture Colin Riba made to me, namely, *biorthogonals are only required to justify languages inspired by classical logic.*

*Acknowledgments.* The idea how to formulate guarded saturated sets came to me during a visit to the Protheo team at LORIA, Nancy in February 2007. Thanks to Frédéric Blanqui and Colin Riba for the invitation. I am also grateful to Thorsten Altenkirch who communicated the type of stream processors to me. Thanks to the anonymous referees for their valuable feedback.

## References

1. Abel, A.: Polarized subtyping for sized types. In: Grigoriev, D., Harrison, J., Hirsch, E.A. (eds.) CSR 2006. LNCS, vol. 3967, pp. 381–392. Springer, Heidelberg (2006)
2. Abel, A.: Semi-continuous sized types and termination. In: Ésik, Z. (ed.) CSL 2006. LNCS, vol. 4207, pp. 72–88. Springer, Heidelberg (2006)
3. Abel, A.: Towards generic programming with sized types. In: Uustalu, T. (ed.) MPC 2006. LNCS, vol. 4014, pp. 10–28. Springer, Heidelberg (2006)
4. Abel, A.: Strong normalization and equi-(co)inductive types. In: Ronchi Della Rocca, S. (ed.) TLCA 2007. LNCS, vol. 4583, pp. 8–22. Springer, Heidelberg (2007)
5. Abel, A., Matthes, R., Uustalu, T.: Iteration schemes for higher-order and nested datatypes. Theor. Comput. Sci. 333, 3–66 (2005)

6. Amadio, R.M., Coupet-Grimal, S.: Analysis of a guard condition in type theory (extended abstract). In: Nivat, M. (ed.) ETAPS 1998 and FOSSACS 1998. LNCS, vol. 1378, pp. 48–62. Springer, Heidelberg (1998)
7. Barthe, G., Frade, M.J., Giménez, E., Pinto, L., Uustalu, T.: Type-based termination of recursive definitions. Math. Struct. in Comput. Sci. 14, 1–45 (2004)
8. Barthe, G., Grégoire, B., Pastawski, F.: CIC^: Type-based termination of recursive definitions in the Calculus of Inductive Constructions. In: Hermann, M., Voronkov, A. (eds.) LPAR 2006. LNCS (LNAI), vol. 4246, pp. 257–271. Springer, Heidelberg (2006)
9. Blanqui, F., Riba, C.: Combining typing and size constraints for checking the termination of higher-order conditional rewrite systems. In: Hermann, M., Voronkov, A. (eds.) LPAR 2006. LNCS (LNAI), vol. 4246, pp. 105–119. Springer, Heidelberg (2006)
10. Ghani, N., Hancock, P., Pattinson, D.: Continuous functions on final coalgebras. Electr. Notes in Theor. Comp. Sci. 164, 141–155 (2006)
11. Hughes, J., Pareto, L., Sabry, A.: Proving the correctness of reactive systems using sized types. In: POPL 1996, pp. 410–423 (1996)
12. Mendler, N.P.: Inductive types and type constraints in the second-order lambda calculus. Annals of Pure and Applied Logic 51, 159–172 (1991)
13. Parigot, M.: Recursive programming with proofs. Theor. Comput. Sci. 94, 335–356 (1992)
14. Parigot, M.: Proofs of strong normalization for second order classical natural deduction. The Journal of Symbolic Logic 62, 1461–1479 (1997)
15. Raffalli, C.: Data types, infinity and equality in system $AF_2$. In: Meinke, K., Börger, E., Gurevich, Y. (eds.) CSL 1993. LNCS, vol. 832, pp. 280–294. Springer, Heidelberg (1994)
16. Riba, C.: On the stability by union of reducibility candidates. In: Seidl, H. (ed.) FOSSACS 2007. LNCS, vol. 4423, pp. 317–331. Springer, Heidelberg (2007)
17. Swierstra, W.: I/O in a dependently typed programming language. Talk presented at TYPES 2007 (2007)

# Static and Dynamic Analysis: Better Together

Sriram K. Rajamani

Microsoft Research India

Static analysis and dynamic analysis have dual properties. Static analysis has high coverage, but is imprecise, and produces false alarms. Dynamic analysis has low coverage, but has high precision. We present lessons learned from three different projects, where we have combined the complementary strengths of static and dynamic analysis to solve interesting problems:

1. The YOGI project [2], which combines static abstraction-refinement and directed testing to validate if software components obey safety properties specified as state machines.
2. The NETRA project [3], which combines static access control configuration analysis and runtime checking to find information flow violations.
3. The CLARITY programming language [1], where a static analysis together with the CLARITY compiler and runtime helps guarantee properties that involve reasoning about asynchrony.

## References

1. Chandrasekaran, P., Conway, C.L., Joy, J.M., Rajamani, S.K.: Programming asynchronous layers with CLARITY. In: FSE 2007, pp. 65–74. ACM Press, New York (2007)
2. Gulavani, B.S., Henzinger, T.A., Kannan, Y., Nori, A.V., Rajamani, S.K.: SYNERGY: A new algorithm for property checking. In: FSE 2006, pp. 117–127. ACM Press, New York (2006)
3. Naldurg, P., Schwoon, S., Rajamani, S.K., Lambert, J.: NETRA: seeing through access control. In: FMSE 2006, pp. 55–66. ACM Press, New York (2006)

Z. Shao (Ed.): APLAS 2007, LNCS 4807, p. 302, 2007.

# The Semantics of "Semantic Patches" in Coccinelle: Program Transformation for the Working Programmer

Neil D. Jones[1] and René Rydhof Hansen[2,*]

[1] DIKU (Computer Science Dept., University of Copenhagen, Denmark)
[2] Dept. of Computer Science, Aalborg University, Denmark

**Abstract.** We rationally reconstruct the core of the *Coccinelle* system, used for automating and documenting collateral evolutions in Linux device drivers. A denotational semantics of the system's underlying *semantic patch language* (SmPL) is developed, and extended to include variables. The semantics is in essence a higher-order functional program and so executable; but is inefficient and limited to straight-line source programs. A richer and more efficient SmPL version is defined, implemented by compiling to the temporal logic CTL-V (CTL with existentially quantified variables ranging over source code parameters and program points; defined using the staging concept from partial evaluation). The compilation is formally proven correct and a model check algorithm is outlined.

## 1 Introduction

A tedious, vital and frequently occurring software engineering job is to carry out *systematic updates to Device Driver code*, often referred to as *software evolution*. Many necessary changes are due to *collateral evolutions*: updates to a given driver that must be made as a consequence of current and substantial changes to library modules that the driver depends on. A change in the API of an external library procedure used by the given driver is a typical example; other common examples include changes in function signatures and data structures used by the driver. Finding all the places where collateral evolutions are needed and then performing the actual update even in a single driver is a non-trivial problem. Changes to accommodate a single library update may involve searching thousands of files and performing hundreds of code changes. This problem needs an automated solution, as it is too frequent and important to be left to inexperienced programmers with traditional text editing and update documentation. See [2,3,5,6,7,8].

*The Coccinelle approach* has demonstrated considerable pragmatic value. Coccinelle is an executable program transformer that has shown its utility, with satisfactory efficiency and expressivity, for large real application problems including

* Supported by the *Coccinelle* project under the Danish Research Council for Technology and Production Sciences.

Z. Shao (Ed.): APLAS 2007, LNCS 4807, pp. 303–318, 2007.

device driver code updates [17]. It develops and applies "Semantic Patch" notation, a concept that abstracts and generalises the practically well-established and frequently used "patches" well-known to the Linux kernel community. Semantic patches are described in the *semantic patch language* SmPL, a domain specific language inspired by the patch notation. In comparison with the usual Linux patches, SmPL is much more versatile and more firmly based in programming language semantics.

Coccinelle has several major components, including ways of *recognising* software patterns frequently occurring in source code (written in C or Java); means for *efficiently performing* the needed pattern recognition using a variant of the temporal logic CTL; and ways to *transform* the recognised code. See [17, 20] for more details and a wide range of applications.

**Analysis: updating source code.** The problem is to make consistent changes to a collection of source programs. An example is to change the way a central function or procedure is called, e.g., to add an extra argument to its parameter list. This requires changing both the function or procedure declaration, and all calls to it.

To avoid struggling from the outset with semantic details of programming languages such as C or Java we take a top-down approach to the problem of updating source programs. Transformation semantics is developed in a language-independent way, carefully side-stepping problems due to inessential but troublesome idiosyncrasies sometimes found in real languages. This approach is able to cope with real-world languages including C and Java [17, 20].

**Linguistic tool:** a transformation *language*, called SmPL in the Coccinelle system. A SmPL transformation consists of source language *patterns*, identifying the source language constructions to be changed; and *insertions and deletions,* marking the changes to be made.

**System tool:** a transformation *engine*. This has two inputs: the source program to be transformed, and the transformation. It produces as output an updated source program. The developments of this paper are based on the following assumptions supported by current practice:

1. We assume that the transformation only describes the part of the source program to be changed, as most of the source program will remain unchanged.
2. Source program insertions or deletions are mainly *order-preserving*, so major textual rearrangements are not needed.
3. There is a need for tokens with *large value ranges*, too large to be listed explicitly. A typical example is an identifier, for instance a variable name, a procedure name, or a constant.

It is essential that Coccinelle be *automatic* (run without human interaction) and *exhaustive* (find all possible places to apply a transformation). Further, the result of transformation should be predictable. Hence Coccinelle must also have a *minimally surprising semantics*, e.g., one free from unexpected pattern matches. As a corollary, Coccinelle must also detect *inconsistent transformation specifications* that perform different transformations, if read in different ways.

**Contribution of the paper.** This "theory-practice border" paper formalises an essential part of SmPL, thus providing a theoretical basis for what has already proven to be a pragmatic success. It is intended to clarify just what it is that semantic patches do (at least a subset of them), and to aid understanding some of the implementational and design challenges that are being met within the Coccinelle project.

Our main contribution is to rationally reconstruct the core of Coccinelle's semantic patch language SmPL, concisely and understandably clarifying a number of points in the core semantics. Our semantics compactly and explicitly describes a practical system, and has been implemented as a functional program.

Coccinelle has shown the utility of the temporal logic CTL [10] *as an intermediate language* to implement SmPL. (As with compiler intermediate languages, users need not know of or be aware of CTL.) In this paper we build *a theoretical bridge*, proving formally that the natural pattern-matching way to read SmPL patterns is equivalent to its CTL implementation.

Expressivity and efficiency of the SmPL patterns of [17] are quite satisfactory in practice. The notation is useful for working software engineers, as it does not require knowing temporal logic such as CTL formulas; or concepts from regular expressions, semantics, finite automata theory, or Prolog. Further, SmPL patterns are much more local than patterns in [11,12,13,14], with less emphasis on computational futures and pasts.

**Related work.** Directly related work on software updating includes [4,11,12, 13,14,16,17,18] by university groups at Nantes (Muller, Padioleau, ...), Copenhagen (Lawall, Hansen, Jones, ...); Oxford (De Moor, Lacey,...); and Stony Brook (Liu, Stoller,...). Papers [4, 16] apply regular expressions to program transformation. Paper [17] is a practice-oriented description of Coccinelle's semantic patches; and [11,12,13,14] apply CTL to program transformation. Compared with [11,13,15,19], the focus of Coccinelle is not compiler optimisation, but software updating. Coccinelle is intentionally *not semantics-preserving*, in contrast to compiler or program transformer works such as [11,14,15]. The reason: Coccinelle may be used to change program functionality, or to fix or to detect bugs.

Papers [11,13] use notation $\mathrm{C} \Rightarrow \mathrm{C}'$ **if** $\phi$ where C is a pattern, C′ is a replacement for C, and the enabling condition for applying the rewrite is given by a formula $\phi$ expressed in the temporal logic CTL-FV. Here $\phi$ may refer to the computational past or future, relative to the occurrence of C.

For reasons of efficiency and usability by a broad software engineering community, Coccinelle does not require familiarity with the sometimes rather subtle nuances of temporal logic. Instead, Coccinelle uses patterns with variables and the "..." operator (explained later) to localise transformation sites.

In our experience, enabling conditions for program transformation seem more naturally expressed using Coccinelle patterns than by using general CTL formulas $\phi$. In principle SmPL may be less expressive than CTL, e.g., it's not clear how to express conditions for some classical compiler optimisations such as constant propagation or live variables. However, if desired, such effects can easily be achieved by using Coccinelle's general scripting framework, discussed in [20].

The Stratego transformation system [1] is less semantics- based than [11,14,15] but more powerful as a rewriting engine, allowing separation of the rewrite rules from strategies for their application.

**Structure of the paper.** The data of a program transformer is a *source program.* A Core-SmPL transformation maps a source program into a target program. Its semantics is first written in the style of denotational semantics or functional programming. For simplicity, a source programs is initially just a *linear sequence of abstract syntax trees*, each attributes such as syntactic type, lexical infomation (e.g., a procedure name or constant value), or application of a value operator (e.g., +, - or assignment).

A more general and realistic source program is a *control flow graph* or CFG: a finite directed graph with program control points as nodes, and whose branching expresses control flow transfers: control divergence, convergence, and loops.

The initial Core-SmPL semantics is extended to such source programs in a perhaps unexpected way: the temporal logic CTL is used as an intermediate language, invisible to the user. This use of CTL is formally proven equivalent to the denotational semantics for programs with linear structure.

A semantic extension is to add pattern (meta-)variables to Core-SmPL, significantly extending its expressivity. The full paper [9] has more details, proofs, and a model checking algorithm for the extended CTL-V.

## 2 Core-SmPL: A Core Language for Semantic Patches

In this section we introduce Core-SmPL, a rational reconstruction of the core of SmPL, and show how it can be used to search for code patterns and to transform programs. In the terminology of the Coccinelle project such specifications are called *semantic patches* which is also the name we adopt in the following.

*Syntax of source and target programs.* We begin with a "linear source program" as a working abstraction of "source program". Later, it will be extended to include not just linear sequencing, but an arbitrary control flow graph or CFG with tests, divergence, convergence and loops.

**Definition 1.** *A* ground term *is a tree structure built from operators. A* linear source program *is a sequence of ground terms. Syntax is straightforward:*

$$\begin{array}{lll} S ::= G_1 G_2 \cdots G_n & & \textit{A program is a sequence of ground terms} \\ G ::= op(G_1, \ldots, G_k) & k = arity(op) : & \textit{Op.'s with right numbers of arguments.} \end{array}$$

*A ground term is a variable-free tree structure built by operators from leaves. Technically a leaf is a 0-ary operator, and may be: a programming language constant; a name, e.g., a program variable or a function name; or a keyword without arguments. Nonleaf operators have positive arities, i.e., 1 or more arguments. Example nonleaf operators include* `+`, `-`, `:=` *(assignment) or* `if`. *For compactness in presentation and examples, we write sequences (inputs to and outputs from our program transformer) without separators, and in infix notation.*

A table that summarises the operators and arities used in the examples:[1]

| Operator | a | b | c | d | e | f | { | } | distance | rate | time | step | + | * | := |
|---|---|---|---|---|---|---|---|---|---|---|---|---|---|---|---|
| Arity | 0 | 0 | 0 | 0 | 0 | 0 | 0 | 0 | 0 | 0 | 0 | 0 | 2 | 2 | 2 |

Symbols from a fixed alphabet such as a, b, c, ..., `step` above are a special case: operators with arity 0. A program with only 0- ary operators is a string over a finite alphabet, as studied for decades in formal language and automata theory.

In real programming languages such as C or Java, the terms are subclassified into syntactic categories such as expression, command, or function declaration; but such distinctions will not be needed in this paper. (Such a classification would be called a *grammar* in compiler terminology, or a *signature* in algebra.)

**Definition 2.** *A* general source program, *or* CFG, *is a binary relation* $\rightarrow$ *on a finite set of* control states *(i.e., program points), each labelled by a ground term.*

The concrete syntax used for semantic patches in the Cocinelle system is similar to but extends the notation used by the `patch` program to specify a program transformation. This patch notation is the de facto standard for communicating proposed changes and updates among the Linux Kernel developers.

| | |
|---|---|
| $P ::= \varepsilon$ | Pattern that matches the empty sequence of terms |
| $\mid\ EP$ | A match for $E$ followed by a match for $P$ |
| $E ::= T$ | Pattern that matches a term $T$ |
| $\mid\ (P_1\ '\|'\ P_2)$ | Match $P_1$ or $P_2$ |
| $\mid\ \ldots$ | Match a sequence of zero, one, or more arbitrary terms |
| $\mid\ -T$ | Delete one $T$: match it, but do not copy it to the output |
| $\mid\ +T$ | Insert $T$ in the output sequence (no matching occurs) |
| $T ::= x$ | A term is like a ground term, but may contain variables |
| $\mid\ op(T_1, \ldots, T_k)$ | $k = arity(op)$: Must have the right numbers of arguments. |
| $x ::= variable$ | A pattern variable |

**Fig. 1.** Syntax of Core-SmPL semantic patches

The pattern "..." matches *any sequence of terms.* This common pattern may be familiar from the patch notation used in the output of the `diff` utility. The variables appearing in a term $T$ not to be confused with source or target program variables; they are *pattern variables* used for matching, essentially the variables or parameters used in [13, 11, 4, 16].

[1] Braces {, } delimit groups of (well-nested!) commands or statements.

*Some Core-SmPL semantics examples.* $\mathcal{T}[\![P]\!](in)$ is the set of target programs that can be obtained by applying pattern $P$ to transform source program *in*. In general, $\mathcal{T}[\![P]\!](in) = \{out_1, out_2, \ldots, out_n\}$ means that pattern $P$ can transform source program *in* into any one target program in the set $\{out_1, out_2, \ldots, out_n\}$.

*Examples with only* 0*-ary operators and no pattern variables.* A special case of a source or target program is a string of symbols (i.e., 0-ary operators) over a finite alphabet $A$. The first example recognises strings over an alphabet $A \supseteq \{\mathtt{a}, \mathtt{b}\}$. The pattern **...abab...** matches strings that contain **abab** as a substring. Viewed as a string transformer, pattern **...abab...** computes the identity transformation on strings that contain **abab** as a substring. It yields the empty set if applied to strings of other forms.

The pattern **...a-ba-b+e+f...** also matches source program strings containing **abab**, but the target string is constructed by deleting the two matched **b**'s from the source, and inserting symbols **e,f** just after the matched part **abab**.

*Examples:* $\mathcal{T}[\![Pattern]\!]$ *(Source- program) = set of transformed programs.*

1. $\mathcal{T}[\![$`...abab...`$]\!]$ `(abcd)` = $\emptyset$
2. $\mathcal{T}[\![$`...abab...`$]\!]$ `(cabababab d)` → `(cababababd)` = {`cababababd`}
3. $\mathcal{T}[\![$`...a-ba-b+e+f...`$]\!]$ `(cababd)` = {`caaefd`}
4. $\mathcal{T}[\![$`...a-ba-b+e+f...`$]\!]$ `(cababgababd)` = {`caaefgaaefd`}
5. $\mathcal{T}[\![$`...a-ba-b+e+f...`$]\!]$ `(cababababd)` = {`caaefababd, cabaaefabd, cababaaefd`}

*Discussion.* For software updating it is important that *all matches* are detected (e.g., if a function's calling mode is to be changed it is vital that all calls be changed to the new format). Example 1 does not match, so the semantics yields the empty set on input **abcd**. Example 2 has three matches in all, but no transformation occurs due to the absence of **+** or **-**. Thus the output is a singleton set, containing only the input sequence. Example 3 removes two **b**'s and adds **ef**. In Example 4 two patterns **abab** are discovered; for each, two **b**'s are removed, and **ef** is added. In examples 3 and 4 all matches are found and the transformation results are well-defined since unique.

Example 5 is problematic as three patterns **abab** are discovered, two of them overlapping. As a result there are in all *three possible* transformed programs. The Coccinelle system only transforms in case $n = 1$ in output $\{out_1, out_2, \ldots, out_n\}$, i.e., the effect of the transformation must be uniquely defined.

*Examples with pattern variables and k-ary operators.* Pattern variables are used to "remember" bits and pieces of the source program and, as it later will be seen, to match positions in the input program. Pattern variables are needed to express realistic source language patterns that contain possibly unbounded data such as function names, parameter names or constants. The Core-SmPL semantic patch notation allows (meta-) variables whose values come from such ranges, and allow testing the source program for equality of such values.

The source language term `distance := rate * time` can be matched with pattern $x$ `:=` $y$ `*` $z$ by an environment that binds pattern variables $x, y, z$ to corresponding bits of the source program, e.g.

$$env = [x \mapsto \texttt{distance}, y \mapsto \texttt{rate}, z \mapsto \texttt{time}]$$

$$\begin{aligned}
\mathcal{T}[\![x \texttt{ := } y\texttt{*}z]\!](\texttt{distance := rate * time}) &= \{\texttt{distance := rate*time}\}\\
\mathcal{T}[\![x \texttt{ := } x\texttt{+}y]\!](\texttt{distance := distance + step}) &= \{\texttt{distance := distance + step}\}\\
\mathcal{T}[\![x \texttt{ := } x\texttt{*}y]\!](\texttt{distance := rate * time}) &= \emptyset\\
&\text{(the empty set, since } \texttt{distance} \neq \texttt{rate}\text{)}
\end{aligned}$$

## 3 Core-SmPL: Executable Transformation Semantics (without pattern variables)

We formalise the meaning of semantic patches by a directly executable semantics for Core-SmPL. This resembles a matcher for regular expressions over strings of terms, extended with *tree transformation* and *variable bindings.* We first develop the semantics for a simplified source language where there are no pattern variables, and a program is simply a string of ground terms, e.g., symbols. We will later generalise to allow variables in patterns, and programs with control transfers such as conditionals and loops.

The Core-SmPL semantic patch semantics is built by adding a transformation component to a string matcher written in continuation-passing style. Its input is a finite term string *in* from the set $GroundTerm^*$, the set of finite strings of ground terms. Its output is the set of all outputs corresponding to *in*: a set $out \subseteq GroundTerm^*$. The set *out* is empty if *in* does not match the pattern.

In the domain definitions of Figure 2 $c$ is a continuation and a pattern meaning is an input-output transformation defined using continuation transformers.

$$\begin{aligned}
&in \in In = GroundTerm^* \quad out \in Out = 2^{GroundTerm^*}\\
&c \in Cont = In \to Out\\
&\mathcal{T}[\![_]\!] : P \to Cont\\
&\mathcal{P}[\![_]\!] : P \to Cont \to Cont\\
&\mathcal{E}[\![_]\!] : E \to Cont \to Cont
\end{aligned}$$

**Fig. 2.** Semantic value domains

Figure 3 contains evaluation rules in a continuation- passing style denotational semantics. This formulation enables a natural and straightforward formalisation of searches for *all* possible matches for a given pattern. In addition, such a formulation lends itself to implementation in a functional language and indeed we have made such a prototype implementation.

Nonterminal $P$ stands for "pattern" and $G$ stands for any ground term. To avoid ambiguity we use ML-like notations to write inputs to and outputs from our program transformer: the empty sequence is represented as [], and $G :: in$ represents the result of putting ground term $G$ at the start of input string $in$.

- I starts the transformation, with an initial continuation $c_0$ that will copy any input that may remain.
- II and III resemble a regular expression matcher, expressed using continuation semantics (it's easy to add a rule for $P^*$ in a way similar to "...").
- III checks to see that the first ground term in the input sequence is $G$. If so, continuation $c$ is applied to the remaining input, and $G$ is added to each output term sequence. If not, no output is produced.
- IV. Deletion works just as $\mathcal{E}[\![G]\!]\ c\ in$ in group II, except that term $G$ is not added to the output sequence. Insertion: term $G$ is added to the output sequence. (No matching is done.)

$I$ :

$$\mathcal{T}[\![P]\!] = \mathcal{P}[\![P]\!]\ c_0 \quad \underline{\text{where}}\ \ c_0\ in = \{in\}$$

$II$ : **Sequences of things**

$$\mathcal{P}[\![\varepsilon]\!]\ c\ in = (c\ in)$$
$$\mathcal{P}[\![\ E\ P\ ]\!]\ c = \mathcal{E}[\![E]\!]\ (\mathcal{P}[\![P]\!]\ c)$$

$III$ : **Single things**

$$\mathcal{E}[\![G]\!]\ c\ [] = \emptyset$$
$$\mathcal{E}[\![G]\!]\ c\ (G' :: in) = \underline{\text{if}}\ G = G'\ \underline{\text{then}}\ \{G :: out \mid out \in (c\ in)\}\ \underline{\text{else}}\ \emptyset$$

$$\mathcal{E}[\![\ P_1 \mid P_2\ ]\!]\ c\ in = (\mathcal{P}[\![P_1]\!]\ c\ in) \cup (\mathcal{P}[\![P_2]\!]\ c\ in)$$

$$\mathcal{E}[\![...]\!]\ c\ in = (c\ in)\ \cup \{G :: out \mid G :: in' = in \text{ and } out \in (\mathcal{E}[\![...]\!]\ c\ in')\}$$

$IV$ : **Deletion, insertion**

$$\mathcal{E}[\![-G]\!]\ c\ [] = \{\}$$
$$\mathcal{E}[\![-G]\!]\ c\ (G :: in) = \underline{\text{if}}\ G = G'\ \underline{\text{then}}\ (c\ in)\ \underline{\text{else}}\ \emptyset$$
$$\mathcal{E}[\![+G]\!]\ c\ in = \{G :: out \mid out \in (c\ in)\}$$

**Fig. 3.** Semantic evaluation rules

## 4 A Practically Better Approach: Compiling SmPL to CTL

The semantics above explains the meanings of SmPL patterns, and can be executed. However Figure 3 applies only to abstract syntax trees, as is usual in denotational semantics. In effect, it makes the unrealistic assumption that a source program is one long ground term sequence.

It also suffers efficiency problems: matching as above is essentially "top-down", repeatedly checking the same goals in slightly different contexts due to non-linear uses of argument $c$. Pattern expression matching can be complex and time-consuming, especially if universal path quantification is used (see [4, 16]).

Because of these and other problems, Coccinelle instead uses instead a two-step approach: SmPL patterns are translated into the temporal logic CTL. This happens "under the hood": users need not know anything about CTL, model checking, etc. We will argue the equivalence of the denotational semantics with the more indirect CTL-based version after a quick review of CTL.

CTL is defined in terms of *transition systems*: directed graphs able naturally to express program control flow graphs (CFGs) with flow divergence, convergence and loops. Compiling into CTL thereby also allows a smooth extension to program control flow graphs, an extension done less systematically in [4, 16].

An immediate advantage is performance: model checkers are known to be fast, with a well-developed theory and practice. Since model checking is done bottom-up, repeated computation is avoided. A further advantage is that the interaction between universal and existential quantification over paths is well-defined in temporal logic, e.g., it does not in principle require extra work to generalise to patterns with alternating path quantifiers.

A final advantage is flexibility: the same CTL language can be used as an intermediate language with different translation schemes. This makes it easier to adapt the Coccinelle approach to applications other than updating and transformation, e.g., bug finding [20].

In the remainder of this paper we mainly focus in using CTL model checking to search for program patterns rather than program transformation. This is motivated by the way Coccinelle works: first model checking is used to find all the relevant program points and then the transformations are performed afterwards. This has proven to be a simple way to avoid ambiguous transformations. It also has the practical advantage that it is significantly simpler to formulate the correctness statements without the transformation component. Extension of CTL (e.g., with transformation operators '+' and '−' giving judgements of the form $\mathcal{M}, s \models \phi \rightarrow \mathcal{M}'$) will be described in a subsequent publication.

*Compiling SmPL into CTL.* We now translate SmPL into CTL instead of executing. To save space we do not repeat the standard semantics of CTL but refer instead to [10]. We will prove that the Core-SmPL semantics of Section 3 is a *symbolic composition* of this transformation semantics with the CTL semantics. For now we use classical CTL without variables, so the $T$ appearing below is an atomic proposition in $AP$: a ground term as in Definition 2. We show later how to allow variables in CTL terms, an idea also used in [13, 11]. To simplify the correctness formulation, we do not here account for transformation by + or -.

Compilation is defined in Figure 4 using functions $\mathcal{T}_{ctl} : P \rightarrow CTL$, $\mathcal{P}_{ctl}[\![\_]\!] : P \rightarrow K \rightarrow CTL$ and $\mathcal{E}_{ctl}[\![\_]\!] : E \rightarrow K \rightarrow CTL$ (note that the $CTL$ and $K$ are also used as types in the figure). Data structure $k \in K$ is related to the continuation functions of the executable semantics of Section 3. For pragmatic reasons, the $K$ data structure distinguishes between two kinds of continuations, denoted `tail` and `after`, representing respectively continuations that are final and continuations that need further work. We defer detailed explanation to [9].

$$k : K = \texttt{tail} \mid \texttt{after}\ CTL$$

$$\mathcal{T}_{ctl}[\![P]\!] = \mathcal{P}_{ctl}[\![P]\!]\ \texttt{tail}$$

$$\mathcal{P}_{ctl}[\![\varepsilon]\!]\ \texttt{tail} = \texttt{true}$$
$$\mathcal{P}_{ctl}[\![\varepsilon]\!]\ (\texttt{after}\ \phi) = \phi$$

$$\mathcal{P}_{ctl}[\![E\ P]\!]k = \mathcal{E}_{ctl}[\![E]\!](\texttt{after}(\mathcal{P}_{ctl}[\![P]\!]k))$$

$$\mathcal{E}_{ctl}[\![G]\!]\ \texttt{tail} = G \qquad \text{ground term } G \text{ regarded as atomic prop.}$$
$$\mathcal{E}_{ctl}[\![G]\!]\ (\texttt{after}\ \phi) = G \wedge AX\phi$$

$$\mathcal{E}_{ctl}[\![P_1 \mid P_2]\!]k = (\mathcal{P}_{ctl}[\![P_1]\!]k) \vee (\mathcal{P}_{ctl}[\![P_2]\!]k)$$

$$\mathcal{E}_{ctl}[\![...]\!]\ \texttt{tail} = AF\ \texttt{exit} \qquad \text{end of the input } (\texttt{exit} \text{ is in Definition 3})$$
$$\mathcal{E}_{ctl}[\![...]\!]\ (\texttt{after}\ \phi) = AF\ \phi \qquad \text{all future states must satisfy } \phi$$

**Fig. 4.** Translation from SmPL into CTL

*Correctness of the compilation to CTL.* We now argue the translation correct by relating the executable semantics of Section 3 to CTL satisfaction of a translated term. As we only consider patterns $P$ without $+$ or $-$, the net semantic effect of $\mathcal{T}[\![P]\!]\ in$ is to transform input $in$ into either $\{in\}$ or $\emptyset$. To state correctness we first define a link between input sequences and transition systems.

**Definition 3.** *Let $in = G_1 G_2 \dots G_n$ be a linear source program: a sequence of ground terms. The corresponding transition system (Figure 5) is denoted $\widehat{in}$. This has states $1, 2, \dots, n, n{+}1$ with labels $L(1) = \{G_1\}, \dots, L(n) = \{G_n\}, L(n{+}1) = \{\texttt{exit}\}$ and transitions $\{1 \to 2, \dots, n \to n+1, n+1 \to n+1\}$.*

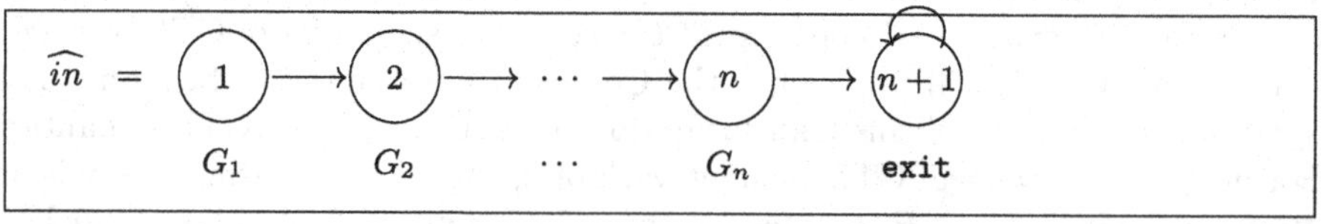


**Fig. 5.** Model for a linear string as source program

**Theorem 1.** *For any linear source program in and pattern $P$ without $+, -$ or variables, we have $\mathcal{T}[\![P]\!]\ in = \{in\}$ if and only if $\widehat{in}, 1 \models \mathcal{T}_{ctl}[\![P]\!]$.*

A definition aids stating a sufficiently strong induction hypothesis:

**Definition 4.** *Relation $c \approx k$ holds if $k = \texttt{tail}$ and $\forall in\ (c(in) = \{in\})$, or if $k = \texttt{after}\ \phi$ and $\forall in\ (\ c(in) = \{in\}$ if and only if $\widehat{in}, 1 \models \phi\ )$.*

We prove this by structural induction on $P$. The desired result follows by structural induction on $P, E$, using the definitions of $\mathcal{P}, \mathcal{P}_{ctl}, \mathcal{E}, \mathcal{E}_{ctl}$ and the following. See the full paper [9] for detailed proof.

**Theorem 2.** *If* $c \approx k$ *it holds that* $\forall P.\ (\ \mathcal{P}[\![P]\!]\ c \approx \mathtt{after}(\mathcal{P}_{ctl}[\![P]\!]\ k)\ )$ *and* $\forall E.\ (\ \mathcal{E}[\![E]\!]\ c \approx \mathtt{after}(\mathcal{E}_{ctl}[\![E]\!]\ k)\ )$.

*Relating regular expressions and CTL.* A natural question: can the translation be extended to allow an arbitrary regular expression in place of $P$? Alas, there seems to be no natural way to translate a general regular pattern $P^*$ into CTL.

## 5 Semantics of Core-SmPL with Pattern Variables

We now enrich Core-SmPL, extending the language of patterns to include pattern variables (essentially the parameters of [16, 4] or meta-variables of [11, 12, 14]). An *environment* parameter holds the values bound to pattern variables.

$$\begin{array}{l} \mathit{In} = \mathit{GroundTerm}^* \quad \mathit{Out} = 2^{\mathit{GroundTerm}^*} \\ c : \mathit{Cont} = \mathit{Env} \rightarrow \mathit{In} \rightarrow \mathit{Out} \quad (c \text{ is a continuation}) \\ \mathcal{T}[\![\_]\!] : P \rightarrow \mathit{In} \rightarrow \mathit{Out} \quad \mathcal{P}[\![\_]\!] : P \rightarrow \mathit{Cont} \rightarrow \mathit{Cont} \quad \mathcal{E}[\![\_]\!] : E \rightarrow \mathit{Cont} \rightarrow \mathit{Cont} \end{array}$$

**Fig. 6.** Semantic value domains for Core-SmPL with variables

The input to a Core-SmPL semantic patch is still a finite sequence $in = G_1G_2 \ldots G_n \in \mathit{GroundTerm}^*$ of ground terms $G_i \in \mathit{GroundTerm}$, and the matcher output is a set of such sequences: a set $out \subseteq \mathit{GroundTerm}^*$, empty if $in$ does not match the pattern. Pattern semantics has to be extended, though, to include bindings of pattern variables. Operations on environments: $env(T)$ denotes the result of replacing every pattern variable $x$ in $T$ by $env(x)$. $env(T)$ is defined only if every $env(x)$ is defined. Updating the environment $env$ with $env'$ is denoted by $env[env']$, i.e., $env[env'](x) = env'(x)$ if $x \in \mathrm{dom}(env')$ and $env[env'] = env(x)$ otherwise. (Note that $\mathrm{dom}(env[env']) = \mathrm{dom}(env) \cup \mathrm{dom}(env')$.)

Further (as in Prolog), $MGU(T_1, T_2)$ denotes the *most general unifier* of $T_1, T_2$. Notation: $MGU(T_1, T_2)$ equals "some $env$" where $env$ is the most general unifier $env$ if it exists, else $MGU(T_1, T_2)$ equals "fail". For SmPL, $T_1$ may contain pattern variables, but $T_2$ will always be a ground term. Here $\mathit{GroundTerm}^*$ and $\mathit{Term}^*$ mean any finite sequence of ground terms and terms respectively.

- I starts, with empty variable environment $env_0$ and initial continuation $c_0$.
- II is just as before except for the extra environment parameter.
- III yields the empty output set on empty input. Otherwise, the first input ground term $G$ is matched against pattern $T$ (after applying the current environment to instantiate its pattern variables). If matching succeeds with $env'$, new bindings found in $env'$ are added to the current environment $env$.

An example: pattern $x{:=}x{+}y$ is successfully matched against program input $\mathtt{di} := \mathtt{di} + \mathtt{st}$ to give new environment bindings $[x \mapsto \mathtt{di}, y \mapsto \mathtt{st}]$:

$$\begin{aligned}&\mathcal{E}[\![x{:=}x{+}y]\!]\ c\ [\,]\ (\mathtt{di} := \mathtt{di} + \mathtt{st}){::}in = \\ &\quad \{(\mathtt{di} := \mathtt{di} + \mathtt{st}){::}out \mid out \in c[x \mapsto \mathtt{di}, y \mapsto \mathtt{st}]\}\end{aligned}$$

– IV. Deletion and insertion are as for Core-SmPL, except the environment is applied to term $T$ as in II.

*An implementation.* These rules have been implemented in a functional programming language, and gave the expected outputs on all this paper's examples. See the full paper [9] for details.

| | |
|---|---|
| $I$: $\mathcal{T}[\![P]\!]$ | $= \mathcal{P}[\![P]\!]\ c_0\ env_0$ <u>where</u> $\mathrm{dom}(env_0) = \emptyset$ and $c_0\ env\ in = \{in\}$ |
| $II$ : **Sequences of things** | |
| $\mathcal{P}[\![\varepsilon]\!]\ c\ env\ in$ | $= c(in)$ |
| $\mathcal{P}[\![\ E\ P\ ]\!]\ c$ | $= \mathcal{E}[\![E]\!]\ (\mathcal{P}[\![P]\!]\ c)$ |
| $III$ : **Single things** | |
| $\mathcal{E}[\![T]\!]\ c\ env\ [\,]$ | $= \{\}$ |
| $\mathcal{E}[\![T]\!]\ c\ env\ (G :: in)$ | $=$ <u>case</u> $MGU(env\ T, G)$ <u>of</u><br>fail : $\{\}$<br>some $env'$ : $\{G :: out \mid out \in (c\ env[env']\ in)\}$ |
| $\mathcal{E}[\![\ P_1 \mid P_2\ ]\!]\ c\ env\ in$ | $= (\mathcal{P}[\![P_1]\!]\ c\ env\ in) \cup (\mathcal{P}[\![P_2]\!]\ c\ env\ in)$ |
| $\mathcal{E}[\![...]\!]\ c\ env\ in$ | $= (c\ in) \cup$<br>$\{G :: out \mid G :: in' = in$ and $out \in (\mathcal{E}[\![...]\!]\ c\ env\ in')\}$ |
| $IV$ : **Deletion, insertion** | |
| $\mathcal{E}[\![-T]\!]\ c\ env\ [\,]$ | $= \{\}$ |
| $\mathcal{E}[\![-T]\!]\ c\ env\ (G :: in)$ | $=$ <u>case</u> $MGU(env\ T, G)$ <u>of</u><br>fail : $\{\}$<br>some $env'$ : $c\ env[env']\ in$ |
| $\mathcal{E}[\![+T]\!]\ c\ env\ in$ | $= \{(env\ T) :: out \mid out \in (c\ env\ in)\}$ |

**Fig. 7.** Semantic evaluation rules with variables

## 6 Semantics of CTL-V with Pattern Variables

The Coccinelle implementation translates SmPL patterns with variables into CTL-V: a CTL extension with quantified variables ranging over fragments from the source program's CFG. The correctness argument of Section 4 was expressed in terms of classical, variable-free, CTL, so some changes are necessary to express correctness of the more general SmPL with pattern variables.

*CTL-V = Staged CTL with quantifiers,* a variant intended to be especially suitable for program manipulation. One extension over classical CTL is (as in

Definition 2) to allow atomic propositions *ap* to have full tree-structured terms as values. The idea is to extend traditional models by allowing a state to be decorated with pieces of source program information, e.g., possibly unbounded data such as function names, parameter names or constants.

These are referred to using *pattern variables* so only a term's top-level syntactic structure need be expressed: a CTL-V atomic proposition may be an arbitrary term, with or without variables. This generalises an approach seen in [13, 12, 11]. (Variables used in a similar way are called *parameters* in [4, 16].) We generalise a bit to allow *explicit quantification*, with existential quantifiers appearing anywhere in a formula.

*CTL-V syntax and its satisfaction relation.* For brevity we just show how CTL-V pattern recognition works, and omit details of how the language and algorithms are extended to carry out program transformation. The development is intended only to clarify the CTL-V semantics, and does not at all account for efficiency issues (e.g., as done in the Coccinelle system).

**Definition 5.** *Let $x$ range over Var, a set of* variables[2]. *A* CTL-V formula *is anything generated by the following context-free grammar, where $ap \in AP$ may be a term containing variables:*

$$\phi ::= ap \mid \neg\phi \mid \phi \wedge \phi \mid \phi \vee \phi \mid AX\phi \mid AF\phi \mid A(\phi U \phi) \mid EX\phi \mid \exists x \phi$$

By Definition 2 the CFG of a source program $P$ is a binary relation $\rightarrow$ on states, each labelled by a single ground term $G$. A pattern-variable value will typically be a fragment of the source program $P$ to be analysed. The set of all possible values is thus the set of all subterms of $P$ , and so *a finite set.* We will henceforth denote this set by $Val = \{v_1, \ldots, v_m\}$.

Before starting with CTL-V-satisfaction and model checking, we need precisely to define the working of substitutions that bind pattern variables. A substitution binds the free variables of a CTL-V-formula $\phi$ to values in *Val*. A term atomic proposition $T$ is true iff $T$ can be unified with $G$.

**Definition 6.** *The* set of free variables $fv(\phi)$ *of CTL-V formula $\phi$ is defined as expected. A formula $\phi$ is* closed *if $fv(\phi) = \emptyset$. A* substitution *is a partial function $\theta : FinSet(Var) \rightarrow Val$ mapping a finite set of CTL-variables to values.*

**Definition 7.** *The* satisfaction *relation $\mathcal{M}, s \models_\theta \phi$ for CTL-V is defined inductively in Figure 8. ($\mathcal{M}$ is elided for brevity.)*

*Staging.* The "silver bullets" of this approach: pattern (meta-)variables, quantification, and the use of two stages. The term "staging" comes from partial evaluation and refers to the *binding times*, i.e., the times at which various things are specified or computed. A key point is that source program-dependent values such as identifiers, although unbounded if one consider arbitrary programs, have a *bounded finite value range* **for any one source program**. Hence $Val$ is a finite value set for the program about to be transformed.

[2] These are names of pattern variables, not program variables.

| | | |
|---|---|---|
| $s \models_\theta T$ | iff | some $\theta = MGU(T, v)$ where $L(s) = \{v\}$ |
| $s \models_\theta \neg\phi$ | iff | not $s \models_\theta \phi$ |
| $s \models_\theta \phi_1 \wedge \phi_2$ | iff | $s \models_\theta \phi_1$ and $s \models_\theta \phi_2$ |
| $s \models_\theta \phi_1 \vee \phi_2$ | iff | $s \models_\theta \phi_1$ or $s \models_\theta \phi_2$ |
| $s \models_\theta AX\phi$ | iff | $\forall\sigma \in \mathbb{P}(s) . \sigma[1] \models_\theta \phi$ |
| $s \models_\theta EX\phi$ | iff | $\exists\sigma \in \mathbb{P}(s) . \sigma[1] \models_\theta \phi$ |
| $s \models_\theta A(\phi_1 U \phi_2)$ | iff | $\forall\sigma \in \mathbb{P}(s) . \exists j \geq 0 .$ $[\forall k . 0 \leq k < j \Rightarrow \sigma[k] \models_\theta \phi_1] \wedge \sigma[j] \models_\theta \phi_2$ |
| $s \models_\theta AF\phi$ | iff | $\forall\sigma \in \mathbb{P}(s) . \exists j \geq 0 . \sigma[j] \models_\theta \phi$ |
| $s \models_\theta \exists x\phi$ | iff | $s \models_{\theta[x \mapsto v_1]} \phi$ or ... or $s \models_{\theta[x \mapsto v_m]}$ |

**Fig. 8.** CTL-V satisfaction relation

*Mapping CTL-V to CTL.* Recall that $Val = \{v_1, \ldots, v_m\}$ and consider the following mapping from CTL-V to CTL:

$$[\![T]\!]\theta = \theta(T) \qquad [\![\phi \wedge \phi']\!]\theta = [\![\phi]\!]\theta \wedge [\![\phi']\!]\theta \qquad [\![\neg\phi]\!]\theta = \neg([\![\phi]\!]\theta)$$
$$[\![\exists x\phi]\!]\theta = [\![\phi]\!]\theta[x \mapsto v_1] \vee \ldots \vee [\![\phi]\!]\theta[x \mapsto v_m]$$

The following theorems establish the correctness of the above mapping and decidability of CTL-V model checking respectively:

**Theorem 3.** *For any $\mathcal{M}, s$ and $\theta$ that closes $\phi$: $\mathcal{M}, s \models [\![\phi]\!]\theta$ iff $\mathcal{M}, s \models_\theta \phi$.*

**Theorem 4.** *It is decidable, given Kripke model $\mathcal{M} = (S, \rightarrow, L)$, state $s \in S$, substitution $\theta$ and CTL-V formula $\phi$, whether $\mathcal{M}, s \models_\theta \phi$.*

In [9] we show a model check algorithm for CTL-V that works because of staging and the corollary finiteness of *Val*. It sidesteps some tricky algorithmic problems involved in an efficient way to implement $\neg\phi, \exists\phi$, as was necessary in [13, 16] (and is also done in Coccinelle).

## 7 Relation to the Coccinelle System

We have made a rational reconstruction of the core of the Coccinelle system. We now briefly review how the real Coccinelle system differs from, and extends, our reconstruction. The most important difference: this paper does not cover the full semantic patch language (SmPL) implemented by Coccinelle.

Other differences are mainly concerned with implementation and issues relating to the underlying models, such as nesting of program structures and matching balanced braces. These particular issues are handled by adding a special atomic proposition, called `Paren`($x$). The `Paren`($x$) proposition is true at some state if the variable $x$ equals the *current nesting level* of program braces. This makes it possible to constrain searches to specific function definition bodies or program block structures, e.g., to skip over the "then" branch of a conditional.

*Efficiency issues.* The Coccinelle system implements a number of optimisations in order to obtain acceptable execution times. These include use of constructive negation for a more efficient implementation of ∃ than in Definition 7; reducing the scope of quantifiers; and a number of low-level implementation techniques. Constructive negation directly encodes "negative information" about variable bindings, i.e., recording that a given variable must not be bound to a certain value. Reducing the scope of quantifiers has the effect of reducing the size and number of environments that have to be propagated by the algorithm.

In practise these optimisations have had a profound effect on execution times.

*Transformation after model checking.* In order to perform program transformations based on successful matches obtained by model checking, the Coccinelle system adds so-called *witness trees* to the CTL-V semantics. These record the variable bindings (substitutions) that led to successful matches. To do transformation some such structure is needed, to record variable bindings that are removed from a substitution when a quantified variable is bound to a value.

## 8 Conclusion

The *Coccinelle* system is a *well-established program transformer* currently being used by practitioners to automate and document collateral evolutions in Linux device drivers. We presented a compact, precise and self-contained semantics of Core-SmPL, in essence a rational reconstruction of the heart of the system. This gives it a solid foundation, one that motivates the structure of the Coccinelle framework, and justifies it theoretically.

Technically: we defined the semantics using continuation-passing style denotational semantics; made a prototype implementation in Haskell; translated SmPL to a novel implementation language (the temporal logic CTL); and formally proved the translation faithful to the denotational semantics. Partial evaluation's "staging" concept was used to define CTL-V, a CTL extension with existentially quantified variables that range over program points and source code parameters. This led to a more complex but practically more expressive and useful version of Core-SmPL. In the full paper [9] a model checking algorithm for CTL-V is outlined and exemplified on a string matching problem.

These results show a pleasing relation between theory and practice, and give descriptions of a complex working practical system. The descriptions are compact and (we hope) comprehensible to outsiders without previous experience with Coccinelle. Ideally, the insights gained here will be of benefit and perhaps even a guide to others with similar goals.

*Acknowledgements.* The authors wish to thank all the people involved with the *Coccinelle* project: Gilles Muller, Yoann Padioleau, Jesper Andersen, Henrik Stuart and, especially, Julia L. Lawall.

## References

1. Bravenboer, M., Kalleberg, K.T., Vermaas, R., Visser, E.: Stratego/XT 0.16. Components for transformation systems. In: PEPM 2006, Charleston, South Carolina (January 2006)
2. Buckley, J., Mens, T., Zenger, M., Rashid, A., Kniesel, G.: Towards a taxonomy of software change. Journal of Software Maintenance and Evolution: Research and Practice 309–332 (2005)
3. Chapin, N., Hale, J.E., Khan, K.M., Ramil, J.F., Than, W.-G.: Types of software evolution and software maintenance. Journal of software maintenance and evolution: Research and Practice 13, 3–30 (2001)
4. De Moor, O., Lacey, D., van Wyk, E.: Universal regular path queries. Higher-order and Symbolic Computation 16(1-2), 15–35 (2003)
5. Dig, D., Johnson, R.: How do APIs evolve? a story of refactoring. Journal of Software Maintenance and Evolution: Research and Practice 18(2), 83–107 (2006)
6. Fiuczynski, M., Grimm, R., Coady, Y., Walker, D.: Patch (1) considered harmful. In: Workshop on Hot Topics in Operating Systems (2005)
7. Fiuczynski, M.E.: Better tools for kernel evolution, please! LOGIN 30(5), 8–10 (2006)
8. Godfrey, M.W., Tu, Q.: Evolution in open source software: A case study. In: ICSM, pp. 131–142 (2000)
9. Hansen, R.R., Jones, N.D.: The semantics of semantic patches in Coccinelle: Program transformation for the working programmer (full paper). Project home page: `http://www.emn.fr/x-info/coccinelle/`
10. Huth, M.R.A., Ryan, M.D.: Logic in Computer Science: Modelling and Reasoning about Systems. Cambridge University Press, Cambridge (2004)
11. Lacey, D., Jones, N.D., Van Wyk, E., Frederiksen, C.C.: Compiler optimization correctness by temporal logic. Higher Order and Symbolic Computation 17(3), 173–206 (2004)
12. Lacey, D.: Program Transformation using Temporal Logic Specifications. PhD thesis, Oxford University Computing Laboratory (2003)
13. Lacey, D., de Moor, O.: Imperative Program Transformation by Rewriting. In: Wilhelm, R. (ed.) CC 2001 and ETAPS 2001. LNCS, vol. 2027, pp. 52–68. Springer, Heidelberg (2001)
14. Lacey, D., Jones, N.D., van Wyk, E., Frederiksen, C.C.: Proving correctness of compiler optimizations by temporal logic. In: POPL 2002, vol. 29, pp. 283–294 (2002)
15. Lerner, S., Millstein, T., Chambers, C.: Automatically proving the correctness of compiler optimizations. In: PLDI 2003, pp. 220–231. ACM Press, New York (2003)
16. Liu, Y.A., Rothamel, T., Yu, F., Stoller, S.D., Hu, N.: Parametric regular path queries. In: PLDI 2004, pp. 219–230 (2004)
17. Padioleau, Y., Hansen, R.R., Lawall, J.L., Muller, G.: Semantic patches for documenting and automating collateral evolutions in Linux device drivers. In: PLOS 2006. Proc. of Workshop on Programming Languages and Operating Systems, p. 10 (2006)
18. Padioleau, Y., Lawall, J.L., Muller, G.: Understanding collateral evolution in Linux device drivers. In: EuroSys 2006, pp. 59–71 (2006)
19. Steffen, B.: Optimal run time optimization proved by a new look at abstract interpretation. In: Ehrig, H., Levi, G., Montanari, U. (eds.) CAAP 1987 and TAPSOFT 1987. LNCS, vol. 249, Springer, Heidelberg (1987)
20. Stuart, H., Hansen, R., Lawall, J.L., Andersen, J., Padioleau, Y., Muller, G.: Towards easing the diagnosis of bugs in OS code. In: PLOS 2007 (to appear, 2007)

# An Efficient SSA-Based Algorithm for Complete Global Value Numbering

Jiu-Tao Nie and Xu Cheng

Peking University, Beijing, China
{njt,chengxu}@mprc.pku.edu.cn

**Abstract.** Global value numbering (GVN) is an important static analysis technique both for optimizing compilers and program verification tools. Existing complete GVN algorithms discovering all Herbrand equivalences are all inefficient. One reason of this is the intrinsic exponential complexity of the problem, but in practice, since the exponential case is quite rare, the more important reason is the huge data structures annotated to every program point and slow abstract evaluations on them site by site. In this paper, we present an SSA-based algorithm for complete GVN, which uses just one global graph to represent all equivalences at different program points and performs fast abstract evaluations on it. This can be achieved because in SSA form, interferences among equivalence relations at different program points can be entirely resolved with dominance information. We implement the new algorithm in GCC. The average proportion of execution time of the new algorithm in the total compilation time is only 0.36%. To the best of our knowledge, this is the first practical complete GVN algorithm.

## 1 Introduction

Global value numbering (GVN) is an important static analysis technique. It detects equivalences of program expressions, which have a variety of applications. Optimizing compilers use this information to detect and eliminate semantic redundant computations [2,14,16,11,15], and useless branches. Program verification tools use it to verify program assertions. Translation validation tools use it to check the validation of program transformations [10], such as the correctness of an optimizer, by discovering equivalences of different programs.

Since checking general equivalence of program expressions is an undecidable problem even when all conditionals are treated as non-deterministic [12], most GVN algorithms treat both all conditionals as non-deterministic and all operators as uninterpreted. The equivalence relation with these restrictions is called *Herbrand equivalence* [13]. The GVN algorithms that can discover all Herbrand equivalences are referred to as *complete* GVN algorithms.

Unfortunately, existing efficient GVN algorithms used in practice are all incomplete. The simple hash-based GVN algorithm fails to detect many kinds of equivalences in the presence of loops and joins. Alpern, Wegman and Zadeck's (AWZ) partition refinement algorithm [1] is based on the static single assignment (SSA) form [4,5]. It treats phi nodes as uninterpreted operators, so equivalences

Z. Shao (Ed.): APLAS 2007, LNCS 4807, pp. 319–334, 2007.

among phi nodes and ordinary expressions can't be discovered. Rüthing, Knoop and Steffen (RKS) improved on AWZ algorithm by incorporating several rewriting rules to remedy this problem [13]. However, their algorithm remains incomplete both for acyclic and cyclic programs [8]. Gargi proposed a set of balanced algorithms that are efficient, but also incomplete [6].

Recently, Gulwani and Necula proposed a randomized polynomial GVN algorithm [7] based on the idea of random interpretation, which involves performing abstract interpretation using randomized data structures and algorithms. This algorithm is complete and efficient. However, unlike other GVN algorithms, there is a small probability that this algorithm deduces false equivalences, i.e. it's not sound. False equivalences are acceptable for program verification tools as long as their appearance probability can be made small enough. However, for compilers this is strictly disallowed.

The obstacle of applying powerful sound and complete GVN algorithms [9,15,8] in practice is their unacceptable low efficiency. Theoretically, all complete GVN algorithms have exponential complexity in the size of the program [8]. To this problem, Gulwani and Necula have proposed a polynomial algorithm that computes all Herbrand equivalences among terms with limited sizes [8]. In practice, choosing the size limitation to the program size is sufficient. Moreover, the exponential case is quite rare in practical programs. Thus, the exponential complexity problem is not really crucial now. The more important reason of the low efficiency of complete GVN algorithms is the huge data structures annotated to every program point and slow abstract evaluations on them site by site [13].

To this problem, we propose a new SSA-based complete GVN algorithm, which uses just one global graph to represent all equivalences at different program points and performs fast abstract evaluations on it. Previous complete GVN algorithms all perform abstract interpretation [3] on ordinary programs. Transforming these algorithms to those working on programs in SSA form is trivial (only need to add abstract interpretation function for phi nodes that can be regarded as copy statements copying values from their operands corresponding to incoming edges to their target). However, we observe that in SSA form, since each variable has only one definition site and its available scope is program points dominated by its definition site, interferences among equivalence relations at different program points can be entirely resolved with dominance information. Therefore, performing abstract evaluations on just one global value number graph is possible. Moreover, using global equivalence representation also greatly speeds up abstract evaluations, since equivalence relation changes caused by each statement only needs to be applied to the global graph once rather than being transferred to all affected local graphs one by one. The difficulty of this achievement is choosing the abstract evaluation order. Naively performing abstract evaluations in an arbitrary order with the global value number graph may cause information inconsistency problem and loss of precision. However, we find that performing abstract evaluations through all edges of a spanning tree of the control flow graph and all other edges separately can conquer this problem.

In the rest of this paper, Section 2 defines the program representation and some relevant notations used in this paper. Section 3 reviews the traditional complete GVN algorithm working on programs not in SSA form. Section 4 extends the basic algorithm to the SSA-based version, and shows how a global value number graph is used to represent all local equivalences. Then, the abstract evaluation order problem is discussed, and the order used by our algorithm is shown to be correct. Section 5 gives implementation details of our algorithm and shows how to restrict it to be polynomial based on the approach proposed in [8]. Section 6 gives experimental results, and Section 7 concludes the paper.

## 2 Program Representation

We use notations $V$, $O$ and $F$ to denote program variable set, operator set, and nonfunctional operation set respectively. For notation simplicity, we also regards constants as variables belonging in $V$. For example,

$$V = \{x_1, x_2, 21, -9, \ldots\} \quad O = \{+, -, \ldots\} \quad F = \{\mathit{load}, \mathit{store}, \mathit{call}, \mathit{branch}, \ldots\}$$

The function $arity : (V \cup O \cup F) \to \omega$ is defined as follows:

$$arity(x) = \begin{cases} 0 & x \in V \\ \text{operands number of } x & x \in O \cup F \end{cases}$$

We assume statements have been decomposed into such a simple form:

$$x_0 = f(x_1, x_2, \ldots, x_{arity(f)}), \text{ where } f \in O \cup F,\ x_i \in V.$$

If $f \in F$, we say that statement/expression is a relevant statement/expression, whose result relies not only on its operands but its position relative to other relevant statements, and it may also cause side effects. For concept unification, we regard parameters and constants as results of hidden relevant statements just after program entry. For a variable $x$, $def(x)$ denotes $x$'s definition statement. For a statement $s$, $lhs(s)$ and $rhs(s)$ denote the left and right hand side expressions of $s$ respectively. For an expression $e$, $Vars(e)$ denotes the set of variables appearing in $e$.

A program $P$ is represented by a directed flow graph $P = (N_P, E_P, \mathit{entry}, \mathit{exit})$. The node set $N_P$ consists of statements, join nodes that merge more than one control flow, and *entry* and *exit* nodes of $P$. The edge set $E_P$ represents non-deterministic control flows. For a node $n$ of a directed multigraph, we use $succ(n)$ to denote the successor sequence of $n$ and $succ(n)[i]$ the $i$-th successor. Correspondingly, $pred(n)$ and $pred(n)[i]$ are for the predecessor sequence and the $i$-th predecessor of $n$.

## 3 Traditional Complete Global Value Numbering

In this section, we review the three components of the traditional complete GVN algorithm as an abstract interpretation problem.

### 3.1 Abstract Semantic Domain

The abstract semantic domain of the GVN problem is the lattice of equivalence relations of expressions. An equivalence relation of expressions can be compactly represented by an annotated directed acyclic graph (DAG), which is called *Structured Partition DAG* (SPDAG) in [15] and *Strong Equivalence DAG* (SED) in [8]. In this paper, we use a similar data structure called *Value Number DAG* (VNDAG) to represent equivalences. A VNDAG is a labeled directed acyclic graph $D = (N_D, E_D, L_D, M_D)$ satisfying:

1. $(N_D, E_D)$ is a directed acyclic graph with node set $N_D$ and edge set $E_D$.
2. $L_D : N_D \to V \cup O \cup \{\bot, \top\}$ is a labeling function satisfying $\forall \nu \in N_D.\ arity(L_D(\nu)) = |succ(\nu)|$.
3. $\forall \nu_1, \nu_2 \in N_D.\ (L_D(\nu_1) = L_D(\nu_2) = l \wedge \forall\ i \in [1, arity(l)].\ succ(\nu_1)[i] = succ(\nu_2)[i]) \to \nu_1 = \nu_2$.
4. $M_D : V \to N_D$ is a function mapping each variable to a node of the DAG.

Every node of a VNDAG represents a value number. A node is labeled by either a variable $x \in V$, indicating that it's a leaf node, or an operator $o \in O$, indicating that it has $arity(o)$ successors, or the special symbols $\bot$ or $\top$. In a VNDAG, there is at most one node with a given label and a given sequence of successors.

For any VNDAG $D$, every value number $\nu \in N_D$ represents a variable set

$$A_D(\nu) = \{x \in V \mid M_D(x) = \nu\}$$

and an expression set

$$T_D(\nu) = \begin{cases} A_D(\nu) & L_D(\nu) \in V \\ A_D(\nu) \cup \{o(t_1, \ldots, t_n) \mid t_i \in T_D(succ(\nu)[i])\} & L_D(\nu) = o \in O \\ \emptyset & L_D(\nu) = \bot \\ \{t \mid Vars(t) \subseteq A_D(\nu)\} & L_D(\nu) = \top \end{cases}$$

Note that $T_D(\nu_\bot)$ is $\emptyset$ and $T_D(\nu_\top)$ contains all expressions whose variables have the value number $\nu_\top$.

We use the notation $D \models t_1 = t_2$ to denote that the VNDAG $D$ implies that expressions $t_1$ and $t_2$ are equivalent. Then, the equivalence of any two expressions represented by VNDAG $D$ is deduced as follows (here $x \in V$, $o \in O$, and $t$, $t_i$ and $t'_i$ denote any expressions):

$$\begin{aligned} D \models x = t \ \text{ iff }\ \{x, t\} \subseteq T_D(M_D(x)) \\ D \models o(t_1, \ldots, t_n) = o(t'_1, \ldots, t'_n) \ \text{ iff }\ D \models t_1 = t'_1 \wedge \ldots \wedge D \models t_n = t'_n \end{aligned}$$

The abstract semantic domain is in fact the lattice $\mathbb{D}$ of all VNDAGs including two special VNDAGs $D_\bot$ denoting the empty relation, and $D_\top$ denoting the universal relation.

For a VNDAG $D$ and a variable $x$, the function $newvn(D, x)$ adds a new node labeled by $x$ to $D$ and returns it. For a non-relevant expression $t$, the following function returns a value number $\nu$ such that $t \in T_D(\nu)$.

$$vn(D, t) = \begin{cases} M_D(t) & t \equiv x \in V \\ find(D, o, vn(D, t_1), \ldots, vn(D, t_n)) & t \equiv o(t_1, \ldots, t_n) \end{cases}$$

where, $find$ returns an existing node with corresponding label and successors, or a newly created one (which is also added to $D$) if such a node is not found. In practice, the VNDAG and $find$ can be implemented with a hash table. Simplifications and normalizations, such as constant folding and expression reassociation can be integrated into $find$ so that more equivalences can be detected.

### 3.2 Abstract Interpretation Function

Each node in $N_P$ of a program $P$ is interpreted by the abstract interpretation function $\theta : N_P \times \mathbb{D} \to \mathbb{D}$ defined as follows:

$$\theta(n, D) = \begin{cases} \text{let } D' = D \text{ in } D'[M_{D'}[newvn(D', x)/x]/M_{D'}] & n \equiv x = f(\ldots) \\ \text{let } D' = D \text{ in } D'[M_{D'}[vn(D', t)/x]/M_{D'}] & n \equiv x = t \\ \text{let } D' = D \text{ in } D' & otherwise \end{cases}$$

The informal meaning of $\theta$ is that: copy $D$ to $D'$ first; then 1) for a relevant statement, add a new node labeled by its left hand side variable to $D'$ and set its value number to the new node, and return the updated $D'$; 2) for a non-relevant statement, get the node of its right hand side expression and set its left hand side variable's value number to that node, and return the updated $D'$; 3) for other nodes (join nodes and *entry* and *exit*), return the unchanged $D'$.

### 3.3 Abstract Evaluation

For a program $P$, each edge $e \in E_P$ is associated with a VNDAG denoted as $vndag(e)$. We use $dest(e)$ to denote the destination node of $e$. For a program node $n \in N_P$, we use $succ_e(n)$ to denote the set of edges whose source node is $n$, and $pred_e(n)$ the set of edges whose destination node is $n$. $D_1 \sqcap D_2$ returns a VNDAG that represents equivalences represented by both $D_1$ and $D_2$ (refer to [8] for the implementation of $\sqcap$). $D_1 \sqsubset D_2$ iff the equivalence relation represented by $D_1$ is a strict subset of that represented by $D_2$. Then, the abstract evaluation algorithm for the complete GVN is given in Figure 1.

```
foreach e ∈ E_P do vndag(e) := D_⊤
worklist := succ_e(entry)
while worklist ≠ ∅ do
    Take e from worklist
    foreach e' ∈ succ_e(dest(e)) do
        D := vndag(e') ⊓ θ(dest(e), vndag(e))
        if D ⊏ vndag(e') then
            vndag(e') := D
            worklist := worklist ∪ {e'}
```

**Fig. 1.** Traditional complete GVN algorithm

# 4 SSA-Based Complete Global Value Numbering

## 4.1 The Trivial SSA-Based Algorithm

In SSA form, every variable has exactly one definition site, and all statements using it as an operand must be dominated by its definition site. This property is achieved by inserting phi nodes at appropriate join nodes and renaming variables for operands and targets of statements and phi nodes [4,5]. The only new notion of the SSA form is the phi node. Thus, to transform the traditional complete GVN to the SSA-based version, we only need to replace join nodes with phi nodes in the program's representation, and define the abstract interpretation function for phi nodes as follows:

$$\theta(x_0 = \phi(x_1, \ldots, x_n), D, i) = \text{let } D' = D \text{ in } D'[M_{D'}[M_{D'}(x_i)/x_0]/M_{D'}]$$

where, the new parameter $i$ is the number of the incoming edge through which the abstract evaluation reaches that phi node. For other nodes, parameter $i$ is ignored. During the abstract evaluation, phi nodes at the same join node are evaluated in parallel, since just evaluating parts of them doesn't make sense.

## 4.2 Use One VNDAG to Represent All Equivalences

With the property of the SSA form, we extend the expression set represented by each VNDAG node by adding a program edge parameter and further extend the equivalence deducing rules so that just one VNDAG can represent all equivalence relations at different program edges. We use the notation *dom* to denote the dominance relation between program nodes or edges. For a program $P$, each edge $e \in E_P$, the expression set

$$T_D(e, \nu) = \{t \in T_D(\nu) \,|\, \forall x \in Vars(t).def(x) \ dom\ e\}$$

contains all expressions represented by $\nu$ and available at $e$. We use the notation $D \models_e t_1 = t_2$ to denote that the VNDAG $D$ implies that expressions $t_1$ and $t_2$ are equivalent at $e$. Then, the equivalence of any two expressions at $e$ represented by $D$ is deduced as follows (here $x \in V$, $o \in O$, and $t$, $t_i$ and $t'_i$ denote any expressions):

$$D \models_e x = t \ \text{ iff } \ \{x, t\} \subseteq T_D(e, M_D(x))$$
$$D \models_e o(t_1, \ldots, t_n) = o(t'_1, \ldots, t'_n) \ \text{ iff } \ D \models_e t_1 = t'_1 \wedge \ldots \wedge D \models_e t_n = t'_n$$

Figure 2 shows a program and the VNDAG representing all Herbrand equivalences in it. For example, we have the following term sets:

$$\begin{aligned} T_D(5) &= \{a_1\} \\ T_D(2) &= \{c_0\} \\ T_D(7) &= \{x_1, z_0\} \cup \{a_1 + c_0\} \\ T_D(L_2, 7) &= \{x_1, z_0, a_1 + c_0\} \end{aligned}$$

Then, we can deduce that $D \models_{L_2} x_1 = z_0$, $D \models_{L_2} x_1 + c_0 = (a_1 + c_0) + c_0$, etc. (RKS-algorithm fails to detect the equivalence of $x_1$ and $z_0$ at $L_2$.) Note that, the only VNDAG represents all Herbrand equivalences at all program edges.

input: $a, b, c$

$x = a + c$

$y = b + c$

$t = a; a = b; b = t$
$t = x; x = y; y = t$
$z = a + c$

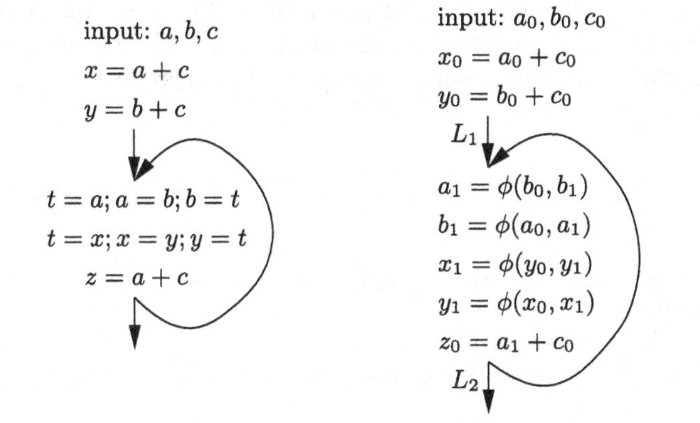

(a) Original program

input: $a_0, b_0, c_0$

$x_0 = a_0 + c_0$

$y_0 = b_0 + c_0$

$L_1$

$a_1 = \phi(b_0, b_1)$
$b_1 = \phi(a_0, a_1)$
$x_1 = \phi(y_0, y_1)$
$y_1 = \phi(x_0, x_1)$
$z_0 = a_1 + c_0$

$L_2$

(b) SSA form of the program

(c) VNDAG of the program

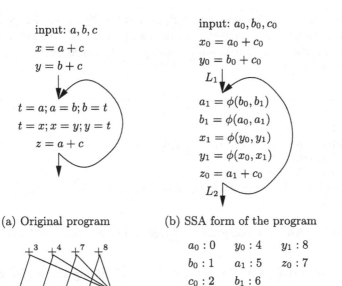

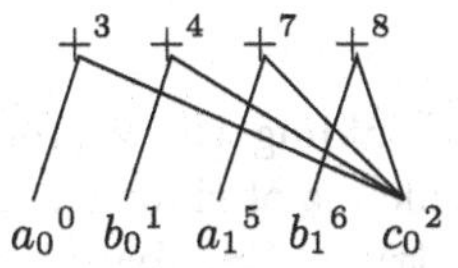

| | | |
|---|---|---|
| $a_0 : 0$ | $y_0 : 4$ | $y_1 : 8$ |
| $b_0 : 1$ | $a_1 : 5$ | $z_0 : 7$ |
| $c_0 : 2$ | $b_1 : 6$ | |
| $x_0 : 3$ | $x_1 : 7$ | |

(d) Value number of each variable $(M_D)$

**Fig. 2.** A program and the VNDAG representing all Herbrand equivalences in it. In (c), the superscript of variable and operator is a unique number representing that node in this figure.

### 4.3 Abstract Evaluation with One Global VNDAG

The hard part is performing abstract evaluations with just one global VNDAG. The naive idea is using the global VNDAG to replace all local VNDAGs appearing in the original abstract evaluation algorithm. Unfortunately, it doesn't always work correctly when joins and loops exist. This is because performing abstract evaluations in an arbitrary order can't ensure that equivalence relations represented by the global VNDAG involved in an operation are always consistent. For example, if the abstract evaluation process reaches a phi node $x_0 = \phi(x_1, x_2)$ through its left incoming edge without touching its right incoming edge, then $x_1$ may have been set to a new equivalence class but $x_2$ is still in the old one. Thus, the meet operation after this node doesn't make sense and generates wrong results.

To solve this problem, we adopt a particular evaluation order since the evaluation order can be arbitrary [9]. The edges of a program $P$ are divided into two subsets: the spanning tree (whose root node is *entry*) edges $E_{tP}$ and others $E_P - E_{tP}$. Now, we use two global VNDAGs $D$ and $D_1$. $D$ is initialized to $D_{\top}$ at the beginning and $D_1$ backups the original $D$ before each evaluation iteration. In the $i$-th evaluation iteration, the $(i-1)$-th (by referring to $D_1$) equivalence relations of edges in $E_P - E_{tP}$ and the $i$-th (by referring to $D$) equivalence relations of edges in $E_{tP}$ are processed in a top-down order of the spanning tree, and the results are saved in $D$. The iteration continues until $D$ reaches the fixed point. Figure 3 gives the formal algorithm. Though two global VNDAGs are used here, one is enough if the algorithm is subtly designed. The next section shows how we achieve this.

```
1  D := D⊤
2  repeat
3      D₁ := D
4      foreach e ∈ E_tP in a top-down order do
5          n := dest(e)
6          let i satisfy that pred_e(n)[i] = e
7          D := θ(n, D₁, 1) ⊓ ... ⊓ θ(n, D₁, |pred_e(n)|) ⊓ θ(n, D, i)
8  until D = D₁
```

Fig. 3. SSA-based complete GVN algorithm with global VNDAG

We show the correctness of this algorithm by building the correspondence between it and the algorithm shown in Figure 4, which is obviously a sound and complete GVN algorithm since compared with the trivial SSA-based algorithm, only the abstract evaluation order is changed (first for non-tree edges and then for tree edges in a top-down order).

```
1  foreach e ∈ E_P do vndag(e) := D⊤
2  repeat
3      foreach e ∈ E_P − E_tP do
4          foreach e' = succ_c(dest(e))[i] do
5              vndag(e') := vndag(e') ⊓ θ(n, vndag(e), i)
6      foreach e ∈ E_tP in a top-down order do
7          foreach e' = succ_c(dest(e))[i] do
8              vndag(e') := vndag(e') ⊓ θ(n, vndag(e), i)
9  until no vndag(e) changed in this iteration
```

Fig. 4. SSA-based complete GVN algorithm with local VNDAGs

To connect a global VNDAG with a set of local VNDAGs, we introduce the function $\eta : \mathbb{D} \times E_P \to \mathbb{D}$. For any global VNDAG $D \in \mathbb{D}$, program edge $e \in E_P$ and any expressions $t_1$ and $t_2$, $\eta(D, e)$ is defined to be a local VNDAG $D' \in \mathbb{D}$ satisfying that $D' \models t_1 = t_2$ iff $D \models_e t_1 = t_2$, i.e. $D'$ is the local VNDAG at $e$ representing the same equivalence relation as $D$ at $e$. Let $R(D)$ denote the equivalence relation represented by $D$, $Na(e)$ denote the set of variables not available at $e$, and for a variable set $X$, $Pairs(X) = \{\langle t_1, t_2 \rangle \mid Vars(t_1) \cap X \neq \emptyset \lor Vars(t_2) \cap X \neq \emptyset\}$. Then, $R(\eta(D, e)) = R(D) - Pairs(Na(e))$. About $\eta$, $\theta$ and $\sqcap$, the following two lemmas hold:

**Lemma 1.** *For any $D_1, D_2 \in \mathbb{D}$, $e \in E_P$, $\eta(D_1 \sqcap D_2, e) = \eta(D_1, e) \sqcap \eta(D_2, e)$.*

*Proof.* We only need to show that the equivalence relations represented by VNDAGs of the two sides are equivalent. $R(\eta(D_1 \sqcap D_2, e)) = R(D_1 \sqcap D_2) - Pairs(Na(e)) = R(D_1) \cap R(D_2) - Pairs(Na(e)) = (R(D_1) - Pairs(Na(e))) \cap (R(D_2) - Pairs(Na(e))) = R(\eta(D_1, e)) \cap R(\eta(D_2, e)) = R(\eta(D_1, e) \sqcap \eta(D_2, e))$. Thus, the proposition holds. □

**Lemma 2.** *For any $e \in E_P$, let $n = dest(e)$, $e' \in succ_e(n)$, then $\eta(\theta(n, D, i), e') = \eta(\theta(n, \eta(D, e), i), e')$.*

*Proof.* Let $\theta_R$ denote the abstract interpretation function on equivalence relations. We omit the first parameter $n$ of $\theta$ and $\theta_R$ for simplicity in this proof since they are all the same. $R(\eta(\theta(\eta(D, e), i), e')) = R(\theta(\eta(D, e), i)) - Pairs(Na(e')) = \theta_R(n, R(D) - Pairs(Na(e)), i) - Pairs(Na(e')) =^a \theta_R(n, R(D), i) - Pairs(Na(e) - \{lhs(n)\}) - Pairs(Na(e')) =^b \theta_R(n, R(D), i) - Pairs(Na(e')) = R(\eta(\theta(D, i), e'))$. In the equation, $=^a$ is because $\theta_R$ only removes and adds equivalence pairs belonging in $Pairs(\{lhs(n)\})$ from and to the input relation. $=^b$ is because $Pairs(Na(e) - \{lhs(n)\}) \subseteq Pairs(Na(e'))$. □

In the new algorithm, each step of interpretation and meet operations on the global VNDAG corresponds to a set of operations on a set of local VNDAGs. The following lemma builds the connection between the new algorithm working on the global VNDAG and that working on local VNDAGs.

**Lemma 3.** *At line 7 of Figure 3, for any $e' \in succ_e(n)$ and $e_j = pred_e(n)[j]$, let $k = |pred_e(n)|$, then $\eta(D, e') = \theta(n, \eta(D_1, e_1), 1) \sqcap \ldots \sqcap \theta(n, \eta(D_1, e_k), k) \sqcap \theta(n, \eta(D, e), i)$*

*Proof.* We omit the first parameter $n$ of $\theta$ for simplicity in this proof since they are all the same.

$$
\begin{aligned}
&R(\eta(D, e')) = R(\eta(\theta(D_1, 1) \sqcap \ldots \sqcap \theta(D_1, k) \sqcap \theta(D, i), e')) \\
&= R(\eta(\theta(\eta(D_1, e_1), 1), e') \sqcap \ldots \sqcap \eta(\theta(\eta(D_1, e_k), k), e') \sqcap \eta(\theta(\eta(D, e), i), e')) \\
&= R(\theta(\eta(D_1, e_1), 1)) \cap \ldots \cap R(\theta(\eta(D_1, e_k), k)) \cap R(\theta(\eta(D, e), i)) - Pairs(Na(e')) \\
&=^a R(\theta(\eta(D_1, e_1), 1)) \cap \ldots \cap R(\theta(\eta(D_1, e_k), k)) \cap R(\theta(\eta(D, e), i)) \\
&= R(\theta(\eta(D_1, e_1), 1) \sqcap \ldots \sqcap \theta(\eta(D_1, e_k), k) \sqcap \theta(\eta(D, e), i))
\end{aligned}
$$

$=^a$ is because that if a variable is available at all predecessors of $e'$, then it must also be available at $e'$. □

The correctness of the new algorithm follows from the following theorem.

**Theorem 1.** *Let $vndag_j(e)$ denote the local VNDAG of the program edge $e$ before the $j$-th iteration of the algorithm in Figure 4. At the beginning of each $j$-th iteration of algorithms in Figure 4 and Figure 3, for any program edge $e$, $\eta(D, e) = vndag_j(e)$.*

*Proof.* When $j = 1$, the proposition holds obviously. Assume that the proposition holds for $j \leq m$ $(m \geq 1)$. When $j = m + 1$, in the $m$-th iteration, after each meet operation in line 7 of Figure 3, due to Lemma 3 and that any changes on $D$ by this meet operation don't affect the equivalence relations represented by $D$ at successor edges of processed tree edges (since removed and added pairs are not available there due to the top-down spanning tree order), by induction on the spanning tree, we can prove that for any $e' \in succ_e(n)$, $\eta(D, e') = \theta(n, \eta(D_1, e_1), 1) \sqcap \ldots \sqcap \theta(n, \eta(D_1, e_k), k) \sqcap \theta(n, \eta(D, e), i) = \theta(n, vndag_m(e_1), 1) \sqcap \ldots \sqcap \theta(n, vndag_m(e_k), k) \sqcap \theta(n, vndag_{m+1}(e), i) = vndag_{m+1}(e')$. After all tree edges are processed, for any $e \in E_P$, $\eta(D, e) = vndag_{m+1}(e)$. □

## 5 Implementation of the New Algorithm

Using the global VNDAG to represent all equivalences not only greatly reduces the data structure size used by the algorithm, but also can greatly speed up the abstract evaluation process. Since all evaluation results are stored in the same VNDAG, only those (rather than all) program nodes that will affect the VNDAG need to be evaluated. Thus, in practice, evaluations are performed along those define-use (DU) chains through spanning tree edges starting from initial program nodes affecting the global VNDAG. The algorithm shown in Figure 5 builds such a kind of DU chains. The variable set $uses(x)$ stores all variables whose definition site is a non-relevant statement referring to $x$ or a phi node referring to $x$ through a spanning tree edge. At the same time, the algorithm also computes the affected basic block set $affected(x)$ for each variable $x$, which stores blocks containing at least one phi node referring to $x$. If the value number of $x$ is changed, phi nodes of blocks in $affected(x)$ must be evaluated.

```
BuildDUChains()
begin
    foreach non-relevant statement x = t do
        foreach y ∈ Vars(t) do
            uses(y) := uses(y) ∪ {x}
    foreach phi node x = φ(x_1, ..., x_n) do
        let b be the containing block of the phi node
        foreach i ∈ [1, n] do
            affected(x_i) := affected(x_i) ∪ {b}
            if (pred(b)[i], b) is a spanning tree edge then
                uses(x_i) := uses(x_i) ∪ {x}
end
```

**Fig. 5.** The algorithm for building define-use chains (*uses*)

Notice that in the algorithm in Figure 3, the only use of VNDAG $D_1$ is computing $D$ at line 7 and testing if $D$ is changed. These two tasks can be achieved without explicitly copying $D$ to $D_1$. We only need to save changes into a variable-value-number pair set *newupdates*. The sub-expression $\theta(n, D_1, 1) \sqcap \ldots \sqcap \theta(n, D_1, |pred_e(n)|)$ at line 7 for all $n = dest(e), e \in E_{tP} \wedge bb(n) \in changed$ are computed by the algorithm shown in Figure 6, and the results are saved in

```
DetectNewUpdates()
begin
    clear newupdates
    foreach b ∈ changed do
        if sorted(b) = false then
            sort phi nodes in b in a topological order of their value numbers in
            the VNDAG
            sorted(b) := true
        foreach phi node x := φ(x_1, ..., x_n) in b do
            ν := Intersect(x, M_D(x_1), ..., M_D(x_n))
            if ν ≠ M_D(x) then
                newupdates := newupdates ∪ {⟨x, ν⟩}
        clear memorize
end
```

**Fig. 6.** The algorithm for detecting new updates

*newupdates* as update pairs. It calls `Intersect` [1] shown in Figure 7 to compute value numbers of phi nodes of each affected blocks (in *changed*), and uses the map *memorize* : $N_D^n \rightarrow N_D$ to build the equivalence relation among them. If and only if the returned value number differs from the original one, the result of the intersection is less than the original equivalence relation, and the new update pair is added to *newupdates*. Phi nodes with leaf value numbers must be processed before others so that these value numbers can be correctly labeled with a unique variable rather than returned as the $\perp$ that denotes the equivalence class containing no available variables. This is achieved by sorting phi nodes in a topological order[2] of their value number nodes in the VNDAG, when their containing blocks are first touched.

The rest part of the expression at line 7 of Figure 3 ($\sqcap\theta(n, D, i)$) is implemented by the algorithm shown in Figure 8. The procedure `SetCounter` shown in Figure 9 counts the number of dependent variables $cnt(x)$ along spanning tree edges for each affected variable $x$. The meet operation is reflected by the condition at line 6, i.e. only if the previous VNDAG deduces that the left hand side variable is equivalent to the right hand side expression, the update should be done for that variable. Then, `UpdateVN` updates value numbers for variables whose *cnt* is set in a topological order of their dependence DAG, and adds affected blocks into *changed*, where new update detection should be performed. To strictly correspond to the algorithm in Figure 3, an additional meet and update process along spanning tree edges should be performed, but it can be omitted since the subsequent process of the main procedure subsumes it.

The main procedure of the new algorithm is shown in Figure 10. It initializes *newupdates* with pairs of targets of relevant statements and unique value

[1] We omit the first parameter of *newvn*, *vn* and *find* since all of them work on the only global VNDAG $D$.

[2] If we attach an increasing sequence number to each value number when they are created, we can use the ascending order of their sequence numbers.

```
Intersect(x, ν1, ..., νn)
begin
    if ν1 = ... = νn then return ν1
    ν := memorize(ν1, ..., νn)
    if ν ≠ nil then return ν
    if ∀i ∈ [1, n].νi = o(μi1, ..., μim) then
        foreach j ∈ [1, m] do
            ξj := Intersect(nil, μ1j, ..., μnj)
        if ∃j ∈ [1, m].ξj = ⊥ then ν := ⊥
        else ν := find(o, ξ1, ..., ξm)
    else ν := ⊥
    if ν = ⊥ and x ≠ nil then ν := newvn(x)
    memorize(ν1, ..., νn) := ν
    return ν
end
```

**Fig. 7.** The algorithm for intersecting value numbers

```
UpdateVN()
begin
    // Count dependence numbers of affected variables
    foreach ⟨x, ν⟩ ∈ newupdates do SetCounter(x)
    // Update M_D for variables in newupdates
    foreach ⟨x, ν⟩ ∈ newupdates do
        cnt(x) := 0
        M_D(x) := ν
        wl := wl ∪ {x}
    // Update M_D for other affected variables
    while wl ≠ ∅ do
        take v from wl
        changed := changed ∪ affected(v)
        foreach x ∈ uses(v) do
            if x is a result of a phi node then
                if cnt(x) = 1 then
                    cnt(x) := 0
                    M_D(x) := M_D(v)
                    wl := wl ∪ {x}
            else
                cnt(x) := cnt(x) − 1
                if cnt(x) = 0 then
                    M_D(x) := vn(rhs(def(x)))
                    wl := wl ∪ {x}
end
```

**Fig. 8.** The algorithm for updating value numbers

```
SetCounter(v)
begin
    cnt(v) := cnt(v) + 1
    // Visit v's successors at the first time
    if cnt(v) = 1 then
        foreach x ∈ uses(v) do
            if x is not a result of phi node or M_D(x) = M_D(v) then
                SetCounter(x)
end
```

**Fig. 9.** The algorithm for setting counters of variables

```
GVN()
begin
    BuildDUChains()
    foreach x ∈ V do M_D(x) := ⊤
    foreach x ∈ V and x is a result of f ∈ F do
        newupdates := newupdates ∪ {⟨x, newvn(x)⟩}
    while newupdates ≠ ∅ do
        UpdateVN()
        DetectNewUpdates()
end
```

**Fig. 10.** The efficient complete GVN algorithm

numbers of them. Then, it updates value numbers of affected variables and detects new updates iteratively until a fixed point is reached.

Figure 11 shows the process of applying our algorithm on the program in Figure 2. The initial *newupdates* comprises pairs of three parameters and leaf value numbers of them. After updating value numbers along DU chains, two new value numbers, $+^3$ and $+^4$ are created and $M_D$ is updated. By applying `Intersect` on phi nodes in the loop body block, all of their value numbers are changed, so four new update pairs are added to *newupdates*. Since *newupdates* is not empty, another iteration runs and the result of the second value number updating is shown in (d). Now, applying `Intersect` on these phi nodes again, we get the same value numbers of them as the last time. Thus, *newupdates* is empty and the algorithm terminates. The resulting VNDAG of the algorithm deduces complete Herbrand equivalences of that program.

The approach used in [8] that restricts the exponential complete GVN to a polynomial GVN that detects equivalences among expressions with limited sizes can be directly adopted in our algorithm. We can set a counter to limit the VNDAG size before calling `Intersect` in `DetectNewUpdates`. In `Intersect`, the counter is decreased by one whenever expressions are decomposed into subexpressions (before line 7 of Figure 7). When the counter is decreased to zero, it simply set the value number variable $\nu$ to $\bot$. Refer to [8] for more details about this approach and its complexity analysis.

$$\{\langle a_0, {a_0}^0\rangle, \langle b_0, {b_0}^1\rangle, \langle c_0, {c_0}^2\rangle\}$$

(a) The *newupdates* before the first iteration

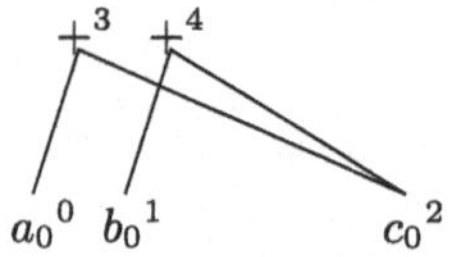


| | | |
|---|---|---|
| $a_0 : 0$ | $y_0 : 4$ | $y_1 : 3$ |
| $b_0 : 1$ | $a_1 : 1$ | $z_0 : 4$ |
| $c_0 : 2$ | $b_1 : 0$ | |
| $x_0 : 3$ | $x_1 : 4$ | |

(b) The VNDAG and $M_D$ after the first iteration

$$\{\langle a_1, {a_1}^5\rangle, \langle b_1, {b_1}^6\rangle, \langle x_1, {a_1}^2 +^7 {c_0}^2\rangle, \langle y_1, {b_1}^6 +^8 {c_0}^2\rangle\}$$

(c) The *newupdates* before the second iteration

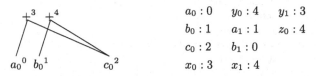

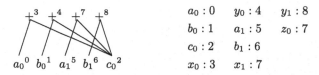

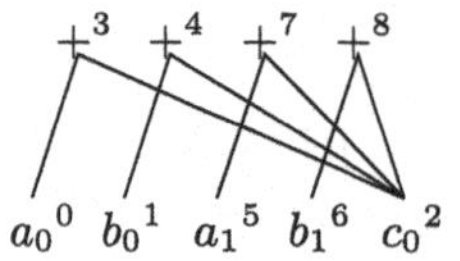


| | | |
|---|---|---|
| $a_0 : 0$ | $y_0 : 4$ | $y_1 : 8$ |
| $b_0 : 1$ | $a_1 : 5$ | $z_0 : 7$ |
| $c_0 : 2$ | $b_1 : 6$ | |
| $x_0 : 3$ | $x_1 : 7$ | |

(d) The VNDAG and $M_D$ after the second iteration

**Fig. 11.** Applying our algorithm on the program in Figure 2

# 6 Experimental Results

We have implemented the new algorithm without VNDAG size restrictions and a semantic code motion algorithm using its result in GCC-4.2.0 as a standard pass. To show the efficiency of the new algorithm, we measured elapsed user times of it and the total compilation, as well as ratios between them, in compiling SPEC CPU2000 on a machine with a 800MHz Pentium-M and 512MB memory. Times are measured by GCC's own timing facility exported in `timevar.h`. The results are shown in Table 1, which indicate that the new GVN algorithm is extremely

**Table 1.** Times (in sec.) spent in GVN and total compilation, as well as ratios between them in compiling SPEC CPU2000

| CINT2000 | gzip | vpr | gcc | mcf | crafty | parser | gap | vortex | bzip2 | twolf |
|---|---|---|---|---|---|---|---|---|---|---|
| CGVN | 0.03 | 0.07 | 0.61 | 0.00 | 0.09 | 0.14 | 0.22 | 0.17 | 0.01 | 0.16 |
| Total | 6.88 | 19.23 | 213.60 | 2.94 | 30.83 | 24.01 | 75.83 | 61.79 | 5.23 | 35.93 |
| Ratio (%) | 0.44 | 0.36 | 0.29 | 0.00 | 0.29 | 0.58 | 0.29 | 0.28 | 0.19 | 0.45 |

| CFP2000 | wupwise | swim | mgrid | applu | mesa | art | equake | facerec | ammp | lucas | fma3d | sixtrack | apsi |
|---|---|---|---|---|---|---|---|---|---|---|---|---|---|
| CGVN | 0.00 | 0.00 | 0.03 | 0.04 | 0.30 | 0.02 | 0.01 | 0.04 | 0.07 | 0.04 | 0.70 | 0.54 | 0.12 |
| Total | 3.09 | 0.71 | 2.08 | 7.58 | 70.58 | 2.13 | 3.08 | 8.78 | 17.68 | 6.00 | 223.23 | 111.15 | 18.50 |
| Ratio (%) | 0.00 | 0.00 | 1.44 | 0.53 | 0.43 | 0.94 | 0.32 | 0.46 | 0.40 | 0.67 | 0.31 | 0.49 | 0.65 |

| Overall | GVN: 3.41 | Total: 950.86 | Ratio: 0.36% |
|---|---|---|---|

fast, and efficient enough to be applied in practice. Notice that this is achieved without VNDAG size restriction, which suggests that the exponential complexity problem almost does not exist in practice.

## 7 Conclusions and Future Works

There are two reasons causing existing complete GVN algorithms inefficient. The first one, the intrinsic exponential complexity problem has been discussed in previous works, but in practice, it is not the important reason (attested by our experiments). This paper conquers the more important and practical reason, the huge data structures and slow abstract evaluations of previous complete algorithms. Based on the SSA form, the new algorithm uses just one global VNDAG to represent all equivalences at different program points and performs fast abstract evaluations on it. The experimental results show that the new algorithm is efficient enough to be applied in practice. To the best of our knowledge, this is the first practical complete GVN algorithm.

In the future, one interesting direction is to generalize this SSA-based approach to apply on other program analysis problems. Another direction is to improve the precision of the basic complete GVN algorithm by considering operator properties, conditionals, memory access instructions and inter-procedural problems.

## References


1. Alpern, B., Wegman, M.N., Zadeck, F.K.: Detecting equality of variables in programs. In: POPL, pp. 1–11 (1988)
2. Briggs, P., Cooper, K.D.: Effective partial redundancy elimination. In: PLDI, pp. 159–170 (1994)
3. Cousot, P., Cousot, R.: Abstract interpretation: A unified lattice model for static analysis of programs by construction or approximation of fixpoints. In: POPL, pp. 238–252 (1977)
4. Cytron, R., Ferrante, J., Rosen, B.K., Wegman, M.N., Zadeck, F.K.: An efficient method of computing static single assignment form. In: POPL, pp. 25–35 (1989)
5. Cytron, R., Ferrante, J., Rosen, B.K., Wegman, M.N., Zadeck, F.K.: Efficiently computing static single assignment form and the control dependence graph. ACM Trans. Program. Lang. Syst. 13(4), 451–490 (1991)
6. Gargi, K.: A sparse algorithm for predicated global value numbering. In: PLDI, pp. 45–56 (2002)
7. Gulwani, S., Necula, G.C.: Global value numbering using random interpretation. In: Jones, N.D., Leroy, X. (eds.) POPL, pp. 342–352. ACM, New York (2004)
8. Gulwani, S., Necula, G.C.: A polynomial-time algorithm for global value numbering. In: Giacobazzi, R. (ed.) SAS 2004. LNCS, vol. 3148, pp. 212–227. Springer, Heidelberg (2004)
9. Kildall, G.A.: A unified approach to global program optimization. In: POPL, pp. 194–206 (1973)
10. Necula, G.C.: Translation validation for an optimizing compiler. In: PLDI, pp. 83–94 (2000)

11. Odaira, R., Hiraki, K.: Partial value number redundancy elimination. In: Eigenmann, R., Li, Z., Midkiff, S.P. (eds.) LCPC 2004. LNCS, vol. 3602, pp. 409–423. Springer, Heidelberg (2005)
12. Reif, J.H., Lewis, H.R.: Symbolic evaluation and the global value graph. In: POPL, pp. 104–118 (1977)
13. Rüthing, O., Knoop, J., Steffen, B.: Detecting equalities of variables: Combining efficiency with precision. In: Cortesi, A., Filé, G. (eds.) SAS 1999. LNCS, vol. 1694, pp. 232–247. Springer, Heidelberg (1999)
14. Simpson, L.T.: Value-Driven Redundancy Elimination. PhD thesis, Rice University (May 1996)
15. Steffen, B., Knoop, J., Rüthing, O.: The value flow graph: A program representation for optimal program transformations. In: Jones, N.D. (ed.) ESOP 1990. LNCS, vol. 432, pp. 389–405. Springer, Heidelberg (1990)
16. van Drunen, T.J.: Partial redundancy elimination for global value numbering. PhD thesis, Purdue University, West Lafayette, IN, USA, Major Professor-Antony L. Hosking (2004)

# A Systematic Approach to Probabilistic Pointer Analysis

Alessandra Di Pierro[1], Chris Hankin[2], and Herbert Wiklicky[2]

[1] University of Verona, Ca' Vignal 2 - Strada le Grazie 15 I-37134 Verona, Italy
[2] Imperial College London, 180 Queen's Gate London SW7 2AZ, UK

**Abstract.** We present a formal framework for syntax directed probabilistic program analysis. Our focus is on probabilistic pointer analysis. We show how to obtain probabilistic points-to matrices and their relational counterparts in a systematic way via Probabilistic Abstract Interpretation (PAI). The analysis is based on a non-standard semantics for a simple imperative language which corresponds to a Discrete-Time Markov Chain (DTMC). The generator of this DTMC is constructed by composing (via tensor product) the probabilistic control flow of the program and the data updates of the different variables at individual program points. The dimensionality of the concrete semantics is in general prohibitively large but abstraction (via PAI) allows for a drastic (exponential) reduction of size.

## 1 Introduction

We investigate a theoretical framework for the systematic construction of a *syntax directed* probabilistic program analysis. We will illustrate our approach based on a simple *imperative* language, **While**, and its probabilistic extension **pWhile**. Our focus is on the systematic derivation of a *probabilistic pointer analysis* within a static memory model, i.e. we do not have dynamically created objects (on a heap). These restrictions are mainly for presentational reasons and we are confident that our basic ideas also apply to other programming paradigms, e.g. object oriented, dynamic objects on a heap, etc.

Our aim is to introduce a *static* analysis, which could provide an alternative to experimental approaches like profiling. As the analysis is probabilistic we were lead to consider a probabilistic language from the start. However, this language subsumes the usual deterministic **While** and our approach thus applies as well to deterministic as to probabilistic programs. It is important to note that even for deterministic programs the analysis gives in general probabilistic results.

The main novel contributions of this study concern the following aspects. (i) We present for the first time a syntax directed construction of the generator of a Markov chain representing the concrete semantics of a **pWhile** program with static pointers. This exploits a tensor product representation which has been studied previously in areas like performance analysis. (ii) Although the concrete semantics is well-defined and based on highly sparse matrices, the use of the tensor product still leads to an exponential increase in its size, i.e. the dimension of

Z. Shao (Ed.): APLAS 2007, LNCS 4807, pp. 335–350, 2007.

the generator matrices. In order to overcome this problem we apply Probabilistic Abstract Interpretation (PAI) – presented first in [1] (see also [2]) – to construct an abstract semantics, i.e. a static program analysis. The fact that PAI is compatible with the tensor product operation allows us to introduce a compositional construction not only of the concrete but also of the abstract semantics with a drastically reduced size. (iii) This leads to a systematic and formal analysis of (dynamic) *branching probabilities* – usually obtained experimentally via profiling or based on various heuristics (see e.g. [3,4] and references therein) – on the basis of abstracted test operators. (iv) Within our framework, we are also able to construct so-called *points-to matrices* which are commonly employed in probabilistic pointer analysis. Furthermore, we will discuss the alternative concept of a *points-to tensor* which provides more precise relational information.

A possible application area of this type of program/pointer analysis could be *speculative optimisation* which recently is gaining importance – not least in modern multi-core environments. The idea here is (i) to execute code "speculatively" based on some *guess*; (ii) then to test at a later stage whether the *guess* was correct; (iii) if it was correct the computation continues, otherwise some repair code is executed. This guarantees that the computation is always correctly performed. The only issue concerns the (average) costs of "repairs". If the *guess* is correct sufficiently often, the execution of the repair code for the cases where it is wrong is amortised. Thus, in the speculative approach the compiler can take advantage of *statistical* (rather than only definite) information when choosing whether to perform an optimisation. The analysis we present would allow for a better exploitation of the 'maybe' case than with classical conservative compiler optimisation, replacing a *possibilistic* analysis by a *probabilistic* one.

## 2 Probabilistic While

We extend the probabilistic **While** language in [5,6] with pointer expressions. In order to keep our treatment simple we allow only for pointers to (existing) variables, i.e. we will not deal with dynamically created objects on a heap.

A program $P$ is made up from a possibly empty list of variable declarations $D$ followed by a statement $S$. Formally, $P ::= D;\ S \mid S$ with $D ::= d;\ D \mid d$. A declaration $d$ fixes the types of the program's variables. Variables can be either basic Boolean or integer variables or pointers of any order $r = 0, 1, \ldots$, i.e.:

$$d ::= \mathtt{x} : t \qquad\qquad t ::= \mathbf{int} \mid \mathbf{bool} \mid *^r t$$

(where we identify $*^0 t$ with $t$).

The syntax of statements is as follows:

$$\begin{aligned} S ::= &\ \mathbf{skip} \mid \mathbf{stop} \mid p \leftarrow e \mid S_1;\ S_2 \mid \mathbf{choose}\ p_1 : S_1\ \mathbf{or}\ p_2 : S_2 \\ &\mid \mathbf{if}\ b\ \mathbf{then}\ S_1\ \mathbf{else}\ S_2\ \mathbf{end\ if} \mid \mathbf{while}\ b\ \mathbf{do}\ S\ \mathbf{end\ while} \end{aligned}$$

In the **choose** statement we allow only for constant probabilities $p_i$ and assume w.l.o.g. that they are normalised, i.e. add up to 1. A pointer expression is a variable prefixed with $r$ dereferencing $*$'s:

$$p \ ::= \ *^r\mathtt{x} \text{ with } \mathtt{x} \in \mathbf{Var}.$$

We allow for higher order pointers, i.e. for pointers to pointers to .... Expressions $e$ are of different types, namely arithmetic expressions $a$, Boolean expressions $b$ and locality expressions (or addresses) $l$. Formally: $e ::= a \mid b \mid l$. Arithmetic expressions are of the form $a ::= n \mid p \mid a_1 \odot a_2$ with $n \in \mathbb{Z}$, $p$ a pointer to an integer, and '$\odot$' representing one of the usual arithmetic operations '+', '−', or '×'. Boolean expressions are defined by $b ::= \text{TRUE} \mid \text{FALSE} \mid p \mid \neg b \mid b_1 \vee b_2 \mid b_1 \wedge b_2 \mid a_1 \lessgtr a_2$, where $p$ is a pointer to a Boolean variable. The symbol '$\lessgtr$' denotes one of the standard comparison operators for arithmetic expressions, i.e. $<, \leq, =, \neq, \geq, >$. Addresses or locality expressions are: $l ::= \mathtt{nil} \mid \&p \mid p$.

The semantics of **pWhile** with pointers follows essentially the standard one for **While** as presented, e.g., in [7]. The only two differences concern (i) the probabilistic choice and (ii) the pointer expressions used in assignments. The operational semantics is given as usual via a transition system on configurations $\langle S, \sigma\rangle$, i.e. pairs of statements and states. To allow for probabilistic choices we label these transitions with probabilities. Except for the **choose** construct these probabilities will always be 1 as all other statements in **pWhile** are deterministic.

A state $\sigma \in$ **State** describes how variables in **Var** are associated to values in **Value** $= \mathbb{Z} + \mathbb{B} + \mathbb{L}$ (with '+' denoting the disjoint union). The value of a variable can be either an integer or a Boolean constant or the address/reference to a(nother) variable, i.e. **State** $=$ **Var** $\rightarrow \mathbb{Z} + \mathbb{B} + \mathbb{L}$.

In the assignments we allow for general pointer expressions (not just basic variables) on the left as well as the right hand side. In order to give a semantics to assignments we therefore need to identify the actual variable a pointer expression on the left hand side of an assignment is referring to. This is achieved via the function $[\![.]\!]$ from **Pointer** × **State** into **Var**, where **Pointer** $= \{*^r\mathtt{x} \mid \mathtt{x} \in \mathbf{Var}, r = 0, 1, \ldots\}$ denotes the set of all pointer expressions, defined as follows:

$$[\![\mathtt{x}]\!]\sigma = \mathtt{x} \qquad\qquad [\![*^r\mathtt{x}]\!]\sigma = [\![*^{r-1}\mathtt{y}]\!]\sigma \text{ if } \sigma(\mathtt{x}) = \&\mathtt{y}.$$

In other words, if we want to find out what variable a pointer expression refers to we either could have the case that $p = \mathtt{x}$ – in which case the reference is immediately to this variable – or $p = *^r\mathtt{x}$ – in which case we have to dereference the pointer to determine the variable $\mathtt{y}$ it points to in the current state $\sigma$ (via $\sigma(\mathtt{x})$). If further dereferencing is needed we continue until we end up with a basic variable. The variable we finally reach this way might still be a pointer, i.e. contain a location rather than a constant, but we only dereference as often as required, i.e. $r$ times. We also do not check whether further dereferencing is possible, i.e. whether $\mathtt{x}$ had been declared a pointer variable of a higher order than $r$ – we assume that either a simple type system rejects malformed programs at compile time, or that the run-time environment raises an exception if there is a violation.

The expressions $a$, $b$, and $l$ (on the right hand side of assignments or as tests in **if** and **while** statements) evaluate to values of type $\mathbb{Z}$, $\mathbb{B}$ and $\mathbb{L}$ in the usual way. The only extension to the standard semantics is caused again when pointers $p$ are part of the expressions. In order to treat this case correctly, we need to determine first the actual variable a pointer refers to and then obtain the value this variable contains in the current state $\sigma$. Again, we do not cover here any type checking, i.e. whether the variable contains ultimately a value of the correct type. If we denote by **Expr** the set of all expressions $e$ then the evaluation function $\mathcal{E}(.)$. is a function from **Expr** $\times$ **State** into $\mathbb{Z} + \mathbb{B} + \mathbb{L}$. The semantics of arithmetic and Boolean expressions is standard. A new kind of expressions return locations in $\mathbb{L}$, either the constant NIL or the address contained in a variable a pointer $p$ refers to, or the address of a variable which a pointer refers to. For these new expressions we define $\mathcal{E}(.)$. as follows:

$$\mathcal{E}(\mathtt{nil})\sigma = \text{NIL} \qquad \mathcal{E}(p)\sigma = \sigma([\![p]\!]\sigma) \qquad \mathcal{E}(\&p)\sigma = \&([\![p]\!]\sigma).$$

Based on the functions $[\![.]\!]$. and $\mathcal{E}(.)$. the semantics of an assignment is given by

$$\langle p \leftarrow e, \sigma\rangle \longrightarrow_1 \langle \mathbf{stop}, \sigma[[\![p]\!]\sigma \mapsto \mathcal{E}(e)\sigma]\rangle.$$

The state $\sigma$ stays unchanged except for the variable the pointer $p$ is referring to (we obtain this information via $[\![.]\!]$.). The value of this variable is changed so that it now contains the value represented by the expression $e$. The rest of the SOS semantics of **pWhile** is quite standard and we will omit here a formal presentation.

## 3 Linear Operator Semantics

In order to study the semantic properties of a **pWhile** program we will investigate the stochastic process which corresponds to the program's executions. More precisely, we will construct the generator of a Discrete Time Markov Chain (DTMC) which represents the operational semantics of the program in question.

### 3.1 Probabilistic Control Flow

We base our construction on a probabilistic version of the *control flow* [7] or *abstract syntax* [8] of **pWhile** programs. The flow $\mathcal{F}(P)$ of a program $P$ is based on a labelled version of $P$. Labelled programs follow the syntax:

$$\begin{aligned} S ::= & \; [\mathbf{skip}]^\ell \mid [\mathbf{stop}]^\ell \mid [p \leftarrow e]^\ell \mid S_1;\, S_2 \mid [\mathbf{choose}]^\ell\, p_1 : S_1 \;\mathbf{or}\; p_2 : S_2 \\ & \mid \mathbf{if}\; [b]^\ell \;\mathbf{then}\; S_1 \;\mathbf{else}\; S_2 \;\mathbf{end\ if} \mid \mathbf{while}\; [b]^\ell \;\mathbf{do}\; S \;\mathbf{end\ while}. \end{aligned}$$

The flow $\mathcal{F}$ is a set of triples $\langle \ell_i, p_{ij}, \ell_j \rangle$ which record the fact that control passes with probability $p_{ij}$ from block $B_i$ to block $B_j$, where a block is of the form $B_i = [\ldots]^{\ell_i}$. We assume label consistency, i.e. the labels on blocks are unique. We denote by $\mathcal{B}(P)$ the set of all blocks and by $\mathcal{L}(P)$ the set of all labels in a program $P$. Except for the **choose** statement the probability $p_{ij}$ is always equal to 1. For the **if** statement we indicate the control step into the **then** branch by underlining the target label; the same is the case for **while** statements.

### 3.2 Concrete Semantics

The generator matrix of the DTMC which we will construct for any given **pWhile** program defines a linear operator – thus we refer to it as a *Linear Operator Semantics* (LOS) – on a vector space based on the labelled blocks and classical states of the program in question. In all generality, the (real) vector space $\mathcal{V}(S,\mathbb{R}) = \mathcal{V}(S)$ over a set $S$ is defined as the formal linear combinations of elements in $S$ which we can also see as tuples of real numbers $x_s$ indexed by elements in $S$, i.e. $\mathcal{V}(X) = \{\langle x_s, s\rangle_{s\in S} \mid x_s \in R\} = \{(x_s)_{s\in S}\}$, with the usual (point-wise) algebraic operations, i.e. scalar multiplication and vector addition.

The probabilistic state of the computation is described via a probability measure over the space of (classical) states $\mathbf{Var} \rightarrow \mathbb{Z} + \mathbb{B} + \mathbb{L}$.

In order to keep the mathematical treatment as simple as possible we will exploit the fact that **Var** and thus $\mathbb{L}$ is finite for any given program. We furthermore restrict the actual range of integer variables to a finite sub-set $\underline{\mathbb{Z}}$ of $\mathbb{Z}$. Although such a finite restriction is somewhat unsatisfactory from a purely theoretical point of view, it appears to be justified in the context of static program analysis (one could argue that any "real world" program has to be executed on a computer with certain memory limitations). As a result, we can restrict our consideration to probability *distributions* on **State** rather than referring to the more general notion of probability *measures*. While in discrete, i.e. finite, probability spaces every measure can be defined via a distribution, the same does not hold any more for infinite state spaces, even for countable ones; it is, for example, impossible to define on the set of rationals in the interval $[0, 1]$ a kind of "uniform distribution" which would correspond to the Lebesgue measure.

*State Space.* As we consider only finitely many variables, $v = |\mathbf{Var}|$, we can represent the space of all possible states $\mathbf{Var} \rightarrow \underline{\mathbb{Z}} + \mathbb{B} + \mathbb{L}$ as the Cartesian product $(\underline{\mathbb{Z}} + \mathbb{B} + \mathbb{L})^v$, i.e. for every variable $\mathbf{x}_i \in \mathbf{Var}$ we specify its associated value in (a separate copy of) $\underline{\mathbb{Z}} + \mathbb{B} + \mathbb{L}$.

As the declarations of variables fix their types, in effect their possible range, we can exploit this information by presenting the (classical) state in a slightly more effective way: $\mathbf{State} = \mathbf{Value}_1 \times \mathbf{Value}_2 \ldots \times \mathbf{Value}_v$ with $\mathbf{Value}_i = \underline{\mathbb{Z}}$, or $\mathbb{B}$ or $\mathbb{L}$. We can go even a step further and exploit the fact that pointers have to refer to variables which represent pointers of a level lower than themselves, i.e. a simple first level pointer must refer to a simple variable, a second level pointer must refer to a first level pointer, etc.; only NIL can be used on all levels. Let us denote by $\mathbb{LZ}_0$ the set of integer variables (plus NIL), by $\mathbb{LB}_0$ the set of Boolean variables (plus NIL), and by $\mathbb{LZ}_l$ and $\mathbb{LB}_l$ the pointer variables which refer to variables in $\mathbb{LZ}_{l-1}$ and $\mathbb{LB}_{l-1}$ (plus NIL) respectively. Obviously, we have $\mathbb{L} = \bigcup_l \mathbb{LZ}_l \cup \bigcup_l \mathbb{LB}_l$.

As the declarations fix the level of a pointer (and its ultimate target type) we can represent the state in a slightly simpler way as $\mathbf{State} = \mathbf{Value}_1 \times \ldots \times \mathbf{Value}_v$ with $\mathbf{Value}_i = \underline{\mathbb{Z}}, \mathbb{B}, \mathbb{LZ}_l$ or $\mathbb{LB}_l$ with $l \geq 1$. We will use the following conventions for the representation of states and state vectors. Given $v$ variables, we will enumerate them according to their pointer level, i.e. first the basic variables, then the $r_1$ simple pointers, then the $r_2$ pointers to pointers, etc. We denote by $r = r_1 + r_2 + \ldots$ the number of all pointer variables. The last component of the state vector corresponds to the label $\ell$.

The distributions which describe the probabilistic state of the execution of a program correspond to (normalised and positive) vectors in $\mathcal{V}(\mathbf{State})$. In terms of vector spaces, the above representation of the classical states can be expressed by means of the *tensor product* construction. We can construct the tensor product of two finite dimensional matrices (or vectors, seen as $1 \times n$ or $n \times 1$ matrices) via the so-called *Kronecker product*: Given an $n \times m$ matrix $\mathbf{A}$ and a $k \times l$ matrix $\mathbf{B}$ then $\mathbf{A} \otimes \mathbf{B}$ is the $nk \times ml$ matrix with entries $(\mathbf{A} \otimes \mathbf{B})_{(i_1-1)\cdot k+i_2,(j_1-1)\cdot l+j_2} = (\mathbf{A})_{i_1,j_1} \cdot (\mathbf{B})_{i_2,j_2}$. The representation of a state as a tuple in the Cartesian product of the sets of values for each variable can be re-formulated in our vector space setting by using the isomorphism $\mathcal{V}(\mathbf{State}) = \mathcal{V}(\mathbf{Value}_1 \times \ldots \times \mathbf{Value}_v) = \mathcal{V}(\mathbf{Value}_1) \otimes \ldots \otimes \mathcal{V}(\mathbf{Value}_v)$.

*Filtering.* In order to construct the concrete semantics we need to identify those states which satisfy certain conditions, e.g. all those states where a variable has a value larger than 5 or where a pointer refers to a particular variable. This is achieved by "filtering" states which fulfill some conditions via *projection operators*, which are concretely represented by diagonal matrices.

Consider a variable $\mathtt{x}$ together with the set of its possible values $\mathbf{Value} = \{v_1, v_2, \ldots\}$, and the vector space $\mathcal{V}(\mathbf{Value})$. The probabilistic state of the variable $\mathtt{x}$ can be described by a distribution over its possible values, i.e. a vector in $\mathcal{V}(\mathbf{Value})$. For example, if we know that $\mathtt{x}$ holds the value $v_1$ or $v_3$ with probabilities $\frac{1}{3}$ and $\frac{2}{3}$ respectively (and no other values) then this situation is represented by the vector $(\frac{1}{3}, 0, \frac{2}{3}, 0, \ldots)$. As we represent distributions by row vectors $\boldsymbol{x}$ the application of a linear map corresponds to a post-multiplication by the corresponding matrix $\mathbf{T}$, i.e. $\mathbf{T}(\boldsymbol{x}) = \boldsymbol{x} \cdot \mathbf{T}$.

We might need to apply a transformation $\mathbf{T}$ to the probabilistic state of the variable $\mathtt{x}_i$ only when a certain condition is fulfilled. We can express such a condition by a predicate $q$ on $\mathbf{Value}_i$. Defining a diagonal matrix $\mathbf{P}$ with $(\mathbf{P})_{ii} = 1$ if $q(v_i)$ holds and 0 otherwise, allows us to "filter out" only those states which fulfill the condition $q$, i.e. $\mathbf{P} \cdot \mathbf{T}$ applies $\mathbf{T}$ only to those states.

*Operators.* The Linear Operator Semantics of **pWhile** is built using a number of basic operators which can be represented by the (sparse) square matrices: $(\mathbf{E}(m,n))_{ij} = 1$ if $m = i \wedge n = j$ and 0 otherwise, and $(\mathbf{I})_{ij} = 1$ if $i = j$ and 0 otherwise. The matrix units $\mathbf{E}(m,n)$ contains only one non-zero entry, and $\mathbf{I}$ is the identity operator. Using these basic building blocks we can define a number of "filters" $\mathbf{P}$ as depicted in Table 1. The operator $\mathbf{P}(c)$ has only one non-zero entry: the diagonal element $\mathbf{P}_{cc} = 1$, i.e. $\mathbf{P}(c) = \mathbf{E}(c,c)$. This operator extracts the probability corresponding to the $c$-th coordinate of a vector, i.e. for $\boldsymbol{x} = (x_i)_i$ the multiplication with $\mathbf{P}(c)$ results in a vector $\boldsymbol{x}' = \boldsymbol{x} \cdot \mathbf{P}(c)$ with only one non-zero coordinate, namely $x'_c = x_c$.

**Table 1.** Test and Update Operators for **pWhile**

$$(\mathbf{P}(c))_{ij} = \begin{cases} 1 \text{ if } i = c = j \\ 0 \text{ otherwise.} \end{cases} \qquad (\mathbf{U}(c))_{ij} = \begin{cases} 1 \text{ if } j = c \\ 0 \text{ otherwise.} \end{cases}$$

$$\mathbf{P}(\sigma) = \bigotimes_{i=1}^{v} \mathbf{P}(\sigma(\mathbf{x}_i)) \qquad \mathbf{U}(\mathbf{x}_k \leftarrow c) = \bigotimes_{i=1}^{k-1} \mathbf{I} \otimes \mathbf{U}(c) \otimes \bigotimes_{i=k+1}^{v} \mathbf{I}$$

$$\mathbf{P}(e = c) = \sum_{\mathcal{E}(e)\sigma = c} \mathbf{P}(\sigma) \qquad \mathbf{U}(\mathbf{x}_k \leftarrow e) = \sum_{c} \mathbf{P}(e = c)\mathbf{U}(\mathbf{x}_k \leftarrow c)$$

$$\mathbf{U}(*^r \mathbf{x}_k \leftarrow e) = \sum_{\mathbf{x}_i} \mathbf{P}(\mathbf{x}_k = \&\mathbf{x}_i)\mathbf{U}(*^{r-1}\mathbf{x}_i \leftarrow e)$$

The operator $\mathbf{P}(\sigma)$ performs a similar test for a vector representing the probabilistic state of the computation. It filters the probability that the computation is in a classical state $\sigma$. This is achieved by checking whether each variable $\mathbf{x}_i$ has the value specified by $\sigma$ namely $\sigma(\mathbf{x}_i)$. Finally, the operator $\mathbf{P}(e = c)$ filters those states where the values of the variables $\mathbf{x}_i$ are such that the evaluation of the expression $e$ results in $c$. The number of (diagonal) non-zero entries of this operator is exactly the number of states $\sigma$ for which $\mathcal{E}(e)\sigma = c$.

The update operators (see Table 1) implement state changes. From an initial probabilistic state $\sigma$, i.e. a distribution over classical states, we get a new probabilistic state $\sigma'$ via $\sigma \cdot \mathbf{U}$.

The simple operator $\mathbf{U}(c)$ implements the deterministic update of a variable $\mathbf{x}_i$: Whatever the value(s) of $\mathbf{x}_i$ are, after applying $\mathbf{U}(c)$ to the state vector describing $\mathbf{x}_i$ we get a point distribution expressing the fact that the value of $\mathbf{x}_i$ is now certainly $c$. The operator $\mathbf{U}(\mathbf{x}_k \leftarrow c)$ puts $\mathbf{U}(c)$ into the context of other variables: Most factors in the tensor product are identities, i.e. most variables keep their previous values, only $\mathbf{x}_k$ is deterministically updated to its new value $c$ using the previously defined $\mathbf{U}(c)$ operator. The operator $\mathbf{U}(\mathbf{x}_k \leftarrow e)$ updates a variable not to a constant but to the value of an expression $e$. This update is realised using the filter operator $\mathbf{P}(e = c)$: For all possible values $c$ of $e$ we select those states where $e$ evaluates to $c$ and then update $\mathbf{x}_k$ to this $c$. Finally, the update operator $\mathbf{U}(*^r\mathbf{x}_k \leftarrow e)$ is used for assignments where we have a pointer on the left hand side. In this case we select those states where $\mathbf{x}_k$ points to another variable $\mathbf{x}_i$ and then update $\mathbf{x}_i$ accordingly. This unfolding of references continues recursively until we end up with a basic variable where we can use the previous update operator $\mathbf{U}(\mathbf{x}_i \leftarrow e)$.

*Semantics.* The Linear Operator Semantics of a **pWhile** program $P$ is defined as the operator $\mathbf{T} = \mathbf{T}(P)$ on $\mathcal{V}(\mathbf{State} \times \mathcal{B}(P))$. This can be seen as a collecting semantics for the program $P$ as it is defined by

$$\mathbf{T}(P) = \sum_{\langle i, p_{ij}, j \rangle \in \mathcal{F}(P)} p_{ij} \cdot \mathbf{T}(\ell_i, \ell_j).$$

**Table 2.** Linear Operator Semantics for **pWhile**

| | |
|---|---|
| $\mathbf{T}(\ell_1,\ell_2) = \mathbf{I} \otimes \mathbf{E}_{\ell_1,\ell_2}$ | for $[\mathbf{skip}]^{\ell_1}$ |
| $\mathbf{T}(\ell_1,\ell_2) = \mathbf{U}(p \leftarrow e) \otimes \mathbf{E}_{\ell_1,\ell_2}$ | for $[\mathrm{p} \leftarrow \mathrm{e}]^{\ell_1}$ |
| $\mathbf{T}(\ell,\ell_t) = \mathbf{P}(b = \text{TRUE}) \otimes \mathbf{E}_{\ell,\ell_t}$ | for $[b]^{\ell}$ |
| $\mathbf{T}(\ell,\ell_f) = \mathbf{P}(b = \text{FALSE}) \otimes \mathbf{E}_{\ell,\ell_f}$ | for $[b]^{\ell}$ |
| $\mathbf{T}(\ell,\ell_k) = \mathbf{I} \otimes \mathbf{E}_{\ell,\ell_k}$ | for $[\mathbf{choose}]^{\ell}$ |
| $\mathbf{T}(\ell,\ell) = \mathbf{I} \otimes \mathbf{E}_{\ell,\ell}$ | for $[\mathbf{stop}]^{\ell}$ |

The meaning of $\mathbf{T}(P)$ is to collect for every triple in the probabilistic flow $\mathcal{F}(P)$ of $P$ its effects, weighted according to the probability associated to this triple. The operators $\mathbf{T}(\ell_i,\ell_j)$ which implement the local state updates and control transfers from $\ell_i$ to $\ell_j$ are presented in Table 2.

Each local operator $\mathbf{T}(\ell_i,\ell_j)$ is of the form $\mathbf{N} \otimes \mathbf{E}(\ell_i,\ell_j)$ where the first factor $\mathbf{N}$ represents a state update or, in the case of tests, a filter operator while the second factor realises the transfer of control from label $\ell_i$ to label $\ell_j$. For the **skip** and **stop** no changes to the state happen, we only transfer control (deterministically) to the next statement or loop on the current (terminal) statement using matrix units $\mathbf{E}$. Also in the case of a **choose** there is no change to the state but only a transfer of control, however the probabilities $p_{ij}$ will in general be different from 1, unlike **skip**. With assignments we have both a state update, implemented using $\mathbf{U}(p \leftarrow e)$, and a control flow step. For tests $b$ we use the filter operator $\mathbf{P}(b = \text{TRUE})$ to select those states which pass the test, and $\mathbf{P}(b = \text{FALSE})$ to select those states which fail it, in order to determine which label the control will pass to.

Note that $\mathbf{P}(b = \text{TRUE}) + \mathbf{P}(b = \text{FALSE}) = \mathbf{I}$, i.e. at any test $b$ every state will cause exactly one (unambiguous) control transfer. We allow in **pWhile** only for constant probabilities $p_i$ in the **choose** construct, which sum up to 1 and as with classical **While** we have no "blocked" configurations (even the terminal **stop** statements 'loop'). It is therefore not necessary to *re-normalise* dynamically the probabilities and it follows easily that:

**Proposition 1.** *The operator* $\mathbf{T}(P)$ *is stochastic for any* **pWhile** *program* $P$, *i.e. the sum of all elements in each row add up to one.*

Thus, $\mathbf{T}$ is indeed the generator of a DTMC. Furthermore, by the construction of $\mathbf{T}$ it also follows immediately that the SOS and LOS semantics are equivalent in the following sense.

**Proposition 2.** *For any* **pWhile** *program* $P$ *and any classical state* $\sigma \in$ **State**, *we have:*

$$\langle S, \sigma\rangle \longrightarrow_p \langle S', \sigma'\rangle \;\; \textit{iff} \;\; (\mathbf{T}(P))_{\langle\sigma,\ell\rangle,\langle\sigma',\ell'\rangle} = p,$$

*where* $\ell$ *and* $\ell'$ *label the first block in the statement* $S$ *and* $S'$, *respectively.*

# 4 Pointer Analysis

In principle, it is possible to construct the concrete linear operator semantics for any **pWhile** program with bounded value ranges for its variables and to analyse this way its properties. However, this remains – as in the classical case – only a hypothetical possibility. Even when using sparse matrix representations it is practically impossible to explicitly compute the semantics of all but very small toy examples. This is not least due to the unavoidable involvement of the tensor product which leads to an exponential growth in the dimension of the operator $\mathbf{T}$. Besides this, there might also be the desire to consider a semantics of a program with unbounded values for variables, in which case we are completely unable to explicitly construct the infinite dimensional operator $\mathbf{T}$. In order to analyse (probabilistic) properties of a program we therefore need to consider an abstract version of $\mathbf{T}$.

## 4.1 Probabilistic Abstract Interpretation

The general approach for constructing simplified versions of a concrete (collecting) semantics via *Abstract Interpretation*, which was introduced by Cousot & Cousot 30 years ago [9], is unfortunately based on order-theoretic and not on linear structures. One can define on a given vector space a number of orderings (lexicographic, etc.) as an additional structure. We could then use this order to compute over- or under-approximations using classical Abstract Interpretation. Though such approximations will always be safe, they might also be quite unrealistic, addressing a *worst case* scenario rather than the *average case* [2]. Furthermore, there is no *canonical* order on a vector space (e.g. the lexicographic order depends on the base). In order to provide probabilistic estimates we have previously introduced, cf. [1,10], a quantitative version of the Cousot & Cousot framework, which we have called *Probabilistic Abstract Interpretation* (PAI).

The PAI approach is based, as in the classical case, on a concrete and abstract domain $\mathcal{C}$ and $\mathcal{D}$ – except that $\mathcal{C}$ and $\mathcal{D}$ are now vector spaces (or in general Hilbert spaces) instead of lattices. We assume that the pair of abstraction and concretisation functions $\alpha : \mathcal{C} \rightarrow \mathcal{D}$ and $\gamma : \mathcal{D} \rightarrow \mathcal{C}$ are again structure preserving, i.e. in our setting they are (bounded) linear maps represented by matrices $\mathbf{A}$ and $\mathbf{G}$. Finally, we replace the notion of a Galois connection by the notion of a Moore-Penrose pseudo-inverse.

**Definition 1.** *Let $\mathcal{C}$ and $\mathcal{D}$ be two finite dimensional vector spaces (or in general, Hilbert spaces) and $\mathbf{A} : \mathcal{C} \rightarrow \mathcal{D}$ a (bounded) linear map between them. The (bounded) linear map $\mathbf{A}^\dagger = \mathbf{G} : \mathcal{D} \rightarrow \mathcal{C}$ is the* Moore-Penrose pseudo-inverse *of $\mathbf{A}$ iff $\mathbf{A} \circ \mathbf{G} = \mathbf{P}_A$ and $\mathbf{G} \circ \mathbf{A} = \mathbf{P}_G$, where $\mathbf{P}_A$ and $\mathbf{P}_G$ denote orthogonal projections (i.e. $\mathbf{P}_A^* = \mathbf{P}_A = \mathbf{P}_A^2$ and $\mathbf{P}_G^* = \mathbf{P}_G = \mathbf{P}_G^2$ where $.^*$ denotes the linear* adjoint *[11, Ch 10]) onto the ranges of $\mathbf{A}$ and $\mathbf{G}$.*

This allows us to construct the closest (i.e. least square) approximation $\mathbf{T}^\# : \mathcal{D} \rightarrow \mathcal{D}$ of $\mathbf{T} : \mathcal{C} \rightarrow \mathcal{C}$ as $\mathbf{T}^\# = \mathbf{G} \cdot \mathbf{T} \cdot \mathbf{A} = \mathbf{A}^\dagger \cdot \mathbf{T} \cdot \mathbf{A} = \alpha \circ \mathbf{T} \circ \gamma$. As our concrete semantics is constructed using tensor products it is important that the

Moore-Penrose pseudo-inverse of a tensor product can easily be computed as follows [12, 2.1,Ex 3]: $(\mathbf{A}_1 \otimes \mathbf{A}_2 \otimes \ldots \otimes \mathbf{A}_n)^\dagger = \mathbf{A}_1^\dagger \otimes \mathbf{A}_2^\dagger \otimes \ldots \otimes \mathbf{A}_n^\dagger$.

*Example 1 (Parity).* Let us consider as abstract and concrete domains $\mathcal{C} = \mathcal{V}(\{-n,\ldots,n\})$ and $\mathcal{D} = \mathcal{V}(\{\text{even},\text{odd}\})$. The abstraction operator $\mathbf{A}_p$ and its concretisation operator $\mathbf{G}_p = \mathbf{A}_p^\dagger$ corresponding to a parity analysis are represented by the following $n \times 2$ and $2 \times n$ matrices (assuming w.l.o.g. that $n$ is even):

$$\mathbf{A}_p^T = \begin{pmatrix} 1\,0\,1\,0\ldots 1 \\ 0\,1\,0\,1\ldots 0 \end{pmatrix} \quad \mathbf{A}_p^\dagger = \begin{pmatrix} \frac{1}{n+1} & 0 & \frac{1}{n+1} & 0 & \ldots & \frac{1}{n+1} \\ 0 & \frac{1}{n} & 0 & \frac{1}{n} & \ldots & 0 \end{pmatrix},$$

where $.^T$ denotes the matrix transpose $(\mathbf{A}^T)_{ij} = (\mathbf{A})_{ji}$. The concretisation operator $\mathbf{A}_p^\dagger$ represents uniform distributions over the $n+1$ even numbers in the range $-n,\ldots,n$ (as the first row) and the $n$ odd numbers in the same range (in the second row).

*Example 2 (Sign).* With $\mathcal{C} = \mathcal{V}(\{-n,\ldots,0,\ldots,n\})$ and $\mathcal{D} = \mathcal{V}(\{-,0,+\})$ we can represent the usual sign abstraction by the following matrices:

$$\mathbf{A}_s^T = \begin{pmatrix} 1\ldots 1\,0\,0\ldots 0 \\ 0\ldots 0\,1\,0\ldots 0 \\ 0\ldots 0\,0\,1\ldots 1 \end{pmatrix} \quad \mathbf{A}_s^\dagger = \begin{pmatrix} \frac{1}{n}\ldots\frac{1}{n}\,0\,0\ldots 0 \\ 0\ldots 0\,1\,0\ldots 0 \\ 0\ldots 0\,0\,\frac{1}{n}\ldots\frac{1}{n} \end{pmatrix}$$

*Example 3 (Forget).* We can also abstract all details of the concrete semantics. Although this is in general a rather unusual abstraction it is quite useful in the context of a tensor product state and/or abstraction. Let the concrete domain be the vector space over any range, i.e. $\mathcal{C} = \mathcal{V}(\{n,\ldots,0,\ldots,m\})$, and the abstract domain a one dimensional space $\mathcal{D} = \mathcal{V}(\{\star\})$. Then the forgetful abstraction and concretisation can be defined by:

$$\mathbf{A}_f^T = (1\,1\,1\ldots 1) \quad \mathbf{A}_f^\dagger = \left(\tfrac{1}{m-n+1}\ \tfrac{1}{m-n+1}\ \tfrac{1}{m-n+1}\ \ldots\ \tfrac{1}{m-n+1}\right)$$

For any matrix $\mathbf{M}$ operating on $\mathcal{C} = \mathcal{V}(\{n,\ldots,0,\ldots,m\})$ the abstraction $\mathbf{A}_f^\dagger \cdot \mathbf{M} \cdot \mathbf{A}_f$ gives a one dimensional matrix, i.e. a single scalar $\mu$. For stochastic matrices, such as our $\mathbf{T}$ generating the DTMC representing the concrete semantics we have: $\mu = 1$. If we consider a tensor product $\mathbf{M} \otimes \mathbf{N}$, then the abstraction $\mathbf{A}_f \otimes \mathbf{I}$ extracts (essentially) $\mathbf{N}$, i.e. $(\mathbf{A}_f \otimes \mathbf{I})^\dagger \cdot (\mathbf{M} \otimes \mathbf{N}) \cdot (\mathbf{A}_f \otimes \mathbf{I}) = \mu\mathbf{N}$.

### 4.2 Abstract Semantics

The abstract semantics $\mathbf{T}^\#$ is constructed exactly like the concrete one, except that we will use abstract tests and update operators. This is possible as abstractions and concretisations distribute over sums and tensor products. More precisely, we can construct $\mathbf{T}^\#$ for a program $P$ as:

$$\mathbf{T}^\#(P) = \sum_{\langle i,p_{ij},j\rangle \in \mathcal{F}(P)} p_{ij} \cdot \mathbf{T}^\#(\ell_i,\ell_j),$$

where the transfer operator along a computational step from label $\ell_i$ to $\ell_j$ can be abstracted "locally". Abstracting each variable separately and using the concrete control flow we get the operator $\mathbf{A} = (\bigotimes_{i=1}^{v} \mathbf{A}_i) \otimes \mathbf{I} = \mathbf{A}_1 \otimes \mathbf{A}_2 \otimes \ldots \otimes \mathbf{A}_v \otimes \mathbf{I}$. Then the abstract transfer operator $\mathbf{T}^{\#}(\ell_i, \ell_j)$ can be defined as $\mathbf{T}^{\#}(\ell_i, \ell_j) = (\mathbf{A}_1^{\dagger}\mathbf{N}_{i1}\mathbf{A}_1)\otimes(\mathbf{A}_2^{\dagger}\mathbf{N}_{i2}\mathbf{A}_2)\otimes\ldots\otimes(\mathbf{A}_v^{\dagger}\mathbf{N}_{iv}\mathbf{A}_v)\otimes\mathbf{E}(\ell_i, \ell_j)$. This operator implements the (abstract) effect to each of the variables in the individual statement at $\ell_i$ and combines it with the concrete control flow.

It is of course also possible to abstract the control flow, or to use abstractions which abstract several variables at the same time, e.g. specifying the abstract state via the difference of two variables.

*Example 4.* Consider the following short program:

**if** $[(\mathrm{x} > 0)]^1$ **then** $[\mathrm{z} \leftarrow \&\mathrm{x}]^2$ **else** $[\mathrm{z} \leftarrow \&\mathrm{y}]^3$ **end if;** $[\mathbf{stop}]^4$

The LOS operator of this program can be straightforwardly constructed as

$$\begin{aligned}\mathbf{T}(P) = {} & \mathbf{P}(\mathrm{x} > 0) \otimes \mathbf{E}(1,2) + \mathbf{P}(\mathrm{x} \leq 0) \otimes \mathbf{E}(1,3) + \\ & + \mathbf{U}(\mathrm{z} \leftarrow \&\mathrm{x}) \otimes \mathbf{E}(2,4) + \mathbf{U}(\mathrm{z} \leftarrow \&\mathrm{y}) \otimes \mathbf{E}(3,4) + \mathbf{I} \otimes \mathbf{E}(4,4).\end{aligned}$$

Here we can see nicely the powerful reduction in size due to PAI. Assuming that x and y take, for example, values in the range $-100, \ldots, +100$ then the concrete semantics requires a $201 \times 201 \times 2 \times 4 = 323208$ dimensional space (as z can point to two variables and there are four program points). The concrete operator $\mathbf{T}(P)$ has about $10^{11}$ entries (although most of them are zero). If we abstract the concrete value of x and y using the sign or parity operators the operator $\mathbf{T}^{\#}(P)$ – constructed exactly in the same way as $\mathbf{T}(P)$ but using smaller, abstract value spaces, requires only a matrix of dimension $3 \times 3 \times 2 \times 4 = 72$ or $2 \times 2 \times 2 \times 4 = 32$, respectively. We can even go one step further and completely forget about the value of y, in which case we need simply a $24 \times 24$ or $16 \times 16$ matrix respectively to describe $\mathbf{T}^{\#}(P)$.

The dramatic reduction in size, i.e. dimensions, achieved via PAI and illustrated by the last example lets us hope that our approach could ultimately lead to scalable analyses, despite the fact that the concrete semantics is so large as to make its construction infeasible. However, further work in the form of practical implementations and experiments is needed in order to decide whether this is indeed the case.

The LOS represents the SOS via the generator of a DTMC. It describes the stepwise evolution of the (probabilistic) state of a computation and does not provide a fixed-point semantics. Therefore, neither in the concrete nor in the abstract case can we guarantee that $\lim_{n\to\infty}(\mathbf{T}(P))^n$ or $\lim_{n\to\infty}(\mathbf{T}(P)^{\#})^n$ always exists. The analysis of a program $P$ based on the abstract operator $\mathbf{T}(P)^{\#}$ is considerably *simpler* than by considering the concrete one but still not entirely trivial. Various properties of $\mathbf{T}(P)^{\#}$ can be extracted by iterative methods (e.g. computing $\lim_{n\to\infty}(\mathbf{T}(P)^{\#})^n$ or some averages). As usual in numerical computation, these methods will converge only for $n \to \infty$ and any result obtained after only a finite number of steps will only be an approximation. However, one can study *stopping criteria* which guarantee a certain quality of this approximation. The development or adaptation of iterative methods and formulation of appropriate stopping criteria might be seen as the numerical analog to the *widening* and *narrowing* techniques of the classical setting.

### 4.3 Abstract Branching Probabilities

The abstract, like the concrete, semantics is based on two types of basic operators, namely abstract update operators $\mathbf{U}^{\#}$ and abstract test operators $\mathbf{P}^{\#}$. As abstract tests introduce probabilistic choices which reflect the probabilities that a test is passed, the abstract semantics will always be probabilistic even if the considered program is deterministic.

*Example 5.* Obviously, the critical element in Example 4 for computing the probabilities of $\mathbf{z}$ pointing to $\mathbf{x}$ or $\mathbf{y}$ is given by the chances that the test $\mathbf{x} > 0$ in label 1 succeeds or fails. These chances depend on the initial (distribution of possible) values of $\mathbf{x}$. In the concrete semantics we can, for example, assume that $\mathbf{x}$ can take initially any value between $-N$ and $+N$ with the same probability, i.e. we could start with the uniform distribution $\boldsymbol{d}_0 = (\frac{1}{2N+1}, \frac{1}{2N+1}, \ldots, \frac{1}{2N+1})$ for $\mathbf{x}$ – or any other distribution. The probability of $\mathbf{z}$ pointing to $\mathbf{x}$ or $\mathbf{y}$ is then: $P(\mathbf{z} = \&\mathbf{x}) = \sum_i (\boldsymbol{d}_0 \cdot \mathbf{P}(\mathbf{x} > 0))_i = \frac{N+1}{2N+1}$ and $P(\mathbf{z} = \&\mathbf{y}) = \sum_i (\boldsymbol{d}_0 \cdot \mathbf{P}(\mathbf{x} \leq 0))_i = \frac{N}{2N+1}$. In other words, if we increase the range, i.e. for $N \to \infty$, the chances of $\mathbf{z}$ pointing to $\mathbf{x}$ or $\mathbf{y}$ are about 50 : 50.

Even in this simple case, the involved matrices, i.e. $\mathbf{P}(\mathbf{x} > 0)$, can become rather large and one might therefore try to estimate the probabilities using PAI. Again the critical element is the abstract test $\mathbf{P}^{\#}(\mathbf{x} > 0) = \mathbf{A}^{\dagger} \cdot \mathbf{P}(\mathbf{x} > 0) \cdot \mathbf{A}$.The abstract test operator $\mathbf{P}^{\#}(\mathbf{x} \leq 0)$ can be computed in the same way or via the fact $\mathbf{P}^{\#}(\mathbf{x} \leq 0) = \mathbf{I} - \mathbf{P}^{\#}(\mathbf{x} > 0)$. For different ranges of $\mathbf{x}$ in $\{-N, \ldots, N\}$ we can construct the abstract test operators for the parity abstraction, i.e. $\mathbf{A} = \mathbf{A}_p$ in Example 1, and the sign abstraction, i.e. $\mathbf{A} = \mathbf{A}_s$ in Example 2. Using the **octave** system [13] we get for $\mathbf{P}_s^{\#} = \mathbf{A}_s^{\dagger} \cdot \mathbf{P}(\mathbf{x} > 0) \cdot \mathbf{A}_s$ and $\mathbf{P}_p^{\#} = \mathbf{A}_p^{\dagger} \cdot \mathbf{P}(\mathbf{x} > 0) \cdot \mathbf{A}_p$:

$$\mathbf{P}_s^{\#} = \begin{pmatrix} 0\,0\,0 \\ 0\,0\,0 \\ 0\,0\,1 \end{pmatrix}, \begin{pmatrix} 0\,0\,0 \\ 0\,0\,0 \\ 0\,0\,1 \end{pmatrix} \text{ and } \begin{pmatrix} 0\,0\,0 \\ 0\,0\,0 \\ 0\,0\,1 \end{pmatrix} \text{ for } N = 1, 2 \text{ and } 10,$$

$$\mathbf{P}_p^{\#} = \begin{pmatrix} 0.00\;0.00 \\ 0.00\;0.50 \end{pmatrix}, \begin{pmatrix} 0.50\;0.00 \\ 0.00\;0.33 \end{pmatrix} \text{ and } \begin{pmatrix} 0.50\;0.00 \\ 0.00\;0.45 \end{pmatrix} \text{ for } N = 1, 2 \text{ and } 10$$

These abstract test operators encode important information about the accuracy of the PAI estimates. Firstly, we observe that the sign abstraction $\mathbf{A}_s$ provides us with stable and correct estimates. As we would expect, we see that the abstract values '–' and 0 never pass the test, while '+' always does, independently of $N$. Secondly, we see that the parity analysis is rather pointless, for large $N$ the test is passed with a 50% chance for **even** as well as **odd** – this expresses just the fact that parity has nothing to do with the sign of a variable. A bit more interesting are the values for $N = 1$ and $N = 2$. If we only consider the concrete values $-1, 0, 1$ for **x** then only even numbers (0 in this set) always fail the test (thus we have a zero entry in the upper left entry) and that it succeeds for the odd numbers, $-1$ and 1, with an even chance; if we consider a larger concrete range, i.e. for $N > 1$, then the chances tend to become $50 : 50$ but due to 0 failing the test, there is a slightly lower chance for even numbers to succeed compared with odd numbers.

As we can see from the example, the abstract test operators $\mathbf{P}^{\#}$ contain information about the probabilities that test succeed for abstract values. This means that the abstract semantics contains estimates of *dynamic* branching probabilities, i.e. depending on the (abstract) state of the computation the probabilities to follow, for example, the **then** or **else** branch will change. One could utilise this information to distinguish between the branching probabilities in different phase of executions; during the initialisation phase of a program the branching probabilities could be completely different from later stages.

However, we can also obtain more conventional, i.e. *static*, branching probabilities for the whole execution of a program. In order to do this we have to provide an initial distribution over abstract values. Using the abstract semantics $\mathbf{T}^{\#}$, we can then compute distributions over abstract values for any program point which in particular provide estimates of the abstract state reaching any test. This amounts to performing a probabilistic forward analysis of the program. Based on the probability estimates for abstract values at a test we can then compute estimates for the branching probabilities in the same way as in the classical case.

With respect to a higher order analysis – such as a pointer analysis – we therefore propose a two-phase analysis: During the first phase the abstract semantics $\mathbf{T}^{\#}$ is used to provide estimates of the probability distributions over abstract values (and thus for the branching probabilities) for every program point; phase two then constructs the actual analysis, e.g. a probabilistic points-to matrix, for every program point. One could interpret phase one also as a kind of program transformation which replaces tests by probabilistic choices.

*Example 6.* For the program in Example 4 the corresponding probabilistic program we have to consider after performing a parity analysis in phase one is:

$$[\textbf{choose}]^1 \ \ (p_\top : [\mathbf{z} \leftarrow \&\mathbf{x}]^2) \ \ \textbf{or} \ \ (p_\perp : [\mathbf{z} \leftarrow \&\mathbf{y}]^3); \ \ [\textbf{stop}]^4$$

where $p_\top$ and $p_\perp$ (which both depend on $N$) are the branching probabilities obtained in phase one.

### 4.4 Probabilistic Points-to Matrix vs. State

The (probabilistic) state in the concrete semantics contains a complete description of the values of all variables as well as the current statement. We can extract information about where pointers (variables) point-to at a certain label by forgetting the value of the basic variables. The same is, of course, also possible with the abstract state. This is achieved via the abstraction $\mathbf{A}_r = \mathbf{A}_f^{\otimes(v-r)} \otimes \mathbf{I}^{\otimes r} \otimes \mathbf{I}$, where $\mathbf{A}_f$ is the "forgetful" abstraction in Example 3 while $v$ and $r$ denote the number of all variables and of all pointer variables, respectively. If we are interested in the pointer structure at a certain program point we can also use the following abstraction:

$$\mathbf{A}_r(\ell) = \mathbf{A}_f^{\otimes(v-r)} \otimes \mathbf{I}^{\otimes r} \otimes \mathbf{A}_f(\ell),$$

where $\mathbf{A}_f(\ell)$ is represented by a column vector (i.e. a $n \times 1$ matrix) with a single non-zero entry $(\mathbf{A}_f(\ell))_{1,\ell} = 1$.

Note that $\mathbf{A}_f(\ell)^\dagger = \mathbf{A}_f(\ell)^T$ and that $\mathbf{A}_f(\ell) \cdot \mathbf{A}_f(\ell)^\dagger = \mathbf{P}(\ell)$ while $\mathbf{A}_f(\ell)^\dagger \cdot \mathbf{A}_f(\ell) = (1)$, i.e. the $1 \times 1$ (identity) matrix.

Given an initial distribution $\boldsymbol{d}_0$ or $\boldsymbol{d}_0^\#$, which represent the initial concrete or abstract values of all variables (and the initial label of the program in question), we can compute the computational state after $n$ computational steps simply by iterating the concrete or abstract semantics $\mathbf{T}$ and $\mathbf{T}^\#$, i.e. $\boldsymbol{d}_n = \boldsymbol{d}_0 \cdot \mathbf{T}^n$ and $\boldsymbol{d}_n^\# = \boldsymbol{d}_0^\# \cdot \mathbf{T}^{\#n}$. Based on these distributions $\boldsymbol{d}_n$ or $\boldsymbol{d}_n^\#$ we can compute also statistical properties of a program, by averaging over a number of iterations, or the final situation, by considering the limit $n \to \infty$.

The typical result of a probabilistic pointer analysis, e.g. [4], is a so-called *points-to* matrix which records for every program point the probability that a pointer variable refers to a particular (other) variable. Using our systematic approach to pointer analysis we can construct such a points-to matrix, concretely or abstractly. However, we can also show that the points-to matrix contains – to a certain extent even in the concrete case – only partial information about the pointer structure of a program.

*Example 7.* Consider the following simple example program:

**if** $[(\mathtt{z}_0 \bmod 2 = 0)]^1$ **then** $[\mathtt{x} \leftarrow \&\mathtt{z}_1]^2$; $[\mathtt{y} \leftarrow \&\mathtt{z}_2]^3$
**else** $[\mathtt{x} \leftarrow \&\mathtt{z}_2]^4$; $[\mathtt{y} \leftarrow \&\mathtt{z}_1]^5$ **end if**; $[\mathbf{stop}]^6$

Any reasonable analysis of this program – assuming a uniform distribution over all possible values of $\mathtt{z}_0$ – will result in the following probabilistic points-to matrix at label 6, i.e. at the end of the program (we write the two rows corresponding to $\mathtt{x}$ and $\mathtt{y}$ as a direct sum):

$$(0,0,0,\frac{1}{2},\frac{1}{2}) \oplus (0,0,0,\frac{1}{2},\frac{1}{2}).$$

This probabilistic points-to matrix states that $\mathtt{x}$ and $\mathtt{y}$ point with probability $\frac{1}{2}$ to $\mathtt{z}_1$ and $\mathtt{z}_2$, but in fact there is a relational dependency between where $\mathtt{x}$ and $\mathtt{y}$ point to. This is detected if we construct the *points-to state* via $\boldsymbol{d}_0 \cdot (\lim_{n\to\infty} \mathbf{T}^{\#n}) \cdot \mathbf{A}_r(6) = \boldsymbol{d}_0 \cdot \lim_{n\to\infty} (\mathbf{A}_p^\dagger \mathbf{T} \mathbf{A}_p)^n \cdot \mathbf{A}_r(6)$. For our example program we get the following *points-to tensor*:

$$\frac{1}{2} \cdot (0,0,0,1,0) \otimes (0,0,0,0,1) + \frac{1}{2} \cdot (0,0,0,0,1) \otimes (0,0,0,1,0)$$

which expresses exactly the fact that (i) there is a 50% chance that $\mathtt{x}$ points to $\mathtt{z}_1$ and $\mathtt{y}$ points to $\mathtt{z}_2$, and that (ii) there is also a 50% chance that $\mathtt{x}$ and $\mathtt{y}$ point to $\mathtt{z}_2$ and $\mathtt{z}_1$, respectively.

For every pointer variable $\mathtt{x}_i$ we can compute the corresponding row in the *points-to matrix* using instead of $\mathbf{A}_r(6)$ the abstraction

$$\mathbf{A}_r(\ell, \mathbf{x}_i) = \mathbf{A}_f^{\otimes(i-1)} \otimes \mathbf{I} \otimes \mathbf{A}_f^{\otimes(v-i+1)} \otimes \mathbf{A}_f(\ell).$$

However, this way we get less information than with the *points-to tensor* above. By a simple dimension argument it's easy to see that, for instance, in our example the points-to matrix has $2 \times 5 = 10$ entries while the points-to state is given by a $5 \times 5 = 25$ dimensional vector.

In fact, it is sufficient to consider the points-to matrix to describe the common state (i.e. distribution) of two pointer variables (seen as random variables) if and only if they are (probabilistically) *independent*, cf e.g. [14, Sect 20]. If two random (pointer) variables are not independent but somehow *correlated*, then we need a points-to tensor to describe the situation precisely. In the classical framework this corresponds exactly to the distinction between *independent* and *relational* analysis. We can combine in our framework both approaches. However – as always – it will depend on the concrete application how much *precision* (provided by the points-to tensor) one is willing to trade in for lower *computational complexity* (the points-to matrix allows for).

## 5 Conclusions and Further Work

We presented a compositional semantics of a simple imperative programming language with a probabilistic choice construct. The executions of a program in this language correspond to a discrete time Markov chain. Important for the syntax directed construction of the generator matrix of this DTMC is the tensor product representation of the probabilistic state. Using a small number of basic filter and update operators we were also able to provide the semantics of pointers (to static variables). Probabilistic Abstract Interpretation, a quantitative generalisation of the classical Cousot & Cousot approach, provided the framework for constructing a "simplified" abstract semantics. Linearity, distributivity and the tensor product enabled us to construct this abstract semantics in the same syntax directed way as the for concrete semantics. Our approach allows for a systematic development and study of various probabilistic pointer analyses. We could, for example, argue that the traditional points-to matrix is not sufficient for providing relational information about the pointer structure of a program.

We used static techniques for estimating execution frequencies. A more common approach is the use of profiles which are derived by running the program on a selection of sample inputs. Our static estimation does not require this separate compilation and is not dependent on the choice of the representative inputs which is a crucial and often very difficult part of the profiling process. Several authors have argued about the advantages of static estimators or program-based branch prediction as opposed to the time-consuming profiling process as a base for program optimisation [15,16,17]. However, since estimates derived from run-time profile information are generally regarded as the most accurate source of information, it is necessary to measure the utility of an estimate provided by static techniques by comparing them with the actual measurements in order to assess their accuracy. We plan to further develop this point in future work; in particular, we plan to exploit the metric intrinsic in the PAI framework for the purpose of measuring the precision of our analyses and to use the mathematical theory of testing and its well-known results (cf. [18]) in order to provide the outcomes of our analyses with a statistical interpretation.

Further work will address various extensions of the current approach: (i) an extension to unbounded value ranges (this will require the reformulation of our framework based on more advanced mathematical structures like measures and Banach/Hilbert spaces), (ii) the introduction of dynamical pointer structures using a heap and a memory allocation function, and (iii) a practical implementation, e.g. by investigating some forms of probabilistic *widening*, of our analysis in order to establish whether it scales, i.e. if it can also be applied to "real world" programs, and provides enough useful information for speculative optimisation.

## References


1. Di Pierro, A., Wiklicky, H.: Concurrent Constraint Programming: Towards Probabilistic Abstract Interpretation. In: PPDP 2000, pp. 127–138 (2000)
2. Di Pierro, A., Hankin, C., Wiklicky, H.: Abstract interpretation for worst and average case analysis. In: Program Analysis and Compilation, Theory and Practice. LNCS, vol. 4444, pp. 160–174. Springer, Heidelberg (2007)
3. Chen, P.S., Hwang, Y.S., Ju, R.D.C., Lee, J.K.: Interprocedural probabilistic pointer analysis. IEEE Trans. Parallel and Distributed Systems 15, 893–907 (2004)
4. Da Silva, J., Steffan, J.G.: A probabilistic pointer analysis for speculative optimizations. In: ASPLOS-XII, pp. 416–425. ACM Press, New York (2006)
5. den Hartog, J., de Vink, E.: Verifying probabilistic programs using a Hoare-like logic. International Journal of Foundations of Computer Science 13, 315–340 (2002)
6. Di Pierro, A., Hankin, C., Wiklicky, H.: On probabilistic techniques for data flow analysis. In: 5th International Workshop on Quantotative Aspects of Programming Languages. Electronic Notes in Computer Science, vol. 190(3), pp. 59–77. Elsevier, Amsterdam (2007)
7. Nielson, F., Nielson, H.R., Hankin, C.: Principles of Program Analysis. Springer, Berlin (1999)
8. Cousot, P., Cousot, R.: Systematic design of program transformation frameworks by abstract interpretation. In: POPL 2002, pp. 178–190 (2002)
9. Cousot, P., Cousot, R.: Abstract Interpretation: A Unified Lattice Model for Static Analysis of Programs by Construction or Approximation of Fixpoints. In: POPL 1977, pp. 238–252 (1977)
10. Di Pierro, A., Wiklicky, H.: Measuring the precision of abstract interpretations. In: Lau, K.-K. (ed.) LOPSTR 2000. LNCS, vol. 2042, pp. 147–164. Springer, Heidelberg (2001)
11. Roman, S.: Advanced Linear Algebra, 2nd edn. Springer, Heidelberg (2005)
12. Ben-Israel, A., Greville, T.: Generalised Inverses, 2nd edn. Springer, Heidelberg (2003)
13. Eaton, J.: Gnu Octave Manual (2002), `http://www.octave.org`
14. Billingsley, P.: Probability and Measure. Wiley & Sons, New York (1978)
15. Wagner, T.A., Maverick, V., Graham, S.L., Harrison, M.A.: Accurate static estimators for program optimization. SIGPLAN Not. 29(6), 85–96 (1994)
16. Ramalingam, G.: Data flow frequency analysis. In: PLDI 1996, pp. 267–277 (1996)
17. Ball, T., Larus, J.R.: Branch prediction for free. SIGPLAN Not. 28, 300–313 (1993)
18. Ferguson, T.S.: Mathematical Statistics. Academic Press, London (1967)

# Complete Lattices and Up-To Techniques*

Damien Pous

LIP: UMR CNRS - ENS Lyon - UCB Lyon - INRIA 5668, France

**Abstract.** We propose a theory of up-to techniques for proofs by coinduction, in the setting of complete lattices. This theory improves over existing results by providing a way to compose arbitrarily complex techniques with standard techniques, expressed using a very simple and modular semi-commutation property.

Complete lattices are enriched with monoid operations, so that we can recover standard results about labelled transitions systems and their associated behavioural equivalences at an abstract, "point-free" level.

Our theory gives for free a powerful method for validating up-to techniques. We use it to revisit up to contexts techniques, which are known to be difficult in the weak case: we show that it is sufficient to check basic conditions about each operator of the language, and then rely on an iteration technique to deduce general results for all contexts.

## Introduction

Coinductive definitions are frequently used in order to define operational or contextual equivalences, in settings ranging from process algebra [11] to functional programming [9,10,17].

This approach relies on Knaster-Tarski's fixpoint theorem [20]: "*in a complete lattice, any order-preserving function has a greatest fixpoint, which is the least upper bound of the set of its post-fixpoints*". Hence, by defining an object $x$ as the greatest fixpoint of an order-preserving function, we have a powerful technique to show that some object $y$ is dominated by $x$: prove that $y$ is dominated by some post-fixpoint. However, in some cases, the least post-fixpoint dominating $y$ can be a "large" object: when reasoning about bisimilarity on a labelled transition system (LTS), the smallest bisimulation relating two processes has to contain all their reducts. Hence, checking that this relation is actually a bisimulation often turns out to be tedious. The aim of up-to techniques, as defined in [11,15], is to alleviate this task by defining functions $f$ over relations such that any bisimulation "up to $f$" is contained in a bisimulation and hence in bisimilarity. These techniques have been widely used [10,19,5,12,17], and turn out to be essential in some cases.

In this paper, we generalise the theory of [15] to the abstract setting of complete lattices [3]. This allows us to ignore the technicalities of LTSs and binary

* This work has been supported by the french project "ModyFiable", funded by ANR ARASSIA.

Z. Shao (Ed.): APLAS 2007, LNCS 4807, pp. 351–366, 2007.

relations, and to obtain a homogeneous theory where we only manipulate objects and order-preserving functions (called maps). The key notion is that of *compatible* maps, i.e., maps satisfying a very simple semi-commutation property. These maps, which correspond to up-to techniques, generalise the "respectful" functions of [15]. They enjoy the same nice compositional properties: we can construct sophisticated techniques from simpler ones. On the other hand, there are cases where compatible maps are not sufficient: we prove in [12] the correctness of a distributed abstract machine, where mechanisms introduced by an optimisation cannot be taken into account by standard techniques relying on compatible maps (e.g., *up to expansion* [1,18]); we have to resort to recent, and more sophisticated techniques [14] relying on termination hypotheses.

The powerful techniques of [14] cannot be expressed by means of compatible maps, which makes it difficult to combine them with other techniques: we have to establish again correctness of each combination. Our first contribution addresses this problem: we give a simple condition ensuring that the composition of an arbitrarily complex correct technique and a compatible map remains correct. While this result is not especially difficult, it greatly enhances both [15], where only compatible maps are considered, and [14], where the lack of compositionality renders the results quite ad-hoc, and their proofs unnecessarily complicated. We illustrate the benefits of this new approach in Sect. 4, by establishing an uncluttered generalisation of one of the main results from [14], and showing how to easily enrich the corresponding up-to technique with standard techniques.

We then refine our framework, by adding monoidal operations to complete lattices, together with a symmetry operator. In doing so, we obtain an abstract, point-free presentation of binary relations, which is well-suited to proofs by diagram chasing arguments. In this setting, an LTS is a collection $(\xrightarrow{\alpha})_{\alpha\in\mathcal{L}}$ of objects, indexed by some *labels*, and strong similarity is the largest object $x$ such that the semi-commutation diagram $(S)$ below is satisfied:

$$(S)\quad \begin{array}{ccc} \cdot & x & \\ \alpha\big\downarrow & \sqsubseteq & \big\downarrow\alpha \\ & x & \cdot \end{array} \qquad\qquad (S_f)\quad \begin{array}{ccc} \cdot & x & \\ \alpha\big\downarrow & \sqsubseteq & \big\downarrow\alpha \\ & f(x) & \cdot \end{array}$$

There is an implicit universal quantification on all labels $\alpha$, so that this diagram should be read $(S): \forall\alpha\in\mathcal{L}, \xleftarrow{\alpha}\cdot x \sqsubseteq x\cdot\xleftarrow{\alpha}$ (where $(\cdot)$ is the law of the monoid, $\sqsubseteq$ is the partial order of the complete lattice, and $\xleftarrow{\alpha}$ denotes the converse of relation $\xrightarrow{\alpha}$). The second diagram, $(S_f)$, illustrates the use of a map $f$ as an up-to technique: "$x$ satisfies $(S)$ up to $f$". Intuitively, if $x \sqsubseteq f(x)$, it will be easier to check $(S_f)$ than $(S)$; the correctness of $f$ should then ensure that $x$ is dominated by some object satisfying $(S)$.

By defining two other notions of diagrams, and using symmetry arguments, we show how to recover in a uniform way the standard behavioural preorders and equivalences (strong and weak bisimilarity, expansion [1]), together with their associated up-to techniques. Notably, we can reduce the analysis of up-to techniques for those two-sided games to the study of their one-sided constituents.

Another advantage of working in this point-free setting is that it encompasses various cases, where objects are not necessarily simple binary relations. This includes *typed bisimulations* [19,7], where processes are related at a given type and/or in a given typing environment; and *environment bisimulations* [17], where environments are used to keep track of the observer's knowledge. Therefore, we obtain standard up-to techniques for these complicated settings, and more importantly, this gives a clear theory to guarantee correctness of up-to techniques that can be specific to these settings.

We then observe that maps over a complete lattice are an instance of complete lattice equipped with monoidal operations satisfying our requirements. We show that compatible maps, which are defined via a semi-commutation property, can be seen as the post-fixpoints of a *functor* (a map over maps). Therefore, our theory provides us for free with up-to techniques for compatible maps. We illustrate the use of such "second-order" techniques by considering up to context techniques; which are well-known for CCS or the $\pi$-calculus [19], and quite hard for functional languages [9,10,17]. Even in the simple case of CCS, (polyadic) contexts have a complex behaviour which renders them difficult to analyse. We show how to use an "up to iteration" technique in order to reduce the analysis of arbitrary contexts to that of the constructions of the language only. While we consider here the case of CCS, the resulting methodology is quite generic, and should be applicable to various other calculi (notably the $\pi$-calculus).

*Outline.* The abstract theory is developed in Sect. 1; we apply it to LTSs and behavioural preorders in Sect. 2. Section 3 is devoted to up to context techniques for CCS; we show in Sect. 4 how to combine a complex technique with compatible maps. We conclude with directions for future work in Sect. 5.

# 1 Maps and Fixpoints in Complete Lattices

## 1.1 Preliminary Definitions

We assume a *complete lattice*, that is, a tuple $\langle X, \sqsubseteq, \bigvee \rangle$, where $\sqsubseteq$ is a partial order over a set $X$ (a reflexive, transitive and anti-symmetric relation), such that any subset $Y$ of $X$ has a *least upper bound* (*lub* for short) that we denote by $\bigvee Y$. A function $f : X \to X$ is *order-preserving* if $\forall x, y \in X\ x \sqsubseteq y \Rightarrow f(x) \sqsubseteq f(y)$; it is *continuous* if $\forall Y \subseteq X,\ Y \neq \emptyset \Rightarrow f(\bigvee Y) = \bigvee f(Y)$. We extend $\sqsubseteq$ and $\bigvee$ pointwise to functions: $f \sqsubseteq g$ if $\forall x \in X,\ f(x) \sqsubseteq g(x)$, and $\bigvee F : x \mapsto \bigvee \{f(x) \mid f \in F\}$ for any family $F$ of functions. In the sequel, we only consider order-preserving functions, which we shall simply call *maps*. For any element $y$ and maps $f, g$, we define the following maps: $\mathrm{id}_X : x \mapsto x$; $\widehat{y} : x \mapsto y$; $f \circ g : x \mapsto f(g(x))$ and $f^\omega \triangleq \bigvee \{f^n \mid n \in \mathbb{N}\}$, where $f^0 \triangleq \mathrm{id}_X$ and $f^{n+1} \triangleq f \circ f^n$. We say that a map $f$ is *extensive* if $\mathrm{id}_X \sqsubseteq f$.

We fix in the sequel a map $s$.

**Definition 1.1.** An *s-simulation* is an element $x$ such that $x \sqsubseteq s(x)$. We denote by $X_s$ the set of all $s$-simulations, *s-similarity* ($\boldsymbol{\nu} s$) is the lub of this set:

$$X_s \triangleq \{x \in X \mid x \sqsubseteq s(x)\} \ , \qquad \boldsymbol{\nu} s \triangleq \bigvee X_s \ .$$

**Theorem 1.2 (Knaster-Tarski [20]).** *$\boldsymbol{\nu} s$ is the greatest fixpoint of $s$: $\boldsymbol{\nu} s = s(\boldsymbol{\nu} s)$.*

## 1.2 Up-To Techniques for Proofs by Coinduction

The previous definition gives the powerful *coinduction* proof method: in order to prove that $y \sqsubseteq \boldsymbol{\nu} s$, it suffices to find some $y'$ such that $y \sqsubseteq y' \sqsubseteq s(y')$. The idea of up-to techniques is to replace $s$ with a map $s'$, such that:

- $s \sqsubseteq s'$ so that there are more $s'$-simulations than $s$-simulations; and
- $\boldsymbol{\nu} s' \sqsubseteq \boldsymbol{\nu} s$ so that the proof method remains correct.

At first, we restrict ourselves to maps of the form $s \circ f$ and focus on the map $f$.

**Definition 1.3.** A map $f$ is *s-correct* if $\boldsymbol{\nu}(s \circ f) \sqsubseteq \boldsymbol{\nu} s$ .
A map $f$ is *s-correct via* $f'$ if $f'$ is an extensive map and $f'(X_{s \circ f}) \subseteq X_s$ .
A map $f$ is *s-compatible* if $f \circ s \sqsubseteq s \circ f$ .

**Proposition 1.4.** (i) *Any s-compatible map $f$ is s-correct via $f^\omega$.*
(ii) *Any map is s-correct iff it is s-correct via some map.*

Intuitively, a map is correct via $f'$ if its correctness can be proved using $f'$ as a "witness function" – these witnesses will be required to establish Prop. 1.10 and Thm. 1.12 below. For example, in the case of an $s$-compatible map $f$, if $x \sqsubseteq s(f(x))$ then $f^\omega(x)$, which is an $s$-simulation, is the witness.

*Remark* 1.5. For any $s$-compatible map $f$, $f(\boldsymbol{\nu} s) \sqsubseteq \boldsymbol{\nu} s$. Hence $s$-compatible maps necessarily correspond to closure properties satisfied by $\boldsymbol{\nu} s$. This is not a sufficient condition: there are maps satisfying $f(\boldsymbol{\nu} s) \sqsubseteq \boldsymbol{\nu} s$ that are not $s$-correct.

**Proposition 1.6.** *The family of s-compatible maps is stable under composition and lubs. It contains the identity, and constant maps $\widehat{x}$ with $x \in X_s$.*

These nice compositional properties are the main motivation behind compatible maps. They do not hold for correct maps (more generally, the map $t = \bigvee \{t \mid \boldsymbol{\nu} t \sqsubseteq \boldsymbol{\nu} s\}$ does not necessarily satisfy $\boldsymbol{\nu} t \sqsubseteq \boldsymbol{\nu} s$). On the other hand, correct maps allow more expressiveness: we can use any mathematical argument in order to prove the correctness of a map; we will for example use well-founded inductions in Sect. 4.

At this point, we have generalised to a rather abstract level the theory developed in [15] (this claim is justified by Sect. 1.4). Thm 1.7, which is our first improvement against [15], allows one to compose correct and compatible maps:

**Theorem 1.7.** *Let $f$ be an s-compatible map, and $g$ an s-correct map via $g'$.*
*If $f$ is g-compatible, then $(g \circ f)$ is s-correct via $(g' \circ f^\omega)$.*

As will be illustrated in Sect. 4, this important result allows one to focus on the heart of a complex technique, so that its proof remains tractable; and then to improve this technique with more standard techniques.

## 1.3 Conjunctions, Symmetry, and Internal Monoid

We now add some structure to complete lattices: conjunctions, which are already supported, symmetry, and monoidal laws.

*Conjunctions.* A complete lattice has both lubs and greatest lower bounds (glb): for any $Y \subseteq X$, $\bigwedge Y \triangleq \bigvee\{x \in X \mid \forall y \in Y,\ x \sqsubseteq y\}$. We extend this definition pointwise to maps. We fix in the sequel a set $S$ of maps and focus on proof techniques for $\bigwedge S$. As will be illustrated in Sect. 2.2, this kind of maps corresponds to coinductive definitions based on a conjunction of several properties.

**Lemma 1.8.** *We have* $X_{\bigwedge S} = \bigcap\{X_s \mid s \in S\}$ *and* $\boldsymbol{\nu}\bigwedge S \sqsubseteq \bigwedge\{\boldsymbol{\nu}s \mid s \in S\}$ .

In general, $\boldsymbol{\nu}\bigwedge S \neq \bigwedge\{\boldsymbol{\nu}s \mid s \in S\}$; for example, in process algebras, 2-simulation and bisimulation do not coincide. Therefore, to obtain results about $\boldsymbol{\nu}\bigwedge S$, it is not sufficient to study the fixpoints $(\boldsymbol{\nu}s)_{s \in S}$ separately.

**Proposition 1.9.** *Any map that is s-compatible for all s in S is* $\bigwedge S$*-compatible.*

Prop. 1.9 deals with compatible maps, and requires that the same map is used for all the components of $S$. We can relax these restrictions by working with correct maps, provided that they agree on a common witness:

**Proposition 1.10.** *Let* $(f_s)_{s \in S}$ *be a family of maps indexed by* $S$ *and let* $f'$ *be an extensive map; let* $S_f \triangleq \{s \circ f_s \mid s \in S\}$.

*If* $f_s$ *is s-correct via* $f'$ *for all s of* $S$*, then* $\boldsymbol{\nu}\bigwedge S_f \sqsubseteq \boldsymbol{\nu}\bigwedge S$.

Although Prop. 1.10 does not define a $\bigwedge S$-correct map, it actually defines an up-to technique for $\bigwedge S$: a priori, $\bigwedge S \sqsubseteq \bigwedge S_f$, so that $\bigwedge S_f$-simulations are easier to construct than $\bigwedge S$-simulations.

*Symmetry.* Let $\bar{\cdot}$ be an order-preserving involution ($\forall x,\ \overline{\overline{x}} = x$). For any map $f$, we define $\overline{f} \triangleq \bar{\cdot} \circ f \circ \bar{\cdot} : x \mapsto \overline{f(\overline{x})}$, and $\overleftrightarrow{f} \triangleq f \wedge \overline{f}$. We call $\overline{x}$ the *converse of* $x$ and we say that an element $x$ (resp. a map $f$) is *symmetric* if $x = \overline{x}$ (resp. $f = \overline{f}$). These definitions yield nice algebraic properties (the key point being that we have $x \sqsubseteq y \Leftrightarrow \overline{x} \sqsubseteq \overline{y}$) and we can relate up-to techniques for $s$ and $\overline{s}$ :

**Proposition 1.11.** *We have* $\overline{X_s} = X_{\overline{s}}$, $\overline{\boldsymbol{\nu}s} = \boldsymbol{\nu}\overline{s}$ *and for any maps* $f, f'$,

(i) $f$ *is s-correct (via* $f'$*) if and only if* $\overline{f}$ *is* $\overline{s}$*-correct (via* $\overline{f'}$*),*
(ii) $f$ *is s-compatible if and only if* $\overline{f}$ *is* $\overline{s}$*-compatible.*

We can finally combine these properties with Prop. 1.10 and reduce the problem of finding up-to techniques for $\overleftrightarrow{s}$ to that of finding up-to techniques for $s$. We illustrate this in Sect. 2.2, by deriving up-to techniques for weak bisimulation from techniques for weak simulation.

**Theorem 1.12.** *For any s-correct map f via a symmetric map,* $\overleftrightarrow{\boldsymbol{\nu}s \circ f} \sqsubseteq \boldsymbol{\nu}\overleftrightarrow{s}$.

**Corollary 1.13.** *Let f be an s-correct map via a symmetric map.*

*If x is symmetric, and* $x \sqsubseteq s(f(x))$*, then* $x \sqsubseteq \boldsymbol{\nu}\overleftrightarrow{s}$.

*Internal monoid.* Suppose that the complete lattice $\langle X, \sqsubseteq, \bigvee\rangle$ is actually a *monoidal complete lattice*, i.e., that $X$ is equipped with an associative product $(\cdot)$ with neutral element $e$, such that:

$$\forall x, y, x', y' \in X,\ x \sqsubseteq x' \wedge y \sqsubseteq y' \Rightarrow x \cdot y \sqsubseteq x' \cdot y' .$$

The *iteration* (resp. *strict iteration*) of an element $x$ is defined by $x^\star \triangleq \bigvee_{n \in \mathbb{N}} x^n$ (resp. $x^+ \triangleq \bigvee_{n>0} x^n$), where $x^0 \triangleq e$ and $x^{n+1} \triangleq x \cdot x^n$. Iterations and product are extended pointwise to maps: $f \mathbin{\hat{\cdot}} g : x \mapsto f(x) \cdot g(x)$, and $f^\star : x \mapsto f(x)^\star$.

**Definition 1.14.** An element $x$ is *reflexive* if $e \sqsubseteq x$; it is *transitive* if $x \cdot x \sqsubseteq x$. We say that $s$ *preserves the monoid* $\langle X, \cdot, e\rangle$ if $e$ is an $s$-simulation and

$$\forall x, y \in X,\ s(x) \cdot s(y) \sqsubseteq s(x \cdot y) .$$

**Proposition 1.15.** *If $s$ preserves the monoid, then:*

(i) *the product of two $s$-simulations is an $s$-simulation;*
(ii) *$s$-similarity ($\boldsymbol{\nu} s$) is reflexive and transitive;*
(iii) *for any $s$-compatible maps $f, g$, $f \mathbin{\hat{\cdot}} g$ and $f^\star$ are $s$-compatible.*

### 1.4 Progressions

While maps and pre-fixpoints are the adequate tool in order to build the previous theory of up-to techniques, it is more convenient in practise to use the following notion of *progression*, which can systematically be turned into a map. This notion facilitates the definition of maps corresponding to the various behavioural preorders we will consider in Sect. 2; moreover, it leads to the important results given in Sect. 1.5 about up-to techniques for compatible maps.

**Definition 1.16.** A *progression* is a binary relation $\rightarrowtail \subseteq X \times X$, such that:

$$\forall x, x', y', y \in X,\ x \sqsubseteq x' \wedge x' \rightarrowtail y' \wedge y' \sqsubseteq y \Rightarrow x \rightarrowtail y ,$$
$$\forall Y \subseteq X,\ \forall z \in X,\ (\forall y \in Y,\ y \rightarrowtail z) \Rightarrow \bigvee Y \rightarrowtail z .$$

We associate to such relation the map $s_{\rightarrowtail} : x \mapsto \bigvee \{y \in X \mid y \rightarrowtail x\}$ .

Relations $\rightarrowtail$ in [15], and $\rightsquigarrow$ in [19] are particular instances of progressions. The main advantages of progressions are the following characterisations of the previous notions:

**Proposition 1.17.** *For any progression $\rightarrowtail$, we have:*

(i) *$\forall x, y \in X,\ x \sqsubseteq s_{\rightarrowtail}(y) \Leftrightarrow x \rightarrowtail y$, and in particular, $x \in X_{s_{\rightarrowtail}}$ iff $x \rightarrowtail x$;*
(ii) *a map $f$ is $s_{\rightarrowtail}$-compatible iff $\forall x, y \in X,\ x \rightarrowtail y \Rightarrow f(x) \rightarrowtail f(y)$ .*
(iii) *$s_{\rightarrowtail}$ preserves the monoid iff $e \rightarrowtail e$ and*

$$\forall x, y, x', y' \in X,\ x \rightarrowtail x' \wedge y \rightarrowtail y' \Rightarrow x \cdot y \rightarrowtail x' \cdot y' .$$

Another practical consequence of (i) is that $\forall x,\ x \sqsubseteq s_{\rightarrowtail}(f(x))$ iff $x \rightarrowtail f(x)$ .

### 1.5 Up-To Techniques for Compatible Maps

Denoting by $X^{\langle X\rangle}$ the set of (order-preserving) maps over $X$, $\langle X^{\langle X\rangle}, \sqsubseteq, \bigvee, \circ, \mathrm{id}_X\rangle$ forms a monoidal complete lattice. Therefore, we can apply the previous theory in order to capture certain properties of maps. In particular, that of being $s$-compatible: for any map $s$, define the following relation over maps:

$$f \overset{s}{\rightsquigarrow} f' \quad \text{if} \quad f \circ s \sqsubseteq s \circ f' \ .$$

Since $s$ is order-preserving, $\overset{s}{\rightsquigarrow}$ is a progression relation, whose simulations are exactly the $s$-compatible maps. Moreover, when $s$ comes from a progression ($s = s_{\rightarrowtail}$), we have $f \overset{s_{\rightarrowtail}}{\rightsquigarrow} f'$ iff $\forall x, y \in X,\ x \rightarrowtail y \Rightarrow f(x) \rightarrowtail f'(y)$ .

**Lemma 1.18.** *For any map $s$, $\overset{s}{\rightsquigarrow}$ preserves the monoid $\langle X^{\langle X\rangle}, \circ, \mathrm{id}_X\rangle$.*

**Theorem 1.19.** *Let $f, g$ be two maps.*

(i) *If the product $(\cdot)$ preserves $s$ and $f \overset{s}{\rightsquigarrow} f^\star$, then $f^\star$ is $s$-compatible.*
(ii) *If $f \overset{s}{\rightsquigarrow} f^\omega$ and $f$ is continuous, then $f^\omega$ is $s$-compatible.*
(iii) *If $f \overset{s}{\rightsquigarrow} g \circ f^\omega$, where $g$ is $s$-compatible, extensive and idempotent ($g \circ g = g$), and $f$ is $g$-compatible, then $g \circ f^\omega$ is $s$-compatible.*

*Proof.* Call *functor* any (order-preserving) map $\varphi$ over maps; we say that a functor is *respectful* when it is compatible w.r.t. $\overset{s}{\rightsquigarrow}$. Recall that $\widehat{g}$ is the constant functor to $g$, and that $(\hat{\circ})$ is the pointwise extension of $(\circ)$ to functors.

(i) By Lemma 1.18 and Prop. 1.15, $\varphi = \widehat{\mathrm{id}_X^\star}\ \hat{\circ}\ \mathrm{id}_{X^{\langle X\rangle}} : f \mapsto f^\star$ is respectful, being the product of two respectful functors:
   – the constant functor to $\mathrm{id}_X^\star$, this map being $s$-compatible by Prop. 1.15;
   – and the identity functor $\mathrm{id}_{X^{\langle X\rangle}}$, which is always respectful.
   Therefore, $f$ is "$s$-compatible up to the respectful functor $\varphi$", so that $\varphi^\omega(f)$ is $s$-compatible, by Prop. 1.4. We finally check that $\varphi^\omega(f) = f^\star$.
(ii) By Lemma 1.18 and Prop. 1.15, the functor $\omega \triangleq \mathrm{id}_{X^{\langle X\rangle}}^\star : f \mapsto f^\omega$ is respectful (iteration $(^\star)$ is done w.r.t $(\circ)$). By Prop. 1.4, $\omega^\omega(f)$ is $s$-compatible, and we check that $\omega^\omega(f) = f^\omega$, $f$ being continuous.
(iii) Using similar arguments, $\varphi = \widehat{g}\ \hat{\circ}\ \omega : f \mapsto g \circ f^\omega$ is respectful, and $\varphi^\omega(f)$ is $s$-compatible. We finally check that $\varphi^\omega(f) = g \circ f^\omega$. ■

The first point generalises [19, Lemma 2.3.16]; we illustrate the use of (ii) and (iii) in Sect. 3. In (iii), the main hypotheses are the progression property and $s$-compatibility of $g$: other hypotheses are only used in order to simplify computations, so that the actual $s$-compatible map we obtain is $g \circ f^\omega$.

## 2 Bisimilarity in Monoidal Lattices with Symmetry

We assume a *continuous monoidal complete lattice with symmetry*, that is, a monoidal complete lattice $\langle X, \sqsubseteq, \bigvee, \cdot, e\rangle$, whose product distributes over arbitrary lubs: ($\forall Y, Z \sqsubseteq X,\ \bigvee Y \cdot \bigvee Z = \bigvee\{y \cdot z \mid y \in Y,\ z \in Z\}$), equipped with a map $\bar{\cdot}$ such that $\forall x,\ \overline{\overline{x}} = x$ and $\forall x, y,\ \overline{x \cdot y} = \overline{y} \cdot \overline{x}$ .

$$
\begin{array}{lll}
\mathbf{s}: & x \rightarrowtail_{\mathbf{s}} y & \text{if } x \sqsubseteq y \text{ and } \forall \alpha \in \mathcal{L},\ \xleftarrow{\alpha} \cdot\, x \sqsubseteq y \cdot \xleftarrow{\alpha}\ ; \\
\mathbf{e}: & x \rightarrowtail_{\mathbf{e}} y & \text{if } x \sqsubseteq y \text{ and } \forall \alpha \in \mathcal{L},\ \xleftarrow{\alpha} \cdot\, x \sqsubseteq y \cdot \xleftarrow{\widehat{\alpha}}\ ; \\
\mathbf{w}: & x \rightarrowtail_{\mathbf{w}} y & \text{if } x \sqsubseteq y \text{ and } \forall \alpha \in \mathcal{L},\ \xleftarrow{\alpha} \cdot\, x \sqsubseteq y \cdot \overset{\widehat{\alpha}}{\Leftarrow}\ ; \\
\mathbf{w}_{\mathrm{t}}: & x \rightarrowtail_{\mathbf{w}_{\mathrm{t}}} y & \text{if } x \sqsubseteq y,\ \xleftarrow{\tau} \cdot\, x \sqsubseteq y \cdot \overset{\widehat{\tau}}{\Leftarrow}\ ,\ \text{and } \forall a \in \mathcal{L}^{\mathrm{v}},\ \xleftarrow{a} \cdot\, x \sqsubseteq y^{\star} \cdot \overset{\widehat{a}}{\Leftarrow}\ .
\end{array}
$$

**Fig. 1.** Maps and progressions for left-to-right simulation-like games

Although we denote by $x, y \dots$ the elements of $X$, they should really be thought of as "abstract relations" so that we shall call them *relations* in the sequel (we employ letters $R, S$ for "set-theoretic relations" of Sect. 3 and 4).

We let $\alpha$ range over the elements of a fixed set $\mathcal{L}$ of *labels*, and we assume a *labelled transition system (LTS)*, that is, a collection $(\xrightarrow{\alpha})_{\alpha \in \mathcal{L}}$ of relations indexed by $\mathcal{L}$. Intuitively, $\xrightarrow{\alpha}$ represents the set of transitions along label $\alpha$. Among the elements of $\mathcal{L}$, we distinguish the *silent action*, denoted by $\tau$; we let $a$ range over the elements of $\mathcal{L}^{\mathrm{v}} \triangleq \mathcal{L} \setminus \{\tau\}$, called *visible labels*. For $\alpha \in \mathcal{L}$ we define the following *weak transition relations*:

$$
\xrightarrow{\widehat{\alpha}} \triangleq \begin{cases} \xrightarrow{\tau} \vee\, e & \text{if } \alpha = \tau\ , \\ \xrightarrow{\alpha} & \text{otherwise}\ ; \end{cases} \qquad \overset{\alpha}{\Rightarrow} \triangleq \xrightarrow{\tau}^{\star} \cdot \xrightarrow{\alpha} \cdot \xrightarrow{\tau}^{\star}\ ; \qquad \overset{\widehat{\alpha}}{\Rightarrow} \triangleq \xrightarrow{\tau}^{\star} \cdot \xrightarrow{\widehat{\alpha}} \cdot \xrightarrow{\tau}^{\star}\ .
$$

Notice the following properties: $\overset{\widehat{\tau}}{\Rightarrow} = \xrightarrow{\tau}^{\star}$, $\overset{\tau}{\Rightarrow} = \xrightarrow{\tau}^{+}$, $\overset{\widehat{a}}{\Rightarrow} = \overset{a}{\Rightarrow}$. The converses of such relations will be denoted by the corresponding reversed arrows.

### 2.1 One-Sided Behavioural Preorders

In order to define behavioural preorders, we construct four maps in Fig. 1, based on four different progressions. Their meaning can be recovered by considering the simulations they define: $\mathbf{s}$ yields strong simulation games, where actions are exactly matched (diagram ($S$) in the introduction); $\mathbf{e}$ yields games corresponding to the left-to-right part of an *expansion* [1,18] game, where it is allowed not to move on silent challenges; and $\mathbf{w}$ yields weak simulations games, where one can answer "modulo silent transitions". The map ($\mathbf{w}_{\mathrm{t}}$) is a variant of $\mathbf{w}$, which allows one to answer up to transitivity on visible challenges. We have $\mathbf{s} \sqsubseteq \mathbf{e} \sqsubseteq \mathbf{w} \sqsubseteq \mathbf{w}_{\mathrm{t}}$, so that $X_{\mathbf{s}} \subseteq X_{\mathbf{e}} \subseteq X_{\mathbf{w}} \subseteq X_{\mathbf{w}_{\mathrm{t}}}$, and $\boldsymbol{\nu}\mathbf{s} \subseteq \boldsymbol{\nu}\mathbf{e} \subseteq \boldsymbol{\nu}\mathbf{w} \subseteq \boldsymbol{\nu}\mathbf{w}_{\mathrm{t}}$.

The following proposition collects standard up-to techniques that can be used with these maps. Maps $\mathbf{s}$ and $\mathbf{e}$ preserve the monoid, so that they enjoy the properties stated in Prop. 1.15: the corresponding greatest fixpoints are reflexive and transitive, and they support the powerful "up to transitivity" technique (i). This is not the case for $\mathbf{w}$: if it was preserving the monoid, the "weak up to weak" technique would be correct, which is not true [18]. We can however show directly that $\mathbf{w}$-simulations are closed under composition ($\cdot$), and that they support "up to expansion" on the left, and "up to weak" on the right (ii). Map $\mathbf{w}_{\mathrm{t}}$ is actually an up-to technique for $\mathbf{w}$: the similarities associated to those maps coincide (iii).

Intuitively, transitivity can be allowed on visible actions, since these are played in a one-to-one correspondence.

**Proposition 2.1.** (i) *The reflexive transitive map* $\mathrm{id}_X^\star$ *is* $\mathbf{s}$*- and* $\mathbf{e}$*-compatible.*
(ii) *For any* $x_e \in X_\mathbf{e}$ *and* $x_w \in X_\mathbf{w}$, *the map* $y \mapsto x_e \cdot y \cdot x_w$ *is* $\mathbf{w}$*-compatible; this map is* $\mathbf{w}_t$*-compatible whenever* $x_e$ *and* $x_w$ *are reflexive.*
(iii) *For any* $\mathbf{w}_t$*-simulation* $x$, $x^\star$ *is a* $\mathbf{w}$*-simulation;* $\boldsymbol{\nu}\mathbf{w}_t = \boldsymbol{\nu}\mathbf{w}$.

## 2.2 Handling Two-Sided Games

To study "reversed games" we just use the converses of the previous maps; for example, the map $\overline{\mathbf{w}}$ defines the same games as $\mathbf{w}$, from right to left: $x$ is a $\overline{\mathbf{w}}$-simulation iff $\overline{x} \rightarrowtail_\mathbf{w} \overline{x}$. Using the results of Sect. 1.3 we can then combine left-to-right maps with right-to-left maps and obtain standard two-sided games:

$$\sim \triangleq \boldsymbol{\nu}\overleftrightarrow{\mathbf{s}} \qquad\qquad \gtrsim \triangleq \boldsymbol{\nu}(\mathbf{e} \wedge \overline{\mathbf{w}}) \qquad\qquad \approx \triangleq \boldsymbol{\nu}\overleftrightarrow{\mathbf{w}}$$

*Strong bisimilarity* ($\sim$) and *weak-bisimilarity* ($\approx$) are symmetric, reflexive and transitive; *expansion* [1,18] ($\gtrsim$) is reflexive and transitive; we have $\sim\ \sqsubseteq\ \gtrsim\ \sqsubseteq\ \approx$ .

Before transferring our techniques from one-sided to two-sided games, we introduce the notion of *closure*, that we use as an abstraction in order to cope with the up-to context techniques we shall define in Sect. 3.

**Definition 2.2.** A *closure* is a continuous, extensive and symmetric map $\mathcal{C}$, such that $\forall x, y \in X,\ \mathcal{C}(x \cdot y) \sqsubseteq \mathcal{C}(x) \cdot \mathcal{C}(y)$ .

**Theorem 2.3.** *Let* $\mathcal{C}$ *be a closure.*

(i) *If* $\mathcal{C}$ *is* $\mathbf{s}$*-compatible,* $x \mapsto (\mathcal{C}(x) \vee \sim)^\star$ *is* $\overleftrightarrow{\mathbf{s}}$*-compatible*
(ii) *If* $\mathcal{C}$ *is* $\mathbf{w}$*-compatible,* $x \mapsto\ \gtrsim \cdot\, \mathcal{C}(x) \cdot \lesssim$ *is* $\overleftrightarrow{\mathbf{w}}$*-compatible.*
(iii) *If* $\mathcal{C}$ *is* $\mathbf{w}$*-compatible,* $x \mapsto\ \gtrsim \cdot\, \mathcal{C}(x) \cdot \approx$ *is* $\mathbf{w}$*-correct via a symmetric map.*
(iv) $\boldsymbol{\nu}\overleftrightarrow{\mathbf{w}_t} = \approx$ .

Intuitively, we may think of $\mathcal{C}(R)$ as being the closure of $R$ under some set of contexts. (i) states that up-to transitivity and contexts is allowed for strong bisimilarity. This corresponds to the left diagram below: if $x$ is symmetric and satisfies this diagram, then $x$ is contained in $\sim$. The standard up to expansion and contexts for weak bisimulation is stated in (ii) and slightly improved in (iii); notice that we need for that to use the notion of correct map: this map is not $\overleftrightarrow{\mathbf{w}}$-compatible. Technique (iii) appears on the second diagram below. Finally, (iv) allows us to work up to transitivity on visible actions; which is depicted on the last two diagrams below ((iii) holds for $\mathbf{w}_t$, provided $\mathcal{C}$ is $\mathbf{w}_t$-compatible, this hypothesis is however problematic, as explained in Sect. 3). We omitted proof techniques for expansion, which can naturally be recovered from up-to techniques for $\mathbf{w}$ and $\mathbf{e}$ using Prop. 1.10.

$$\begin{array}{ll} \alpha \in \mathcal{L} & a \in \mathcal{L}^{\mathrm{v}} \\ \overline{\tau} = \tau & \overline{\overline{a}} = a \\ \multicolumn{2}{l}{p ::= \mathbf{0} \mid \alpha.p \mid p|p \mid (\nu a)p \mid !p} \end{array} \qquad \frac{p \xrightarrow{\alpha} p'}{p \mid q \xrightarrow{\alpha} p' \mid q} \qquad \frac{q \xrightarrow{\alpha} q'}{p \mid q \xrightarrow{\alpha} p \mid q'} \qquad \frac{p \xrightarrow{a} p' \quad q \xrightarrow{\overline{a}} q'}{p \mid q \xrightarrow{\tau} p' \mid q'}$$

$$\frac{}{\alpha.p \xrightarrow{\alpha} p} \qquad \frac{p \xrightarrow{\alpha} p'}{(\nu a)p \xrightarrow{\alpha} (\nu a)p'} \alpha \neq a, \overline{a} \qquad \frac{!p \mid p \xrightarrow{\alpha} p'}{!p \xrightarrow{\alpha} p'}$$

**Fig. 2.** Calculus of Communicating Systems (CCS)

## 3 Congruence and Up to Context Techniques in CCS

We now look at "up to context" techniques, which provide an example of application of the results from Sect. 1.5. We need for that to instantiate the previous framework: contexts do not make sense in a point-free setting. We study the case of (sum-free) CCS [11], whose syntax and semantics are recalled in Fig. 2. The sum operator could easily be added; it is omitted here for lack of space. Moreover, we chose replication (!) rather than recursive definitions in order to get an algebra which is closer the $\pi$-calculus.

We denote by $\mathcal{P}$ the set of processes, and we let $R, S$ range over the set $\mathcal{R}$ of binary relations over $\mathcal{P}$. We write $p \mathrel{R} q$ when $\langle p, q\rangle$ belongs to $R$. We denote by $I$ the reflexive relation: $\{\langle p,p\rangle \mid p \in \mathcal{P}\}$. The composition of $R$ and $S$ is the relation $R \cdot S \triangleq \{\langle p, r\rangle \mid \exists q,\ p \mathrel{R} q \text{ and } q \mathrel{S} r\}$; the converse of $R$ is $\overline{R} \triangleq \{\langle p, q\rangle \mid q \mathrel{R} p\}$. We finally equip relations with set-theoretic inclusion ($\subseteq$) and union ($\bigcup$), so that $\langle \mathcal{R}, \subseteq, \bigcup, \cdot, I, \bar{\cdot}\rangle$ forms a monoidal complete lattice with symmetry.

For any natural number $n$, a *context with arity* $n$ is a function $c : \mathcal{P}^n \to \mathcal{P}$, whose application to a $n$-uple of processes $p_1, \dots, p_n$ is denoted by $c[p_1, \dots, p_n]$. We associate to such context the following map (which is actually a closure):

$$\lfloor c \rfloor : R \mapsto \{\langle c[p_1, \dots, p_n],\ c[q_1, \dots, q_n]\rangle \mid \forall i \leq n,\ p_i \mathrel{R} q_i\}$$

This notation is extended to sets $C$ of contexts, by letting $\lfloor C \rfloor \triangleq \bigcup_{c \in C} \lfloor c \rfloor$ .

**Definition 3.1.** We define the following *initial* contexts:

$$\mathbf{0} : p \mapsto \mathbf{0} \qquad | : p, q \mapsto p|q \qquad \alpha. : p \mapsto \alpha.p \qquad (\nu a) : p \mapsto (\nu a)p \qquad ! : p \mapsto !p$$

We gather these in the set $C_i \triangleq \{\mathrm{id}_{\mathcal{P}}, \mathbf{0}, |, !\} \cup \{\alpha. \mid \alpha \in \mathcal{L}\} \cup \{(\nu a) \mid a \in \mathcal{L}^{\mathrm{v}}\}$, and we call *closure under CCS contexts* the map $\mathcal{C}_{ccs} \triangleq \lfloor C_i \rfloor^{\omega}$ .

*Initial vs. Monadic Contexts.* $\mathcal{C}_{ccs}(R)$ is actually the closure of $R$ under arbitrary polyadic CCS contexts: we can show that $p \mathrel{\mathcal{C}_{ccs}(R)} q$ iff $p$ and $q$ can be obtained by replacing some occurrences of $\mathbf{0}$ in a process with processes related by $R$. A different approach is adopted in [19]: the family $C_m$ of *monadic CCS contexts* is defined; it consists in arbitrary CCS contexts, where the argument is used at most once. The map $\mathcal{C}_{ccs}$ can then be recovered by transitive closure: we have $\mathcal{C}_{ccs} \subseteq \lfloor C_m \rfloor^{\star}$. It has to be noticed that polyadic contexts cannot be avoided when we study the correctness of such maps: the monadic replication context (!)

"evolves" by reduction into a polyadic context. In order to be able to consider only monadic contexts, a lemma corresponding to Thm 1.19(i) is used in [19], so that the proof in the strong case – reformulated into our setting – amounts to proving $\lfloor C_m \rfloor \overset{\mathbf{s}}{\leadsto} \lfloor C_m \rfloor^\star$, i.e., $\forall c \in C_m$, $\lfloor c \rfloor \overset{\mathbf{s}}{\leadsto} \lfloor C_m \rfloor^\star$, which is done by structural induction on context $c$ (recall that $f \overset{\mathbf{s}}{\leadsto} f'$ iff $R \rightarrowtail_{\mathbf{s}} S$ entail $f(R) \rightarrowtail_{\mathbf{s}} f'(S)$). This approach does not scale to the weak case however, where up to transitivity is not correct, so that Thm 1.19(i) cannot no longer be used. Therefore, [19] suggests to work with polyadic contexts from the beginning, which is tedious and happens to require more attention than expected, as will be shown below.

Focusing on initial contexts makes it possible to reach $\mathcal{C}_{ccs}$ by iteration (Thm 1.19(ii)) rather than transitive closure, so that the extension to the weak case is not problematic. Moreover, initial contexts are much simpler than monadic contexts: the argument is almost at the top of the term, so that it is really easy to figure out the transitions of $c[p_1, \ldots, p_n]$. We give a detailed proof of the following theorem to illustrate the benefits of this approach.

**Theorem 3.2.** *The closure $\mathcal{C}_{ccs}$ is* s*-compatible.*

*Proof.* By Thm.1.19(ii), it suffices to show $\lfloor C_i \rfloor \overset{\mathbf{s}}{\leadsto} \mathcal{C}_{ccs}$, i.e., $\forall c \in C_i$, $\lfloor c \rfloor \overset{\mathbf{s}}{\leadsto} \mathcal{C}_{ccs}$. We study each context of $C_i$ separately, and we show

$$\lfloor \mathrm{id}_{\mathcal{P}} \rfloor = \mathrm{id}_{\mathcal{R}} \overset{\mathbf{s}}{\leadsto} \mathrm{id}_{\mathcal{R}} \qquad \lfloor \mathbf{0} \rfloor \overset{\mathbf{s}}{\leadsto} \lfloor \mathbf{0} \rfloor \qquad \lfloor \alpha. \rfloor \overset{\mathbf{s}}{\leadsto} \mathrm{id}_{\mathcal{R}}$$

$$\lfloor (\nu a) \rfloor \overset{\mathbf{s}}{\leadsto} \lfloor (\nu a) \rfloor \qquad \lfloor | \rfloor \overset{\mathbf{s}}{\leadsto} \lfloor | \rfloor \qquad \lfloor ! \rfloor \overset{\mathbf{s}}{\leadsto} \lfloor | \rfloor^\omega \circ (\lfloor ! \rfloor \cup \mathrm{id}_{\mathcal{R}})$$

(all maps used on the right of the above progression are contained in $\mathcal{C}_{ccs}$). Let $R, S$ such that $R \rightarrowtail_{\mathbf{s}} S$, in each case, we suppose $u \lfloor c \rfloor(R)\ v$ and $u \xrightarrow{\alpha} u'$, and we have to find some $v'$ such that $v \xrightarrow{\alpha} v'$ and $u' \lfloor c' \rfloor(S)\ v'$.

$\mathrm{id}_{\mathcal{R}}$, $\lfloor \mathbf{0} \rfloor$: straightforward.

$\lfloor \alpha. \rfloor$: $u = \alpha'.p \xrightarrow{\alpha} u'$, $v = \alpha'.q$ with $p\ R\ q$. Necessarily, $\alpha = \alpha'$ and $u' = p$. We hence have $v = \alpha.q \xrightarrow{\alpha} q$, with $p\ \mathrm{id}_{\mathcal{R}}(S)\ q$, (recall that $R \rightarrowtail_{\mathbf{s}} S$ entails $R \subseteq S$).

$\lfloor (\nu a) \rfloor$: $u = (\nu a)p \xrightarrow{\alpha} u'$, $v = (\nu a)q$ with $p\ R\ q$. Inferences rules impose $u' = (\nu a)p'$ where $p \xrightarrow{\alpha} p'$ and $\alpha \neq a, \overline{a}$. Since $p\ R\ q$, we obtain $q'$ such that $q \xrightarrow{\alpha} q'$ and $p'\ S\ q'$, and we check that $v \xrightarrow{\alpha} v' = (\nu a)q'$, with $u' \lfloor (\nu a) \rfloor(S)\ v'$.

$\lfloor | \rfloor$: $u = p_1|p_2 \xrightarrow{\alpha} u'$, $v = q_1|q_2$ with $p_1\ R\ q_1$ and $p_2\ R\ q_2$. According to the inference rules in the case of a parallel composition, there are three cases:

- $u' = p_1'|p_2$ with $p_1 \xrightarrow{\alpha} p_1'$. Since $R \rightarrowtail_{\mathbf{s}} S$, $q_1 \xrightarrow{\alpha} q_1'$ with $p_1'\ S\ q_1'$. We check that $v \xrightarrow{\alpha} v' = q_1'|q_2$ and $u' \lfloor | \rfloor(S)\ v'$ (again we use $R \rightarrowtail_{\mathbf{s}} S \Rightarrow R \subseteq S$).
- $u' = p_1|p_2'$ with $p_2 \xrightarrow{\alpha} p_2'$, which is identical to the previous case.
- $u' = p_1'|p_2'$ with $p_1 \xrightarrow{a} p_1'$, $p_2 \xrightarrow{\overline{a}} p_2'$, and $\alpha = \tau$. We have $q_1 \xrightarrow{a} q_1'$ $q_2 \xrightarrow{\overline{a}} q_2'$ with $p_1'\ S\ q_1'$ and $p_2'\ S\ q_2'$; so that $v \xrightarrow{\tau} v' = q_1'|q_2'$ and $u' \lfloor | \rfloor(S)\ v'$.

$\lfloor ! \rfloor$: this case is handled in the proof of Thm 3.3 below, so that we omit it here. ∎

$$R = \{\langle a, (\nu b)(b.a|\bar{b})\rangle, \langle b.a, b\rangle, \langle(\nu b)(b|\bar{b}), \mathbf{0}\rangle, \langle(\nu b)\mathbf{0}, \mathbf{0}\rangle\}$$
$$c : p \mapsto (\nu b)(p|\bar{b})$$

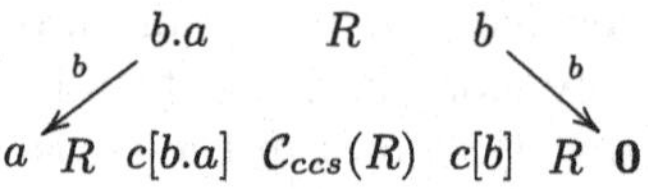


**Fig. 3.** Closure $\mathcal{C}_{ccs}$ is not $\mathbf{w}_t$-correct

Contrarily to what is announced in [19, Lem. 2.4.52], $\mathcal{C}_{ccs}$ is not $\mathbf{w}$-compatible: consider for example $R = \{\langle \tau.a, a\rangle\} \cup I$; although $R \rightarrowtail_{\mathbf{e}} R$, $\mathcal{C}_{ccs}(R) \rightarrowtail_{\mathbf{e}} \mathcal{C}_{ccs}(R)$ does not hold: the challenge $!\tau.a|a \xleftarrow{\tau} !\tau.a \ \lfloor ! \rfloor(R) \ !a$ cannot be answered in $\mathcal{C}_{ccs}(R)$ since $!a$ cannot move; we first have to rewrite $!a$ into $!a|a$. This is possible up to $\sim$: unfolding of replications is contained in strong similarity. [19] should thus be corrected by working modulo unfolding of replications, the corresponding proof would be *really* tedious however. In our setting, it suffices to use Thm. 1.19(iii): we work "up to iteration and a compatible map".

**Theorem 3.3.** *$R \mapsto \sim \cdot \mathcal{C}_{ccs}(R) \cdot \sim$ is an* $\mathbf{e}$- *and* $\mathbf{w}$-*compatible closure.*

*Proof ($\mathbf{w}$-compatibility).* Take $g : r \mapsto \sim \cdot R \cdot \sim$ ; $g$ is $\mathbf{w}$-compatible, extensive and idempotent; moreover, $\mathcal{C}_{ccs}$ being $\mathbf{s}$-compatible, $\mathcal{C}_{ccs}(\sim) \subseteq \sim$, and $\mathcal{C}_{ccs}$ is $g$-compatible. Hence, by Thm.1.19(iii), it suffices to show $\forall c \in C_i$, $\lfloor c \rfloor \overset{\mathbf{w}}{\rightsquigarrow} g \circ \mathcal{C}_{ccs}$.

Like previously, $\lfloor \mathbf{0} \rfloor \overset{\mathbf{w}}{\rightsquigarrow} \lfloor \mathbf{0} \rfloor$, $\lfloor | \rfloor \overset{\mathbf{w}}{\rightsquigarrow} \lfloor | \rfloor$, $\lfloor \alpha. \rfloor \overset{\mathbf{w}}{\rightsquigarrow} \mathrm{id}_{\mathcal{R}}$, and $\lfloor (\nu a) \rfloor \overset{\mathbf{w}}{\rightsquigarrow} \lfloor (\nu a) \rfloor$; we detail the case of the replication, for which we need the map $g$. Consider $R, S$ such that $R \rightarrowtail_{\mathbf{w}} S$, we have to show $\lfloor ! \rfloor(R) \rightarrowtail_{\mathbf{w}} \sim \cdot \mathcal{C}_{ccs}(S) \cdot \sim$. Suppose that $p \ R \ q$ and $!p \xrightarrow{\alpha} p'$; there are two cases:

- $p' = !p|p^k|p_0|p^{k'}$ with $p \xrightarrow{\alpha} p_0$ ($p^k$ denotes the parallel composition of $k$ copies of $p$). Since $R \overset{\mathbf{w}}{\rightsquigarrow} S$, we deduce $q \overset{\widehat{\alpha}}{\Rightarrow} q_0$ with $p_0 \ S \ q_0$. There are two cases:
  - $q \overset{\alpha}{\Rightarrow} q_0$, and we check that $!q \overset{\alpha}{\Rightarrow} q' = !q|q^k|q_0|q^{k'}$, where $p' \ \mathcal{C}_{ccs}(S) \ q'$.
  - $q = q_0$ (and $\alpha = \tau$), in that case, $!q$ cannot move, this is where we have reason modulo $\sim$: $!q \sim q' = !q|q^{k+1+k'}$, and $p' \ \mathcal{C}_{ccs}(S) \ q' \sim !q$.
- $p' = !p|p^k|p_0|p^{k'}|p_1|p^{k''}$ with $p \xrightarrow{a} p_0$ and $p \xrightarrow{\bar{a}} p_1$ ($\alpha = \tau$). Since $R \overset{\mathbf{w}}{\rightsquigarrow} S$, we deduce $q \overset{a}{\Rightarrow} q_0$ and $q \overset{\bar{a}}{\Rightarrow} q_1$ with $p_0 \ S \ q_0$ and $p_1 \ S \ q_1$. We check that $!q \overset{\tau}{\Rightarrow} q' = !q|q^k|q_0|q^{k'}|q_1|q^{k''}$, where $p' \ \mathcal{C}_{ccs}(S) \ q'$. ■

**A Negative Result.** Rather surprisingly, $\mathcal{C}_{ccs}$ is not $\mathbf{w}_t$-correct: a counterexample [16] is depicted on Fig. 3, where $R$ is not contained in $\mathbf{w}_t$-similarity while $R$ is a $(\mathbf{w}_t \circ \mathcal{C}_{ccs})$-simulation. The point is that $\lfloor | \rfloor \overset{\mathbf{w}_t}{\rightsquigarrow} \mathcal{C}_{ccs}$ does not hold: since parallel composition is able to "transform" two visible actions into a silent action, up to transitivity is brought from visible challenges – where it is allowed by $\mathbf{w}_t$, to silent challenges – where it is not

This shows that maps inducing the same fixpoint (recall that $\boldsymbol{\nu}\mathbf{w} = \boldsymbol{\nu}\mathbf{w}_t$) may define different sets of compatible or correct maps. At a pragmatic level, this reveals the existence of a trade-off between the ability to use up to context and up to transitivity. More importantly, it shows that from the point of view of up-to techniques, weak bisimilarity is different from "strong bisimilarity on the weak LTS ($\overset{\widehat{\alpha}}{\Rightarrow}$)": the relation $R$ from Fig. 3 also satisfies $\forall \alpha$, $\overset{\widehat{\alpha}}{\Leftarrow} \cdot R \subseteq \mathcal{C}_{ccs}(R)^\star \cdot \overset{\widehat{\alpha}}{\Leftarrow}$ .

## 4 Going Beyond Expansion: Termination Hypotheses

In recent work [14], we proved that we can use up to transitivity and go beyond expansion – even on silent challenges – provided that some termination hypotheses are satisfied. In this section, we generalise the most important of these techniques (that has actually been used in [12]), and show how to integrate it with previously defined techniques. We say that a relation $\succ$ *terminates* if there exists no infinite sequence $(p_i)_{i\in\mathbb{N}}$ such that $\forall i \in \mathbb{N},\ p_i \succ p_{i+1}$ .

**Theorem 4.1.** *Let $R, S$ be two relations; suppose that $S^+ \cdot \stackrel{\tau}{\Rightarrow}$ terminates.*

$$\textit{If } S \subseteq R \textit{ and } \begin{cases} \stackrel{\tau}{\leftarrow} \cdot R \subseteq S^\star \cdot R \cdot \stackrel{\hat{\tau}}{\Leftarrow} \\ \forall a \in \mathcal{L}^{\mathrm{v}},\ \stackrel{a}{\leftarrow} \cdot R \subseteq R^\star \cdot \stackrel{a}{\Leftarrow} \end{cases} \quad \textit{then} \quad R^\star \textit{ is a } \mathbf{w}\textit{-simulation.}$$

The proof is given in appendix; intuitively, this theorem allows reasoning up to transitivity, provided that the pairs used in transitivity position in silent challenges (those collected in relation $S$) satisfy a termination property. Restricted to the case $R = S \cup I$, this corresponds to [14, Thm. 3.13]. This generalisation, which may seem useless, makes the result much more tractable in practise: the termination requirement refers only to the part of $R$ that is actually used in silent challenges, to rewrite the left-hand-side process. Therefore, we can enlarge $R$ according to our need, without having to bother with the termination of $S^+ \cdot \stackrel{\tau}{\Rightarrow}$ . Notably, and unlike in [14], $S^\star$ is not required to be a $\mathbf{w}$-simulation by itself. Also remark that the termination requirement does not entail the termination of $S$ or $\stackrel{\tau}{\rightarrow}$, which makes it realistic in practise. An application, where this kind of requirement comes from the termination of $\stackrel{\tau}{\rightarrow}$ and the fact that $S$ does not interfere with the termination argument is described in [12].

In order to integrate this technique into our setting, we have to define a map that enforces the termination hypothesis. We achieve this by using an external relation that will satisfy the termination hypothesis: let $\succ$ be a transitive relation and define $t_\succ : R \mapsto (R \cap \succ)^\star \cdot R$.

**Corollary 4.2.** *If $\succ \cdot \stackrel{\tau}{\Rightarrow}$ terminates, then $t_\succ$ is $\mathbf{w}$- and $\mathbf{w}_t$-correct via $\mathrm{id}^\star_{\mathcal{R}}$.*

It, then suffices to establish the following (elementary) properties, so that we can combine this correct map with standard compatible maps, using Thm. 1.7.

**Lemma 4.3.** *Let $\mathcal{C}$ be a closure such that $\mathcal{C}(\succ) \subseteq \succ$, let $S$ be a reflexive relation. The maps $\mathcal{C}$, $R \mapsto S$ and $R \mapsto R \cdot S$ are $t_\succ$-compatible.*

**Theorem 4.4.** *Let $\mathcal{C}$ be a $\mathbf{w}$-compatible closure such that $\mathcal{C}(\succ) \subseteq \succ$. If $\succ \cdot \stackrel{\tau}{\Rightarrow}$ terminates, $R \mapsto ((\mathcal{C}(R) \cup \approx) \cap \succ)^\star \cdot \mathcal{C}(R) \cdot \approx$ is $\mathbf{w}$-correct via a symmetric map.*

This theorem also holds for $\mathbf{w}_t$; it is however unclear whether there are interesting $\mathbf{w}_t$-compatible closures, as explained in Sect. 3. We conclude by considering *elaboration* ($\gtrsim$) [2], which is another coinductively defined preorder contained in $\approx$. We have shown in [13] that this preorder can be used as an up-to technique for $\approx$, when $\stackrel{\tau}{\rightarrow}$ terminates. Using our theory, we can combine this result with up to context: if $\xrightarrow{\tau}$ terminates, so does $\gtrapprox \cdot \stackrel{\tau}{\Rightarrow}$ [13, Lemma 2.5]; we can moreover show that elaboration is a congruence w.r.t CCS contexts, so that $\gtrapprox$ naturally satisfies the requirements of Thm. 4.4.

**Corollary 4.5.** *In finite (replication free) CCS, map* $R \mapsto \gtrapprox \cdot \mathcal{C}_{ccs}(R) \cdot \approx$ *is* $\mathbf{w}$*-correct via a symmetric map.*

## 5 Related and Future Work

*Termination in the point-free setting.* We would like to investigate whether the presentation of the techniques exploiting termination arguments and well-founded induction (Sect. 4) can be lifted to the point-free setting of Sect. 2. Results from [4], in the setting of *relation algebras*, are really encouraging: terminating relations can be characterised at a point-free level, and this property can be related to corresponding well-founded induction principles. Notably, Newman's Lemma, whose proof uses the same ingredients as our proof of Lemma A.1 (e.g., diagram chasing and well-founded induction), can be proved at the corresponding abstraction level. Relation algebras are slightly more restrictive than our setting however: they require a completely distributive complete lattice (e.g., that arbitrary lubs distribute over arbitrary glbs) and a "modular identity law".

*Termination and contexts.* In order to use Théorème. 4.4 with a closure $(\mathcal{C})$, we have to check that relation $\succ$, which ensures the termination requirement $(\succ \cdot \stackrel{\tau}{\Rightarrow})$, is closed under $\mathcal{C}$ $(\mathcal{C}(\succ) \subseteq \succ)$. This hypothesis is automatically satisfied by elaboration, which is a pre-congruence; however, we would like to investigate more generally how to obtain such pre-congruences satisfying the termination requirement. This is a common question in rewriting theory; we plan to study whether tools from this domain (rewrite orders, dependency pairs, interpretations) can be adapted to our case, where the termination property is about the composition of the relation with silent transitions, rather than about the relation itself.

*Congruence properties.* In the case of sum-free CCS, which we studied in Sect. 3, bisimilarities are congruences w.r.t all contexts. Such situations are not so common in concurrency theory, where we often have to close bisimilarity under some contexts, in order to obtain a congruence [19,6]. Our setting seems well-suited to analyse such situations at a rather abstract level: given a closure $\mathcal{C}$, representing the congruence property to be satisfied, we can define its adjoint as the map $\mathcal{C}^\circ : x \mapsto \bigvee\{y \mid \mathcal{C}(y) \sqsubseteq x\}$. We have $\mathcal{C}^\circ \circ \mathcal{C} = \mathcal{C}$, $\mathcal{C} \circ \mathcal{C}^\circ = \mathcal{C}^\circ$, so that $\mathcal{C}(x) \sqsubseteq y$ iff $x \sqsubseteq \mathcal{C}^\circ(y)$; therefore, $\mathcal{C}^\circ$ maps any element $x$ to the largest congruence dominated by $x$. For example, $\mathcal{C}^\circ(\boldsymbol{\nu}\overleftrightarrow{\mathbf{w}})$ is the largest congruence contained in weak bisimilarity. Another standard approach consists in closing the relation under contexts, after each step of the bisimulation games; in doing so, we obtain *barbed congruence* [8,6], which is both a congruence, and a bisimulation. We can capture this approach by considering $\boldsymbol{\nu}\left(\overleftrightarrow{\mathbf{w}} \wedge \mathcal{C}^\circ\right)$. We would like to study whether up-to techniques can be developed in order to reduce the number of contexts to be considered in such cases, and to have a better understanding of the interactions between "game maps" like $\mathbf{w}$ and "congruent maps" like $\mathcal{C}^\circ$.

**Acknowledgements.** The author is very grateful to Daniel Hirschkoff and Davide Sangiorgi for helpful discussions and suggestions. Moreover, he would like to acknowledge Tom Hirschowitz for an initial idea which lead to Thm. 1.7.

## References

1. Arun-Kumar, S., Hennessy, M.: An efficiency preorder for processes. Acta Informatica 29(9), 737–760 (1992)
2. Arun-Kumar, S., Natarajan, V.: Conformance: A precongruence close to bisimilarity. In: Proc. Struct. in Concurrency Theory, Springer, London (1995)
3. Davey, B., Priestley, H.: Introduction to Lattices and Order. Cambridge University Press, Cambridge (1990)
4. Doornbos, H., Backhouse, R., van der Woude, J.: A calculational approach to mathematical induction. Theoretical Computer Science 179(1–2), 103–135 (1997)
5. Fournet, C., Lévy, J.-J., Schmitt, A.: An asynchronous, distributed implementation of mobile ambients. In: Watanabe, O., Hagiya, M., Ito, T., van Leeuwen, J., Mosses, P.D. (eds.) TCS 2000. LNCS, vol. 1872, pp. 348–364. Springer, Heidelberg (2000)
6. Fournet, C., Gonthier, G.: A hierarchy of equivalences for asynchronous calculi. Journal of Logic and Algebraic Programming 63(1), 131–173 (2005)
7. Hennessy, M., Rathke, J.: Typed behavioural equivalences for processes in the presence of subtyping. Math. Struct. in Computer Science 14(5), 651–684 (2004)
8. Honda, K., Yoshida, N.: Kohei Honda and Nobuka Yoshida. Theoretical Computer Science 151(2), 437–486 (1995)
9. Howe, D.J.: Proving congruence of bisimulation in functional programming languages. Information and Computation 124, 103–112 (1996)
10. Lassen, S.B.: Relational reasoning about contexts. In: Gordon, A.D., Pitts, A.M. (eds.) Higher Order Operational Techniques in Semantics, Cambridge University Press, Cambridge (1998)
11. Milner, R.: Communication and Concurrency. Prentice-Hall, Englewood Cliffs (1989)
12. Pous, D.: On bisimulation proofs for the analysis of distributed abstract machines. In: Montanari, U., Sannella, D. (eds.) Proc. TGC 2006. LNCS, vol. 4661, Springer, Heidelberg (2007)
13. Pous, D.: Weak bisimulation up to elaboration. In: Baier, C., Hermanns, H. (eds.) CONCUR 2006. LNCS, vol. 4137, pp. 390–405. Springer, Heidelberg (2006)
14. Pous, D.: New up-to techniques for weak bisimulation. In: Caires, L., Italiano, G.F., Monteiro, L., Palamidessi, C., Yung, M. (eds.) ICALP 2005. LNCS, vol. 3580, Springer, Heidelberg (2005)
15. Sangiorgi, D.: On the bisimulation proof method. Journal of Math. Struct. in Computer Science 8, 447–479 (1998)
16. Sangiorgi, D.: Personal communication (2006)
17. Sangiorgi, D., Kobayashi, N., Sumii, E.: Environmental bisimulations for higher-order languages. In: LICS 2007, pp. 293–302. IEEE Computer Society Press, Los Alamitos (2007)
18. Sangiorgi, D., Milner, R.: The problem of "weak bisimulation up to. In: Cleaveland, W.R. (ed.) CONCUR 1992. LNCS, vol. 630, pp. 32–46. Springer, Heidelberg (1992)
19. Sangiorgi, D., Walker, D.: The $\pi$-calculus: a Theory of Mobile Processes. Cambridge University Press, Cambridge (2001)
20. Tarski, A.: A lattice-theoretical fixpoint theorem and its applications. Pacific Journal of Mathematics 5(2), 285–309 (1955)

# A Proof of Theorem 4.1

We give the proof of Thm 4.1; this requires a technical lemma expressing the commutation property on which the technique relies.

**Lemma A.1.** *Let $R, S, \rightarrow$ and $\hookrightarrow$ be four relations. If $S \subseteq R$, and $S^+ \cdot \rightarrow^+$ terminates, then*

$$\begin{cases} \leftarrow \cdot R \subseteq S^\star \cdot R \cdot \leftarrow^\star & \text{(H)} \\ \hookleftarrow \cdot R \subseteq R^\star \cdot \hookleftarrow \cdot \leftarrow^\star & \text{(H}'\text{)} \end{cases} \quad \textit{entail} \quad \hookleftarrow \cdot \leftarrow^\star \cdot R^\star \subseteq R^\star \cdot \hookleftarrow \cdot \leftarrow^\star .$$

*Proof.* We actually prove $\hookleftarrow \cdot \leftarrow^\star \cdot R \subseteq R^\star \cdot \hookleftarrow \cdot \leftarrow^\star$, which leads to the desired result by a simple induction. We proceed by well-founded induction over $\langle \mathcal{P}, \mathbb{N} \rangle$, equipped with the lexicographic product of $\stackrel{\tau}{\Rightarrow} \cdot S^+$ and the standard ordering of natural numbers, which are two well-founded relations (the termination of $\stackrel{\tau}{\Rightarrow} \cdot S^+$ is equivalent to that of $S^+ \cdot \stackrel{\tau}{\Rightarrow}$). We use the predicate $\varphi(u, n)$:

"for any $p, p_0', q$, $u \rightarrow^\star p \rightarrow^n \cdot \hookrightarrow p_0'$ and $p \mathrel{R} q$ entail $p_0' \mathrel{R^\star} \cdot \hookleftarrow \cdot \leftarrow^\star q$."

- if $n = 0$, then $\varphi(u, n)$ holds by using the commutation hypothesis (H');
- otherwise, take $p_0$ such that $p \rightarrow p_0 \rightarrow^{n-1} \cdot \hookrightarrow p_0'$, and apply the first commutation hypothesis (H) to $p_0 \hookleftarrow \cdot \leftarrow p \mathrel{R} q$: there exist $k > 0$ and $p_1, \ldots, p_k$ such that $q \rightarrow^\star \cdot \hookrightarrow p_k$, $p_{k-1} \mathrel{R} p_k$ and $\forall i \in [1; k-1]$, $p_{i-1} \mathrel{S} p_i$.
  We now define by an internal induction a sequence $(p_i')_{0<i\leq k}$ such that we have $\forall i \in [1; k]$, $p_{i-1} \mathrel{R^\star} p_i' \hookleftarrow \cdot \leftarrow^\star p_i$.
  - if $i = 1$, we apply the external induction hypothesis: $\varphi(u, n-1)$, to $p_0' \hookleftarrow \cdot \leftarrow^{n-1} p_0 \mathrel{R} p_1$ (recall that $S \subseteq R$): there exists $p_1'$ such that $p_0' \mathrel{R^\star} p_1'$ and $p_1 \rightarrow^\star \cdot \hookrightarrow p_1'$.
  - otherwise, $i > 1$, we suppose that the sequence is constructed until $i - 1$, and we remark that $u \rightarrow^+ \cdot S^+ p_{i-1}$, so that we can obtain $p_i'$ by applying the external induction hypothesis, $\varphi(p_{i-1}, m_{i-1})$, to $p_{i-1}' \hookleftarrow \cdot \leftarrow^{m_{i-1}} p_{i-1} \mathrel{R} p_i$ ($m_{i-1}$ is the number of steps between $p_{i-1}$ and $p_{i-1}'$).

  We can conclude: we have $p_0' \mathrel{R^\star} p_k' \hookleftarrow \cdot \leftarrow^\star q$.
  This case of the proof is summed up below in a diagrammatic way:

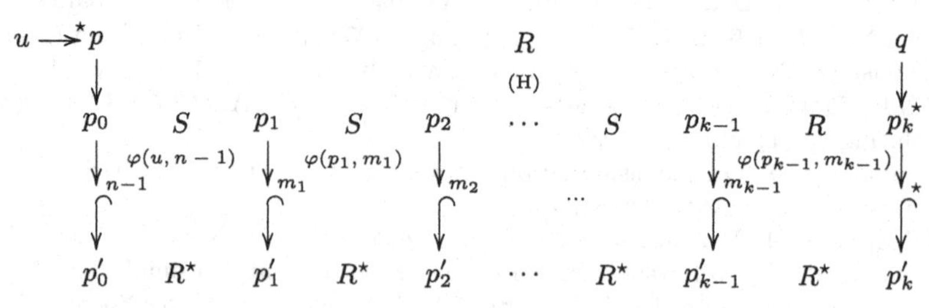


■

*Proof of Theorem 4.1.* We first apply Lemma A.1 with $\rightarrow = \stackrel{\tau}{\rightarrow}$ and $\hookrightarrow = I$, so that we obtain $\stackrel{\widehat{\tau}}{\Leftarrow} \cdot R^\star \subseteq R^\star \cdot \stackrel{\widehat{\tau}}{\Leftarrow}$ .

This leads to $\stackrel{\widehat{\tau}}{\Leftarrow} \cdot \stackrel{a}{\leftarrow} \cdot R \subseteq R^\star \cdot \stackrel{\widehat{a}}{\Leftarrow}$ , so that we can apply Lemma A.1 again, with $\rightarrow = \stackrel{\tau}{\rightarrow}$ and $\hookrightarrow = \stackrel{a}{\rightarrow} \cdot \stackrel{\widehat{\tau}}{\Rightarrow}$, to obtain $\stackrel{\widehat{a}}{\Leftarrow} \cdot R^\star \subseteq R^\star \cdot \stackrel{\widehat{a}}{\Leftarrow}$ . ■

# A Trace Based Bisimulation for the Spi Calculus: An Extended Abstract

Alwen Tiu

Computer Sciences Laboratory
Australian National University

**Abstract.** A notion of open bisimulation is formulated for the spi calculus, an extension of the $\pi$-calculus with cryptographic primitives. In this formulation, open bisimulation is indexed by pairs of symbolic traces, which represent the history of interactions between the environment with the pairs of processes being checked for bisimilarity. The use of symbolic traces allows for a symbolic treatment of bound input in bisimulation checking which avoids quantification over input values. Open bisimilarity is shown to be sound with respect to testing equivalence, and futher, it is shown to be an equivalence relation on processes and a congruence on finite processes.

## 1 Introduction

The spi-calculus [2] is an extension of the $\pi$-calculus [9] with crytographic primitives. This extension allows one to model cryptographic protocols and, via a notion of observational equivalence called *testing equivalence*, one can express security properties that a protocol satisfies. Testing equivalence is usually defined by quantifying the environment with which the processes interact: roughly, to show that two processes are testing equivalent, one shows that the two processes exhibit the same traces under arbitrary observers. As in the $\pi$-calculus, bisimulation techniques have been defined to check the observational equivalence of processes that avoids quantification over all possible observers. Unlike the $\pi$-calculus, in order to capture security notions such as secrecy, bisimulation in the spi-calculus needs to take into account the states of the environment (e.g., public networks) in its interaction with the processes being checked for equivalence. This gives rise to a more refined notion of equivalence of actions in the definition of bisimulation. In the $\pi$-calculus, to check whether two processes are bisimilar, one checks that an action by one process is matched by an equivalent action by the other process, and their continuations possess the same property. The differences between bisimulations for the $\pi$- and the spi-calculus lie in the interpretation of "equivalent actions". Consider the processes $P = (\nu x)\bar{a}\langle\{b\}_x\rangle.0$ and $Q = (\nu x)\bar{a}\langle\{c\}_x\rangle.0$. $P$ is a process that can output on channel $a$ a message $b$, encrypted with a fresh key $x$, and terminates, while $Q$ outputs a message $c$ encrypted with $x$ on the same channel. In the standard definitions of bisimulation for the $\pi$-calculus, e.g., late or early bisimulation [9], these two processes are not

Z. Shao (Ed.): APLAS 2007, LNCS 4807, pp. 367–382, 2007.

bisimilar since they perform (syntactically) distinct actions. In the spi-calculus, when one is concerned only with whether an intruder (in its interaction with $P$ and $Q$) can discover the message being encrypted, the two actions by $P$ and $Q$ are essentially equivalent; the intruder does not have access to the key $x$, hence cannot access the underlying messages.

Motivated by the above observation, different notions of bisimulation have been proposed, among others *framed bisimulation* [1], *environment-sensitive bisimulation* [4], *hedged bisimulation* [6], etc. (see [6] for a review on these bisimulations). All these notions of bisimulation share a similarity in that they are all indexed by some sort of structure representing the "knowledge" of the environment. This structure is called differently from one definition to another. We shall use the rather generic term *observer theory*, or *theory* for short, to refer to the knowledge structure used in this paper, which is just a finite set of pairs of messages. A theory represents the pairs of messages that are obtained through the interaction between the environment (observer) and the pairs of processes in the bisimulation set. The pairs of messages in the theory represent equivalent messages, from the point of view of the observer. This observer theory is then used as a theory in a deductive system for deducing messages (or actions) equivalence. Under this theory, equivalent messages need not be syntactically equivalent.

A main difficulty in bisimulation checking for spi-processes is in dealing with the input actions of the processes, where one needs to check that the processes are bisimilar for all equivalent pairs of input messages. One way of dealing with the infinite quantification is through a symbolic technique where one delays the instantiations of input values until they are needed. This technique has been applied to hedged bisimulation by Borgström et al.[5]. Their work on symbolic bisimulation for the spi-calculus is, however, mainly concerned with obtaining a sound approximation of hedged bisimulation, and less with studying meta-level properties of the symbolic bisimulation as an equivalence relation. *Open bisimulation* [10], on the other hand, makes use of the symbolic handling of input values, while at the same time maintains interesting meta-level properties, such as being a congruence relation on processes. Open bisimulation has so far been studied for the $\pi$-calculus and its extension to the spi-calculus has not been fully understood. There is a recent attempt at formulating an open-style bisimulation for the spi-calculus [8], which is shown to be sound with respect to hedged bisimulation. However, no congruence results have been obtained for this notion of open bisimulation. We propose a different formulation of open bisimulation, which is inspired by hedged bisimulation. A collection of *up-to techniques* are defined, and shown to be sound. These up-to techniques can be used to finitely check the bisimilarity of processes in some cases and, more importantly, they are used to show that open bisimilarity is a congruence on finite spi-processes. The latter allows for compositional reasoning about open bisimilarity.

A crucial part in theories of environment-sensitive bisimulation is that of the consistency of the observer theory. A consistent theory guarantees that the induced equality on messages satisfies the usual axioms of equality, most importantly, transitivity. A difficulty in formulating open bisimulation is in finding a good symbolic representation of observer theories. One needs to make sure that the symbolic observer theories in the bisimulation set can be properly instantiated to consistent theories. The symbolic representation of observer theories used in this paper is based on Boreale's *symbolic traces* [3]. A symbolic trace is a compact representation of a set of traces of a process, where the input values are represented by parameters (which are essentially names). Associated with a symbolic trace is a notion of consistency, i.e., it should be possible to instantiate the symbolic trace to a set of concrete traces. The definition of open bisimulation in Section 4 is indexed by pairs of symbolic traces, called *bi-traces.* A symbolic trace is essentially a list, and the position of a particular name in the list constraints its possible instantiations. In this sense, its position in the list enforces an implicit scoping of the name. Bi-traces are essentially observer theories with added structures. The notion of consistency of bi-traces is therefore based on the notion of consistency for observer theories, with the added constraint on the possible instantiations of names in the bi-traces. The latter gives rise to the notion of respectful substitutions, much like the same notion that appears in the definition of open bisimulation for the $\pi$-calculus.

A good definition of open bisimulation for the spi-calculus should naturally address the issue of name distinction. As in the definition of open bisimulation for the $\pi$-calculus, the fresh names extruded by a bound output action of a process should be considered distinct from all other pre-existing names. We employ a syntactic device to encode this distinction implicitly. We extend the language of processes with a countably infinite set of *rigid names.* Rigid names are not subject to instantiations and therefore cannot be identified by substitutions. Note that it is possible to formulate open bisimulation without the use of rigid names, at a price of an added complexity. The role of rigid names will be clear when we discuss open bisimulation in Section 4.

*Outline of the paper.* Section 2 reviews some notations and the operational semantics for the spi-calculus. Section 3 presents the notion of observer theories along with its properties. Section 4 defines the bi-trace structure and open bisimulation, and states its soundness with respect to testing equivalence. Section 5 defines several up-to techniques for open bisimulation. The main purpose of these techniques is to show that open bisimilarity is closed under parallel composition and respectful substitutions, from which the soundness of open bisimulation and its congruence results follow. Section 6 shows that open bisimilarity is an equivalence relation on processes and also a congruence relation on finite spi-processes without rigid names. Section 7 concludes the paper and outlines some directions for future work. The detailed proofs are omitted but they can be found in the extended version of the paper [11].

## 2 The Spi Calculus

In this section we review the syntax and the operational semantics for the spi-calculus, following its original presentation as in [2]. We consider a more restricted language, i.e., the one with only the pairing and encryption operators.

We assume that the reader has some familiarity with the spi-calculus, so the meaning of various constructs of the calculus will not be explained in detail.

We assume a denumerable set of names, denoted with $\mathcal{N}$. We use $m$, $n$, $x$, $y$, and $z$ to range over names. In order to simplify the presentation of open bisimulation, we introduce another infinite set of names which we call *rigid names*, denoted with $\mathcal{RN}$, which are assumed to be of a distinct syntactic category from names. Rigid names are a purely syntactic device to simplify presentation. It can be thought of as names which are created when restricted names in processes are extruded in their transitions. Rigid names embody a notion of *distinction*, as in open bisimulation for the $\pi$-calculus [10], in the sense that they cannot be instantiated, thus cannot be identified with other rigid names. Rigid names are ranged over by bold lower-case letters, e.g., as in **a**, **b**, **c**, etc.

Messages in the spi calculus are given by the following grammar:

$$M, N ::= x \mid \mathbf{a} \mid \langle M, N \rangle \mid \{M\}_N$$

where $\langle M, N \rangle$ denotes a pair consisting of messages $M$ and $N$, and $\{M\}_N$ denotes the message $M$ encrypted with the key $N$. The set of processes is defined by the grammar:

$$\begin{array}{rl} P, Q, R ::= & 0 \mid \bar{M}\langle N \rangle.P \mid M(x).P \mid P|Q \mid (\nu x)P \mid\ !P \\ & \mid\ [M = N]P \mid \text{let } \langle x, y \rangle = M \text{ in } P \mid \text{case } L \text{ of } \{x\}_N \text{ in } P \end{array}$$

The names $x$ and $y$ in the restriction, the 'let' and the 'case' constructs are binding occurences. We assume the usual $\alpha$-equivalence on process expressions. Given a syntactic expression $E$, e.g., a process, a set of process, pairs, etc., we write $\mathrm{fn}(E)$ to denote the set of free names in $E$. Likewise, $\mathrm{rn}(E)$ denote the set of rigid names in $E$. We call a process $P$ *pure* if there are no occurrences of rigid names in $P$.

*A substitution* is a mapping from names to messages. Substitutions are ranged over by $\theta$, $\sigma$ and $\rho$. The domain of substitutions is defined as $\mathrm{dom}(\theta) = \{x \mid \theta(x) \neq x\}$. We consider only substitutions with finite domains. The substitution with empty domain is denoted by $\epsilon$. We often enumerate the mappings of a substitution on its finite domain, using the notation $[M_1/x_1, \cdots, M_n/x_n]$. Substitutions are generalised straightforwardly to mappings between terms (processes, messages, etc.), with the usual proviso that the free names in the substitutions do not become bound as a result of the applications of the substitutions. Applications of substitutions to terms (processes or messages) are written in postfix notation, e.g., as in $M\theta$. Composition of two substitutions $\theta$ and $\sigma$, written $(\theta \circ \sigma)$, is defined as follows: $M(\theta \circ \sigma) = (M\theta)\sigma$. Given a substitution $\theta$ and a finite set of names $V$, we denote with $\theta_{\restriction V}$ the substitution which coincides with $\theta$ on the set $V$, and is the identity map everywhere else.

We use the operational semantics of the spi calculus as it is given in [1], with one small modification: we allow communication channels to be arbitrary messages, instead of just names. We do this in order to get a simpler formulation of open bisimulation in Section 4, since we do not need to keep track of certain constraints related to channel names.

$$\frac{}{M(x).P \xrightarrow{M} (x)P} \qquad \frac{}{\bar{M}\langle N\rangle.P \xrightarrow{\overline{M}} \langle N\rangle P} \qquad \frac{P > Q \quad Q \xrightarrow{\alpha} A}{P \xrightarrow{\alpha} A} \qquad \frac{P \xrightarrow{\alpha} A}{P \mid Q \xrightarrow{\alpha} A \mid Q}$$

$$\frac{P \xrightarrow{M} F \quad Q \xrightarrow{\overline{M}} C}{P \mid Q \xrightarrow{\tau} F@C} \qquad \frac{Q \xrightarrow{\overline{N}} C \quad P \xrightarrow{N} F}{P \mid Q \xrightarrow{\tau} C@F} \qquad \frac{Q \xrightarrow{\alpha} A}{P \mid Q \xrightarrow{\alpha} P \mid A} \qquad \frac{P \xrightarrow{\alpha} A \quad m \notin \mathrm{fn}(\alpha)}{(\nu m)P \xrightarrow{\alpha} (\nu m)A}$$

**Fig. 1.** The operational semantics of the spi calculus

The one-step transition relations are not relating processes with processes, rather processes with *agents*. The latter is presented using the notion of *abstraction* and *concretion* of processes. Abstractions are expressions of the form $(x)P$ where $P$ is a process and the construct $(x)$ binds free occurences of $x$ in $P$, and concretions are expressions of the form $(\nu\vec{x})\langle M\rangle P$ where $M$ is a message and $P$ is a process. Agents are ranged over by $A$, $B$ and $C$. As with processes, we call an agent $A$ *pure* if $\mathrm{rn}(A) = \emptyset$.

To simplify the presentation of the operational semantics, we define compositions between processes and agents as follows. In the definition below we assume that $x \notin \{\vec{y}, z\} \cup \mathrm{fn}(R)$ and $\{\vec{y}\} \cap \mathrm{fn}(R) = \emptyset$.

$$(\nu x)(z)P \triangleq (z)(\nu x)P, \qquad R \mid (x)P \triangleq (x)(R \mid P),$$
$$(\nu x)(\nu\vec{y})\langle M\rangle Q \triangleq (\nu x, \vec{y})\langle M\rangle Q, \text{ if } x \in \mathrm{fn}(M)$$
$$(\nu x)(\nu\vec{y})\langle M\rangle Q \triangleq (\nu\vec{y})\langle M\rangle(\nu x)Q, \text{ if } x \notin \mathrm{fn}(M)$$
$$R \mid (\nu\vec{y})\langle M\rangle Q \triangleq (\nu\vec{y})\langle M\rangle(R \mid Q)$$

The dual composition $A \mid R$ is defined symmetrically.

Given an abstraction $F = (x)P$ and a concretion $(\nu\vec{y})\langle M\rangle Q$, where $\{\vec{y}\} \cap \mathrm{fn}(P) = \emptyset$, the *interactions* of $F$ and $C$ are defined as follows.

$$F@C \triangleq (\nu\vec{y})(P[M/x] \mid Q) \qquad C@F \triangleq (\nu\vec{y})(Q \mid P[M/x])$$

We define a reduction relation $>$ on processes as follows:

$$!P > P \mid !P \qquad \text{let } \langle x, y\rangle = \langle M, N\rangle \text{ in } P > P[M/x][N/y]$$
$$[M = M]P > P \qquad \text{case } \{M\}_N \text{ of } \{x\}_N \text{ in } P > P[M/x]$$

The operational semantics of the spi calculus is given in Figure 1. The action $\alpha$ can be either the silent action $\tau$, a term $M$, or a *co-term* $\overline{M}$, where $M$ is a term. We note that as far as the operational semantics is concerned, there is no distinction between a name and a rigid name; both can be used as channel names and as messages.

*Testing equivalence.* In order to define testing equivalence, we first define the notion of a *barb*. A barb is an input or an output channel on which a process can communicate. We assume that barbs contain no rigid names. We denote the reflexive-transitive closure of the silent transition $\xrightarrow{\tau}$ with $\xrightarrow{\tau}{}^*$.

**Definition 1.** *Two pure processes $P$ and $Q$ are said to be* testing equivalent, *written $P \sim Q$, when for every pure process $R$ and every barb $\beta$, if*

$$P \mid R \xrightarrow{\tau}{}^{*} P' \xrightarrow{\beta} A$$

*for some $P'$ and $A$, then $Q \mid R \xrightarrow{\tau}{}^{*} Q' \xrightarrow{\beta} B$ for some $Q'$ and $B$, and vice versa.*

Notice that testing equivalence is defined for pure processes only, therefore our definition of testing equivalence coincides with that in [2].

## 3 Observer Theory

An *observer theory* is just a finite set of pairs of messages. These pairs of messages denote the pairs of indistinguishable messages from the observer point of view. We adopt the convention that *all* names are entities known to the observer. Rigid names, on the other hand, may or may not be known to the observer, depending on whether they are present in the observer theory.

Associated with an observer theory are certain proof systems representing the deductive capability of the observer. These proof systems allow for derivation of new knowledge from existing ones. Observer theories are ranged over by $\Gamma$ and $\Delta$. We often refer to observer theory simply as *theory*. Given a theory $\Gamma$, we write $\pi_1(\Gamma)$ to denote the set $\{M \mid \exists N.(M,N) \in \Gamma\}$, and likewise, $\pi_2(\Gamma)$ to denote the set $\{N \mid \exists M.(M,N) \in \Gamma\}$. The observer can encrypt and decrypt messages it has in order to either analyze or syntesize messages to deduce the equality of messages. This deductive capability is presented as a proof system in Figure 2. This proof system is a straightforward adaptation of the standard proof systems for message analysis and synthesis, usually presented in a natural-deduction style, e.g., as found in [3], to sequent calculus. We find sequent calculus a more natural setting to prove various properties of observer theories. The sequent $\Gamma \vdash M \leftrightarrow N$ means that the messages $M$ and $N$ are indistinguishable in the theory $\Gamma$. We shall often write $\Gamma \vdash M \leftrightarrow N$ to mean that the sequent $\Gamma \vdash M \leftrightarrow N$ is derivable using the rules in Figure 2. Notice that in the proof system in Figure 2, two names are indistinguishable if they are syntactically equal. This reflects the fact that names are entities known to the observer.

It is useful to consider the set of messages that can be constructed by an observer in its interaction with a particular process. This synthesis of messages follows the inference rules given in Figure 3. The symbol $\Sigma$ denotes a finite set of messages. We overload the symbols $\vdash$ and $\vdash$ to denote, respectively, sequents and derivability relation of messages given a set of messages. The rules for message synthesis are just a projection of the rules for message equivalence.

A nice feature of the sequent calculus formulation is that in any derivation of a judgment, every judgment in the derivation contains only subterms occuring in the judgment at the root of the derivation tree. This gives us immediately a bound on the depth of the derivation tree, hence the decidability of the proof systems.

$$\frac{x \in \mathcal{N}}{\Gamma \vdash x \leftrightarrow x}\ var \qquad \frac{}{\Gamma, (M, N) \vdash M \leftrightarrow N}\ id \qquad \frac{\Gamma \vdash M \leftrightarrow M' \quad \Gamma \vdash N \leftrightarrow N'}{\Gamma \vdash \langle M, N\rangle \leftrightarrow \langle M', N'\rangle}\ pr$$

$$\frac{\Gamma, (\langle M_1, N_1\rangle, \langle M_2, N_2\rangle), (M_1, M_2), (N_1, N_2) \vdash M \leftrightarrow N}{\Gamma, (\langle M_1, N_1\rangle, \langle M_2, N_2\rangle) \vdash M \leftrightarrow N}\ pl$$

$$\frac{\Gamma \vdash M \leftrightarrow M' \quad \Gamma \vdash N \leftrightarrow N'}{\Gamma \vdash \{M\}_N \leftrightarrow \{M'\}_{N'}}\ er$$

$$\frac{\Gamma' \vdash N_1 \leftrightarrow N_2 \quad \Gamma', (M_1, M_2), (N_1, N_2) \vdash M \leftrightarrow N}{\Gamma, (\{M_1\}_{N_1}, \{M_2\}_{N_2}) \vdash M \leftrightarrow N}\ el$$

**Fig. 2.** Proof system for deriving message equivalence. In the rule *el*, $\Gamma'$ is the set $\Gamma \cup \{(\{M_1\}_{N_1}, \{M_2\}_{N_2})\}$.

$$\frac{x \in \mathcal{N}}{\Sigma \vdash x}\ var \qquad \frac{}{\Sigma, M \vdash M}\ id \qquad \frac{\Sigma \vdash M \quad \Sigma \vdash N}{\Sigma \vdash \langle M, N\rangle}\ pr \qquad \frac{\Sigma \vdash M \quad \Sigma \vdash N}{\Sigma \vdash \{M\}_N}\ er$$

$$\frac{\Sigma, \langle M, N\rangle, M, N \vdash R}{\Sigma, \langle M, N\rangle \vdash R}\ pl \qquad \frac{\Sigma, \{M\}_N \vdash N \quad \Sigma, \{M\}_N, M, N \vdash R}{\Sigma, \{M\}_N \vdash R}\ el$$

**Fig. 3.** Proof system for message synthesis

**Proposition 2.** *Given any $\Gamma$, $\Sigma$, $M$ and $N$, it is decidable whether the judgments $\Gamma \vdash M \leftrightarrow N$ and $\Sigma \vdash M$ hold.*

*Consistency of observer theory.* Recall that the motivation behind the notion of message equivalence $\leftrightarrow$ is for it to replace syntactic equality in the definition of bisimulation. Since the relation $\leftrightarrow$ is parameterised upon an observer theory, we shall investigate under what conditions an observer theory gives rise to a well-behaved relation $\leftrightarrow$ . In the literature of bisimulation for the spi calculus, this notion is usually referred to as the *consistency* property of observer theories. We define an abstract notion of theory consistency, based on the entailment relation $\vdash$ defined previously. We later show that this abstract notion of consistency is equivalent to a more concrete one which is finitely checkable.

**Definition 3.** *A theory $\Gamma$ is* consistent *if for every $M$ and $N$, if $\Gamma \vdash M \leftrightarrow N$ then the following hold:*

1. *$M$ and $N$ are of the same type of expressions, i.e., $M$ is a pair (an encrypted message, a (rigid) name) if and only if $N$ is.*
2. *If $M = \{M_1\}_{M_2}$ and $N = \{N_1\}_{N_2}$ then $\pi_1(\Gamma) \vdash M_2$ implies $\Gamma \vdash M_2 \leftrightarrow N_2$ and $\pi_2(\Gamma) \vdash N_2$ implies $\Gamma \vdash M_2 \leftrightarrow N_2$.*
3. *For any $R$, $\Gamma \vdash M \leftrightarrow R$ implies $R = N$ and $\Gamma \vdash R \leftrightarrow N$ implies $R = M$.*

The first condition in Definition 3 states that the equality relation $\leftrightarrow$ respects types, i.e., it is not possible that an operation (pairing, encryption) on $M$ succeeds while the same operation on $N$ fails. The second condition states that both projections of the theory contain "equal" amount of knowledge, e.g., it is not possible that one message decrypts while the other fails to. The third condition states the unicity of $\leftrightarrow$ .

*Characterisation of consistent theories.* The notion of consistency as defined in Definition 3 is not obvious to check since it involves quantification over all equivalent pairs of messages. We show that a theory can be reduced to a certain normal form for which there exist finitely checkable properties that entail consistency of the original theory. For this purpose, we define a rewrite relation on theories.

**Definition 4.** *The rewrite relation $\longrightarrow$ on observer theories is defined as follows:*

$$\begin{aligned} \Gamma, (\langle M, N\rangle, \langle M', N'\rangle) &\longrightarrow \Gamma, (M, M'), (N, N') \\ \Gamma, (\{M\}_N, \{M'\}_{N'}) &\longrightarrow \Gamma, (M, M'), (N, N') \\ & \quad \text{if } \Gamma, (\{M\}_N, \{M'\}_{N'}) \vdash N \leftrightarrow N'. \end{aligned}$$

*A theory $\Gamma$ is* irreducible *if $\Gamma$ cannot be rewritten to any other theory. $\Gamma$ is an irreducible form of another theory $\Gamma'$ if $\Gamma$ is irreducible and $\Gamma' \longrightarrow^* \Gamma$.*

The rewrite relation on theories defined above can be shown to be terminating and confluent, hence every theory $\Gamma$ has a unique irreducible form, which we denote here with $\Gamma\Downarrow$ . Moreover, the reduction can be shown to preserve consistency. Therefore to check the consistency of a theory, it is enough to check its irreducible form.

**Proposition 5.** *A theory $\Gamma$ is consistent if and only if $\Gamma\Downarrow$ satisfies the following conditions: if $(M, N) \in \Gamma\Downarrow$ then*

**(a)** *$M$ and $N$ are of the same type of expressions,*
**(b)** *if $M = \{M_1\}_{M_2}$ and $N = \{N_1\}_{N_2}$ then $\pi_1(\Gamma\Downarrow) \not\vdash M_2$ and $\pi_2(\Gamma\Downarrow) \not\vdash N_2$.*
**(c)** *for any $(U, V) \in \Gamma\Downarrow$, $U = M$ if and only if $V = N$.*

*Closure under substitutions.* The entailment relation $\vdash$ is in general not closed under arbitrary substitutions, the reason being the inclusion of the *var*-rule. Using this rule, we can prove, for instance, $\emptyset \vdash x \leftrightarrow x$. Now if we substitute **a** for $x$, where **a** is some rigid name, we do not have $\emptyset \vdash \mathbf{a} \leftrightarrow \mathbf{a}$, since the *var*-rule does not apply to rigid names.

We shall often work with substitution pairs in the following sections. Application of a substitution pair $\vec{\theta} = (\theta_1, \theta_2)$ to a pair of terms $(M, N)$ is defined to be $(M\theta_1, N\theta_2)$. This extends straightforwardly to application of substitution pairs to sets or lists of pairs. The following lemma gives a class of substitutions under which the entailment relation is preserved.

**Lemma 6.** *Let $\Gamma \vdash M \leftrightarrow N$ and let $\vec{\theta} = (\theta_1, \theta_2)$ be a substitution pair such that for all $x \in fn(\Gamma, M, N)$ it holds that $\Gamma\vec{\theta} \vdash \theta_1(x) \leftrightarrow \theta_2(x)$. Then $\Gamma\vec{\theta} \vdash M\theta_1 \leftrightarrow N\theta_2$.*

## 4 Open Bisimulation

Open bisimulation for the spi-calculus to be presented in this section is similar to other environment-sensitive bisimulations, in the sense that it is also indexed by some structure representing the knowledge of the environment. A candidate for representing this knowledge is the observer theory presented earlier. However, since the crucial feature of open bisimulation is the symbolic representation of input values, extra structures need to be added to observer theories to capture dependencies between various symbolic input values at different stages of bisimulation checking. The notion of *symbolic traces* as defined in [3] conveniently captures this sort of dependency. Open bisimulation is indexed by pairs of a variant of symbolic traces, called *bi-traces*. The important properties we need to establish regarding bi-traces are that they can be soundly interpreted as observer theories, and they behave well with respect to substitutions of input values.

In the following, we use the notation $[x_1, \ldots, x_n]$ to denote a list whose elements are $x_1, \ldots, x_n$. The empty list is denoted by $[]$. Concatenation of a list $l_1$ with another list $l_2$ is denoted with $l_1.l_2$, if $l_2$ is appended to the end of $l_1$. If $l_2$ is a singleton list, say $[x]$, then we write $l_1.x$ instead of $l_1.[x]$, likewise $x.l_1$ instead of $[x].l_1$.

**Definition 7.** *An* I/O pair *is a pair of messages marked with* $i$ *(indicating input) or* $o$ *(indicating output), i.e., it is of the form* $(M, N)^i$ *or* $(M, N)^o$*. A* bi-trace *is a* list *of I/O message pairs, ranged over by* $h$*. We denote with* $\pi_1(h)$ *the list obtained from* $h$ *by taking the first components of the pairs in* $h$*. The list* $\pi_2(h)$ *is defined analogously. Bi-traces are subject to the following restriction: if* $h = h_1.(M, N)^o.h_2$ *then* $fn(M, N) \subseteq fn(h_1)$*. If* $h$ *is* $[(M_1, N_1)^{l_1}, \ldots, (M_k, N_k)^{l_k}]$ *then the* inverse *of* $h$*, written* $h^{-1}$*, is the list* $[(N_1, M_1)^{l_1}, \ldots, (N_k, M_k)^{l_k}]$*. We write* $\{h\}$ *to denote the set* $\{(M, N) \mid (M, N)^i \in h \text{ or } (M, N)^o \in h\}$*.*

The underlying idea in the bi-trace representation is that *names are symbolic values.* This explains the requirement that the free names of an output pair in a bi-trace must appear before the output pair. In other words, input values (i.e., names) are created only at input pairs.

Given a bi-trace $h$, the underlying set $\{h\}$ is obviously an observer theory, hence bi-traces are essentially theories with added structures. As in symbolic traces [3], bi-traces consistency needs to take into account the fact that their instantiations correspond to concrete traces. Consistency conditions for bi-traces are more complicated since we need extra conditions ensuring the consistency of the underlying observer theory. We first define a notion of respectful substitutions for bi-traces, which is later used to define the notion of consistency for bi-traces. In the following we shall write $h \vdash M \leftrightarrow N$, instead of a more type-correct version $\{h\} \vdash M \leftrightarrow N$, when we consider an equivalent pair of messages under the theory obtained from a bi-trace $h$. Application of a substitution pair $(\theta_1, \theta_2)$ to a bi-trace is defined element-wise in a straightforward way.

**Definition 8.** *A substitution pair* $\vec{\theta} = (\theta_1, \theta_2)$ respects *a bi-trace* $h$ *if whenever* $h = h_1.(M, N)^i.h_2$*, then for every* $x \in fn(M, N)$ *it holds that* $h_1\vec{\theta} \vdash x\theta_1 \leftrightarrow x\theta_2$*.*

**Definition 9.** *We define the notion of* consistent bi-traces *inductively on the length of bi-traces as follows:*

1. *The empty bi-trace is consistent.*
2. *If $h$ is a consistent bi-trace then $h.(M,N)^i$ is also a consistent bi-trace, provided that $h \vdash M \leftrightarrow N$.*
3. *If $h$ is a consistent bi-trace, then $h' = h.(M,N)^o$ is a consistent bi-trace, provided that for every $h$-respectful substitution pair $\vec{\theta}$, if $h\vec{\theta}$ is a consistent bi-trace then $\{h'\vec{\theta}\}$ is a consistent theory.*

The requirement that every input pair be deducible from its predecessors in the bi-trace captures the dependency of the names of the input pair on their preceding input/output pairs. At this point, it is instructive to examine the case where the elements of bi-traces are pairs of names or rigid names. Consider for example the bi-trace $(x,x)^i.(\mathbf{a},\mathbf{a})^o.(y,y)^i.(\mathbf{b},\mathbf{b})^o$. There is a respectful substitution that identifies $x$ and $y$, or $y$ with $\mathbf{a}$, but there are no respectful substitutions that identify $x$ with $\mathbf{a}$, $y$ with $\mathbf{b}$ nor $\mathbf{a}$ with $\mathbf{b}$. Thus this bi-trace captures a restricted notion of distinction [10]. Rigid names encode an implicit distinction: no two rigid names can be identified by substitutions, whereas the position of names encode their respective scopes.

Note that in item (3) in Definition 9, we quantify over all respectful substitutions. This is unfortunate from the viewpoint of bisimulation checking but it is unavoidable if we want the notion of consistency to be closed under respectful substitutions. Consider the bi-trace:

$$(\mathbf{a},\mathbf{a})^o.(\mathbf{b},\mathbf{b})^o.(x,x)^i.(\{x\}_\mathbf{k},\{\mathbf{a}\}_\mathbf{k})^o.(\{\mathbf{b}\}_\mathbf{k},\{x\}_\mathbf{k})^o.$$

If we drop the quantification on respectful substitutions, then this trace would be considered consistent. Under the respectful substitution pair $([\mathbf{b}/x],[\mathbf{b}/x])$, however, the above bi-trace becomes

$$(\mathbf{a},\mathbf{a})^o.(\mathbf{b},\mathbf{b})^o.(\mathbf{b},\mathbf{b})^i.(\{\mathbf{b}\}_\mathbf{k},\{\mathbf{a}\}_\mathbf{k})^o.(\{\mathbf{b}\}_\mathbf{k},\{\mathbf{b}\}_\mathbf{k})^o$$

which gives rise to an inconsistent theory.

**Definition 10.** *A* traced process pair *is a triple $(h,P,Q)$ where $h$ is a bi-trace, $P$ and $Q$ are processes such that fn$(P,Q) \subseteq$ fn$(h)$. Let $\mathcal{R}$ be a set of traced process pairs. We write $h \vdash P\ \mathcal{R}\ Q$ to denote the fact that $(h,P,Q) \in \mathcal{R}$. $\mathcal{R}$ is consistent if for every $h \vdash P\ \mathcal{R}\ Q$, $h$ is consistent. The inverse of $\mathcal{R}$, written $\mathcal{R}^{-1}$, is the set $\{(h^{-1},Q,P) \mid (h,P,Q) \in \mathcal{R}\}$. $\mathcal{R}$ is* symmetric *if $\mathcal{R} = \mathcal{R}^{-1}$.*

**Definition 11.** *A bi-trace $h$ is called a* universal bi-trace *if $h$ consists only of input-pairs of names, i.e., it is of the form $(x_1,x_1)^i.\cdots.(x_n,x_n)^i$, where each $x_i$ is a name.*

**Definition 12.** Open bisimulation. *A set of traced process pairs $\mathcal{R}$ is a* strong open bisimulation *if $\mathcal{R}$ is consistent and symmetric, and if $h \vdash P\ \mathcal{R}\ Q$ then for all substitution pair $\vec{\theta} = (\theta_1,\theta_2)$ that respects $h$, the following hold:*

1. *If* $P\theta_1 \xrightarrow{\tau} P'$ *then there exists* $Q'$ *such that* $Q\theta_2 \xrightarrow{\tau} Q'$ *and* $h\vec{\theta} \vdash P' \mathcal{R} Q'$.
2. *If* $P\theta_1 \xrightarrow{M} (x)P'$, *where* $x \notin fn(h\vec{\theta})$, *and* $\pi_1(h\vec{\theta}) \vdash M$ *then there exists* $Q'$ *such that* $Q\theta_2 \xrightarrow{N} (x)Q'$ *and* $h\vec{\theta}.(M,N)^i.(x,x)^i \vdash P' \mathcal{R} Q'$.
3. *If* $P\theta_1 \xrightarrow{\bar{M}} (\nu\vec{x})\langle M'\rangle P'$, *and* $\pi_1(h\vec{\theta}) \vdash M$ *then there exist* $N$, $N'$ *and* $Q'$ *such that* $Q\theta_2 \xrightarrow{\bar{N}} (\nu\vec{y})\langle N'\rangle Q'$, *and*

$$h\vec{\theta}.(M,N)^i.(M'[\vec{\mathbf{c}}/\vec{x}], N'[\vec{\mathbf{d}}/\vec{y}])^o \vdash P'[\vec{\mathbf{c}}/\vec{x}] \mathcal{R} Q'[\vec{\mathbf{d}}/\vec{y}],$$

*where* $\{\vec{\mathbf{c}}, \vec{\mathbf{d}}\} \cap rn(h\vec{\theta}, P\theta_1, Q\theta_2) = \emptyset$.

*We denote with* $\approx_o$ *the union of all open bisimulations. We say that* $P$ *and* $Q$ *are* strong open $h$-bisimilar, *written* $P \sim_o^h Q$, *if* $(h, P, Q) \in \approx_o$. *They are said to be* strong open bisimilar, *written* $P \sim_o Q$, *if* $rn(P,Q) = \emptyset$ *and* $P \sim_o^h Q$ *for a universal bi-trace* $h$.

Notice that in the bound output case, the restricted names in the concretions are replaced by fresh rigid names. Notice also that strong open bisimilarity $\sim_o$ is defined on pure processes, i.e., those processes without free occurrences of rigid names. We now show that open bisimilarity is sound with respect to testing equivalence. Its proof follows straightforwardly from the fact that open bisimilarity is closed under parallel composition (see Section 5 and Section 6).

**Theorem 13.** Soundness. *If* $P \sim_o Q$ *then* $P \sim Q$.

## 5 Up-To Techniques

We define several up-to techniques for open bisimulation. The main purpose of these techniques is to prove congruence results for open bisimilarity, in particular, closure under parallel composition, and to prove soundness of open bisimilarity with respect to testing equivalence. Up-to techniques are also useful in checking bisimulation since in certain cases it allows one to finitely demonstrate bisimilarity of processes. The proof techniques used in this section derive mainly from the work of Boreale et al. [4]. We first need to introduce several notions, parallel to those in [4], and adapting their up-to techniques to open bisimulation.

Open bisimilarity for the spi-calculus is not closed under parallel composition with arbitrary processes, since these extra processes might introduce inconsistency into the observer theory or may reveal other knowledge that causes the composed processes to behave differently. Therefore, in defining closure under parallel composition, we need to make sure that the processes we are composing with do not reveal or add any extra information for the observer. This is done by restricting the composition to processes obtained by instantiating pure processes with the current knowledge of the observer. This is defined via a notion of equivalent substitutions.

**Definition 14.** *Let* $h$ *be a consistent bi-trace. Given two substitutions* $\theta_1$ *and* $\theta_2$, *we say that* $\theta_1$ *is* $h$*-equivalent to* $\theta_2$, *written* $\theta_1 \leftrightarrow_h \theta_2$, *if* $dom(\theta_1) = dom(\theta_2)$

*and for every $x \in dom(\theta_1)$, we have $h \vdash x\theta_1 \leftrightarrow x\theta_2$ and $fn(x\theta_1, x\theta_2) \subseteq fn(h)$. A substitution $\sigma$* extends *$\theta$, written $\theta \preceq \sigma$, if $\sigma(x) = \theta(x)$ for every $x \in dom(\theta)$.*

The next lemma is crucial to the soundness of up-to parallel composition. It shows that one-step transitions for pure processes are invariant under equivalent substitutions.

**Lemma 15.** *Let $h$ be a consistent bi-trace, let $\sigma_1$ and $\sigma_2$ be substitutions such that $\sigma_1 \leftrightarrow_h \sigma_2$, and let $R$ be a process such that $fn(R) \subseteq dom(\sigma_1)$ and $rn(R) = \emptyset$. If $R\sigma_1 \xrightarrow{M} R'$ then there exist $\sigma_1 \preceq \sigma_1'$, $\sigma_2 \preceq \sigma_2'$, $U$ and $Q$ such that $\sigma_1' \leftrightarrow_h \sigma_2'$, $fn(U, Q) \subseteq dom(\sigma_1')$, $rn(U, Q) = \emptyset$, $M = U\sigma_1'$, $R' = Q\sigma_1'$ and $R\sigma_2 \xrightarrow{U\sigma_2'} Q\sigma_2'$.*

We need a few relations on bi-traces to describe the up-to techniques.

**Definition 16.** *The relations $<_i$, $<_o$ and $<_f$ on bi-traces are defined as follows. Given two bi-traces $h$ and $h'$:*

- weakening: *$h <_w h'$ holds if $h = h_1.h_2$ and $h' = h_1.(M, N)^*.h_2$, where $* \in \{i, o\}$ and $fn(M, N) \subseteq fn(h_1)$,*
- contraction: *$h <_c h'$ holds if $h = h_1.(M, N)^*.h_2$ and $h' = h_1.h_2$, where $* \in \{i, o\}$, and $h_1 \vdash M \leftrightarrow N$, and*
- flex-rigid: *$h <_f h'$ holds if $h = h_1.(\mathbf{c}, \mathbf{c})^o.h_2[\mathbf{c}/x]$, $h' = h_1.(x, x)^i.h_2$, $x \notin fn(h_1)$ and $\mathbf{c} \notin rn(h_1.h_2)$.*

*The reflexive-transitive closures of $<_w$, $<_c$ and $<_f$ are denoted, respectively, by $\sqsubseteq_w$, $\sqsubseteq_c$ and $\sqsubseteq_f$ . If $h \sqsubseteq_f h'$ then $h = h'\theta$ for a unique substitution $\theta$ with $dom(\theta) \subseteq fn(h')$. We denote this substitution with $\theta_{h,h'}$.*

Reading from right-to-left, the above relations read as follows: The relation $<_w$ removes an arbitrary pair from the bi-trace (hence possibly reducing the knowledge of the observer). The relation $<_c$ adds a redundant pair, i.e., one which is deducible from the current knowledge, hence adding no extra knowledge. The relation $<_f$ replaces a variable input pair with a fresh output pair of rigid names. It does not increase the knowledge of the observer, since the added pair is fresh value, but it does limit the possible respectful substitutions, since the fresh output pair cannot be substituted (they are rigid names). Thus, going from right to left in the relations, the knowledge of the observer does not increase.

In the following, the notation $\equiv$ denotes the structural equivalence on processes as defined in [2].

**Definition 17.** *Given a set of consistent traced process pairs $\mathcal{R}$, define $\mathcal{R}_t$, for $t \in \{\equiv, w, c, s, i, f, r, p\}$, as the least relations containing $\mathcal{R}$ which satisfy the following rules:*

1. *up to structural equivalence:* $\dfrac{P \equiv P', Q \equiv Q' \text{ and } h \vdash P' \mathcal{R}\, Q'}{h \vdash P\, \mathcal{R}_{\equiv}\, Q} \equiv$
2. *up to weakening:* $\dfrac{h \vdash P\, \mathcal{R}\, Q,\ h' \sqsubseteq_w h \text{ and } h' \text{ is consistent}}{h' \vdash P\, \mathcal{R}_w\, Q} w$

3. *up to contraction:* $\dfrac{h \vdash P\ \mathcal{R}\ Q,\ h' \sqsubseteq_c h \text{ and } h' \text{ is consistent}}{h' \vdash P\ \mathcal{R}_c\ Q}\ c$

4. *up to substitutions:* $\dfrac{h \vdash P\ \mathcal{R}\ Q \text{ and } \vec{\theta} = (\theta_1, \theta_2) \text{ respects } h}{h\vec{\theta} \vdash P\theta_1\ \mathcal{R}_s\ Q\theta_2}\ s$

5. *up to injective renaming of rigid names:*

$$\frac{h \vdash P\ \mathcal{R}\ Q,\ \rho_1 \text{ and } \rho_2 \text{ are injective renaming on rigid names}}{h(\rho_1, \rho_2) \vdash P\rho_1\ \mathcal{R}_i\ Q\rho_2}\ i$$

6. *up to flex-rigid reversal of names:* $\dfrac{h \vdash P\ \mathcal{R}\ Q,\ h' \sqsubseteq_f h}{h' \vdash P\theta_{h',h}\ \mathcal{R}_f\ Q\theta_{h',h}}\ f$

7. *up to restriction:* $\dfrac{h \vdash P[\vec{\mathbf{c}}/\vec{x}]\ \mathcal{R}\ Q[\vec{\mathbf{d}}/\vec{y}],\quad \{\vec{\mathbf{c}}\} \cap rn(\pi_1(h), P) = \emptyset,\quad \{\vec{\mathbf{d}}\} \cap rn(\pi_2(h), Q) = \emptyset,\quad \{\vec{x}, \vec{y}\} \cap fn(h) = \emptyset}{h \vdash (\nu\vec{x})P\ \mathcal{R}_r\ (\nu\vec{y})Q}\ r$

8. *up to parallel composition:*

$$\frac{h \vdash P\ \mathcal{R}\ Q,\quad h' \text{ is consistent},\ h' \sqsubseteq_c h,\ \sigma_1 \leftrightarrow_{h'} \sigma_2,\quad fn(R) \subseteq dom(\sigma_1),\ rn(R) = \emptyset,\ A \equiv (P \mid R\sigma_1) \text{ and } B \equiv (Q \mid R\sigma_2).}{h' \vdash A\ \mathcal{R}_p\ B}\ p$$

Strong open bisimulation up to structural equivalence *is defined similarly to Definition 12, except that we replace the relation $\mathcal{R}$ in items (1), (2) and (3) in Definition 12 with $\mathcal{R}_\equiv$. Strong open bisimulation up to weakening, contraction, substitutions, injective renaming, flex-rigid reversal, restrictions and parallel composition are defined analogously.*

In those rules that concern weakening, contraction and flex-rigid reversal of names, the observer knowledge in the premise is always equal or greater than its knowledge in the conclusion. In other words, if the observer cannot distinguish two processes using its current knowledge, it cannot do so either in a reduced knowledge. In the rule for parallel composition, we allow only processes that can introduce no extra information to the observer. Notice that in the rule, for technical reason, we need to contract the bi-trace $h$ to allow $R\sigma_i$ to contain new names not already in $h$.

**Proposition 18.** *Let $\mathcal{R}$ be an open bisimulation up to structural equivalence (respectively, weakening, contraction, etc.). Then $\mathcal{R} \subseteq \mathcal{R}_\equiv \subseteq\ \approx_o$ (respectively, $\mathcal{R} \subseteq \mathcal{R}_t \subseteq\ \approx_o$, for $t \in \{w, c, s, i, f, r, p\}$).*

*Example 19.* This example demonstrates the use of the up-to techniques in proving bisimilarity. This example is adapted from a similar one in [5]. Let $P$ and $Q$ be the following processes:

$$P = \mathbf{a}(x).(\nu k)\bar{\mathbf{a}}\langle\{x\}_k\rangle.(\nu m)\bar{\mathbf{a}}\langle\{m\}_{\{\mathbf{a}\}_k}\rangle.\bar{m}\langle\mathbf{a}\rangle.0$$

$$Q = \mathbf{a}(x).(\nu k)\bar{\mathbf{a}}\langle\{x\}_k\rangle.(\nu m)\bar{\mathbf{a}}\langle\{m\}_{\{\mathbf{a}\}_k}\rangle.[x = \mathbf{a}]\bar{m}\langle\mathbf{a}\rangle.0$$

Let $\mathcal{R}$ be the least set such that:

$$\begin{array}{l}(\mathbf{a},\mathbf{a})^o \vdash P\ \mathcal{R}\ Q, \quad (\mathbf{a},\mathbf{a})^o.(x,x)^i \vdash P_1\ \mathcal{R}\ Q_1,\\ (\mathbf{a},\mathbf{a})^o.(x,x)^i.(\{x\}_{\mathbf{k}},\{x\}_{\mathbf{k}})^o \vdash P_2\ \mathcal{R}\ Q_2,\\ (\mathbf{a},\mathbf{a})^o.(x,x)^i.(\{x\}_{\mathbf{k}},\{x\}_{\mathbf{k}})^o.(\{\mathbf{m}\}_{\{\mathbf{a}\}_{\mathbf{k}}},\{\mathbf{m}\}_{\{\mathbf{a}\}_{\mathbf{k}}})^o \vdash P_3\ \mathcal{R}\ Q_3,\\ (\mathbf{a},\mathbf{a})^o.(\mathbf{a},\mathbf{a})^i.(\{\mathbf{a}\}_{\mathbf{k}},\{\mathbf{a}\}_{\mathbf{k}})^o.(\{\mathbf{m}\}_{\{\mathbf{a}\}_{\mathbf{k}}},\{\mathbf{m}\}_{\{\mathbf{a}\}_{\mathbf{k}}})^o.(\mathbf{m},\mathbf{m})^i.(\mathbf{a},\mathbf{a})^o \vdash 0\ \mathcal{R}\ 0,\end{array}$$

where

$$\begin{array}{c}P_1 = (\nu k)\bar{\mathbf{a}}\langle\{x\}_{\mathbf{k}}\rangle.(\nu m)\bar{\mathbf{a}}\langle\{m\}_{\{\mathbf{a}\}_{\mathbf{k}}}\rangle.\bar{m}\langle\mathbf{a}\rangle.0,\\ Q_1 = (\nu k)\bar{\mathbf{a}}\langle\{x\}_{k}\rangle.(\nu m)\bar{\mathbf{a}}\langle\{m\}_{\{\mathbf{a}\}_{k}}\rangle.[x=\mathbf{a}]\bar{m}\langle\mathbf{a}\rangle.0,\\ P_2 = (\nu m)\bar{\mathbf{a}}\langle\{m\}_{\{\mathbf{a}\}_{\mathbf{k}}}\rangle.\bar{m}\langle\mathbf{a}\rangle.0, \quad Q_2 = (\nu m)\bar{\mathbf{a}}\langle\{m\}_{\{\mathbf{a}\}_{\mathbf{k}}}\rangle.[x=\mathbf{a}]\bar{m}\langle\mathbf{a}\rangle.0,\\ P_3 = \bar{\mathbf{m}}\langle\mathbf{a}\rangle.0,\ Q_3 = [x=\mathbf{a}]\bar{\mathbf{m}}\langle\mathbf{a}\rangle.0.\end{array}$$

Let $\mathcal{R}'$ be the symmetric closure of $\mathcal{R}$. Then it is easy to see that $\mathcal{R}'$ is an open bisimulation up-to contraction and substitutions. For instance, consider the traced process pair $h \vdash \bar{\mathbf{m}}\langle\mathbf{a}\rangle.0\ \mathcal{R}'\ [x=\mathbf{a}]\bar{\mathbf{m}}\langle\mathbf{a}\rangle.0$
where $h = (\mathbf{a},\mathbf{a})^o.(x,x)^i.(\{x\}_{\mathbf{k}},\{x\}_{\mathbf{k}})^o.(\{\mathbf{m}\}_{\{\mathbf{a}\}_{\mathbf{k}}},\{\mathbf{m}\}_{\{\mathbf{a}\}_{\mathbf{k}}})^o$. Let $\vec{\theta} = (\theta_1,\theta_2)$ be an $h$-respectful substitution. Since $x$ is the only name in $h$, we have

$$h\vec{\theta} = (\mathbf{a},\mathbf{a})^o.(s,t)^i.(\{s\}_{\mathbf{k}},\{t\}_{\mathbf{k}})^o.(\{\mathbf{m}\}_{\{\mathbf{a}\}_{\mathbf{k}}},\{\mathbf{m}\}_{\{\mathbf{a}\}_{\mathbf{k}}})^o,$$

where $s = x\theta_1$ and $t = x\theta_2$. We have to check that every detectable action from $\bar{\mathbf{m}}\langle\mathbf{a}\rangle.0$ can be matched by $[t=\mathbf{a}]\bar{\mathbf{m}}\langle\mathbf{a}\rangle.0$. If $t \neq \mathbf{a}$, then $s \neq \mathbf{a}$ (by the consistency of $h\vec{\theta}$), therefore, $\pi_1(h\vec{\theta}) \not\vdash \mathbf{m}$, i.e., the action $\mathbf{m}$ is not detected by the environment, so this case is trivial. If $t = \mathbf{a}$, then $s = \mathbf{a}$ and $h\vec{\theta} \vdash \mathbf{m} \leftrightarrow \mathbf{m}$, so both $P_3\theta_1$ and $Q_3\theta_2$ can make a transition on channel $\mathbf{m}$. Their continuation is the traced process pair

$$(\mathbf{a},\mathbf{a})^o.(\mathbf{a},\mathbf{a})^i.(\{\mathbf{a}\}_{\mathbf{k}},\{\mathbf{a}\}_{\mathbf{k}})^o.(\{\mathbf{m}\}_{\{\mathbf{a}\}_{\mathbf{k}}},\{\mathbf{m}\}_{\{\mathbf{a}\}_{\mathbf{k}}})^o.(\mathbf{m},\mathbf{m})^i.(\mathbf{a},\mathbf{a})^o \vdash 0\ \mathcal{R}'\ 0$$

which is in the set $\mathcal{R}'$, hence also in $\mathcal{R}'_{cs}$ (up-to contraction and substitution on $\mathcal{R}'$). Therefore by Proposition 18, $(\mathbf{a},\mathbf{a})^o \vdash P \approx_o Q$. □

## 6 Congruence Results for Open Bisimilarity

In this section we show that the relation $\sim_o$ on pure processes is an equality relation (reflexive, symmetric, transitive) and is closed under arbitrary pure process contexts without replication. To show reflexivity, we define a bisimulation set indexed by *reflexive bi-traces*. Reflexive bi-traces are consistent bi-traces such that its first and second projections are the same list.

**Lemma 20.** *The following set is an open bisimulation:*

$$\{(h,P,P) \mid (h,P,P) \textit{ is a traced process pair, } h \textit{ is consistent and reflexive}\}.$$

To show transitivity, we first need to define composition of bi-traces.

**Definition 21.** Composition of bi-traces. *Two bi-traces can be composed if they have the same length and match element wise. More precisely, given two bi-traces*

$$h_1 = [(R_1, T_1)^{p_1}, \cdots, (R_m, T_m)^{p_m}]$$

$$h_2 = [(U_1, V_1)^{q_1}, \cdots, (U_n, V_n)^{q_n}]$$

*we say $h_1$ is* left-composable *to $h_2$ (equivalently, $h_2$ is* right-composable *to $h_1$) if and only if $m = n$ and $T_k = U_k$ and $p_k = q_k$ for every $k \in \{1, \ldots, n\}$. Their composition, written $h_1 \circ h_2$, is $[(R_1, V_1)^{p_1}, \cdots, (R_m, V_m)^{p_m}]$*

The important properties of composition are that it preserves consistency and that it behaves well with respect to respectful substitutions. The latter is made precise in the following lemma.

**Lemma 22.** Separating substitution. *Let $h_1$ and $h_2$ be consistent and composable bi-traces such that $h_1 \circ h_2$ is also consistent. Let $(\theta_1, \theta_2)$ be a substitution pair that respects $h_1 \circ h_2$. Then there exists a substitution $\rho$ such that $(\theta_1, \rho)$ respects $h_1$ and $(\rho, \theta_2)$ respects $h_2$.*

Given two sets of traced process pairs $\mathcal{R}_1$ and $\mathcal{R}_2$, their composition, written $\mathcal{R}_1 \circ \mathcal{R}_2$, is the set

$$\{(h_1 \circ h_2, P, R) \mid h_1 \vdash P \; \mathcal{R} \; Q,\ h_2 \vdash Q \; \mathcal{R}_2 \; R \text{ and } h_1 \text{ is left-composable with } h_2\}.$$

**Lemma 23.** *If $\mathcal{R}_1$ and $\mathcal{R}_2$ are open bisimulations then $\mathcal{R}_1 \circ \mathcal{R}_2$ is also an open bisimulation.*

**Theorem 24.** *The relation $\sim_o$ is an equivalence relation on pure processes.*

*Proof.* It follows straightforwardly from Lemma 20, Lemma 23 and Definition 12.

We now proceed to showing that it is also a congruence, for *finite* pure processes. This follows almost directly from Proposition 18.

**Theorem 25.** *The relation $\sim_o$ is a congruence on finite pure processes.*

## 7 Conclusion and Future Work

We have shown a formulation of open bisimulation for the spi-calculus. In this formulation, bisimulation is indexed by pairs of symbolic traces that concisely encode the history of the interaction between the environment with the processes being checked for bisimilarity. We show that open bisimilarity is a congruence for finite pure processes and is sound with respect to testing equivalence. For the latter, we note that with some minor modifications, we can also show soundness of open bisimilarity with respect to barbed congruence. Our formulation is directly inspired by hedged bisimulation [6]. In fact, open bisimilarity can be shown to be sound with respect to hedged bisimulation. Comparison with hedged bisimulation and other formulations of bisimulation for the spi-calculus is left for future work.

It would be interesting to see how the congruence results extend to the case with replications or recursions. This will probably require a more general definition of the rule for up-to parallel composition. The definition of open bisimulation and the consistency of bi-traces make use of quantification over respectful substitutions. We will investigate whether there is a finite characterisation of consistent bi-traces. One possibility is to use a symbolic transition system, i.e., a transition system parameterised upon certain logical constraints, the solution of which should correspond to respectful substitutions. Some preliminary study in this direction is done in [7] for a variant of open bisimulation based on hedged bisimulation. Since the bi-trace structure we use is a variant of symbolic traces, we will also investigate whether the techniques used for symbolic traces analysis [3] can be adapted to our setting.

*Acknowledgment.* The author thanks the anonymous referees for their comments on earlier versions of the paper.

## References

1. Abadi, M., Gordon, A.D.: A bisimulation method for cryptographic protocols. Nord. J. Comput. 5(4), 267–303 (1998)
2. Abadi, M., Gordon, A.D.: A calculus for cryptographic protocols: The spi calculus. Information and Computation 148(1), 1–70 (1999)
3. Boreale, M.: Symbolic trace analysis of cryptographic protocols. In: Orejas, F., Spirakis, P.G., van Leeuwen, J. (eds.) ICALP 2001. LNCS, vol. 2076, pp. 667–681. Springer, Heidelberg (2001)
4. Boreale, M., Nicola, R.D., Pugliese, R.: Proof techniques for cryptographic processes. SIAM Journal of Computing 31(3), 947–986 (2002)
5. Borgström, J., Briais, S., Nestmann, U.: Symbolic bisimulation in the spi calculus. In: Gardner, P., Yoshida, N. (eds.) CONCUR 2004. LNCS, vol. 3170, pp. 161–176. Springer, Heidelberg (2004)
6. Borgström, J., Nestmann, U.: On bisimulations for the spi calculus. Mathematical Structures in Computer Science 15(3), 487–552 (2005)
7. Briais, S.: A symbolic characterisation of open bisimulation for the spi calculus. Technical Report LAMP-REPORT-2007-002, École Polytechnique Fédérale de Lausanne (2007)
8. Briais, S., Nestmann, U.: Open bisimulation, revisited. Electr. Notes Theor. Comput. Sci. 154(3), 109–123 (2006)
9. Milner, R., Parrow, J., Walker, D.: A calculus of mobile processes, Part II. Information and Computation, pp. 41–77 (1992)
10. Sangiorgi, D.: A theory of bisimulation for the $\pi$-calculus. Acta Informatica 33(1), 69–97 (1996)
11. Tiu, A.: A trace based bisimulation for the spi calculus. (2007), Preprint, available on `http://rsise.anu.edu.au/~tiu/tbisim.pdf`

# CCS with Replication in the Chomsky Hierarchy: The Expressive Power of Divergence

Jesús Aranda[1,*], Cinzia Di Giusto[2], Mogens Nielsen[3], and Frank D. Valencia[4]

[1] Universidad del Valle, Colombia and LIX École Polytechnique, France
jesus.aranda@lix.polytechnique.fr
[2] Dip. Scienze dell'Informazione, Università di Bologna, Italy
digiusto@cs.unibo.it
[3] BRICS, University of Aarhus, Denmark
mn@brics.dk
[4] CNRS and LIX École Polytechnique, France
frank.valencia@lix.polytechnique.fr

**Abstract.** A remarkable result in [4] shows that in spite of its being less expressive than CCS w.r.t. weak bisimilarity, $CCS_!$ (a CCS variant where infinite behavior is specified by using replication rather than recursion) is Turing powerful. This is done by encoding Random Access Machines (RAM) in $CCS_!$. The encoding is said to be *non-faithful* because it may move from a state which can lead to termination into a divergent one which do not correspond to any configuration of the encoded RAM. I.e., the encoding is not termination preserving.

In this paper we study the existence of faithful encodings into $CCS_!$ of models of computability *strictly less* expressive than Turing Machines. Namely, grammars of Types 1 (Context Sensitive Languages), 2 (Context Free Languages) and 3 (Regular Languages) in the Chomsky Hierarchy. We provide faithful encodings of Type 3 grammars. We show that it is impossible to provide a faithful encoding of Type 2 grammars and that termination-preserving $CCS_!$ processes can generate languages which are not Type 2. We finally show that the languages generated by termination-preserving $CCS_!$ processes are Type 1 .

## 1 Introduction

The study of concurrency is often conducted with the aid of process calculi. A common feature of these calculi is that they treat processes much like the $\lambda$-calculus treats computable functions. They provide a language in which the structure of *terms* represents the structure of processes together with a *reduction* relation to represent computational steps. Undoubtedly Milner's CCS [9], a calculus for the modeling and analysis of synchronous communication, remains a standard representative of such calculi.

Infinite behaviour is ubiquitous in concurrent systems. Hence, it ought to be represented by process terms. In the context of CCS we can find at least two representations of them: *Recursive definitions* and *Replication*. Recursive process definitions take the form $A(y_1, \ldots, y_n)$ each assumed to have a unique, possibly recursive, *parametric*

* The work of Jesús Aranda has been supported by COLCIENCIAS (Instituto Colombiano para el Desarrollo de la Ciencia y la Tecnología "Francisco José de Caldas") and INRIA Futurs.

Z. Shao (Ed.): APLAS 2007, LNCS 4807, pp. 383–398, 2007.

*process definition* $A(x_1, \ldots, x_n) \stackrel{\texttt{def}}{=} P$. The intuition is that $A(y_1, \ldots, y_n)$ behaves as $P$ with each $y_i$ replacing $x_i$. Replication takes the form $!P$ and it means $P \mid P \mid \cdots$; an unbounded number of copies of the process $P$ in parallel. An interesting result is that in the $\pi$-calculus, itself a generalization of CCS, parametric recursive definitions can be encoded using replication up to weak bisimilarity. This is rather surprising since the syntax of $!P$ and its description are so simple. In fact, in [3] it is stated that in CCS recursive expressions are more expressive than replication. More precisely, it is shown that it is impossible to provide a weak-bisimulation preserving encoding from CCS with recursion, into the CCS variant in which infinite behaviour is specified only with replication. From now on we shall use CCS to denote CCS with recursion and $\text{CCS}_!$ to the CCS variant with replication.

Now, a remarkable expressiveness result in [4] states that, in spite of its being less expressive than CCS in the sense mentioned above, $\text{CCS}_!$ is Turing powerful. This is done by encoding (Deterministic) Random Access Machines (RAM) in $\text{CCS}_!$. Nevertheless, the encoding is not *faithful* (or deterministic) in the sense that, unlike the encoding of RAMs in CCS, it may introduce computations which do not correspond to the expected behaviour of the modeled machine. Such computations are forced to be *infinite* and thus regarded as non-halting computations which are therefore ignored. Only the finite computations correspond to those of the encoded RAM.

A crucial observation from [4] is that to be able to force wrong computation to be infinite, the $\text{CCS}_!$ encoding of a given RAM can, during evolution, move from a state which may terminate (i.e. weakly terminating state) into one that cannot terminate (i.e., strongly non-terminating state). In other words, the encoding does not *preserve (weak) termination* during evolution. It is worth pointing that since RAMs are deterministic machines, their faithful encoding in CCS given in [3] does preserve weak termination during evolution. A legitimate question is therefore: What can be encoded with termination-preserving $\text{CCS}_!$ processes?

**This work.** We shall investigate the expressiveness of $\text{CCS}_!$ processes which indeed preserve (weak) termination during evolution. This way we disallow the technique used in [4] to unfaithfully encode RAMs.

A sequence of actions $s$ (over a finite set of actions) performed by a process $P$ specifies a sequence of interactions with $P$'s environment. For example, $s = a^n.\bar{b}^n$ can be used to specify that if $P$ is input $n$ $a$'s by environment then $P$ can output $n$ $b$'s to the environment. We therefore find it natural to study the expressiveness of processes w.r.t. sequences (or patterns) of interactions (languages) they can describe. In particular we shall study the expressiveness of $\text{CCS}_!$ w.r.t. the existence of termination-preserving encodings of grammars of Types 1 (Context Sensitive grammars), 2 (Context Free grammars) and 3 (Regular grammars) in the Chomsky Hierarchy whose expressiveness corresponds to (non-deterministic) Linear-bounded, Pushdown and Finite-State Automata, respectively. As elaborated later in the related work, similar characterizations are stated in the Caucal hierarchy of transition systems for other process algebras [2].

It worth noticing that by using the non termination-preserving encoding of RAM's in [3] we can encode Type 0 grammars (which correspond to Turing Machines) in $\text{CCS}_!$.

Now, in principle the mere fact that a computation model fails to generate some particular language may not give us a definite answer about its computation power. For a trivial example, consider a model similar to Turing Machines except that the machines always print the symbol $a$ on the first cell of the output tape. The model is essentially Turing powerful but fails to generate $b$. Nevertheless, our restriction to termination-preserving processes is a natural one, much like restricting non-deterministic models to deterministic ones, meant to rule out unfaithful encodings of the kind used in [4]. As matter of fact, Type 0 grammars can be encoded by using the termination-preserving encoding of RAMs in CCS [3].

**Contributions.** For simplicity let us use $\mathrm{CCS}_!^{-\omega}$ to denote the set of $\mathrm{CCS}_!$ processes which preserve weak termination during evolution as described above. We first provide a language preserving encoding of Regular grammars into $\mathrm{CCS}_!^{-\omega}$. We also prove that $\mathrm{CCS}_!^{-\omega}$ processes can generate languages which cannot be generated by any Regular grammar. Our main contribution is to show that it is *impossible* to provide language preserving encodings from Context-Free grammars into $\mathrm{CCS}_!^{-\omega}$. Conversely, we also show that $\mathrm{CCS}_!^{-\omega}$ can generate languages which cannot be generated by any Context-free grammar. We conclude our classification by stating that all languages generated by $\mathrm{CCS}_!^{-\omega}$ processes are context sensitive. The results are summarized in Fig. 1.

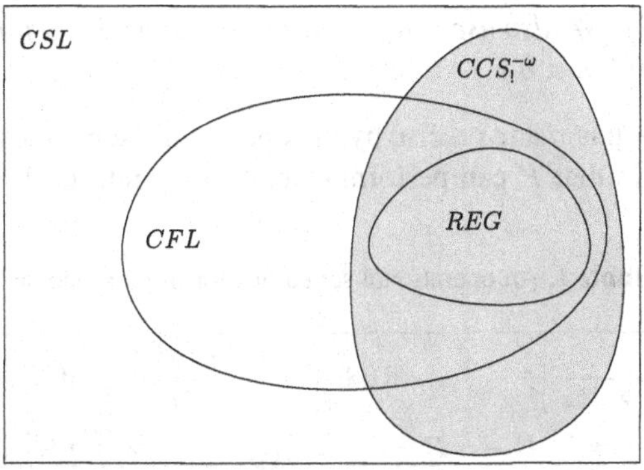


**Fig. 1.** Termination-Preserving $\mathrm{CCS}_!$ Processes ($\mathrm{CCS}_!^{-\omega}$) in the Chomsky Hierarchy

**Outline of the paper.** This paper is organized as follows. Section 2 introduces the CCS calculi under consideration. We then discuss in Section 3 how unfaithful encodings are used in [4] to provide an encoding of RAM's. We prove the above-mentioned results in Section 4. Finally, some concluding remarks are given in Section 5.

## 2 Preliminaries

In what follows we shall briefly recall the CCS constructs and its semantics as well as the $\mathrm{CCS}_!$ calculus.

### 2.1 The Calculi

**Finite CCS.** In CCS, processes can perform actions or synchronize on them. These actions can be either offering port *names* for communication, or the so-called *silent*

action $\tau$. We presuppose a countable set $\mathcal{N}$ of port *names*, ranged over by $a, b, x, y \ldots$ and their primed versions. We then introduce a set of *co-names* $\overline{\mathcal{N}} = \{\overline{a} \mid a \in \mathcal{N}\}$ disjoint from $\mathcal{N}$. The set of *labels*, ranged over by $l$ and $l'$, is $\mathcal{L} = \mathcal{N} \cup \overline{\mathcal{N}}$. The set of *actions* $Act$, ranged over by $\alpha$ and $\beta$, extends $\mathcal{L}$ with a new symbol $\tau$. Actions $a$ and $\overline{a}$ are thought of as *complementary*, so we decree that $\overline{\overline{a}} = a$. We also decree that $\overline{\tau} = \tau$.

The processes specifying finite behaviour are given by:

$$P, Q \ldots := 0 \mid \alpha.P \mid (\nu a)P \mid P \mid Q \tag{1}$$

Intuitively 0 represents the process that does nothing. The process $\alpha.P$ performs an action $\alpha$ then behaves as $P$. The restriction $(\nu a)P$ behaves as $P$ except that it can offer neither $a$ nor $\bar{a}$ to its environment. The names $a$ and $\bar{a}$ in $P$ are said to be *bound* in $(\nu a)P$. The *bound names* of $P$, $bn(P)$, are those with a bound occurrence in $P$, and the *free names* of $P$, $fn(P)$, are those with a not bound occurrence in $P$. The set of names of $P$, $n(P)$, is then given by $fn(P) \cup bn(P)$. Finally, $P \mid Q$ represents parallelism; either $P$ or $Q$ may perform an action, or they can also synchronize when performing complementary actions.

**Notation 1.** *We shall write the summation* $P + Q$ *as an abbreviation of the process* $(\nu u)(\overline{u} \mid u.P \mid u.Q)$. *We also use* $(\nu a_1 \ldots a_n)P$ *as a short hand for* $(\nu a_1) \ldots (\nu a_n)P$. *We often omit the "0" in* $\alpha.0$.

The above description is made precise by the operational semantics in Table 1. A transition $P \xrightarrow{\alpha} Q$ says that $P$ can perform $\alpha$ and evolve into $Q$. In the literature there

**Table 1.** An operational semantics for finite processes

$$\text{ACT}\ \frac{}{\alpha.P \xrightarrow{\alpha} P} \qquad \text{RES}\ \frac{P \xrightarrow{\alpha} P'}{(\nu a)P \xrightarrow{\alpha} (\nu a)P'}\ \text{if } \alpha \notin \{a, \overline{a}\}$$

$$\text{PAR}_1\ \frac{P \xrightarrow{\alpha} P'}{P \mid Q \xrightarrow{\alpha} P' \mid Q} \qquad \text{PAR}_2\ \frac{Q \xrightarrow{\alpha} Q'}{P \mid Q \xrightarrow{\alpha} P \mid Q'}$$

$$\text{COM}\ \frac{P \xrightarrow{l} P' \quad Q \xrightarrow{\overline{l}} Q'}{P \mid Q \xrightarrow{\tau} P' \mid Q'}$$

are at least two alternatives to extend the above syntax to express infinite behaviour. We describe them next.

### 2.2 Parametric Definitions: CCS and CCS$_p$

A typical way of specifying infinite behaviour is by using parametric definitions [10]. In this case we extend the syntax of finite processes (Equation 1) as follows:

$$P, Q, \ldots := \ldots \mid A(y_1, \ldots, y_n) \tag{2}$$

Here $A(y_1, \ldots, y_n)$ is an *identifier* (also *call*, or *invocation*) of arity $n$. We assume that every such an identifier has a unique, possibly recursive, *definition* $A(x_1, \ldots, x_n) \stackrel{\text{def}}{=}$

$P_A$ where the $x_i$'s are pairwise distinct, and the intuition is that $A(y_1, \ldots, y_n)$ behaves as its *body* $P_A$ with each $y_i$ replacing the *formal parameter* $x_i$. For each $A(x_1, \ldots, x_n) \stackrel{\text{def}}{=} P_A$, we require $fn(P_A) \subseteq \{x_1, \ldots, x_n\}$.

Following [5], we should use $\text{CCS}_\text{p}$ to denote the calculus with parametric definitions with the above syntactic restrictions.

*Remark 1.* As shown in [5], however, $\text{CCS}_\text{p}$ is equivalent w.r.t. strong bisimilarity to the standard CCS. We shall then take the liberty of using the terms CCS and $\text{CCS}_\text{p}$ to denote the calculus with parametric definitions as done in [10].

The rules for $\text{CCS}_\text{p}$ are those in Table 1 plus the rule:

$$\text{CALL}\ \frac{P_A[y_1, \ldots, y_n/x_1, \ldots, x_n] \xrightarrow{\alpha} P'}{A(y_1, \ldots, y_n) \xrightarrow{\alpha} P'}\ \text{if } A(x_1, \ldots, x_n) \stackrel{\text{def}}{=} P_A \tag{3}$$

As usual $P[y_1 \ldots y_n/x_1 \ldots x_n]$ results from replacing every free occurrence of $x_i$ with $y_i$ renaming bound names in $P$ wherever needed to avoid capture.

### 2.3 Replication: $\text{CCS}_!$

One simple way of expressing infinite is by using replication. Although, mostly found in calculus for mobility such as the $\pi$-calculus and mobile ambients, it is also studied in the context of CCS in [3,5].

For replication the syntax of finite processes (Equation 1) is extended as follows:

$$P, Q, \ldots := \ldots \mid !P \tag{4}$$

Intuitively the process $!P$ behaves as $P \mid P \mid \ldots \mid P \mid !P$; unboundedly many $P$'s in parallel. We call $\text{CCS}_!$ the calculus that results from the above syntax The operational rules for $\text{CCS}_!$ are those in Table 1 plus the following rule:

$$\text{REP}\ \frac{P \mid !P \xrightarrow{\alpha} P'}{!P \xrightarrow{\alpha} P'} \tag{5}$$

## 3 The Role of Strong Non-termination

In this section we shall single out the fundamental non-deterministic strategy for the Turing-expressiveness of $\text{CCS}_!$. First we need a little notation.

**Notation 2.** *Define* $\stackrel{s}{\Longrightarrow}$, *with* $s = \alpha_1 \ldots \alpha_n \in \mathcal{L}^*$, *as*

$$(\xrightarrow{\tau})^* \xrightarrow{\alpha_1} (\xrightarrow{\tau})^* \ldots (\xrightarrow{\tau})^* \xrightarrow{\alpha_n} (\xrightarrow{\tau})^*.$$

*For the empty sequence* $s = \epsilon$, $\stackrel{s}{\Longrightarrow}$ *is defined as* $(\xrightarrow{\tau})^*$.

We shall say that a process generates a sequence of non-silent actions $s$ if it can perform the actions of $s$ in a finite maximal sequence of transitions. More precisely:

**Definition 1 (Sequence and language generation).** *The process $P$ generates a sequence $s \in \mathcal{L}^*$ if and only if there exists $Q$ such that $P \stackrel{s}{\Longrightarrow} Q$ and $Q \stackrel{\alpha}{\not\longrightarrow}$ for any $\alpha \in Act$. Define the language of (or generated by) a process $P$, $L(P)$, as the set of all sequences $P$ generates.*

The above definition basically states that a sequence is generated when no reduction rule can be applied. It is inspired by language generation of the model of computations we are comparing our processes with. Namely, formal grammars where a sequence is generated when no rewriting rule can be applied.

As we shall see below (strong) non-termination plays a fundamental role in the expressiveness of CCS$_!$. We borrow the following terminology from rewriting systems:

**Definition 2 (Termination).** *We say that a process $P$ is* (weakly) terminating *(or that it can terminate) if and only if there exists a sequence $s$ such that $P$ generates $s$. We say that $P$ is* (strongly) non-terminating, *or that it* cannot terminate *if and only if $P$ cannot generate any sequence.*

The authors in [4] show the Turing-expressiveness of CCS$_!$, by providing a CCS$_!$ encoding $[\![\cdot]\!]$ of Random Access Machines (RAMs) a well-known Turing powerful deterministic model [11]. The encoding is said to be *unfaithful* (or non-deterministic) in the following sense: Given $M$, during evolution $[\![M]\!]$ may make a transition, by performing a $\tau$ action, from a weakly terminating state (process) into a state which do not correspond to any configuration of $M$. Nevertheless such states are strongly non-terminating processes. Therefore, they may be thought of as being configurations which cannot lead to a halting configuration. Consequently, the encoding $[\![M]\!]$ does not *preserve (weak) termination* during evolution.

*Remark 2.* The work [4] considers also guarded-summation for CCS$_!$. The results about the encodability of RAM's our work builds on can straightforwardly be adapted to our guarded-summation free CCS$_!$ fragment.

Now rather than giving the full encoding of RAMs in CCS$_!$, let us use a much simpler example which uses the same technique in [4]. Below we encode a typical context sensitive language in CCS$_!$.

*Example 1.* Consider the following processes

$$\begin{aligned} P &= (\nu\, k_1, k_2, k_3, u_b, u_c)(\,\overline{k_1} \mid \overline{k_2} \mid Q_a \mid Q_b \mid Q_c) \\ Q_a &= !k_1.a.(\overline{k_1} \mid \overline{k_3} \mid \overline{u_b} \mid \overline{u_c}) \\ Q_b &= k_1.!k_3.k_2.u_b.b.\overline{k_2} \\ Q_c &= k_2.(!u_c.c \mid u_b.DIV) \end{aligned}$$

where $DIV = !\tau$. It can be verified that $L(P) = \{a^n b^n c^n\}$. Intuitively, in the process $P$ above, $Q_a$ performs (a sequence of actions) $a^n$ for an arbitrary number $n$ (and also produces $n$ $u_b$'s). Then $Q_b$ performs $b^m$ for an arbitrary number $m \leq n$ and each time it produces $b$ it consumes a $u_b$. Finally, $Q_c$ performs $c^n$ and diverges if $m < n$ by checking if there are $u_b$'s that were not consumed. □

**The Power of Non-Termination.** Let us underline the role of strong non-termination in Example 1. Consider a run

$$P \stackrel{a^n b^m}{\Longrightarrow} \ldots$$

Observe that the name $u_b$ is used in $Q_c$ to test if $m < n$, by checking whether some $u_b$ were left after generating $b^m$. If $m < n$, the non-terminating process $DIV$ is triggered and the extended run takes the form

$$P \stackrel{a^n b^m c^n}{\Longrightarrow} \stackrel{\tau}{\longrightarrow} \stackrel{\tau}{\longrightarrow} \ldots$$

Hence the sequence $a^n b^m c^n$ arising from this run (with $m < n$) is therefore not included in $L(P)$.

**The tau move.** It is crucial to observe that there is a $\tau$ transition arising from the moment in which $\overline{k_2}$ chooses to synchronize with $Q_c$ to start performing the $c$ actions. One can verify that if $m < n$ then the process just before that $\tau$ transition is weakly terminating while the one just after is strongly non-terminating. □

Formally the class of termination-preserving processes is defined as follows.

**Definition 3 (Termination Preservation).** *A process $P$ is said to be (weakly) termination-preserving if and only if whenever $P \stackrel{s}{\Longrightarrow} Q \stackrel{\tau}{\longrightarrow} R$:*

- *if $Q$ is weakly terminating then $R$ is weakly terminating.*

*We use $CCS_!^{-\omega}$ to denotes the set of $CCS_!$ processes which are termination-preserving.*

One may wonder why only $\tau$ actions are not allowed in Definition 3 when moving from a weakly terminating state into a strongly non-terminating one. The next proposition answers to this.

**Proposition 1.** *For every $P, P', \alpha \neq \tau$ if $P \stackrel{\alpha}{\longrightarrow} P'$ and $P$ is weakly terminating then $P'$ must be weakly terminating.*

*Proof (Outline).* As a mean of contradiction let $P'$ be a strongly non-terminating process such that $P \stackrel{\alpha}{\longrightarrow} P'$ where $\alpha \neq \tau$. Let $\gamma$ be an arbitrary maximal sequence of transitions from $P$. Since $P \stackrel{\alpha}{\longrightarrow} P'$, the action $\alpha$ will be performed in $\gamma$ as a visible action or in a synchronization with its complementary action $\bar{\alpha}$. In the synchronization case, one can verify that there exists another maximal sequence $\gamma'$ identical to $\gamma$ except that in $\gamma'$, $\alpha$ and $\bar{\alpha}$ appear as visible actions instead of their corresponding synchronization. Therefore, there exists a sequence $P \stackrel{t_1}{\Longrightarrow} Q \stackrel{\alpha}{\longrightarrow} R \stackrel{t_2}{\Longrightarrow}\not\rightarrow$ (Fig. 2). From $P \stackrel{t_1}{\Longrightarrow} Q \stackrel{\alpha}{\longrightarrow} R$ and $P \stackrel{\alpha}{\longrightarrow} P'$, we can show that $P \stackrel{\alpha}{\longrightarrow} P' \stackrel{t_1}{\Longrightarrow} R \stackrel{t_2}{\Longrightarrow}\not\rightarrow$ (Fig. 3) thus contradicting the assumption that $P'$ is a strongly non-terminating process. □

We conclude this section with a proposition which relates preservation of termination and the language of a process.

**Proposition 2.** *Suppose that $P$ is terminating-preserving and that $L(P) \neq \emptyset$. For every $Q$, if $P \stackrel{s}{\Longrightarrow} Q$ then $\exists s'$ such that $s.s' \in L(P)$.*

*Proof.* Let $Q$ an arbitrary process such that $P \stackrel{s}{\Longrightarrow} Q$. Since $L(P) \neq \emptyset$ then $P$ is weakly terminating. From Definition 3 and Proposition 1 it follows that $Q$ is weakly terminating. Hence there exists a sequence $s'$ such that $P \stackrel{s}{\Longrightarrow} Q \stackrel{s'}{\Longrightarrow} R \not\rightarrow$ and thus from Definition 1 we have $s.s' \in L(P)$ as wanted. □

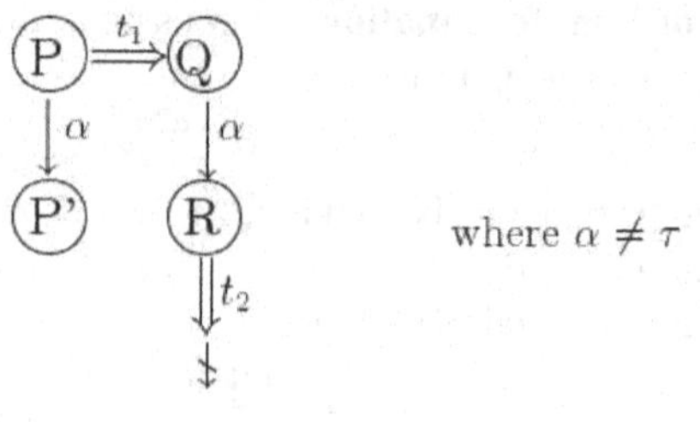


**Fig. 2.** Alternative evolutions of $P$ involving $\alpha$

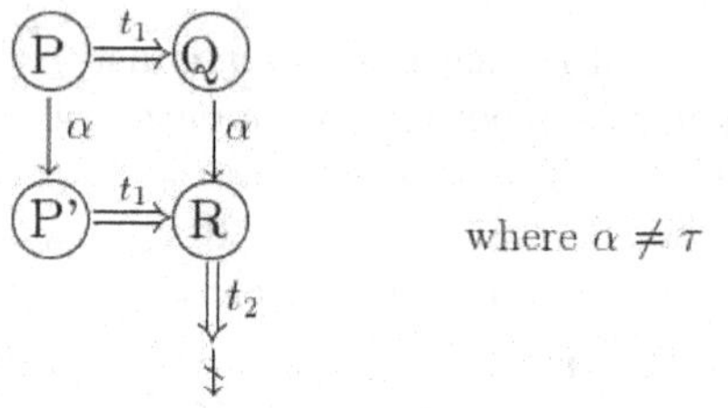


**Fig. 3.** Confluence from $P$ to R

# 4 $CCS_!$ and Chomsky Hierarchy

In this section we study the expressiveness of termination-preserving $\mathrm{CCS}_!$ processes in the Chomsky hierarchy. Recall that, in a strictly decreasing expressive order, Types 0, 1, 2 and 3 in the Chomsky hierarchy correspond, respectively, to unrestricted-grammars (Turing Machines), Context Sensitive Grammars (Non-Deterministic Linear Bounded Automata), Context Free Grammars (Non-Deterministic PushDown Automata), and Regular Grammars (Finite State Automata).

We assume that the reader is familiar with the notions and notations of formal grammars. A grammar is a quadruple $G = (\Sigma, N, S, P)$ where $\Sigma$ are the terminal symbols, $N$ the non-terminals, $S$ the initial symbol, $P$ the set of production rules. The language of (or generated by) a formal grammar $G$, denoted as $L(G)$, is defined as all those strings in $\Sigma^*$ that can be generated by starting with the start symbol $S$ and then applying the production rules in $P$ until no more non-terminal symbols are present.

## 4.1 Encoding Regular Languages

Regular Languages ($REG$) are those generated by grammars whose production rules can only be of the form $A \rightarrow a$ or $A \rightarrow a.B$. They can be alternatively characterized as those recognized by regular expressions which are given by the following syntax:

$$e = \emptyset \mid \epsilon \mid a \mid e_1 + e_2 \mid e_1.e_2 \mid e^*$$

where $a$ is a terminal symbol.

**Definition 4.** *Given a regular expression e, we define* $[\![e]\!]$ *as the* $CCS_!$ *process* $(\nu\, m)$ $([\![e]\!]_m \mid m)$ *where* $[\![e]\!]_m$*, with* $m \notin fn([\![e]\!])$*, is inductively defined as follows:*

$$
\begin{array}{ll}
[\![\emptyset]\!]_m = & DIV \\
[\![\epsilon]\!]_m = & \overline{m} \\
[\![a]\!]_m = & a.\overline{m} \\
[\![e_1 + e_2]\!]_m = & \begin{cases} [\![e_1]\!]_m & \text{if } L(e_2) = \emptyset \\ [\![e_2]\!]_m & \text{if } L(e_1) = \emptyset \\ [\![e_1]\!]_m + [\![e_2]\!]_m & \text{otherwise} \end{cases} \\
[\![e_1.e_2]\!]_m = & (\nu\, m_1)([\![e_1]\!]_{m_1} \mid m_1.[\![e_2]\!]_m) \text{ with } m_1 \notin fn(e_1) \\
[\![e^*]\!]_m = & \begin{cases} \overline{m} & \text{if } L(e) = \emptyset \\ (\nu\, m')(\overline{m'} \mid !m'.[\![e]\!]_{m'} \mid m'.\overline{m}) \text{ with } m' \notin fn(e) & \text{otherwise} \end{cases}
\end{array}
$$

*where* $DIV = !\tau$.

*Remark 3.* The conditionals on language emptiness in Definition 4 are needed to make sure that the encoding of regular expressions always produce termination-preserving processes. To see this consider the case $a+\emptyset$. Notice that while $[\![a]\!] = a$ and $[\![\emptyset]\!] = DIV$ are termination-preserving, $a + DIV$ is not. Hence $[\![e_1 + e_2]\!]$ cannot be defined as $[\![e_1]\!] + [\![e_2]\!]$. Since the emptiness problem is decidable for regular expressions, it is clear that given e, $[\![e]\!]$ can be effectively constructed.

The following proposition, which can be proven by using induction on the structure of regular expressions, states the correctness of the encoding.

**Proposition 3.** *Let* $[\![e]\!]$ *as in Definition 4. We have* $L(e) = L([\![e]\!])$ *and furthermore* $[\![e]\!]$ *is termination-preserving.*

From the standard encoding from Type 3 grammars to regular expressions and the above proposition we obtain the following result.

**Theorem 3.** *For every Type 3 grammar G, we can construct a termination-preserving* $CCS_!$ *process* $P_G$ *such that* $L(G) = L(P_G)$*.*

The converse of the theorem above does not hold; Type 3 grammars are strictly less expressive.

**Theorem 4.** *There exists a termination-preserving* $CCS_!$ *process P such that* $L(P)$ *is not Type 3.*

The above statement can be shown by providing a process which generates the typical $a^n b^n$ context-free language. Namely, let us take

$$P = (\nu\, k, u)(\overline{k} \mid !(k.a.(\overline{k} \mid \overline{u})) \mid k.!(u.b)).$$

One can verify that $P$ is termination-preserving and that $L(P) = a^n b^n$.

### 4.2 Impossibility Result: Context Free Languages

Context-Free Languages (CFL) are those generated by Type 2 grammars: grammars where every production is of the form $A \to \gamma$ where $A$ is a non-terminal symbol and $\gamma$ is a string consisting of terminals and/or non-terminals.

We have already seen that termination-preserving CCS$_!$ process can encode a typical CFL language such as $a^n b^n$. Nevertheless, we shall show that they cannot in general encode Type 2 grammars.

The nesting of restriction processes plays a key role in the following results CCS$_!$.

**Definition 5.** *The maximal number of nesting of restrictions $|P|_\nu$ can be inductively given as follows:*

$$|(\nu\, x)P|_\nu = 1 + |P|_\nu \qquad |P \mid Q|_\nu = max(|P|_\nu, |Q|_\nu)$$
$$|\alpha.P|_\nu = |!P|_\nu = |P|_\nu \qquad |0|_\nu = 0$$

A very distinctive property of CCS$_!$ is that the maximal nesting of restrictions is invariant during evolution.

**Proposition 4.** *Let P and Q be CCS$_!$ processes. If $P \overset{s}{\Longrightarrow} Q$ then $|P|_\nu = |Q|_\nu$.*

*Remark 4.* In CCS because of the *unfolding* of recursive definitions the nesting of restrictions can increase unboundedly during evolution[1]. E.g., consider $A(a)$ where $A(x) \stackrel{\text{def}}{=} (\nu\, y)(x.\bar{y}.R \mid y.A(x))$ (see Section 2.2) which has the following sequence of transitions $A(a) \overset{aaa...}{\Longrightarrow} (\nu y)(R \mid (\nu y)(R \mid (\nu y)(R \mid \ldots)))$ □

Another distinctive property of CCS$_!$ is that if a CCS$_!$ process can perform a given action $\beta$, it can always do it by performing a number of actions bounded by a value that depends only on the size of the process. In fact, as stated below, for a significant class of processes, the bound can be given solely in terms of the maximal number of nesting of restrictions.

Now, the above statement may seem incorrect since as mentioned earlier CCS$_!$ is Turing expressive. One may think that $\beta$ above could represent a termination signal in a TM encoding, then it would seem that its presence in a computation cannot be determined by something bounded by the syntax of the encoding. Nevertheless, recall that the Turing encoding in [4] may wrongly signal $\beta$ (i.e., even when the encoded machine does not terminate) but it will diverge afterwards.

The following section is devoted to some lemmas needed for proving our impossibility results for CCS$_!$ processes.

**Trios-Processes**

For technical reasons we shall work with a family of CCS$_!$ processes, namely *trios-processes*. These processes can only have prefixes of the form $\alpha.\beta.\gamma$ . The notion of trios was introduced for the $\pi$-calculus in [14] . We shall adapt trios and use them as a technical tool for our purposes.

[1] Also in the $\pi$-calculus [15], an extension of CCS$_!$ where names are communicated, the nesting of restrictions can increase during evolution due to its name-extrusion capability.

We shall say that a CCS$_!$ process $T$ is a *trios-process* iff all prefixes in $T$ are *trios*; i.e., they all have the form $\alpha.\beta.\gamma$ and satisfy the following: If $\alpha \neq \tau$ then $\alpha$ is a *name* bound in $T$, and similarly if $\gamma \neq \tau$ then $\gamma$ is a *co-name* bound in $T$. For instance $(\nu l)(\tau.\tau.\bar{l} \mid l.a.\tau)$ is a trios-process. We will view a trio $l.\beta.\bar{l}$ as linkable node with incoming link $l$ from another trio, outgoing link $\bar{l}$ to another trio, and contents $\beta$.

Interestingly, the family of trios-processes can capture the behaviour of arbitrary CCS$_!$ processes via the following encoding:

**Definition 6.** *Given a CCS$_!$ process $P$, $[\![P]\!]$ is the trios-process $(\nu\, l)(\tau.\tau.\bar{l} \mid [\![P]\!]_l)$ where $[\![P]\!]_l$, with $l \notin n(P)$, is inductively defined as follows:*

$$\begin{array}{ll} [\![0]\!]_l = & 0 \\ [\![\alpha.P]\!]_l = & (\nu\, l')(l.\alpha.\overline{l'} \mid [\![P]\!]_{l'}) \text{ where } l' \notin n(P) \\ [\![P \mid Q]\!]_l = & (\nu\, l', l'')(l.\overline{l'}.\overline{l''} \mid [\![P]\!]_{l'} \mid [\![P]\!]_{l''}) \text{ where } l', l'' \notin n(P) \cup n(Q) \\ [\![!P]\!]_l = & (\nu\, l')(!l.\overline{l'}.\bar{l} \mid ![\![P]\!]_{l'}) \text{ where } l' \notin n(P) \\ [\![(\nu\, x)P]\!]_l = & (\nu\, x)[\![P]\!]_l \end{array}$$

Notice that the trios-process $[\![\alpha.P]\!]_l$ encodes a process $\alpha.P$ much like a linked list. Intuitively, the trio $l.\alpha.\overline{l'}$ has an outgoing link $l$ to its continuation $[\![P]\!]'_l$ and incoming link $l$ from some previous trio. The other cases can be explained analogously. Clearly the encoding introduces additional actions but they are all silent—i.e., they are synchronizations on the bound names $l, l'$ and $l''$.

Unfortunately the above encoding is not invariant w.r.t. language equivalence because the replicated trio in $[\![!P]\!]_l$ introduces divergence. E.g, $L((\nu x)!x) = \{\epsilon\}$ but $L([\![(\nu x)!x]\!]) = \emptyset$. It has, however, a pleasant invariant property: *weak bisimilarity*.

**Definition 7 (Weak Bisimilarity).** *A* (weak) simulation *is a binary relation $\mathcal{R}$ satisfying the following: $(P, Q) \in \mathcal{R}$ implies that:*

- *if $P \stackrel{s}{\Longrightarrow} P'$ where $s \in \mathcal{L}^*$ then $\exists Q' : Q \stackrel{s}{\Longrightarrow} Q' \wedge (P', Q') \in \mathcal{R}$.*

*The relation $\mathcal{R}$ is a* bisimulation *iff both $\mathcal{R}$ and its converse $\mathcal{R}^{-1}$ are -simulations. We say that $P$ and $Q$ are* (weak) bisimilar, *written $P \approx Q$ iff $(P, Q) \in \mathcal{R}$ for some bisimulation $\mathcal{R}$.*

**Proposition 5.** *For every CCS$_!$ process $P$, $P \approx [\![P]\!]$ where $[\![P]\!]$ is the trios-process constructed from $P$ as in Definition 6.*

Another property of trios is that if a trios-process $T$ can perform an action $\alpha$, i.e., $T \stackrel{s.\alpha}{\Longrightarrow}$, then $T \stackrel{s'.\alpha}{\Longrightarrow}$ where $s'$ is a sequence of actions whose length bound can be given solely in terms of $|T|_\nu$.

**Proposition 6.** *Let $T$ be a trios-process such that $T \stackrel{s\cdot\beta}{\Longrightarrow}$. There exists a sequence $s'$, whose length is bounded by a value depending only on $|T|_\nu$, such that $T \stackrel{s'\cdot\beta}{\Longrightarrow}$.*

We conclude this technical section by outlining briefly the main aspects of the proof of the above proposition. Roughly speaking, our approach is to consider a minimal sequence of visible actions $t = \beta_1 \ldots . \beta_m$ performed by $T$ leading to $\beta$ (i.e., $P \stackrel{t}{\Longrightarrow}$

and $\beta_m = \beta$) and analyze the *causal dependencies* among the (*occurrences* of) the actions in this $t$. Intuitively, $\beta_j$ depends on $\beta_i$ if $T$, while performing $t$, could not had performed $\beta_j$ without performing $\beta_i$ first. For example in

$$T = (\nu l)(\nu l')(\nu l'')(\tau.a.\bar{l} \mid \tau.b.\bar{l'} \mid l.l'.\bar{l''} \mid l''.c.\tau)$$

$\beta = c$, $t = abc$, we see that $c$ depends on $a$ and $b$, but $b$ does not depend on $a$ since $T$ could had performed $b$ before $a$.

We then consider the unique directed acyclic graph $G_t$ arising from the transitive reduction[2] of the partial ordered induced by the dependencies in $t$. Because $t$ is minimal, $\beta$ is the only sink of $G_t$.

We write $\beta_i \rightsquigarrow_t \beta_j$ ($\beta_j$ depends directly on $\beta_i$) iff $G_t$ has an arc from $\beta_i$ to $\beta_j$. The crucial observation from our restrictions over trios is that if $\beta_i \rightsquigarrow_t \beta_j$ then (the trios corresponding to the occurrences of) $\beta_i$ and $\beta_j$ must occur in the scope of a restriction process $R_{ij}$ in $T$ (or in some evolution of $T$ while generating $t$). Take e.g, $T = \tau.a.\tau \mid (\nu\, l)(\tau.b.\bar{l} \mid l.c.\tau)$ with $t = a.b.c$ and $b \rightsquigarrow c$. Notice that the trios corresponding to the actions $b$ and $c$ appear within the scope of the restriction in $T$

To give an upper bound on the number of nodes of $G_t$ (i.e., the length of $t$), we give an upper bound on its length and maximal in-degree. Take a path $\beta_{i_1} \rightsquigarrow_t \beta_{i_2} \ldots \rightsquigarrow_t \beta_{i_u}$ of size $u$ in $G_t$. With the help of the above observation, we consider sequences of restriction processes $R_{i_1 i_2} R_{i_2 i_3} \ldots R_{i_{u-1} i_u}$ such that for every $k < u$ the actions $\beta_{i_k}$ and $\beta_{i_{k+1}}$ (i.e., the trios where they occur) must be under the scope of $R_{i_k i_{k+1}}$. Note that any two different restriction processes with a common trio under their scope (e.g. $R_{i_1 i_2}$ and $R_{i_2 i_3}$) must be nested, i.e., one must be under the scope of the other. This induces tree-like nesting among the elements of the sequence of restrictions. E.g., for the restrictions corresponding to $\beta_{i_1} \rightsquigarrow_t \beta_{i_2} \rightsquigarrow_t \beta_{i_3} \rightsquigarrow_t \beta_{i_4}$ we could have a tree-like situation with $R_{i_1 i_2}$ and $R_{i_3 i_4}$ being under the scope of $R_{i_2 i_3}$ and thus inducing a nesting of at least two. We show that for a sequence of restriction processes, the number $m$ of nesting of them satisfies $u \leq 2^m$. Since the nesting of restrictions remains invariant during evolution (Proposition 4) then $u \leq 2^{|T|_\nu}$. Similarly, we give an upper bound $2^{|T|_\nu}$ on the indegree of each node $\beta_j$ of $G_t$ (by considering sequences $R_{i_1 j}, \ldots, R_{i_m j}$ such that $\beta_{i_k} \rightsquigarrow \beta_j$, i.e having common trio corresponding to $\beta_j$ under their scope). We then conclude that the number of nodes in $G_t$ is bounded by $2^{|T|_\nu \times 2^{|T|_\nu}}$.

**Main Impossibility Result**

We can now prove our main impossibility result.

**Theorem 5.** *There exists a Type 2 grammar $G$ such that for every termination-preserving CCS$_!$ process $P$, $L(G) \neq L(P)$.*

*Proof.* It suffices to show that no process in CCS$_!^{-\omega}$ can generate the CFL $a^n b^n c$. Suppose, as a mean of contradiction, that $P$ is a CCS$_!^{-\omega}$ process such that $L(P) = a^n b^n c$.

Pick a sequence $\rho = P \stackrel{a^n}{\Longrightarrow} Q \stackrel{b^n c}{\Longrightarrow} T \not\rightarrow$ for a sufficiently large $n$. From Proposition 5 we know that for some $R$, $[\![P]\!] \stackrel{a^n}{\Longrightarrow} R \stackrel{b^n c}{\Longrightarrow}$ and $R \approx Q$ . Notice that $R$ may not

[2] The transitive reduction of a binary relation $r$ on $X$ is the smallest relation $r'$ on $X$ such that the transitive closure of $r'$ is the same as the transitive closure of $r$.

be a trios-process as it could contain prefixes of the form $\beta.\gamma$ and $\gamma$. However, such prefixes into $\tau.\beta.\gamma$ and $\tau.\tau.\gamma$, we obtain a trios-process $R'$ such that $R \approx R'$ and $|R|_\nu = |R'|_\nu$. We then have $R' \stackrel{b^n \cdot c}{\Longrightarrow}$ and, by Proposition 6, $R' \stackrel{s' \cdot c}{\Longrightarrow}$ for some $s'$ whose length is bounded by a constant $k$ that depends only on $|R'|_\nu$. Therefore, $R \stackrel{s' \cdot c}{\Longrightarrow}$ and since $R \approx Q$, $Q \stackrel{s' \cdot c}{\Longrightarrow} D$ for some $D$. With the help of Proposition 4 and from Definition 6 it is easy to see that $|R'|_\nu = |R|_\nu = |[\![P]\!]|_\nu \leq 1 + |P| + |P|_\nu$ where $|P|$ is the size of $P$. Consequently the length of $s'$ must be independent of $n$, and hence for any $s'' \in \mathcal{L}^*$, $a^n s' c s'' \notin L(P)$. Nevertheless $P \stackrel{a^n}{\Longrightarrow} Q \stackrel{s' \cdot c}{\Longrightarrow} D$ and therefore from Proposition 2 there must be at least one string $w = a^n s' c w' \in L(P)$; a contradiction. □

It turns out that the converse of Theorem 5 also holds: Termination-preserving CCS$_!$ processes can generate non CFL's. Take

$$P = (\nu\, k, u)(\overline{k} \mid !k.a.(\overline{k} \mid \overline{u})) \mid k.!u.(b \mid c))$$

One can verify that $P$ is termination-preserving. Furthermore, $L(P) \cap a^*b^*c^* = a^n b^n c^n$, hence $L(P)$ is not a CFL since CFL's are closed under intersection with regular languages. Therefore:

**Theorem 6.** *There exists a termination-preserving CCS$_!$ process $P$ such that $L(P)$ is not a CFL.*

Now, notice that if we allow the use of CCS$_!$ processes which are not termination-preserving, we can generate $a^n b^n c$ straightforwardly by using a process similar to that of Example 1.

*Example 2.* Consider the process $P$ below:

$$\begin{aligned}
P &= (\nu\, k_1, k_2, k_3, u_b)(\,\overline{k_1} \mid \overline{k_2} \mid Q_a \mid Q_b \mid Q_c) \\
Q_a &= !k_1.a.(\overline{k_1} \mid \overline{k_3} \mid \overline{u_b}) \\
Q_b &= k_1.!k_3.k_2.u_b.b.\overline{k_2} \\
Q_c &= k_2.(c \mid u_b.DIV)
\end{aligned}$$

where $DIV = !\tau$. One can verify that $L(P) = \{a^n b^n c\}$. □

**Termination-Preserving CCS.** Type 0 grammars can be encoded by using the termination-preserving encoding of RAMs in CCS given in [3]. However, the fact that preservation of termination is not as restrictive for CCS as it is for CCS$_!$ can also be illustrated by giving a simple termination-preserving encoding of Context-Free grammars.

**Theorem 7.** *For every type 2 grammar $G$, there exists a termination-preserving CCS process $P_G$, such that $L(P_G) = L(G)$.*

*Proof Outline.* For simplicity we restrict ourselves to Type 2 grammars in Chomsky normal form. All production rules are of the form $A \rightarrow B.C$ or $A \rightarrow a$. We can encode the productions rules of the form $A \longrightarrow B.C$ as the recursive definition $A(d) \stackrel{\text{def}}{=} (\nu\, d')(B(d') \mid d'.C(d))$ and the terminal production $A \longrightarrow a$ as the definition $A(d) \stackrel{\text{def}}{=} a.\overline{d}$. Rules with the same head can be dealt with using the summation $P + Q$. One can verify that, given a Type 2 grammar $G$, the suggested encoding generates the same language as $G$.

Notice, however, that there can be a grammar $G$ with a non-empty language exhibiting derivations which do not lead to a sequence of terminal (e.g., $A \longrightarrow B.C$, $A \longrightarrow a$, $B \longrightarrow b$, $C \longrightarrow D.C$,$D \longrightarrow d$). The suggested encoding does not give us a termination-preserving process. However one can show that there exists another grammar $G'$, with $L(G) = L(G')$ whose derivations can always lead to a final sequence of terminals . The suggested encoding applied to $G'$ instead, give us a termination-preserving process. □

### 4.3 Inside Context Sensitive Languages (CSL)

Context-Sensitive Languages (CSL) are those generated by Type 1 grammars. We shall state that every language generated by a termination-preserving CCS$_!$ process is context sensitive.

The next proposition reveals a key property of any given termination-preserving CCS$_!$ process $P$ which can be informally described as follows. Suppose that $P$ generates a sequence $s$ of size $n$. By using a technique similar to the proof of Theorem 5 and Proposition 6, we can prove that there must be a trace of $P$ that generates $s$ with a total number of $\tau$ actions bounded by $kn$ where $k$ is a constant associated to the size of $P$. More precisely,

**Proposition 7.** *Let $P$ be a termination-preserving CCS$_!$ process. There exists a constant $k$ such that for every $s = \alpha_1 \ldots \alpha_n \in L(P)$ then there must be a sequence*

$$P(\stackrel{\tau}{\longrightarrow})^{m_0} \stackrel{\alpha_1}{\longrightarrow} (\stackrel{\tau}{\longrightarrow})^{m_1} \ldots (\stackrel{\tau}{\longrightarrow})^{m_{n-1}} \stackrel{\alpha_n}{\longrightarrow} (\stackrel{\tau}{\longrightarrow})^{m_n} \not\longrightarrow$$

*with $\Sigma_{i=0}^{n} m_i \leq kn$.*

Now recall that context-sensitive grammars are equivalent to linear bounded non-deterministic Turing machines. That is a non-deterministic Turing machine with a tape with only $kn$ cells, where $n$ is the size of the input and $k$ is a constant associated with the machine. Given $P$, we can define a non-deterministic machine which simulates the runs of $P$ using the semantics of CCS$_!$ and which uses as many cells as the total number of performed actions, silent or visible, multiplied by a constant associated to $P$. Therefore, with the help of Proposition 7, we obtain the following result.

**Theorem 8.** *If $P$ is a termination-preserving CCS$_!$ process then $L(P)$ is a context-sensitive language.*

Notice that from the above theorem and Theorem 5 it follows that the languages generated by termination-preserving CCS$_!$ processes form a proper subset of context sensitive languages.

## 5 Related and Future Work

The closest related work is that in [3,4] already discussed in the introduction. Furthermore in [3] the authors also provide a discrimination result between $CCS_!$ and CCS by showing that the divergence problem (i.e., given $P$, whether $P$ has an infinite sequence of $\tau$ moves) is decidable for the former calculus but not for the latter.

In [5] the authors study replication and recursion in CCS focusing on the role of name scoping. In particular they show that $CCS_!$ is equivalent to CCS with recursion with static scoping. The standard CCS in [9] is shown to have dynamic scoping. A survey on the expressiveness of replication vs recursion is given in [13] where several decidability results about variants of $\pi$, CCS and Ambient calculi can be found. None of these works study replication with respect to computability models less expressive than Turing Machines.

In [12] the authors showed a separation result between replication and recursion in the context of temporal concurrent constraint programming (tccp) calculi. They show that the calculus with replication is no more expressive than finite-state automata while that with recursion is Turing Powerful. The semantics of tccp is rather different from that of CCS. In particular, unlike in CCS, processes interact via the shared-memory communication model and communication is asynchronous.

In the context of calculi for security protocols, the work in [6] uses a process calculus to analyze the class of ping-pong protocols introduced by Dolev and Yao. The authors show that all nontrivial properties, in particular reachability, become undecidable for a very simple recursive variant of the calculus.The authors then show that the variant with replication renders reachability decidable. The calculi considered are also different from CCS. For example no restriction is considered and communication is asynchronous.

There is extensive work in process algebras and rewriting transition systems providing expressiveness hierarchies similar to that of Chomsky as well as results closely related to those of formal grammars. For example work involving characterization of regular expression w.r.t. bisimilarity include [7,8] and more recently [1]. An excellent description is provided in [2]. These works do not deal with replication nor the restriction operator which are fundamental to our study.

As for future work, it would be interesting to investigate the decidability of the question whether a given $CCS_!$ process $P$ preserves termination. A somewhat complementary study to the one carried in this paper would be to investigate what extension to $CCS_!$ is needed for providing faithful encoding of RAMs. Clearly the extension with recursion is sufficient but there may be simpler process constructions from process algebra which also do the job.

**Acknowledgments.** We would like to thank Maurizio Gabbrielli and Catuscia Palamidessi for their suggestions on previous versions of this paper.

We are indebted to Nadia Busi for providing helpful comments, suggestions and information to complete this work. Her influential research on expressiveness is inspirational to us: may she rest in peace.

## References


1. Baeten, J.C.M., Corradini, F.: Regular expressions in process algebra. In: LICS 2005, pp. 12–19. IEEE Computer Society Press, Washington, DC, USA (2005)
2. Burkart, O., Caucal, D., Moller, F., Steffen, B.: Verification on infinite structures ch. 9, pp. 545–623. Elsevier, North-Holland (2001)
3. Busi, N., Gabbrielli, M., Zavattaro, G.: Replication vs. recursive definitions in channel based calculi. In: Baeten, J.C.M., Lenstra, J.K., Parrow, J., Woeginger, G.J. (eds.) ICALP 2003. LNCS, vol. 2719, pp. 133–144. Springer, Heidelberg (2003)
4. Busi, N., Gabbrielli, M., Zavattaro, G.: Comparing recursion, replication, and iteration in process calculi. In: Díaz, J., Karhumäki, J., Lepistö, A., Sannella, D. (eds.) ICALP 2004. LNCS, vol. 3142, pp. 307–319. Springer, Heidelberg (2004)
5. Giambiagi, P., Schneider, G., Valencia, F.D.: On the expressiveness of infinite behavior and name scoping in process calculi. In: Walukiewicz, I. (ed.) FOSSACS 2004. LNCS, vol. 2987, pp. 226–240. Springer, Heidelberg (2004)
6. Huttel, H., Srba, J.: Recursion vs. replication in simple cryptographic protocols. In: Vojtáš, P., Bieliková, M., Charron-Bost, B., Sýkora, O. (eds.) SOFSEM 2005. LNCS, vol. 3381, pp. 175–184. Springer, Heidelberg (2005)
7. Kanellakis, P.C., Smolka, S.A.: CCS expressions finite state processes, and three problems of equivalence. Inf. Comput. 86(1), 43–68 (1990)
8. Milner, R.: A complete inference system for a class of regular behaviours. J. Comput. Syst. Sci. 28(3), 439–466 (1984)
9. Milner, R.: Communication and Concurrency. International Series in Computer Science. Prentice Hall, Englewood Cliffs (1989) SU Fisher Research 511/24
10. Milner, R.: Communicating and Mobile Systems: the $\pi$-calculus. Cambridge University Press, Cambridge (1999)
11. Minsky, M.: Computation: finite and infinite machines. Prentice-Hall, Englewood Cliffs (1967)
12. Nielsen, M., Palamidessi, C., Valencia, F.: On the expressive power of concurrent constraint programming languages. In: PPDP 2002, pp. 156–167. ACM Press, New York (2002)
13. Palamidessi, C., Valencia, F.D.: Recursion vs replication in process calculi: Expressiveness. Bulletin of the EATCS 87, 105–125 (2005)
14. .Parrow, J.: Trios in concert. In: Plotkin, G., Stirling, C., Tofte, M. (eds.) Proof, Language and Interaction: Essays in Honour of Robin Milner, pp. 621–637. MIT Press, Cambridge (2000)
15. Sangiorgi, D., Walker, D.: PI-Calculus: A Theory of Mobile Processes. Cambridge University Press, New York (2001)

# Call-by-Name and Call-by-Value in Normal Modal Logic

Yoshihiko Kakutani

Department of Information Science, University of Tokyo
kakutani@is.s.u-tokyo.ac.jp

**Abstract.** This paper provides a call-by-name and a call-by-value calculus, both of which have a Curry-Howard correspondence to the minimal normal logic **K**. The calculi are extensions of the $\lambda\mu$-calculi, and their semantics are given by CPS transformations into a calculus corresponding to the intuitionistic fragment of **K**. The duality between call-by-name and call-by-value with modalities is investigated in our calculi.

## 1 Introduction

Modal logics have a long history since logics with strict implications, and are now widely accepted both theoretically and practically. Especially, studies of modal logics by Kripke semantics [18] are quite active and a large number of results exist, for example, [7] is a textbook about such studies. Since Kripke semantics concern only provability, equality on proofs is less studied on modal logics compared with traditional logics.

It is well-known that the intuitionistic propositional logic exactly corresponds to the simply typed $\lambda$-calculus: formulae as types and proofs as terms. Such a correspondence is called a Curry-Howard correspondence after Howard's work [15]. A Curry-Howard correspondence enables us to study equality on proofs computationally. Though the correspondence can be extended to higher-order and predicate logics as shown in [3], we investigate only propositional logics in this paper. The aim of this study is to give a proper calculus that have a Curry-Howard correspondence to the modal logic **K**. Through a Curry-Howard correspondence, any type system can be regarded as a logic by forgetting terms. In this sense, modal logics are contributing to practical studies for programming languages, *e.g.*, staged computations [8] and information flow analysis [23]. Since **K** is known as a minimal modal logic, this paper focuses on **K** rather than **S4**.

Before defining a calculus for **K**, we consider the intuitionistic fragment of **K**, which is called **IK** in this paper. In Section 2, the calculus for **IK** is defined as a refinement of Bellin *et al.*'s calculus [4] rather than Martini and Masini's[22]. Our calculus is sound and complete for the categorical semantics given in [4]. The study [19] about simply typed $\lambda$-calculus and cartesian closed categories is a typical study of categorical semantics. Categorical semantics of modal logics are studied by Bierman and de Paiva, and Bellin *et al.* in [6] and [4]. Their semantics are based on studies about semantics of linear logics (*e.g.*, [29] and [5]) since the exponential of the linear logic [12] is a kind of **S4** modality.

Z. Shao (Ed.): APLAS 2007, LNCS 4807, pp. 399–414, 2007.

A Curry-Howard correspondence between the classical propositional logic and the $\lambda$-calculus with continuations was provided in [13] by Griffin. Parigot has proposed the $\lambda\mu$-calculus as a calculus for the classical logic in [26]. Now, kinds of $\lambda\mu$-calculi exist and some of them are defined by CPS transformations. A CPS transformation was originally introduced in [11], and the relation between call-by-value and CPS semantics was first studied by Plotkin in [27]. De Groote defines a CPS transformation on a call-by-name $\lambda\mu$-calculus in [9], but in this paper, we adopt Selinger's CPS transformation [30], which is an extension of Hofmann and Streicher's [14]. In Section 3, we provide a call-by-name $\lambda\mu$-calculus with a box modality, which has a Curry-Howard correspondence to **K**, by the CPS semantics into the calculus for **IK** defined in Section 2. A call-by-value $\lambda\mu$-calculus is provided in [25] by Ong and Stewart. We define a call-by-value calculus for **K** also as an extension of Selinger's call-by-value $\lambda\mu$-calculus [30] via the CPS transformation in Section 4.

The duality between call-by-name and call-by-value is an important property of the classical logic. The duality on a programming language with first-class continuations was first formalized by Filinski in [10]. It has been formalized on the $\lambda\mu$-calculi in [30] by Selinger, and reformulated as sequent calculi in [34] by Wadler. In [16], the duality is developed with recursion by the author. In Section 5, we study such duality on the classical modal logic **K**.

In addition, we investigate the logic **S4** with the CPS semantics. It is shown in Section 6 that a diamond modality is a monad in call-by-name **S4**.

### Notations

We introduce notations specific to this paper.

- The symbol "$\equiv$" denotes the $\alpha$-equivalence.
- We may omit superscripted and subscripted types if they are trivial.
- A notation "$\overrightarrow{M}$" is used for a sequence of meta-variables "$M_1, \ldots, M_n$". Hence, an expression "$\overrightarrow{M}, \overrightarrow{N}$" stands for the concatenation of $\overrightarrow{M}$ and $\overrightarrow{N}$.
- For a unary operator $\Phi(-)$, we write "$\Phi(\overrightarrow{M})$" for "$\Phi(M_1), \ldots, \Phi(M_n)$".
- We write "$\overrightarrow{N}(\theta\overrightarrow{x}.M)$" for "$N_1(\theta x_1.\cdots N_n(\theta x_n.M)\cdots)$" and "$[\overrightarrow{a}](\theta\overrightarrow{x}.M)$" for "$[a_1](\theta x_1.\cdots[a_n](\theta x_n.M)\cdots)$", where $\theta$ is $\lambda$ or $\mu$.
- We write "$\neg\tau$" for "$\tau \to \bot$".

## 2 Calculus for Intuitionistic Normal Modal Logic

In this section, we study the intuitionistic modal logic **IK**. Intuitionism of a diamond modality is not trivial, for example, [33] gives an account of it, but this section focuses on the box fragment of **IK**. We call also this fragment itself **IK** in this paper. A diamond modality is investigated in a classical logic after the next section.

It is well-known that the $\lambda$-calculus with conjunctions and disjunctions exactly corresponds to the intuitionistic propositional logic. Therefore, we extend

**Table 1.** Typing rules of λ□-calculus

$$\frac{}{\Gamma \vdash \alpha^\tau : \tau} \qquad \frac{}{\Gamma, x:\tau, \Gamma' \vdash x : \tau}$$

$$\frac{}{\Gamma \vdash \langle\rangle : \top} \qquad \frac{}{\Gamma \vdash []_\tau : \bot \to \tau}$$

$$\frac{\Gamma, x:\sigma \vdash M : \tau}{\Gamma \vdash \lambda x^\sigma. M : \sigma \to \tau} \qquad \frac{\Gamma \vdash M : \sigma \to \tau \quad \Gamma \vdash N : \sigma}{\Gamma \vdash MN : \tau}$$

$$\frac{\Gamma \vdash M_1 : \tau_1 \quad \Gamma \vdash M_2 : \tau_2}{\Gamma \vdash \langle M_1, M_2\rangle : \tau_1 \wedge \tau_2} \qquad \frac{\Gamma \vdash M : \tau_1 \wedge \tau_2}{\Gamma \vdash \pi_j M : \tau_j}$$

$$\frac{\Gamma, x_1 : \sigma_1 \vdash M_1 : \tau \quad \Gamma, x_2 : \sigma_2 \vdash M_2 : \tau}{\Gamma \vdash [\lambda x_1^{\sigma_1}. M_1, \lambda x_2^{\sigma_2}. M_2] : \sigma_1 \vee \sigma_2 \to \tau} \qquad \frac{\Gamma \vdash M : \tau_j}{\Gamma \vdash \iota_j M : \tau_1 \vee \tau_2}$$

$$\frac{x_1 : \sigma_1, \ldots, x_n : \sigma_n \vdash M : \tau \quad \Gamma \vdash N_1 : \Box\sigma_1 \quad \cdots \quad \Gamma \vdash N_n : \Box\sigma_n}{\Gamma \vdash \texttt{box}\,\langle x_1^{\sigma_1}, \ldots, x_n^{\sigma_n}\rangle\ \texttt{be}\ \langle N_1, \ldots, N_n\rangle\ \texttt{in}\ M : \Box\tau}$$

the λ-calculus with a box construct. Our calculus, called the λ□-calculus, is a refinement of Bellin *et al.*'s calculus given in [4]. The difference from Bellin *et al.*'s is discussed in [17].

**Definition 1.** *The λ□-calculus is defined as follows. Types* $\tau$ *and terms* $M$ *are defined by*

$$\begin{aligned}\tau &::= p \mid \tau \to \tau \mid \top \mid \tau \wedge \tau \mid \bot \mid \tau \vee \tau \mid \Box\tau \\ M &::= \alpha^\tau \mid x \mid \lambda x^\tau. M \mid MM \mid \langle\rangle \mid \langle M, M\rangle \mid \pi_1 M \mid \pi_2 M \\ &\mid []_\tau \mid [\lambda x^\tau. M, \lambda x^\tau. M] \mid \iota_1 M \mid \iota_2 M \\ &\mid \texttt{box}\,\langle x^\tau, \ldots, x^\tau\rangle\ \texttt{be}\ \langle M, \ldots, M\rangle\ \texttt{in}\ M\end{aligned}$$

*where* $p$*,* $c$*, and* $x$ *range over type constants, constants, and variables, respectively. A variable* $x_i$ *occurring freely in* $M$ *is bound in the term* $\texttt{box}\,\langle x_1, \ldots, x_n\rangle \texttt{be}\ \langle N_1, \ldots, N_n\rangle\ \texttt{in}\ M$*. The typing rules are given in Table 1. The equality is defined by the axioms given in Table 2. In the table, an equation* $M = N$ *means that two derivable judgments* $\Gamma \vdash M : \tau$ *and* $\Gamma \vdash N : \tau$ *are equal for any* $\Gamma$ *and* $\tau$*. A theory including the equality of the λ□-calculus is called a λ□-theory.*

Note that all free variables of $M$ are covered by $\overrightarrow{x}$ when the term $\texttt{box}\,\langle\overrightarrow{x}\rangle\ \texttt{be}\ \langle\overrightarrow{N}\rangle\ \texttt{in}\ M$ is typable. It means that each box encloses a proof.

Since the λ□-calculus has essentially the same syntax as the calculus defined in [4], we can show that our calculus corresponds to the intuitionistic modal logic.

Let **IK** be an intuitionistic Hilbert system with the axiom $\Box(\sigma \to \tau) \to \Box\sigma \to \Box\tau$ and the box inference rule. The λ□-calculus can be regarded as a natural deduction by forgetting terms. It is shown as follows that our logic is equivalent to **IK** with respect to provability. The box inference rule of **IK** is simulated by

$$\frac{\vdash M : \tau}{\vdash \texttt{box}\,\langle\rangle\ \texttt{be}\ \langle\rangle\ \texttt{in}\ M : \Box\tau}$$

**Table 2.** Axioms of $\lambda\square$-calculus

$(\lambda x. M)N = M\{N/x\}$

$\lambda x. Mx = M$ $\qquad\qquad\qquad\qquad\qquad\qquad$ if $x \notin \mathbf{FV}(M)$

$\langle\rangle = M$

$\pi_j\langle M_1, M_2\rangle = M_j$

$\langle\pi_1 M, \pi_2 M\rangle = M$

$[] = M$

$[\lambda x_1. M_1, \lambda x_2. M_2](\iota_j N) = (\lambda x_j. M_j)N$

$[\lambda x_1. M(\iota_1 x_1), \lambda x_2. M(\iota_2 x_2)] = M$ $\qquad\qquad$ if $x_1, x_2 \notin \mathbf{FV}(M)$

$\mathbf{box}\,\langle x\rangle\,\mathbf{be}\,\langle M\rangle\,\mathbf{in}\,x = M$

$\mathbf{box}\,\langle \vec{w}, x, \vec{z}\rangle\,\mathbf{be}\,\langle \vec{Q}, \mathbf{box}\,\langle \vec{y}\rangle\,\mathbf{be}\,\langle \vec{L}\rangle\,\mathbf{in}\,N, \vec{P}\rangle\,\mathbf{in}\,M$

$\qquad = \mathbf{box}\,\langle \vec{w}, \vec{y}, \vec{z}\rangle\,\mathbf{be}\,\langle \vec{Q}, \vec{L}, \vec{P}\rangle\,\mathbf{in}\,M\{N/x\}$ $\qquad$ if $|\vec{w}| = |\vec{Q}|$

and the distributivity is realized by the judgment

$$\vdash \lambda f'. \lambda x'. \mathbf{box}\,\langle f, x\rangle\,\mathbf{be}\,\langle f', x'\rangle\,\mathbf{in}\,fx : \square(\sigma \to \tau) \to \square\sigma \to \square\tau$$

in our logic. Conversely, **IK** simulates our typing rule as

$$\frac{\dfrac{\dfrac{\sigma_1, \ldots, \sigma_n \vdash \tau}{\vdash \sigma_1 \to \cdots \to \sigma_n \to \tau}}{\dfrac{\vdash \square(\sigma_1 \to \cdots \to \sigma_n \to \tau)}{\dfrac{\Gamma \vdash \square(\sigma_1 \to \cdots \to \sigma_n \to \tau)}{\Gamma \vdash \square\sigma_1 \to \square(\sigma_2 \to \cdots \to \sigma_n \to \tau)} \qquad \Gamma \vdash \square\sigma_1}}}{\dfrac{\Gamma \vdash \square(\sigma_2 \to \cdots \to \sigma_n \to \tau)}{\dfrac{\vdots}{\dfrac{\dfrac{\Gamma \vdash \square(\sigma_n \to \tau)}{\Gamma \vdash \square\sigma_n \to \square\tau} \qquad \Gamma \vdash \square\sigma_n}{\Gamma \vdash \square\tau}}}}$$

We can also show more directly that our logic corresponds to the sequent calculus formulation of **IK** proposed in [35].

According to the above encoding, it is not trivial whether an exchange rule commutes with a box operation. Therefore, we distinguish such symmetricity from other axioms although it is common to consider proofs up to exchanges.

**Definition 2.** *In a $\lambda\square$-theory, $\square$ is symmetric if the equation*

$$\mathbf{box}\,\langle \vec{w}, x, y, \vec{z}\rangle\,\mathbf{be}\,\langle \vec{Q}, N, L, \vec{P}\rangle\,\mathbf{in}\,M$$

$$= \mathbf{box}\,\langle \vec{w}, y, x, \vec{z}\rangle\,\mathbf{be}\,\langle \vec{Q}, L, N, \vec{P}\rangle\,\mathbf{in}\,M \qquad if\ |\vec{w}| = |\vec{Q}|$$

*is satisfied.*

Our axiomatization is justified logically via the Curry-Howard correspondence: the equation

$$\mathtt{box}\,\langle x\rangle\ \mathtt{be}\ \langle M\rangle\ \mathtt{in}\ x = M$$

says that a trivial boxed proof can be removed, and the equation

$$\begin{aligned}&\mathtt{box}\,\langle \overrightarrow{w}, x, \overrightarrow{z}\rangle\ \mathtt{be}\ \langle \overrightarrow{Q}, \mathtt{box}\,\langle \overrightarrow{y}\rangle\ \mathtt{be}\ \langle \overrightarrow{L}\rangle\ \mathtt{in}\ N, \overrightarrow{P}\rangle\ \mathtt{in}\ M\\ &= \mathtt{box}\,\langle \overrightarrow{w}, \overrightarrow{y}, \overrightarrow{z}\rangle\ \mathtt{be}\ \langle \overrightarrow{Q}, \overrightarrow{L}, \overrightarrow{P}\rangle\ \mathtt{in}\ M\{N/x\}\end{aligned}$$

says that adjacent boxes can be combined into one box. In addition, Abe characterizes the $\lambda\Box$-calculus by a standard translation into the intuitionistic predicate logic in [1]. Computational meaning of the $\lambda\Box$-calculus is shown as follows.

We consider categorical models of **IK** along the line of [4]. Because Kripke semantics cover provability but not proofs themselves, they are not suitable for our aim. Since our calculus is an extension of the simply typed $\lambda$-calculus, a model of the $\lambda\Box$-calculus should be a cartesian closed category with finite coproducts. ([19] provides a deep analysis of the $\lambda$-calculus and cartesian closed categories.) In addition, the $\lambda\Box$-calculus requires a modality. Roughly speaking, the modality behaves like a functor and is characterized by the axiom $\Box\sigma \wedge \Box\tau \rightarrow \Box(\sigma \wedge \tau)$, which is an adjoint of $\Box(\sigma \rightarrow \tau) \rightarrow \Box\sigma \rightarrow \Box\tau$. Assuming that this axiom is parametric, the modality is just *a monoidal endofunctor* with respect to cartesian products. (Fundamental properties of monoidal categories are found in [20].) Hence, a model of **IK** is naturally considered a cartesian closed category with a lax monoidal endofunctor with respect to cartesian products.

An interpretation is given in the usual manner: a type is interpreted as an object and a judgment is interpreted as a morphism. Let a bicartesian closed category $\mathcal{C}$ have a monoidal endofunctor $\Box$ with a natural transformation $\mathtt{m}_{A,B} : \Box A \times \Box B \rightarrow \Box(A \times B)$ and $\mathtt{m}_\top : \top \rightarrow \Box\top$. We write $\mathtt{m}^*$ as a composite of $\mathtt{m}_{A,B}$'s or $\mathtt{m}_\top$. An interpretation $[\![-]\!]$ of the $\lambda\Box$-calculus into $\mathcal{C}$ is defined inductively by $[\![\Box\sigma]\!] = \Box[\![\sigma]\!]$ and

$$\begin{aligned}&[\![\Gamma \vdash \mathtt{box}\,\langle \overrightarrow{x}\rangle\ \mathtt{be}\ \langle \overrightarrow{N}\rangle\ \mathtt{in}\ M : \Box\tau]\!]\\ &= [\![\Gamma]\!] \xrightarrow{\langle g_1,\ldots,g_n\rangle} \Box[\![\sigma_1]\!] \times \cdots \times \Box[\![\sigma_n]\!] \xrightarrow{\mathtt{m}^*} \Box([\![\sigma_1]\!] \times \cdots \times [\![\sigma_n]\!]) \xrightarrow{\Box f} \Box[\![\tau]\!]\\ &\quad \text{where } g_i = [\![\Gamma \vdash N_i : \Box\sigma_i]\!] \text{ and } f = [\![x_1 : \sigma_1, \ldots, x_n : \sigma_n \vdash M : \tau]\!].\end{aligned}$$

**Theorem 3.** *The $\lambda\Box$-calculus is sound and complete for the class of bicartesian closed categories with monoidal endofunctors.*
*The $\lambda\Box$-calculus with symmetric $\Box$ is sound and complete for the class of bicartesian closed categories with symmetric monoidal endofunctors.*

*Proof.* The soundness is shown by induction as usual. The former box axiom holds because a functor preserves identities. The latter box axiom holds because of the naturality of $\mathtt{m}$.

The completeness is shown by construction of the term model. The functor conditions are derived from the former box axiom and a special case of the latter axiom. A natural transformation is given by $\lambda x.(\texttt{box}\,\langle y_1, y_2\rangle\ \texttt{be}\ \langle \pi_1 x, \pi_2 x\rangle\ \texttt{in}\ \langle y_1, y_2\rangle)$ and its properties follow from the latter box axiom. □

In fact, the term model in the above proof is an initial model, so we can get a result about internal languages in addition. Because of the space limitation, we omit a discussion about the category of λ□-theories along the line of [19]. The notion of equivalence on categories with monoidal endofunctors follows [21].

**Definition 4.** *The internal language of a bicartesian closed category $\mathcal{C}$ with a monoidal endofunctor is a λ□-theory whose type constants consist of objects of $\mathcal{C}$ and whose constants consist of morphisms of $\mathcal{C}$ such that the canonical interpretation is sound and complete.*

**Proposition 5.** *A bicartesian closed category with a monoidal endofunctor is equivalent to the term model of its internal language.*

One might expect a monoidal endofunctor to be strong, *i.e.*, to preserve products, but it can be reminded of the intuitionistic modal logic **IS4**. A model of the box fragment of **IS4** is a cartesian closed category with a monoidal comonad as mentioned by Bierman and de Paiva in [6]. Here, a monoidal comonad is a lax monoidal functor but not a strong monoidal functor in general. If the modality of **IK** is required to be strong monoidal, a model of **IS4** cannot be a model of **IK**. Therefore, we do not require the modality to be strong monoidal. Nevertheless it is possible to consider a strong monoidal functor in our calculus.

**Definition 6.** *In a λ□-theory, □ is strong if the equations*

$$\begin{aligned}
&\texttt{box}\,\langle \vec{w}, x, \vec{z}\rangle\ \texttt{be}\ \langle \vec{Q}, N, \vec{P}\rangle\ \texttt{in}\ M \\
&\quad = \texttt{box}\,\langle \vec{w}, \vec{z}\rangle\ \texttt{be}\ \langle \vec{Q}, \vec{P}\rangle\ \texttt{in}\ M && \textit{if } |\vec{w}| = |\vec{Q}| \\
&\texttt{box}\,\langle \vec{w}, x, y, \vec{z}\rangle\ \texttt{be}\ \langle \vec{Q}, N, N, \vec{P}\rangle\ \texttt{in}\ M \\
&\quad = \texttt{box}\,\langle \vec{w}, x, \vec{z}\rangle\ \texttt{be}\ \langle \vec{Q}, N, \vec{P}\rangle\ \texttt{in}\ M\{x/y\} && \textit{if } |\vec{w}| = |\vec{Q}|
\end{aligned}$$

*are satisfied.*

The soundness and completeness of the λ□-calculus with strong □ are proved in the same way as Theorem 3.

**Theorem 7.** *The λ□-calculus with strong (resp. strong symmetric) □ is sound and complete for the class of bicartesian closed categories with strong (resp. strong symmetric) monoidal functors.*

It is also possible to define the linear version of the λ□-calculus if we restrict occurrence of every free variable to only once. Because in fact the proof of Theorem 3 does not depend on properties of cartesian products, also the linear calculus enjoys the theorem: the linear λ□-calculus is sound and complete for the class of monoidal closed categories with monoidal endofunctors.

*Remark 8.* This paper is overall motivated by equality on proofs and does not address reductions, but the author proposes a reduction system for the implication fragment of the λ□-calculus in [17]. The strong normalizability, the confluency, and the subformula property of the calculus has been proved in [17].

**Table 3.** Typing rules of $\lambda\mu\Box$-calculus

$$\frac{}{\Gamma \vdash \alpha^{\tau} : \tau \mid \Delta} \qquad \frac{}{\Gamma, x:\tau, \Gamma' \vdash x : \tau \mid \Delta} \qquad \frac{}{\Gamma \vdash \langle\rangle : \top \mid \Delta}$$

$$\frac{\Gamma, x:\sigma \vdash M : \tau \mid \Delta}{\Gamma \vdash \lambda x^{\sigma}.\, M : \sigma \to \tau \mid \Delta} \qquad \frac{\Gamma \vdash M : \sigma \to \tau \mid \Delta \quad \Gamma \vdash N : \sigma \mid \Delta}{\Gamma \vdash MN : \tau \mid \Delta}$$

$$\frac{\Gamma \vdash M_1 : \tau_1 \mid \Delta \quad \Gamma \vdash M_2 : \tau_2 \mid \Delta}{\Gamma \vdash \langle M_1, M_2\rangle : \tau_1 \wedge \tau_2 \mid \Delta} \qquad \frac{\Gamma \vdash M : \tau_1 \wedge \tau_2 \mid \Delta}{\Gamma \vdash \pi_j M : \tau_j \mid \Delta}$$

$$\frac{\Gamma \vdash M : \bot \mid a:\tau, \Delta}{\Gamma \vdash \mu a^{\tau}.\, M : \tau \mid \Delta} \qquad \frac{\Gamma \vdash M : \tau \mid \Delta, a:\tau, \Delta'}{\Gamma \vdash [a]M : \bot \mid \Delta, a:\tau, \Delta'}$$

$$\frac{\Gamma \vdash M : \bot \mid a_1:\tau_1, a_2:\tau_2, \Delta}{\Gamma \vdash \mu(a_1^{\tau_1}, a_2^{\tau_2}).\, M : \tau_1 \vee \tau_2 \mid \Delta} \qquad \frac{\Gamma \vdash M : \tau_1 \vee \tau_2 \mid \Delta, a_1:\tau_1, a_2:\tau_2, \Delta'}{\Gamma \vdash [a_1, a_2]M : \bot \mid \Delta, a_1:\tau_1, a_2:\tau_2, \Delta'}$$

$$\frac{x_1:\sigma_1, \ldots, x_n:\sigma_n \vdash M : \tau \mid \quad \Gamma \vdash N_1 : \Box\sigma_1 \mid \Delta \quad \cdots \quad \Gamma \vdash N_n : \Box\sigma_n \mid \Delta}{\Gamma \vdash \mathtt{box}\, \langle x_1^{\sigma_1}, \ldots, x_n^{\sigma_n}\rangle\ \mathtt{be}\ \langle N_1, \ldots, N_n\rangle\ \mathtt{in}\ M : \Box\tau \mid \Delta}$$

## 3 Call-by-Name Calculus for Normal Modal Logic

We have defined a calculus for the intuitionistic modal logic in the previous section. This section provides a calculus corresponding to the classical normal modal logic **K**. Our calculus is defined as an extension of Selinger's version [30] of the $\lambda\mu$-calculus, which has a Curry-Howard correspondence to the classical logic. The semantics of the calculus is given by a CPS transformation to the $\lambda\Box$-calculus.

For abbreviation, we may write $\lambda\langle x_1, x_2\rangle.\, M$ for $\lambda y.\, (\lambda x_1.\, \lambda x_2.\, M)(\pi_1 y)(\pi_2 y)$ and $[M_1, M_2]$ for $[\lambda y_1.\, M_1 y_1, \lambda y_2.\, M_2 y_2]$ in the $\lambda\Box$-calculus.

**Definition 9.** *The call-by-name $\lambda\mu\Box$-calculus is defined as follows. Types $\tau$ and terms $M$ are defined by*

$$\begin{aligned} \tau &::= p \mid \tau \to \tau \mid \top \mid \tau \wedge \tau \mid \bot \mid \tau \vee \tau \mid \Box\tau \\ M &::= \alpha^{\tau} \mid x \mid \lambda x^{\tau}.\, M \mid MM \mid \langle\rangle \mid \langle M, M\rangle \mid \pi_1 M \mid \pi_2 M \\ &\quad\ \mid \mu a^{\tau}.\, M \mid [a]M \mid \mu(a^{\tau}, a^{\tau}).\, M \mid [a, a]M \\ &\quad\ \mid \mathtt{box}\, \langle x^{\tau}, \ldots, x^{\tau}\rangle\ \mathtt{be}\ \langle M, \ldots, M\rangle\ \mathtt{in}\ M \end{aligned}$$

*where $p$, $c$, $x$, and $a$ range over type constants, constants, variables, and control variables, respectively. The typing rules are given in Table 3. The equality is defined by the transformation $[\![-]\!]_{\mathrm{n}}$ to the $\lambda\Box$-calculus with a type constant $\mathtt{R}$ given in Table 4. We write $M =_{\mathrm{n}} N$ for $[\![M]\!]_{\mathrm{n}} = [\![N]\!]_{\mathrm{n}}$ when $M$ and $N$ have the same type.*

A typing derivation of $x_1{:}\sigma_1, \ldots, x_n{:}\sigma_n \vdash M : \tau \mid a_1{:}\tau_1, \ldots, a_m{:}\tau_m$ in the $\lambda\mu\Box$-calculus is regarded as a natural deduction style derivation of $\sigma_1, \ldots, \sigma_n, \neg\tau_1, \ldots, \neg\tau_m \vdash \tau$. By the same reason as in the intuitionistic case, it can be seen that the $\lambda\mu\Box$-calculus corresponds to the classical modal logic **K** with respect to provability.

**Table 4.** CBN CPS transformation

$$p^\circ \equiv p \qquad (\Box\tau)^\circ \equiv \Box(\tau^\circ \to \mathtt{R}) \to \mathtt{R}$$
$$(\neg\sigma)^\circ \equiv \sigma^\circ \to \mathtt{R} \qquad (\sigma \to \tau)^\circ \equiv (\sigma^\circ \to \mathtt{R}) \wedge \tau^\circ \text{ if } \tau \not\equiv \bot$$
$$\top^\circ \equiv \bot \qquad (\tau_1 \wedge \tau_2)^\circ \equiv {\tau_1}^\circ \vee {\tau_2}^\circ$$
$$\bot^\circ \equiv \top \qquad (\tau_1 \vee \tau_2)^\circ \equiv {\tau_1}^\circ \wedge {\tau_2}^\circ$$

$$
\begin{aligned}
[\![\alpha]\!]_{\mathrm{n}} &\equiv \alpha \\
[\![x]\!]_{\mathrm{n}} &\equiv x \\
[\![\lambda x.\, M]\!]_{\mathrm{n}} &\equiv \lambda x.\, [\![M]\!]_{\mathrm{n}}\langle\,\rangle \text{ if } M : \bot \\
&\equiv \lambda\langle x, k\rangle.\, [\![M]\!]_{\mathrm{n}} k \text{ o.w.} \\
[\![MN]\!]_{\mathrm{n}} &\equiv \lambda k.\, [\![M]\!]_{\mathrm{n}}[\![N]\!]_{\mathrm{n}} \text{ if } MN : \bot \\
&\equiv \lambda k.\, [\![M]\!]_{\mathrm{n}}\langle [\![N]\!]_{\mathrm{n}}, k\rangle \text{ o.w.} \\
[\![\langle\,\rangle]\!]_{\mathrm{n}} &\equiv [\,] \\
[\![\langle M_1, M_2\rangle]\!]_{\mathrm{n}} &\equiv [[\![M_1]\!]_{\mathrm{n}}, [\![M_2]\!]_{\mathrm{n}}] \\
[\![\pi_j M]\!]_{\mathrm{n}} &\equiv \lambda k.\, [\![M]\!]_{\mathrm{n}}(\iota_j k) \\
[\![\mu a.\, M]\!]_{\mathrm{n}} &\equiv \lambda a.\, [\![M]\!]_{\mathrm{n}}\langle\,\rangle \\
[\![[a]M]\!]_{\mathrm{n}} &\equiv \lambda k.\, [\![M]\!]_{\mathrm{n}} a \\
[\![\mu(a_1, a_2).\, M]\!]_{\mathrm{n}} &\equiv \lambda\langle a_1, a_2\rangle.\, [\![M]\!]_{\mathrm{n}}\langle\,\rangle \\
[\![[a_1, a_2]M]\!]_{\mathrm{n}} &\equiv \lambda k.\, [\![M]\!]_{\mathrm{n}}\langle a_1, a_2\rangle \\
[\![\mathtt{box}\ \langle\vec{x}\rangle\ \mathtt{be}\ \langle\vec{N}\rangle\ \mathtt{in}\ M]\!]_{\mathrm{n}} &\equiv \lambda k.\, [\![\vec{N}]\!]_{\mathrm{n}}(\lambda\vec{x'}.\, k(\mathtt{box}\ \langle\vec{x}\rangle\ \mathtt{be}\ \langle\vec{x'}\rangle\ \mathtt{in}\ [\![M]\!]_{\mathrm{n}}))
\end{aligned}
$$

$$\frac{x_1 : \sigma_1, \ldots, x_n : \sigma_n \vdash M : \tau \mid a_1 : \tau_1, \ldots, a_m : \tau_m}{x_1 : {\sigma_1}^\circ \to \mathtt{R}, \ldots, x_n : {\sigma_n}^\circ \to \mathtt{R}, a_1 : {\tau_1}^\circ, \ldots, a_m : {\tau_m}^\circ \vdash [\![M]\!]_{\mathrm{n}} : \tau^\circ \to \mathtt{R}}$$

Unlike the intuitionistic case, call-by-name classical disjunctions are not coproducts. (Our formulation of disjunctions is based on Selinger's [30], but it is possible to define the calculus along the line of [28].) Instead of case functions and injections, we use the syntax sugar

$$
\begin{aligned}
&[\lambda x_1^{\sigma_1}.\, M_1, \lambda x_2^{\sigma_2}.\, M_2] \\
&\quad \equiv \lambda x^{\sigma_1 \vee \sigma_2}.\, \mu b^{\tau}.\, [b]((\lambda x_1^{\sigma_1}.\, M_1)(\mu a_1^{\sigma_1}.\, [b]((\lambda x_2^{\sigma_2}.\, M_2)(\mu a_2^{\sigma_2}.\, [a_1, a_2]x)))) \\
&\iota_j M \equiv \mu(a_1^{\tau_1}, a_2^{\tau_2}).\, [a_j]M \ \text{ where } a_1, a_2 \notin \mathtt{FV}(M).
\end{aligned}
$$

These abbreviations are applied to also the call-by-value $\lambda\mu\Box$-calculus given in the next section.

*Remark 10.* In the definition of the CPS transformation, the cases of abstractions and applications depend on the types, but such dependency is not essential for the semantics. It is just a technical requirement for the syntactic duality shown in Section 5.

The equality is defined by the CPS transformation, so it is not trivial which kind of equation holds. We show some equations which hold in the $\lambda\mu\Box$-calculus but do not hold in the ordinary $\lambda\mu$-calculus. (Of course, equations that hold in the ordinary $\lambda\mu$-calculus hold in the $\lambda\mu\Box$-calculus.)

**Proposition 11.** *The following equations hold in the call-by-name $\lambda\mu\Box$-calculus.*

$$\mathtt{box}\,\langle x\rangle\ \mathtt{be}\ \langle M\rangle\ \mathtt{in}\ x =_{\mathrm{n}} M$$

$$\mathtt{box}\,\langle \vec{w}, x, \vec{z}\rangle\ \mathtt{be}\ \langle \vec{Q}, \mathtt{box}\,\langle\vec{y}\rangle\ \mathtt{be}\ \langle\vec{L}\rangle\ \mathtt{in}\ N, \vec{P}\rangle\ \mathtt{in}\ M$$
$$=_{\mathrm{n}} \mathtt{box}\,\langle \vec{w}, \vec{y}, \vec{z}\rangle\ \mathtt{be}\ \langle \vec{Q}, \vec{L}, \vec{P}\rangle\ \mathtt{in}\ M\{N/x\} \qquad \textit{if } |\vec{w}| = |\vec{Q}|$$

$$\mathtt{box}\,\langle \vec{x}\rangle\ \mathtt{be}\ \langle \mu a.\, N, \vec{P}\rangle\ \mathtt{in}\ M$$
$$=_{\mathrm{n}} \mu b.\, N\{[b](\mathtt{box}\,\langle\vec{x}\rangle\ \mathtt{be}\ \langle -, \vec{P}\rangle\ \mathtt{in}\ M)/[a]-\}$$

*where* $\{C/[a]-\}$ *means the substitution of* $C\{M\}$ *for* $[a]M$*,* $C\{\mu a.\,[a,b]M\}$ *for* $[a,b]M$*, and* $C\{\mu a.\,[b,a]M\}$ *for* $[b,a]M$*.*

*Proof.* Straightforwardly. Note that $[\![M\{N/x\}]\!]_{\mathrm{n}} \equiv [\![M]\!]_{\mathrm{n}}\{[\![N]\!]_{\mathrm{n}}/x\}$ holds. □

The fact, that the $\lambda\mu\Box$-calculus satisfies box axioms of the $\lambda\Box$-calculus, means that the modality in the $\lambda\mu\Box$-calculus is a monoidal functor.

*Remark 12.* □ is neither symmetric nor strong in the $\lambda\mu\Box$-calculus even if □ is symmetric and strong in the target of the CPS transformation.

Though the $\lambda\mu\Box$-calculus does not have a diamond modality primitively, we can define a construct for a diamond modality. Let $\Diamond\tau$ be $\neg\Box\neg\tau$. Define syntax sugar by

$$\mathtt{dia}\,\langle\vec{a}\rangle\ \mathtt{be}\ \langle\vec{N}\rangle\ \mathtt{in}\ M$$
$$\equiv \lambda k.\, \vec{N}(\lambda\vec{x'}.\, k(\mathtt{box}\,\langle\vec{x}\rangle\ \mathtt{be}\ \langle\vec{x'}\rangle\ \mathtt{in}\ \mu b.\, \vec{x}(\mu\vec{a}.\,[b]M)))$$

for terms $M$ and $\vec{N}$ such that $\vdash M : \neg\tau \mid a_1 : \sigma_1, \ldots, a_n : \sigma_n$ and $\Gamma \vdash N_j : \neg\Diamond\sigma_j \mid \Delta$ hold. Then the judgment

$$\Gamma \vdash \mathtt{dia}\,\langle a_1^{\sigma_1}, \ldots, a_n^{\sigma_n}\rangle\ \mathtt{be}\ \langle N_1, \ldots, N_n\rangle\ \mathtt{in}\ M : \neg\Diamond\tau \mid \Delta$$

is derivable. This $\mathtt{dia}\,\langle\vec{a}\rangle\ \mathtt{be}\ \langle\vec{N}\rangle\ \mathtt{in}\ M$ is a dual form of $\mathtt{box}\,\langle\vec{x}\rangle\ \mathtt{be}\ \langle\vec{N}\rangle\ \mathtt{in}\ M$ in the sense of Section 5. A formula $\Diamond(\tau_1 \vee \tau_2) \to \Diamond\tau_1 \vee \Diamond\tau_2$, which means distributivity of $\Diamond$ to $\vee$, is inherited by the term

$$\lambda x.\, \mu(a_1', a_2').\, (\mathtt{dia}\,\langle a_1, a_2\rangle\ \mathtt{be}\ \langle [a_1'], [a_2']\rangle\ \mathtt{in}\ [[a_1], [a_2]])x$$

where we write just $[a]$ for $\lambda x.\, [a]x$. It is remarkable that the family of these terms is not a natural transformation. One can find more properties of $\Diamond$ through the duality.

In a similar way, we can consider another modality $\Box'\tau \equiv \neg\neg\Box\neg\neg\tau$ and

$$\begin{aligned}
&\texttt{box}'\,\langle\overrightarrow{x}\rangle\;\texttt{be}\;\langle\overrightarrow{N}\rangle\;\texttt{in}\;M\\
&\quad\equiv \texttt{dia}\,\langle\overrightarrow{a}\rangle\;\texttt{be}\;\langle\overrightarrow{N}\rangle\;\texttt{in}\;\lambda k.\,[\overrightarrow{a}](\lambda\overrightarrow{x}\,.\,kM)\\
&\quad=_{\mathrm{n}} \lambda h.\,\overrightarrow{N}(\lambda\overrightarrow{y'}\,.\,h(\texttt{box}\,\langle\overrightarrow{y}\rangle\;\texttt{be}\;\langle\overrightarrow{y'}\rangle\;\texttt{in}\;\overrightarrow{y}(\lambda\overrightarrow{x}\,.\,M)))
\end{aligned}$$

for terms $M$ and $\overrightarrow{N}$ such that $x_1 : \sigma_1, \ldots, x_n : \sigma_n \vdash M : \tau \mid$ and $\Gamma \vdash N_j : \Box'\sigma_j \mid \Delta$ hold. Because $\neg\neg\tau$ is not isomorphic to $\tau$ in general in the classical logic, $\Box'\tau$ is not isomorphic to $\Box\tau$ in the $\lambda\mu\Box$-calculus. However, $\Box'$ acts like $\Box$; the following is a formal description of this fact.

**Theorem 13.** *Define the transformation* $\overline{-}$ *on the* $\lambda\mu\Box$*-calculus by* $\overline{\Box\tau} \equiv \Box'\tau$ *and* $\overline{\texttt{box}\,\langle\overrightarrow{x}\rangle\;\texttt{be}\;\langle\overrightarrow{N}\rangle\;\texttt{in}\;M} \equiv \texttt{box}'\,\langle\overrightarrow{x}\rangle\;\texttt{be}\;\langle\overrightarrow{\overline{N}}\rangle\;\texttt{in}\;\overline{M}$*. For* $\lambda\mu\Box$*-terms* $M$ *and* $N$*,* $M =_{\mathrm{n}} N$ *holds if and only if* $\overline{M} =_{\mathrm{N}} \overline{N}$ *holds.*

*Proof.* Consider the transformation on the $\lambda\Box$-calculus that sends $[\![M]\!]_{\mathrm{n}}$ to $[\![\overline{M}]\!]_{\mathrm{n}}$, *i.e.*, $\Box$ to $(\Box((- \to \mathtt{R}) \to \mathtt{R}) \to \mathtt{R}) \to \mathtt{R}$. The claim of the theorem is nothing less than this transformation preserves and reflects the equality. One can show the left-to-right implication by checking all the axioms. The right-to-left implication holds because the functor $(- \to \mathtt{R}) \to \mathtt{R}$ is injective in the $\lambda\Box$-calculus. $\Box$

## 4 Call-by-Value Calculus for Normal Modal Logic

In this section, we provide a call-by-value calculus which is dual to the call-by-name $\lambda\mu\Box$-calculus. A formal statement of the duality is given in the next section. The call-by-value calculus is an extension of Selinger's call-by-value version [30] of the $\lambda\mu$-calculus, and hence an extension of the $\lambda_{\mathrm{c}}$-calculus [24].

**Definition 14.** *The call-by-value* $\lambda\mu\Box$*-calculus has the same syntax as the call-by-name* $\lambda\mu\Box$*-calculus. The equality of the call-by-value* $\lambda\mu\Box$*-calculus is defined by the transformation* $[\![-]\!]_{\mathrm{v}}$ *given in Table 5. We write* $M =_{\mathrm{v}} N$ *for* $[\![M]\!]_{\mathrm{v}} = [\![N]\!]_{\mathrm{v}}$ *when* $M$ *and* $N$ *have the same type.*

Since the call-by-value $\lambda\mu\Box$-calculus has the same syntax as the call-by-name, it is trivial that the call-by-value calculus Curry-Howard corresponds to **K**.

For an axiomatization of the call-by-value calculus, we need to define the set of values. Values $V$ and evaluation contexts $E$ are defined by

$$\begin{aligned}
V ::= {} & \alpha^\tau \mid x \mid \lambda x^\tau.\,M \mid \langle\rangle \mid \langle V, V\rangle \mid \pi_1 V \mid \pi_2 V\\
& \mid [\lambda x^\tau.\,M, \lambda x^\tau.\,M] \mid [\lambda x^\tau.\,V, \lambda x^\tau.\,V]V \mid \iota_1 V \mid \iota_2 V\\
& \mid \texttt{box}\,\langle x^\tau, \ldots, x^\tau\rangle\;\texttt{be}\;\langle V, \ldots, V\rangle\;\texttt{in}\;M\\
E ::= {} & - \mid EM \mid VE \mid \langle E, M\rangle \mid \langle V, E\rangle \mid \pi_1 E \mid \pi_2 E \mid [a]E \mid [a, a]E\\
& \mid \texttt{box}\,\langle x^\tau, \ldots, x^\tau\rangle\;\texttt{be}\;\langle V, \ldots, V, E, M, \ldots, M\rangle\;\texttt{in}\;M
\end{aligned}$$

**Table 5.** CBV CPS transformation

$$p^\bullet \equiv p \qquad (\Box\tau)^\bullet \equiv (\Box((\tau^\bullet \to \mathtt{R}) \to \mathtt{R}) \to \mathtt{R}) \to \mathtt{R}$$
$$(\neg\sigma)^\bullet \equiv \sigma^\bullet \to \mathtt{R} \qquad (\sigma \to \tau)^\bullet \equiv (\sigma^\bullet \wedge (\tau^\bullet \to \mathtt{R})) \to \mathtt{R} \text{ if } \tau \not\equiv \bot$$
$$\top^\bullet \equiv \top \qquad (\tau_1 \wedge \tau_2)^\bullet \equiv {\tau_1}^\bullet \wedge {\tau_2}^\bullet$$
$$\bot^\bullet \equiv \bot \qquad (\tau_1 \vee \tau_2)^\bullet \equiv {\tau_1}^\bullet \vee {\tau_2}^\bullet$$

$$\begin{aligned}
[\![\alpha]\!]_{\mathrm{v}} &\equiv \lambda k.\, k\alpha \\
[\![x]\!]_{\mathrm{v}} &\equiv \lambda k.\, kx \\
[\![\lambda x.\, M]\!]_{\mathrm{v}} &\equiv \lambda k.\, k(\lambda x.\, [\![M]\!]_{\mathrm{v}}[\,]) \text{ if } M : \bot \\
&\equiv \lambda k.\, k(\lambda\langle x, h\rangle.\, [\![M]\!]_{\mathrm{v}} h) \text{ o.w.} \\
[\![MN]\!]_{\mathrm{v}} &\equiv \lambda k.\, [\![M]\!]_{\mathrm{v}}[\![N]\!]_{\mathrm{v}} \text{ if } MN : \bot \\
&\equiv \lambda k.\, [\![M]\!]_{\mathrm{v}}(\lambda y.\, [\![N]\!]_{\mathrm{v}}(\lambda z.\, y\langle z, k\rangle)) \text{ o.w.} \\
[\![\langle\,\rangle]\!]_{\mathrm{v}} &\equiv \langle\,\rangle \\
[\![\langle M_1, M_2\rangle]\!]_{\mathrm{v}} &\equiv \lambda k.\, [\![M_1]\!]_{\mathrm{v}}(\lambda y_1.\, [\![M_2]\!]_{\mathrm{v}}(\lambda y_2.\, k\langle y_1, y_2\rangle)) \\
[\![\pi_j M]\!]_{\mathrm{v}} &\equiv \lambda k.\, [\![M]\!]_{\mathrm{v}}(\lambda y.\, k(\pi_j y)) \\
[\![\mu a.\, M]\!]_{\mathrm{v}} &\equiv \lambda a.\, [\![M]\!]_{\mathrm{v}}[\,] \\
[\![[a]M]\!]_{\mathrm{v}} &\equiv \lambda k.\, [\![M]\!]_{\mathrm{v}} a \\
[\![\mu(a_1, a_2).\, M]\!]_{\mathrm{v}} &\equiv \lambda k.\, [\![M]\!]_{\mathrm{v}}\{\lambda y_1.\, k(\iota_1 y_1), \lambda y_2.\, k(\iota_2 y_2)/a_1, a_2\}[\,] \\
[\![[a_1, a_2]M]\!]_{\mathrm{v}} &\equiv \lambda k.\, [\![M]\!]_{\mathrm{v}}[a_1, a_2]
\end{aligned}$$

$$[\![\mathtt{box}\,\langle\vec{x}\rangle\,\mathtt{be}\,\langle\vec{N}\rangle\,\mathtt{in}\,M]\!]_{\mathrm{v}} \equiv$$
$$\lambda k.\, [\![\vec{N}]\!]_{\mathrm{v}}(\lambda\vec{g}.\, k(\lambda h.\, \vec{g}(\lambda\vec{f'}.\, h(\mathtt{box}\,\langle\vec{f}\rangle\,\mathtt{be}\,\langle\vec{f'}\rangle\,\mathtt{in}\,\lambda l.\, \vec{f}(\lambda\vec{x}.\, [\![M]\!]_{\mathrm{v}} l)))))$$

$$\frac{x_1 : \sigma_1, \ldots, x_n : \sigma_n \vdash M : \tau \mid a_1 : \tau_1, \ldots, a_m : \tau_m}{x_1 : {\sigma_1}^\bullet, \ldots, x_n : {\sigma_n}^\bullet, a_1 : {\tau_1}^\bullet \to \mathtt{R}, \ldots, a_m : {\tau_m}^\bullet \to \mathtt{R} \vdash [\![M]\!]_{\mathrm{v}} : (\tau^\bullet \to \mathtt{R}) \to \mathtt{R}}$$

and we use also $W$ as a meta-variable for values. In addition, we use the syntax sugar

$$\mathtt{let}\,x\,\mathtt{be}\,N\,\mathtt{in}\,M \equiv (\lambda x.\, M)N$$
$$\mathtt{let}\,\vec{x}\,\mathtt{be}\,\vec{N}\,\mathtt{in}\,M \equiv \mathtt{let}\,x_1\,\mathtt{be}\,N_1\,\mathtt{in}\cdots\mathtt{let}\,x_n\,\mathtt{be}\,N_n\,\mathtt{in}\,M$$

as usual. Syntax sugar about disjunctions is used in the definition of values, but it is possible to introduce $[M_1, M_2]$ and $\iota_j M$ as primitive syntax instead of $\mu(a_1, a_2).\, M$ and $[a_1, a_2]M$ in the call-by-value calculus as noted in [31].

In our definition, there is a value that has a redex exterior to abstractions, but it is not serious because we are not focusing on reductions. Our notion of values is based on semantical effect-freeness: a value is interpreted to a form $\lambda k.\, kV$. There is room for improvement if we consider not an equality but a reduction system or other semantics.

**Proposition 15.** *The following equations hold in the call-by-value $\lambda\mu\Box$-calculus.*

$$E\{M\} =_{\mathrm{v}} \mathtt{let}\, x\, \mathtt{be}\, M\ \mathtt{in}\ E\{x\} \qquad \text{if } x \notin \mathtt{FV}(E)$$

$$\mathtt{box}\,\langle x\rangle\ \mathtt{be}\ \langle M\rangle\ \mathtt{in}\ x =_{\mathrm{v}} M$$

$$\mathtt{box}\,\langle \vec{z}, x\rangle\ \mathtt{be}\ \langle \vec{P}, \mathtt{box}\,\langle \vec{y}\rangle\ \mathtt{be}\ \langle \vec{L}\rangle\ \mathtt{in}\ N\rangle\ \mathtt{in}\ M$$
$$=_{\mathrm{v}} \mathtt{box}\,\langle \vec{z}, \vec{y}\rangle\ \mathtt{be}\ \langle \vec{P}, \vec{L}\rangle\ \mathtt{in}\ \mathtt{let}\, x\, \mathtt{be}\, N\ \mathtt{in}\ M$$

$$\mathtt{box}\,\langle \vec{w}, x, \vec{z}\rangle\ \mathtt{be}\ \langle \vec{W}, \mathtt{box}\,\langle \vec{y}\rangle\ \mathtt{be}\ \langle \vec{N}\rangle\ \mathtt{in}\ V, \vec{P}\rangle\ \mathtt{in}\ M$$
$$=_{\mathrm{v}} \mathtt{box}\,\langle \vec{w}, \vec{y}, \vec{z}\rangle\ \mathtt{be}\ \langle \vec{W}, \vec{N}, \vec{P}\rangle\ \mathtt{in}\ M\{V/x\} \qquad \text{if } |\vec{w}| = |\vec{W}|$$

*where $V$ and $W_j$ are values.*

*Proof.* First we show the following fact by induction: for any value $V$, there is a term $V'$ such that $[\![V]\!]_{\mathrm{v}} = \lambda k.\, kV'$. This fact enables us to show $[\![E\{M\}]\!]_{\mathrm{v}} = \lambda k.\, [\![M]\!]_{\mathrm{v}}(\lambda x.\, [\![E\{x\}]\!]_{\mathrm{v}}k)$ by induction. Also the last equation is derived from the fact. Other equations are proved straightforwardly. □

Commutativity between $\mu$ abstractions and boxed applications is derived from the first equation:

$$\mathtt{box}\,\langle \vec{x}\rangle\ \mathtt{be}\ \langle \vec{W}, \mu a.\, N, \vec{P}\rangle\ \mathtt{in}\ M$$
$$=_{\mathrm{v}} \mathtt{let}\, y\, \mathtt{be}\, \mu a.\, N\ \mathtt{in}\ \mathtt{box}\,\langle \vec{x}\rangle\ \mathtt{be}\ \langle \vec{W}, y, \vec{P}\rangle\ \mathtt{in}\ M$$
$$=_{\mathrm{v}} \mu b.\, N\{[b](\mathtt{let}\, y\, \mathtt{be} - \mathtt{in}\ \mathtt{box}\,\langle \vec{x}\rangle\ \mathtt{be}\ \langle \vec{W}, y, \vec{P}\rangle\ \mathtt{in}\ M)/[a]-\}$$
$$=_{\mathrm{v}} \mu b.\, N\{[b](\mathtt{box}\,\langle \vec{x}\rangle\ \mathtt{be}\ \langle \vec{W}, -, \vec{P}\rangle\ \mathtt{in}\ M)/[a]-\}$$

where the last two lines hold by the ordinary call-by-value equality. Unlike the call-by-name case, Proposition 15 means that $\Box$ in the call-by-value calculus is monoidal only on values.

We define the diamond structure $\Diamond\tau$ and $\mathtt{dia}\,\langle \vec{a}\rangle\,\mathtt{be}\,\langle \vec{N}\rangle\ \mathtt{in}\ M$ in the call-by-value $\lambda\mu\Box$-calculus as just the same syntax sugar as in the call-by-name. Such syntax is used for the duality in the next section.

*Remark 16.* For the duality, we adopt a complex transformation as semantics: $[\![-]\!]_{\mathrm{v}}$ is defined in order that

$$(\Box\tau)^{\bullet} \equiv (\Box((\tau^{\bullet} \to \mathtt{R}) \to \mathtt{R}) \to \mathtt{R}) \to \mathtt{R}$$

holds. If we ignore the duality, we can reduce the transformation such that

$$(\Box\tau)^{\bullet} \equiv \Box((\tau^{\bullet} \to \mathtt{R}) \to \mathtt{R})$$

holds. It can be proved that this simpler translation gives the same equality as the original one.

**Table 6.** Transformation from CBV to CBN

$$\lceil p \rceil \equiv p \qquad \lceil \neg\sigma \rceil \equiv \neg\lceil \sigma \rceil$$

$$\lceil \sigma \to \tau \rceil \equiv \neg(\lceil \sigma \rceil \vee \neg\lceil \tau \rceil) \text{ if } \tau \not\equiv \bot$$

$$\lceil \top \rceil \equiv \bot \qquad \lceil \tau_1 \wedge \tau_2 \rceil \equiv \lceil \tau_1 \rceil \vee \lceil \tau_2 \rceil$$

$$\lceil \bot \rceil \equiv \top \qquad \lceil \tau_1 \vee \tau_2 \rceil \equiv \lceil \tau_1 \rceil \wedge \lceil \tau_2 \rceil$$

$$\lceil \Box\tau \rceil \equiv \Diamond\lceil \tau \rceil$$

$$\lceil \mathtt{box}\,\langle \overrightarrow{x} \rangle\,\mathtt{be}\,\langle \overrightarrow{N} \rangle\,\mathtt{in}\,M \rceil \equiv \mathtt{dia}\,\langle \overrightarrow{x} \rangle\,\mathtt{be}\,\langle \lceil \overrightarrow{N} \rceil \rangle\,\mathtt{in}\,\lceil M \rceil$$

$$\frac{x_1 : \sigma_1, \ldots, x_n : \sigma_n \vdash M : \tau \mid a_1 : \tau_1, \ldots, a_m : \tau_m}{a_1 : \lceil \tau_1 \rceil, \ldots, a_m : \lceil \tau_m \rceil \vdash \lceil M \rceil : \neg\lceil \tau \rceil \mid x_1 : \lceil \sigma_1 \rceil, \ldots, x_n : \lceil \sigma_n \rceil}$$

**Table 7.** Transformation from CBN to CBV

$$\lfloor p \rfloor \equiv p \qquad \lfloor \neg\sigma \rfloor \equiv \neg\lfloor \sigma \rfloor$$

$$\lfloor \sigma \to \tau \rfloor \equiv \neg\lfloor \sigma \rfloor \wedge \lfloor \tau \rfloor \text{ if } \tau \not\equiv \bot$$

$$\lfloor \top \rfloor \equiv \bot \qquad \lfloor \tau_1 \wedge \tau_2 \rfloor \equiv \lfloor \tau_1 \rfloor \vee \lfloor \tau_2 \rfloor$$

$$\lfloor \bot \rfloor \equiv \top \qquad \lfloor \tau_1 \vee \tau_2 \rfloor \equiv \lfloor \tau_1 \rfloor \wedge \lfloor \tau_2 \rfloor$$

$$\lfloor \Diamond\tau \rfloor \equiv \Box\lfloor \tau \rfloor$$

$$\lfloor \mathtt{dia}\,\langle \overrightarrow{x} \rangle\,\mathtt{be}\,\langle \overrightarrow{N} \rangle\,\mathtt{in}\,M \rfloor \equiv \lambda k.\,\lfloor \overrightarrow{N} \rfloor(\lambda \overrightarrow{x'}.\,k(\mathtt{box}\,\langle \overrightarrow{x} \rangle\,\mathtt{be}\,\langle \overrightarrow{x'} \rangle\,\mathtt{in}\,\mu a.\,\lfloor M \rfloor(\lambda y.\,[a]y)))$$

$$\frac{a_1 : \tau_1, \ldots, a_m : \tau_m \vdash M : \sigma \mid x_1 : \sigma_1, \ldots, x_n : \sigma_n}{x_1 : \lfloor \sigma_1 \rfloor, \ldots, x_n : \lfloor \sigma_n \rfloor \vdash \lfloor M \rfloor : \neg\lfloor \sigma \rfloor \mid a_1 : \lfloor \tau_1 \rfloor, \ldots, a_m : \lfloor \tau_m \rfloor}$$

## 5 Duality Between Call-by-Name and Call-by-Value

It is known that there exists a duality between call-by-name and call-by-value in languages with control operators, *e.g.*, [10] and [30]. In this section, we observe such duality on the $\lambda\mu\Box$-calculus. Since our calculi are extensions of Selinger's $\lambda\mu$-calculi, we show the duality along the line of [30].

For readability of the duality, we use meta-variables $a$ and $x$ for variables and control variables of the call-by-name $\lambda\mu\Box$-calculus, respectively.

Table 6 gives the transformation from the call-by-value to the call-by-name $\lambda\mu\Box$-calculus. Other cases than the box case are omitted in the table because they are essentially the same as Selinger's [30]. It is shown that the call-by-value CPS transformation coincides with the call-by-name one via this transformation.

**Theorem 17.** *For any type $\tau$ and any term $M$ of the call-by-value $\lambda\mu\Box$-calculus, $\tau^\bullet \equiv \lceil \tau \rceil^\circ$ and $[\![M]\!]_{\mathrm{v}} = [\![\lceil M \rceil]\!]_{\mathrm{n}}$ hold.*

*Proof.* By induction. □

On the other hand, a transformation from the call-by-name to the call-by-value can not be defined totally. We just define the transformation from the $\Diamond$ fragment of the call-by-name $\lambda\mu\Box$-calculus to the call-by-value $\lambda\mu\Box$-calculus by Table 7. Since the type of $[\![M]\!]_\mathrm{n}$ does not match the type of $[\![\lfloor M \rfloor]\!]_\mathrm{v}$, the dual of the previous theorem is the following.

**Theorem 18.** *For any type $\tau$ and any term $M$ of the $\Diamond$ fragment of the call-by-name $\lambda\mu\Box$-calculus, $\tau^\circ \equiv \lfloor \tau \rfloor^\bullet$ and $[\![M]\!]_\mathrm{n} = \lambda x.\, [\![\lfloor M \rfloor]\!]_\mathrm{v}(\lambda k.\, kx)$ hold.*

*Proof.* By induction. □

It follows from Theorem 17 and 18 that the call-by-value $\lambda\mu\Box$-calculus and the $\Diamond$ fragment of the call-by-name $\lambda\mu\Box$-calculus are in bijective correspondence in some sense. Moreover,

$$\lfloor \mathtt{box}'\,\langle \overrightarrow{a} \rangle\ \mathtt{be}\ \langle \overrightarrow{N} \rangle\ \mathtt{in}\ M \rfloor =_\mathrm{v} \mathtt{dia}\,\langle \overrightarrow{a} \rangle\ \mathtt{be}\ \langle \lfloor \overrightarrow{N} \rfloor \rangle\ \mathtt{in}\ \lfloor M \rfloor$$

holds. Hence, there exists a bijective correspondence between the $\Box'$ fragment of the call-by-name $\lambda\mu\Box$-calculus and the $\Diamond$ fragment of the call-by-value $\lambda\mu\Box$-calculus. By Theorem 13 in Section 3, we can conclude that the call-by-name $\lambda\mu\Box$-calculus and the $\Diamond$ fragment of the call-by-value $\lambda\mu\Box$-calculus are in bijective correspondence.

## 6 Extensions

We add type-indexed families of constants $\{\varepsilon_\sigma : \Box\sigma \to \sigma\}$ and $\{\delta_\sigma : \Box\sigma \to \Box\Box\sigma\}$ with the axioms

$$\begin{aligned}
&\varepsilon(\mathtt{box}\,\langle \overrightarrow{x} \rangle\ \mathtt{be}\ \langle \overrightarrow{N} \rangle\ \mathtt{in}\ M) = M\{\varepsilon\overrightarrow{N}/\overrightarrow{x}\}\\
&\delta(\mathtt{box}\,\langle \overrightarrow{x} \rangle\ \mathtt{be}\ \langle \overrightarrow{N} \rangle\ \mathtt{in}\ M) = \mathtt{box}\,\langle \overrightarrow{y} \rangle\ \mathtt{be}\ \langle \delta\overrightarrow{N} \rangle\ \mathtt{in}\ \mathtt{box}\,\langle \overrightarrow{x} \rangle\ \mathtt{be}\ \langle \overrightarrow{y} \rangle\ \mathtt{in}\ M\\
&\delta(\delta M) = \mathtt{box}\,\langle x \rangle\ \mathtt{be}\ \langle \delta M \rangle\ \mathtt{in}\ \delta x\\
&\varepsilon(\delta M) = \mathtt{box}\,\langle x \rangle\ \mathtt{be}\ \langle \delta M \rangle\ \mathtt{in}\ \varepsilon x = M
\end{aligned}$$

to the $\lambda\Box$-calculus. A model of this calculus is a bicartesian closed category with a monoidal comonad, that is, a model of the box fragment of **IS4**. Also to the $\lambda\mu\Box$-calculus, we add families $\{\varepsilon_\sigma : \Box\sigma \to \sigma\}$ and $\{\delta_\sigma : \Box\sigma \to \Box\Box\sigma\}$. Then, it is obvious that this calculus corresponds to **S4** with respect to provability. The semantics are given by

$$\begin{aligned}
&[\![\varepsilon]\!]_\mathrm{n} \equiv \lambda\langle x, k\rangle.\, x(\lambda y.\, \varepsilon y k)\\
&[\![\delta]\!]_\mathrm{n} \equiv \lambda\langle x, k\rangle.\, x(\lambda y.\, k(\mathtt{box}\,\langle z \rangle\ \mathtt{be}\ \langle \delta y \rangle\ \mathtt{in}\ \lambda h.\, hz))\\
&[\![\varepsilon]\!]_\mathrm{v} \equiv \lambda k.\, k(\lambda\langle x, h\rangle.\, x(\lambda y.\, \varepsilon y h))\\
&[\![\delta]\!]_\mathrm{v} \equiv \lambda k.\, k(\lambda\langle x, h\rangle.\, h(\lambda l.\, x(\lambda y.\, l(\mathtt{box}\,\langle z \rangle\ \mathtt{be}\ \langle \delta y \rangle\ \mathtt{in}\ \lambda m.\, m(\lambda n.\, nz))))).
\end{aligned}$$

Unfortunately, $\Box$ is not a comonad in the call-by-name calculus because

$$\varepsilon(\mathtt{box}\,\langle x \rangle\ \mathtt{be}\ \langle N \rangle\ \mathtt{in}\ M) \neq_\mathrm{n} M\{\varepsilon N/x\}$$

in general. On the other hand, in the call-by-value calculus, the equations

$$\varepsilon(\texttt{box}\,\langle x\rangle\,\texttt{be}\,\langle N\rangle\,\texttt{in}\,M) =_{\text{v}} \texttt{let}\,x\,\texttt{be}\,\varepsilon N\,\texttt{in}\,M$$
$$\delta(\texttt{box}\,\langle x\rangle\,\texttt{be}\,\langle N\rangle\,\texttt{in}\,M) =_{\text{v}} \texttt{box}\,\langle y\rangle\,\texttt{be}\,\langle \delta N\rangle\,\texttt{in}\,\texttt{box}\,\langle x\rangle\,\texttt{be}\,\langle y\rangle\,\texttt{in}\,M$$
$$\delta(\delta M) =_{\text{v}} \texttt{box}\,\langle x\rangle\,\texttt{be}\,\langle \delta M\rangle\,\texttt{in}\,\delta x$$
$$\varepsilon(\delta M) =_{\text{v}} \texttt{box}\,\langle x\rangle\,\texttt{be}\,\langle \delta M\rangle\,\texttt{in}\,\varepsilon x =_{\text{v}} M$$

hold, and hence $\Box$ is a comonad (but not a monoidal comonad). Through the duality, one can conclude that $\Diamond$ is a monad in the call-by-name calculus.

In [6], Bierman and de Paiva propose a monad as a model of $\Diamond$ in **IS4**. Our semantics matches their observation. An **S4** extension of the dual calculus [34] along the line of dual context calculi (*e.g.*, [2]) is provided in [32] by Shan. Since the $\lambda\mu$-calculus has a bijective correspondence to the dual calculus, the $\lambda\mu\Box$-calulus remains to be formalized in the dual calculus and to be compared with Shan's calculus.

## References


[1] Abe, T.: Completeness of modal proofs in first-order predicate logic. Computer Software, JSSST Journal (to appear)

[2] Barber, A.: Dual intuitionistic linear logic. Technical report, LFCS, University of Edinburgh (1996)

[3] Barendregt, H.P.: Lambda calculi with types. In: Abramski, S., Gabbay, D.M., Maibaum, T.S.E. (eds.) Handbook of Logic in Computer Science, vol. 2, pp. 117–309. Oxford University Press, Oxford (1992)

[4] Bellin, G., de Paiva, V.C.V., Ritter, E.: Extended Curry-Howard correspondence for a basic constructive modal logic. In: Proceedings of Methods for Modalities (2001)

[5] Bierman, G.M.: What is a categorical model of intuitionistic linear logic. In: Dezani-Ciancaglini, M., Plotkin, G. (eds.) TLCA 1995. LNCS, vol. 902, pp. 78–93. Springer, Heidelberg (1995)

[6] Bierman, G.M., de Paiva, V.C.V.: On an intuitionistic modal logic. Studia Logica 65(3), 383–416 (2000)

[7] Blackburn, P., de Rijke, M., Venema, Y.: Modal Logic. Cambridge University Press, Cambridge (2001)

[8] Davies, R., Pfenning, F.: A modal analysis of staged computation. Journal of the ACM 48(3), 555–604 (2001)

[9] de Groote, P.: A cps-translation of the $\lambda\mu$-calculus. In: Tison, S. (ed.) CAAP 1994. LNCS, vol. 787, pp. 85–99. Springer, Heidelberg (1994)

[10] Filinski, A.: Declarative continuations and categorical duality. Master's thesis, Computer Science Department, University of Copenhagen (1989)

[11] Fischer, M.: Lambda calculus schemata. In: Proving Assertions about Programs, pp. 104–109. ACM Press, New York (1972)

[12] Girard, J.-Y.: Linear logic. Theoretical Computer Science 50(1), 1–102 (1987)

[13] Griffin, T.G.: A formulae-as-types notion of control. In: Principles of Programming Languages, pp. 47–58. ACM Press, New York (1990)

[14] Hofmann, M., Streicher, T.: Continuation models are universal for $\lambda\mu$-calculus. In: Logic in Computer Science, pp. 387–397. IEEE Computer Society Press, Los Alamitos (1997)

[15] Howard, W.A.: The formulae-as-types notion of construction. In: Essays on Combinatory Logic, Lambda Calculus and Formalism, pp. 479–490. Academic Press, London (1980)
[16] Kakutani, Y.: Duality between call-by-name recursion and call-by-value iteration. In: Bradfield, J.C. (ed.) CSL 2002 and EACSL 2002. LNCS, vol. 2471, pp. 506–521. Springer, Heidelberg (2002)
[17] Kakutani, Y.: Calculi for intuitionistic normal modal logic. In: Proceedings of Programming and Programming Languages (2007)
[18] Kripke, S.: Semantic analysis of modal logic I, normal propositional logic. Zeitschrift für Mathemathische Logik und Grundlagen der Mathematik 9, 67–96 (1963)
[19] Lambek, J., Scott, P.J.: Introduction to Higher-Order Categorical Logic. Cambridge University Press, Cambridge (1986)
[20] Mac Lane, S.: Categories for the Working Mathematician, 2nd edn. Springer, Heidelberg (1997)
[21] Maietti, M.E., Maneggia, P., de Paiva, V.C.V., Ritter, E.: Relating categorical semantics for intuitionistic linear logic. Applied Categorical Structures 13(1), 1–36 (2005)
[22] Martini, S., Masini, A.: A computational interpretation of modal proofs. In: Proof Theory of Modal Logics, pp. 213–241. Kluwer Academic Publishers, Dordrecht (1996)
[23] Miyamoto, K., Igarashi, A.: A modal foundation for secure information flow. In: Proceedings of Foundations of Computer Security (2004)
[24] Moggi, E.: Computational lambda-calculus and monads. In: Logic in Computer Science, pp. 14–23. IEEE Computer Society Press, Los Alamitos (1989)
[25] Ong, C.-H.L., Stewart, C.A.: A Curry-Howard foundation for functional computation with control. In: Principle of Programming Languages, pp. 215–227. ACM Press, New York (1997)
[26] Parigot, M.: $\lambda\mu$-calculus: an algorithmic interpretation of classical natural deduction. In: Voronkov, A. (ed.) LPAR 1992. LNCS, vol. 624, pp. 190–201. Springer, Heidelberg (1992)
[27] Plotkin, G.D.: Call-by-name, call-by-value and the lambda calculus. Theoretical Computer Science 1(2), 125–159 (1975)
[28] Pym, D., Ritter, E.: On the semantics of classical disjunction. Journal of Pure and Applied Algebra 159(2,3), 315–338 (2001)
[29] Seely, R.A.G.: Linear logic, $*$-autonomous categories and cofree coalgebras. In: Categories in Computer Science and Logic. Contemporary Mathematics, vol. 92, pp. 371–389. AMS (1989)
[30] Selinger, P.: Control categories and duality: on the categorical semantics of the lambda-mu calculus. Mathematical Structures in Computer Science 11(2), 207–260 (2001)
[31] Selinger, P.: Some remarks on control categories. Manuscript (2003)
[32] Shan, C.-C.: A computastional interpretation of classical S4 modality. In: Proceedings of Intuitionistic Modal Logics and Applications (2005)
[33] Simpson, A.K.: The Proof Theory and Semantics of Intuitionistic Modal Logics. PhD thesis, University of Edinburgh (1993)
[34] Wadler, P.: Call-by-value is dual to call-by-name. In: International Conference on Functional Programming, pp. 189–201. ACM Press, New York (2003)
[35] Wijesekera, D.: Constructive modal logic I. Annals of Pure and Applied Logic 50, 271–301 (1990)

# Call-by-Value Is Dual to Call-by-Name, Extended

Daisuke Kimura

National Institute of Informatics
Tokyo, 101-8430, Japan
kmr@nii.ac.jp

**Abstract.** We extend Wadler's work that showed duality between call-by-value and call-by-name by giving mutual translations between the $\lambda\mu$-calculus and the dual calculus. We extend the $\lambda\mu$-calculus and the dual calculus through two stages. We first add a fixed-point operator and an iteration operator to the call-by-name and call-by-value systems respectively. Secondly, we add recursive types, $\top$, and $\bot$ types to these systems. The extended duality between call-by-name with recursion and call-by-value with iteration has been suggested by Kakutani. He followed Selinger's category-theoretic approach. We completely follow Wadler's syntactic approach. We give mutual translations between our extended $\lambda\mu$-calculus and dual calculus by extending Wadler's translations, and also show that our translations form an equational correspondence, which was defined by Sabry and Felleisen. By composing our translations with duality on the dual calculus, we obtain a duality on our extended $\lambda\mu$-calculus. Wadler's duality on the $\lambda\mu$-calculus was an involution, and our duality on our extended $\lambda\mu$-calculus is also an involution.

## 1 Introduction

In the last twenty years, a line of work, including that of Filinski [3], Griffin [5], Parigot [9], Ong and Stewart [8], Barbanera and Berardi [1], Selinger [13], Curien and Herbelin [2], and Wadler [14,15] extended the Curry-Howard isomorphism to classical logic, and concluded that call-by-value is dual to call-by-name in the sense of de Morgan duality.

Selinger showed a duality between call-by-value and call-by-name by a category theoretical approach, and gave a duality transformation for Parigot's $\lambda\mu$-calculus. Kakutani [7] investigated the duality between call-by-name recursion and call-by-value iteration by the same approach as Selinger, and extended Selinger's duality by giving translations between the call-by-name $\lambda\mu$-calculus with a fixed-point operator and the call-by-value one with an iteration operator.

Wadler [15] pointed out that Selinger's duality is *not* involutive, *i.e.*, it needed two distinct translations from call-by-name into call-by-value and from call-by-value into call-by-name. Moreover, the compositions of these maps do not preserve types up to identity, but only up to isomorphism. The similar problem can be found in Kakutani's duality, too.

Wadler also showed a duality between call-by-value and call-by-name, but it was involutive. A key point of his approach was that he replaced implication $A \supset B$ by

Z. Shao (Ed.): APLAS 2007, LNCS 4807, pp. 415–430, 2007.

$\neg A \vee B$ under call-by-name, or $\neg(A \& \neg B)$ under call-by-value. Since there is a clean and involutive duality on conjunction, disjunction, and negation, Wadler finally gave an involutive version of duality between the call-by-name and call-by-value $\lambda\mu$-calculi.

Wadler's approach is as follows. Firstly, he introduced the dual calculus that corresponds to Gentzen's classical sequent calculus. The dual calculus has an explicit and involutive duality. The translation $(-)^{\circ}$ captures this duality, and translates from call-by-name into call-by-value and vice-versa. Secondly, he gave translations $(-)^{*}$ and $(-)_{*}$ between the $\lambda\mu$-calculus and the dual calculus, and showed that these translations form an *equational correspondence* (defined by Sabry and Felleisen [12]) with respect to call-by-value (and also call-by-name) equations. Finally, by composing $(-)^{*}$, $(-)_{*}$, and $(-)^{\circ}$, he derived a duality transformation $(-)_{\circ}$ from the $\lambda\mu$-calculus to itself, which takes a call-by-value equation to a call-by-name one and vice-versa.

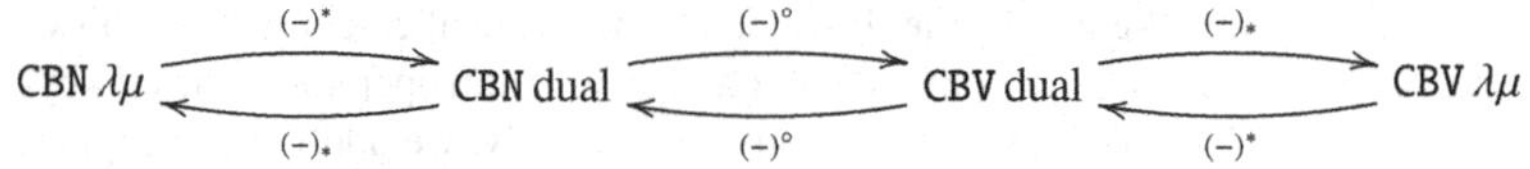


We take the same approach as Wadler. We extend the $\lambda\mu$ and dual calculi, and show that Wadler's result can be expanded into our extended systems. The extension is performed by the following two steps. (i) We extend the $\lambda\mu$-calculi with a call-by-name fixed-point operator and a call-by-value iteration operator. The call-by-name dual calculus is extended with a fixed-point operator, and the call-by-value one is extended with a co-fixed-point operator, which is dual to the fixed-point operator. (ii) We further extend these systems with recursive types, unit, and counit types.

Our first contribution in this paper is that we refine Kakutani's duality into an involutive one. Kakutani introduced fixed-point and iteration operators as constants. Since these operators act on functions, his formulation requires implication. We give a slightly, but not essentially, different formulation without implications. By this modification, Wadler's duality can be naturally expanded into our extended systems.

Our second contribution is that we extend Wadler's duality with recursive types, unit type, and counit type. The existence of these types enables us to encode several important data types, such as types of natural numbers, booleans, lists, streams. In section 6, we demonstrate that natural numbers and booleans are dually encoded in our call-by-name and call-by-value systems. Our duality exchanges the unit type with the counit type, and recursive types are self-dual. This duality yields a duality of natural numbers and booleans. Let $(k)_v$ and $(k)_n$ be encoded natural numbers of $k$ in the call-by-value and call-by-name codings respectively, then our duality translates $(k)_v$ into $(k)_n$ and vice-versa. Furthermore, this duality of natural numbers induces a duality of programs on natural numbers (Theorem 5): a call-by-name program on natural numbers is dual to a call-by-value program that returns the same values as the original one.

The paper is organized as follows. In section 2 we briefly review Wadler's previous work [15]. In section 3 we extend the call-by-value $\lambda\mu$ and dual calculi by adding an iteration and a co-fixed-point operators respectively, and also extend the call-by-name calculi by adding fixed-point operators. We show that Wadler's equational correspondence can be expanded into these extended systems (Theorem 2). In section 4 we further add unit, counit, and recursive types to the $\lambda\mu$ and dual calculi, extend the translations between the $\lambda\mu$ and dual calculi, and show that they form an equational correspondence

$$A,B ::= X \mid A\&B \mid A \vee B \mid \neg A \mid A \supset B \qquad \text{(Types)}$$
$$M,N,O ::= x \mid \langle M,N\rangle \mid \texttt{fst}\,M \mid \texttt{snd}\,N \mid \mu(\alpha,\beta).S \mid \mu\alpha.S \mid \lambda x.S \mid \lambda x.M \mid OM \qquad \text{(Terms)}$$
$$S,T ::= [\alpha]M \mid [\alpha,\beta]M \mid OM \qquad \text{(Statements)}$$
$$V,W ::= x \mid \langle V,W\rangle \mid \texttt{fst}\,V \mid \texttt{snd}\,W \mid \mu(\alpha,\beta).[\alpha]V \mid \mu(\alpha,\beta).[\beta]W \mid \lambda x.S \mid \lambda x.M \qquad \text{(Values)}$$
$$E ::= \{-\} \mid \langle E,N\rangle \mid \langle V,E\rangle \mid \texttt{fst}\,E \mid \texttt{snd}\,E \mid EM \mid VE \qquad \text{(Evaluation contexts)}$$
$$D ::= [\alpha]E \mid [\alpha,\beta]E \mid EM \mid VE \qquad \text{(Statement contexts)}$$

**Fig. 1.** The syntax of the $\lambda\mu$-calculus

(Theorem 3). In section 5 we obtain our extended duality from the results of the previous section. In section 6 we discuss some applications of our results. Using unit, counit, and recursive types, we encode natural numbers and booleans in our calculi, and yield a duality of natural numbers and booleans from our extended duality. Finally, we obtain a duality of programs on natural numbers (Theorem 5).

## 2 Preliminaries

### 2.1 The $\lambda\mu$-calculus

The $\lambda\mu$-calculus was first introduced by Parigot [9] as an extension of the $\lambda$-calculus with the notion of continuations. In this subsection, we define the syntax of the $\lambda\mu$-calculus. We consider the two variants of this calculus, call-by-value and call-by-name. Our version of the $\lambda\mu$-calculus is based on Wadler's [15].

The $\lambda\mu$-calculus consists of types and expressions. Let $X, Y, Z, \ldots$ range over type variables, $A, B, \ldots$ range over types, $x, y, z, \ldots$ range over variables, and $\alpha, \beta, \gamma, \ldots$ range over covariables. An expression of the $\lambda\mu$-calculus is either a term (denoted by $O, M, N$) or a statement (denoted by $S, T$). For the call-by-value system, we define values (denoted by $V$, $W$), evaluation contexts (denoted by $E$), and statement contexts (denoted by $D$). The syntax of the $\lambda\mu$-calculus is summarized in Figure 1.

A typing judgment of the $\lambda\mu$-calculus takes either the form $\Gamma \rightharpoonup \Delta \mid M : A$ or the form $\Gamma \mid S \mid\!\rightharpoonup \Delta$, where $\Gamma$ denotes a $\lambda$-context, i.e., $x_1 : A_1, \ldots, x_n : A_n$ and $\Delta$ denotes a $\mu$-context, i.e., $\alpha_1 : B_1, \ldots, \alpha_m : B_m$. The typing rules of the $\lambda\mu$-calculus are given in Wadler's paper [15].

The call-by-value equalities (denoted by $=_v$) and the call-by-name equalities (denoted by $=_n$) of the $\lambda\mu$-calculus are defined from the axioms listed in Figure 2 and 3 respectively. Note that expressions like $[N/x]$ and $[\beta/\alpha]$ are usual substitutions for free variable $x$ and covariable $\alpha$ respectively, but an expression like $[D\{-\}/[\alpha]\{-\}]$, called a mixed substitution, acts all free name $\alpha$ and recursively replaces $[\alpha]M$, $[\alpha,\beta]M$ and $[\beta,\alpha]M$ by $D\{M\}$, $D\{\mu\alpha.[\alpha,\beta]M\}$ and $D\{\mu\alpha.[\beta,\alpha]M\}$ respectively. The more formal definition of the mixed substitution is given in [13] and [15].

Wadler showed that implication can be defined in terms of the other connectives.

**Proposition 1 (Wadler(2005)).** *Under call-by-value, implication can be defined as follows:*

| | | | | |
|---|---|---|---|---|
| $(\beta\&_1)$ | $\mathtt{fst}\langle V, W\rangle$ | $=_v$ | $V$ | |
| $(\beta\&_2)$ | $\mathtt{snd}\langle V, W\rangle$ | $=_v$ | $W$ | |
| $(\beta\vee)$ | $[\alpha',\beta']\mu(\alpha,\beta).S$ | $=_v$ | $S[\alpha'/\alpha,\beta'/\beta]$ | |
| $(\beta\neg)$ | $(\lambda x.S)V$ | $=_v$ | $S[V/x]$ | |
| $(\beta\supset)$ | $(\lambda x.M)V$ | $=_v$ | $M[V/x]$ | |
| $(\beta\mu)$ | $[\alpha']\mu\alpha.S$ | $=_v$ | $S[\alpha'/\alpha]$ | |
| $(\eta\&)$ | $V : A\&B$ | $=_v$ | $\langle \mathtt{fst} V, \mathtt{snd}\, V\rangle$ | |
| $(\eta\vee)$ | $M : A \vee B$ | $=_v$ | $\mu(\alpha,\beta).[\alpha,\beta]M$ | ($\alpha,\beta$: fresh) |
| $(\eta\neg)$ | $V : \neg A$ | $=_v$ | $\lambda x.Vx$ | ($x$: fresh) |
| $(\eta\supset)$ | $V : A \supset B$ | $=_v$ | $\lambda x.Vx$ | ($x$: fresh) |
| $(\eta\mu)$ | $M$ | $=_v$ | $\mu\alpha.[\alpha]M$ | ($\alpha$: fresh) |
| (name) | $D\{M\}$ | $=_v$ | $(\lambda x.D\{x\})M$ | ($x$: fresh) |
| (comp) | $D\{(\lambda x.N)M\}$ | $=_v$ | $(\lambda x.D\{N\})M$ | |
| $(\varsigma)$ | $D\{\mu\alpha.S\}$ | $=_v$ | $S[D\{-\}/[\alpha]\{-\}]$ | |

**Fig. 2.** The equality axioms of the call-by-value $\lambda\mu$-calculus

| | | | | |
|---|---|---|---|---|
| $(\beta\&_1)$ | $\mathtt{fst}\langle M, N\rangle$ | $=_n$ | $M$ | |
| $(\beta\&_2)$ | $\mathtt{snd}\langle M, N\rangle$ | $=_n$ | $N$ | |
| $(\beta\vee)$ | $[\alpha',\beta']\mu(\alpha,\beta).S$ | $=_n$ | $S[\alpha'/\alpha,\beta'/\beta]$ | |
| $(\beta\neg)$ | $(\lambda x.S)N$ | $=_n$ | $S[N/x]$ | |
| $(\beta\supset)$ | $(\lambda x.M)N$ | $=_n$ | $M[N/x]$ | |
| $(\beta\mu)$ | $[\alpha']\mu\alpha.S$ | $=_n$ | $S[\alpha'/\alpha]$ | |
| $(\eta\&)$ | $M : A\&B$ | $=_n$ | $\langle \mathtt{fst} M, \mathtt{snd}\, M\rangle$ | |
| $(\eta\vee)$ | $M : A \vee B$ | $=_n$ | $\mu(\alpha,\beta).[\alpha,\beta]M$ | ($\alpha,\beta$: fresh) |
| $(\eta\neg)$ | $M : \neg A$ | $=_n$ | $\lambda x.Mx$ | ($x$: fresh) |
| $(\eta\supset)$ | $M : A \supset B$ | $=_n$ | $\lambda x.Mx$ | ($x$: fresh) |
| $(\eta\mu)$ | $M$ | $=_n$ | $\mu\alpha.[\alpha]M$ | ($\alpha$: fresh) |
| $(\varsigma\&_1)$ | $\mathtt{fst}(\mu\alpha.S)$ | $=_n$ | $\mu\beta.S[[\beta]\mathtt{fst}\{-\}/[\alpha]\{-\}]]$ | |
| $(\varsigma\&_2)$ | $\mathtt{snd}(\mu\alpha.S)$ | $=_n$ | $\mu\beta.S[[\beta]\mathtt{snd}\{-\}/[\alpha]\{-\}]$ | |
| $(\varsigma\vee)$ | $[\beta,\gamma]\mu\alpha.S$ | $=_n$ | $S[[\beta,\gamma]\{-\}/[\alpha]\{-\}]$ | |
| $(\varsigma\neg)$ | $(\mu\alpha.S)M$ | $=_n$ | $S[\{-\}M/[\alpha]\{-\}]$ | |
| $(\varsigma\supset)$ | $(\mu\alpha.S)M$ | $=_n$ | $\mu\beta.S[[\beta]\{-\}M/[\alpha]\{-\}]$ | |

**Fig. 3.** The equality axioms of the call-by-name $\lambda\mu$-calculus

$$A \supset B \equiv \neg(A\&\neg B) \quad \lambda x.N \equiv \lambda z.(\lambda x.(\mathtt{snd}\, z)N)(\mathtt{fst}\, z) \quad OM \equiv \mu\beta.O\langle M, \lambda y.[\beta]y\rangle$$

*By this definition, $(\beta\supset)$, $(\eta\supset)$ and the other equations for functions are validated, and a function abstraction is a value.*

**Proposition 2 (Wadler(2005)).** *Under call-by-name, implication can be defined as follows:*

$$A \supset B \equiv \neg A \vee B \quad \lambda x.N \equiv \mu(\gamma,\beta).[\gamma]\lambda x.[\beta]N \quad OM \equiv \mu\beta.(\mu\gamma.[\gamma,\beta]O)M$$

*By this definition, $(\beta\supset)$, $(\eta\supset)$ and $(\varsigma\supset)$ are validated.*

| | | |
|---|---|---|
| $A, B$ | $::= X \mid A\&B \mid A \vee B \mid \neg A \mid A \supset B$ | (Types) |
| $M, N$ | $::= x \mid \langle M, N\rangle \mid \langle M\rangle\texttt{inl} \mid \langle N\rangle\texttt{inr} \mid [K]\texttt{not} \mid \lambda x.M \mid (S).\alpha$ | (Terms) |
| $K, L$ | $::= \alpha \mid [K, L] \mid \texttt{fst}[K] \mid \texttt{snd}[L] \mid \texttt{not}\langle M\rangle \mid M@K \mid x.(S)$ | (Coterms) |
| $S, T$ | $::= M \bullet K$ | (Statements) |
| $V, W$ | $::= x \mid \langle V, W\rangle \mid \langle V\rangle\texttt{inl} \mid \langle W\rangle\texttt{inr} \mid [K]\texttt{not} \mid \lambda x.M$ <br> $\mid (V \bullet \texttt{fst}[\alpha]).\alpha \mid (W \bullet \texttt{snd}[\beta]).\beta$ | (Values) |
| $P, Q$ | $::= \alpha \mid [P, Q] \mid \texttt{fst}[P] \mid \texttt{snd}[Q] \mid \texttt{not}\langle M\rangle \mid M@P$ <br> $\mid x.(\langle x\rangle\texttt{inl} \bullet P) \mid y.(\langle y\rangle\texttt{inr} \bullet Q)$ | (Covalues) |
| $E$ | $::= \{-\} \mid \langle E, N\rangle \mid \langle V, E\rangle \mid \langle E\rangle\texttt{inl} \mid \langle E\rangle\texttt{inr}$ | (Evaluation contexts) |
| $F$ | $::= \{-\} \mid [L, F] \mid [F, P] \mid \texttt{fst}[F] \mid \texttt{snd}[F]$ | (Coevaluation contexts) |

**Fig. 4.** The syntax of the dual calculus

## 2.2 The Dual Calculus

The dual calculus (DC) is a term calculus, which corresponds to the classical sequent calculus. Wadler first gave it as a reduction system in [14], and later introduced as an equation system in [15]. In this paper, we consider the equation system in his latter paper.

DC consists of types and expressions. Types, variables, and covariables of DC are the same as those of the $\lambda\mu$-calculus. An expression is either a term (denoted by $M$, $N$), a coterm (denoted by $K$, $L$), or a statement (denoted by $S$, $T$). We also need notions of values (denoted by $V$, $W$) and evaluation contexts (denoted by $E$) for the call-by-value calculus, and notions of covalues (denoted by $P$, $Q$) and co-evaluation contexts (denoted by $F$) for the call-by-name calculus. They are summarized in Figure 4.

A typing judgment of DC takes either the form $\Gamma \rightarrow \Delta \mid M : A$, the form $K : A \mid \Gamma \rightarrow \Delta$ or the form $\Gamma \mid S \mapsto \Delta$, where $\Gamma$ denotes a context, i.e., $x_1 : A_1, \ldots, x_n : A_n$ and $\Delta$ denotes a cocontext, i.e., $\alpha_1 : B_1, \ldots, \alpha_m : B_m$. The typing rules of the dual calculus are given in Wadler's paper [15].

The call-by-value equalities (denoted by $=^v$) and the call-by-name equalities (denoted by $=^n$) of DC are defined from the axioms listed in Figure 5 and 6 respectively.

As before, implication of DC can be defined in terms of the other connectives.

**Proposition 3 (Wadler(2005)).** *Under call-by-value, implication can be defined as follows:*

$$A \supset B \equiv \neg(A\&\neg B)$$
$$\lambda x.N \equiv [z.(z \bullet \texttt{fst}[x.(z \bullet \texttt{snd}[\texttt{not}\langle N\rangle])])]\texttt{not} \qquad M@K \equiv \texttt{not}\langle\langle M, [K]\texttt{not}\rangle\rangle$$

*By this definition, $(\beta \supset)$, $(\eta \supset)$ and the other equations for functions are validated, and a function abstraction is a value.*

**Proposition 4 (Wadler(2005)).** *Under call-by-name, implication can be defined as follows:*

$$A \supset B \equiv \neg A \vee B$$
$$\lambda x.N \equiv (\langle[x.(\langle N\rangle\texttt{inr} \bullet \gamma)]\texttt{not}\rangle\texttt{inl} \bullet \gamma).\gamma \qquad M@K \equiv [\texttt{not}\langle M\rangle, K]$$

| | | | | |
|---|---|---|---|---|
| $(\beta\&_1)$ | $\langle V, W\rangle \bullet \mathtt{fst}[K]$ | $=^v$ | $V \bullet K$ | |
| $(\beta\&_2)$ | $\langle V, W\rangle \bullet \mathtt{snd}[L]$ | $=^v$ | $W \bullet L$ | |
| $(\beta\vee_1)$ | $\langle V\rangle\mathtt{inl} \bullet [K, L]$ | $=^v$ | $V \bullet K$ | |
| $(\beta\vee_2)$ | $\langle W\rangle\mathtt{inr} \bullet [K, L]$ | $=^v$ | $W \bullet L$ | |
| $(\beta\neg)$ | $[K]\mathtt{not} \bullet \mathtt{not}\langle M\rangle$ | $=^v$ | $M \bullet K$ | |
| $(\beta\supset)$ | $\lambda x.N \bullet (M@K)$ | $=^v$ | $M \bullet x.(N \bullet K)$ | |
| $(\beta R)$ | $(S).\alpha \bullet K$ | $=^v$ | $S[K/\alpha]$ | |
| $(\beta L)$ | $V \bullet x.(S)$ | $=^v$ | $S[V/x]$ | |
| $(\eta\&)$ | $V : A\&B$ | $=^v$ | $\langle (V \bullet \mathtt{fst}[\alpha]).\alpha, (V \bullet \mathtt{snd}[\beta]).\beta\rangle$ | $(\alpha, \beta$: fresh) |
| $(\eta\vee)$ | $K : A \vee B$ | $=^v$ | $[x.(\langle x\rangle\mathtt{inl} \bullet K), y.(\langle y\rangle\mathtt{inr} \bullet K)]$ | ($x$, $y$: fresh) |
| $(\eta\neg)$ | $V : \neg A$ | $=^v$ | $[x.(V \bullet \mathtt{not}\langle x\rangle)]\mathtt{not}$ | ($x$: fresh) |
| $(\eta\supset)$ | $V : A \supset B$ | $=^v$ | $\lambda x.((V \bullet (x@\beta)).\beta))$ | ($x$: fresh) |
| $(\eta R)$ | $M$ | $=^v$ | $(M \bullet \alpha).\alpha$ | ($\alpha$: fresh) |
| $(\eta L)$ | $K$ | $=^v$ | $x.(x \bullet K)$ | ($x$: fresh) |
| (name) | $E\{M\} \bullet K$ | $=^v$ | $M \bullet x.(E\{x\} \bullet K)$ | ($x$: fresh) |

**Fig. 5.** The equality axioms of the call-by-value dual calculus

*By this definition, $(\beta\supset)$, $(\eta\supset)$, and the other equations for functions are validated, and a function application is a covalue.*

Wadler introduced the translation $(-)^*$ from $\lambda\mu$ into DC, and its inverse translation $(-)_*$. The formal definitions of his translations are given in Figure 7 and 8. He showed that these translations preserve typing relations, and form an *equational correspondence* with respect to the call-by-value (resp. call-by-name) equations. The original notion of equational correspondence was given by Sabry and Felleisen [12]. We apply this notion on the several extended systems of $\lambda\mu$ and DC.

**Definition 1 (equational correspondence).** *Let $\lambda\mu+$ and DC+ be extended systems of $\lambda\mu$ and DC respectively, and let $=_+$ and $=^+$ be equations of $\lambda\mu+$ and DC+ defined on them. Suppose a translation $(-)^{\circledast}$ from $\lambda\mu+$ into DC+ is an extension of $(-)^*$, and a translation $(-)_{\circledast}$ from DC+ into $\lambda\mu+$ is an extension of $(-)_*$. We say that the pair of translations $((-)^{\circledast}, (-)_{\circledast})$ forms an equational correspondence with respect to $(=_+, =^+)$ if the following four conditions hold.*
(Soundness):

$$M =_+ N \text{ implies } M^{\circledast} =^+ N^{\circledast}, \quad \text{and} \quad S =_+ T \text{ implies } S^{\circledast} =^+ T^{\circledast}$$

for any terms $M$ and $N$, and statements $S$ and $T$ of $\lambda\mu+$.
(Completeness):

$$M =^+ N \text{ implies } M_{\circledast} =_+ N_{\circledast},$$
$$K =^+ L \text{ implies } K_{\circledast}\{O\} =_+ L_{\circledast}\{O\}, \text{ and}$$
$$S =^+ T \text{ implies } S_{\circledast} =_+ T_{\circledast},$$

for any terms $M$, coterms $K$, and statements $S$ of DC+, and any term $O$ of $\lambda\mu+$.

| | | | | |
|---|---|---|---|---|
| $(\beta\&_1)$ | $\langle M,N\rangle \bullet \mathtt{fst}[P]$ | $=^n$ | $M \bullet P$ | |
| $(\beta\&_2)$ | $\langle M,N\rangle \bullet \mathtt{snd}[Q]$ | $=^n$ | $N \bullet Q$ | |
| $(\beta\vee_1)$ | $\langle M\rangle\mathtt{inl} \bullet [P,Q]$ | $=^n$ | $M \bullet P$ | |
| $(\beta\vee_2)$ | $\langle Q\rangle\mathtt{inr} \bullet [P,Q]$ | $=^n$ | $N \bullet Q$ | |
| $(\beta\neg)$ | $[K]\mathtt{not} \bullet \mathtt{not}\langle M\rangle$ | $=^n$ | $M \bullet K$ | |
| $(\beta\supset)$ | $\lambda x.N \bullet (M@K)$ | $=^n$ | $M \bullet x.(N \bullet K)$ | |
| $(\beta R)$ | $(S).\alpha \bullet P$ | $=^n$ | $S[P/\alpha]$ | |
| $(\beta L)$ | $M \bullet x.(S)$ | $=^n$ | $S[M/x]$ | |
| $(\eta\&)$ | $M : A\&B$ | $=^n$ | $\langle(M \bullet \mathtt{fst}[\alpha]).\alpha, (M \bullet \mathtt{snd}[\beta]).\beta\rangle$ | ($\alpha,\beta$: fresh) |
| $(\eta\vee)$ | $P : A \vee B$ | $=^n$ | $[x.(\langle x\rangle\mathtt{inl} \bullet P), y.(\langle y\rangle\mathtt{inr} \bullet P)]$ | ($x$, $y$: fresh) |
| $(\eta\neg)$ | $P : \neg A$ | $=^n$ | $\mathtt{not}\langle([\alpha]\mathtt{not} \bullet P).\alpha\rangle$ | ($\alpha$: fresh) |
| $(\eta\supset)$ | $M : A \supset B$ | $=^n$ | $\lambda x.((M \bullet (x@\beta)).\beta))$ | ($x$: fresh) |
| $(\eta R)$ | $M$ | $=^n$ | $(M \bullet \alpha).\alpha$ | ($\alpha$: fresh) |
| $(\eta L)$ | $K$ | $=^n$ | $x.(x \bullet K)$ | ($x$: fresh) |
| (name) | $M \bullet F\{K\}$ | $=^n$ | $(M \bullet F\{\alpha\}).\alpha \bullet K$ | ($\alpha$: fresh) |

**Fig. 6.** The equality axioms of the call-by-name dual calculus

| | | | | | |
|---|---|---|---|---|---|
| $(x)^*$ | $\equiv$ | $x$ | $(\langle M,N\rangle)^*$ | $\equiv$ | $\langle M^*, N^*\rangle$ |
| $(\mathtt{fst}\,O)^*$ | $\equiv$ | $(O^* \bullet \mathtt{fst}[\alpha]).\alpha$ | $(\mathtt{snd}\,O)^*$ | $\equiv$ | $(O^* \bullet \mathtt{snd}[\beta]).\beta$ |
| $(\mu(\alpha,\beta).S)^*$ | $\equiv$ | $(\langle(\langle(S)^*.\beta\rangle\mathtt{inr} \bullet \gamma).\alpha\rangle\mathtt{inl} \bullet \gamma).\gamma$ | $([\alpha,\beta]M)^*$ | $\equiv$ | $M^* \bullet [\alpha,\beta]$ |
| $(\lambda x.S)^*$ | $\equiv$ | $[x.(S)^*]\mathtt{not}$ | $(OM)^*$ | $\equiv$ | $O^* \bullet \mathtt{not}\langle M^*\rangle$ |
| $(\mu\alpha.S)^*$ | $\equiv$ | $(S^*).\alpha$ | $([\alpha]M)^*$ | $\equiv$ | $M^* \bullet \alpha$ |
| $(\lambda x.M)^*$ | $\equiv$ | $\lambda x.M^*$ | $(OM)^*$ | $\equiv$ | $(O^* \bullet (M^*@\beta)).\beta$ |

**Fig. 7.** The translation $(-)^*$ from the $\lambda\mu$-calculus into DC

(Reloading property (1)):

$$(M^{\circledast})_{\circledast} =_+ M \quad \text{and} \quad (S^{\circledast})_{\circledast} =_+ S$$

for any term $M$ and statement $S$ of $\lambda\mu$+.
(Reloading property (2)):

$$(M_{\circledast})^{\circledast} =^+ M, \quad (K_{\circledast}\{O\})^{\circledast} =^+ O^{\circledast} \bullet K, \quad \text{and} \quad (S_{\circledast})^{\circledast} =^+ S$$

for any term $M$, coterm $K$, and statement $S$ of DC+, and any term $O$ of $\lambda\mu$+.

**Theorem 1 (Wadler (2005)).** *(1)* $((-)^*, (-)_*)$ *forms equational correspondence with respect to the call-by-value equations* $(=_v, =^v)$.
*(2)* $((-)^*, (-)_*)$ *forms equational correspondence with respect to the call-by-name equations* $(=_n, =^n)$.

# 3 Extension with Fixed-Point and Iteration

## 3.1 The $\lambda\mu$-calculus with Fixed-Point and Iteration Operators

In this subsection, we extend the call-by-name $\lambda\mu$-calculus by adding a *fixed-point operator* (called $\lambda\mu_n^{+\mathtt{fix}}$), and extend the call-by-value one by adding an *iteration operator* (called $\lambda\mu_v^{+\mathtt{loop}}$).

| | | | | | |
|---|---|---|---|---|---|
| $(x)_*$ | $\equiv$ | $x$ | $(\alpha)_*\{O\}$ | $\equiv$ | $[\alpha]O$ |
| $(\langle M,N\rangle)_*$ | $\equiv$ | $\langle M_*,N_*\rangle$ | $([K,L])_*\{O\}$ | $\equiv$ | $L_*\{\mu\beta.K_*\{\mu\alpha.[\alpha,\beta]O\}\}$ |
| $(\langle M\rangle\mathtt{inl})_*$ | $\equiv$ | $\mu(\alpha,\beta).[\alpha]M_*$ | $(\mathtt{fst}[K])_*\{O\}$ | $\equiv$ | $K_*\{\mathtt{fst}\,O\}$ |
| $(\langle N\rangle\mathtt{inr})_*$ | $\equiv$ | $\mu(\alpha,\beta).[\beta]N_*$ | $(\mathtt{snd}[L])_*\{O\}$ | $\equiv$ | $L_*\{\mathtt{snd}\,O\}$ |
| $([K]\mathtt{not})_*$ | $\equiv$ | $\lambda x.K_*\{x\}$ | $(\mathtt{not}\langle M\rangle)_*\{O\}$ | $\equiv$ | $OM_*$ |
| $(\lambda x.M)_*$ | $\equiv$ | $\lambda x.M_*$ | $(M@K)_*\{O\}$ | $\equiv$ | $K_*\{OM_*\}$ |
| $((S).\alpha)_*$ | $\equiv$ | $\mu\alpha.S_*$ | $(x.S)_*\{O\}$ | $\equiv$ | $(\lambda x.S_*)O$ |

$$(M \bullet K)_* \equiv K_*\{M_*\}$$

**Fig. 8.** The translation $(-)_*$ from DC into the $\lambda\mu$-calculus

The syntax of the $\lambda\mu_n^{+\mathtt{fix}}$-calculus is defined by adding $\mathtt{fix}\,x.M$ to the terms of the $\lambda\mu$-calculus. $\mathtt{fix}$ is a fixed point operator, which binds $x$ in $M$. The syntax of the $\lambda\mu_v^{+\mathtt{loop}}$-calculus is defined by adding $\mathtt{loop}\,x.M$ to the terms of the $\lambda\mu$-calculus. $\mathtt{loop}$ is a iteration operator, which binds $x$ in $M$.

The additional typing rules and the equality axioms are as follows:

$$\frac{\Gamma, x : A \rightharpoonup \Delta \mid M : A}{\Gamma \rightharpoonup \Delta \mid \mathtt{fix}\,x.M : A}\,(\mathrm{fix}) \qquad \frac{\Gamma, x : A \rightharpoonup \Delta \mid M : A}{\Gamma \rightharpoonup \Delta \mid \mathtt{loop}\,x.M : \neg A}\,(\mathrm{loop})$$

and

$$\begin{array}{ll} (\mathrm{fix}) & \mathtt{fix}\,x.M =_n (\lambda x.M)\mathtt{fix}\,x.M \\ (\mathrm{loop}) & \mathtt{loop}\,x.M =_v \lambda x.((\mathtt{loop}\,x.M)M) \end{array}$$

Our formulation of fixed-point and iteration operators is slightly, but not essentially, different from Kakutani's one [7]. He introduced them as constants, and so needed implication. On the other hand, our formulation does not need implication. Since duality in this paper is not defined for implication (see section 5), our formulation of fixed-point and iteration operators is more suitable for seeing duality between them.

### 3.2 The Dual Calculus with Fixed-Point and Co-fixed-Point Operators

We extend the call-by-name dual calculus by adding a fixed-point operator, obtaining thus $\mathrm{DC}_n^{+\mathtt{fix}}$, and extend the call-by-value calculus by adding a co-fixed-point operator, obtaining thus $\mathrm{DC}_v^{+\mathtt{cofix}}$. The co-fixed-point operator is the dual one of the fixed-point operator.

We define the syntax of $\mathrm{DC}_n^{+\mathtt{fix}}$ by adding $\mathtt{fix}\,x.\langle M\rangle$ to the terms of DC , and the syntax of $\mathrm{DC}_v^{+\mathtt{cofix}}$ by adding $\mathtt{cofix}\,\alpha.[K]$ to the coterms of DC . The additional typing rules and the equality axioms are as follows:

$$\frac{\Gamma, x : A \rightarrow \Delta \mid M : A}{\Gamma \rightarrow \Delta \mid \mathtt{fix}\,x.\langle M\rangle : A}\,(\mathrm{fix}) \qquad \frac{K : A \mid \Gamma \rightarrow \Delta, \alpha : A}{\mathtt{cofix}\,\alpha.[K] : A \mid \Gamma \rightarrow \Delta}\,(\mathrm{cofix})$$

and

$$\begin{array}{lll} (\mathrm{fix}) & (\mathtt{fix}\,x.\langle M\rangle) \bullet P =^n (\mathtt{fix}\,x.\langle M\rangle) \bullet x.(M \bullet P) & (P : \mathrm{covalue}) \\ (\mathrm{cofix}) & V \bullet (\mathtt{cofix}\,\alpha.[K]) =^v (V \bullet K).\alpha \bullet (\mathtt{cofix}\,\alpha.[K]) & (V : \mathrm{value}) \end{array}$$

Intuitively, $\texttt{fix}\, x.\langle M\rangle$ is a fixed-point of $\lambda x.M$ in the call-by-name dual calculus. In fact, $\texttt{fix}\, x.\langle M\rangle$ is equal to $M[^{\texttt{fix}\, x.\langle M\rangle}/_x]$ under the call-by-name equation:

$$\begin{aligned}\texttt{fix}\, x.\langle M\rangle &=^n ((\texttt{fix}\, x.\langle M\rangle) \bullet \alpha).\alpha =^n ((\texttt{fix}\, x.\langle M\rangle) \bullet x.(M \bullet \alpha)).\alpha \\ &=^n (M[^{\texttt{fix}\, x.\langle M\rangle}/_x] \bullet \alpha).\alpha =^n M[^{\texttt{fix}\, x.\langle M\rangle}/_x]\end{aligned}$$

Dually, $\texttt{cofix}\, \alpha.[K]$ is equal to $K[^{\texttt{cofix}\, \alpha.[K]}/_\alpha]$ under the call-by-value equation.

### 3.3 Translations

In this subsection, we extend Wadler's translations $(-)^*$ and $(-)_*$ between $\lambda\mu$ and DC. We first consider the languages $\lambda\mu^{+\texttt{fix}+\texttt{loop}}$ with both $\texttt{fix}$ and $\texttt{loop}$ and $\texttt{DC}^{+\texttt{fix}+\texttt{cofix}}$ with both $\texttt{fix}$ and $\texttt{cofix}$. Then we give translations $(-)^{*_1}$ and $(-)_{*_1}$ between $\lambda\mu^{+\texttt{fix}+\texttt{loop}}$ and $\texttt{DC}^{+\texttt{fix}+\texttt{cofix}}$ as extensions of $(-)^*$ and $(-)_*$ respectively. $(-)^{*_1}$ is defined as follows:

$$\begin{aligned}(\texttt{fix}\, x.M)^{*_1} &\equiv \texttt{fix}\, x.\langle M^{*_1}\rangle, \\ (\texttt{loop}\, x.M)^{*_1} &\equiv [\,\texttt{cofix}\, \alpha.[x.(M^{*_1} \bullet \alpha)]\,]\texttt{not}.\end{aligned}$$

The other clauses are similar to the definition of $(-)^*$. On the other hand, $(-)_{*_1}$ is defined as follows:

$$\begin{aligned}(\texttt{fix}\, x.\langle M\rangle)_{*_1} &\equiv \texttt{fix}\, x.M_{*_1} \\ (\texttt{cofix}\, \alpha.[K])_{*_1}\{O\} &\equiv (\texttt{loop}\, x.(\mu\alpha.K_{*_1}\{x\}))O\end{aligned}$$

The other clauses are similar to the definition of $(-)_*$.

Note that the images of $\lambda\mu_n^{+\texttt{fix}}$ and $\lambda\mu_v^{+\texttt{loop}}$ by $(-)^{*_1}$ are $\texttt{DC}_n^{+\texttt{fix}}$ and $\texttt{DC}_v^{+\texttt{cofix}}$ respectively. Similarly, the images of $\texttt{DC}_n^{+\texttt{fix}}$ and $\texttt{DC}_v^{+\texttt{cofix}}$ by $(-)_{*_1}$ are $\lambda\mu_n^{+\texttt{fix}}$ and $\lambda\mu_v^{+\texttt{loop}}$ respectively.

The extended translations also preserve typing relations.

**Proposition 5.** (1) $(-)^{*_1}$ *preserves typing relations, that is,*

$$\begin{aligned}\Gamma \rightharpoonup \Delta \mid M : A \text{ implies } \Gamma \rightarrow \Delta \mid M^{*_1} : A, \\ \Gamma \mid S \mapsto \Delta \text{ implies } \Gamma \mid S^{*_1} \mapsto \Delta\end{aligned}$$

*for any terms $M$ and statement $S$ of $\lambda\mu^{+\texttt{fix}+\texttt{loop}}$.*
(2) $(-)_{*_1}$ *preserves typing relations, that is,*

$$\begin{aligned}\Gamma \rightarrow \Delta \mid M : A \text{ implies } \Gamma \rightharpoonup \Delta \mid M_{*_1} : A, \\ K : A \mid \Gamma \rightarrow \Delta \text{ and } \Gamma \rightharpoonup \Delta \mid O : A \text{ implies } \Gamma \mid K_{*_1}\{O\} \mapsto \Delta. \\ \Gamma \mid S \mapsto \Delta \text{ implies } \Gamma \mid S_{*_1} \mapsto \Delta\end{aligned}$$

*for any term $M$, coterm $K$, and statement $S$ of $\texttt{DC}^{+\texttt{fix}+\texttt{cofix}}$, and term $O$ of $\lambda\mu^{+\texttt{fix}+\texttt{loop}}$.*

The main result of this section is the following theorem.

**Theorem 2.** (i) $((-)^{*_1}, (-)_{*_1})$ *forms an equational correspondence with respect to the call-by-value equations.*
(ii) $((-)^{*_1}, (-)_{*_1})$ *forms an equational correspondence with respect to the call-by-name equations.*

*Proof.* Soundness of (i) and (ii) can be shown by the inductions on $=_v$ and $=_n$ respectively. We show the case of (loop)-rule:

$$
\begin{aligned}
(\texttt{loop}\, x.M)^{*1} &\equiv [\,\texttt{cofix}\,\alpha.[x.(M^{*1} \bullet \alpha)]\,]\texttt{not} =^{v}_{(\eta L)} [\,z.(z \bullet \texttt{cofix}\,\alpha.[x.(M^{*1} \bullet \alpha)])\,]\texttt{not} \\
&=^{v}_{(\text{cofix})} [\,z.((z \bullet x.(M^{*1} \bullet \alpha)).\alpha \bullet \texttt{cofix}\,\alpha.[x.(M^{*1} \bullet \alpha)])\,]\texttt{not} \\
&=^{v}_{(\beta R)} [\,z.(z \bullet x.(M^{*1} \bullet \texttt{cofix}\,\alpha.[x.(M^{*1} \bullet \alpha)]))\,]\texttt{not} \\
&=^{v}_{(\eta L)} [\,x.(M^{*1} \bullet \texttt{cofix}\,\alpha.[x.(M^{*1} \bullet \alpha)])\,]\texttt{not} \\
&=^{v}_{(\beta_\neg)} [\,x.(\,[\,\texttt{cofix}\,\alpha.[(M^{*1} \bullet \alpha)]\,]\texttt{not} \bullet \texttt{not}\langle M^{*1}\rangle\,)\,]\texttt{not} \\
&\equiv [\,x.(\,(\texttt{loop}\,x.M)^{*1} \bullet \texttt{not}\langle M^{*1}\rangle\,)\,]\texttt{not} \\
&\equiv (\,\lambda x.(\texttt{loop}\,x.M)M\,)^{*1}
\end{aligned}
$$

Completeness of (i) and (ii) can be shown by the inductions on $=^v$ and $=^n$ respectively. We show the case of (cofix)-rule:

$$
\begin{aligned}
(V \bullet (\texttt{cofix}\,\alpha.[K]))_{*1} &\equiv (\texttt{cofix}\,\alpha.[K])_{*1}\{V_{*1}\} \equiv (\texttt{loop}\,x.(\mu\alpha.K_{*1}\{x\}))V_{*1} \\
&=^{(\text{loop})}_{v} (\lambda x.((\texttt{loop}\,x.(\mu\alpha.K_{*1}\{x\}))\mu\alpha.K_{*1}\{x\}))V_{*1} \\
&=_v (\texttt{loop}\,x.(\mu\alpha.K_{*1}\{x\}))\mu\alpha.K_{*1}\{V_{*1}\} \equiv (\texttt{cofix}\,\alpha.[K])_{*1}\{\,\mu\alpha.K_{*1}\{V_{*1}\}\} \\
&\equiv ((V \bullet K).\alpha \bullet (\texttt{cofix}\,\alpha.[K]))_{*1}
\end{aligned}
$$

Reloading property (1) of (i) and (ii) can be shown by the inductions on $M$ and $S$ respectively. We show the case of $(\texttt{loop}\,x.M)$:

$$
\begin{aligned}
((\texttt{loop}\,x.M)^{*1})_{*1} &\equiv [\,\texttt{cofix}\,\alpha.[x.(M^{*1} \bullet \alpha)]\,]\texttt{not}_{*1} \equiv \lambda z.(\texttt{cofix}\,\alpha.[x.(M^{*1} \bullet \alpha)])_{*1}\{z\} \\
&\equiv \lambda z.(\texttt{loop}\,y.(\mu\alpha.(x.(M^{*1} \bullet \alpha))_{*1}\{y\}))z \equiv \lambda z.(\texttt{loop}\,y.(\mu\alpha.(\lambda x.[\alpha](M^{*1})_{*1})y))z \\
&\overset{I.H.}{=_v} \lambda z.(\texttt{loop}\,y.(\mu\alpha.(\lambda x.[\alpha]M)y))z =^{(\beta_\neg)}_{v} \lambda z.(\texttt{loop}\,x.(\mu\alpha.[\alpha]M))z \\
&=^{(\eta\mu)}_{v} \lambda z.(\texttt{loop}\,x.M)z =^{(\text{loop})}_{v} \lambda z.(\lambda x.(\texttt{loop}\,x.M)M)z =^{(\beta_\neg)}_{v} \lambda z.(\texttt{loop}\,z.M)M \\
&\equiv \texttt{loop}\,x.M
\end{aligned}
$$

Reloading property (2) of (i) and (ii) can be shown by the inductions on $M$ and $S$ respectively. We show the case of $(\texttt{cofix}\,\alpha.[K])$:

$$
\begin{aligned}
((\texttt{cofix}\,\alpha.[K])_{*1}\{O\})^{*1} &\equiv ((\texttt{loop}\,x.(\mu\alpha.K_{*1}\{x\}))O)^{*1} \equiv (\texttt{loop}\,x.(\mu\alpha.K_{*1}\{x\}))^{*1} \bullet \texttt{not}\langle O^{*1}\rangle \\
&\equiv [\,\texttt{cofix}\,\beta.[x.(\,(K_{*1}\{x\})^{*1}.\alpha \bullet \beta\,)]\,]\texttt{not} \bullet \texttt{not}\langle O^{*1}\rangle \\
&=^{v}_{(\beta_\neg)} O^{*1} \bullet \texttt{cofix}\,\beta.[x.(\,(K_{*1}\{x\})^{*1}.\alpha \bullet \beta\,)] \overset{I.H.}{=^{v}} O^{*1} \bullet \texttt{cofix}\,\beta.[x.((x \bullet K).\alpha \bullet \beta)\,)] \\
&=^{v}_{(\beta_R)} O^{*1} \bullet \texttt{cofix}\,\alpha.[x.(x \bullet K)\,)] =^{v}_{(\eta_L)} O^{*1} \bullet \texttt{cofix}\,\alpha.[K]
\end{aligned}
$$

## 4 Extension with Recursive Types, and ⊤, ⊥ Types

In this section, we further extend Wadler's results by adding ⊤, ⊥, and recursive types ($\texttt{rec}\,X.A$) to the $\lambda\mu$-calculi and the dual calculi. Intuitively, ⊤ type means the unit type, and ⊥ type means the counit type. By this extension, we can define many important data types, such as boolean, natural numbers, lists, and streams. For example, under the call-by-value system, boolean type can be defined by $\top \vee \top$, and natural numbers type can be defined by $\texttt{rec}\,X.(\top \vee X)$.

### 4.1 The $\lambda\mu$-calculus with Recursive Types, and $\top$, $\bot$ Types

In this subsection, we extend the $\lambda\mu_v^{+\mathtt{loop}}$ and $\lambda\mu_n^{+\mathtt{fix}}$-calculi by adding $\top$, $\bot$, and recursive types. The extended systems are called $\lambda\mu_v^{+\mathtt{loop}+\{\top,\bot\}+\mathtt{rec}}$ and $\lambda\mu_n^{+\mathtt{fix}+\{\top,\bot\}+\mathtt{rec}}$. We also consider the general syntax (without equations) $\lambda\mu^{+\mathtt{fix}+\mathtt{loop}+\{\top,\bot\}+\mathtt{rec}}$ with both of $\mathtt{fix}$ and $\mathtt{loop}$. The syntax of $\lambda\mu^{+\mathtt{fix}+\mathtt{loop}+\{\top,\bot\}+\mathtt{rec}}$ (resp. $\lambda\mu_v^{+\mathtt{loop}+\{\top,\bot\}+\mathtt{rec}}$, $\lambda\mu_n^{+\mathtt{fix}+\{\top,\bot\}+\mathtt{rec}}$) is defined by adding

$$\begin{aligned} A, B &::= \ldots \mid \top \mid \bot \mid \mathtt{rec}\, X.A \\ M, N, O &::= \ldots \mid * \mid \mathtt{fold}(M) \mid \mathtt{unfold}(M) \\ S, T &::= \ldots \mid [\bot]M \end{aligned}$$

to the types, terms, and statements of $\lambda\mu^{+\mathtt{fix}+\mathtt{loop}}$ (resp. $\lambda\mu_v^{+\mathtt{loop}}$, $\lambda\mu_n^{+\mathtt{fix}}$). We also extend the definition of values and evaluation contexts of the call-by-value calculus by adding

$$\begin{aligned} V, W &::= \ldots \mid * \mid \mathtt{fold}(V), \\ E &::= \ldots \mid \mathtt{fold}(E) \mid \mathtt{unfold}(E). \end{aligned}$$

The additional typing rules are

$$\frac{}{\Gamma \rightharpoonup \Delta \mid * : \top}(\top) \qquad \frac{\Gamma \rightharpoonup \Delta \mid M : A[^{\mathtt{rec}\, X.A}/X]}{\Gamma \rightharpoonup \Delta \mid \mathtt{fold}(M) : \mathtt{rec}\, X.A}(\mathtt{fold})$$

$$\frac{\Gamma \rightharpoonup \Delta \mid M : \bot}{\Gamma \mid [\bot]M \vdash\!\rightharpoonup \Delta}(\bot) \qquad \frac{\Gamma \rightharpoonup \Delta \mid M : \mathtt{rec}\, X.A}{\Gamma \rightharpoonup \Delta \mid \mathtt{unfold}(M) : A[^{\mathtt{rec}\, X.A}/X]}(\mathtt{unfold}),$$

the additional equality axioms for call-by-name are

$$\begin{array}{llr} (\top) & M =_n * & (M : \top) \\ (\bot) & [\alpha]M =_n [\bot]M & (M : \bot) \\ (\beta_{rec}) & \mathtt{unfold}(\mathtt{fold}(M)) =_n M & \\ (\varsigma_{rec}) & \mathtt{unfold}(\mu\alpha.S) =_n \mu\beta.S\,[[\beta]\mathtt{unfold}(-)/[\alpha]\{-\}], & \end{array}$$

and the additional equality axioms for call-by-value are

$$\begin{array}{llr} (\top) & V =_v * & (V : \top) \\ (\bot) & [\alpha]M =_v [\bot]M & (M : \bot) \\ (\beta_{rec}) & \mathtt{unfold}(\mathtt{fold}(V)) =_v V\,. & \end{array}$$

### 4.2 The Dual Calculus with Recursive Types, and $\top$, $\bot$ Types

In this subsection, we extend $\mathtt{DC}_v^{+\mathtt{cofix}}$ and $\mathtt{DC}_n^{+\mathtt{fix}}$ by adding $\top$, $\bot$, and recursive types. The extended systems are called $\mathtt{DC}_v^{+\mathtt{cofix}+\{\top,\bot\}+\mathtt{rec}}$ and $\mathtt{DC}_n^{+\mathtt{fix}+\{\top,\bot\}+\mathtt{rec}}$. For the dual calculus, we consider the general syntax (without equations) $\mathtt{DC}^{+\mathtt{fix}+\mathtt{cofix}+\{\top,\bot\}+\mathtt{rec}}$ with both of $\mathtt{fix}$ and $\mathtt{cofix}$.

The syntax of $\mathtt{DC}^{+\mathtt{fix}+\mathtt{cofix}+\{\top,\bot\}+\mathtt{rec}}$ (resp. $\mathtt{DC}_v^{+\mathtt{cofix}+\{\top,\bot\}+\mathtt{rec}}$, $\mathtt{DC}_n^{+\mathtt{fix}+\{\top,\bot\}+\mathtt{rec}}$) is defined by adding

$$\begin{array}{ll} A,B ::= \ldots \mid \top \mid \bot \mid \mathtt{rec}\,X.A & \\ M,N ::= \ldots \mid * \mid \langle M\rangle\mathtt{in} & K,L ::= \ldots \mid \Box \mid \mathtt{in}[K] \\ V,W ::= \ldots \mid * \mid \langle V\rangle\mathtt{in} & P,Q ::= \ldots \mid \Box \mid \mathtt{in}[P] \end{array}$$

to the types, terms, coterms, values, and covalues of $\mathsf{DC}^{+\mathtt{fix}+\mathtt{cofix}}$ (resp. $\mathsf{DC}_v^{+\mathtt{cofix}}$, $\mathsf{DC}_n^{+\mathtt{fix}}$). The additional typing rules and the equality axioms are as follows:

$$\frac{}{\Gamma \to \Delta \mid * : \top}\,(\top) \qquad \frac{}{\Box : \bot \mid \Gamma \to \Delta}\,(\bot)$$

$$\frac{\Gamma \to \Delta \mid M : A[^{\mathtt{rec}X.A}/X]}{\Gamma \to \Delta \mid \langle M\rangle\mathtt{in} : \mathtt{rec}\,X.A}\,(\mathtt{rec}\,R) \qquad \frac{K : A[^{\mathtt{rec}X.A}/X] \mid \Gamma \to \Delta}{\mathtt{in}[K] : \mathtt{rec}\,X.A \mid \Gamma \to \Delta}\,(\mathtt{rec}\,L)$$

and

| | $\mathsf{DC}_n^{+\mathtt{fix}+\{\top,\bot\}+\mathtt{rec}}$ | $\mathsf{DC}_v^{+\mathtt{cofix}+\{\top,\bot\}+\mathtt{rec}}$ | |
|---|---|---|---|
| $(\top)$ | $M =^n *$ | $V =^v *$ | $(M,V : \top)$ |
| $(\bot)$ | $P =^n \Box$ | $K =^v \Box$ | $(P,K : \bot)$ |
| $(\beta_{rec})$ | $\langle M\rangle\mathtt{in} \bullet \mathtt{in}[P] =^n M \bullet P$ | $\langle V\rangle\mathtt{in} \bullet \mathtt{in}[K] =^v V \bullet K$ | |
| (name) | $M \bullet \mathtt{in}[K] =^n (M \bullet \mathtt{in}[\alpha]).\alpha \bullet K$ | $\langle M\rangle\mathtt{in} \bullet K =^v M \bullet x.(\langle x\rangle\mathtt{in} \bullet K)$ | |

### 4.3 Translations

We give the translation $(-)^{*2}$ from $\lambda\mu^{+\mathtt{fix}+\mathtt{loop}+\{\top,\bot\}+\mathtt{rec}}$ into $\mathsf{DC}^{+\mathtt{fix}+\mathtt{cofix}+\{\top,\bot\}+\mathtt{rec}}$ by extending $(-)^{*1}$:

$$\begin{array}{ll} (*)^{*2} \equiv * & ([\bot]M)^{*2} \equiv M^{*2} \bullet \Box \\ (\mathtt{fold}(M))^{*2} \equiv \langle M^{*2}\rangle\mathtt{in} & (\mathtt{unfold}(M))^{*2} \equiv (M^{*2} \bullet \mathtt{in}[\alpha]).\alpha \end{array}$$

for any term $M$ of $\lambda\mu^{+\mathtt{fix}+\mathtt{loop}+\{\top,\bot\}+\mathtt{rec}}$. The other clauses are similar to the translation $(-)^{*1}$. We also consider the extended inverse translation $(-)_{*_2}$, which is the inverse of $(-)^{*2}$ from $\mathsf{DC}^{+\mathtt{fix}+\mathtt{cofix}+\{\top,\bot\}+\mathtt{rec}}$ into $\lambda\mu^{+\mathtt{fix}+\mathtt{loop}+\{\top,\bot\}+\mathtt{rec}}$. This inverse translation is defined by extending the translation $(-)_{*_1}$:

$$\begin{array}{ll} (*)_{*_2} \equiv * & (\Box)_{*_2}\{O\} \equiv [\bot]O \\ (\langle M\rangle\mathtt{in})_{*_2} \equiv \mathtt{fold}(M_{*_2}) & (\mathtt{in}[K])_{*_2}\{O\} \equiv K_{*_2}\{\mathtt{unfold}(O)\} \end{array}$$

for any term $M$ and coterm $K$ of $\mathsf{DC}^{+\mathtt{fix}+\mathtt{cofix}+\{\top,\bot\}+\mathtt{rec}}$, and term $O$ of $\lambda\mu^{+\mathtt{fix}+\mathtt{loop}+\{\top,\bot\}+\mathtt{rec}}$. The other clauses are similar to the translation $(-)_{*_1}$.

The extended translations also preserve typing relations, and form an equational correspondence.

**Theorem 3.** (i) $((-)^{*2}, (-)_{*_2})$ *forms an equational correspondence with respect to the call-by-value equations.*
(ii) $((-)^{*2}, (-)_{*_2})$ *forms an equational correspondence with respect to the call-by-name equations.*

*Proof.* Soundness, completeness, and the reloading properties can be shown by the straightforward inductions. Note that (name)-rule is needed when we show the reloading property (2):

$$\begin{aligned} ((\mathtt{in}[K])_{*_2}\{O\})^{*2} &\equiv (K_{*_2}\{\mathtt{unfold}(O)\})^{*2} \overset{I.H.}{=^n} (\mathtt{unfold}(O))^{*2} \bullet K \\ &\equiv (O^{*2} \bullet \mathtt{in}[\alpha]).\alpha \bullet K =^n_{(name)} O^{*2} \bullet \mathtt{in}[K] \end{aligned}$$

$$(X)^\circ \equiv X \quad (\neg A)^\circ \equiv \neg A^\circ \quad (A\&B)^\circ \equiv B^\circ \vee A^\circ \quad (A \vee B)^\circ \equiv B^\circ \& A^\circ$$
$$(\top)^\circ \equiv \bot \quad (\bot)^\circ \equiv \top \quad (\mathtt{rec}\, X.A)^\circ \equiv \mathtt{rec}\, X.A^\circ$$

$$(x)^\circ \equiv x \quad (\alpha)^\circ \equiv \alpha \quad (M \bullet K)^\circ \equiv K^\circ \bullet M^\circ$$
$$(\langle M,N\rangle)^\circ \equiv [N^\circ, M^\circ] \quad (\langle M\rangle\mathtt{inl})^\circ \equiv \mathtt{snd}[M^\circ] \quad (\langle N\rangle\mathtt{inr})^\circ \equiv \mathtt{fst}[N^\circ] \quad ([K]\mathtt{not})^\circ \equiv \mathtt{not}\langle K^\circ\rangle$$
$$([K,L])^\circ \equiv \langle L^\circ, K^\circ\rangle \quad (\mathtt{fst}[K])^\circ \equiv \langle K^\circ\rangle\mathtt{inr} \quad (\mathtt{snd}[L])^\circ \equiv \langle L^\circ\rangle\mathtt{inl} \quad (\mathtt{not}\langle M\rangle)^\circ \equiv [M^\circ]\mathtt{not}$$
$$(*)^\circ \equiv \Box \quad ((S).\alpha)^\circ \equiv \alpha.(S^\circ) \quad (\mathtt{fix}\, x.\langle M\rangle)^\circ \equiv \mathtt{cofix}\, x.[M^\circ] \quad (\langle M\rangle\mathtt{in})^\circ \equiv \mathtt{in}[M^\circ]$$
$$(\Box)^\circ \equiv * \quad (x.(S))^\circ \equiv (S^\circ).x \quad (\mathtt{cofix}\, \alpha.[K])^\circ \equiv \mathtt{fix}\, \alpha.\langle K^\circ\rangle \quad (\mathtt{in}[K])^\circ \equiv \langle K^\circ\rangle\mathtt{in}$$

**Fig. 9.** Extended duality of the dual calculus

# 5 Duality

We discuss the duality of the dual calculus and the $\lambda\mu$-calculus, and show that Wadler's duality can be expanded into our extended systems. From this section, we translate away any occurrences of implications by using Wadler's results (proposition 1, 2, 3, and 4), since duality is not defined for implication. We suppose that $\{x, y, z \ldots\}$ and $\{\alpha, \beta, \gamma \ldots\}$ are two disjoint sets of meta-variables, and one is the set of variables and the other is the set of covariables.

## 5.1 Duality of the Extended Dual Calculus

The essential feature of DC is its duality: variables are dual to covariables, terms are dual to coterms, values are dual to covalues, and statements are self-dual. Wadler gave the duality translation $(-)^\circ$ from DC into itself, which captures this duality. Our extended versions of DC are designed to preserve this duality. Indeed, we can extend the duality translation $(-)^\circ$ from $\mathrm{DC}^{+\mathtt{fix}+\mathtt{cofix}+\{\top,\bot\}+\mathtt{rec}}$ into itself as displayed in Figure 9. This extended duality translation also satisfies the similar properties to the original one.

**Proposition 6 (Duality of the extended dual calculus).** (1) $(-)^\circ$ *preserves typing relation of* $\mathrm{DC}^{+\mathtt{fix}+\mathtt{cofix}+\{\top,\bot\}+\mathtt{rec}}$.
(2) $(-)^\circ$ *is an involution up to identity, that is,*

$$(A^\circ)^\circ \equiv A, \quad (M^\circ)^\circ \equiv M, \quad (K^\circ)^\circ \equiv K, \quad (S^\circ)^\circ \equiv S$$

*for any type A, term M, coterm K, statement S of* $\mathrm{DC}^{+\mathtt{fix}+\mathtt{cofix}+\{\top,\bot\}+\mathtt{rec}}$.
(3) $(-)^\circ$ *takes the call-by-value equalities in* $\mathrm{DC}_v^{+\mathtt{cofix}+\{\top,\bot\}+\mathtt{rec}}$ *into the call-by-name equalities in* $\mathrm{DC}_n^{+\mathtt{fix}+\{\top,\bot\}+\mathtt{rec}}$, *and vice versa:*

$$M =^v N \text{ iff } M^\circ =^n N^\circ, \quad K =^v L \text{ iff } K^\circ =^n L^\circ, \quad S =^v T \text{ iff } S^\circ =^n T^\circ$$

## 5.2 Duality of the Extended $\lambda\mu$-calculus

By composing our translations in this paper, we obtain the extended duality translation between $\lambda\mu_v^{+\mathtt{loop}+\{\top,\bot\}+\mathtt{rec}}$ and $\lambda\mu_n^{+\mathtt{fix}+\{\top,\bot\}+\mathtt{rec}}$.

**Definition 2.** *The duality translation* $(-)_\circ$ *from* $\lambda\mu^{+\mathtt{fix}+\mathtt{loop}+\{\top,\bot\}+\mathtt{rec}}$ *into itself is defined as follows:*

| | |
|---|---|
| $(X)_\circ \equiv X$ | |
| $(\top)_\circ \equiv \bot$ | $(\bot)_\circ \equiv \top$ |
| $(A\&B)_\circ \equiv B_\circ \vee A_\circ$ | $(A \vee B)_\circ \equiv B_\circ \& A_\circ$ |
| $(\neg A)_\circ \equiv \neg A_\circ$ | $(\mathtt{rec}\, X.A)_\circ \equiv \mathtt{rec}\, X.A_\circ$ |
| $(x)_\circ\{O\} \equiv [x]O$ | $(\langle M,N\rangle)_\circ\{O\} \equiv N_\circ\{\mu\beta.M_\circ\{\mu\alpha.[\beta,\alpha]O\}\}$ |
| $(\mathtt{fst}\, M)_\circ\{O\} \equiv (\lambda x.M_\circ\{\mu(\alpha,\beta).[\beta]x\})O$ | $(\mathtt{snd}\, N)_\circ\{O\} \equiv (\lambda y.N_\circ\{\mu(\alpha,\beta).[\alpha]y\})O$ |
| $(\lambda x.S)_\circ\{O\} \equiv O(\mu x.S_\circ)$ | $(OM)_\circ \equiv O_\circ\{\lambda x.M_\circ\{x\}\}$ |
| $(\mu\alpha.S)_\circ\{O\} \equiv (\lambda\alpha.S_\circ)O$ | $([\alpha]M)_\circ \equiv M_\circ\{\alpha\}$ |
| $(\mu(\alpha,\beta).S)_\circ\{O\} \equiv (\lambda z.(\lambda\alpha.(\lambda\beta.S_\circ)(\mathtt{fst}\, z))(\mathtt{snd}\, z))O$ | $([\alpha,\beta]M)_\circ \equiv M_\circ\{\langle\beta,\alpha\rangle\}$ |
| $(\mathtt{fix}\, x.M)_\circ\{O\} \equiv \mathtt{loop}\, z.((\mu x.M_\circ\{z\})O)$ | $(\mathtt{loop}\, x.M)_\circ\{O\} \equiv O(\mathtt{fix}\, \alpha.(\mu x.M_\circ\{\alpha\}))$ |
| $(*)_\circ\{O\} \equiv [\bot]O$ | $([\bot]M)_\circ \equiv M_\circ\{*\}$ |
| $(\mathtt{fold}(M))_\circ\{O\} \equiv M_\circ\{\mathtt{unfold}(O)\}$ | $(\mathtt{unfold}(M))_\circ\{O\} \equiv M_\circ\{\mathtt{fold}(O)\}$ |

**Fig. 10.** Extended duality of the $\lambda\mu$-calculus

$$A_\circ \equiv A^\circ, \quad M_\circ\{O\} \equiv ((M^{*_2})^\circ)_{*_2}\{O\}, \quad S_\circ \equiv ((S^{*_2})^\circ)_{*_2}$$

*for any type A, terms M and O, and statement S of* $\lambda\mu^{+\mathtt{fix}+\mathtt{loop}+\{\top,\bot\}+\mathtt{rec}}$.

This extended duality translation $(-)_\circ$ is given in Figure 10, and it has similar properties to Wadler's original one.

**Theorem 4 (Duality of the extended $\lambda\mu$-calculus).** (1) $(-)_\circ$ *preserves typing relation of* $\lambda\mu^{+\mathtt{fix}+\mathtt{loop}+\{\top,\bot\}+\mathtt{rec}}$.
(2) $(-)_\circ$ *is an involution up to equalities, that is,*

$$(M_\circ\{O\})_\circ =_v O_\circ\{M\}, \quad \mu\alpha.(M_\circ\{\alpha\})_\circ =_v M, \quad (S_\circ)_\circ =_v S \quad \text{in } \lambda\mu_v^{+\mathtt{loop}+\{\top,\bot\}+\mathtt{rec}},$$

*for any term M and statement S of* $\lambda\mu_v^{+\mathtt{loop}+\{\top,\bot\}+\mathtt{rec}}$, *and term O of* $\lambda\mu_n^{+\mathtt{fix}+\{\top,\bot\}+\mathtt{rec}}$,

$$(M_\circ\{O\})_\circ =_n O_\circ\{M\}, \quad \mu\alpha.(M_\circ\{\alpha\})_\circ =_n M, \quad (S_\circ)_\circ =_n S \quad \text{in } \lambda\mu_n^{+\mathtt{fix}+\{\top,\bot\}+\mathtt{rec}}$$

*for any term Mand statement S of* $\lambda\mu_n^{+\mathtt{fix}+\{\top,\bot\}+\mathtt{rec}}$, *and term O of* $\lambda\mu_v^{+\mathtt{loop}+\{\top,\bot\}+\mathtt{rec}}$.
(3) $(-)_\circ$ *takes the call-by-value equalities in* $\lambda\mu_v^{+\mathtt{loop}+\{\top,\bot\}+\mathtt{rec}}$ *into the call-by-name equalities in* $\lambda\mu_n^{+\mathtt{fix}+\{\top,\bot\}+\mathtt{rec}}$, *and vice versa:*

$$M =_v N \text{ iff } M_\circ\{O\} =_n N_\circ\{O\}, \quad S =_v T \text{ iff } S_\circ =_n T_\circ$$

*for any term M and statement S of* $\lambda\mu_v^{+\mathtt{loop}+\{\top,\bot\}+\mathtt{rec}}$, *and term O of* $\lambda\mu_n^{+\mathtt{fix}+\{\top,\bot\}+\mathtt{rec}}$,

$$M =_n N \text{ iff } M_\circ\{O\} =_v N_\circ\{O\}, \quad S =_n T \text{ iff } S_\circ =_v T_\circ$$

*for any term M and statement S of* $\lambda\mu_n^{+\mathtt{fix}+\{\top,\bot\}+\mathtt{rec}}$, *and term O of* $\lambda\mu_v^{+\mathtt{loop}+\{\top,\bot\}+\mathtt{rec}}$.

## 6 Applications

Since our extended $\lambda\mu$-calculi have unit, counit, and recursive types, some important data types can be represented in our calculi. For example, under call-by-value, boolean and natural number types can be coded in this way.

$$\texttt{bool}_v \equiv \top \vee \top, \quad \texttt{true}_v \equiv \mu(\alpha,\beta).[\alpha]*, \quad \texttt{false}_v \equiv \mu(\alpha,\beta).[\beta]*,$$
$$\texttt{nat}_v \equiv \texttt{rec}\, X.(\top \vee X), \quad (0)_v \equiv \texttt{fold}(\mu(\alpha,\beta).[\alpha]*), \quad (k+1)_v \equiv \texttt{fold}(\mu(\alpha,\beta).[\beta](k)_v),$$
$$\texttt{Succ}_v(M) \equiv \texttt{fold}(\mu(\alpha,\beta).[\beta]M), \quad \texttt{Pred}_v(M) \equiv \mu\beta.[\alpha,\beta]\texttt{unfold}(M)$$

for any natural number $k$. We can easily see that $\texttt{Succ}_v((k)_v) =_v (k+1)_v$ and $\texttt{Pred}_v((k+1)_v) =_v (k)_v$ for any natural number $k$. However, this coding does not work under call-by-name, since we have $(0)_v =_n (1)_v$ from $* =_n \mu\alpha.[\beta](0)_v$ (where $\alpha : \top, \beta : \texttt{nat}_v$), and $\texttt{true}_v =_n \texttt{false}_v$ from $* =_n \mu\alpha.[\beta]*$ (where $\alpha, \beta : \top$). Kakutani [7] gave another coding in his call-by-name $\lambda\mu$-calculus. We interpret his call-by-name coding for our call-by-name system as follows.

$$\texttt{bool}_n \equiv \neg(\bot \& \bot), \quad \texttt{true}_n \equiv \lambda x.[\bot]\texttt{snd}\, x, \quad \texttt{false}_n \equiv \lambda y.[\bot]\texttt{fst}\, y$$
$$\texttt{nat}_n \equiv \neg\texttt{rec}\, X.(X \& \bot), \quad (k)_n \equiv \lambda x.[\bot]\texttt{snd}((\texttt{unfold fst})^k(\texttt{unfold}(x))),$$
$$\texttt{Succ}_n(M) \equiv \lambda z.M\, \texttt{fst}(\texttt{unfold}(z)), \quad \texttt{Pred}_n(M) \equiv \lambda z.M\, \texttt{fold}(\langle z, \texttt{snd}(\texttt{unfold}(z))\rangle)$$

where $(\texttt{unfold fst})^k(M)$ is defined by $(\texttt{unfold fst})^0(M) \equiv M$ and $(\texttt{unfold fst})^{k+1}(M) \equiv (\texttt{unfold fst})^k(\texttt{unfold}(\texttt{fst}\, M))$. The call-by-name and call-by-value codings are converted to each other by our duality translation. Let $O$ be a term of $\lambda\mu_v^{+\texttt{loop}+\{\top,\bot\}+\texttt{rec}}$, $O'$ be a term of $\lambda\mu_n^{+\texttt{fix}+\{\top,\bot\}+\texttt{rec}}$, and $k$ be a natural number, then

$$\neg(\texttt{bool}_v)_\circ \equiv \texttt{bool}_n, \quad \neg(\texttt{nat}_v)_\circ \equiv \texttt{nat}_n,$$
$$(\texttt{true}_n)_\circ\{O\} =_v O\,\texttt{true}_v, \quad (\texttt{true}_v)_\circ\{O'\} =_n \texttt{true}_n\, O',$$
$$(\texttt{false}_n)_\circ\{O\} =_v O\,\texttt{false}_v, \quad (\texttt{false}_v)_\circ\{O'\} =_n \texttt{false}_n\, O',$$
$$((k)_n)_\circ\{O\} =_v O\,(k)_v, \quad ((k)_v)_\circ\{O'\} =_n (k)_n\, O'.$$

If we have a program $P : A \supset B$, its dual program $P_\circ : B_\circ \supset A_\circ$ is defined by $\lambda\alpha.\mu x.(Px)_\circ\{\alpha\}$, and $(P_\circ)_\circ$ is equal to $P$ up to the call-by-value (and also call-by-name) equality. Moreover, we can convert a program $P : \texttt{nat}_v \supset \texttt{nat}_v$ and $Q : \texttt{nat}_n \supset \texttt{nat}_n$ to $P_\dagger : \texttt{nat}_n \supset \texttt{nat}_n$ and $Q_\sharp : \texttt{nat}_v \supset \texttt{nat}_v$ by defining $P_\dagger \equiv \lambda x.\lambda y.x(P_\circ y)$ and $Q_\sharp \equiv \lambda x.\mu\alpha.((Q_\circ \lambda y.[\alpha]y)x)$ respectively. These converted programs have essentially the same behavior as the original ones.

**Theorem 5.** *(1)* $(P_\dagger)_\sharp =_v P$*, and* $(Q_\sharp)_\dagger =_n Q$*,*
*(2)* $P(k)_v =_v (l)_v$ *iff* $P_\dagger(k)_n =_n (l)_n$*, and* $Q(k)_n =_n (l)_n$ *iff* $Q_\sharp(k)_v =_v (l)_v$
*for any terms* $P : \texttt{nat}_v \supset \texttt{nat}_v$*,* $Q : \texttt{nat}_n \supset \texttt{nat}_n$*, and natural numbers* $k$ *and* $l$*.*

## 7 Conclusion

Selinger [13] showed the duality between the call-by-name $\lambda\mu$-calculus and the call-by-value one, and Kakutani [7] extended Selinger's duality by adding a fixed-point operator and an iteration operator to the call-by-name and call-by-value $\lambda\mu$-calculus, respectively. Wadler pointed out that Selinger's (and also Kakutani's) duality is *not* involutive, and gave an involutive duality on the $\lambda\mu$-calculus by defining implication in terms of the other connectives rather than by taking it primitive one. We showed that Wadler's duality can be extended to the duality between the call-by-name $\lambda\mu$-calculus with a fixed-point operator and recursive types, and the call-by-value one with an iteration operator and recursive types. Our duality is also involutive, and shows a cleaner relationship between the fix-point operator and the iteration operator.

The existence of recursive types, unit, and counit types enables us to encode important data types. In the last section, we demonstrated that natural numbers and booleans are dually encoded in our call-by-name and call-by-value systems. Moreover, the duality of natural numbers yields a duality of programs on natural numbers, as claimed in our final theorem.

We hope that the duality and the results in this paper will have useful applications to practical programming languages.

## Acknowledgment

This work is greatly influenced by Wadler's and Kakutani's original work. The author is grateful to them. The author also thank Makoto Tatsuta, Kazushige Terui, and Makoto Kanazawa for their comments and encouragement.

## References

1. Barbanera, F., Berardi, S.: A symmetric lambda calculus for classical program extraction. Information and Computation 125(2), 103–117 (1996)
2. Curien, P.-L., Herbelin, H.: The duality of computation. In: ICFP 2000. Proc. of the Fifth ACM SIGPLAN International Conference on Functional Programming, Montreal, Canada, pp. 233–243. ACM Press, New York (2000)
3. Filinski, A.: Declarative continuations and categorical duality. Master's thesis, Univ. of Copenhagen (1989)
4. Filinski, A.: Recursion from iteration. Lisp and Symbolic Computation 7(1), 11–38 (1994)
5. Griffin, T.G.: A formulae-as-types notion of control. In: Proc. of the 1990 Principles of Programming Languages Conference, pp. 47–58. IEEE Computer Society Press, Los Alamitos (1990)
6. Hofmann, M., Streicher, T.: Completeness of continuation models for $\lambda\mu$-calculus. Information and Computation 179(2), 332–355 (2002)
7. Kakutani, Y.: Duality between call-by-name recursion and call-by-value iteration. Master's thesis, Kyoto University (2001)
8. Ong, C.-H.L., Stewart, C.A.: A Curry-Howard foundation for functional computation with control. In: Proc. of the Symposium on Principles of Programming Languages, pp. 215–227 (1997)
9. Parigot, M.: $\lambda\mu$-calculus: an algorithmic interpretation of classical natural deduction. In: Voronkov, A. (ed.) LPAR 1992. LNCS, vol. 624, pp. 190–201. Springer, Heidelberg (1992)
10. Pierce, B.C.: Types and Programming Languages. MIT Press, Cambridge (2002)
11. Pym, D., Ritter, E.: On the semantics of classical disjunction. Journal of Pure and Applied Algebra 159, 315–338 (2001)
12. Sabry, A., Felleisen, M.: Reasoning about programs in continuation-passing style. Lisp and Symbolic Computation 6(3/4), 289–360 (1993)
13. Selinger, P.: Control categories and duality: on the categorical semantics of the lambda-mu calculus. In: Mathematical Structures in Computer Science, pp. 207–260 (2001)
14. Wadler, P.: Call-by-Value is Dual to Call-by-Name. In: International Conference on Functional Programming, Uppsala, Sweden, pp. 25–29 (2003)
15. Wadler, P.: Call-by-Value is Dual to Call-by-Name – Reloaded. In: Rewriting Techniques and Applications, Nara, Japan, pp. 185–203. Springer, Heidelberg (2005)

# Author Index

# Author Index

# Lecture Notes in Computer Science

Sublibrary 2: Programming and Software Engineering

For information about Vols. 1–4184
please contact your bookseller or Springer

Vol. 4824: A. Paschke, Y. Biletskiy (Eds.), Advances in Rule Interchange and Applications. XIII, 243 pages. 2007.

Vol. 4807: Z. Shao (Ed.), Programming Languages and Systems. XI, 431 pages. 2007.

Vol. 4789: M. Butler, M.G. Hinchey, M.M. Larrondo-Petrie (Eds.), Formal Methods and Software Engineering. VIII, 387 pages. 2007.

Vol. 4767: F. Arbab, M. Sirjani (Eds.), International Symposium on Fundamentals of Software Engineering. XIII, 450 pages. 2007.

Vol. 4764: P. Abrahamsson, N. Baddoo, T. Margaria, R. Messnarz (Eds.), Software Process Improvement. XI, 225 pages. 2007.

Vol. 4762: K.S. Namjoshi, T. Yoneda, T. Higashino, Y. Okamura (Eds.), Automated Technology for Verification and Analysis. XIV, 566 pages. 2007.

Vol. 4758: F. Oquendo (Ed.), Software Architecture. XVI, 340 pages. 2007.

Vol. 4757: F. Cappello, T. Herault, J. Dongarra (Eds.), Recent Advances in Parallel Virtual Machine and Message Passing Interface. XVI, 396 pages. 2007.

Vol. 4753: E. Duval, R. Klamma, M. Wolpers (Eds.), Creating New Learning Experiences on a Global Scale. XII, 518 pages. 2007.

Vol. 4749: B.J. Krämer, K.-J. Lin, P. Narasimhan (Eds.), Service-Oriented Computing - ICSOC 2007. XIX, 629 pages. 2007.

Vol. 4748: K. Wolter (Ed.), Formal Methods and Stochastic Models for Performance Evaluation. X, 301 pages. 2007.

Vol. 4741: C. Bessière (Ed.), Principles and Practice of Constraint Programming - CP 2007. XV, 890 pages. 2007.

Vol. 4735: G. Engels, B. Opdyke, D.C. Schmidt, F. Weil (Eds.), Model Driven Engineering Languages and Systems. XV, 698 pages. 2007.

Vol. 4716: B. Meyer, M. Joseph (Eds.), Software Engineering Approaches for Offshore and Outsourced Development. X, 201 pages. 2007.

Vol. 4680: F. Saglietti, N. Oster (Eds.), Computer Safety, Reliability, and Security. XV, 548 pages. 2007.

Vol. 4670: V. Dahl, I. Niemelä (Eds.), Logic Programming. XII, 470 pages. 2007.

Vol. 4652: D. Georgakopoulos, N. Ritter, B. Benatallah, C. Zirpins, G. Feuerlicht, M. Schoenherr, H.R. Motahari-Nezhad (Eds.), Service-Oriented Computing ICSOC 2006. XVI, 201 pages. 2007.

Vol. 4634: H. Riis Nielson, G. Filé (Eds.), Static Analysis. XI, 469 pages. 2007.

Vol. 4615: R. de Lemos, C. Gacek, A. Romanovsky (Eds.), Architecting Dependable Systems IV. XIV, 435 pages. 2007.

Vol. 4610: B. Xiao, L.T. Yang, J. Ma, C. Muller-Schloer, Y. Hua (Eds.), Autonomic and Trusted Computing. XVIII, 571 pages. 2007.

Vol. 4609: E. Ernst (Ed.), ECOOP 2007 – Object-Oriented Programming. XIII, 625 pages. 2007.

Vol. 4608: H.W. Schmidt, I. Crnković, G.T. Heineman, J.A. Stafford (Eds.), Component-Based Software Engineering. XII, 283 pages. 2007.

Vol. 4591: J. Davies, J. Gibbons (Eds.), Integrated Formal Methods. IX, 660 pages. 2007.

Vol. 4589: J. Münch, P. Abrahamsson (Eds.), Product-Focused Software Process Improvement. XII, 414 pages. 2007.

Vol. 4574: J. Derrick, J. Vain (Eds.), Formal Techniques for Networked and Distributed Systems – FORTE 2007. XI, 375 pages. 2007.

Vol. 4556: C. Stephanidis (Ed.), Universal Access in Human-Computer Interaction, Part III. XXII, 1020 pages. 2007.

Vol. 4555: C. Stephanidis (Ed.), Universal Access in Human-Computer Interaction, Part II. XXII, 1066 pages. 2007.

Vol. 4554: C. Stephanidis (Ed.), Universal Acess in Human Computer Interaction, Part I. XXII, 1054 pages. 2007.

Vol. 4553: J.A. Jacko (Ed.), Human-Computer Interaction, Part IV. XXIV, 1225 pages. 2007.

Vol. 4552: J.A. Jacko (Ed.), Human-Computer Interaction, Part III. XXI, 1038 pages. 2007.

Vol. 4551: J.A. Jacko (Ed.), Human-Computer Interaction, Part II. XXIII, 1253 pages. 2007.

Vol. 4550: J.A. Jacko (Ed.), Human-Computer Interaction, Part I. XXIII, 1240 pages. 2007.

Vol. 4542: P. Sawyer, B. Paech, P. Heymans (Eds.), Requirements Engineering: Foundation for Software Quality. IX, 384 pages. 2007.

Vol. 4536: G. Concas, E. Damiani, M. Scotto, G. Succi (Eds.), Agile Processes in Software Engineering and Extreme Programming. XV, 276 pages. 2007.

Vol. 4530: D.H. Akehurst, R. Vogel, R.F. Paige (Eds.), Model Driven Architecture - Foundations and Applications. X, 219 pages. 2007.

Vol. 4523: Y.-H. Lee, H.-N. Kim, J. Kim, Y.W. Park, L.T. Yang, S.W. Kim (Eds.), Embedded Software and Systems. XIX, 829 pages. 2007.

Vol. 4498: N. Abdennahder, F. Kordon (Eds.), Reliable Software Technologies - Ada-Europe 2007. XII, 247 pages. 2007.

Vol. 4486: M. Bernardo, J. Hillston (Eds.), Formal Methods for Performance Evaluation. VII, 469 pages. 2007.

Vol. 4470: Q. Wang, D. Pfahl, D.M. Raffo (Eds.), Software Process Dynamics and Agility. XI, 346 pages. 2007.

Vol. 4468: M.M. Bonsangue, E.B. Johnsen (Eds.), Formal Methods for Open Object-Based Distributed Systems. X, 317 pages. 2007.

Vol. 4467: A.L. Murphy, J. Vitek (Eds.), Coordination Models and Languages. X, 325 pages. 2007.

Vol. 4454: Y. Gurevich, B. Meyer (Eds.), Tests and Proofs. IX, 217 pages. 2007.

Vol. 4444: T. Reps, M. Sagiv, J. Bauer (Eds.), Program Analysis and Compilation, Theory and Practice. X, 361 pages. 2007.

Vol. 4440: B. Liblit, Cooperative Bug Isolation. XV, 101 pages. 2007.

Vol. 4408: R. Choren, A. Garcia, H. Giese, H.-f. Leung, C. Lucena, A. Romanovsky (Eds.), Software Engineering for Multi-Agent Systems V. XII, 233 pages. 2007.

Vol. 4406: W. De Meuter (Ed.), Advances in Smalltalk. VII, 157 pages. 2007.

Vol. 4405: L. Padgham, F. Zambonelli (Eds.), Agent-Oriented Software Engineering VII. XII, 225 pages. 2007.

Vol. 4401: N. Guelfi, D. Buchs (Eds.), Rapid Integration of Software Engineering Techniques. IX, 177 pages. 2007.

Vol. 4385: K. Coninx, K. Luyten, K.A. Schneider (Eds.), Task Models and Diagrams for Users Interface Design. XI, 355 pages. 2007.

Vol. 4383: E. Bin, A. Ziv, S. Ur (Eds.), Hardware and Software, Verification and Testing. XII, 235 pages. 2007.

Vol. 4379: M. Südholt, C. Consel (Eds.), Object-Oriented Technology. VIII, 157 pages. 2007.

Vol. 4364: T. Kühne (Ed.), Models in Software Engineering. XI, 332 pages. 2007.

Vol. 4355: J. Julliand, O. Kouchnarenko (Eds.), B 2007: Formal Specification and Development in B. XIII, 293 pages. 2006.

Vol. 4354: M. Hanus (Ed.), Practical Aspects of Declarative Languages. X, 335 pages. 2006.

Vol. 4350: M. Clavel, F. Durán, S. Eker, P. Lincoln, N. Martí-Oliet, J. Meseguer, C. Talcott, All About Maude - A High-Performance Logical Framework. XXII, 797 pages. 2007.

Vol. 4348: S. Tucker Taft, R.A. Duff, R.L. Brukardt, E. Plödereder, P. Leroy, Ada 2005 Reference Manual. XXII, 765 pages. 2006.

Vol. 4346: L. Brim, B.R. Haverkort, M. Leucker, J. van de Pol (Eds.), Formal Methods: Applications and Technology. X, 363 pages. 2007.

Vol. 4344: V. Gruhn, F. Oquendo (Eds.), Software Architecture. X, 245 pages. 2006.

Vol. 4340: R. Prodan, T. Fahringer, Grid Computing. XXIII, 317 pages. 2007.

Vol. 4336: V.R. Basili, H.D. Rombach, K. Schneider, B. Kitchenham, D. Pfahl, R.W. Selby (Eds.), Empirical Software Engineering Issues. XVII, 193 pages. 2007.

Vol. 4326: S. Göbel, R. Malkewitz, I. Iurgel (Eds.), Technologies for Interactive Digital Storytelling and Entertainment. X, 384 pages. 2006.

Vol. 4323: G. Doherty, A. Blandford (Eds.), Interactive Systems. XI, 269 pages. 2007.

Vol. 4322: F. Kordon, J. Sztipanovits (Eds.), Reliable Systems on Unreliable Networked Platforms. XIV, 317 pages. 2007.

Vol. 4309: P. Inverardi, M. Jazayeri (Eds.), Software Engineering Education in the Modern Age. VIII, 207 pages. 2006.

Vol. 4294: A. Dan, W. Lamersdorf (Eds.), Service-Oriented Computing – ICSOC 2006. XIX, 653 pages. 2006.

Vol. 4290: M. van Steen, M. Henning (Eds.), Middleware 2006. XIII, 425 pages. 2006.

Vol. 4279: N. Kobayashi (Ed.), Programming Languages and Systems. XI, 423 pages. 2006.

Vol. 4262: K. Havelund, M. Núñez, G. Roşu, B. Wolff (Eds.), Formal Approaches to Software Testing and Runtime Verification. VIII, 255 pages. 2006.

Vol. 4260: Z. Liu, J. He (Eds.), Formal Methods and Software Engineering. XII, 778 pages. 2006.

Vol. 4257: I. Richardson, P. Runeson, R. Messnarz (Eds.), Software Process Improvement. XI, 219 pages. 2006.

Vol. 4242: A. Rashid, M. Aksit (Eds.), Transactions on Aspect-Oriented Software Development II. IX, 289 pages. 2006.

Vol. 4229: E. Najm, J.-F. Pradat-Peyre, V.V. Donzeau-Gouge (Eds.), Formal Techniques for Networked and Distributed Systems - FORTE 2006. X, 486 pages. 2006.

Vol. 4227: W. Nejdl, K. Tochtermann (Eds.), Innovative Approaches for Learning and Knowledge Sharing. XVII, 721 pages. 2006.

Vol. 4218: S. Graf, W. Zhang (Eds.), Automated Technology for Verification and Analysis. XIV, 540 pages. 2006.

Vol. 4214: C. Hofmeister, I. Crnković, R. Reussner (Eds.), Quality of Software Architectures. X, 215 pages. 2006.

Vol. 4204: F. Benhamou (Ed.), Principles and Practice of Constraint Programming - CP 2006. XVIII, 774 pages. 2006.

Vol. 4199: O. Nierstrasz, J. Whittle, D. Harel, G. Reggio (Eds.), Model Driven Engineering Languages and Systems. XVI, 798 pages. 2006.

Vol. 4192: B. Mohr, J.L. Träff, J. Worringen, J. Dongarra (Eds.), Recent Advances in Parallel Virtual Machine and Message Passing Interface. XVI, 414 pages. 2006.